ROMAN LITERARY
THEORY AND CRITICISM

ROMAN LITERARY THEORY AND CRITICISM

A STUDY IN TENDENCIES

BY THE REV.
J. F. D'ALTON, M.A., D.D., D.LITT.

NEW YORK
RUSSELL & RUSSELL · INC

1962

FIRST PUBLISHED IN 1931
REISSUED, 1962, BY RUSSELL & RUSSELL, INC.
BY ARRANGEMENT WITH THE AUTHOR
L. C. CATALOG CARD NO: 62-10683

PREFACE

THESE STUDIES are being offered to the public in the hope that they provide some contribution to the history of Roman Literary Theory and Criticism. When the subject first attracted me, I had no well-defined plan for its treatment before my mind. Eventually, I decided to confine myself to such aspects of it as would serve to illustrate the main tendencies in the work of Roman critics. The early period, though our knowledge of it is so fragmentary, is valuable, not only as showing the actual problems then engaging the attention of critics, but as supplying evidence of the reactions of Hellenistic theory upon the Romans. A chapter is devoted to a discussion of the problem of Style as it presented itself to the Romans, both because the problem has an intrinsic interest of its own, and because a discussion of it helps us to comprehend better Cicero's standpoint in many of his criticisms. In propounding their theory of Style, especially in the sphere of oratory, the Romans were in the main dependent on the Greeks. One could not hope to deal adequately with all the complexities of this problem within the limits of a single chapter, but such features of it as I have studied, will serve to show the trend of ancient theory towards a somewhat rigid formulism. When we turn to Cicero, we find in him a good example of stereotyped and conventional criticism, while his quarrel with the Atticists is of particular interest, not only as revealing a conflict of ideals with regard to oratorical prose, but as showing how potent was the spell cast by Greek models upon the Romans. In

those characteristics of Horatian criticism that I have
examined, one may see the strength of Classicism, as well
as its limitations. In my chapter on the Ancients and
Moderns I have touched on many aspects of literary theory
among the Romans, and have endeavoured to illustrate the
more important phases in the struggle between Tradition
and Experiment in Roman literature down to the days of
Fronto. In another chapter I have dealt with the predominant position of Rhetoric in ancient times, and have
considered its influence in the spheres of poetry and history.
My final chapter is designed to present a review of the
prominent points that have emerged in the course of our
survey, and an estimate of their value in the general
history of Criticism. Throughout, either in the text or in
the notes, I have aimed, as far as the plan of the work
would permit, at showing the interrelation of Greek and
Roman literary theory. The captions I have employed in
the various chapters should help to make clear the principal
topics treated, and obviate the necessity of an elaborate
table of contents.

Even within the limits which I prescribed for myself, I
was compelled to exercise a principle of selection. I had
to omit altogether certain questions that attracted me, and
had to be content with a summary treatment of others. If
the book had not grown beyond the proportions originally
designed, and if the question of scale had not seriously to be
considered, I would have liked, for instance, to deal more
fully with other aspects of the problem of Style, and with
the importance in Roman criticism of writers such as the
two Senecas, Petronius, and Quintilian. Especially, I
would have wished to discuss more thoroughly the reactions of Hellenistic theory upon the Romans. The
Hellenistic age seems to me to hold the key to much Roman
criticism. It was then most of all that the tendency became
manifest to stereotype the laws of certain poetic genres, and

to fetter rhetoric with conventional rules. The fragments
of Philodemus have helped to throw some light on the
character of poetic theory in that age, but unfortunately
there are still many gaps in our knowledge of the period.
This circumstance alone makes us regret that so much
has been lost of the critical works of Accius, Aelius Stilo,
and Varro, who were probably in large measure heirs to the
Hellenistic tradition. From Cicero and Quintilian we
might reconstruct the main outlines of Hellenistic rhetoric,
though one might profitably pursue the further task of
isolating the distinctively Roman elements in these authors.
There are, indeed, many fascinating questions that call for
treatment. A systematic history of Roman literary theory
and criticism has yet to be written. Professor Saintsbury
in his monumental work has discussed the broader aspects
of Roman criticism, and has dealt with its more prominent
figures. His vast erudition, his freshness of outlook, and
his independence of judgment, make us wish that he had
been able to give us a more detailed treatment of the
Roman section of his subject. My own studies will, I hope,
be of assistance to those who choose to labour in this field.
They may, at any rate, profit by my shortcomings.

I have selected the main title for the work, because
amongst the Romans theory and criticism generally went
hand in hand. They exhibit little in the way of impres-
sionist criticism. Most of their criticism might be styled
judicial or dogmatic. In poetry the critic found existing
well-defined laws for many of the genres, in rhetoric he was
confronted with a stereotyped scheme, and relying on the
authority of these he plied his trade. The poets themselves
often speculated on the laws of their craft. It was not felt
that there was any impassable barrier between criticism and
creation, or that the corruption of the poet was inevitable
on the generation of the critic.

I hope I have acknowledged adequately my obligations

to those modern authors whose works I have found useful
in individual points in the course of these studies, even
though I have had to differ from some of their conclusions.
There are other obligations that weigh heavily upon me.
I find it difficult to express, as I would wish, my deep sense
of gratitude to Professor Tierney of University College,
Dublin, and to my colleague, Father J. Duff, for their
generous assistance at every stage of the work. They made
many helpful suggestions, and lightened considerably for
me the labour of correction. I feel that I trespassed unsparingly on their time and patience. Professor Semple of
University College, Dublin, was kind enough to read most
of the work in proof, and his wide knowledge of Roman
literature proved of great value to me at many points.
Finally, I desire to thank my colleague, Dr. Lucey, and
my old pupil, Rev. M. Brennan of Knockbeg College, who
helped me unstintingly in the arduous task of proof-
reading.

J. F. D.

August, 1931.

CONTENTS

AUTHOR'S NOTE

THE following abbreviations have been used in the Notes :—
Val. = Valmaggi.
A.K. = Die antike Kunstprosa (Norden).
K. = Keil, Grammatici Latini.
Sp. = Spengel, Rhetores Graeci.
Philod. = Philodemus, Rhetorica (Sudhaus).

N.B.—The Italics used in quotations are in every case my own.

CHAPTER I

THE AWAKENING OF THE CRITICAL SPIRIT

A T FIRST sight it would seem that there is little in the early period of Roman literature to reward the investigations of one who seeks to recount, even in summary fashion, the development of criticism in Rome. Roman literature was almost barren, until it began to draw its inspiration from the Greeks, and was touched by some of their divine fire. Even if we allow for a body of native[1] poetry, yet there was little either in this, or in the religious formulæ so common in early Rome, that could inspire one to formulate the rules of artistic production. Criticism pre-supposes a certain stage of culture, a certain advance in self-consciousness, and above all a standard of comparison. The author of the treatise *On the Sublime* says happily[2]: ἡ γὰρ τῶν λόγων κρίσις πολλῆς ἐστι πείρας τελευταῖον ἐπιγέννημα. The Romans at this period had not the long experience requisite for successful criticism, but they were gradually growing in self-consciousness, and a standard of comparison came into their possession when they first began to experience the beauty of Greek literature. Early Roman literature was, it is true, largely a transcript from the Greek, but even thus, problems would arise for the Roman writers when they endeavoured to estimate the difficulties of their task, and the measure of success achieved.

Of the poets Livius Andronicus and Naevius, who first came under Greek influence, we have only a few fragments extant. They must have been wholly en-
Livius and Naevius grossed in the task of moulding the intractable material of the Latin tongue into a poetical medium that would reproduce something at least

[1] Cf. Cic. Tusc. Disp., I. 3, Br. 75 ; Livy, VII. 2. 4 ; Val. Max., II. 4. 4 ; cf. Steuart, The Annals of Quintus Ennius, p. 163 *et seq.* ; the author's Horace and his Age, p. 254 *et seq.*
[2] C. 6.

of the beauty of their Greek originals. Their art was largely
the art of the translator, and naturally one of the first
problems that would present itself to them, was how success
in such an art could best be attained, and what was to be
their relation to their models. Their remains are so fragmentary, that we cannot tell if they busied themselves with
such questions. Naevius, indeed, was more than a translator, and worked on original lines in his *Bellum Punicum*
and his " Praetextae". He was the founder of the historical
Epic at Rome, and moreover, as we know, he was the first
Roman poet to employ " contamination " in his adaptations
from the Greek drama. He was a man of independent
character, with much of the innate pride of the Campanian.
It is doubtful if the epitaph which Gellius quotes[1] as having
been written by himself, is authentic, but it may reflect
something of his personal pride in his achievement in
having transformed Latin into a flexible medium of expression. The vivid picture[2] of the coquette in his comedy
Tarentilla, would alone suffice to show how plastic Latin
had already become in his hands.

Plautus worked at high pressure, intent, Horace tells us,
on acquiring a fortune. He did not concern himself with
the theoretical problems of his art, though,
as we shall see,[3] he censures certain stage
conventions and certain weaknesses of the Comic drama in
terms, however, that may be derived from his Greek originals. Moreover, in one important passage[4] he deals with the
poet's power of fiction, his search for the " light that never
was on sea or land," and his capacity for creating poetic faith.[5]

Ennius   In the person of Ennius we come to a
poet who is thoroughly self-conscious, and
imbued with a high esteem[6] for his lofty calling. It is not

Plautus

---

[1] I. 24; it says that after his death " oblitei Romae loquier Latina lingua."
[2] *Vide* Pascal, Scritti Varii, p. 49, on the authorship of the passage.
[3] *Vide infra*, p. 9.
[4] Pseudolus, 401 *et seq.*: " qui quaerit quod nusquam est gentium, repperit tamen."
[5] The "repperit tamen " suggests that the poet is able to engender " a
willing suspension of disbelief;" cf. Saintsbury, A History of Criticism, Vol.
III, p. 208.
[6] Cic. Pro Archia, 18 : " noster ille Ennius sanctos appellat poetas."

surprising that he furnishes us with the first definite example of literary criticism amongst the Romans. His was
an original and forceful personality, so intensely proud of
its achievements that it was being ever tempted into self-
revelation. Though Homer, his prototype,[1] was so im-
personal, Ennius, even in his great Epic, cannot refrain
from striking the personal note.[2] When he came to Rome,
he was fortunate enough to enjoy[3] the patronage of some of
the leading Romans. He took pride[4] in his newly-acquired
Roman citizenship, and approached his task of writing an
epic of Roman achievements, filled with admiration for the
qualities[5] that had built up the greatness of the Eternal
City. He used to declare[6] that he possessed three hearts,
because of his mastery of Greek, Oscan, and Latin, but for
him all else was subordinated to the Latin heart, and to his
task of singing the glories of Rome. He is confident that
he has performed the task in a manner so worthy, that his
Epic will win fame[7] throughout the world. In one of his
Satires the poet speaks[8] of the " flaming verses " that he
offers to men from the very core of his being.

All this is evidence of a forceful genius, conscious of
attempting and achieving great things in the
world of poetry. It prepares us, too, for
the famous verses[9] in the *Annales*, in which
he decries the crude efforts of his predecessors who sang

Criticism of
his predeces-
sors

[1] Cic. De Fin. I. 3. 7 ; Sen. Ep. 108. 34 ; cf. Duckett, Studies in Ennius, p. 40.

[2] Cf. his references to his old age, Valmaggi, Q. Ennio, fr. 268 ; Steuart,
op. cit., Bk. XVI, fr. 2 ; cf. Gellius, XVII. 21. 43 ; Cic. Cato Major, 141 ;
Aelius Stilo (Gellius, XII. 4) looked on the Servilius fragment also as a piece
of self-revelation ; *vide infra*, p. 295 ; cf. Vahlen, Ennianae Poesis Reliquiae,
Ann. VII. 234.

[3] Cic. Cato Major, 10, Pro Archia, 22, 27 ; Nepos, Cato, I. 4.

[4] Val., fr. 313 : " nos sumus Romani qui fuimus ante Rudini."

[5] Val., fr. 305 : " moribus antiquis res stat Romana virisque "; cf.
Vahlen, 500, 537, 546, 547, 550.

[6] Gellius, XVII. 17. 1.

[7] Val., fr. 8 (where the text is somewhat doubtful) " (per) populos
terrasque poemata nostra cluebunt "; cf. the words of Ennius' epitaph :
" volito vivos per ora hominum "; cf. Cic. Cato Major, 73.

[8] " Enni poeta salve, qui mortalibus versus propinas flammeos medul-
litus " ; cf. Nonius (Mueller), Vol. I. p. 45, *ib*. p. 201.

[9] Cf. Cic. Br. 71, 76, Or. 171 ; Varro, De L. L., VII. 36 ; Q. IX. 4. 115 ;
cf. Val., fr. 123 ; Steuart, Bk. VII, fr. 5, *ib*. Excursus II, p. 163 *et seq*.

in Saturnian verse, but who had never like himself unlocked
the secret of the Muses. No one before him, he tells us,
was " dicti studiosus," a conscious artist in language. The
poet may have had here in mind a body of native poetry
that existed before the Romans came under Greek influence,
but it is more probable that he had Naevius principally in
view, who like himself had written an historical Epic, but
in Saturnian verse. Cicero is indignant that he should thus
attempt to disparage the merits of Naevius, whose work, if
not as polished as that of Ennius, at least showed promise
of high achievement. Ennius was, in fact, indebted to the
older poet in many things, and implicitly at least paid a
tribute to the value of Naevius' Epic, when, in recounting
the various campaigns of Rome, he had omitted[1] to deal
with the First Punic War, as having already been treated
by his predecessor.

But, apart from such a tribute, Ennius was convinced
that he himself had made a striking advance on all who had
gone before him. Livius and Naevius had
His own achievements also fallen under the spell of the Greeks, but
Ennius evidently felt that he had drunk more
deeply than they at the fountain-head[2] of the true Hellenic
tradition. The famous dream,[3] conceived under Pythagorean
influence, in which Homer appeared to the Latin poet, and
revealed that his soul had passed into him, is evidence of
Ennius' belief that through his works the spirit of the
Homeric Epic had migrated to Roman soil. He adapted
the machinery of Homer's mythology to his own Epic, and,

---

[1] Cic. Br. 76 ; there is no reason to doubt the substantial accuracy
of Cicero's statement here, though Ennius certainly touched on certain
aspects of the First Punic War ; cf. Norden, Ennius und Vergilius, p.
63 *et seq.*, 148, 171 ; Steuart, op. cit., p. 149 ; Vahlen, Introd., p. 179
et seq.
[2] His invocation of the Muses instead of the Camenae is significant ; Val.,
fr. I ; cf. Varro, Satirae, Riese, p. 183, XXII : " Pacuvi discipulus dicor,
porro is fuit Enni, Ennius Musarum " ; Prop. III. 3, 6.
[3] Val., frs. 2–3 ; Steuart, Bk. I. 2–5 (with notes) ; cf. Lucr., I. 123
et seq. ; Cic. De Rep., VI. 10. 10 ; Hor. Ep., II. 1. 50 ; Persius, Sat., VI.
10 (with Scholiast's notes) ; Fronto (ed. Haines), Vol. I. pp. 94, 98, 204;
vide infra, p. 48.

true to Homeric tradition, had chosen the hexameter[1] as the metre of the poem. He thus regarded himself as the Latin Homer,[2] and in that spirit set about the task of fashioning from Latin a garb that would be worthy of his theme. A true lover of Homer would, however, find the Roman poet too lavish in his employment of devices, some of which were legitimate in poetry, but others alien to its nature. The fragments[3] of the *Annales* furnish us with examples of alliteration, homoeoteleuton, antithesis, isokolon, internal assonance, and play upon words. If the poem were extant as a whole, we would probably find that such devices were very extensively employed. In this, Ennius was probably in part influenced by Greek rhetoric, though he could find examples of alliteration and internal assonance in the old Italian carmina[4], while his predecessors, Naevius and Plautus[5], were addicted to many of these devices. Ennius himself would probably consider that his greatest contribution to the poetical language of Rome lay in his use of single words. Suetonius[6] mentions, only to reject, a tradition which credited him with treatises entitled *De Metris*, and *De Litteris Syllabisque*, but, though the tradition may have no foundation, it is clear that he regarded himself as more concerned than his predecessors for the niceties of language. To the mind of Lucretius[7] he was the first who succeeded in importing into Latium the glory of Greek poetry. Cicero pays a tribute[8] to his choice of ornate and appropriate words, while Horace commends[9] him for having enriched the

---

[1] Livius had already employed the hexameter in the hymn to Diana in his tragedy Ino; cf. Ribbeck, Tragicorum Latinorum Reliquiae, p. 3; Leo, Geschichte der röm. Literatur, p. 71.

[2] His admirers spoke of him as " alter Homerus ", Hor. Ep. II. 1. 50; cf. Lucilius, fr. 1189 (ed. Marx).

[3] Cf. Val., fr. 150; Steuart, Bk. VIII. fr. 2, Bk. VI. fr. 9; such devices are frequent also in his tragedies.

[4] *Vide* Lejay, Histoire de la Littérature Latine, p. 141 *et seq.*, 151 *et seq.*, for examples ; *vide infra*, p. 454.

[5] Bacchides, 1086 *et seq.*, furnishes some typical examples.

[6] De Gram., C. I.

[7] I. 117.

[8] De Or. I. 154 ; cf. Or. 36, where Cic. quotes some critic as admiring him, " quod non discedit a communi more verborum."

[9] A.P. 56.

Latin language. Ennius allows himself a generous licence in the coinage of words, and sought by his many new compounds[1] to impart to Latin something of the splendour and richness of Homeric diction. He was happier in his coinages than Pacuvius, whose monstrous creations[2] were derided by many critics. The purism of the Augustan age in general rejected such compounds, but the influence of Ennius on many of the later poets is proof of his success in giving an appropriate dress to his Epic, and in developing and enriching the language of poetry among the Romans. He clearly rejoiced in the felicity of some of his phrases.[3] Apart, however, from his diction, he did much to stabilise[4] the laws of the Latin hexameter, though he exhibited a certain monotony in his verse, and allowed himself licences which later poets avoided. The genius of Virgil succeeded in avoiding monotony by the variation of the feet, and by a skilful use of the caesura and of periodic structure, while his feeling for rhythm enabled him to awaken new harmonies from the hexameter, but even Ennius could produce effects of rhythm[5] and word painting remarkable in so early a poet. In view of all that he accomplished, his conviction that he had surpassed his predecessors is not surprising. His criticism of them implies that, as compared with them, he himself was " dicti studiosus," and it may be taken too as evidence of a belief that, to the limit of his powers, he was trying to grapple with the most serious problem facing a poet at the time, that of transforming a language of comparative crudeness into a medium of artistic expression.

Terence occupies no inconsiderable place in the history of criticism at Rome. The prologue of his first play, the

---

[1] e.g. altitonans, altivolans, velivolus, bellipotens, suaviloquens ; Naevius, too, furnishes examples of such coinages, e.g., suavisonus, frundifer, arquitenens.

[2] *Vide infra*, p. 50.

[3] Val., frs. 37, 89 : stellis fulgentibus aptum ; cf. fr. 202 : " nox stellis ardentibus apta."

[4] Mueller, Q. Ennius, p. 218 *et seq.* ; Norden, Aen., Bk. VI. p. 418 *et seq.*

[5] Val. fr. 296 : " labitur uncta carina," etc. ; fr. 262 : " it eques et plausu cava concutit ungula terram "; cf. fr. 152 ; Steuart, Bk. VI, fr. 9 *et seq.*

Andria, which may[1] have been written for the second per-
formance of the piece, places us at once in
Literary pole- an atmosphere of literary polemic. It is a
mic in Terence
prologue distinct from the play, which he was
compelled to write, not for the purpose of unfolding the
plot of his piece, but of answering the abuse of a " malevo-
lent old poet." By this note of polemic he brought his
prologue into line with the parabasis of the Old Comedy.

In the opening[2] of the *Andria* prologue, as well as in the
prologues to the *Heautontimorumenos* and the *Phormio,*
Terence speaks as if Luscius Lanuvinus were his only
enemy, but other passages[3] make it clear that Luscius was
not alone in his opposition. It is evident that these opponents
formed a close corporation of their own, and were jealous
of the sudden rise of a new star.[4] Their jealousy naturally
increased, as the success of the young dramatist became
assured. Luscius Lanuvinus and his circle obviously
claimed to be superior critics,[5] and may have belonged to
the official guild of poets,[6] the " collegium poetarum " as
it came to be styled, which traced its origin to Livius
Andronicus. Terence, backed by the powerful influence of
aristocratic friends, could afford to stand aloof from this
official guild, but the literary quarrels that ensued, shed
much light on the character of the " genus irritabile vatum,"
and on the bitterness that prevailed in the literary coteries
of the time. It is clear that Terence's enemies made determined[7] but unsuccessful efforts to discourage him from his
labours. The young dramatist asserts[8] the right of every

[1] Schanz, Röm. Litteraturgeschichte, I. 1. p. 141; Meyer, Quaestiones
Terentianae, p. 41 *et seq.*; however, Luscius Lanuvinus may have come to
a knowledge of the piece, when the aediles purchased it; cf. Eun. Prol. 20.
[2] Prol. 6; cf. Heauton. Prol. 22, Phormio, Prol., *passim.*
[3] Andria, Prol. 15 : " isti vituperant "; *ib.* 21 : " istorum obscuram
diligentiam "; cf. Hecyra, Prol. II. 54, Adelphi, 2, 15, Heauton. Prol. 27.
[4] Heauton. Prol. 23.
[5] Andria, Prol. 17 : " faciuntne intellegendo ut nihil intellegant."
[6] Cf. E. G. Sihler, The Collegium Poetarum at Rome, Am. Jour. of
Phil., XXVI. 1905, p. 1 *et seq.*; originally it was styled " collegium scri-
barum et histrionum "; cf. Plaut. Asin. 746, where scriba = poeta ; *vide
infra,* p. 50.
[7] Phormio, Prol. I *et seq.*
[8] *Ib.* 16.

man to compete for the prize, where the arts of the Muses
are concerned. He does not wish the drama to become the
monopoly[1] of a small circle. It may be reasonably con-
jectured[2] that the poet Caecilius was beset with opposition
similar to that which Terence encountered, and had to
struggle against similar malignity.

Terence was thus forced by circumstances to indulge in
literary polemic in his prologues, but even from the first
He eschews the
Prologue of
exposition he seems to have ruled out[3] the prologue of
exposition as an inartistic device, though
many regarded[4] exposition as the proper
function of the prologue. In the prologue to the *Adelphi* he
warns the spectators not to expect to hear beforehand the
plot of the piece, which will be revealed to them within the
play, partly by narrative, partly by action. The prologue
of exposition was the special creation of Euripides, who,
with his tendency to modify the old legends, found it particularly useful for purposes of clearness. We should like to
have more knowledge of the practice followed in their
prologues by the New Comedy writers, but the extraordinary
variety of Plautus' prologues may (in so far as they are
genuine) be a reflex[5] of his Greek originals. Some of Plautus'
comedies have no prologue, but, where he employs one, it
was customary with him to reveal[6] in it the outlines of the
plot. However, from the prologues of two of his plays,
the *Asinaria* and *Trinummus*,[7] he expressly excludes ex-

---

[1] Hecyra, Prol. II. 46 : " nolite sinere per vos artem musicam recidere
ad paucos "; Norwood, The Art of Terence, p. 139, interprets this passage
as an expression of Terence's desire to uplift the popular taste in comedy, but
the other interpretation seems to suit better the circumstances of the poet at
the time.

[2] Cf. Hecyra, Prol. II. 21 *et seq.* ; *vide infra*, p. 17.

[3] Andria, Prol. 6, Adelphi, Prol. 22.

[4] Terence seems to reflect this view in Andria, Prol. 6 ; cf. Donatus *ad loc.*,
Wessner, Vol. I. p. 43 ; Eugraphius *ad loc.* : " non ut argumentum narret,
quod prologorum est *semper* officium."

[5] Cf. Leo, Plautinische Forschungen, p. 215 ; Fabia, Les Prologues de
Térence, p. 77 *et seq.* ; Michaut, Sur les Trétaux latins, p. 153 *et seq.*

[6] Cf. Menaechmi, Prol. 14 *et seq.*

[7] Prol. 16 : " sed de argumento ne expectetis fabulae "; cf. fragments of
Vidularia, Prol. 10 ; the Asinaria prologue may, however, have been composed after Plautus' time.

position, because there were no serious complications in these comedies. At times the prologues of Plautus are delivered by gods or allegorical personages, and are occasionally pronounced[1] after the opening of the play. The employment by Menander[2] of Ἄγνοια, Ἥρως Θεός, and Ἔλεγχος, to pronounce his prologues, shows that the use of such allegorical personages was a favourite device with the Greek writers of the New Comedy. Such prologues, apart from their utilitarian purpose, were beloved by many as investing the drama with an element of beauty and mystery. Yet Terence[3] by deliberate choice renounced all such possibilities for effect, and preferred the more delicate and subtle economy of making his exposition within the compass of the play. His opponents, whether it was that they regarded the other types of prologue as a source of beauty, or considered that Terence was not being faithful enough to his originals, were evidently averse to the innovation of the young dramatist.[4] They declared that only for the attacks of Luscius he would never have succeeded in writing a prologue.

Naturally, the polemical character of his prologues was not to their liking. It is difficult to say how far Terence found a precedent for such polemics in the **Polemic in the New Comedy** Greek writers of the New Comedy,[5] though traces of literary quarrels are not wanting in them. Plautus, probably under their influence, furnishes us with some instances of literary criticism and polemic, as when in his prologue to the *Amphitruo*[6] he deals with the nature of Tragi-Comedy, or in the *Menæchmi*[7] reflects on

[1] Cf. the Cistellaria and Miles Gloriosus.

[2] Allison, Menander, pp. 204, 296 ; Legrand, The New Greek Comedy, p. 389 ; Capps, Four Plays of Menander, p. 152 ; Terzaghi, Fabula, p. 175 *et seq.*

[3] Evanthius, De Comoedia, III. 2, Wessner, Vol. I. p. 18; cf. Donatus ad Hecyra, 58, ad Andria, 28.

[4] Phormio, Prol. 13.

[5] Cf. Dziatzko-Kauer, Adelphoe, p. 26 ; Legrand, op. cit., p. 403, on Antiphanes' Prologue to the Ποίησις, and on the Strassburg Prologue ; C. R. Post, The Dramatic Art of Menander, Harvard Studies, Vol. 24. p. 128, on the question of personal satire in Diphilus.

[6] 51 *et seq.*

[7] Prol. 7 *et seq.*

the custom prevailing among writers of Comedy of placing
the scene at Athens, or in the *Captivi*[1] makes a special plea
for a play that lacks many of the stock characters, and is free
from salacious elements. Again, in the *Mercator*[2] we find
him ridiculing the extravagance of the stage lovers. But
Plautus discusses no really subtle matters of dramatic technique, and in his prologues generally endeavours to speak
to the capacity of his audience. Their prolix and witty
character was designed to tickle the ears of the groundlings.
Terence seems to have taken much less account of his
audience, or else he would have abstained from discussing
critical problems, and have had recourse to the prologue of
exposition to facilitate the understanding of the play.

Both from him and from Plautus we get many side-lights
on the crude taste of Roman play-goers of the time.[3] The
appeal to the audience for a favourable hear-
The Roman audience ing was, of course, part of the " captatio
benevolentiae,"[4] at which the prologues with
their rhetorical character aimed, but the din and disorder
among the spectators, and their predilection for lower forms
of amusement, must have placed a severe strain on the
actors of a Roman comedy, and have made such appeals[5]
necessary. Even in later ages[6] at Rome, there is evidence of
the depraved tastes of the play-going public, and its lack of
appreciation for the drama. Terence in his day had bitter
experience of its crudeness in the double failure of his
Hecyra, and he gives[7] us a vivid picture of the difficulties,

---

[1] Prol. 55 *et seq.*; Leo, Plaut. Forsch., p. 217, Legrand, op. cit., p. 408,
argue for the polemical character of the Vidularia prologue, but it is too
mutilated to allow any decisive argument to be drawn from it.

[2] I. 3 *et seq.*

[3] Even at Athens complaints were sometimes made of the dullness of the
audience ; cf. Philemon on ἀκροατὴς ἀσύνετος (Kock, fr. 143).

[4] Cf. the appeal of Ἄγνοια in Menander, Allison, p. 208.

[5] Cf. the Prologues to the Captivi and Poenulus ; cf. Eun. Prol. 44,
Phormio, Prol. 30 ; Michaut, op. cit., pp. 24, 449–450.

[6] Cicero, however, speaks of the quickness of the audience to detect a
false quantity, De Or. III. 196, Or. 173 ; cf. Dionys., De Comp. Verb.,
C. XI ; the audience in Cicero's day was more cultured, but the level of
appreciation for the drama was still low ; cf. the author's Horace and his
Age, pp. 289–90.

[7] Hecyra, Prol. I. 4 ; II. 34 *et seq.*

including " clamor mulierum,"[1] against which the actors
had to struggle. The play of bustle and action, with an
element of broad farce, had most attraction for such an
audience, so that Ambivius was forced to make a special
plea[2] for a favourable hearing of the *Heautontimorumenos*, a
play of quiet movement (fabula stataria). An audience of
this character would require material help[3] to understand
anything in the nature of a complicated plot, especially in a
play with a recognition scene. In spite of all this, Terence
chose to renounce the prologue of exposition, and to discuss
questions of literary and dramatic interest before a body of
playgoers who would be little likely to appreciate such
delicate problems. Though he endeavours at times to conciliate them, and pays them the compliment of appointing
them judges in the dispute between himself and his opponents, yet it looks as if his primary appeal was to the
intellectuals of his day, and especially to those of his own
literary circle. His appeal being such, he could afford to
abandon the prologue of exposition, because it was at the
best an inartistic device. Moreover, he had faith[4] in his
own ability to overcome the difficulties of exposition by other
means.

In spite, however, of his confidence, Terence did not
always solve the problem of exposition in the most artistic
way. It is, indeed, one of the most formid-
able problems[5] that the dramatist has to face,
as it requires no little skill to effect it in a
natural and unobtrusive manner. Some modern dramatists
continue to give exposition of necessary details till the play
is far advanced, but the Ancients as a rule confined their
exposition to the opening scenes. The old commentators
on Terence remarked his fondness for employing a " pro-

*The problem
of exposition*

---

[1] Norwood, op. cit., p. 98, suggests that possibly the women were scanda-
lized by the favourable picture of the courtesan Bacchis in the play ; *vide
infra*, p. 21.

[2] Prol. 35 ; cf. Fabia, op. cit., p. 211 *et seq.*

[3] Plautus at times gives a double exposition, as in the Captivi.

[4] Adelphi, Prol. 22 *et seq.*, is evidence of such confidence.

[5] Cf. Archer, Playmaking, C. VIII ; Clayton Hamilton, Problems of the
Playwright, pp. 14–5 ; cf. Legrand, op. cit., p. 412 *et seq.*, on exposition in
the Greek dramatists ; Lucas, Tragedy, p. 81 *et seq.*

sopon protaticon,"[1] a character whose chief function in the play was to facilitate the task of exposition. Such were the characters of Sosia[2] in the *Andria*, Philotis and Syria in the *Hecyra*, and Davus in the *Phormio*. For the use of such characters the poets of the New Comedy were again indebted to Euripides.[3] Exposition within the play could be made either through monologue or dialogue, but, as his ancient commentators remarked, Terence showed a preference for dramatic dialogue.[4] Terence's commentators did not seè that even the employment of the " prosopon protaticon " had its defects, as it was difficult to eliminate an element of improbability from the introduction of such a character. However, the attention which these commentators gave to Terence's method of exposition, shows that they regarded it as an advance on the crude device of the narrative prologue. How far Terence was indebted to the Greek originals for the " prosopon protaticon " it would be difficult to say. It is probable that Apollodorus had recourse to it, and that in this respect Terence, both in the *Phormio*[5] and *Hecyra*, was following closely in his footsteps. It is significant enough that there is no clearly established instance of the " prosopon protaticon " in Menander,[6] who may have regarded it as a mark of inferior dramatic technique, and certainly would hardly have commended Terence's extensive use of it.

There was evidently, also, a conflict of ideals between Terence and his opponents as to the freedom with which the Greek originals should be handled. The question was one that would naturally arise at a period, when Roman literature was so

Relation to the Greek models

[1] Evanthius, De Fabula, Wessner, Vol. ·1, p. 19: "προτατικὰ πρόσωπα, id est personas extra argumentum accersitas quibus Terentius saepe utitur."

[2] Donatus ad Andria, 28; *ib.* 172: " peracta narratione jam persona Sosiae non erat necessaria "; cf. ad Phormio, 35, ad Hecyra, 58.

[3] Leo, Plaut. Forsch., p. 244; *ib.* p. 194, on the use of ' prosopa protatica' in Plautus.

[4] Donatus ad Andria, 28: " ut agi res magis quam narrari videantur."

[5] Donatus, ad Phormio, 49–50.

[6] Capps, op. cit, pp. 6, 27, believes that the character of Geta in the Hero is an instance of it, but the play is too fragmentary to allow of any definite conclusion; cf. Leo, Plaut. Forsch., p. 243.

dependent on the Greek, and it was at that time one of the most important problems in criticism. Luscius Lanuvinus and his followers believed in pedantic accuracy[1] in dealing with the Greek models. Their own translations were exact, but their Latin style was poor. Terence did not favour such close adherence to his originals, though in the *Adelphi*[2] he confesses to having taken a passage word for word from Diphilus, and introduced it into his play. In such a close translation he was following the practice of his opponents and, possibly, by thus openly avowing it, he hoped to minimise in their eyes the offence of " contamination." In his first play he had practised contamination, and this was made the basis of one of the most serious charges brought against him.

The term " contaminare " etymologically means to bring one thing into relation with another, while it has the secondary[3] sense of defiling. As a term in criticism it was probably new, and seems to have been first[4] employed as such by Luscius and his friends. The word was used to describe the practice of fusing together scenes from two or more Greek originals, though Donatus applies[5] the term to the transference of a single thought from another play. Terence's practice seems to have been confined as a rule to the fusion of *two* originals, though his enemies tried to create the impression[6] that it went much further. When accused of contamination in the *Andria*, he does not deny the charge. He admits having transferred from the *Perinthia*, another play of Menander not dissimilar in plot, whatever he found

"Contamina-
tion"

---

[1] Andria, Prol. 21 : " istorum obscuram diligentiam "; Eun. Prol. 7 : " qui bene vortendo et easden scribendo male "; Kunst, Studien zur grie-chisch-römischen Komödie, p. 66.

[2] Prol. 11 ; *vide infra*, p. 20.

[3] Cf., however, Donatus ad Andria, 16 : " *proprie* est manibus luto plenis aliquid attingere "; cf. Meyer, op. cit., p. 14 *et seq.*

[4] Andria, Prol. 15 : " in eo disputant contaminari non decere fabulas."

[5] Ad Andria, 959 : " hanc sententiam totam Menandri de Eunucho transtulit, et hoc est quod dicitur ' contaminari non decere fabulas '."

[6] Heauton. Prol. 17 : " multas contaminasse Graecas, dum facit paucas Latinas "; however, the addition of the characters Byrria and Charinus to the Andria, especially if they were taken from a dramatist other than Menan-der, would go to confirm this charge ; *vide infra*, p. 14 n. 2.

suitable for his purpose. The *Andria* of Menander had for its opening scene a monologue spoken by an old man, while his *Perinthia* opened with a dialogue between Simo and his wife. Terence adopted[1] the dialogue form, but with a change in which for the person of the wife he substituted that of the freedman Sosia. Donatus tells us[2] of another addition made to the play in the characters of Byrria and Charinus, introduced to serve as a foil to Pamphilus and Davus, and to make the piece more varied and complex. Terence's introduction[3] in this comedy of a second love intrigue throws some light on the purpose of contamination, and its value in enriching the action of a play, and imparting to it greater movement and more diversity of interest. He was certainly a successful contaminator, and was so skilful in welding the alien elements to his play that, without the help of his own admissions and the guidance of Donatus, the jointings would remain undetected.

It is clear from the prologue to the *Heautontimorumenos* that Terence's opponents had charged him with an exten-

The ' Eunuch '   sive[4] employment of contamination. There is, however, no specific charge of contamination made against the *Heautontimorumenos* itself, though modern[5] commentators have tried to find evidence of it in the play. But from the prologue[6] to the *Eunuch* we learn that Terence's old enemies are again active. Luscius had been allowed to examine the play after it had been purchased by the aediles, and during the rehearsal he proclaimed that Terence was a plagiarist, and had taken his characters of the captain and the parasite from an old play, the *Flatterer*,

---

[1] Donatus ad Andria, 14.

[2] Ad Andria, 301 : " has personas addidit fabulae ; nam non sunt apud Menandrum "; D. possibly means not in the Andria of Menander ; cf. Fabia, op. cit., p. 182 ; Norwood, op. cit., p. 31, regards these characters as dramatically useless.

[3] Cf. Donatus ad Andria, 977 ; Evanthius, De Fabula, III, 9.

[4] Though Terence so far had published only two plays, the Andria and the Hecyra.

[5] Cf. Schanz, I. i. p. 147, for a discussion of the question ; Gaffiot, Revue de Phil., 1904, p. 128 *et seq.*, having weighed the pros and cons, leaves the question undecided ; cf. Fabia, op. cit., p. 188 *et seq.*

[6] 20 *et seq.*

already adapted by Naevius and Plautus. Terence converted the offence from one of plagiarism into one of contamination, by admitting that he had transferred the characters[1] of the parasite and braggart soldier from Menander's *Kolax* to his present play, but denying all knowledge of any previous representation of the play on the Roman stage. He seems to have selected the characters as typical[2] of the New Comedy,[3] but probably, too, from a desire to pander somewhat to the tastes of his audience, as Plautus so often does, by introducing an element of buffoonery and broad farce. He effected other changes in the *Eunuch*, for instance in the names[4] borne by certain of his characters. He, moreover, introduced the character of Antipho[5] to eliminate the long monologue in which Chaerea recounts his misdeeds, substituting for it a more dramatically effective dialogue. There are traces, too, of certain changes in characterisation,[6] so that many indications point to an extensive[7] use of contamination in this play, unless we give credit to the originality of the Roman dramatist for some of the alterations effected.

The *Adelphi*, modelled on Menander, is also a play in which Terence admits contamination. On this occasion he

The "Adelphi"

took over a scene from another dramatist, Diphilus, whose play, the *Synapothnescontes*, had been turned into Latin by Plautus under the title of *Commorientes*. At the opening of the original play of Diphilus was a scene, in which a young girl was forcibly carried off from a slave-dealer. This scene had not been used by Plautus, and Terence thought himself justified in

---

[1] Gnatho and Thraso; cf. Donatus ad Eun. 228.

[2] *Vide* Norwood, op. cit., p. 66 *et seq.*, on the Thraso scenes; cf. Fabia, op. cit., p. 183; Ribbeck, Alazon, p. 37 *et seq.*; cf. Menander, Περικειρομένη, 234 *et seq.* (Capps, p. 175), for a mock siege similar to that in the Eunuch.

[3] Lamachus was typical of the " miles gloriosus " in the Old Comedy.

[4] Cf. Schol. ad Persius, V. 161; Davus, Chaerestratus, Chrysis, appear as Parmeno, Phaedria, and Thais; cf. Donatus ad Eun. 971.

[5] Cf. Donatus ad Eun. 539.

[6] Donatus ad 507: " haec persona (Chremes) apud Menandrum adulescentis rustici est "; *ib.* ad 689, for a misunderstanding of Menander on Terence's part.

[7] *Vide* Leo, Geschichte der röm. Lit., p. 243.

embodying[1] it (translated word for word) in the *Adelphi*.
The audience is asked to judge whether his proceeding was
plagiarism[2] (*furtum*), or the recovery of an episode that had
been lost through the negligence of Plautus. Evidently
Terence did not regard his action as plagiarism, inasmuch
as the scene in question had never before been represented
on the Roman stage. Varro, we are told,[3] preferred
Terence's opening in the *Adelphi* to that of Menander, which
indicates that Terence here also had departed from his
original, at least in details. Though attempts[4] have been
made to detect in what respects he diverged from Menander,
they have not been successful, and it is probable that, if any
considerable alterations had been made, Donatus would have
noted them. The latter does, however, indicate[5] slight
changes effected by Terence both here and in other parts of
the play. The most important change of all concerned the
forced marriage[6] of Micio to Sostrata at the close of the play.
While Micio in Menander offers no opposition to the
marriage, in the Latin version he shows himself adverse to
the proposal. Various views[7] have been put forward as to
the dramatic propriety of the incident, but it was really an
effective stroke on Terence's part to exhibit Micio as caught
in the meshes of his own complacency, and compelled to
live up to his usual standard of easy indulgence. The
incident is a proof that the Roman dramatist, at any rate in
details, could strike out on original lines, not content with
a mere slavish imitation of his originals.

Terence, in face of his opponents' charges, not merely
admits contamination, but declares[8] that he will practise it

---

[1] Scene 155–208; cf. Dziatko-Kauer, Adelphoe, Introd., p. 11; *vide*
Norwood, op. cit., p. 126, on the Sannio passages.

[2] Evidently Terence's opponents had raised the cry of plagiarism.

[3] Suetonius, Life of Terence, 2.

[4] *Vide* Dziatzko-Kauer, op. cit., Introd., p. 12 ; Legrand, op. cit., p. 277.

[5] Cf. Adelphi, 275 : " Menander mori illum (i.e. Ctesipho) voluisse
fingit, Terentius profugere "; cf. ad 43, 81, 351.

[6] Donatus, ad 938 : " apud Menandrum senex de nuptiis non gravatur :
ergo Terentius εὑρετικῶς "; Lessing, by taking " gravatur " as passive,
wished to eliminate from Menander all question of Micio's marriage.

[7] Norwood, op. cit., p. 129.

[8] Heauton. Prol. 19–20.

again.   He evidently realised to the full its value for imparting richness,[1] variety,[2] and animation to his plays, and
must have felt that it was a field in which
The value of contamination the Roman imitators of Greek models had
scope for originality, above all if it were practised, as he himself had practised it, by the deft and artistic fusion of different originals.   It is not surprising then that contamination was favoured almost from the time when Roman literature first became imitative, so that Terence, in support of his own practice, was able to appeal[3] to the example set by Naevius, Plautus, and Ennius.   We are not in a position to judge of Naevius' success as a " contaminator."   Ennius[4] probably had recourse to contamination both in his comedies and tragedies.   Plautus[5] never acquired the same skill in it as Terence.   Caecilius has been credited[6] with not employing it, but the proofs adduced—the omission of his name by Terence from the list of those who had practised it, and Varro's award[7] of the palm to him for pre-eminence " in argumentis "—cannot be regarded as conclusive.   Contamination is quite compatible with excellence in plot construction.   Terence's sympathetic[8] reference to Caecilius gives no support to the theory that the latter was definitely on the side of Luscius in opposing contamination.   In fact, the second prologue of the *Hecyra*

---

[1] It has been suggested that some scenes at least, in which more than three actors appear, are the result of contamination, but this, of course, can only be taken as a conjecture ; cf. Legrand, op. cit., p. 294 ; Flickinger, The Greek Theater and its Drama, p. 188.

[2] It is interesting to note that there is no evidence of contamination in the Hecyra and Phormio, based on Apollodorus ; Terence probably considered them varied enough in themselves.

[3] Andria, Prol. 18 ; Heauton. Prol. 20.

[4] *Vide* Leo, Gesch. der röm. Lit., p. 193 ; Fabia, op. cit., p. 195 *et seq.*

[5] Legrand, op. cit., p. 48 *et seq.*, 280 ; Dziatzko-Hauler, Phormio, Introd., pp. 8–9 ; Leo, Plaut. Forsch., p. 99 *et seq.*, 169 *et seq.* ; cf. Jachmann in Χάριτες (1911), p. 249 *et seq.*, for an examination of contamination in the Poenulus.

[6] *Vide* Legrand, op. cit., p. 283 ; Schanz, op. cit., I. i. p. 133 ; Leo, op. cit., p. 100.

[7] " In argumentis Caecilius poscit palmam "; cf. Riese, Varronis Satiræ, p. 191.

[8] Hecyra, Prol. II. 14 *et seq.*

seems rather to suggest that Caecilius had to face malignant criticism from the same source which sought to thwart Terence's own ambitions. The comparison which Gellius[1] institutes between the *Plocium* of Caecilius and that of Menander, shows that the Latin poet could handle his originals with a certain freedom, even though his alterations did not always tend to approximate to the grace and charm of the Greek dramatist. This, however, is not the place to enter on the larger problem of the general attitude of the Roman dramatists to their Greek models. The question of contamination was merely one aspect of the problem, but one of considerable importance for the dramatists of the early period.

Plagiarism was another of the problems raised by Terence's opponents, and one that, as part of the general **Plagiarism** question of Imitation,[2] is not without its interest in the history of criticism among the Ancients. In Roman literature we find it explicitly raised for the first time in Terence's prologues.[3] Charges of plagiarism abounded among the Greeks, and an extensive[4] literature περὶ κλοπῆς grew up in course of time. As an offset to accusations of plagiarism stood the many claims[5] made to priority of invention. Aristophanes[6] in his own day roundly charged some of his rivals with plagiarism, and they responded with similar charges against him. At a later period, when the works of the Classical authors were studied more intensively, even though plagiarism had not taken place, parallels between various authors were construed as such, so that poets, historians, orators, and philosophers were all involved in the charge. Cicero accuses[7] Ennius of borrowing from Naevius, or of thieving, if he denies the debt.

[1] II. 23.
[2] *Vide infra*, p. 426 *et seq.*
[3] Eun. 23 ; Adelphi, 13.
[4] *Vide* Stemplinger, Das Plagiat in der griechischen Literatur, especially Part I.
[5] Aristoph. Clouds, 546 *et seq.*, Wasps, 784, Eccles. 578 ; Verg. Georg. III. 40 ; Hor. Ep., I. 19. 21 *et seq.* ; Prop. III. 1. 3.
[6] Clouds, 554 ; cf. Stemplinger, op. cit., p. 12.
[7] Br. 76 ; cf. De Fin. I. 3. 7, on his borrowings from Homer ; *ib.* V. 74, on plagiarism amongst the Stoics.

As we know from Macrobius, the " furta Vergiliana "[1] were a favourite topic amongst the enemies of the poet.

The Ancients, as a rule, though they condemned[2] barefaced plagiarism, had much less rigorous notions about **Similarity of motifs in the New Comedy** imitation than prevail in modern times. Terence, as we have seen,[3] when charged with plagiarism in the *Eunuch*, rebuts the charge by declaring that he did not know that the *Flatterer*, from which he had taken the characters of the braggart captain and the parasite, had already been adapted by Naevius and Plautus. He might well have claimed the right to set himself in rivalry with these two poets, but he evidently did not regard it as proper to make use of a play already presented to the Roman public. At the same time, he asserts[4] his right to introduce into his play characters similar to those employed by the poets who had gone before him ; for here he was confronted with a difficulty which lay in the path of all the writers of the New Comedy, the similarity[5] of motifs in their dramas, and the recurrence of so many stock characters, which laid them peculiarly open to the charge of plagiarism.[6] We are then not surprised to hear of the resemblance, noted by Sidonius Apollinaris,[7] between the *Hecyra* (derived from Apollodorus) and the *Epitrepontes* of Menander, nor need we wonder at the many parallelisms[8] in thought and incident in Terence's *Eunuch* and Menander's *Periceiromene*. Terence's declaration[9] " nul-

---

[1] *Vide infra*, pp. 289, 305.

[2] *Vide infra*, p. 428 *et seq.*

[3] *Vide supra*, p. 15.

[4] Eun. Prol. 35 *et seq.*

[5] Terence himself notes the similarity of plot in Menander's Andria and Perinthia ; cf. Andria, Prol. 11 ; cf. Stemplinger, op. cit., pp. 140–1 ; Terzaghi, Fabula, p. 131 *et seq.*, on the double titles in Greek Comedy.

[6] For charges of plagiarism against Menander himself, *vide* Stemplinger, pp. 7, 35–6 ; Legrand, op. cit., p. 238, quotes Xenarchus (a poet of the Middle Comedy) as saying that fishmongers have more fertile imaginations than poets ; cf. Kock, Xenarchus, fr. 7.

[7] Ep. IV. 12. 1 ; cf. Capps, op. cit., p. 36 *et seq.*, 108 ; Wilamowitz-Moellendorff, Menander, Das Schiedsgericht, p. 133.

[8] Cf. Περικειρομένη, 224, 234 *et seq.*, 355, 633 (*vide* Capps ad loc) ; Eun. 187, 771, 814, 753.

[9] Eun. Prol. 41.

lumst jam dictum quod non sit dictum prius," might serve
as a defence even for the plagiarist, but it was a defence
especially appropriate to a poet of the New Comedy, who
found it difficult to move out of the " vilem patulumque
orbem " marked out by those who had preceded him.

In the *Adelphi*,[1] Terence had once more to face the charge
of plagiarism, and he counters it by declaring that he simply
used a scene from the *Synapothnescontes* of
Diphilus which Plautus had omitted in
his version of that play. Here again he evidently considered it the fitting thing to abstain from adapting a scene already represented on the Roman stage. Hence
his insistence in many of his prologues[2] that his comedies
are new to the Roman public. He throws some light, however, on the Roman attitude to the Greek originals by his
further statement[3] that he translated the scene in question
word for word from Diphilus. The Roman dramatist,
though he might avoid a scene adapted by his predecessors,
thought it within his right to translate his Greek model as
literally as he pleased. In this instance Terence cannot claim
even the measure of originality left open to a translator who
gives a free[4] version, and reproduces the sense and not
merely the words of the original. However, his own practice, his defence of contamination, and the many details in
which he is noted by Donatus as modifying his originals,
show that in general he allowed himself a much larger
measure of freedom than in the Diphilus scene.

We have referred already to the difficulties[5] felt by
Terence with regard to the similarity of the
themes that were constantly recurring in
the New Comedy, and the impossibility
of avoiding characters and situations already found in his

The rights of the dramatist

*Stock charac-
ters and stage
conventions*

---

[1] *Vide supra*, p. 15.

[2] Heauton. Prol. 4 (cf. Eugraphius *ad loc.*), *ib.* 7, 29 ; Phormio, Prol. 24,
Adelphi, Prol. 12.

[3] Adelphi, Prol. 11 ; *vide supra*, p. 13.

[4] Cf. Cicero, De Off. II. 60, De opt. gen. 14, Acad. Post., 10 ; contrast De Fin. I. 4, III. 15 ; Hor. A.P. 133, on mechanical reproduction ;
vide Stemplinger, op. cit., p. 210 *et seq.* ; Leo, Plaut. Forsch., p. 77 *et seq.*,
for some interesting remarks on the Roman art of translation ; *vide infra*,
p. 429.   [5] Cf. Eun. Prol. 35 *et seq.*

predecessors. The slave, especially the bustling slave,[1] was one of the stock characters[2] of the New Comedy that by his farcical conduct could always be relied on to make a strong appeal to an unlettered audience. Terence himself had employed him on occasion,[3] but it is evident that he at times felt the irksomeness of dealing always with such conventional types of character. The *Heautontimorumenos* is a drama of quiet action.[4] Ambivius, in the prologue, pleads with the audience to give it a fair hearing, as he does not wish to play eternally[5] rôles that demand boisterous acting. There is here a reaction against such rôles as much on the part of the dramatist as on the part of the leading actor. In the *Hecyra*, Terence has given us the reverse[6] of some of the usual characters of comedy, especially in his sympathetic portrait of Bacchis. Gnatho[7] claims that he himself has invented something new in the art of the parasite, and discarded old methods. We see again a reaction[8] against the publicity usual in comedies, when Pamphilus and Bacchis determine to keep their secret to themselves. Terence, too, has his thrust[9] at the old device, designed to relieve the embarrassment of lovers, of proving that the girl involved

[1] Cf. Heauton. Prol. 31 *et seq.*, where Terence charges Luscius with a breach of decorum in making the crowd give way before a bustling slave ; cf. Calphurnius (quoted by Fabia, p. 272) : " in hoc notatur adversarius, qui decorem personae non servaverit."

[2] Cf. Plautus, Mercator, 111 *et seq.*, Amphitruo, Prol. 62 *et seq.*, *ib.* 986 *et seq.*; Curculio, 281 *et seq.*; cf. Hor. Ep. II. 1. 171 ; Q. XI. 3. 112 ; Apul. Flor. XVI. 64 ; Dieterich, Pulcinella, pp. 26–7, on such conventional types.

[3] Phormio, 179, Adelphi, 299 (with Donatus' notes).

[4] *Vide supra*, p. 11 ; contrast the Phormio ; cf. Donatus, Phormio, praef. 2 : " haec igitur tota motoria est."

[5] Heauton. Prol. 37 *et seq.*

[6] Cf. Donatus ad Hecyra, 727 : " meretrix loquitur et senex, et quod est admirabilius, bona meretrix, mitis senex, ut intellegas laborasse Terentium ut et a lege comicorum recederet," etc. ; Evanthius, De. Com., III. 4 (Wessner, Vol. I. p. 19) : " solus ausus est . . . etiam contra praescripta comica meretrices interdum non malas introducere "; cf. Thais, Eun. 197 *et seq.*; Norwood, op. cit., p. 93.

[7] Eun. 247.

[8] Hecyra, 866 : " non placet fieri hoc item ut in comoediis, omnia omnes ubi resciscunt."

[9] Andria, 220 *et seq.*

was a free-born Athenian citizen. The poets of the New Comedy, moreover, were alive to the limitations of the ancient stage, and the conventions that were necessary in view of such limitations. Terence in a passage of the *Andria*,[1] where the instructions which Lesbia should have given at the bedside of Glycerium, are shouted from the street, gives us a clear indication of the difficulties felt by a dramatist when faced with the necessity of representing an indoor[2] scene.

Plautus, too, as we have seen,[3] had his moments of reaction against certain conventions of the drama, and against the monotonous repetition of similar[4] characters and situations. He makes[5] a special claim for the *Captivi* that it excludes many of the stock characters of Comedy. Aristophanes,[6] in his own day, could ridicule the stale jokes and outworn devices of the poets of the Old Comedy, though he himself was not above employing them on occasion. If we had more extensive remains of the Greek poets of the New Comedy, we would probably find that the note of polemic and reaction in Plautus and Terence against conventional elements could, in some measure at least, be traced back to their models. The Strassburg Prologue[7] furnishes a specimen of such polemic in its criticism of the long rambling explanations of the Θεοὶ προλογίζοντες. Antiphanes, in his prologue to Ποίησις,[8] indulges in irony when criticising the writers of tragedy, and must have dealt in a similar spirit with many other matters relating to the drama. But, apart from all this, the Roman writers themselves would

Reaction against conventions

---

[1] 490 *et seq.* ; cf. Legrand, op. cit., p. 346 *et seq.* ; Montague, Dramatic Values, p. 126 *et seq.*, on the difficulties presented by stage conventions.

[2] Cf. Plautus, Aul. II. 1. 14.

[3] *Vide supra*, p. 9.

[4] On the " miles gloriosus " in comedy, cf. Ribbeck, Alazon, p. 26 *et seq.*, 55 *et seq.*

[5] Prol. 57–8 : " hic neque perjurus leno est, nec meretrix mala, neque miles gloriosus."

[6] Clouds, 540 *et seq.*, Wasps, 58 *et seq.*, Peace, 739 *et seq.*, Frogs, 1 *et seq.*

[7] Legrand, op. cit., p. 403 ; Wilamowitz-Moellendorff, Das Schiedsgericht, p. 146.

[8] Cf. Kock, Comicorum Atticorum Fragmenta, Antiphanes, fr. 191.

have felt, as they advanced, the irksomeness of dealing constantly with conventional characters and situations, and of having to employ devices that could be saved from absurdity only by signal skill on the part of the dramatist.

His opponents[1] cast the reproach against Terence that he was a new-comer in the world of letters, and relied for his success on the talent of his friends, and not on his own abilities. The reproach was evidently inspired by the jealousy felt by the guild of professional poets on the score of Terence's achievements, and of the influence which he enjoyed with the cultured nobles of the day. Terence tactfully refrains from denying the charge directly, and even declares that the accusation is an honour to him, as it is evidence that he enjoys the confidence of distinguished patrons. The tradition[2] that he was helped by his friends in the composition of his plays long persisted with certain variations and additions, some attributing the authorship of them to the younger Scipio, others to Laelius. Santra, however, was of the opinion that both these were too young to have aided Terence, who, if he had needed help, would rather have appealed for it to poets and scholars such as Sulpicius Gallus, Q. F. Labeo, and M. Popillius. Terence may have enjoyed the patronage of these latter, but the tradition[3] of his friendship with Scipio and the members of the Scipionic circle is still better authenticated. These, with their strong literary instincts, could have given Terence the benefit of advice and helpful criticism. The whole episode is interesting as indicating the rise of the coterie spirit in Roman literature. We have already[4] seen reasons for believing that

The authorship of Terence's plays

[1] Heauton. Prol. 22 *et seq.*; Adelphi, Prol. 15 *et seq.*

[2] Cic. Ad Att. VII. 3. 10; however, in De Amic. 89, he makes Laelius say : " quod in Andria familiaris meus dicit "; cf. Q. X. 1. 99 ; Suet., Life of Terence, 3–4 ; Vallegius (quoted by Donatus in his addition to Suetonius' Life, Wessner, Vol. I. p. 9) evidently regards Scipio as the author of the plays.

[3] Cf. Suet., Life, i. *ib.* 5, with quotations from Porcius Licinus (who as a follower of Marius shows his bias against the aristocracy) ; Donatus ad Adelphi, Prol. 15 ; Dziatzko-Hauler, Phormio, p. 21.

[4] *Vide supra*, p. 11.

Terence's primary appeal was not so much to the unlettered Roman public, as to the members of a select circle. His decided preference for Menander in his choice of models, the purity and elegance of his style, the restraint of his dialogue, his skill in character drawing, the absence in him of Plautus' boisterous vigour, were all calculated to make a strong appeal to a chosen and cultured few.

Luscius Lanuvinus, like Terence, chose Menander as one of his models, but reproduced him with pedantic accuracy, and marred[1] the beauty of his original by his defective style. Terence evidently felt that his own style[2] was something new in Rome. It was limpid and unadorned, remarkable for its correct and elegant diction, and thus was capable of transferring to Latin much of the lucid charm of Menander. The tributes[3] that Caesar and Cicero paid to him in later days, emphasise especially the choiceness and purity of his diction. In this quality of his we can discern the influence of the Scipionic circle, which laboured for the ideal of correct Latinity. We might call Terence's style " plain," without being bound[4] to the full significance of the word, as it is used in the division of the oratorical styles. The ancient critics were, however, much preoccupied with the categories of rhetorical styles, and it is interesting to note that Varro[5] considers Terence rather as a representative of the Middle Style, while Cicero, too, attributes to him qualities[6] which are characteristic of that style with its aim of giving delight. Both these critics looked upon him as a representative of it,

Terence's style

---

[1] *Vide supra,* p. 13.

[2] Cf. Heauton. Prol. 46 : " in hac est pura oratio "; Fabia, op. cit., p. 259, curiously interprets : " dans cette pièce il n'y a que discours "; in Cic. De Or. III. 37–8, Ad Her. IV. 12. 17, " Latinus " and " purus " are identified ; cf. καθαρός with its connotation of elegant, accurate, lucid ; Dionys. De Lysia, 2, De Comp. Verb. C. I ; Geigenmueller, Quaestiones Dionysianæ, p. 13 ; cf. Cic. Br. 274, where " purus " signifies lucid.

[3] " Puri sermonis amator " (Caesar); " lecto sermone " (Cicero) ; Q. X. 1. 99, calls his writings " elegantissima."

[4] Even though Luscius speaks of his plays as " tenui oratione ".

[5] Gellius, VII. 14. 6 : " mediocritatis Terentium "; cf. Leo, Gesch. der röm. Lit., Vol. I. p. 252 *et seq.*; *vide infra,* p. 467.

[6] " Quiddam come loquens atque omnia dulcia dicens "; cf. De Or. II. 129, on " lenitas " as an attribute of the Middle style.

probably owing to his success in character-drawing.[1]
Luscius, however, was dissatisfied with Terence's style,
which he regarded[2] as too plain and unadorned. Chiefly for
that reason, he considered his compositions trivial, and
meagre in their content. In comparison with Plautus and
Caecilius,[3] he would find his language less rich and varied,
exhibiting as it did little effort[4] at rhetorical colouring. He
would miss in him Plautus' vigour and vivacity, and probably also the scenes of heightened emotion to which he
himself was partial.

There was evidently a fundamental difference of opinion
between Terence and his opponents regarding not only the
The spirit of   style, but the elements appropriate to Com-
Comedy   edy. Among the ancient critics generally, it
seems to have been felt that the former
lacked the fire[5] necessary to portray emotion ; but,
whatever his natural powers may have been, he evidently
wished to avoid emotional passages that might border on the
tragic, and aimed at keeping clearly delimited the boundaries[6]
between the genres of Comedy and Tragedy. Evanthius has
well described[7] this quality in his plays : " ejus fabulae eo
sunt temperamento, ut neque extumescant ad tragicam
celsitudinem, neque abjiciantur ad mimicam vilitatem."
Luscius, in objecting to Terence's plain style, displays his
ignorance, says Donatus,[8] inasmuch as he condemns a style

---

[1] Cic. Or. 128 : "illud superius (ἠθικόν) come, jucundum, ad bene-
volentiam conciliandam paratum "; *vide infra*, p. 127 ; for Varro's judgment
on T. cf. Funaioli, Gram. Rom. Fragmenta, Vol. I, p. 203 ; cf. Cic. De
Inv., I. 27, who illustrates from T. " narratio quae versatur in personis."

[2] Phormio, Prol. 4–5 : " quas antehac fecit fabulas, tenui esse oratione
et scriptura levi."

[3] To whom Varro ascribes pre-eminence in πάθη; cf. Hor. Ep. II. 1.
59, on his " gravitas ".

[4] Except in his Prologues ; *vide infra*, p. 455.

[5] Cf. Cicero : " Menandrum in medium nobis sedatis vocibus effers ";
Caesar speaks of his " lenia scripta " (Fiske, Lucilius and Horace, p. 83,
wrongly reads " levia scripta ") ; Leo, Gesch. der röm. Lit., p. 254, interprets Caesar's reference to "lenia scripta " as placing Terence in the category
of the Plain style, but Cic. De Or., II. 129 (which he quotes), tells against
this view.   [6] Cic. De opt. gen. I. 1 ; Hor. A.P. 89.

[7] De Fabula, III. 5 ; *vide infra*, p. 403.

[8] Ad Phormio, Prol. 5.

especially suited to Comedy, which as a " species vitae "
demanded something akin to the language of everyday life.
He himself had a fondness for a richer and loftier style, just
as he favoured scenes of strong emotion. Terence condemns[1]
a scene in one of his comedies in which a young man, presumably a lover, is driven in his disappointment into
frenzied hallucinations. Such a scene, exhibited in sober
earnest, was in Terence's view alien to the spirit of Comedy,
which, however, for comic effect, may at times indulge in a
travesty of the lofty style. This latter was a favourite device
of Aristophanes[2] to raise a laugh, while some of his keenest
criticisms of the poets were delivered by way of parody.
Rhinthon had specialised in "hilaro-tragoediae," which relied for their effect on the incongruities that resulted from
setting the lofty personages of tragedy amidst the scenes of
common life. Plautus, probably in imitation of him, composed the *Amphitruo*, a Tragi-comedy as he called it,[3] which
gave abundant scope for a mock tragic style, while elsewhere[4] he parodies the elevated diction of Ennius. But, even
apart from parody, Comedy will occasionally choose to
raise[5] its tone above the speech of ordinary life in a passage
of heightened emotion. Terence, like his great prototype
Menander, has his elevated moments,[6] especially when he
portrays the grief of lovers, but his criticism of Luscius
shows that he was alive to the danger that such scenes might
easily transcend the limits of Comedy. With a clear conception of the genre in which he worked, and a fine sense

[1] Phormio, Prol. 6; cf. Eugraphius ad loc: "qui affectus a comoediis
longe videtur alienus"; cf. Plautus, Mercator, 931 *et seq.*, Menaechmi, 835
et seq.; Leo, Plaut. Forsch., p. 162, sees in the scene traces of a dream motif.
[2] Knights, 623 *et seq.*, Peace, 136; cf. Guglielmino, La Parodia nella
Commedia Greca Antica, p. 61 *et seq.*
[3] Prol. 59: "faciam ut commixta sit tragi-comoedia"; cf. *ib.* 51:
"post argumentum hujus eloquar tragoediae"; cf. Michaut, op. cit., p. 128
et seq.; Dieterich, Pulcinella, p. 27.
[4] Bacchides, 932; cf. Pseudolus, 707: "ut paratragoedat carnufex";
Kunst, op. cit., p. 124; Donatus describes Eun. 590 as a parody of Ennius;
cf. Ribbeck, Tragicorum Rom. Reliquiae, p. 57.
[5] Hor. A.P. 93, had Terence evidently in his mind.
[6] Cf. Donatus ad Adelphi, 790: "O Coelum, O Terra, O Maria Nep-
tuni!" *ib.* 610; Menander, Σαμία, 110, 328, is rather in the mock-
tragic style; *vide* Legrand, op. cit., p. 481; Capps, op. cit., p. 278.

of the style that was appropriate to it, he, as a rule, laboured to keep his plays on the level of ordinary life, and avoid everything in thought or diction that might savour of the tragic.[1]

Thus the prologues of Terence have raised many interesting problems, some of them, such as the question of exposition, concerned with the technique of the drama, others indicating the difficulties the New Comedy writers had to contend with in dealing with material that had become hackneyed and conventional. Certain aspects of the problem of imitation were discussed, and not the least interesting point in the prologues was the manifestation of a divergence of ideals regarding the subjects and style of Comedy.

We have already referred to the tradition of Terence's connection with the Scipionic Circle. The circle, apart from Terence and Lucilius, may seem to be of small importance for our purpose, as it gives us little in the way of explicit criticism, but yet the ideals that inspired it are indicative of a point of view that, indirectly at any rate, must have influenced the course of Roman criticism. We can form a fairly accurate estimate of its members from contemporary and subsequent writers. Laelius next to Scipio was the soul of it, and the friendship[2] of these two men was justly celebrated in antiquity. Lucilius[3] gives us a picture of Scipio's being escorted home by a host of friends, amongst them the poet himself, while he reveals the names of some members of the circle, when, in an ironical mood, he sets[4] forth the readers to whom he most wishes to appeal in his writings.

But it is Cicero that gives us most light on the composi-

---

[1] Cf. Donatus' tributes to him, Andria, 106, Hecyra, 281, Adelphi, 541 ; cf. Praef. to Phormio : " et in affectibus constituta paene majoribus quam comicus stylus posceret, nisi quod arte poetae omnia moderata sunt."

[2] Cic. De Or. II. 22, Lael. 104, *ib.* 4, 33, Br. 84–85, De Off. I. 108, De Rep. I. 18 ; Hor. Sat. II. 1. 72 ; Val. Max. VIII. 8. 1 ; Sen. Ep. 95. 72.

[3] Fr. 1142 (Marx, C. Lucilii Carminum Reliquiae) : " ibat forte domum ; sequimur multi atque frequentes."

[4] Frs. 592–594, ed. Marx, whose order I follow, unless otherwise indicated.

tion of this coterie. He found in it the embodiment of
many of his own ideals. Its desire to effect
**Its members
and ideals** a union on sane lines between Greek and
Roman culture would especially appeal to
him, while in its members he found enshrined the noblest
traditions of Republican Rome. In the *De Republica* he
brings them together to discuss the best form of constitution, and introduces[1] us to many of Scipio's associates,
Q. Tubero, Scipio's nephew, Furius Philus, Rutilius, Sp.
Mummius, Q. Scaevola, the historian C. Fannius, and the
jurist M. Manilius. Probably Sulpicius Gallus,[2] though
not present, shared their ideals. In the same work Cicero
gives us glimpses[3] of the relation between Scipio, Polybius,
and Panaetius. With the circle was associated also Diogenes
the Stoic, the master[4] of Laelius. In the dialogue *Laelius*,
fittingly consecrated to the praise of friendship, Cicero has
introduced as speakers Laelius himself, C. Fannius, and
Q. Mucius Scaevola, who help to reveal[5] something of the
spirit that inspired Scipio and his friends. In others[6] of his
works also, Cicero found a congenial topic in the Scipionic
circle, as if he realised that herein lay his ideal of all that
was best in Roman culture. The friendship of Scipio with
many of his associates must have been cemented by their
common military service[7] in the camp before Numantia.

Philosophers, statesmen, poets, orators, historians, were
thus found in this coterie, which in many respects is one
of the most interesting phenomena in the
**The attractions
of Hellenism** cultured life of Rome, especially when we
consider the period in which it flourished.
The Romans had already begun to learn the beauties of

[1] De Rep. I. c. IX, XI–XII ; cf. Laelius, 14.

[2] De Rep. I. 21 ; cf. Pro Muraena, 66.

[3] De Rep. I. 15, *ib.* 34, II. 27, IV. 3. 3.

[4] De Fin. II. 24 ; cf. Schmekel, Die Philosophie der mittleren Stoa,
p. 443.

[5] Cf. Laelius, 6, 14, 33, 69 : " saepe enim excellentiae quaedam sunt,
qualis erat Scipionis in nostro, ut ita dicam, grege "; *ib.* 101.

[6] Pro Archia, 16, De Or. II. 154, De Leg. Agr. II. 64, De Fin. II. 24–25,
V. 2.

[7] De Rep. I. 17 (Rutilius) ; Vell. II. 9. 3 (Lucilius) ; Gellius, II. 13. 3
(Sempronius Asellio, the historian, though he is not mentioned by Cicero
as belonging to the circle) ; cf. Marx, op. cit., Introd. pp. 24–25.

Greek literature, even though it was through the often distorted medium of translation. Greek rhetoric and philosophy had penetrated[1] into Rome, and had aroused the suspicion and hostility of the more conservative-minded amongst the Romans. The elder Cato detested the Greeks, and was the uncompromising foe[2] of Hellenism, or at least of such aspects of it as he believed to be detrimental to the true Roman spirit. It is clear[3] that he himself had a good knowledge of Greek, whilst a later tradition,[4] inspired probably by some Philhellenist, liked to represent him as converted in his old age to the charm of Greek studies.

In spite of this atmosphere of hostility, Aemilius Paulus, Scipio's father, an enlightened[5] man for his age, was himself an enthusiastic Hellenist, and aimed[6] at imparting to his sons the best that Greek culture could bestow. He brought the philosopher Metrodorus from Athens to teach them, and reserved for their use the library of Perseus, whom he had conquered at Pydna. Soon after Pydna, the historian Polybius came to Rome as one of the Achaean hostages, and before long an intimacy[7] sprang up between him and the sons of Aemilius Paulus, which in the case of Scipio ripened into a close friendship. Polybius probably had no small influence upon Scipio. He was a Stoic of high moral standards and robust virtue, and, though a patriotic Greek, he could warn[8] his friend against the dangerous and cor-

Scipio's education

[1] The Epicurean philosophers, Alcaeus and Philiscus, were expelled in 173 B.C., Athenaeus (ed. Kaibel), XII, 68 ; a decree was passed against rhetoricians and philosophers, 161 B.C.; cf. Gellius, XV. 11. 1 ; Suet. De Rhet. I.

[2] Pliny, N.H., 29. 6–7 ; Plutarch, M. Cato, c. 22 ; Goldbacher, Der Hellenismus in Rom., p. 18 et seq. ; Baldi, Die Gegner der griech. Bildung, p. 7 et seq.

[3] Vide Polybius, XXXV. 6 ; Plut. M. Cato, c. 9, 12 ; cf. Colin, Rome et la Grèce, pp. 590–591.

[4] Cic. Cato Major, 3, 26, 38, De Rep. VI. I. 1 (Teubner), Acad. Pr. 5 ; Nepos, Cato, 3 ; Plut. M. Cato, 2.

[5] Cic. Br. 80, De Rep. I. 23 ; Polybius, XXX. 10 (Loeb. ed.).

[6] Polybius, XXXI. 22 et seq. ; Plut. Aem. Paulus, 6 ; Livy, 45. 41 ; cf. E. Lincke, P. Cor. Scipio Ämilianus, pp. 4–5.

[7] Polybius, XXXI. 23 et seq. ; Vell. I. 13.

[8] Cf. Polyb. XXXIX. 1.

rupting elements in Greek civilisation. He soon became imbued with an intense admiration[1] for the qualities that had raised Rome to her position of pre-eminence, and some at least of the views[2] attributed to Scipio in Cicero's *De Republica* may be traced to him as well as to Panaetius.

In the year 155 B.C. another event occurred that must have given a new zest to the Hellenic leanings of Scipio and

The Embassy of 155 B.C. his associates. The three philosophers, Carneades the Academic, Critolaus the Peripatetic, and Diogenes the Stoic, came to Rome on an embassy[3] to plead the cause of Athens, which was being arraigned for her harsh treatment of Oropus. Gellius quotes[4] two members of the Scipionic circle, Polybius and Rutilius, on the effect created by the different styles of oratory of the three philosophers, and the vivid impression they left upon their hearers. Cato urged that the ambassadors be dismissed without delay. His hostility[5] had been awakened in part by the torrential eloquence[6] of of Carneades, but still more by his sceptical tendencies. He must have appeared to Cato as the very embodiment of the Sophistic spirit. Cicero makes Furius Philus argue against justice in the *De Republica*[7] in the style of Carneades. Still, it was not he, but Diogenes the Stoic, as we shall see, that exercised the more lasting influence on Scipio and his associates.

In later years a pupil of Diogenes, Panaetius, whom

Panaetius Cicero extols[8] as the greatest of the Stoics, was the predominant influence in the Scipionic circle. He lived in close intimacy[9] with Scipio, who

---

[1] Polyb. I. 1.5, *ib*. 12. 7, 20. 10; cf. Hahn, Rom und Romanismus, p. 40 *et seq.*

[2] Cf. De Rep. I. 34; cf. Sabine and Smith, Cicero on the Commonwealth, Introd. p. 33 *et seq.*, 57 *et seq.*, 92.

[3] De Or. II. 155, Tusc. Disp. IV. 5, Acad. Pr. 137.

[4] VII. 14. 8 *et seq.*; cf. Macrob. Sat. I. V. 14 *et seq.*

[5] Pliny, N. H. VII. 30; Plut. M. Cato, 22; cf. Cic. De Rep. III. 6. 9 (cf. Lactantius, Inst. Div. V. 14).

[6] Lucilius, fr. 31, pays a striking tribute to his eloquence; cf. Lactantius, loc. cit.; Gellius, VII. 14. 10; Philostr. V. S. 486; *vide infra.*, p. 159.

[7] III. 5. 8 *et seq.*

[8] Acad. Pr. 107, De Off. II. 51, De Div. II. 97.

[9] De Off. I. 90, II. 76, De Rep. I. 15, *ib*. 34, Tusc. Disp. I. 81, Acad. Pr. 5, Ad Att. IX. 12; Vell. I. 13. 3.

became his pupil, and was the friend and master[1] of Laelius. Cicero mentions[2] also his instruction of, or his intimacy with, others of Scipio's adherents. Panaetius was a man of wide sympathies, who did much to soften[3] the rigour of primitive Stoicism, and adapt the tenets of his philosophical creed to the needs of the average Roman. He was an eclectic, who thought it possible to be a good Stoic without unwavering devotion either to the Stoic paradoxes, or to Stoic dialectic.[4] He was a professed admirer[5] of Plato, and it was probably from him that he derived a feeling for style uncommon in his sect. Like Polybius he must have influenced the political views[6] of Scipio and his friends. He must also have helped to consolidate the ideal[7] of " humanitas " within the Scipionic circle, though Terence[8] had already given expression to it in its widest sense. The word " humanitas " is one of the most complex words in Latin, as it embraces in its meaning almost every intellectual and moral quality that should distinguish the refined and cultured gentleman. The aspect of it that connoted wide culture[9] and broad sympathies, would appeal especially to Scipio and his friends, and would help to counteract the dangers of a narrow and doctrinaire Stoicism. Laelius, in particular, was given the title of " Sapiens,"[10] but it is clear[11] that in him, with his unvarying gaiety and easy charm of

[1] De Fin. II. 24, IV. 23.
[2] Br. 101 (C. Fannius) ; ib. 114, De Off. III. 10 (Rutilius) ; Acad. Pr. 135, De Fin. IV. 23, Tusc. Disp. IV. 4 (Q. Tubero) ; cf. De Or. III. 78.
[3] De Fin. IV. 79 : " nec acerbitatem sententiarum nec disserendi spinas probavit " ; cf. Schmekel, op. cit., p. 439 et seq. ; Horace and his Age, p. 85 et seq.
[4] De Off. II. 35.
[5] De Fin. IV. 79 ; cf. Susemihl, Gesch. der griech. Lit. Vol. II. pp. 67, 77, for his acquaintance with the Attic orators ; Plut. Dem. 13 ; cf. Schmekel, op. cit., p. 205 et seq., 231 et seq.
[6] De Rep. I. 34.
[7] De Or. II. 154 ; cf. Fiske, Lucilius and Horace, p. 73 et seq. ; Reitzenstein, Werden und Wesen der Humanität, p. 7 et seq. ; Schneidewin, Die antike Humanität, p. 28 et seq.
[8] Heauton. 77.
[9] Tus. Disp. I. 5, IV. 5 ; Gellius, VII. 12. 4.
[10] Cic. Laelius, 5–6, De Off. II. 40, III. 16 ; Sen. Ep. 95. 72 ; Lucil. fr. 1236 ; Plut. Tib. Gr. 8.
[11] De Or. II. 22, ib 286, De Off. I. 90, 108 ; Hor. Sat. II. 1. 72.

manner, it did not connote anything of the severity, morose-
ness, and extravagant pretensions of the "Sapiens"
of the Stoic paradoxes.[1] Cicero emphasises[2] the fact that
the teaching of Panaetius had generally a softening and
humanising influence on the members of the Scipionic
circle, though Scipio's nephew Tubero[3] modelled himself
rather according to the uncompromising standards of the
early Stoics.

On the other hand his culture and philosophy sat lightly[4]
and gracefully on Scipio. He, moreover, avoided the
danger of Graecomania, which was a serious
peril for young Romans who, thirsting for
self-improvement, came under the seductive
influence of Greek literature and philosophy. The heady
wine of Greek culture proved too potent a beverage for
many of these enthusiasts. Cato had occasion[5] to reprove
A. Postumius Albinus, who preferred to write his history
in Greek, while apologising for his defects of style in that
language. Lucilius, as we shall see, will furnish us with a
typical example of the Graecomaniac in Albucius. Both
Polybius and Panaetius would probably act as a restraining
influence on Scipio. Both of them might warn him of the
dangerous elements in Greek culture, while from Polybius
in particular, if he had need of it, he could have learned to
admire the great qualities of his own race. It would be
interesting to speculate on Cato's influence upon Scipio.
Cicero tells[6] us of their friendship, and of Scipio's reverence
for the old man. From Cato's constant invectives against
the dangers of the new civilisation Scipio might well have
imbibed a distrust of excessive and indiscriminate enthusiasm for Greek studies. Greece had much to give that could

The dangers of
Graecomania

[1] Cicero, Paradoxa ; Arnim, Stoicorum Veterum Fragmenta, Vol. III.
p. 146 *et seq.*
[2] Pro Murena, 66 ; cf. Laelius, 18, 48, 77 ; however, in De Off.
I. 108, Cic. considers Scipio in comparison with Laelius as showing " ambitio
major, vita tristior."
[3] *Vide infra.*, p. 165.
[4] De Or. III. 87.
[5] Gellius, XI. 8 ; Macrob. Sat. Praef. 14 ; cf. Cic. Acad. Pr. 137 ;
Polyb. XXXIX. 1. 5.
[6] De Inv. I. 5, De Rep. II. 1, Cato Major, 3–4 ; cf. Plut. M. Cato, 20.

beautify and ennoble Roman life, but it could also contribute[1] much that could corrupt and degrade. Signs were
not wanting that already the old Roman love of simplicity
and frugality was being undermined by contact with other
peoples. His reforms in the camp at Numantia, as well as
his spoken utterances, are evidence[2] that Scipio was the
sworn foe of indiscipline, luxury, and effeminacy, and, in
fact, of every novelty[3] that could demoralise the youth of
Rome. It is clear that he wished to conserve above all
the " mos majorum,"[4] the traditional virtues and outlook
of his Roman forefathers. It was probably this characteristic of his, combined with the high moral tone of his
speeches, that made him a favourite author[5] with Marcus
Aurelius. Possibly with a touch of the irony for which he
was famous, Scipio rather under-estimates his own pro-
ficiency in Greek studies, but he is sincere, when in the
same context[6] he declares that he owes more to practical
experience and home training than to acquired learning.
Though enthusiasm for Greek studies prevailed in the
Scipionic circle, yet such enthusiasm[7] was always tempered
by common sense. Its ideal[8] was the happy union of the
practical virtues of the Roman statesman with the theoretical
culture of Greece, but it took care that Roman civilisation
was to be ennobled and not demoralised by the gifts the
Greeks could bestow. How far Scipio was removed from
Graecomania is evident from the fact that, when he conquered Carthage, he restored the works of art[9] he found
there to the Sicilians, from whom the Carthaginians had
plundered them.

[1] De Rep. IV. 4.

[2] Lucilius, frs. 389 et seq., 407 et seq. ; cf. Cichorius, Untersuchungen
zu Lucilius, p. 303 et seq. ; cf. Gellius, VII. 12. 4 ; Polyb. XXXI. 25 et seq.

[3] Macrob. Sat. III. 14. 6 et seq. ; cf. De Rep. II. 4. 7, on the danger of
maritime cities so acquiring evil customs from abroad " ut nihil possit in
patriis institutis manere integrum " ; ib. IV. 10. 10.

[4] Gellius, IV. 20. 10, V. 19. 15.

[5] Fronto (ed. Haines), I. p. 138.

[6] De Rep. I. 36 ; cf. Gwynn, Roman Education, p. 56 et seq.

[7] De Rep. I. 30, II. 29.

[8] Ib. III. 5 : " ad domesticum majorumque morem etiam hanc a Socrate
adventiciam doctrinam adhibuerunt."

[9] Cic. In Verrem, De Signis, 73–74 ; cf. Colin, op. cit., p. 556 (with
inscription there quoted).

We have now to examine other aspects of the Scipionic circle that more nearly concern the question of criticism.

The ideal of "Latinitas" It is evident that the ideal of pure Latinity was one that was strongly cherished by that coterie. Lucilius[1] rails at Scipio for his learned affectation in the use of the form " pertisum " instead of " pertaesum." The incident is of importance as showing the influence of Analogy[2] even in those early years. Here, indeed, was a case in which Analogy and Purism went hand in hand. The theories of the Stoic Diogenes[3] were probably a powerful factor in this purist movement. He laid special stress on Ἑλληνισμός as an element in style, and dealt with the various faults against correctness such as impropriety of diction, barbarisms,[4] and solecisms. The Romans of Scipio's coterie naturalised such conceptions in their own ideal of " Latinitas." Terence, as we have seen, laid claim to pure Latinity, while Cicero pays[5] his tribute to the purity of speech that prevailed in the time of Scipio, and that characterised both him and Laelius. Purity of Latin was a tradition in their families, so that even the women[6] exhibited this characteristic. Cicero pays homage,[7] too, for his good Latinity to another member of the circle, Furius Philus, who according to Porcius Licinus[8] was an intimate friend of Terence.

The Stoics, in fact, were in general interested in the theory of grammar and language, and at Pergamum[9]

[1] Fr. 963 : " quo facetior videare et scire plus quam ceteri " ; cf. Cic. Or. 159.

[2] Cf. Festus, 273, on Scipio's " rederguisse " ; cf. Q. I. 7. 25 ; Norden, Die antike Kunstprosa, Vol. I. p. 186 ; Reitzenstein, M. Terentius Varro, p. 90, curiously denies such influence ; *vide infra*, p. 40.

[3] Arnim, op. cit., Vol. III. p. 210 *et seq. ; vide infra*, p. 41.

[4] *Vide infra*, p. 78.

[5] Br. 252, 258 ; cf. Gellius, II. 20. 5 : " Scipionem omnium aetatis suae purissime locutum."

[6] De Or. III. 45, Br. 211, 252.

[7] Br. 108.

[8] Suet. Life of Terence, c. I ; cf. Schanz, op. cit., I. 1. pp. 334–335.

[9] *Vide* Striller, De Stoicorum Studiis Rhetoricis, p. 3 ; Brzoska, De Canone Decem Oratorum, p. 56 *et seq. ;* cf. Susemihl, op. cit., II. p. 494, for the connection of Panaetius with Crates and Pergamum ; cf. *ib.* I. p. 5, II. 4 *et seq.*

especially had united grammatical and rhetorical studies.

Stoic theories of language They concerned themselves with the origin, nature, and growth of language. Cicero refers[1] to their fondness for inventing new words, and for distinguishing[2] ambiguous words in accordance with the principles of their Dialectic. They contributed much towards the fixing of grammatical terminology.[3] They held the theory[4] that language was a natural growth, not a matter of convention ; hence their insistence[5] on the use of the natural and appropriate word (κυριολεξία) for each thing, and the view, held by some of them at least, " nihil esse obscoenum, nihil turpe dictu." Still, Stoics like Panaetius evidently shrank[6] from the logical consequences of the position, maintained with all its implications by the Cynics and by certain Stoics, that " naturalia non sunt obscoena." The theory of the Stoics that language was a natural growth led them to occupy themselves with etymology,[7] as they believed that the real meaning of a word was to be found in its origin. We shall later see the influence of such theories on Lucilius, but they had their influence, too, upon Scipio, if one may judge from fragments of his speeches[8] which show what nice distinctions he could make in the use of words.

The preference for the Plain style But more interesting than such questions of grammar and language is the general preference for the Plain style shown by the orators of the Scipionic circle. Here again Stoic influence was at work. The Stoics, in formulating their theory of ora-

[1] De Fin. III. 15, IV. 7, Br. 118.

[2] De Or. II. 111, Or. 115 ; Gellius, XI. 12. 1 ; Hermagoras, who was under Stoic influence, is taxed by Q. with " affectata subtilitas circa nomina rerum," Q. III. 11. 21.

[3] Q. I. 4, 19 ; cf. Dionys. De Comp. Verb. c. 2.

[4] *Vide* Steinthal, Geschichte der Sprachwissenschaft, Vol. II. p. 141 ; Reitzenstein, Scipio Aemilianus und die stoische Rhetorik, p. 156 *et seq.*

[5] Cic. Ad Fam. IX. 22. 1 : " Placet Stoicis suo quamque rem nomine appellare."

[6] De Off. I. 127–128 ; cf. De Or. II. 252 ; Schneidewin, op. cit., p. 103.

[7] De Off. I. 23 ; cf. Laelius, 26 : " Amor ex quo amicitia nominata est ;" Reitzenstein, Scipio Aem. p. 156, with examples quoted from Varro.

[8] Cf. Gellius, VII. 11. 9, for his distinction of " nequitia " and " malitia ; " *ib.* 12. 5, where he plays on the words " vinosus " and " virosus".

torical style,[1] were probably in reaction against the excessive embellishment of Sophistic oratory, and its concern for victory at all costs rather than for truth.   Diogenes, in particular,[2] would have helped to familiarise the members of Scipio's circle with the Stoic theory of Style.   He enumerated the virtues[3] of Style as correctness of language, clearness, conciseness, aptness, and ornament that rose above the level of vulgar speech.   The Stoics from the very nature of their theory of Style would not be inclined to lay much stress on positive ornament.[4]   Their tendency was towards unimpassioned oratory, marked especially by the quality of conciseness.   The strength of Diogenes himself lay in Dialectic, and the plainness of his style, as compared with that of his fellow-ambassadors, was noted by the Romans.[5] Panaetius also was another influence that helped to establish the ideal of the Plain style in the Scipionic circle.   He elaborated the theory of the " sermo,"[6] which found its best illustration in the conversations of Socrates and his friends.   Its language was akin to the speech of everyday life, and its whole spirit was opposed to the stately and impassioned style of oratory (contentio).   With the " sermo " was associated a certain quiet type of ironic humour, half playful, half serious, that again is found in its purest form in the conversations of Socrates.[7]

Fannius has left on record[8] that such irony was char-

---

[1] *Vide infra*, p. 161 *et seq.*

[2] *Vide* Fiske, op. cit., p. 78 *et seq.*

[3] Diog. Laert. VII. 59 ; cf. Cic. Part. Or. 19, where the Stoic list of virtues is somewhat modified ; Volkmann, Die Rhetorik der Griechen und Römer, p. 158.

[4] For their relation to certain of the Figures, *vide* Smiley, Seneca and the Stoic theory of Style, p. 53 *et seq.*

[5] Cic. De Or. II. 157–159: " genus sermonis . . . exile, aridum, concisum, ac minutum "; Gellius, VII. 14. 10: " modesta Diogenes ac sobria," *ib. :* " violenta et rapida Carneades dicebat, scita et teretia Critolaus."

[6] De Off. I. 132, 134, II. 48 ; cf. Or. 64, 109, De Rep. I. 10. 16 : " leporem Socraticum subtilitatemque sermonis "; De Or. I. 32, 35, 255, III. 203, Acad. Pr. 74 ; cf. Ad Her. III. 13. 23 ; Reitzenstein (Scipio Aem.), pp. 154–155 ; Fiske, op. cit., p. 84 *et seq.*

[7] De Off. I. 108, Br. 292 ; Q. IX. 2. 46.

[8] De Or. II. 270, 272, Br. 299, Acad. Pr. 16.

acteristic of Scipio, whose oratory was spiced, too, with
other forms of wit. We may fairly con-
Scipio's ora-
tory clude from Cicero that irony was a quality
that marked Scipio's public speaking[1] no
less than his private conversations. Cicero, moreover,
records[2] the fact of his predilection for Xenophon, whose
style was plain and almost conversational in tone. The
Ancients paid many tributes[3] to the eloquence of Scipio,
but both he and Laelius tried to get their effects in a style[4]
slightly exalted above the tone of ordinary conversation.
Several fragments[5] of Scipio's oratory have survived.
Though at times he indulges in careful periodic structure,
and shows a leaning towards certain figures[6] such as climax
and anaphora, yet there is evidence[7] in him, too, of a fondness for short clauses, questions, and definitions, such as
would be in harmony with the spirit of Stoic Dialectic,
while the general tone of the fragments shows much of
the casual ease of ordinary conversation.

Cicero extols the eloquence of Laelius in many passages,[8]
and places him even above Scipio as an orator, even though
his style was somewhat more archaic. It
Laelius as
orator was he who composed the funeral oration on
the occasion of Scipio's death, though it
was delivered by the latter's nephew.[9] Like Scipio, Laelius
showed a preference for a plain,[10] unemotional type of

[1] Though Reitzenstein, op. cit., p. 149, thinks this uncertain.

[2] Tusc. Disp. II. 62, Cato Major, 59, Ad Q. Fr. I. 1. 23.

[3] De Or. I. 215, Br. 82 *et seq.*, De Off. I. 116, Pro Murena, 58 ; Vell.
II. 9. 1.

[4] De Or. I. 255 : " qui omnia sermone conficerent paulo intentiore " ;
however, Cic. Lael. 96, suggests other qualities in Scipio's oratory.

[5] Gellius, II. 20. 6, V. 19. 15, VII. 11. 9, 12. 5 ; Macrob. Sat. III.
14. 6 ; cf. Cima, L'Eloquenza Latina, p. 115 *et seq. ;* Meyer, Oratorum
Romanorum Fragmenta, p. 101 *et seq.*

[6] Cf. Lucilius, fr. 1133 (with Marx's note), on the merit of these two figures.

[7] Cf. Gellius, VII. 11. 9.

[8] De Or. I. 35, 59, 215, Br. 82–84, Lael. 96, De Rep. III. 42, De Nat.
Deorum, III. 43.

[9] Tubero in De Or. II. 341, Q. Fab. Maximus in Pro Murena, 75 ;
cf. Schol. Bobb. ad Pro Milone, VII. 16 ; Meyer, op. cit., p. 99.

[10] De Or. I. 255, *ib.* III. 28 : " lenitatem Laelius " ; Q. XII. 10. 39,
speaks of Scipio and Laelius as " veluti Attici Romanorum," with their
plain style evidently in mind.

oratory, and like him, too, he was distinguished for his wit.[1]
Cicero, on the authority of Rutilius, a member of the
Scipionic circle, relates an incident[2] that well illustrates
Laelius' temperament as an orator, and the effect of his
Stoic training upon him. He was engaged to appear for
the publicani in connection with the affair in the forest of
Sila.   On both occasions on which he pleaded, his speech
was marked by choice diction and careful composition, but
it failed of success, because it lacked the fire of emotion.
On Laelius' own suggestion the case was entrusted to
Servius Galba, a more emotional orator,[3] who gained a
verdict for the publicani by the passion and vehemence of
his pleading.

The effect of Stoic training on the Scipionic circle is
seen, too, in the plain style[4] adopted by Spurius Mummius,
                         while a similar plainness was characteristic
Effect of Stoic   both of the historical style and the oratory
training
                         of Fannius,[5] the opponent of C. Gracchus.
I shall deal in a later chapter with other Stoic orators who
were associates of Scipio, but in general, as we shall see
when we come to treat of Lucilius, the Scipionic circle was
hostile to rhetoric that was artificial and over-ornate.   It
was probably this spirit that actuated Mummius in his
hostility[6] to the rhetoricians.   We cannot determine exactly how far Polybius, in his opposition[7] to the highly
coloured and rhetorical manner of historical writing, was
moved by his own temperament and conception of history,

---

[1] Cic. Ad Fam. IX. 15. 2, De Or. II. 286.

[2] Br. 85 et seq.

[3] Cic. Br. 89, contrasts the two styles of oratory : " una subtiliter disputandi ad docendum, altera graviter agendi ad animos audientium permo-
vendos."

[4] Br. 94 ; cf. Ad Att. XIII. 6. 4, on Mummius as a letter-writer.

[5] Br. 99–101 ; Cicero was mistaken in supposing that there were two
Fannii ; cf. Kroll, ad loc. ; Ad Att. XII. 5. 3, XVI. 13 c. 2 quoted by him ;
cf. De Or. III. 183 ; Cima, op. cit., pp. 125–126, on F's speech " De
sociis et nomine Latino ;" on Fannius as historian, vide infra, p. 517.

[6] Cf. De Rep. V. 9. 11 (quoted from Nonius) ; cf. ib. the quotation
from Ammianus Marcellinus, the context of which is unfortunately obscure ;
both quotations are interesting in view of Diogenes' hostility to Rhetoric ;
cf. Philodemus, Rhetorica, I. 346, II. 99.

[7] Vide infra, p. 501 et seq.

or how far he was influenced by the stylistic theories of the Stoics.

It is sometimes claimed[1] that the poet Pacuvius, and the historian Coelius Antipater, both friends[2] of Laelius, were members of the circle, but both of them ran counter to ideals held sacred by Scipio and his friends. Pacuvius was sharply criticised by Lucilius for the distorted character of his style, while in purity[3] of speech he fell far short of the rigorous standard of the Scipionic circle. Coelius, who had almost certainly come under Asianist influence, was essentially the type of the rhetorical[4] historian that would not be likely to find favour with those who were acquainted with Polybius' views on history, and who were habituated to Stoic standards of criticism. The Scipionic circle has given us little in the way of explicit criticism, but I have thought it well to treat of it at some length, because it upheld theories and ideals that left their mark on its own and succeeding generations, and that, indirectly at least, must have influenced the course of Roman criticism.

We must, however, deal in some detail with one of its members, Lucilius, who was amongst the most original

Lucilius   writers of early Rome. Unfortunately we possess only fragments of his work, for the most part mutilated and obscure, but still giving sufficient light to enable us to see that he was no unimportant figure in the development of criticism at Rome.

Lucilius' friendship with Scipio must have begun early ; it must have been further consolidated during his service in the Numantine war,[5] and soon ripened into that charming intimacy to which reference[6] is made in later times. He made Scipio's quarrels his own, and attacked unsparingly his personal enemies. His friendship with Laelius, " sophos ille," as he calls him,[7] must have been equally marked ;

---

[1] *Vide* Lincke, op. cit., pp. 8–9.
[2] Lael. 24, Or. 230
[3] Br. 258.
[4] *Vide infra*, p. 514 *et seq.*
[5] Cf. frs. 405, 467 *et seq.* ; Cichorius, op. cit., p. 29 *et seq.* ; *vide supra*, p. 28.
[6] Schol. ad Hor. Sat. II. 1. 71 ; cf. fr. 1138–1142.
[7] Fr. 1236.

yet Lucilius, though a member of the Scipionic circle, maintained a certain degree of independence in his relations with it. He probably aimed at making his primary appeal to its adherents, but in a jesting mood he defines[1] the class of readers by whom he desires his works to be read. He does not write for the uncultured, but neither does he wish to submit his works to the rigorous criticism of the "intellegentsia" (doctissimi). He declares that he will address himself to the plain people rather than subject his writings to the ordeal of being tested by such learned men as Scipio and Rutilius.

We[2] have already referred to his raillery of Scipio for his over-nicety in the use of the form "pertisum." Still there is evidence[3] that Lucilius himself felt the **Lucilius and Analogy** influence of the movement towards Analogy. He did not, however, adopt the standpoint of the rigid Analogist, but like Varro in later days tried to hold the balance between "ratio" and "consuetudo." Quintilian lays it down[4] that speech is based on reason,[5] antiquity, authority, and usage. The Analogist took account[6] of the origin and nature of a language, and in case of doubt had a standard of comparison by which he could test the validity of a particular form, and render himself immune from the caprice of irrational custom. The Anomalist took account of existing usage, and the possibilities of development in a living language. He refused to be bound by rigid laws that could only arrest the natural evolution of speech. Irregularities might occur, but they were pardoned as the outcome of a vigorous living growth. Custom was ever changing, and might consecrate what the Analogist would regard as corrupt and abnormal elements. One

[1] De Or. II. 25, Br. 99, De Fin. I. 3. 7 ; Pliny, N.H. Praef. 7 ; cf. Marx, frs. 592 *et seq.* ; Fiske, op. cit., p. 71.

[2] *Vide supra*, p. 34.

[3] Frs. 356–357 ; cf. Q. I. 6. 8, on L's use of the form "fervit."

[4] I. 6. 1.

[5] "Ratio" was the guiding principle of the Analogist ; Gellius, XV. 8. 4, speaks of it more fully as "ratio proportionis" ; cf. Q. I. 6. 3.

[6] On the question of Analogy and Anomaly, *vide* Colson, Quintilian, Book I, especially his notes on I. 6. 1 *et seq.*, *ib.* pp. 175–176 ; also his article, The Analogist and Anomalist Controversy, C. Q. XIII. 1, Jan., 1919.

might argue[1] that custom, too, was at the basis of Analogy,[2] but it was not the custom of the Present with all its vagaries, so much as the custom[3] of approved authors, or at any rate a custom that took account of the original form of the language, and showed due respect for the opinions of the learned.

While Lucilius may not have wished to conform absolutely to the inexorable standards of speech imposed by **His purism** Scipio, for all that, he could not escape from the purist atmosphere of his circle. It was this that impelled him to criticise[4] the provincialisms in the speech of Vettius. In another fragment[5] he rails at the rustic pronunciation of the praetor Caecilius. Probably a similar spirit of criticism may have inspired his reference[6] to the Bruttii, who spoke a mixture of Greek and Oscan. In a fragment,[7] the purpose of which is obscure, he reflects on the use of unusual words, and may be criticising from the standpoint of the purist a fault of style in the writings of some opponent.[8] His reference[9] to the numerous kinds of solecisms shows that he was concerning himself with defects of speech, in accordance with the theories of the Stoic Diogenes. All this would indicate that, in theory at least, Lucilius paid homage to the ideal of Latinitas, while his criticism of provincial peculiarities of speech is interest-

[1] Varro, De L. Lat. IX. 2 et seq., X. 74; Cic. Br. 261, where we have the contrast of " consuetudo vitiosa et corrupta " and " pura et incorrupta consuetudo " (of the Analogist); Q. I. 6. 16; Gellius, II. 25. 5; vide infra, p. 80.

[2] At all events, the moderate Analogist took account of it.

[3] Here, of course, the factor of " auctoritas " would be operative.

[4] Q. I. 5. 56; Marx, fr. 1322, refers the criticism to Vettius Philocomus (Suet. De Gr. 2); Cichorius, however, justly remarks that this Vettius was a Greek, who would hardly be imbued with Latin provincialisms (op. cit., p. 348).

[5] Fr. 1130; cf. Varro, De L. L. VII. 96 (Spengel); the " Caecilius " referred to is probably C. Caecilius Metellus Caprarius, with whom Scipio came into conflict at Numantia; cf. Gerlach, C. Lucilii Saturarum Reliquiae, Introd., p. 40; Cic. De Or. II. 267.

[6] Fr. 1124; cf. Ennius, Annales, 496 (Vahlen); Porphyrio ad Hor. Sat. I. 10. 30.

[7] Fr. 650.

[8] Possibly Accius; cf. Cichorius, op. cit., p. 127 et seq.; vide infra, p. 50.

[9] Fr. 1100; cf. fr. 1215; Q. I. 5. 50; Fiske, op. cit., p. 107 et seq.; vide supra, p. 34.

ing, as showing that as early as the time of Scipio the notion[1] of " urbanitas " was beginning to be evolved in the intellectual circles of Rome.

It is doubtful, however, if Lucilius' own practice would have satisfied the rigid purists.   The large admixture[2] of
Greek words to be found in his *Satires* would
The practice of probably have offended[3] their susceptibili-
Lucilius ties, though we must remember that many
of these words are to be found in passages[4] in which Lucilius aims at parody, or is endeavouring to ridicule the affectations of the cultured society of his day.   In their context such words are particularly effective.[5]   His use of Oscan[6] words, or words from the soldiers' argot,[7] would also run counter to the ideas of the stricter purists.   Lucilius, though he might prescribe a standard of purity for other genres, wished his *Satires* to be a transcript from life, and evidently aimed at reproducing faithfully the language peculiar[8] to each occupation and profession that came within the range of his writings.

The fragments of Lucilius' ninth book raise some important questions, and provide further evidence of his culture
and his diversity of interests.   He mani-
Lucilius and festly dealt there[9] with the cacophonous
Hellenistic effects of certain letters, especially " s " and
theory
" r," thus showing his appreciation for euphony[10] as an

[1] The name came later, as we know from Cicero and Varro.

[2] *Vide* Gerlach, op. cit., Introd. p. 129 *et seq.*

[3] Cic. De Off. I. 111 ; Fiske, op. cit., p. 339 ; *vide infra*, p. 80.

[4] Frs. 13–18, where Lucilius, from the national standpoint, is really condemning those who affect Greek words instead of Latin ; *ib.* fr. 71 ; in fr. 84 *et seq.* he is railing at the affectation of men like Albucius ; cf. fr. 540, where parody is evidently intended ; *vide* Suess, Petronii Imitatio Sermonis Plebei, p. 21 *et seq.*, for a collection of the relevant passages.

[5] Scipio, too, was able to make effective use of Greek words in his speeches ; cf. " chiridota," " crotola," etc.

[6] Frs. 1249, 1318.

[7] *Vide* Marx's Index on " sermo castrensis."

[8] Fronto (Haines), I. p. 4 : " Lucilium (elegantem) in cujusque artis ac negotii propriis (verbis)."

[9] Frs. 377–381 ; Fiske, op. cit., p. 110, refers in this connection to fr. 386, which he takes as dealing with " junctura," though there it is rather a question of " ordo ;" cf. fr. 1168, on " euphona ;" *vide infra*, p. 88.

[10] *Vide infra*, p. 397, on the importance of euphony in Hellenistic theory.

element in style. The distinction that he draws[1] between " poema " and " poesis " is of particular interest, as indicating that he was acquainted with the discussions[2] of the problem in the Hellenistic theory[3] of poetry. He illustrates " poesis " (an extended work of many parts exhibiting unity as a whole) by the *Annales* of Ennius as well as by the *Iliad*, and thus pays a tribute to the fame already enjoyed by the Roman Epic.

Other fragments of the same book go to confirm the suggestion that he was speculating on the problems of grammar and language in the spirit of the Stoic members of his circle. This is evidenced, too, by his fondness[4] for etymology. Moreover, the question of orthography was then being debated, and Lucilius entered the lists with views[5] opposed to those of Accius.[6] His practice of writing " puerei " for the nominative plural, " pueri " for the genitive singular, may, as Kroll suggests,[7] be due to Stoic influence, and to the belief that, the word being an image of the thing, the plural should be longer than the singular.

His interest in language

Like the other members of the Scipionic circle, Lucilius could hardly have escaped such influence, but it is equally clear that, like Horace in later days, he was unwilling to swear allegiance to any single school. His general philosophic position has no interest for us except as an indication of the independence of his character, and as evidence of his standpoint in his criticism of the life around him. His friendship[8] with Clitomachus

Stoic influence

[1] Fr. 338 *et seq. ;* cf. Varro, Satires (Parmeno), Riese, p. 190 ; Nonius, Mueller, II. p. 13.

[2] Cf. Jensen, Philodemos, p. 29, Col. XI, where also the Iliad is used to illustrate the difference between ποίησις and ποίημα ; *ib.* p. 103 cf. Diomede, G. L. (Keil), p. 473 (there quoted) for the distinction between poetica, poema, poesis ; *vide infra*, p. 470.

[3] We have to look for more than Stoic influence here, which Striller op. cit., pp. 47–48, considers as alone operative.

[4] Cf. fr. 437, on the derivation of "tragoedia" ; fr. 452, on "iners"; fr 1340.

[5] Frs. 352 *et seq. ;* cf. Q. I. 7. 15, 19.

[6] Who introduced the custom of writing a long vowel by doubling (e.g. paastores).

[7] Studien zum Verständniss der röm. Lit. p. 104.   [8] Cic. Acad. Pr. 1c2

(a pupil of Carneades), who dedicated a work to him, shows that the poet, possibly from his student days, had connections with the Academy. His reference[1] to the succession of Polemon as leader of the Academy, and the fine tribute he pays[2] to the power of Carneades' eloquence, point in the same direction. For all that, he could not evade the influence of the Stoics. We find in his *Satires* many echoes[3] of their doctrines, such as reflections on the self-sufficiency of virtue, the limitation of our needs, the insatiable greed for material possessions displayed by men who have not attained to the wisdom of the Sapiens. In the longest[4] of the fragments preserved to us, he has given us, in language more than usually studied and exalted, a picture of virtue essentially Stoic in colouring. It is possible to detect in some[5] of the fragments the direct influence of Panaetius. The *Satires* contain, also, many elements of popular[6] Cynic and Stoic philosophy, as developed in the Χρεία and Διατριβή. Lucilius, however, cannot refrain from more than one jibe[7] at that impossible figure of Stoicism, the Sapiens, who was in theory the embodiment of every virtue and perfection. In a similar spirit Horace in later days could find material[8] for ridicule in the Ideal Sage, and in the paradoxes of Stoicism. Still, we need not be surprised at finding Stoic colouring in the writings of Lucilius, because Stoicism, with its high ideals and its lofty code of morality, was a secure standpoint for the Satirist who chose to set himself up as a censor of the vices of his age.

[1] Frs. 754–756 ; Cichorius, op. cit., p. 46, interprets fr. 753 as a dispute between an Epicurean and a member of the Academy.

[2] Fr. 31 ; *vide supra*, p. 30.

[3] Frs. 550, 554, 558, 700–701, 1178, on " furor " ; cf. Porphyrio ad Hor. Sat. II. 3. 41 ; cf. fr. 658.

[4] Fr. 1326 ; cf. Lact. Inst. Div. VI. 5. 2.

[5] Cf. fr. 738 (with Marx's note), *ib.* 1337–1338 ; Cic. De Off. I. 58 (quoted by Marx).

[6] Fiske, op. cit., c. III, gives an admirable account of the influence of such popular forms of philosophising on Lucilius and Horace ; cf. Oltramare, Les Origines de la Diatribe Romaine, p. 91 *et seq.*

[7] Frs. 515, 747, 1225.

[8] Sat. I. 3. 124 *et seq.*, II. 3 *passim*, II. 7. 83 *et seq.*, Ep. I. 1. 106 *et seq.* ; cf. Cic. Pro Murena, 61 *et seq.*

Lucilius in his second book[1] gives us an account of the famous quarrel between Albucius and Mucius Scaevola,[2]

The quarrel of Scaevola and Albucius the Augur, which resulted in the latter being put on trial for extortion on his return from Asia. The fragments bearing on the incident have many points of interest for the history of Roman criticism. Scaevola was best known for his pre-eminence as a jurist,[3] a pre-eminence that was traditional in his family. Cicero studied law under his guidance, and, as a proof of his admiration for him, introduced him as one of the speakers in the first book of the *De Oratore*, in the *Laelius*, and in the *De Republica*. As a Stoic,[4] and a pupil of Panaetius, and in accordance with the tenets of his philosophy an orator of the Plain style,[5] he distrusted emotional eloquence, and all the embellishments of rhetoric. Albucius was an Epicurean,[6] and though the members of his sect as a rule despised[7] the higher culture, and showed little aptitude for eloquence, and little regard for the graces of speech, Albucius seems to have been meticulous in his efforts to give distinction to his oratory. Lucilius represents Mucius as ridiculing his affected and artificial style, and as comparing the order and setting of his words to a tesselated pavement, in which the cubes are wrought into a cunning and intricate pattern. This description of an artificial style is one of Lucilius' happiest efforts in criticism, and it evidently struck the imagination of Cicero, who reproduces it on three[8] distinct occasions. In the *Orator* he uses it to illustrate and condemn a laboured style of composition that fails to conceal its art. Albucius apparently departed from

[1] Frs. 84 *et seq.*; cf. Cic. De Or. II. 281, Br. 102.
[2] Cf. Cic. De Or. I. 72; Persius I. 114, on L's attitude to Scaevola.
[3] De Or. I. 35, 200, 234, Br. 102, 212, Lael. I. 1, Phil. VIII. 31.
[4] De Or. I. 43, 45, 75.
[5] De Or. I. 214, 234.
[6] Br. 131, De Nat. Deor. I. 93; the reference in Fronto, II. 48, seems to be to Abuccius, not Albucius; (for Abuccius, cf. Varro, R. R. III. 2. 17, III. 6. 6).
[7] De Or. III. 63, 78, De Fin. I. 26, II. 27.
[8] De Or. III. 171, Br. 274 (in his criticism of Calidius), Or. 149; cf. Pliny, N. H. 36. 185; Q. IX. 4. 113.

the usual[1] word order, and possibly too, like Hegesias[2] and many of the Asiatic orators, affected a series of short clauses highly rhythmical in character. Scaevola threatens that he will call upon the aid of his son-in-law Crassus, the distinguished orator, to oppose the rhetorical flights of Albucius, possibly with a hint that Crassus himself indulged in a style[3] of oratory too florid and high-flown. It is probably criticism such as this that evoked the tribute of the elder Pliny, when he declared that Lucilius was the first Roman[4] to exhibit a flair for style, a tribute that is almost tantamount to saying that he was the first genuine literary critic in Rome.

Scaevola, in defending himself against the charge of extortion, gave an account, which is of some interest, of the origin of Albucius' enmity towards him.

Graecomania

It arose when, on the occasion of their meeting at Athens, he ridiculed the Graecomania[5] of Albucius, and his ridicule was re-echoed by all who followed in the Praetor's train. This is interesting as shedding light on the ideals of Scipio and his associates. They did not, like Albucius and similar frenzied enthusiasts, yield themselves wholly to the spell of things Greek, nor despise[6] the products of native genius, but sought to engraft upon these the finest elements they could borrow from the Greeks.

The incident of Scaevola and Albucius is important also as showing Lucilius' interest in oratorical style. It is not

Lucilius' interest in rhetoric

impossible that the poet, especially in his picture of the Council of the gods, ridiculed[7] some of the rhetorical devices employed in oratory. In one fragment he seems to refer to the brazen

[1] Marx compares Cic. Or. 230, on Coelius Antipater.

[2] *Vide infra*, p. 214; cf. Theon, Progym. II. 71 (Spengel), on some followers of Epicurus who were addicted to such a style.

[3] *Vide infra*, p. 183.

[4] N. H. Praef. 7 : " qui primus condidit stili nasum."

[5] Cic. Br. 131 : " doctus enim Graecis T. Albucius vel potius plane Graecus"; De Fin. I. 9, De Prov. Consul. 15 : " Graecum hominem ac levem."

[6] Cf. Cic. De Fin. I. 10, on " tam insolens domesticarum rerum fastidium"; *vide supra*, p. 32.

[7] Fr. 26 ; Marx regards it as ridiculing the exordium of some orator ; fr. 603, may refer to the orator's employment of " commiseratio "; cf.

effrontery of some orator[1] who sought to compensate by
boldness of tongue for his lack of other qualities.   As an
offset to such a picture we may refer to a dictum of Lucilius,
quoted[2] by Cicero, that no one can be worthy of the name of
orator who is not versed[3] in all the liberal arts.   In this
dictum he may be giving expression to an ideal of his own,
or possibly to an ideal that was held by many members[4] of
his circle.   There is another important fragment,[5] in which
he ridicules the affectations of contemporary rhetoric.   In
writing to a friend, to chide him for his failure to visit him
during an illness, he unconsciously gave expression to a
" homoioteleuton."[6]   Such a silly and puerile Isocratic
device may, he thinks, offend the susceptibilities of his
friend, who evidently had a refined taste which rejected
such rhetorical ornaments.   It is interesting to note that
the figure of " homoioteleuton," which is one of the Gorgianic figures,[7] is here associated with the name of Isocrates,[8]
who came under the influence of the Sicilian school.   These
figures were afterwards employed to a tasteless excess by
the Asianist orators.   Possibly, Lucilius in this fragment,
though he calls the figure Isocratic, may have in mind some
writer[9] or orator who came under Asianist influence, rather
than one who directly imitated Isocrates.   The orators of
the Scipionic circle who were nurtured on Stoic ideals, who
followed the Plain style of oratory, and valued especially

fr. 908, where " epiphoni " shows acquaintance with the terms of the
rhetorical schools.

[1] Fr. 385, Bk. X ; Cichorius, p. 298, notes in this connection the statement in the Life of Persius that he was inspired by this book of Lucilius to
" recentium poetarum et oratorum insectatio."

[2] De Or. I. 72.

[3] This is interesting in view of Cicero's own discussion of the culture of
the orator.

[4] Cf. however, De Or. I. 165, where Mucius, in reference to the ideal of
culture for the orator sketched by Crassus, says : " in oratoris vero instru-
mento tam lautam supellectilem nunquam videram."

[5] Fr. 181 ; cf. Gellius, XVIII. 8.

[6] " Quem nolueris quem visere debueris."

[7] Gellius, loc. cit., speaks as if Lucilius had ridiculed all the Gorgianic
figures.

[8] *Vide infra*, p. 100.

[9] Such as Coelius Antipater ; *vide infra*, p. 515.

clearness, brevity, and restraint, would naturally have rejected[1] all such gaudy embellishment, but independently of these, Lucilius, with his fine feeling for style, would have despised devices that in practice led so many writers into puerile extravagance. Another point of interest in this fragment is the fact of Lucilius' acquaintance with the terms of Greek literary criticism. The term μειρακιώδης[2] is expressly applied to the Gorgianic figures by Dionysius,[3] who in thus employing it was evidently following the lead of some of his predecessors. This passage from Lucilius is, as far as I know, the earliest instance of the use of such critical terms amongst the Romans.

Lucilius also directed his criticism against contemporary poets,[4] notably the writers of Tragedy. We have seen traces of his interest in the *Annales* of Ennius, which he employed to illustrate "poesis," but whether his reference[5] to the Roman Epic poet as "alter Homerus" is to be taken seriously is more than doubtful. It is probable, indeed, that Lucilius is ridiculing the claim made by the poet at the beginning of the *Annales*, that Homer's spirit had passed into him. Horace tells[6] us that Lucilius railed at certain verses of Ennius as wanting in dignity. Servius has preserved[7] for us one instance of such raillery, in which the older poet's phrase "splendet et horret" is changed by Lucilius into "horret et alget." It is more than probable that much of the latter's criticism of Ennius was conducted indirectly by way of parody of his Epic style. Parody is

Criticism of contemporary poets

[1] Cic. Or. 84, excludes such figures from the Plain style of oratory.

[2] This reading, adopted by Marx, seems almost certain ; Aristotle's use of ληρώδης (Rhet. III. 13. 5) seems also to weigh in favour of his reading "hoc lerodes " instead of " ochlerodes."

[3] De Isocr. 12, 13, De Thucyd. 46, Ad Pomp. c. 2, Ep. II. Ad Ammaeum, c. 17 ; περὶ ὕψους, III. 4, describes τὸ μειρακιῶδες as the antithesis of the Sublime ; Arist. Rhet. III. 11. 16, uses the term rather in the sense of " juvenile."

[4] Hor. Sat. I. 10. 53–54 ; cf. Gellius, XVII. 21. 49.

[5] Fr. 1189 (quoted from St. Jerome's Commentary in Michaeam) ; *vide supra*, p. 4.

[6] Sat. I. 10. 54.

[7] Ad Aen. XI. 601 ; Luc. fr. 1190 ; Macrob. Sat. VI. 4. 6, who attributes the phrase to the " Scipio."

one of the most subtle weapons in the armoury of the Satirist as well as of the writer[1] of Comedy, and such writers can find a perennial source of laughter in the application of a phrase of epic dignity to a trivial and commonplace subject.   There is plenty of evidence[2] of imitations of Ennius in Lucilius, who had particularly wide scope for a parody of that poet's Epic style in his mock-heroic account[3] of the Council[4] of the gods convened on the death of Lupus. In certain fragments[5] we have echoes also of Ennius' Tragic diction, probably again reproduced by way of parody.

It is, indeed, evident that Lucilius was the sworn foe of the bombastic style[6] of the writers of Tragedy, and that

The Tragic style of Pacuvius he castigated their turgid language with unsparing ridicule.   Pacuvius, though a friend of Laelius, was the object of many bitter

attacks.   The fastidiousness of Lucilius revolted against the contorted character[7] of the tragedian's prologues.   Moreover, the marvel of winged snakes described by Pacuvius, presented a welcome butt for his ridicule.[8]   We find[9] many parodies of that writer in the Satirist, who seems to have directed his attention[10] in particular to his strange compounds, and to the unusual words employed by him. Lucilius' own good taste would have risen in spontaneous

[1] Cf. Starkie, Acharnians, Introd. p. 45 *et seq. ; vide supra*, p. 26.

[2] Frs. 939, 996, 1000, 1008, 1021, 1314, 1316 (cf. Cichorius, p. 348), 1323 (with Marx's notes).

[3] Bk. I ; cf. especially frs. 4, 18, 28 ; cf. Ennius, Annales, 37–42 (Valmaggi) ; Servius ad Aen. X. 104.

[4] Cf. Weinreich, Senecas Apocolocyntosis, pp. 36, 94, 99, 127, for affinities between Seneca and Lucilius.

[5] Frs. 870–872 ; cf. Cic. Tus. Disp. I. 107 ; Ribbeck, Trag. Lat. Rel. 309–310.

[6] Cf. Fr. 388 ; cf. περὶ ὑψους,, III. 1, where a passage from Aeschylus is severely criticised from this point of view.

[7] Fr. 875.

[8] Fr. 587 ; cf. Ribbeck, op. cit., 397 ; Cic. De Inv. I. 27, De Rep. III. 9. 14 (there quoted) ; cf. the criticism of Aeschylus' marvels in Aristoph. Frogs, 937 *et seq.*

[9] Fr. 597 (with Marx's note), 599 *et seq.*, 653 ; cf. Ribbeck, 112.

[10] Fr. 212 ; cf. Ribbeck, 408 ; Q. I. 5. 67–70 ; Varro, De L. L. V. 7 ; fr. 608 " monstrificabile " ; cf. Persius, I. 78 ; fr. 654 " contemnificus," fr. 677 " repedare " ; cf. Ribbeck, 400 ; in fr. 1108, " grandaevus " may be an echo of Pacuvius' ". grandaevitas " (Ribbeck, 162).

protest against the excesses of the Tragic style as exemplified in Pacuvius, but his criticism of his language was undoubtedly influenced in part by the ideal of pure Latinity
so highly prized in the circle of Scipio. Pacuvius, in his
endeavour to reproduce something of the stateliness and
splendour of his Greek originals, allowed himself much
licence in the way of new forms[1] and compounds which
were rejected by the Purists[2] of his own and succeeding
ages. In the hands of most of the early poets Latin was a
flexible medium, which became more rigid, as the views of
the Purists prevailed. Cicero pays some generous compli-
ments[3] to Pacuvius, but he criticises[4] him for his defective
Latinity. In the same context he had paid a tribute to
Scipio and Laelius for the purity of their Latin, and with
them he contrasts the defects of Caecilius and Pacuvius,[5]
as if for the moment he was adopting as a standard of
judgment the point of view of Lucilius and his associates
in the Scipionic circle.

There is evidence, too, in Lucilius of a keen polemic[6]
against the poet Accius. We have already seen that he

**Polemic
against
Accius**

was opposed to the innovations in orthography introduced by Accius. The latter
belonged to the professional guild[7] of poets,
and a great statue of him had been erected in the temple of
the Muses, where the " collegium poetarum " usually held
its meetings. Lucilius[8] seems to have ridiculed his vanity
and pretensions in having the statue erected. Accius did

---

[1] Varro attributed " ubertas " to him ; cf. Gellius, VII. 14. 6 ; Kroll,
Studien, p. 100 *et seq.*

[2] *Vide infra*, p. 83.

[3] De Or. I. 246, II. 187, Or. 36, De opt. gen. I. 2.

[4] Br. 258 : " nam illorum (i.e. Scipio and Laelius) aequales Caecilium
et Pacuvium male locutos videmus."

[5] Of course, in the context it is evident that the publication of Caesar's
" De Analogia " had given a new prominence to the question of correct
Latinity ; *vide infra*, p. 243.

[6] Cf. Porphyrio ad Hor. Sat. I. 10. 53 ; Luc. attacked Accius, especially
in books 3, 9, and 10 of his Satires ; cf. Gellius, XVII. 21. 49.

[7] Pliny, N. H. 34. 19 ; Val. Max. III. 7. 11 ; cf. Lucilius, fr. 1028, for
a possible reference to the guild of poets ; Cichorius, op. cit., p. 205 ; *vide
supra*, p. 7.

[8] Fr. 794 (with Marx's note).

not belong to the Scipionic circle, but enjoyed[1] the patronage of D. Brutus Callaicus.   On the other hand, Lucilius
held himself aloof from the guild of poets, and thereby
earned their enmity.   In later days Horace, from his coign
of vantage in the circle of Maecenas, directed some of his
bitterest satire against the mutual admiration of the professional poets.

We must remember that Accius was not only a poet, but
a critic as well.   He was, in fact, the first Roman to devote

Accius as critic   whole works expressly to questions of criticism.   In his *Pragmatica*[2] he seems to have
dealt mainly with the problems of the
theatre.   His chief critical work was the *Didascalica*,[3] of
which unfortunately only a few fragments have survived.
The work, which was in nine books, was evidently of wide
range, and dealt with many questions of a literary-historical
character concerning both Greek and Latin literature.   It
is possible that Accius endeavoured to work out the history
of both literatures on parallel lines.   He was interested in
chronology, though some of his attempts to establish it were
unhappy, as he blunders[4] over the relative dates of Homer
and Hesiod, giving Hesiod priority in time.   Cicero,[5] relying probably on Varro's[6] authority, has to correct his
erroneous date (197 B.C.) for the representation of the first
play of Livius Andronicus.   Accius dealt, too, with Greek[7]
Tragedy, and we know from Gellius[8] that he was interested
in the plays of Plautus.   A fragment[9] from the ninth book
of the *Didascalica*, addressed to Baebius, was seemingly

---

[1] Cic. Pro Archia, 27, Br. 107 ; Val. Max. VIII. 14. 2.

[2] Funaioli, op. cit., Vol. I. p. 27.

[3] *Ib.* p. 25 *et seq. ;* cf. Leo, Gesch. der röm. Lit. p. 386 *et seq. ;* Marx's
article "Accius" in Pauly–Wissowa.

[4] Gellius, III. 11. 4.

[5] Br. 72–73, Tusc. Disp. I. 3, Cato Major, 50 ; cf. Hendrickson, A
Pre-Varronian chapter in Literary History, A. J. Phil. XIX, 1898, p. 285
et seq. ; Leo, Plaut. Forsch. p. 66 *et seq.*

[6] Gellius, XVII. 21. 42 *et seq.*

[7] Funaioli, Didascalica, fr. 6 : " sed Euripidis, qui choros temerius in
fabulis," where he evidently glances at the irrelevancy of some of Euripides'
Choral odes ; cf. Aristotle, Poetics, c. 18.

[8] III. 3. 1, *ib.* 9.

[9] Funaioli, fr. 8 ; *vide infra*, p. 402.

part of an introduction to his treatment of the various genres of poetry. To judge from the bitterness of the polemic directed against him by Lucilius, it is not improbable that in his review of the several kinds of poetry, he had criticised the *Satires* of his contemporary. Lucilius was not the inventor of Satire, but he had given it a new character by infusing into it a spirit of invective, and also showed himself an innovator by his employment of the hexameter, in which metre alone many of his *Satires* were written. Whether such innovations were criticised by Accius, it is impossible to decide. What is more probable is that Accius contrasted the genre of Tragedy, wherein lay his own greatest glory,[1] with the genre in which Lucilius laboured. To one who aimed at sublimity[2] in language, the somewhat crude and vulgar diction of Satire, that was often redolent of the soil, would seem unworthy of an educated man,[3] while its general tone would be accounted commonplace[4] in comparison with the stateliness of Tragedy. Lucilius on his side mocked,[5] as we have seen, at the extravagant word-painting and turgid style of Tragedy, and evidently wished to win popular favour[6] in a different sphere of literature. He has many reminiscences[7] of the style of Tragedy, and some distinct echoes of Accius, probably intended as parodies of that poet. It is probable also that, as in the case of Pacuvius, Lucilius criticised him from the standpoint of the purists, and found fault[8] with certain strange forms and new compounds employed by his rival.

[1] Cf. Cic. Pro Plancio, 59, Pro Sestio, 120; Ovid, Am. I. 15. 19; Vell. I. 17. 1, II. 9. 2; Q. X. 1. 97.

[2] His admirers styled him " altus "; cf. Hor. Ep. II. 1. 56; *vide infra*, p. 299.

[3] It is possible that Lucil. fr. 649, may refer to such a polemic.

[4] Cf. Luc. fr. 608 : " nunc ignobilitas his mirum ac monstrificabile "; note frs. 628–630, in which Luc. contrasts his own aims with those of some rival, possibly Accius; cf. Cichorius, op. cit., pp. 129–130.

[5] Frs. 586 *et seq.*

[6] Cf. fr. 1013, where he boasts of his fame.

[7] Frs. 170, 276 " cortinipotentis," 507, suggestive of Accius (cf. Marx's note); cf. Birt, Zwei politische Satiren, p. 83 *et seq.*

[8] Fr. 650 may well be referred to such a criticism; cf. Varro, De L.L. V. 21, X. 70, on Accius' fondness for Greek endings; cf. Cic. Tusc. Disp. III. 20 (quoting Accius) : " male Latine videtur, sed praeclare Accius."

It is clear from all this that Lucilius had little taste for the grand style of Tragedy, which to him savoured of unreality. There is evidence that he pointed the contrast between his own work and that of the Tragedians, and that for himself he claimed above all the quality of sincerity.[1] Horace, a keen critic of the poet in other respects, upholds this claim, and tells[2] us that his life was mirrored in his writings, as if it were written on a votive tablet. Lucilius makes no ambitious claims for his *Satires*. Satire like Comedy is a mirror of life, and, being so, will not as a rule aim at elevation of style. Hence the names that he employs to describe his *Satires*, are significant. He does not appear to have used the title " satura," but he applies to them the word " schedium "[3] which is suggestive of improvisation,[4] and exclusive of effort to attain to the niceties of style. He employs[5] two other terms, " ludus " and " sermo," that throw light on the ideal at which he was aiming. " Ludus " is suggestive[6] of the half-playful tone of his *Satires*. The element of invective is prominent in him, but it is clear from his use of this term that he regarded himself as capable of employing the " ridiculum "[7] as well as the " acre."

The laws of Satire

The other title "sermo "[8] is even more significant, though it is difficult to decide whether Lucilius used it with a full consciousness of its implications, as they appear in contemporary[9] and later theory. With the " sermo," as we have seen, was associated a certain type of restrained and refined humour

The qualities of the " sermo "

[1] Fr. 590 : " ego ubi quem ex praecordiis ecfero versum."

[2] Sat. II. 1. 30 *et seq.*

[3] Fr. 1279 ; cf. Hor. Sat. I. 4. 9 *et seq.*, on Luc's faculty for speedy composition ; *ib.* I. 10. 60 ; Petron. Satyr. 4 : " schedium humilitatis Lucilianae " ; cf. Suess, op. cit., p. 89 *et seq. ; vide infra*, p. 377.

[4] Cf. Arist. Poet. 4, 1448. 6, on αὐτοσχεδιάσματα as a characteristic of primitive poetry.

[5] Fr. 1039 : " ludo ac sermonibus nostris."

[6] *Vide infra*, p. 358.

[7] *Vide infra*, p. 365.

[8] Fiske. op. cit., p. 90 *et seq.*, p. 118, has a very full treatment of the term, though he possibly reads into its use in Lucilius a greater import than it will bear.

[9] *Vide supra*, p. 36.

which often masqueraded under the guise of seriousness, and which was seen at its best in the conversation of Socrates[1] with its play of delicate irony. Cicero's discussion in the *De Officiis* of the various types of humour, the liberal and illiberal jest, and the quality of humour suited to the " sermo," was probably based on the theories of Panaetius,[2] and it is natural to conclude that such theories were discussed in the Scipionic circle, and that Scipio himself was indebted to his master for some at least of the characteristics of his humour. Horace in after days came under the influence of such theories. For him, as we shall see in a later chapter,[3] the title " sermo " was of first importance as helping to define both the style and humour of the Satiric genre, as he conceived it. It was indicative of the easy,[4] informal, and discursive character of his *Satires*, that were couched in a style akin to the speech of everyday life. It might also be used to describe the half-playful, half-serious criticism of human failings, and the mixture of the moralising of the philosopher and the shrewdness of the common-sense man, that were characteristic of the Διατριβαί of Bion,[5] who exercised no little influence on Roman Satire. Horace, when charged[6] with excessive venom and bitterness in his *Satires*, naturally endeavoured to formulate the quality of humour appropriate to the " sermo." He took pains to distinguish the Satirist from the slanderer and the buffoon. He demanded in particular that Satire be characterised by urbanity and restraint, by a mixture of grave and gay, and an absence of coarse and malignant wit. He denied that he himself was a slanderer, and sought to soothe the resentment of his victims by saying that his writings were intended to be read only by a few, not scattered broad-

[1] Lucilius' reference (fr. 709) to " Socratici carti " is interesting, but too obscure to draw any conclusion from it.

[2] Cf. De Off. II. 60: " quem multum in his libris secutus sum, non interpretatus."

[3] *Vide infra*, p. 374.

[4] Ad Her. III. 23: " sermo est oratio remissa et finitima cotidianae locutioni."

[5] Hor. Ep. II. 2. 60; cf. Fiske, op. cit., p. 178 *et seq.*, for his relation to Roman Satire; Oltramare, op. cit., *passim.*

[6] *Vide infra*, p. 354.

cast to the city. He declared, moreover, that he did not seek to wound for the sake of wounding, that he would attack only when attacked, and that his chief aim was to correct his own faults.

Even from the mutilated fragments of his work, it is clear that Lucilius in his own day had to submit to charges[1]
Lucilius' de- similar to those brought against Horace, of
fence of his making indiscriminate and envenomed at-
Satires tacks on citizens, of wishing to wound them
and defame their characters, and of assailing them with all the bitterness of the Cynic. Those who were pilloried by him, naturally asked[2] why should the manner in which they regulated their lives concern him. In endeavouring to answer[3] them Lucilius, too, evidently attempted to define the laws according to which he laboured in the genre of Satire. He seems to have set up, as Horace did later, a comparison between Satire and Comedy as a " species vitae,"[4] and to have denied to himself the title of poet. He declared[5] that his desire was not to play the part of slan-derer, but of social reformer. His claim to be a social reformer would in the eyes of later theorists bring him into line with the poets of the Old Comedy,[6] and thus make him a representative of the liberal jest.[7] It is interesting to note that Cicero emphasises[8] the refined and elegant character of Lucilius' wit. Horace, however, though he applies the epithet " facetus " to him, would regard him as lacking in the restraint[9] that should mark a delicate and urbane wit, and as too often employing invective[10] where playful banter

[1] *Vide infra*, p. 355.
[2] Frs. 1017 *et seq.*
[3] Fr. 1027.
[4] Frs. 1028–1029 : " ea quae speciem vitae esse putamus " ; cf. Fiske, op. cit., p. 288 ; *vide infra*, p. 374.
[5] Frs. 1030–1034 ; cf. Hor. Sat. II. 1. 70.
[6] Hor. Sat. I. 4. 1 *et seq.* ; Persius, I. 123 *et seq.* ; however, *vide infra*, p. 366.
[7] *Vide infra*, p. 362.
[8] De Or. I. 72, II. 25, III. 171, De Fin. I. 3. 7 : " urbanitas summa " ; cf. Ad Fam. IX. 15. 2, on Lucilius as a type of the " Romani veteres atque urbani sales " ; cf. Hor. Sat. I. 10. 65.
[9] *Vide infra*, p. 364 *et seq.*
[10] Cf. Sat. I. 10. 14–15.

would be more effective. Later critics,[1] too, were fond of emphasising the quality of biting invective in Lucilius. Juvenal in particular, for whom the element of invective was the vital breath of Satire, would naturally be inclined to stress this quality in the older Satirist. He regards himself as his lineal descendant, but it is doubtful if Lucilius would have shown much sympathy with Juvenal's grand manner, or with his ambitious rhetoric that at times sounds so hollow and unreal. Invective that is fierce and sustained, will naturally issue in a vehement[2] rhetorical style that is raised above the ordinary speech of men. Lucilius indulged in stinging invective, especially where political opponents[3] were concerned, and thus would have been carried at times into a style more elevated in tone than the usual level of his *Satires*. Still, the fact that he spoke of his writings as " Sermones," would indicate that his mind was fixed on another ideal, though, as I have said, it is not easy to decide from the fragments that survive how far he used the term[4] with a consciousness of its full import (in respect both of style and humour) as it was discussed in the Scipionic circle, and reflected in Horace's use of it in later times. However, Lucilius' conception of his *Satires* as a " species vitae," would of itself demand an unadorned[5] and unambitious style akin to the speech of everyday life. Several of the later critics[6] lay stress on the plain and commonplace character of his *Satires*. As regard humour, his use of the term

[1] Persius, I. 114 ; Q. X. 1. 94 ; Juv. I. 165 ; Macrob. Sat. III 16. 17 : " acer et violentus poeta."

[2] Cic's distinction between " sermo " and " contentio " is here important; cf. De Or. III. 177, Or. 64, De Off. I. 132, II. 48 ; Fiske, op. cit., p. 114 *et seq.*, Grant, The Ancient Rhetorical Theories of the Laughable, p. 131 *et seq.*, treat very fully of this point, though they are inclined to force the discussion too much into the conventional moulds of Rhetoric.

[3] Hor. Sat. II. 1. 67 *et seq. ;* Persius, I. 115.

[4] Fr. 1039 is the most vital fragment in regard to the special meaning of the term ; the phrase " sermonibus differre " which he elsewhere (frs. 1015–1016) uses, seems to have had a fairly general application ; cf. the phrase " differor sermone miser " used by Caecilius (Gellius, II. 23. 10).

[5] Independently of any rhetorical theory of the Plain style, such as Fiske postulates ; *vide infra*, p. 467.

[6] Gellius, VII. 14, 6, where Varro sets him down as a type of " gracilitas ; Petron. Satyr. 4 ; Fronto, II. p. 48, styles him " gracilis."

" ludus " to describe his writings, indicates that he himself was convinced that he could at times abandon the weapon of invective for the more subtle weapon of playful raillery.

Lucilius evidently felt that the genre of Satire was best suited to his talents, and that he was not gifted with the inspired qualities which would enable him **His incapacity for Epic** to essay a more sublime form of poetry.

Hence he is insistent on his incapacity to compose an Epic. He addresses certain verses[1] to a young historian who was engaged in writing the history of Ancient Rome. The allocation[2] of the fragments is difficult. In them, however, Lucilius seems to have urged the historian to abandon his labour of writing Ancient History, and to concentrate on an epic poem dealing with the campaign of Popilius Laenas, and the exploits of Scipio in the Numantine War, while he proclaims[3] his own unfitness for so formidable a task. There is another series of fragments[4] in which Lucilius once again refers to warlike exploits. He was seemingly desirous[5] of celebrating such exploits in epic strain, and for the moment tries to rise to something of the sublimity of the epic poet, but soon he feels that the wings of his inspiration are beginning to droop, and suddenly desists[6] from the attempt. All this finds a close parallel in Horace, who had been urged[7] by Trebatius Testa to write an Epic dealing with the exploits of Octavian. Though like Lucilius he adopts the epic manner for a brief space, he realised[8] that his genius was not fitted for such a task. It was a cardinal principle with Horace that the poet should not apply himself to a theme beyond his powers. Lucilius

[1] Frs. 612 *et seq.*, 625 *et seq. ;* the historian may have been Julius Congus, as Marx conjectures.

[2] Cichorius, op. cit., p. 113 *et seq.*, takes frs. 620–622, 627, as addressed by Lucilius to the historian ; *ib.* p. 31 *et seq. ;* cf. Fiske, op. cit., p. 374 *et seq.*

[3] Fr. 622.

[4] Frs. 1079 *et seq.*, which, as Cichorius conjectures (p. 183), may be addressed to C. Sempronius Tuditanus, Consul 129 B.C., and commander in the Istrian War.

[5] Frs. 1080–1085, 1094 ; cf. 1008.

[6] Fr. 1086 : " his te versibus interea contentus teneto."

[7] Sat. II. 1. 11 *et seq.*

[8] *Vide infra,* p. 415.

evidently saw the value of the same principle for one whose work is to bear the impress of sincerity. He was aware that men are endowed by nature with different gifts and different inclinations,[1] and felt that the poet above all should not attempt to bear a burden too heavy for his shoulders. One wonders if here again Lucilius is not showing evidence of the influence of Panaetius. As part of the law of Decorum, Panaetius (who, we take it, is reproduced by Cicero[2]) declares that each one should have a proper estimate of his own natural abilities, and show himself a keen judge of his own merits and defects. Lucilius was ready to do this, but was also ready to play the rôle of candid critic[3] to his friends, and avoid unmerited commendation of them, such as is given by some interested flatterer, whose praise is as insincere as the grief of hired mourners at a funeral.

The fragments of Lucilius are often obscure, and it would not be wise to raise too heavy a superstructure on them, even by way of conjecture. They are, however, sufficiently illuminating to enable us to see that their author holds a not unimportant place in the history of Roman criticism. He shows a fine appreciation for the faults of style both in tragedy and oratory. His associations with the Scipionic circle may have helped him here, but it is probable that Lucilius, original and independent character that he was, would on his own account have merited the tribute paid to him by the Elder Pliny as a critic of discerning taste. He had clearly some knowledge of Greek criticism and rhetorical theory, while we have seen evidence of his acquaintance with Hellenistic theorising on poetry. Moreover, his fragments are of no small interest as showing some attempt to define, under the stress of polemic it is true, the nature and the laws of the genre in which he worked.

With the ideals of the Scipionic circle one is naturally

---

[1] Frs. 628–630.

[2] De Off. I. 114.

[3] Fr. 611 (adopting Marx's reading), 717, 953–955 ; cf. Cic. Lael. 44, on the rôle of the candid friend ; Hor. A.P. 425 *et seq.*, for a close imitation of Lucilius ; cf. Cichorius, op. cit., p. 116 *et seq. ;* Fiske, op. cit., p. 458 *et seq. ; vide infra,* p. 382.

tempted to compare those of Catulus, who like Scipio
The culture gathered round him a number of literary
and ideals of men. Here again we meet with little in the
Catulus way of explicit criticism, but, if Cicero's
account of Catulus may be taken as historically accurate,
it is clear that he had theories on style that show affinity
with those of Scipio and his associates. Catulus was himself a poet[1] who, at least in one epigram, made Callimachus
his model. He was a friend of the improvisatori,[2] Archias
and Antipater of Sidon. He dedicated[3] a volume of autobiography to the poet Furius Antias, probably with the idea
that Furius would incorporate the material in his *Annales*,
an Epic poem designed as a continuation of the *Annales* of
Ennius. When dealing[4] with the question of the flute-
player, by whose aid C. Gracchus regulated his voice when
delivering a speech, Cicero appeals to the testimony of
Licinius, whom he styles a client of Catulus, and a " lit-
teratus homo."[5] Catulus' half-brother was C. Julius Caesar
Strabo, and to both of them Cicero assigned important
rôles in the coterie of literary men whom he gathered together to discuss the problems of the *De Oratore*. All this
serves to show how wide were the literary interests of
Catulus. He, in fact, helped to carry on the cultural traditions of the Scipionic circle. Cicero,[6] who pays many tributes
to the integrity of his character, calls[7] him " almost a second
Laelius," and represents[8] him as intimate with Scipio and

[1] Cf. Cic. De Nat. Deor. I. 79, for his epigram on Roscius : Pliny,
Ep. V. 3. 5 ; Gellius, XIX. 9. 10, 14 ; Apul. Apol. 9.

[2] Pro Archia, 6, 19 ; Archias wrote a poem on the Cimbric War, but
from what standpoint it is difficult to say, as he was also a friend of Marius ;
cf. De Or. III. 194 ; Q. X. 7. 19.

[3] Cic. Br. 132 ; cf. Peter, Historicorum Rom. Reliquiae, Vol. I. p.
cclxii *et seq.*, *ib.* p. 191 *et seq.*

[4] De Or. III. 225 *et seq.* ; Büttner, Porcius Licinus, p. 80 *et seq.*, identifies this Licinius with Porcius Licinus, but his evidence is by no means
conclusive.

[5] Cf. Suet. De Gr. 3, on the purchase by Catulus, and manumission of
Lutatius Daphnis, the grammarian.

[6] Pro Murena, 36, Pro Plancio, 12, Pro Sestio, 101, De Domo Sua,
113–114, De Nat. Deor. III. 80 ; cf. De Or. III. 9, on his death.

[7] Tusc. Disp. V. 56.

[8] De Or. II. 154–155.

his friends, and filled with admiration for their qualities.
It is evident that he shared their ideals for the union[1] of
Greek and Roman culture, while he embodied in his own
person the best elements of Hellenism. He had mastered[2]
Greek so thoroughly, that he was able to reproduce the
delicacy and charm of the language. In the *De Oratore*
his authority is highly valued, when some question[3] of
Greek erudition arises that requires a specialist's knowledge.
He contrasts[4] the literary qualities of the Greek and Roman
historians to the disadvantage of the latter. He was also
an ardent student of philosophy, and, though influenced[5]
by the scepticism of Carneades, he yet proclaims[6] his
admiration of Aristotle. With such a wide range of intellectual interests, Catulus was naturally on the side of
those who demanded[7] the most comprehensive culture in
the orator, and herein probably lay the secret of his admiration[8] for the eloquence of Crassus. However, his devotion
to Hellenism was not the blind devotion of the Graecomaniac, but of one that could discern[9] the weak elements in
Hellenic culture, and estimate the hollowness of the Greek
charlatan.

There are other characteristics in him that remind us of
Scipio and the members of his circle. Like Scipio his
learning sat upon him easily,[10] and without
His affinity any trace of ostentation. Crassus pays him[11]
with Scipio a remarkable tribute, when he declares that
so pure was his Latin, that he seemed in that age to be the

[1] Cic. Br. 132, describes him as " non antiquo illo more sed hoc nostro
. . . eruditus," *vide infra*, p. 175.

[2] De Or. II. 28.

[3] Cf. De Or. II. 151, 154, on Greek Philosophy in Italy ; *ib*. III. 126
et seq., on the history of the Sophists ; cf. III. 21.

[4] *Ib*. II. 51, 54.

[5] Acad. Pr. 148 ; Reid, Introd. p. 39, considers the younger Catulus as
the mouthpiece of his father's views ; cf. Acad. Pr. 12, *ib*. 18.

[6] De Or. II. 152, III. 182, 187.

[7] *Ib*. II. 363.

[8] *Ib*. II. 233, III. 82, 131, 228.

[9] *Ib*. II. 19, 75–76 ; he was evidently not enamoured of some of the
later developments of Greek Rhetoric with its minute attention to rules.

[10] Cic. De Off. I. 133.

[11] De Or. III. 29 ; cf. Br. 132.

only master of pure Latinity. He was remarkable,[1] too, for the refined character of his pronunciation. His words were uttered with a charm and sweetness that were free from all affectation. He did not mumble his words, but pronounced them naturally, without seeking to gain distinctness by staccato effects. He seems to have paid particular attention to the purity[2] of his vowel sounds, and to have avoided those broad sounds that were common in old Latin, and were still maintained in peasant speech.[3] The result was a softness and sweetness that contrasted strongly with the broadness of the rustic " brogue " affected by Cotta. The charm of Catulus' pronunciation was in part native to him, but, as Cicero[4] makes it clear, it was in part also the outcome of a scientific study of Greek sounds. In all this Catulus was probably carrying on the traditions[5] of the Scipionic circle. Another point of interest is that, both by the purity of his language, and the refined character of his pronunciation, he was helping to put on a firm foundation the ideal of " urbanitas."[6]

In his fondness for a plain style of oratory, he again reminds us of a characteristic of the Scipionic circle. It is **His preference** true that at times he used rare forms[7] to **for the Plain** give distinction to his prose, while Fronto[8] **style** found an element of bombast in a letter[9] of his written to celebrate his exploits. He himself, however,

[1] De Or. III. 42, Br. 133, 259 ; Q. XI. 3. 35.

[2] Q. loc. cit. also lays stress on his pronunciation of combinations of consonants such as occur in words like pellexit, collegit, etc.

[3] Cf. " speca " for " spica," " vea " for " via " ; Varro, R. R. I. 2. 14, 48. 2 ; Cic. De Or. III. 46, Br. 137.

[4] Br. 259 ; Cotta in contrast to Catulus " se valde dilatandis litteris a similitudine Graecae locutionis abstraxerat " ; cf. De Or. III. 42 : "verum id (i.e. the characteristics of Catulus' pronunciation) adfert ratio, docent litterae, confirmat consuetudo et legendi et loquendi " ; Catulus' half-brother, J. Caesar, showed great care in the transcription and pronunciation of Greek names, e.g. " Tecmessa " for the older form " Tecumessa " ; cf. Büttner, op. cit., p. 166.

[5] In view of De Or. III. 45, Büttner, p. 163, surely exaggerates in calling Catulus a pioneer in the matter of pronunciation.

[6] *Vide infra*, p. 244.   [7] Cf. De Or. III. 153.

[8] II. p. 142 (Haines).

[9] Peter, op. cit., Vol. I. p. cclxiv, conjectures that this is to be identified with the " liber " mentioned by Cic. Br. 132.

characterises his style[1] of oratory in a way that suggests the orator of the plain style, who was restrained in delivery, and did not aim at emotional effects. He praises[2] Crassus' discourse on prose rhythm, but on the other hand Crassus is afraid[3] lest his precepts about euphony may seem to him artificial and puerile, as if he were averse to such over-niceness in the writing of prose. Cicero records[4] the interesting fact that his volume of autobiography was written in the style of Xenophon, an author beloved by the younger Scipio. When we take this into account, and consider the element of humour[5] that was diffused amidst his gravity, and recollect the characteristics of his oratory,[6] as they are described for us especially by Cicero, it is not too much to assume that Catulus' prose style may have been influenced by the theories[7] of the Scipionic circle.

It is interesting to note that Julius Caesar Strabo presented similar characteristics. As well as being an orator, he was a Tragic poet,[8] though from his

Julius Caesar Strabo character one would expect him to have achieved greater success as a writer of Comedies. He was famous[9] as a wit, and was selected by Cicero to propound the theory of the " Laughable " in the *De Oratore*. He appealed to the latter as introducing a new note into Roman oratory, but he, too, seems merely to have continued the tradition of the Scipionic circle. His speeches were carefully composed, but neither in his oratory,[10]

---

[1] De Or. II. 74 ; *ib.* 28, for his qualities of " subtilitas " and " elegantia "; cf. II. 86, III. 29.

[2] *Ib.* III. 187 ; Büttner, however, p. 170, is wrong in ascribing to Catulus an intimate knowledge of the laws of prose rhythm.

[3] De Or. III. 172–173 ; Büttner, loc. cit., takes " puerile " in the sense of elementary, but surely in view of the whole context (171 *et seq.*) Cicero is thinking rather of τὸ μειρακιῶδες, as it was used in Greek criticism.

[4] Br. 132.

[5] De Or. III. 29 ; cf. II. 255, 278.

[6] Cic. *ib.* II. 44, mentions the interesting fact that his panegyric on his mother was the first ever delivered on a woman.

[7] *Vide supra*, p. 36, on the theory of the " sermo."

[8] Ribbeck, Die röm. Tragödie, pp. 610–612, Trag. Lat. Reliquiae, p. 194.

[9] De Or. II. 98, 216, 231, 276, Br. 177, 216, Tusc. Disp. V. 55, De Off. I. 108.

[10] Br. 177 : " minime . . . vehemens."

nor in his dramas, did he aim at being forceful. Cicero expressly relates[1] of him that in the law courts he was able by his conversational style of speaking to prevail over the more ambitious and emotional oratory of other advocates. He evidently regarded this quiet, conversational style[2] as the most fitting medium for his humorous sallies. He thus compensated for his lack of vigour by his ready wit, and by his divine gift of humour which radiated throughout his oratory, and enabled[3] him to mingle grave and gay without impairing the dignity of his subject. He first won fame when he prosecuted Albucius[4] on behalf of the Sardinians, but he, too, was drawn into the vortex of party politics,[5] and suffered the fate[6] of so many of the aristocracy. There is thus much both in Catulus and his half-brother that renders it probable that they were influenced by the theories of style prevailing in the Scipionic circle, and were in a measure heirs to its traditions.

In this early period we have seen indications of an attempt at a systematic criticism of poetry in the *Didascalica* of Accius. Porcius Licinus, who was[7] himself a poet, turned his attention to a similar task. Gellius quotes[8] from him a fragment of verse in which he declares that Poetry first winged its flight in the Second Punic War to the fierce and warlike people of Romulus. It seems clear that Porcius is ignoring the native Camenae, and viewing the beginnings of Roman poetry from the standpoint of the Hellenist, but he leaves us in doubt as to whom he will assign the honour of being the first Roman poet. It is probable that, in thus placing

Porcius Licinus

[1] De Off. I. 133 ; note his contrast of " sermo " and " contentio."

[2] It was probably the union of the conversational tone and the play or humour that constituted the novelty of his style in Cicero's eyes, though both Scipio and Laelius must have exhibited similar characteristics.

[3] De Or. III. 30.

[4] De Off. II. 50 ; cf. Suet. J. C. 55, for Caesar's imitation of him ; Meyer, Or. Rom. pp. 160–162.

[5] Br. 226, *ib.* 305, on his " accuratae contiones " ; De Har. Resp. 43.

[6] De Or. III. 10, Br. 307.

[7] Gellius, XIX. 9. 10, 13.

[8] XVII. 21. 45 ; cf. Büttner op. cit., p. 50 *et seq.* ; cf. Lucr. I. 117 *et seq.* (there quoted), where Ennius is described as the first Roman to win the glory of a true poet, inspired by the Muses of Helicon ; *vide infra*, p. 283.

the beginnings of Roman poetry in the Second Punic War, he was merely following the false chronology[1] of Accius, who held that Livius Andronicus came to Rome after the capture of Tarentum in 209 B.C., and produced his first play in 197 B.C.   Horace, in later days, again probably following the lead of Accius, adopted[2] a similar chronology. To judge by the fragment referred to above, Porcius Licinus seems to have written a metrical treatise *De Poetis*, giving an account of the development of poetry in Rome up to his own time.   Varro preserves[3] from him a fragment referring to Ennius, while from Cicero[4] we have his criticism of the poet Atilius, whom he styled a " ferreus scriptor."   This criticism is an indication that he judged the poets from the aesthetic standpoint, and probably took into account their success or failure in reproducing the polish and charm of their Greek models.   His longest fragment,[5] also in verse, may possibly come from the same treatise, and deals with the relations of Terence to his patrons in the Scipionic circle.   It contains nothing of interest from the point of view of literary criticism, as it leaves obscure even the literary relationship of Terence to his friends, but its wealth of innuendo[6] is proof of a strong anti-aristocratic bias, and tells against Büttner's view that Licinus belonged to the circle of Catulus.

Volcacius Sedigitus, whom the Elder Pliny styles " illustris in poetica,"[7] affords another instance of a critic's interest in the history of Roman poetry.   He

The Canon of Sedigitus wrote a metrical treatise *De Poetis*, from which Gellius[8] has preserved his famous Canon of the Roman Comic poets.   Like Accius, and like

---

[1] *Vide supra*, p. 51.

[2] Ep. II. 1. 156 *et seq.*;   cf. Hendrickson, A Pre-Varronian chapter, p. 293.

[3] De L. L. V. 163.

[4] De Fin. I. 5 ; cf. Ad Att. XIV. 20. 3, where Atilius is styled " poeta durissimus," probably, as Büttner suggests, an echo of Porcius' criticism.

[5] *Vide* Suet. Life of Terence, c. I.

[6] Even the verses, as reconstructed by Büttner, p. 32, with such daring, will not remove the rock of offence.

[7] N.H. XI. 244.

[8] XV. 24.

Varro at a later date, he evidently[1] busied himself with the problem of determining the authentic plays of Plautus. All the fragments of his writings that have been preserved, deal with the Comic dramatists, though the title of his work as given by Gellius seems to indicate that he did not confine his attention to these alone. The references[2] to him in Suetonius' Life of Terence give grounds for the presumption that he dealt with the life and works of each of the poets of Comedy. The text[3] of his reference to Terence's *Hecyra* is so uncertain, that we cannot determine whether he wished to place it last among Terence's plays, as being the weakest, or to refer to its failure on the stage, though the context in which Suetonius quotes him, is in favour of the latter view. His chief importance, however, in the history of Roman criticism lies in his Canon of the Comic poets. This is of special interest as showing the influence[4] of criticism, as it was practised at Pergamum, and at Alexandria by such men as Aristophanes[5] of Byzantium and Aristarchus, who aimed at arranging the chief poets in each genre according to the order of their merit. Such Canons were framed from a study of the various genres, and tended not only to stereotype the laws of the genres, but to set the seal of pre-eminence on certain writers and their works to the exclusion[6] of others scarcely less deserving of recognition. Thus there was danger that advance would be barred to any innovating genius. The Canon usually, we may presume, included only those writers who had stood the test of time, but it might easily become a mechanical form of criticism, especially if the framer of

[1] Gellius, III. 3. 1.

[2] C. 2, 4, 5.

[3] *Ib.* c. 2 ; cf. Büttner, op. cit., p. 37 *et seq.*, for MS. readings, and attempts at emendation ; Schanz, op. cit., I. 1. p. 226.

[4] For traces of such " Canons " cf. Petr. Satyr. 2 : " Pindarus novemque lyrici " ; Sen. Ep. 27. 6 ; Q. I. 4. 3, X. 1. 54, 59, 61, 76 ; cf. Usener, Dionysii Halicarnassensis, etc., p. 130 *et seq. ;* Hartmann, De Canone Decem Oratorum, p. 2 *et seq. ;* Sandys, A History of Classical Scholarship, Vol. I. p. 119 *et seq.*, 130.

[5] Cf. Vitruv. VII. Praef. 5 *et seq.*

[6] Hor. Sat. I. X. 34 : " insanius ac si magnas Graecorum malis implere catervas," may have had such " Canons " before his mind, and be suggesting here that the ranks of the mighty Greeks were closed once and for all.

it had no clear or definite criterion of judgment. The consecration of certain names in the various genres of Greek literature would naturally have tempted the Romans to do likewise for their own literature, and also to set up a parallelism between their own writers and the Greek writers who had laboured in the corresponding genre, and had been deified by inclusion in the Canon.

We cannot be sure of Volcacius' date, but he seemingly desired to construct a Canon that would vie[1] with some of the Alexandrian Canons. His taste was catholic enough to include almost all the writers of Comedy[2] down to his own day. In this he presents a striking contrast to Quintilian who, viewing Comedy as a weak element in Roman literature, mentions[3] only Plautus, Terence, and Caecilius amongst the writers of "Palliatae." It is evident from Volcacius that the relative merits of the Roman Comic writers was a question that was being debated in the literary circles of his day, so that he sets out to dispel all doubt, and deliver what is equivalent to an ex cathedra pronouncement.[4] It is not easy to determine what criterion of judgment he employed. He awards the palm to Caecilius for his characteristics of broad farce and his affinity with the Mime.[5] We may presume that Plautus was assigned the second place, because he exhibited similar qualities. In the case of Naevius, who comes third on the list, and who is characterised by the words " qui fervet," we are faced by another standard of judgment. At first sight the words seem to suggest Naevius' power of stirring the

The aim of Sedigitus

---

[1] Brzoska, op. cit., p. 79, suggests that he may have adopted the number ten in imitation of the Canon of Orators ; this view, of course, pre-supposes that the Canon of orators was then in existence.

[2] Volcacius, however, deals only with the writers of Palliatae.

[3] Q. X. 1. 99 ; Vell. I. 17. 1, mentions only Caecilius, Terence, and Afranius, as representatives of Roman Comedy.

[4] Cf. Cic. De opt. gen. I. 2 : " itaque licet dicere et Ennium summum epicum poetam, si cui ita videtur, et Pacuvium tragicum, et Caecilium fortasse comicum " ; cf. Q. X. 1. 99.

[5] Reading " mimico " ; cf. Gellius, II. 23. 12, on his version of Menander's Plocium : " et alia nescio quae mimica inculcavit " ; Reich, Der Mimus, Vol. I. p. 337 et seq., on the relation of Caecilius to the Mime.

emotions, and remind us of Varro's criticism[1] of the Comic poets Trabea, Atilius, and Caecilius, but it is possible that Volcacius had in mind the poet's passionate temperament, which led him to attack[2] some of the leading men in Rome with something of the bitter invective of the Old Comedy. Whether, in placing the remaining writers of Comedy, Volcacius kept before him the criteria already employed, or whether he was actuated merely by personal predilection, it is impossible to decide. Terence, who lacked the farcical element so prominent in Plautus, is placed sixth[3] on the list, though his admirers might find consolation in the fact that the last place but one is assigned to his old adversary Luscius Lanuvinus. Volcacius evidently either wished to complete his roll of ten, or else felt himself at a loss for a standard of judgment, when he determined to include Ennius at the close of his list " causa antiquitatis."

[1] Cf. Charisius, G. L. I. p. 241 (Keil) : " πάθη vero Trabea, inquit, Atilius, Caecilius facile moverunt."

[2] Cf. Gellius, III. 3. 15, VI. 8. 5 ; Aug. De Civ. Dei, II. 12.

[3] Cf. Suet. Life of Terence, c. 5.

CHAPTER II

ASPECTS OF THE PROBLEM OF STYLE

THE QUESTION of Style, as propounded in Classical theory, is so complex and varied that one could never hope to deal adequately with it within the limits of a single chapter. Hence my aim will be nothing more than to treat of certain aspects of it which seem to me to have a special interest. When I speak of the Classical theory of style, I do not wish to suggest that the Ancients had any clear-cut theory that could embrace the subject as a whole. To discover a final solution of the problem of style would have been for them a task as elusive and as baffling as it is for the Moderns. The Ancient theorists, however, accustomed to the definite precepts and formulas of the Rhetorical schools, would not perhaps have been as much dismayed by the problem as the modern critics who endeavour to arrive at a solution of the mystery. In Rome, as time went on, the influence of Greek rhetorical theory helped to stereotype certain views and classifications of style that in particular predominated in the realm of oratory.

We are all familiar with the classification of oratorical styles into the Plain, the Middle, and the Grand. In Latin literature it makes its first appearance in the **The three oratorical styles** *Auctor ad Herennium*.[1] It figures largely in Cicero's rhetorical works,[2] and is adopted by Quintilian[3] and later authors.[4] Among the Greek theorists Dionysius makes effective use of it in dealing[5] with Demosthenes, whose supremacy as an orator was considered to lie in his mastery over all three styles.

[1] IV. 8. 11.
[2] De Or. III. 177, 199, 212, Or. 20–21, 75 *et seq.*
[3] X. 1. 44, XII. 10. 58 *et seq.*
[4] Gellius, VII. 14. 1 *et seq.* ; Fronto, I. 104.
[5] De Dem. c. 33 ; cf. *ib.* 8.

Now when or with whom[1] this classification of styles originated is still a debated question.   It is clear, of course,

Origin of the classification that certain broad distinctions of style were generally noted in Greek oratory. Isocrates emphasises[2] the contrast between the splendour and elaborateness of his own style, and the plainness of forensic eloquence, especially such as dealt with private cases. Aristotle makes a pregnant observation with an important bearing on the styles of forensic oratory, when he declares[3] that a case should be fought out on the facts alone, and that the orator should not have recourse to devices for persuasion, or to adventitious appeals to the emotions.   Such an ideal might be realised in a community of philosophers,[4] but appeals to the feelings, the use of language charged with emotion, a display of histrionic power on the part of the speaker, are rendered almost inevitable by the depravity of the audience, or the perverse nature of constitutions.[5]   Aristotle's ideal[6] may have demanded nothing more than a mere argumentative treatment of the facts of a case, without reference to a positive[7] oratorical style.   Its importance, however, lies in the fact that it had its influence on his pupil Theophrastus,[8] and on the Stoics, who held[9] that the true function of the orator was to instruct (docere), and to argue from the facts of his case without any appeal to the emotions.   It was in turn

[1] Volkmann, op. cit., p. 532, with little to support his view, suggests that such a classification may go back to Antisthenes ; cf. Diog. Laert. VI. 15 ; cf. Hendrickson's important article, " The Origin and Meaning of the Ancient Characters of Style," A. J. Phil. Vol. XXVI. 3, 1905, p. 249 *et seq.*

[2] Panegyr. 11 ; note the contrast of ἀφελῶς and ἐπιδεικτικῶς ; cf. Panath. 11, περὶ ἀντιδ. 2–3.

[3] Rhet. III. 1. 5 ; cf. *ib.* I. 1. 3, III. 14. 8, on the use of the exordium ; cf. Lucian, Anacharsis, 19.

[4] Cf. Q. II. 17. 28.

[5] Rhet. III. 1. 4.

[6] Cf. Kroll, Randbemerkungen, Rhein. Mus. 1907, p. 86 *et seq.*

[7] i.e., the Plain style in contradistinction to the Grand ; still we are within measurable distance of a distinction between the two styles.

[8] Cf. Mayer, Theophrastus, p. 14 (quoting Ammonius) on the distinction between λόγος πρὸς τὰ πράγματα and λόγος πρὸς τοὺς ἀκροωμένους ; Mayer is certainly wrong in adducing as a parallel Aristotle's distinction between γραφικὴ and ἀγωνιστικὴ λέξις.

[9] *Vide infra*, p. 161 *et seq.*

through Stoic[1] influence that an ideal of the philosophic style was developed, as something essentially plain, contemptuous of the graces of rhetoric, aiming at logical acumen, and concerned more with the matter than with the manner.   Again, mainly under Stoic influence, arose the contrast[2] between the quiet, even, almost conversational flow of the philosopher's discourse, and the grand, impetuous manner of the orator, whose aim is to rouse the emotions of his audience.   Stoic theories had their inevitable reaction on the oratory of the school, and resulted in a style characterised by dialectical subtlety and studied plainness.

Our discussion so far has revealed a number of influences that must have contributed not a little to the formulation of the Plain style, as we find it set forth in Cicero,[3] though on the other hand the study by the critics of an orator such as Lysias must have helped considerably towards its definition.   The language employed[4] by the orator of the Plain style was akin to the speech of everyday life, and the power of close reasoning demanded from him was emphasised especially when such a style was brought into relation with his function of instructing[5] the judge on the facts of his case, and of setting forth his proofs.   The more complete was the formulation of the Plain style, the more was the contrast heightened between it and the Grand style.

The formulation of the Plain style

Returning to Aristotle, we find[6] in him another important distinction between the style suited for delivery in actual debate, whether in forensic or deliberative oratory, and the style suited to a written composition.   The latter was

---

[1] *Vide infra*, p. 139.

[2] Cf. the contrast between " sermo " and " contentio."

[3] Or. 75 *et seq.*, Br. 201, 317 ; cf. Ad Her. IV. 8. 11 ; Demetr. 190 *et seq.*, where Lysias is quoted in illustration.

[4] Or. 76, *ib*. 77 : " non ingratam negligentiam de re hominis magis quam de verbis laborantis," *ib*. 196, on the use of Iambic rhythms in the Plain style ; cf. Dionys. De Lysia, 3, 13, De Dem. 2, on Lysias as an exponent of it.

[5] Cic. Or. 20, De Or. II. 215, De opt. gen. 5 ; Q. X. 10. 1. 78 (on Lysias), XII. 10. 58–59.

[6] Rhet. III. 12, on γραφικὴ and ἀγωνιστικὴ λέξις ; cf. Cic. Or. 37 *et seq.* ; Demetr. 193 ; Isocr. Phil. 25 *et seq.*

primarily intended to be read, and could embrace within
its fold such branches of literature as poetry,
history, and "epideictic" exercises[1] in oratory,
which were designed for display and for
the pleasure[2] of the hearers. Such exer-
cises included[3] the various kinds of panegyrical oratory,
which were permitted to indulge in almost unlimited ornament and elaboration. All the resources of rhetoric could
be lavished[4] on such themes, as they had no practical aim.
They held a place analogous to the Fine[5] as compared with
the useful arts. The epideictic orator[6] in his own sphere
enjoyed almost as much licence as the poet in regard to his
choice of words, and the boldness of his figures, while he
was left practically unfettered in the use of amplification,
and in the rhythmical structure of his periods. The
epideictic style then, in its use of rhetorical ornament, might
be regarded as a heightening[7] of the Grand style as it was
employed by the orator in real debate. With the aim of
epideictic oratory Aristotle contrasts[8] the practical aim of
the speaker who pleads a cause before a public assembly
(deliberative oratory), or a case before the law-courts
(forensic oratory). As regards the styles of these latter
orators, he introduces[9] a subtle distinction in respect of
the audiences before whom they plead. The style of the
forensic speaker must be the more finished,[10] as he addresses
a smaller audience, just as we expect more exact perfection

Written com-
positions and
the style of ac-
tual debate

---

[1] Rhet. III. 12. 6: ἡ μὲν οὖν ἐπιδεικτικὴ λέξις γραφικωτάτη; cf.
Philod. Rhet. I. 122, II. 79; Hermogenes, περὶ ἰδ. (Spengel), II. 417, on
panegyrical style in the broadest sense; Q. III. 8. 63.

[2] Cic. De Or. I. 81, II. 341, Or. 42, 65, on Sophistic Rhetoric; cf.
Arist. Rhet. I. 3. 1 *et seq.;* Thucy. III. 38, where Cleon compares the
Athenians to θεαταὶ σοφιστῶν.

[3] Cf. Q. III. 7. 1, on Roman usage in this matter.

[4] Q. VIII. 3. 11, XI. 1. 48; Isocr. περὶ ἀντιδ. 46 *et seq.*

[5] Cf. Cic. De Or. I. 118.

[6] Cic. Or. 38 *et seq.,* 207; Q. IX. 4. 130; Arist. Rhet. I. 9. 40, on the
use of amplification in epideictic oratory; Demetr. 120, 301.

[7] Cf. Fronto, I. p. 104, where he says that there is practically no place
for the Plain style in epideictic oratory.

[8] Rhet. I. 3. 1.

[9] *Ib.* III. 12. 5; the distinction is a matter of perspective.

[10] It must be especially so, says A., if he pleads before a single judge.

of detail in a picture that is to be viewed at close range.   As a general condition for style, Aristotle demands that it be clear and becoming.   With the introduction of this principle of Decorum,[1] he thus finds place for many nuances of style, which must be in harmony with a speaker's character, emotions, and the magnitude of the issue at stake.

Aristotle could thus envisage various styles, but he makes no attempt to formulate the doctrine of the three styles, as it appears in later theory.   This

**Did Theophra-
stus formulate
the three
styles ?** doctrine is usually associated with the name of his pupil Theophrastus, who according to Dionysius[2] considered Thrasymachus as the representative of the Middle style, and so must have had before his mind the concept of the other two oratorical styles,[3] the Plain and the Grand.   With much plausibility Hendrickson[4] has argued that Theophrastus concerned himself not with defining a Middle style, but the " Mean " ($\mu\acute{\epsilon}\sigma\sigma\tau\eta s$)[5] in which the perfection of all good style lay. Dionysius confounded this doctrine of Theophrastus with the doctrine of the three styles current in his own day.   It is interesting to note that he considers[6] the Middle style the most excellent of the three, but he more than once uses[7] language with regard to it that suggests the Peripatetic Mean of style.   The $\mu\acute{\epsilon}\sigma\sigma\tau\eta s$ defined by Theophrastus constituted the ideal style, inasmuch as it avoided excess,[8] whether on the side of baldness or over-ornateness, and at the same time connoted adherence to the principle of

---

[1] *Vide infra*, p. 114 *et seq.*

[2] De Dem, 3 : $\tau\rho\acute{\iota}\tau\eta\ \lambda\acute{\epsilon}\xi\epsilon\omega s\ <\iota\delta\acute{\epsilon}a>\ .\ .\ .\ \mathring{\eta}\nu\ \mathring{\eta}\ \mu\iota\kappa\tau\acute{\eta}\ \tau\epsilon\ \kappa\alpha\grave{\iota}\ \sigma\acute{\upsilon}\nu\theta\epsilon\tau\sigma s$ $\grave{\epsilon}\kappa\ \tau\sigma\acute{\upsilon}\tau\omega\nu\ \tau\mathring{\omega}\nu\ \delta\upsilon\epsilon\hat{\iota}\nu$;   cf. Mayer, op. cit., p. 6.

[3] Cf. De Dem. c. I–II.

[4] The Peripatetic Mean of Style, and the Three Stylistic Characters, A.J. Phil. Vol. XXV. 2, 1904, p. 125 *et seq.* ; cf. Stroux, De Theophrasti Virtutibus Dicendi, p. 108 *et seq.*

[5] According to the Peripetetic theory, virtue lay in the " Mean " ; this, as we shall see, was at the basis of the doctrine of Decorum.

[6] De Dem. 34 ; cf. De C. V. 24, on $\mathring{\alpha}\rho\mu\sigma\nu\acute{\iota}\alpha\ \epsilon\mathring{\upsilon}\kappa\rho\alpha\tau\sigma s$.

[7] De Dem. 3 (on Thrasymachus' style) : $\epsilon\mathring{\iota}\ \delta\grave{\eta}\ \pi\eta\gamma\acute{\eta}\ \tau\iota s\ \mathring{\eta}\nu\ \mathring{\sigma}\nu\tau\omega s\ \tau\mathring{\eta}s$ $\mu\epsilon\sigma\acute{\sigma}\tau\eta\tau\sigma s$.

[8] Cf. Demetr. 114, 222, on Theoph's precepts against excess ; Dionys. De Lysia, 14, for his criticism of such faults in Lysias ; Cic. De Or. III. 184, on moderation in prose rhythm ; Ad Fam. XVI. 17. 1.

Decorum which is imperative for every good style. It seems probable that the doctrine of the three styles was elaborated at a later date, when the theory of Imitation began to be in vogue, and when various Attic orators, differing in style, were being proposed[1] as models. It was convenient then to have categories into which could be fitted orators such as Lysias, Isocrates, and Demosthenes, who exhibited such divergent characteristics. A fundamental difference[2] was felt to exist between the Plain and the Grand styles. It was an easy step to conceive a style intermediate[3] between these two, and regarded by some as partaking of the excellencies of both. This Middle style became a convenient category to which could be relegated certain orators and writers that did not seem to fit easily into either of the other two categories. However, a serious problem arose when it became necessary to define the characteristics of this style. Dionysius evidently realised[4] the difficulty of the problem, with the result that he sometimes classes[5] together orators such as Lysias and Thrasymachus that were usually supposed to have little affinity with each other. Hence some critics found a way out by identifying the Middle style with the " genus floridum,"[6] the distinguishing characteristics of which were smoothness and charm.

But difficulty was experienced not only in assigning positive characteristics to this style, but in defining the faulty style corresponding to it, so that critics, in des-

[1] Especially after the rise of Asianist oratory, and the setting in of the Atticist reaction.

[2] Recognised by some critics as *the* fundamental difference in styles ; Demetr. 36 ; cf. Cic. Br. 201, Or. 196, where the two styles are contrasted without reference to a Middle style ; De Or. II. 215 (on officia oratoris) : " docere judicem possunt, commovere non posunt ; in quo sunt omnia."

[3] Cic. Or. 21 ; Gellius, VII. 14. 3.

[4] Cf. De C.V. c. 21, 24, for his difficulty in naming the ἁρμονία εὔκρατος ; here, of course, he is dealing with composition, but the problem was an analogous one.

[5] De Isaeo, 20.

[6] Cf. Cic. Or. 96 : " florens . . . orationis genus " (here brought into relation with the style of the Sophists) ; Q. XII 10. 58 ; the corresponding Greek term was γλαφυρός or ἀνθηρός ; cf. Dionys. De Dem. 40 ; Demetr. 36.

cribing the latter, were forced to take refuge in vague
The corres- and indefinite terms.[1] The characteristics of
ponding defec- the other two styles were securely established,
tive styles so that it was easy to describe the corresponding faulty styles. The Plain style[2] might easily degenerate by
excess into one that was dry and attenuated. The Grand
style through lack of restraint was prone[3] to pass into one
that was tasteless, bombastic, exaggerated, and unreal in its
passion. The orator of the Grand style had at his command
all the resources of rhetoric, elevated diction, wealth of
figures, the use of commonplaces and amplification, but as
he had a practical end[4] in view, he was at times expected to
abandon[5] the grand manner, and exhibit a certain moderation, if he wished to impress the audience with his sincerity.

The doctrine of the three styles, which was primarily
designed to characterise various types of oratory, in time
The three came to be applied to other branches of
styles in literature, to poetry[6] as well as prose. In
practice the sphere of oratory the division became
important, when it was adapted to the theory of the " officia
oratoris," according to which it was the orator's duty[7] to
instruct, delight, and move his audience. The Plain
style, with its predominant qualities of clearness and
logical subtlety, was best suited to the purposes of instruction. When the Middle style became identified with the
" genus floridum," with its characteristics of smoothness
and charm, it was naturally assigned the task of giving
pleasure[8] to, or winning over an audience. The orator

[1] Auct. ad Her. IV. 11. 16, calls it " fluctuans et dissolutum " ; Demetr.
186, calls this defective style κακόζηλος.

[2] Ad Her. loc. cit. ; Cic. Br. 202 ; Pliny, Ep. I. 20. 21 ; Gellius, VII.
14. 5 ; Demetr. 236 *et seq.*

[3] Ad Her. IV. 10. 15 ; Br. 202 ; Hor. A.P. 27 : " professus grandia
turget " ; Pliny, Ep. VII. 12. 4 ; Q. XII. 10. 80 ; cf. Arist. Rhet. III. 3, on
τὰ ψυχρά, which are mostly faults of excess in the Grand style ; Demetr.
114 *et seq.* ; περὶ ὕψους, III. 3 ; *vide infra*, p. 240.

[4] As compared with the epideictic orator.

[5] Or. 99.

[6] *Vide infra*, p. 467.

[7] Cic. De Or. II. 72, 115, 121, 128, 310, Br. 276, Or. 69, De opt. gen. 5 ;
Q. III. 5. 2, XI. 1. 6, XII. 10. 59, 70.

[8] Delectare or conciliare ; De Or. II. 182 *et seq.*, 216, Or. 128.

however, could point to his greatest achievements as effected through the medium of the Grand style, which was calculated[1] to play at will upon the feelings[2] of an assembly. Cicero and Quintilian[3] considered this style to be supreme, just as they considered that to stir the emotions was the highest function of the orator. Both these authors are viewing the problem from a standpoint[4] different from that of Dionysius, who weighed the intrinsic merits of the styles, and held that the Middle style, compounded[5] as it was of the other two, was the most excellent. As we shall see, Cicero, in his dispute with the Atticists, laid emphasis on the fact that representatives of all three styles were to be found amongst the Attic orators, and that the supreme orator is he who, like Demosthenes, is master of them all, and can employ them as the occasion demands.

Analogous to this division of style was another[6] which sprang up after the rise of the Atticist controversy, and the consequent reaction against Asianism. Ac-

Atticism, Asianism, the Rhodian school

cording to this, at one extreme stood Attic plainness, correctness, and restraint, at the other Asiatic oratory marked by impurity of diction, over-ornateness, and redundancy, while to the orators of the Rhodian school was assigned a place intermediate[7] between the two. Asianists like Hegesias claimed[8] to follow Attic models, but the difference that separated the Attic and Asianist orators was emphasised[9] particularly

---

[1] Cf. Cic. De Or. I. 60, II. 178, 215, Or. 97 ; Q. XI. 1. 85, XII. 10. 61 et seq.

[2] Cf. Cic. Or. 128 et seq., on παθητικόν.

[3] De Or. I. 94 ; Q. IV. 5. 6, XII. 10. 63.

[4] That of the " officia oratoris."

[5] De Dem. c. 3, ib. 34 ; the method of " compounding " is not easy to conceive, inasmuch as the Plain and Grand styles were considered as standing at opposite poles ; hence Dionysius sometimes speaks of the Middle style as standing midway between the other two ; cf. Cic. De Or. III. 199 : " quae particeps utriusque generis quadam mediocritate laudatur " ; this compromise is in Cicero's best style ; cf. Or. 21 ; Q. XII. 10. 58.

[6] Q. XII. 10. 16 : "et antiqua quidem illa divisio inter Atticos atque Asianos."

[7] Cic. Br. 52, Or. 25.

[8] Br. 286.

[9] Note how the contrast is put in Q. loc. cit. ; it is, of course, reminiscent of Cic's controversy with the Atticists, but Q. evidently assigns it an older date.

by the extreme Atticists, who claimed that the Plain style of oratory was the only genuine Attic style. Some critics invested the Rhodian school with an almost fictitious importance. Aeschines was credited with the founding of the school, but many of its orators took Hyperides[1] as their model, and were not conspicuously successful in their imitation of him. Cicero was naturally inclined to exaggerate[2] the importance of the Rhodian school out of deference to his old master Molon.

We find at times a four-fold classification of styles. Demetrius to the three styles generally recognised added a fourth, which he called the "forcible."[3]

A four-fold division of styles

The characteristics ascribed to this style were probably in the main derived from a study of the oratory of Demosthenes,[4] whose dominant quality was considered to be his vehemence.[5] Philodemus, too, in his Rhetorica[6] seems to have before his mind a four-fold classification, though his meaning is hard to divine owing to the defective condition of the text. Amongst the Latin writers, Macrobius presents us with a four-fold division[7] which exhibits at least one unusual feature, and is illustrated by authors as diverse as Cicero, Sallust, Fronto, and Pliny. It was something of an achievement in criticism for Macrobius to discover examples of all his four styles in Virgil.

It was, of course, inevitable that theorists, if only as an exercise in ingenuity, would begin to refine on the tradi-

---

[1] Dionys. De Din. 8.

[2] Cf. Sandys, Cic. Orator, Introd. p. 37 ; Q. XII. 10. 18, however, clearly implies that the same critics who originated the division of oratory into Attic and Asiatic, were responsible for assigning a separate existence to the Rhodian school.

[3] περὶ ἑρμην. 36, on the χαρακτὴρ δεινός ; cf. Rhys Roberts, Introd. p. 34, ib. p. 61, with quotation from Syrianus.

[4] Demetr. illustrates the "forcible" style mostly from him ; cf. 246, 248, 253, 263, 270, 272–3, 278–80 ; cf. Hermog. περὶ ἰδ. Sp. II. 268, 389.

[5] On his δεινότης, cf. Dionys. De Dem. 10 ; περὶ ὕψους, 12. 4, 34. 4 ; Cic. De Or. III. 28 ; Q. X. 1. 76, XII. 10. 23.

[6] Rhet. I. p. 165, col. IV ; Hubbell, The Rhetorica of Philodemus, p. 298, ascribes a threefold classification to Philod. without any reference to the difficulties of the text.

[7] Sat. V. 1. 7 : " copiosum, breve, siccum, pingue et floridum."

tional classification, but such attempts betoken also a
Drawbacks of recognition of the fact that it is difficult to
rigid cate- fit every writer into a rigid category. The tra-
gories
ditional classification was useful when one was
propounding a theory of imitation, and indicating possible
models, but an author like Quintilian felt its limitations,
and is forced[1] to admit that eloquence with its diversity of
types cannot be confined within the limits of the three
recognised forms. Many nuances[2] may be discovered
within these three forms, and almost innumerable species
exhibiting subtle shades of difference.

Theophrastus, who was concerned with the problem of style
in general, demanded[3] four " virtues," or essential qualities
in every good style, viz., clearness, correctness,
The "virtues" ornateness,[4] and appropriateness. His teach-
of style
ing is echoed with more or less fidelity by
Latin authors.[5] The Stoics,[6] who aimed above all at
plainness, and shunned elaborate ornament, added a fifth
virtue, brevity. But in other respects too, the critics began
to refine upon the teaching of Theophrastus. Dionysius,
who enlarges the list of virtues,[7] makes a distinction between
those that are essential (ἀναγκαῖαι), and those that are superadded (ἐπίθετοι), and includes clearness, correctness, and conciseness,[8] in the first category. Elsewhere,[9] however, he
declares that Decorum is the most important of all the virtues, and we find that in reality almost all his " superadded "
virtues can be reduced to either Decorum or ornateness.

[1] XII. 10. 66 *et seq.*
[2] Cf. Cic. Or. 20, for some of these nuances.
[3] Cic. Or. 79.
[4] The degree of this would be determined by the Law of Decorum.
[5] Auct. ad Her. IV. 12. 17, requires elegantia (=Latinitas+explanatio),
compositio, dignitas ; Cic. De Or. I. 144, III. 37 ; Q. VIII. 1. 1 ; cf. I. 5. 1,
where a threefold division is adopted (emendata, dilucida, ornata), " apte
dicere " being considered under the head of " ornatus " ; *ib.* XI. 3. 30, where
the doctrine of the " virtues " is applied to delivery.
[6] *Vide supra*, p. 70 ; cf. Cic. Part. Or. 19, where the Stoic " brevitas "
is enjoined.
[7] De Thucyd. c. 22, Ep. ad Pomp. c. 3 ; cf. Cic. Or. 139, on " dicendi
quasi virtutes " ; Stroux, op. cit., p. 9 *et seq.*
[8] His study of Lysias (cf. c. 4) was probably the dominating influence here.
[9] De Lysia, 9.

Now Theophrastus propounded his doctrine of the virtues as applicable to style in general, but those who adopted the threefold division of style, were compelled to have recourse to the device of distributing[1] the virtues over the various styles.   Cicero, for instance, associates the virtues of correctness, clearness, and appropriateness with the Plain style, but denies it ornateness, which he assigns[2] in part to the Middle, and in its entirety to the Grand style.

The first essential of every good style was to exhibit correct usage.[3]   This, indeed, as Aristotle had proclaimed,[4] was the foundation of all style.   According

The virtue of correctness   to Cicero,[5] no orator deserves admiration for speaking correct Latin, which should[6] be the distinguishing mark of every true-born Roman citizen. He lays[7] down in a general way that the requirements of Latinitas demand a choice of words above reproach, and correctness of grammatical construction.   The Stoics, in particular, had dealt[8] with the question of correct usage, and had treated extensively of the specific violations of it through " barbarisms " and " solecisms."   Ordinarily, " barbarism " was a term applied[9] to a fault in single words, while " solecisms " were deemed to occur in connected[10] speech, but authors[11] were not always in agreement in their definitions of these terms.   Apart, however, from such technical distinctions, cultured Romans would as a rule be in agreement in judging violations of idiom or grammatical

---

[1] Cf. Dionys. De Dem. 34.

[2] *Vide infra*, p. 85.

[3] Ἑλληνισμός, or Latinitas, as the case might be ; cf. Ad Her. IV. 12. 17 ; De Or. III. 37 *et seq.*, Br. 258, De opt. gen. 4.

[4] Rhet. III. 5. 1 : ἔστι δ'ἀρχὴ τῆς λέξεως τὸ Ἑλληνίζειν.

[5] De Or. III. 52, Br. 140, 261.

[6] Yet, as we shall see, in C's criticism of many orators in the Brutus, " Latine loqui " is mentioned as one of their merits ; *vide infra*, p. 246.

[7] De Or. III. 40.

[8] On the Stoics and Ἑλληνισμός, cf. Reitzenstein, M. Terentius Varro, pp. 90–92 ; *vide supra*, pp. 34, 41 ; cf. Funaioli, op. cit., p. 46.

[9] Q. I. 5. 5 *et seq.*

[10] e.g., faults of syntax or idiom.

[11] For Aristotle's use of them, cf. Rhet. III. 5. 1 (with Cope's note), *ib.* 7 ; for traces of controversy, cf. Philod. Rhet. I. 154–155 ; Q. I. 5. 16, 34 ; Gellius, V. 20 ; Suess, op. cit., p. 59 *et seq.*

construction.[1] A more serious problem would arise when the choice of words was involved, as an author who believed himself to be secure in the matter of correct usage, had to run the gauntlet of the Purists, whose ideals were high, and whose demands could be exacting in the extreme.

From the days of the Scipionic circle, as we have seen, there were men like Scipio himself, Terence, Laelius, and Catulus, who aimed at being " puri sermonis amatores," and who were ready to condemn breaches[2] of correctness. The Purist movement was particularly strong in Cicero's day.[3] The Atticists of Calvus' circle laid great stress on integrity of speech, while the cause of correct Latinity was no less vigorously espoused by others. Caesar's dictum[4] banning the " inauditum atque insolens verbum " would probably have served as a watch-word for many of the Purists. But at times it must have been no easy matter to determine what should be the criterion of correct usage,[5] where the choice of a particular word was concerned. Cicero, especially in his speeches, was as a rule scrupulously careful in his choice of words, but, for all that, critics[6] were found to carp at him for breaches of correctness and propriety. Except on rare occasions,[7] he adhered to the principle of Anomaly, following the guidance of custom (" consuetudo "), and thus in his choice of certain *forms* would have offended the rigid Analogists. It is, however, not always easy to decide in what sense Cicero employs the word " consuetudo." On occasion he seems to indicate by it the natural growth of

The Purist movement

[1] The champions of Analogy and Anomaly would, however, often dispute about individual grammatical forms ; Cic. Or. 159 *et seq.* ; Q. I. 6. 42.

[2] Cf. Varro, De L. L. VI. 59, where Aelius Stilo and " senes aliquot " condemned the use of " novissimus " for " extremus " ; cf. Gellius, X. 21.

[3] *Vide infra*, p. 243 *et seq.*

[4] Gellius, I. 10. 4 ; Augustus, though he had regard for elegance of speech, was not disposed to be a pedantic purist ; cf. Q. I. 6. 19 ; Suet. Aug. 86 *et seq.* ; Gellius, X. 24. 2.

[5] The Stoics (Diog. Laert. VII. 59) define Ἑλληνισμός as φράσις ἀδιάπτωτος ἐν τῇ τεχνικῇ καὶ μὴ εἰκαίᾳ συνηθείᾳ ; they evidently had in mind the usage of the cultured.

[6] *Vide infra.* p. 246.

[7] Ad Att. VI. 2. 3 ; *vide infra*, p. 243.

language based on prevailing custom,[1] the vagaries of which the Analogists sought to correct by their own peculiar principle (ratio). But, especially as regards choice of words, when Cicero at other times speaks of " consuetudo," he seems to have in mind the usage[2] that had been sealed by the approval of the cultured few, or of recognised authors.[3] Probably, as regards choice of words, the usage of the cultured (whether Analogists or Anomalists) who had regard for purity of diction, would differ little in practice.

In Cicero's day arose the concept[4] of " urbanitas," according to which the usage of cultured society in Rome itself was taken as the standard of correctness. Cicero evidently had in view the practice of educated circles in Rome, when, with certain limitations, he enjoins upon the orator to employ " verba usitata,"[5] and to avoid unusual words[6] that would offend the susceptibilites of the Purists. The champions of correctness would naturally object to the impurities[7] of ordinary speech, and to the employment of vulgar words,[8] though the use of a vulgar word that was expressive, was at times[9] considered effective from the stylist's point of view. The Purists, too, would rule out the use of foreign words, and, though many of them, like Messalla, were ardent Hellenists, they forbade[10] the inter-

The concept of " urbanitas "

---

[1] Cic. Or. 157, 159, 161, where he speaks of " indocta consuetudo "; cf. Hor. A.P. 71–72 ; Q. I. 6. 1, 3 ; *vide supra*, pp. 40–41.

[2] Cf. De Or. III. 150, on "consuetudo bene loquendi ; " Or. 153 : " consuetudo elegans Latini sermonis " ; cf. De Or. III. 170, where " consuetudo " by itself seems to be used in this sense.

[3] Cf. De Or. III. 39, on the reading of good authors and its effect on Latinity ; cf. Q. I. 6. 2, I. 4. 4.

[4] Or at any rate the name for the concept ; *vide infra*, p. 244.

[5] De Or. III. 39, *ib.* 49 ; cf. Q. I. 5. 71 ; Suet. De Gr. 10, on the precept of Ateius Philologus.

[6] Cf. Br. 274, 284, De opt. gen. 7–8.

[7] Cf. Tac. Dial. 32, on " cotidiani sermonis foeda ac pudenda vitia."

[8] Cic. De Or. III. 97, 150, on " abjecta verba " ; cf. Sen. Controv. IV. pr. 9, VII. pr. 3 ; Gellius, XIX. 13. 3.

[9] *Vide infra*, p. 88.

[10] Cf. Hor. Sat. I. 10. 20, *ib.* 29 (with Scholiast's note) ; Cic. De Off. I. 111, Tus. Disp. I. 15 ; Suet. Tib. 71.

mixture of Greek words in Latin. Again, as the concept of
" urbanitas " took definite shape, the Purists were ready[1] to
condemn provincialisms, and proclaim the superiority of
the Latin spoken at Rome.

Two classes of unusual words, archaisms and new coinages, call for more than a passing mention. Archaisms
Archaisms   could be employed for stylistic effect, but
the Purists would generally be rigid in their
exclusion of such words, especially those that seemed to
have become obsolete. It must at times have been a serious
difficulty to determine whether or not a word had become
obsolete, as language was constantly subject to decay.[2]
There were words like Cato's " lurchinabundus," that were
definitely excluded. Quintilian, who enjoins[3] as a practical
rule the employment of the newest of the old words and
the oldest of the new, forbade[4] students to draw their words
from remote and forgotten ages. Cicero's injunctions[5]
about obsolete words are somewhat vague, though in his
precepts he evidently kept before his mind the usage[6] of
cultured society in Rome. It would, however, be interesting to discover if the Purists would accept some of the old
words to which he himself was partial.[7]

The question of new coinages[8] must have also been
sharply debated, as the Purists[9] would look askance at such
New Coinages   novelties. It is clear, of course, that in a
subject like Philosophy which dealt with
concepts new to the Romans, an author was forced either

[1] *Vide infra*, p. 244.

[2] Cic. De Or. III. 153 ; Hor. A.P. 61 ; Sen. Ep. 58. 2 ; Q. VIII. 6. 32 ;
X. 2. 13.

[3] I. 6. 41 ; Ben Jonson, a close student of Q., re-echoes the rule ; cf.
Spingarn, Critical Essays, Vol. I. p. 38.

[4] I. 6. 40, VIII. 3. 25 ; " nec ex ultimis tenebris repetenda."

[5] De Or. III. 33, 150.

[6] Cf. De Or. III. 39, where he forbids words " quibus jam consuetudo
nostra non utitur."

[7] De Or. III. 153 ; cf. Q. VIII. 3. 26–27.

[8] Cf. Cic. De Or. III. 149, 152 ; Q. I. 5. 3, VIII. 3. 24 ; Fronto, II. 114,
from his own peculiar standpoint, condemns neologisms.

[9] Still, Q. VIII. 3. 34, mentions " reatus " as having been coined by
Messalla ; *vide infra*, p. 261.

to coin new words,[1] or to borrow them from the Greek.[2] Cicero hopes[3] that use will soften words of his own invention such as " beatitas " and " beatitudo." A Roman writer was faced with a similar difficulty, when he attempted to express in Latin the technical[4] terms of Greek Grammar or Rhetoric. But, while concessions might be made to those who were dealing with the learned sciences, the writer of oratorical prose,[5] whose appeal was essentially popular, was censured for the use of novel words. A writer of outstanding authority might succeed[6] in getting a new word accepted, but innovations in language such as Sisenna[7] was guilty of, were condemned. An author had to take account of the laws of good usage,[8] if he wished to get a novel word accepted as current coin.[9] Such a word might be wholly new, or else be a new derivative or compound.[10] The Romans felt that,[11] especially in the formation of compounds, the Greeks enjoyed a great advantage in the flexibility of their language, though some of them were at times criticised[12] for their coinages. When Latin was little developed as a literary language, the early Roman poets, having to

[1] De Fin. III. 4 et seq., IV. 7, on the Stoic practice; Acad. Post. 5, 24, Acad. Pr. 17 ; vide infra, p. 204.

[2] Acad. Post. 25, De Fin. III. 15 ; Q. II. 14. 4.

[3] De N. D. I. 95 ; cf. Q. VIII. 3. 32 ; Sen. Ep. 58. 6, makes a plea for " essentia ", attributing the authorship of it to Cicero ; cf., however, Q. II. 14. 2, VIII. 3. 33.

[4] Cf. Cic. Br. 162 ; Q. I. 6. 28, II. 14. 1 et seq. ; vide infra, p. 203 et seq.

[5] Cic. Phil. XIII. 43 ; Q. VIII. 3. 35, where Celsus forbids the orator to coin new words.

[6] Q. I. 4. 4, I. 6. 1, 11.

[7] Br. 259–260 ; S's adherence to Analogy seems to have led him to some strange forms ; cf. Q. I. 5. 13, VIII. 3. 35 ; Gellius, II. 25. 9, XI. 15. 7, XII. 15 ; Sen. Ep. 114. 10, notes the passion for new coinage in his own day ; cf. Gellius, I. 15. 18 (on Sallust) ; Suet. De Gr. 22.

[8] De Or. III. 170 ; cf. Demetr. 96 et seq.

[9] Cf. Fronto, II. 54 : " oratori cavendum ne quod novum verbum ut aes adulterinum percutiat."

[10] Cic. De Or. III. 154, Part. Or. 16 ; Q. I. 5. 65 et seq.

[11] Q. I. 5. 70, VIII. 3. 30, 6. 31 et seq. ; cf. Demetr. 95, on Homer as a word-maker.

[12] Ar. Rh. III. 3. 1, on some extravagant compounds used by the Sophists ; cf. Dionys. Ad Pomp. c. 2, on Plato.

create a poetical vocabulary, attempted to impart to their own tongue something of the richness of Greek by their many new coinages. They were not, however, always successful, as is proved by the derision which greeted the efforts of Pacuvius.[1] Some of the succeeding poets were assiduous word-makers, and though the results of their labours may have appealed to the archaists[2] of a later age, they also were often severely criticised.[3] The absence of an established tradition amongst the Romans that could pave the way for these experiments, was a difficulty, while the Purists constantly intervened to arrest such developments in the language. Quintilian gives warning[4] of the danger that lies in the path of one who would coin a new word. He bewails[5] the failure of the Romans to expand their language even by way of new compounds, and, in declaring that in this matter they were too morbidly self-critical, he gives us an index of the restrictive influence of the Purists.

According to the scheme of Theophrastus, the second virtue of style was clearness. Aristotle evidently regarded[6] it as the great essential of every good style, and its importance is emphasised by later theorists.[7] Even Epicurus, who was charged with being indifferent to the niceties of style, laid stress[8] on the paramount need of perspicuity. The Stoics, who eschewed ornateness of speech, and from the utilitarian[9] standpoint regarded language primarily as a vehicle for

The virtue of clearness

---

[1] *Vide supra*, p. 49 ; cf. Cic. Or. 164.

[2] Gellius, XV. 25, XVI. 7, XIX. 7.

[3] *Ib*. XVIII. 11.

[4] I. 5. 71 ; *vide infra*, p. 391.

[5] VIII. 3. 31, 33, *ib*. 6. 31–32.

[6] Rhet. III. 2. 1, where he demands clearness as the essential ἀρετή ; *ib*. 6, *ib*. c. 5, where many of his precepts concern clearness; III. 12. 6, Poet. 22. 1, *ib*. 4, where metaphor is said to achieve both clearness and distinction of style.

[7] Cic. De Or. I. 144, III. 37, De Fin. III. 19 ; Q. II. 3. 8 : " prima est eloquentiae virtus perspicuitas," VIII. 1. 22 ; Dionys. De Lys. 4.

[8] *Vide infra*, p. 159.

[9] Varro, De L. L. VIII. 26 (evidently from a Stoic source) : " omnis oratio cum debeat dirigi ad utilitatem, ad quam tum denique pervenit, si est aperta et brevis ; cf. Q. XII. 10. 40.

the expression of thought, naturally demanded clearness as
one of the chief virtues of style.   The question arose as to
how clearness could best be achieved.   As far as it depended
on the selection of words, Aristotle had already given the
lead in declaring[1] that it could be secured especially by the
use of words usually employed and naturally adapted to
designate things.   His precept was repeated by later
theorists, both Greek[2] and Roman,[3] who regarded the
employment of such ordinary[4] and " natural " speech as the
easiest road to perspicuity.   Quintilian comments[5] on the
obscurity that arises from the use of unusual words, such as
obsolete or dialect words, or technical terms.   Obscurity
might arise also from breaches of correctness,[6] from an
author's eagerness for brevity[7] and condensation, or from
defective composition.[8]   This latter point, however, was
dealt with only in a passing way, as clearness was supposed
to follow naturally from the use of ordinary language, as
it was customarily employed by men.

When the doctrine of the three oratorical styles was
evolved, the virtue of clearness became associated especially
with the Plain style,[9] which was supposed to
Clearness in be based chiefly on the speech of every-
the Plain style day life.[10]   We can witness a natural extension of this doctrine to certain divisions of a speech, when

[1] Rhet. III. 2. 2, on κύρια ὀνόματα ; Poet. c. 22.

[2] Demetr. 190, 192 ; Dionys. De Lysia, 4.

[3] Ad Her. IV. 12. 17 ; De Or. III. 49, *ib.* 149 : <verba> " propria
. . . . paene una nata cum rebus ipsis " ; Q. I. 5. 71, VIII. 2. 3 *et seq.*

[4] As a rule, " verba propria " and " usitata " would be identical, but the
Roman theorists sometimes distinguished them, as a word might be " pro-
prium " but " inusitatum ", inasmuch as it had become obsolete ; cf. Ad Her.
loc. cit. ; De Or. III. 150, Or. 80 ; in De Or. II. 329, Cicero mentions
" usitata " alone as conducive to clearness ; cf. Q. IV. 2. 36.

[5] VIII. 2. 12 *et seq.* ; cf. Cic. De Or. III. 50.

[6] Aris. Rhet. III. 5, shows the relation of clearness to correctness ; cf.
Philod. Rhet. I. 156–159.

[7] *Vide infra*, p. 478.

[8] Cic. De Or. III. 49 ; Q. VIII. 2. 14 *et seq.* ; Demetr. 192 *et seq.*

[9] Cic. Or. 79 ; Demetr. 191, 203.

[10] Or. 76, 85 ; Q. VIII. 3. 87 ; of course, ordinary metaphors
would enter into this style ; Or. 81 ; cf. De Or. III. 155 ; Ar. Rhet.
III. 2. 6.

theorists insisted[1] on clearness as essential to the " narratio," and to the exposition of a speaker's proofs.

Hitherto we have dealt with the two " virtues " of style that could lay claim[2] to no special merit, and that might **The virtue of** well be expected in the speech of every **ornateness** educated man. A more serious[3] task confronted the author who sought to rise[4] above the level of ordinary speech, and write what might be called artistic prose. It is in the accomplishment of such a task that a writer's genius is most fully displayed, while an orator who can transcend[5] the commonplace, and attain to distinction and sublimity, is sure to arouse the enthusiasm of his audience. It is the virtue of " ornateness " (united, however, with that of Decorum), that in the eyes of the Ancients constituted what we commonly call Style. Theophrastus seems[6] to have dealt with the virtue as a unit, but those who, like Cicero, followed the doctrine of the three styles, resolved[7] it into the elements of charm and grandeur. The attribute of charm came to be associated in particular with the Middle style[8], while the virtue in its entirety was assigned to the Grand Style. Theophrastus laid it down[9] that the source of ornateness and distinction in style lay in the choice[10] of words, in composition, and the employment

[1] Cic. De Or. II. 329; Q. IV. 2. 31, 36, V. 14. 33, XI. 1. 6.

[2] Cf. Cic. De Or. III. 38; Q. VIII. 3. 1.

[3] De Or. III. 52–53, 91.

[4] Cf. Diog. Laert. VII. 59 : κατασκευή δὲ ἐστι λέξις ἐκπεφευγυῖα τὸν ἰδιωτισμόν ; ib. 60, on Poseidonius' view.

[5] Br. 123, Or. 97 ; Q. VIII. 3. 2 et seq. ; cf. περὶ ὕψους, c. 35, for some interesting remarks on this subject.

[6] Cf. De Or. III. 37 ; Theophrastus' term for " ornatus " may have been κατασκευή, a term used later in this sense by the Stoics ; probably, as Stroux, op. cit., p. 37, suggests, Cicero is endeavouring to find an equivalent for κατασκευή in his " quasi supellex " (Or. 79).

[7] Or. 79 : " ornatum illud suave et adfluens," corresponding to ἡδύ and μεγαλοπρεπές in the Greek ; cf. Arist. Rhet. III. 12. 6 ; Q. IV. 2. 63, for the use of these terms by Theodectes.

[8] Or. 91 ; Q. XII. 10. 60 ; cf. Part. Or. 21–22, for aspects of " suavitas " that bring it into association rather with the Grand style ; vide supra, p. 73.

[9] Dionys. De Isocr. 3 ; cf. De Thucyd. 22–23, De C. V. c. 16, where Th. is quoted on the choice of beautiful words ; Demetr. 173.

[10] ἐκλογὴ ὀνομάτων, ἁρμονία or σύνθεσις, σχήματα, would thus all be grouped under the head of " ornatus."

of figurative speech, and his doctrine was substantially reproduced by later theorists.[1]

We have dealt already with the choice of words from the
standpoint of correctness, but the problem had to be
viewed from a different angle when a writer
Choice of was aiming at ornateness. He had to con-
words as an
aid to style sider the means by which he could rise
above the dead level[2] of ordinary speech, or elevate ordinary
language to a higher[3] power. The ancient theorists laid[4]
it down in a general way that a selection of the best words
was one of the first essentials for a writer who wished to
attain distinction. Such a careful selection was especially
necessary where it was a question of the language in common
use, or where a choice of synonyms was involved. It was
recognised that one word might have a higher stylistic
value than another, though the Ancients do not seem[5] to
have approximated to Flaubert's doctrine of the " mot
juste," " the idea[6] of some pre-existent adaptation between
a relative somewhere in the world of thought and its cor-
relative in the world of language." But some writers made
the quest of words an endless labour, and developed in
their task a morbid self-criticism,[7] and what Quintilian
happily styles[8] an " incredibile verborum fastidium," that
rejected a large part of current speech. Something of this
morbidness may be detected in the Roman Atticists,[9] and

---

[1] Auct. ad Her. IV. 12. 17, deals with " compositio " and " dignitas "
(=use of figures) ; Cic. De Or. III. 149 *et seq.*, 201, Br. 69, 274–275, Or.
134–236, Part. Or. 72 ; Q. VIII. 3. 15 *et seq.*, 40 *et seq. ;* Fronto, II. 78 ;
Demetr. 38 *et seq.*, 59, where the Figures are ranged under the head of
composition ; περὶ ὕψους, c. 8, 30.

[2] Ar. Rhet. III. 2. 2, Poet, 22, 1 : <λέξις> ἐξαλλάττουσα τὸ
ἰδιωτικόν ; Dionys. De Dem. 10, 15 ; Demetr. 77 ; Cic. Part. Or. 17.

[3] Ad Her. IV. 31. 42 : " ut ab usitata potestate verborum recedatur."

[4] De Or. I. 151, III. 150 *et seq.*, Br. 250, Or. 227 : " optimis sententiis
verbisque lectissimis dicere," De opt. gen. 4 ; Q. IX. 4. 60, X. 1. 6, *ib.*
3. 5 ; Dionys. De C. V. c. 25.

[5] *Vide infra*, p. 350, where I have suggested that Fronto has some anticipation of it ; Q. X. 5. 5, seems definitely against it.

[6] Pater, Appreciations, Style, p. 27.

[7] Q. VIII. pr. 31, X. 3. 10 *et seq.*   [8] VIII. 3. 23, cf. *ib.* 2. 2.

[9] Cic. Br. 283, on Calvus, though C's chief anxiety was to attain correctness.

in a later writer such as Fronto, who for his own purposes was constantly engaged[1] in tracking words to their lair.

One of the fundamental problems then for the successful stylist was to evade triteness of expression, and impart an air of distinction to his writing. As Aristotle saw,[2] there was a psychological basis for this ; for, while familiarity breeds contempt, men are admirers of what is remote from the ordinary. The use of ordinary speech will achieve clarity, but for distinction and ornateness something more is required,[3] such as the employment of metaphors, epithets, compound, rare,[4] or strange words. The poet, or the orator in an impassioned speech,[5] will be allowed a certain licence in the use of all these devices, but Aristotle realised[6] that a passage composed wholly of such words would be nothing better than a riddle or a jargon. By means of such a vocabulary a prose-writer could certainly transcend the ordinary, and even produce something wholly bizarre, which would, however, exhibit nothing of the sanity and restraint demanded by the ancient instinct for decorum. Gorgias and his brother Sophists achieved the unfamiliar by an immoderate use[7] of poetical diction, artificial figures, epithets, elaborate compounds,[8] harsh and far-fetched metaphors, but they passed altogether beyond the limits of good taste, and failed to recognise that such devices may be an ornament, if used in moderation,[9] but can only disfigure style, if indulged in to excess. The Roman writers on style knew the value of the rare word,[10] but they had learnt also the lesson of moderation.

How to achieve distinction

[1] *Vide infra*, p. 318.

[2] Rhet. III. 2. 3 ; cf. Demetr. 60 ; Q. VIII. 6. 51.

[3] Ar. Rhet. III. 2. 2, 5, *ib*. 10. 2, Poet. 22. 1 ; Dionys. De C. V. c. 3.

[4] Such as archaic, newly-coined, dialect, or foreign words.

[5] Rhet. III. 7. 11.

[6] Poet. 22. 2.

[7] Rhet. III. 1. 9, *ib*. c. 3, for various faults common in Sophistic prose ; cf. Demetr. 112, 115 *et seq.* ; Dionys. De Lys. 3 ; περὶ ὕψους., III. 2 ; Diod. XII. 53 ; Cic. Or. 39 ; Q. IX. 3. 74 ; *vide infra*, p. 441.

[8] Cf. Rhet. III. 2. 5, *ib*. 3. 1, Poet. 22. 10 ; Demetr. 91 *et seq.*, 143.

[9] Cf. Rhet. III. 12. 6, where a judicious blend of τὸ εἰωθός and τὸ ξενικόν is held up as the ideal.

[10] Cf. Cic. De Or. III. 39, 153.

Following the Greek theorists, they distinguished[1] words
into those that were natural and ordinary, and those that

Beauty in words

were unusual, such as archaisms, new coinages, or foreign words (from the Italic[2]
dialects, or the languages of other peoples).
The writer who aimed at leaving on his work the impress
of distinction, had in the employment of the " verba
propria " to exercise a principle of selection. He was
bound to avoid[3] vulgar, mean, or trivial words, though at
times[4] a slang expression might be effective owing to its
vividness and force. But apart from such words, it often
happens that, when a choice of synonyms is offered in the
ordinary language, there are certain words that attract us
by their natural beauty[5] and charm. Words such as these
constitute " the peculiar light of thought."[6] The Ancients
generally measured the beauty of a word by the force of its
appeal to the ear. Being addicted to the habit of reading
aloud or declaiming, they were sensitive[7] to the musical
qualities of language. As Cicero put it[8] : " voluptati autem
aurium morigerari debet oratio." Hence sprang the many
exhortations[9] to the stylist to employ " verba sonantia,"
words that would satisfy the ear by their euphony. The
prose writer, however, was not to exercise the same exquisite
care as the poet[10] in the selection of musical language, and
was warned[11] to avoid choosing words for their sound value

[1] Cic. De Or. III. 149, 170, 201, Or. 80, Part. Or. 16–17 ; Q. I. 5. 3,
55, 71, VIII. 3. 24 *et seq. ;* cf. Mart. Cap. (ed. Dick) pp. 250–251.

[2] Though Q. I. 5. 56, is prepared to regard these as of native origin.

[3] Cic. De Or. III. 150 ; Q. VIII. 3. 17 ; Dionys. De C. V. c. 16, where
μικρὰ καὶ ταπεινὰ ὀνόματα are ruled out ; *vide supra*, p. 80.

[4] Q. VIII. 3. 21, X. 1. 9 ; Gellius, XVII. 2. 21 ; Fronto, II. 80 ;
Mart. Cap. p. 250 ; περὶ ὕψους, 31. 1.

[5] Cic. De Or. III. 125, Br. 216 ; Pliny, Ep. I. 16. 2 ; Q. X. 1. 6 ; Fronto,
II. 78, *ib.* 134, on "verba delenifica" ; Arist. Rhet. III. 2. 13 ; Demetr. 173.

[6] περὶ ὕψους, 30. 1.

[7] *Vide infra*, pp. 98, 103.

[8] Or. 159.

[9] Or. 80 ; Q. I. 5. 4, on " vocalitas," IX. 4. 58 ; Gellius, XIII. 20. 1.

[10] Or. 163, where Cicero shows his appreciation of the " Miltonic ring "
of certain proper names.

[11] Cic. De Or. I. 51 ; cf. Or. 68 (where the poets are in question) ;
Q. VIII. pr. 18 *et seq.*

alone.   I need not dwell on the tendency of the Romans to
prefer particular grammatical forms[1] for the sake of euphony,
or on the part that the quest of euphony must have played
in developing certain forms in their language.   A more
interesting question is the sensitiveness manifested by
both Greeks[2] and Romans to the musical or unmusical
qualities of certain letters of the alphabet, as these were
the elements out of which words were formed.   They found
some letters pleasing[3] in sound, and others disagreeable.
Both Greeks and Romans considered the " s "[4] sound unpleasing, while the Romans found cacophonous, especially
in certain combinations, their own letters " x,"[5] " f,"[6] and
" m," which Quintilian styles[7] the " mugiens littera." They
were sensitive then to the sound values of certain letters,
and consequently to the effect of sonorous or rugged words,[8]
which they could employ as expressive of different emotions,
thus[9] adapting the sound to the sense.   To render composition beautiful they sought out sonorous words, or,
if a word or syllable was naturally harsh, they endeavoured
to mask its harshness by subtly interweaving[10] it with a more
melodious sound.   But they realised, too, that words in
themselves rugged could often be effectively employed to

[1] Such as scripsere, vitasti, quadrigae ; cf. Cic. Or. 153 et seq. ; Q. I. 5.
42, IX. 4. 59 ; Gellius, II. 17. 3 ; cf. Hever, De Praeceptis Rom. Euphonicis, where this aspect of the problem is well illustrated.

[2] Dionys. De C. V. c. 14–16, is especially important in this connection.

[3] Cf. Q. VIII. 3. 16, on " litterae melius sonantes " ; Demetr. 174, on
the pleasing sound of " l " and " n ", ib. 176 ; ib. 70 et seq., on vowel
values.

[4] Dionys. De C. V. c. 14 ; Eurip's famous line (Medea, 476) was often
ridiculed ; cf., however, Rhys Roberts' interesting note (Dionys. loc. cit.)
on the effective use sometimes made of sigmatism both in prose and verse ;
cf. Q. IX. 4. 38, XII. 10. 32 ; Mart. Cap. pp. 253–254 ; vide supra, p. 42.

[5] Cic. Or. 153 ; Q. IX. 4. 37 ; Hever, op. cit., pp. 16–18 ; St. August.
De Dial. c. 6–7 (there quoted).

[6] Cic. Or. 163 ; Q. XII. 10. 29 ; cf. I. 4. 14.

[7] XII. 10. 31.

[8] Demetr. 49, 176.

[9] Dionys. De C. V. c. 16 ; Hermog. περὶ ἰδ. Sp. II. 297 et seq. ; Q.
VIII. 3. 17, IX. 4. 130–131 (where, however, it is rather a question of
rhythm) ; cf. Norden, Aen. VI. p. 414 et seq., on word-painting in the poets ;
here, of course, the question of composition would largely enter in.

[10] Dionys. De C. V. c. 12.

convey an emotion of horror, or a suggestion of grandeur or intensity.   Such weighing and testing of even individual letters may seem a meticulous labour, but care about such minutiae contributed to the perfection of style, as was realised by a modern master[1] who was keenly alive to the finer delicacies and harmonies of language.

Apart from sonorous words, an author who aimed at distinction had another instrument to hand in the rare word,[2] the skilful use of which was regarded as one **The value of** of the great ornaments of style.   Such a **the rare word** word might be one habitually used by the poets,[3] but in speaking of rare words the Roman theorists as a rule[4] had in mind those that were either archaic or newly-coined.   An archaic word that has all the charm of novelty when revived, may still appeal[5] by its old associations, while in the eyes of many it has been invested[6] by its antiquity with a subtle atmosphere of beauty and majesty. The poets[7] recognised the stylistic value of many of these old words, and enjoyed a larger licence in their use than the prose-writer, but even they were not[8] conceded an un-restricted licence.   Dryden, in his Preface[9] to the Fables, gives a sound rule for their use in saying : " when an ancient word for its sound and significancy deserves to be revived, I have that reasonable veneration for antiquity to restore it."   Virgil, with the instinct of the supreme artist, knew[10] how to make effective use of archaisms, and convert

---

[1] R. L. Stevenson, in his essay " On some technical elements of style in Literature."

[2] In spite of the restrictions of the Purists.

[3] De Or. III. 153.

[4] Cf., however, Q. I. 5. 55 *et seq.*, for another class of rare words taken from a dialect, or a foreign language ; cf. VIII. 1. 2, for the Purist standpoint.

[5] Cf. Raleigh, Style, p. 32 *et seq.*, for an interesting analysis of the appeal of archaisms.

[6] Q. I. 6. 1, 39–41.

[7] Or. 202 ; cf. Dio Chrys. XII. 60, on Homer's use of them ; *vide infra*, p. 479.

[8] Cf. Gellius, XVI. 7. 4.

[9] *Vide* Vaughan, English Literary Criticism, p. 79.

[10] Q. I. 7. 18, VIII. 3. 24 ; cf. IX. 3. 14 ; Macrob. Sat. VI. 4. 1 *et seq. ; vide infra*, p. 390, on Horace's use of archaisms.

them into a genuine ornament of style.   The prose-writer was reminded that his privileges were restricted, and he was warned[1] to be sparing in his use of such words.   The orator of the Plain[2] style especially was urged to be restrained in the employment of them, while Quintilian favours[3] their exclusion from such parts of a speech as the exordium, and the statement of facts and proofs, where a speaker has other aims than to entrance an audience with the beauty of his style.   The legitimate use of archaic words as a stylistic device forms a striking contrast to the affectation[4] of them which caused men, either in their veneration for antiquity, or their desire to escape from familiar forms of expression, to rifle the works of the Ancients for antiquated diction.

The newly-coined word was another ornament that had to be used in prose with the strictest economy[5].   Com-

Restrictions   pound words[6] might find a place at times in elevated or impassioned prose, but care had to be taken that they were not too elaborate or extravagant. In general, the poets were considered[7] to enjoy a licence of their own in the use of new coinages, but, as we have seen,[8] limits were set even to their privileges.   More stringent conditions still were laid down for the prose-writer, who in his new formations was bound[9] to respect existing usage and pay homage to the demands of euphony, while if he was an orator of the Plain style,[10] he had to be particularly sparing in his use of such an ornament.

---

[1] De Or. III. 201, Or. 80 ; cf. Gellius, XIII. 20. 22, on Cicero's sparing use of archaisms ; cf. Dionys. De Thucyd. 52, on Th's use of them.

[2] Cic. Or. 81.

[3] IV. 1. 58, XI. 1. 6.

[4] *Vide infra*, p. 272 *et seq.*

[5] Ad Her. IV. 31. 42 ; Cic. De Or. III. 201.

[6] Cf. Ar. Rhet. III. 2. 5, 3. 1, 3, 7. 11 ; Ar. in some at least of these passages has newly-formed compounds in mind ; elaborate compounds were considered especially suitable to the Dithyramb, Poet. 22. 10 ; Demetr. 91 *et seq. ;* cf. Aristoph. Clouds, 335 *et seq.*, for a parody of the dithyrambic style ; dithyrambic compounds in prose were condemned ; Dionys. De Dem. 29, De Din. 8.

[7] Cic. Or. 68, 202 ; Fronto, I. p. 218.

[8] *Vide supra*, p. 83.

[9] Cic. De Or. III. 170.   [10] *Vide infra*, p. 120.

The ancient theorists generally regarded[1] the effective use of metaphor as one of the chief sources of charm and grandeur in style.   Some of them dealt with the subject in connection with the choice of words, but others[2] rather in relation to composition, especially when a series of metaphors was involved.   Again, others ranged them under the general head of Figures,[3] though those who aimed at a nice discrimination were careful to class them amongst the Tropes.[4]

The use of metaphor

Aristotle considers[5] that the making of good metaphors is one of the great marks of original genius.   The writer who strikes out a metaphor for the first time, shows himself endowed with a power of intuition[6] which can detect resemblances unperceived by his less gifted brethren.   Some resemblance must exist between the object to which the metaphorical expression was originally applied in its ordinary sense, and the object to which it is now applied in its transferred sense. Hence the Ancients were fond[7] of emphasising the relation between the metaphor and the simile, and of styling the former a compressed simile.   They therefore conceived some similarity or " proportion "[8] to be the necessary basis of every good metaphor.   Aristotle at times[9] classifies metaphors so as to include more[10] than we commonly understand by the term, but he is careful to indicate his

Aristotle on metaphor

[1] Arist. Rhet. III. 2. 8 ; Demetr. 78 ; De Or. III. 159.

[2] Q. VIII. 3. 38 : " translata probari nisi in contextu sermonis non possunt " ; cf. Cic. De Or. III. 166–167.

[3] Cf. Ad Her. IV. 34. 45, where they are classed as " exornationes verborum."

[4] Q. gives us some idea of the difficulties of classification ; VIII. 6. 1, IX. 1. 5, 9.

[5] Poet. 22. 9.

[6] Cf. Middleton Murry, The Problem of Style, p. 12, for an interesting discussion of the nature of metaphor.

[7] Ar. Rhet. III. 4. 1, *ib.* 10. 2–3, *ib.* 11. 13 ; Demetr. 80 ; Q. VIII. 6. 8.

[8] Rhet. III. 2. 9, *ib.* 4. 4, Poet. 21. 6 ; Cic. De Or. III. 162 : " fugienda est dissimilitudo," Or. 134, De opt. gen. 4.

[9] Rhet. III. 10. 7 ; cf. his classification, Poet. 21. 2.

[10] E. G. Synechdoche and Metonymy ; cf. Cope, An Introduction to Aristotle's Rhetoric, p. 374 *et seq.*

preference for the " proportional " metaphor. He is particularly interesting when he sets[1] out to analyse the intellectual pleasure derived from a good metaphor. He refers it to the enjoyment always afforded by the acquisition of new knowledge. The poet or prose-writer who forges an original metaphor, opens up a new perspective, and establishes an affinity between things that seemed hitherto unrelated. The hearer derives from the metaphor a peculiar pleasure of his own, which is rooted mainly in the element of surprise when a hitherto unnoticed resemblance is revealed. If the resemblance thus disclosed is comparatively obvious,[2] there can be little pleasure afforded either to the author of the metaphor, or to those who hear it. Again, it is evident that, if the resemblance is obscure or remote,[3] the writer who seeks to establish it, may derive a certain pleasure from the exercise of his ingenuity, but too often he will leave his readers baffled in their search for his meaning. The poet[4] by his use of bold metaphors may exercise his ingenuity in this way, or with his finer vision of things may detect resemblances which are scarcely perceptible to meaner mortals, but the prose-writer was forbidden to use " far-fetched "[5] metaphors based on a merely obscure resemblance. Again, the law of Decorum intervened to prohibit harsh[6] and inappropriate metaphors, which arose particularly from an exaggerated disproportion[7] between the objects involved. This was a fault especially common among the early Sophists,[8] and in the schools of declamation at Rome.

[1] Rhet. III. 10. 2 *et seq.*, *ib.* 11. 5 *et seq.*

[2] Metaphors should be drawn ἀπὸ οἰκείων καὶ μὴ φανερῶν ; cf. Rhet. III. 10. 6 ; *ib.* 4, for his remarks on the " superficial " enthymeme.

[3] Rhet. III. 2. 12 ; cf., however, his remarks on the relation between metaphor and enigma ; cf. Demetr. 102.

[4] In this respect, Q. VIII. 6. 17–18, contrasts the licence allowed in poetry and in prose ; *vide infra*, p. 446.

[5] Ar. Rhet. III. 3. 4, 10. 6 ; Cic. De Or. III. 163 ; Q. identifies " harsh " and " far-fetched " metaphors.

[6] Demetr. 83, 84, 116 ; Ad Her. IV. 10. 15.

[7] Such a lack of proportion might, however, be designed for the purpose of magnifying or belittling a person or object ; cf. Rhet. III. 2. 9–10 ; Cic. De Or. III. 164.

[8] περὶ ὕψους, III. 2 ; cf. Hermog. περὶ ἰδ. Sp. II. p. 292.

Cicero like Aristotle[1] deals with the intellectual pleasure
that springs from the use of metaphor, but he is not always
so happy in his treatment of the theme,
Cicero on   though he follows Aristotle in the main.   In
metaphor   metaphor, he tells[2] us, we pass by the obvious
to something which is not obvious.   There is a swift transition of thought, delightful in itself, in which the mind is
transported, as it were, to a strange sphere, while the hearer
enjoys the pleasure of having to make a new mental excur-
sion under the guidance of the author.   Above all, a good
metaphor has the effect of putting an object vividly[3] before
our eyes.   This was achieved especially by the so-called
" active "[4] metaphor, which was at its best in endowing
inanimate[5] things with life.

We are reminded[6] that men employ metaphors in ordinary conversation, while even the rustic has homely metaphors of his own.   Such metaphors would be
The range of   almost invariably those that have become well
metaphor   established in a language, or those that have
become " faded," and have lost their first bloom of originality.   They are based on a resemblance now so obvious
that they afford but moderate pleasure, and little serve to
enhance the charm of style.   Many of these ordinary metaphors were contrived in the first instance to supply[7] the deficiencies of language, but it is the bold metaphor,[8] springing from a writer's intuitive power to detect the latent resemblances in things, that adds to the beauty and sublimity both[9]

[1] De Or. III. 160 *et seq.*, Or. 134.

[2] His phrase " ingeni specimen est quoddam transilire ante pedes posita
et alia longe repetita sumere " suggests rather the " far-fetched " metaphor.

[3] There is a certain pleasure derived, too, from the conciseness of metaphor,
De Or. III. 158.

[4] Demetr. 81–82 ; cf. Ar. Rhet. III. 11. 1 *et seq.*

[5] Q. VIII. 6. 11 ; cf. *ib.* 9–10, 13, for his classification of metaphors.

[6] Rhet. III. 2. 6 ; Demetr. 86–87 ; De Or. III. 155, Or. 81–82 ;
Q. VIII. 6. 6 ; cf. Mart. Cap. p. 252 ; the similarity of the examples used
for illustration should be noted.

[7] Cic. De Or. III. 159, Or. 92 ; Q. VIII. 6. 5 ; Mart. Cap. p. 251.

[8] De Or. III. 156 ; Q. VIII. 6. 11.

[9] Modern critics no less strongly insist on metaphor as a vital element in
Style ; cf. Middleton Murry, op. cit., pp. 12, 83, 119–120 ; Raleigh,
op. cit., p. 56.

of poetry and of prose. The prose writer, however, was warned to exercise restraint, if he wished to convert the use of metaphor into a genuine ornament of style. Excess,[1] whether in the character or the number of his metaphors, was regarded as a serious defect, though it was difficult at times to determine when[2] an author had overstepped the limits. The poet had privileges of his own, but metaphors were freely[3] allowed in any lofty and impassioned prose passage, where metaphorical language would seem to be the fitting medium for the expression of the writer's emotions. Vehement passion will excuse almost the boldest metaphor even in prose, though writers were sometimes[4] advised to employ certain devices to soften its boldness, if it seemed too hazardous. Those who distinguished the three oratorical styles marked off[5] by nice gradations the licence in metaphor granted to their several representatives.

Next after the choice of words as a constituent of style, the Ancients considered[6] of prime importance the artistic

Composition structure or "composition" of continuous speech, what the author of the treatise *On the Sublime* calls[7] "the harmony of that speech implanted by nature in man." Language in its crude state could be moulded[8] according to a writer's fancy, and composition was considered to have the power of fashioning the rough elements of speech into a thing of grace and beauty.[9] In its highest manifestation, it could make itself the fitting mouthpiece of the sublime,[10] while, even in the hands of

---

[1] Ar. Rhet. III. 3. 4 ; Demetr. 78 *et seq. ;* περὶ ὕψους, III. 2, 32. 7 ; De Or. III. 164 *et seq.,* De opt. gen. 4 ; Ad Fam. XVI. 17. 1 ; Q. VIII. 6. 14.

[2] De Or. III. 201 : " ut translatis frequenter utamur " ; Or. 134 : " ex omnique genere frequentissimae translationes erunt."

[3] περὶ ὕψους, 32. 1, 4.

[4] Demetr. 80 ; περὶ ὕψους, 32. 3.

[5] Or. 81–82 ; cf. Q. XI. 1. 6 ; Or. 92 (on the Middle style), *ib.* 134, on the ideal orator, whose greatest glory would be won in the Grand style.

[6] De Or. I. 17 ; Q. IX. 4. 1 *et seq.*

[7] 39. 3.

[8] De Or. III. 177.

[9] Demetr. 139, 179 *et seq.*

[10] περὶ ὕψους, c. 8. 1, *ib.* 39.

writers with no special endowments, it could assure[1] to language compactness, smoothness, and evenness of flow. In general, the aim[2] of composition was to invest speech with beauty and charm, and when directed by a skilful hand it could, by the subtle interweaving of sounds, conceal[3] the commonplace character of a word, or veil its harshness, while it had the power, too, of evoking the latent harmonies of language. Dionysius goes so far as to declare that the chief difference between poet and poet, between orator and orator, is the skill with which they arrange their words. The Ancients, however, recognised that the art of composition might easily degenerate into artifice, if an over-scrupulous care were expended on it, and they condemned the writer, who, as Lucilius[4] happily puts it, seeks to imitate the intricate pattern of a mosaic in the nicety of his style. Many reacted against such refinements, and in their devotion to " natural " speech considered[5] the whole art of composition to be anathema.

The Romans, as a rule, followed the Greek theorists in dealing with composition, but, though alive to the musical qualities of their own tongue, they do not often exhibit that appreciation of the delicate nuances of language which is one of the great attractions of Dionysius' treatise on *Literary Composition*. In laying down his rules for composition, Quintilian demands[6] that as far as possible the natural order of the words be followed, but this demand is to yield to the higher law of euphony. For the Roman theorists the " apta junctura " meant[7] particularly the avoidance of hiatus and the harsh collocation of sounds. Hiatus was generally considered a defect, as it left a gap in speech, which in consequence seemed to labour in its march ; but,

The avoidance of hiatus

---

[1] Ad Her. IV. 12. 18 ; De Or. III. 172, Br. 96, De opt. gen. 5.

[2] Dionys. De C. V. c. 10 *et seq.* ; Q. IX. 4. 9.

[3] Dionys, op. cit., c. 3–4 ; περὶ ὕψους, 40. 2 ; cf. Hor. A.P. 46–48, on the effect of " callida junctura."

[4] *Vide supra*, p. 45.

[5] Q. IX. 4. 3 *et seq.* ; *vide infra*, p. 326.

[6] IX. 4. 27 : " rectus ordo, apta junctura, numerus opportune cadens," are the three great essentials ; *ib.* 22.

[7] De Or. III. 171 *et seq.*, 201, Or. 149 *et seq.*

as Quintilian says,[1] it is not to be regarded as a serious crime, though some forms[2] of it were more offensive than others to Roman ears. At times it might[3] even have the effect of grandeur and a certain impressive[4] harshness. The Roman stylists never sought to avoid hiatus with the same laboured care as Isocrates and Theopompus, who strove to banish it from their writings with a zeal that was generally reprobated[5] by the critics. They even considered[6] that an occasional hiatus might serve to indicate the pleasing negligence of one who was more concerned with his matter than with his manner.

We have seen already[7] how important the Romans considered the choice of euphonious words as an aid to style,

The quest of euphony but euphony could be secured also by skill in composition. The nature of letters and syllables, says Quintilian,[8] cannot be changed, but much depends on their compatibility with each other. The Greeks[9] were especially alive to the need of avoiding collocations of discordant sounds, and to the possibility of rendering speech euphonious by the skilful fusion of harsh and soft sounds, and the juxtaposition of words that are naturally musical with those that are cacophonous. The Romans, too, were not insensible to the music of speech, and strove[10] to avoid the clashing of harsh consonants, and the unpleasing effect of a similar syllable at the end of one word and the beginning of the next. They also found disagreeable[11] a succession of monosyllables, or long polysyllabic words, and a series of sentences ending with

[1] IX. 4. 35.
[2] e.g. the clashing of two short vowels.
[3] Q. IX. 4. 36.
[4] Demetr. 299.
[5] Or. 151 ; Demetr. 68 ; Dionys. De C. V. c. 19, De Isocr. c. 2 ; cf. Isocr. τέχνη, fr. 7 ; *vide infra*, p. 496.
[6] Or. 77 ; Q. IX. 4. 37.
[7] *Vide supra*, p. 88 *et seq.*
[8] IX. 4. 91.
[9] Dionys. De C. V. c. 12.
[10] *Vide supra*, p. 89 ; cf. Q. IX. 4. 37 *et seq.*, on the clashing of " s " and " x," and combinations such as " ars studiorum."
[11] Q. IX. 4. 42 ; Ad Her. IV. 12. 18.

similar cadences, terminations, and inflexions. It was, however, recognised as possible to go so far in the quest after
smoothness as to render one's style feeble and nerveless.[1]
Quintilian warns[2] us that we must not in our anxiety for
euphony reject an effective and appropriate word that may
seem to impair the even flow and rhythm of our sentence.
The Greeks, manipulating a flexible language, often, as
we have seen, aimed at adopting sound to sense by their
choice of suggestive words, but they also sought to express
various emotions by their supreme skill in intermingling
words of varied tone and colour. In their composition, they
deliberately at times contrived to secure harsh effects[3] for
the sake of impressiveness. Virgil, consummate artist that
he was, is said[4] to have interspersed through the *Aeneid*
some rough and unpolished verses as being suggestive of
the archaic and rugged grandeur of Ennius.

The precepts already dealt with concerning the avoidance
of hiatus and the harsh collocations of sounds, and the
Prose rhythm   need of euphony, show how constant was
the appeal to the ear, when the Ancients
aimed at the niceties of style. Particularly in oratorical
prose, the judgment[5] of the ear is frequently invoked, as
the orator must attend to his delivery,[6] and aim at effects
that will be attractive to his audience. Especially important
was the judgment of the ear where prose rhythm was involved, an ornament that in the eyes of many critics[7] lifted
speech above the level of natural and primitive utterance,
and constituted one of the greatest instruments for moulding language into artistic form. The primitive writers at
times stumbled by chance[8] into rhythmical speech, but it

---

[1] Hor. A.P. 26 : " sectantem levia nervi deficiunt " ; cf. Q. IX. 4. 142.
[2] IX. 4. 144.
[3] Demetr. 48-49, 246, 255 ; cf. Hever, op. cit., p. 51 *et seq.*, on cacosyntheton.
[4] *Vide infra*, p. 290.
[5] Ad Her. IV. 14. 21, 23. 32 ; Cic. Or. 150 *et seq.*, 159, 162, 198–199,
203 ; Q. IX. 4. 116; Gellius, XIII. 20. 22 *et seq.*
[6] Q. IX. 4. 138: "sic fere componendum quomodo pronuntiandum erit."
[7] Cf. Cic. De Or. III. 53, 173 *et seq.*, 181, Or. 169 *et seq.*, 185, 229 ;
cf. Q. IX. 4. 4 *et seq.*
[8] De Or. III. 198, Or. 170, 177, 186 ; cf. *ib.* 219 ; Q. IX. 4. 16, takes
a different view with regard to some of the early Greek writers.

was left to those of a later age to make a scientific study
of prose rhythm, which, as Cicero puts it,[1] " extrema linia-
menta orationi attulit." There is a natural instinct[2] for
rhythm in man, which finds expression most readily in
music and the dance ; but it was discovered, too, that
language could be adapted to satisfy this need. Verse in
particular had served to minister to such an instinct. Strong
emotion generally tends to express itself in rhythmical
language, and verse with its regularly recurring rhythms
had shown itself to be the greatest vehicle of emotional
utterance. The prose writer soon discovered that this
rhythmical element constituted one of the great sources of
charm in the poet, and found[3] that by it he could give an
emotional colouring to his own style, and impart to it an
added pleasure. It is significant, indeed, that writers, in
their first attempt to set prose on the path of beauty, turned
to the poets to learn the secret of their appeal. A writer
such as Gorgias strove to imitate[4] the elegance and splendour of the poet's diction, and he and his brother Sophist,
Thrasymachus, aimed[5] at transferring to prose something
of the rhythmical effect of verse. Gorgias sought[6] to achieve
this especially by the arrangement of carefully balanced
antithetical clauses, often heightened by the jingle[7] of
similar terminations. Cicero frequently emphasises[8] the
fact that the Gorgianic figures are one of the sources of
rhythm in prose, apart from any combination of metrical
feet. With the latter form of prose rhythm was associated
especially the name of Thrasymachus, who earned[9] the
title of its inventor. The poets had already taught the

[1] Or. 187.

[2] De Or. III. 196–197, Or. 168, 173, 177–178 ; Q. IX. 4. 10, *ib.* 139 ;
cf. Jensen, Philodemos, pp. 150–151.

[3] Ad Her. IV. 32. 44 ; De Or. III. 173–174, Or. 67, 174 ; Q. IX. 4.
52 *et seq.*

[4] *Vide supra*, p. 87.

[5] Cic. Or. 39 ; cf. Philostr. V. S. (Loeb ed.) 601, on the style of Apollonius.

[6] Cf. Polheim, Die lateinische Reimprosa, p. 134 *et seq.*

[7] The jingle of paronomasia was also sought ; cf. Cic. Or. 84.

[8] Or. 38, 164 *et seq.*, 175, 202, 219–220.

[9] In Or. 175, Cic. corrects De Or. III. 173, where the credit is given to
Isocrates ; cf. Q. IX. 4. 87, on Thrasymachus' discovery of the " paean."

lesson of the musical and emotional value of the various metrical feet when skilfully interwoven, and prose found that it could win a new ornament and a new beauty by its own adaptation of the same feet.[1]   However, both Gorgias and Thrasymachus, as if elated with their discoveries, passed all reasonable bounds in their application, and made their prose so highly rhythmical that it resembled[2] too closely the metrical scheme of the poets.   Isocrates employed many of the devices of these Sophists to enhance the beauty of his prose, though he sought,[3] especially in his later years, to temper their extravagances and his own early excesses, and above all to counteract the suggestion of a definite metrical scheme by the use of an ampler period.

It thus came to be recognised that rhythm was one of the chief embellishments particularly of oratorical prose, but one that must be employed judiciously and unobtrusively.   An orator would defeat his object, if his pursuit of rhythmical effects became apparent,[4] or if he sought[5] for rhythm at the sacrifice of more important things.   Quintilian warns[6] his pupils to avoid anything like a too formal measurement of feet or syllables, and to be content with a general rhythmical effect.   There were legitimate devices[7] which a writer was entitled to employ for the sake of rhythm, but he was bound to avoid unnatural[8] transpositions of words, and mere padding.[9]   It was above all essential that an orator should conceal his art, and so he had to guard against monotony[10] in the use of a particular rhythm, and against excess[11] of rhythmical effects generally.

The limits of rhythm in oratorical prose

[1] Cic. Or. 188 : " nullus est igitur numerus extra poeticos ; " *ib.* 227.

[2] Or. 39–40, 175–176.

[3] Or. 40 *et seq.*; Q. IX. 3. 74 ; cf. *ib.* III. 1. 13 ; Philostr. V. S. 503 ; *vide infra*, p. 242.

[4] Or. 209, 213, 218 ; cf. περὶ ὕψους, 41. 1.

[5] Q. IX. 4. 137.   [6] *Ib.* 112–115, *ib.* 56.

[7] Q. IX. 4. 26–27, *ib.* 58–60, 117.

[8] Ad Her. IV. 32. 44 ; Or. 229 ; Q. IX. 4. 28 ; cf., however, VIII. 6. 62 *et seq.*

[9] Or. 230 ; Q. IX. 4. 58 ; cf. Dionys. De Isocr. 3.

[10] Particularly in forensic oratory ; cf. Or. 207–208, 215, 221, 231 Q. IX. 4. 142 ; cf. De Or. III. 192 ; Ar. Rhet. III. 8. 1.

[11] Or. 40, 195 ; Demetr. 118 ; Dionys. De Isocr. 12.

The feet employed by the writer of prose were identical with those of poetry, but the poet in his verse elaborated a

The character of prose rhythm rigid metrical scheme, and wrought his rhythms into a definite pattern. Prose had no stereotyped pattern of its own. All kinds of feet could enter[1] into its wide domain, and these within limits had to be judiciously selected for particular effects. Prose was bound above all things to maintain the appearance of being free and unfettered[2] by the restraints of verse. Hence the ancient critics[3] generally condemned a writer who allowed a verse, or a portion of a verse to steal into his prose. Everything suggestive of a definite metrical scheme was to be excluded[4] The defect was all the more serious if the latter portion of a verse occurred in the cadence of a period, or the first portion at the beginning, though in spite of all precautions metrical phrases, or even complete verses, may slip unawares into the prose of even the most careful writers.

The Ancients had learned from their study of the poets the emotional value[5] of different rhythms. Particularly in

The emotional value of different rhythms oratory, they strove to adapt the rhythmical character of their language to their feelings at the moment, as well as to the nature of the subject which they were treating. There were measures that were considered stately or ignoble, slow or rapid, languid and effeminate or the reverse ; measures, too, that seemed to limp and halt. It was a commonplace that spondaic rhythms produced the impression of gravity and stability, while iambic measures were considered[6] expressive of vigour and impetuosity. A succession[7] of short syllables

[1] Cic. Or. 189, 195 ; Q. IX. 4. 83, 87, 89.

[2] De Or. III. 184 ; cf. Q. IX. 4. 53.

[3] De Or. III. 175–176, *ib.* 182, on the danger of a succession of dactyls as suggestive of the hexameter, Or. 172, 189–190, 194, 220 ; Ar. Rhet. III. 8. 1 ; Isocr. τέχνη, fr. 7a (Sheehan) ; Dionys. De C. V. c. 25.

[4] Q. IX. 4. 72, 75–76, 109, 111.

[5] Or. 212 ; Q. IX. 4. 66, 69, 91 *et seq.*, 116 *et seq.*, 131–139 ; Ar. Rhet. III. 8. 4 *et seq.;* Demetr. 38, 42 ; Dionys. De C. V. c. 17–18 ; περὶ ὕψους, 39–41.

[6] Q. IX. 4. 136, 141.

[7] Q. *ib.* 66, compares their effect to a child's rattle.

was indicative, indeed, of speed, but lacking in dignity, and so out of place in elevated prose. Sir Walter Raleigh in a felicitous phrase speaks[1] of the " pert intrusion on a solemn thought of a flight of short syllables twittering like a flock of sparrows." The preponderance of these short syllables helped to constitute those dancing, effeminate, and agitated rhythms,[2] that marred the dignity of lofty prose. Some authors,[3] in their anxiety to avoid any suggestion of enervated rhythm, changed the natural word-order to secure the effect of harshness. Again, there were rhythms that were considered[4] naturally noble and dignified, and by the deft intermixture of these a writer could hide the ignoble character of the meaner rhythms. An author had thus to hand a varied selection of rhythms from which to draw in fashioning the harmony of his period, and in determining whether its march[5] was to be slow and solemn, or swift and impetuous. By a skilful manipulation of the material at his disposal he could weave patterns of many designs, and, what was especially effective for the orator, vary continuously the cadence of his periods. To achieve such variety, or fail to achieve it, was the glory or despair of the prose writer. The law of Decorum enjoined upon the orator to adapt the character[6] of his speech to the subject he was treating. This entailed not only a suitable choice of thought and diction, but a delivery suited to the various portions of his address. The rhythmical qualities of his speech could help him materially in securing[7] an appropriate delivery. To the artist in prose it made a world of difference whether his theme was one of panegyric or of deliberative oratory, whether he was exhibiting the impassioned indignation of the prosecutor, or as counsel for defence seeking to win the favour of the court by the conciliatory tone of his speech. Exordium, proofs, refutation, statement of facts, peroration,

---

[1] Style, p. 16.
[2] Q. IX. 4. 6, 106, 140 ; Dionys. De C. V. c. 18 (on Hegesias).
[3] Q. IX. 4. 31, 142 ; cf. Demetr. 48 (on Thucydides).
[4] Cic. Or. 191.
[5] Or. 201.
[6] Even the rhythmical character ; cf. Or. 180 ; Q. IX. 4. 126, 130 et seq.
[7] Q. IX. 4. 138–139.

passages of flattery or entreaty, to produce their fullest effect, should move on different rhythmical planes.

It is evident that the theory of prose rhythm, as developed by the Ancients, was designed primarily for oratorical prose,[1] though in any form of elevated prose an author[2] might seek for rhythmical effects to lend colour to his style. The prevalence of rhetorical training in ancient times would serve to extend the application of the theory to other styles,[3] while every writer will unconsciously favour certain rhythms, particularly in the cadence of his sentences. But prose rhythm was in its origin contrived as an appeal to the ear, and thus could be used with finest effect by the orator. Cicero, however, in portraying the orator of the Plain style,[4] makes him eschew rhythm altogether. This is interesting as an attempt to propound a theory of prose void of emotional content, and primarily intended to appeal[5] to the intellect. On the other hand, the orator of the Grand style could indulge freely in rhythm in his effort to entrance his audience, and play upon their feelings. If Cicero[6] is not exaggerating, the Roman audience was particularly sensitive to the harmonies of speech. It was keenly alive to language that seemed to be broken and halting, while it was ever ready to applaud a period that ended with an effective cadence. The structure of the period as a whole was important, and Cicero is fond[7] of contrasting the effect of a period well compacted and rounded to a rhythmical close, with a loose,

The appeal of rhythm especially in oratory

[1] Cf. Cic. Or. 67 et seq., ib., 77, where he speaks of " oratorii numeri " ; ib. 166 ; Q. IX. 4. 13, 52.

[2] Cf. Demetr. 183, on Plato ; Dionys. De C. V. c. 18, analyses the rhythms of passages from Plato and Thucydides (from their " Funeral speeches," however).

[3] Q. IX. 4. 18, 129, on the historical style ; ib. 20–21, on the more humble styles of Dialogues and Epistles.

[4] Or. 77, ib. 84, where the Gorgianic figures are excluded from this style ; cf. Q. IX. 4. 17, on the style of Lysias.

[5] According to some the proper function of prose ; cf. Ar. Rhet. III. 1. 6, on the style of scientific exposition ; Cic. Or. 20 (on the Plain style) : " omnia docentes et dilucidiora non ampliora facientes."

[6] De Or. III. 196, 198, Or. 168, 178, 197, 214 ; cf. Q. IX. 4. 7 et seq. ; vide supra, p. 88.

[7] De Or. III. 190, Or. 228, 232–233, 235 ; περὶ ὕψους, 40. 1 et seq.

straggling, badly-knit style.[1]   He emphasises,[2] too, how the
beauty of style is disfigured, when the framework of the
period is dissolved.   But, apart from the question of beauty,
a period forming a compact rhythmical unit rendered easier[3]
the orator's task of delivery.

There were different types of periods,[4] some simple and
severe, others complex, consisting of a series of " membra "
Restrictions   welded together in due subordination so as
imposed upon to form a harmonious whole.   These different
the orator   types could be adapted[5] in accordance with
the different purposes of the orator.   In demonstrative[6]
oratory the full periodic structure, with its richest elaboration and most expansive rhythms, could be employed without restriction ; but in forensic cases,[7] where the orator's
aim was practical, the elaborate embroidery of the period
had to be employed with restraint, and resorted to mostly
in impassioned and elevated passages.   Its unrestricted use
in such cases might easily betray the secret of an orator's
art.   Hence, to secure variety, the period had to be abandoned at times for shorter clauses[8] (incisa, membra), which,
resembling a series of rapid thrusts, were especially suited
to argumentative passages that required a display of vigour
and pugnacity.   These shorter clauses, more particularly
the " membra," had rhythms[9] of their own.   In the larger
and more complex unit of the period the rhythmical character of the opening[10] was important, while the middle portions[11] required less care.   Of supreme importance, however,

---

[1] The contrast of the periodic and disjointed styles was, of course, a
commonplace ; cf. Q. IX. 4. 19 ; Ar. Rhet. III. 9.

[2] Cf. Q. IX. 4. 14.   [3] De Or. III. 181–182.

[4] Cf. Ar. Rhet. III. 9. 5.

[5] Q. IX. 4. 124 et seq., 128, 134 ; cf. Dionys. De C. V. c. 19.

[6] Or. 37, 207–208 ; Q. IX. 4. 130 ; vide supra, p. 71.

[7] Or. 209 et seq. ; vide infra, p. 133.

[8] De Or. III. 186, Or. 211–212, 221 et seq. ; cf. Br. 162, on Crassus'
practice ; Q. IX. 4. 126.

[9] De Or. III. 190, Or. 213, 216, 222 et seq. ; Q. IX. 4. 67 ; cf. ib. 122,
where he denies rhythmical completeness to the " incisum."

[10] De Or. III. 182 ; cf. however, 192.

[11] It is interesting to note that Dionys. De C. V. c. 18, analyses the rhythmical character of passages from Thucydides, Plato, and Demosthenes, from
beginning to end.

was the closing cadence, the very citadel of style, as Quintilian calls it,[1] wherein both orator and declaimer can win their chief renown. The close should be impressive, without any suggestion of harshness or abruptness ; hence the preference shown for long syllables[2] in that position. The orator had to avoid, too, the appearance of monotony by varying[3] the rhythm of the " clausula." If he is constantly employing the same cadences, there is a danger that his trick of rhythm may become apparent, and that the audience may turn[4] his efforts to derision by anticipating the endings of his periods. There was all the more need of care, as rhythmical effects come readily to an orator of long practice, so that even in extempore speaking[5] he is able to achieve them.

There was fairly general agreement among the Ancients that certain rhythms were stately, and others ignoble and un-**The subjective nature of rhythm** dignified. We do not, however, find amongst either the Greek or Latin theorists on style such general agreement as to the particular rhythm that formed the most appropriate close. In his use of rhythm an author had in the last resort to appeal to his ear, the judgment[6] of which was essentially subjective. Hence we find amongst the Romans differences of individual taste, and more marked differences still in the preferences for particular rhythms shown by the Greek as compared with the Latin writers who dealt with such problems. In this latter fact would be operative not merely divergences of taste, but also difference in race and in the genius of two languages, for the regular intonations and sentence accent would be dissimilar in Greek and Latin. The Greeks, for instance, showed a preference[7] for the paean, especially in certain positions, but both Cicero[8] and Quintilian[9] favour

---

[1] IX. 4. 62 ; cf. *ib.* 57 ; Or. 199.

[2] Or. 194 ; Q. IX. 4. 106.

[3] De Or. III. 191–193, Or. 213, 218, 231 ; cf. Q. IX. 4. 143.

[4] Ar. Rhet. III. 8. 1 ; περὶ ὕψους, 41. 2.

[5] Q. IX. 4. 114 ; cf. De Or. III. 194, Or. 200.

[6] Q. IX. 4. 118–120.

[7] Cic. De Or. III. 193, Or. 191, 193–194, 218 ; Q. IX. 4. 87 ; Ar. Rhet. III. 8. 4–5 ; Demetr. 38 *et seq.* ; Dionys. however, shows no marked preference for it.

[8] Or. 212–215, 224, 231.   [9] IX. 4. 110–111.

other rhythms. The Asianist orators[1] were fond of ending
with a double trochee, and Cicero, too, is partial to this
rhythm, though he realised the danger of using it to excess.
I need, however, pursue no further this aspect of the problem.
Enough has been said to indicate what diversity of taste
could enter into the application to prose of an element so
subjective as rhythm.

Next after the choice of words, and the artistic structure
of continuous speech, the Ancients relied much for the
elevation of their style on the embellishment

The Figures   afforded by the various Figures of thought
and diction. Many[2] of them considered that in the Figures
lay some magic power to enhance the beauty and sublimity
of either poetry or prose. The orator in particular set great
store by them, and no scheme of rhetorical training was
regarded as complete without an exhaustive survey[3] of the
many Figures which the ingenuity[4] of rhetoricians had
discovered or devised. An effective use of such ornament
was considered[5] one of the great glories of the orator. The
Figures serve[6] to give variety to style, to bring to light the
latent powers of language, or even to invest it with a new
power, while they help to transform it into a fitting vehicle
for the expression of thoughts of the widest range and loftiest
sublimity. The Figures of diction, diverging from the
ordinary path of simple and direct expression, impart to
style an element of the unfamiliar. As Quintilian puts[7] it,
they obviate the tedium of customary everyday speech, and
save us from commonplace language. Amongst these were

---

[1] *Ib.* 103, 105.

[2] Ad Her. IV. 11. 16 : " omne genus orationis . . . dignitate adficiunt
exornationes " ; De Or. III. 200 ; Fronto, II. 86 ; Aquila Romanus,
Halm, Rhet. Lat. Vol. I. pp. 22–23 ; Demetr. 140–142 ; Dionys. De C. V.
c. 19 ; περὶ ὕψους, 8. 1, on Figures as a source of the Sublime ; cf. Norden,
A. K. I. p. 50.

[3] Ad Her. IV. 13. 18 *et seq.* ; Cic. De Or. c. 53–54, Or. 134 *et seq.* ;
Q. VIII. 6 (on Tropes), IX. c. 1–3.

[4] For special treatises on them, cf. Q. IX. 1. 18, *ib.* 2. 102, on Gorgias,
who was followed in Latin by Rutilius Lupus ; *ib.* 3. 38, 46–47, 89 ; cf.
Halm, op. cit., Vol. I. pp. 3–77.

[5] Cic. Br. 140–141, Or. 136 ; Pliny, Ep. III. 13. 3.

[6] Cf. Q. IX. 1. 21, *ib.* 2. 59, 63.

[7] IX. 3. 3 ; cf. Ad Her. IV. 31. 42.

to be found many striking Figures that, when wielded by a great orator, helped[1] to focus the attention of his audience, and keep it from flagging. The Figures of thought,[2] however, were an even more potent instrument for exciting emotion, strengthening a pleader's arguments, making his proofs more convincing, and winning the favour of judge or audience. Many of these latter[3] served to vary and enliven oratory, but in general they affected[4] only indirectly the formal elements of style.

Real bewilderment arose when it became necessary to determine the number of possible Figures, and define their scope. We are indebted to Quintilian for one of the best discussions of this element of style, a discussion that is moderate and well reasoned, and that shows an insight into the psychological basis of many of the Figures. He divides[5] the Figures of diction into those that depend on the (grammatical) form of language, and those that arise from a particular arrangement of words. The first class especially seems capable of being multiplied indefinitely, so that according to Quintilian,[6] there is a Figure corresponding to every species of solecism. There are Figures, too, that have faded,[7] and have almost ceased to be such through the attrition of common use. Again, as regards the Figures of thought, the title of Figure was often given to a device,[8] or form of proof, that any skilled pleader might well have used in the course of his argument. Quintilian himself seems[9] to realise the difficulty of giving the honoured name of Figure to some of these ordinary devices, but he salves his con-

The multiplicity of Figures

---

[1] Q. IX. 3. 27, 66.

[2] Q. IX. 1. 19–21, *ib.* 2. 26.

[3] Q. IX. 2. 29 *et seq.*, on Personification.

[4] Cf., however, Q. IX. 2. 96.

[5] IX. 3. 2.

[6] IX. 3. 11, *ib.* 14, 17, on " archaic " Figures and those derived from Graecisms ; cf. Gellius, XV. 14 ; Q. IX. 3. 90, admits that more Figures of speech may yet be discovered.

[7] *Ib.* IX. 3. 4, 13.

[8] Devices such as prolepsis, exclamation, amplification, digression, repetition, etc. ; cf. Q. IX. 2. 16, 27, 55, 61, 63, 100, 103 *et seq.*, 106–107.

[9] IX. 2. 4 *et seq.* ; cf. *ib.* 91, 98–99.

science by declaring[1] that they are such only, if art assists in their designing. Some went so far as to declare[2] that there are as many types of Figures as there are kinds of emotion.

The formidable list of Figures that we meet with in special treatises and in the hand-books of Rhetoric, must have been the result of the accretions of many generations. The poets had employed numerous Figures which owed their beauty and effectiveness to the fact that they were rooted in genuine emotion. It was an obvious task for their commentators to tabulate and classify the Figures they employed, but it seems to have been left to the perverted ingenuity of rhetorical theorists to refine upon the old Figures, to devise new ones, to invent new names,[3] and even to give the title of Figure to many turns of thought and speech that hardly deserved the name. The number of genuine Figures could in reality[4] be reduced to a comparatively small compass, but the rhetoricians would thereby be deprived of an exercise ground for their ingenuity, while the commentators on the poets would be condemned to silence on many passages, where nothing is left to them but the discovery of a Figure.

The ingenuity of the Rhetoricians

No subject, in fact, evoked a greater display of scholastic subtlety than the Figures, or gave rise to more numerous and seemingly interminable disputes. Those who dealt with them, hotly discussed[5] the distinction between Tropes and Figures, and quarrelled regarding the species,[6] number, and classification

Controversy regarding the Figures

[1] IX. 2. 27.

[2] IX. 1. 23 ; *ib.* 25, on Cicero's view.

[3] Cf. Q. IX. 1. 18, *ib.* 22, on the many names of Figures invented by the Greeks ; cf. IX. 3. 54, 99 ; Dionys. De C. V. c. 8, says the Figures are perhaps innumerable ; περὶ ὕψους, 16. 1, where the author says he will deal only with a few Figures that produce elevation of style ; cf. Saintsbury, op. cit., Vol. I. p. 102.

[4] Q. IX. 1. 22.

[5] Q. VIII. 6. 1 *et seq.*, IX. 1. 2 *et seq.* ; Cic. Br. 69, seems to have been the first Roman to distinguish Trope and Figure ; cf. Laurand, Étude sur le Style, etc., p. 296 ; Causeret, Étude, p. 176 *et seq.* ; Volkmann, Die Rhetorik, pp. 415–416.

[6] Q. VIII. 6. 43, 58, IX. 1. 7, on Irony as Trope and Figure.

of Tropes. Similar disputes[1] arose regarding the Figures proper, some holding that there are only Figures of speech, others maintaining that there are none but Figures of thought. Doubts were raised[2] as to what constituted a particular Figure, or as to whether[3] a particular Figure was a Figure of speech or a Figure of thought. Again, difficulties[4] arose as to whether a particular phenomenon of language should be classed as a Trope or a Figure. Cicero[5] regales us with a rather jejune list of the various Figures, shorter, however, in the *Orator* than in the *De Oratore*, but even his great authority was not sufficient to insure that his classification would pass unchallenged. In all this discussion the fixing of nomenclature must have always presented a serious problem to the Romans, especially in cases where the Greek terms were not adopted. The *Auctor ad Herennium* exhibits a formidable array of Figures, and makes a brave attempt to cope with the difficulties of terminology, but many of the names he employs are peculiar[6] to himself, or at least used in a peculiar sense. There was often thus a wide divergence[7] in terminology, which must have added to the general confusion, and which certainly increased the perplexity of the student.

I have drawn largely on Quintilian in this brief discussion of the Figures.[8] He, while he appreciates their value as an element of style, if properly employed, is
The proper use of Figures careful to issue a warning against their abuse. With such a wealth of ornament ready to hand, there was danger that the budding orator, and even

[1] Q. IX. 1. 10 *et seq.*, *ib.* 15.

[2] Q. IX. 2. 32, 3. 60, 76, *ib.* 97, where Q. declares himself in the dark as to what Cicero meant by " relatio."

[3] Q. IX. 2. 101, *ib.* 3. 88, 98.

[4] Q. IX. 3. 91, classes Hyperbaton as a Trope (cf. VIII. 6. 62) ; Caecilius called it a Figure.

[5] Q. IX. 1. 26 *et seq.*, reproduces verbatim Cicero's treatment of the Figures.

[6] Cf. his use of frequentatio, transgressio, conformatio, significatio ; Cicero, however, in De Or. c. 53–54, adopts many of his terms.

[7] Cf. Q. IX. 2. 22, 54, 3. 45, 49, 81 ; Rutilius Lupus adheres to the Greek terms, but others, such as Aq. Romanus and Rufinianus, show divergences in their efforts to find Latin equivalents.

[8] I use " Figure " here as a general term to include Trope as well.

the aspirant to poetic honours whose work was not quickened by the breath of inspiration, might grasp at the embellishment afforded by the Figures, and apply it indiscriminately. Figures, to be effective, had to be used in moderation.[1] There were many who overloaded[2] their style with such ornament, thus rendering it tasteless and frequently obscure. They indulged in excessive use of metaphors,[3] often harsh and over-bold, and scattered pointless epithets[4] indiscriminately through their prose. It was felt to be especially important to refrain from a constant and monotonous use[5] of the same Figure, while more than ordinary caution had to be exercised in employing Figures,[6] the art of which became so obvious as to seem laboured and unnatural. This was particularly true of the " Gorgianic " Figures,[7] which, if used sparingly and unobtrusively, could contribute much towards elegance of style. They were capable of heightening the beauty of prose by their rhythmical qualities, while a good antithesis[8] had a logical value of its own. Gorgias,[9] however, having discovered the potentialities of such devices, marred their effect by an immoderate use of them. Others[10] followed his lead, lured probably by the very ease with

---

[1] Ad Her. IV. 15. 22 ; Q. IX. 2. 72, 3. 4, 27, 100 *et seq.* ; Demetr. 67 ; περὶ ὕψους, 17 ; *vide infra*, p. 132.

[2] Aq. Rom. 30, 42 ; cf. Dionys. De Lys. 3, De Isocr. 3.

[3] Q. VIII. 6. 14, 16 *et seq.*

[4] *Ib.* 40–42 ; cf. Ar. Rhet. III. 3. 3, for this fault in the Sophist Alcidamas.

[5] Cf. Dionys. De C. V. c. 19, on this defect in Isocr. and his followers ; cf. Ad Her. IV. 31. 42.

[6] Q. IX. 3. 5, on figurae "secretae et extra vulgarem usum positae; " *ib.* 54, on Climax ; cf. Ad Her. IV. 27. 38 (on " disjunctio ").

[7] Ad Her. IV. 12. 18, *ib.* 22. 32 ; Cic. De Or. III. 206 ; Q. IX. 3. 74 ; Aq. Rom. 21 *et seq.* ; cf. Philod. Rhet. I. 162, II. 258 ; Dionys. De C. V. c. 23, for their use in the λέξις γλαφυρὰ ; *vide supra*, p. 99.

[8] Ar. Rhet. III. 9. 8, *ib.* 9, on the other Gorgianic figures ; cf. *ib.* 10. 5, 11. 9 ; Anaximenes, 26–28.

[9] Some at least of the " Gorgianic " figures existed prior to Gorgias ; cf. Lamb, Clio Enthroned, c. 5 ; Polheim, op. cit., p. 138 *et seq.* ; Navarre, Essai sur la Rhétorique Grecque, c. 3–4 ; cf. Thompson, Plato's Gorgias, p. 247 *et seq.*, Immisch, Gorgiae Helena, for fragments of Gorgias.

[10] Isocr. Panath, 2 ; Demetr. 247, 250 ; Dionys. De Isocr. 2, De Lys. 14, Ad Amm. II. 2 ; Cic. Or. 38, 176 ; Gellius, XVIII. 8 ; cf. Aq. Rom. 21 ; Polheim, op. cit., p. 148 *et seq.*

which such Figures could be formed in Greek and Latin owing to the similarity of inflexions.

In many of the strictures that Quintilian passes on the abuse of Figures, it is clear that he has in mind conditions

Abuses   prevalent in his own day, especially in the schools of declamation. The declaimers cultivated a style that was tawdry, and were ready to seek their effects even at the sacrifice of clearness,[1] good sense, and propriety. There were Figures that were regarded as suitable to particular styles.[2] There were on the other hand Tropes and Figures so bold that as a rule[3] they were left as a monopoly to the poets, or sparingly used in the most elevated prose. The declaimers, however, provided they could attain even a counterfeit brilliance, were prepared[4] to employ even the boldest and harshest Figures. Quintilian probably has chiefly them in mind, when he speaks[5] of those who, regardless of the weight of their subject-matter and the force of their thought, distort even empty words into figurative shapes. In the same context he gets to the root of the matter, when he declares that it is as absurd to pursue Figures without regard to the subject, as to aim at deportment and gesture without reference to the body. If a writer errs in this way, it means that his Figures are thrown[6] in as mere external ornament. They are not grounded in genuine emotion, but are mere excrescences that have no vital connection[7] with the author's thought, and can never be woven into its texture.

The majority of the ancient theorists who dealt with the Figures, are content to give a bare enumeration of them, adding a short definition and an illustration of each,

[1] Q. VIII. 2. 20–21; *vide infra*, p. 211 *et seq.*, for Seneca's picture of the declaimers.

[2] Cf. Fronto, II. 158.

[3] Q. VIII. 6. 19, 24–25, 29–30, 59–61.

[4] *Ib.* IX. 2. 81; on their excesses in the use of " sententiae," *vide infra*, p. 336.

[5] IX. 3. 100, cf. *ib.* 5; Sen. Controv. I. pr. 22–23.

[6] Cf. Saintsbury, op. cit., I. p. 53.

[7] Cf. Middleton Murry, op. cit., pp. 10–12, 83, for some interesting remarks on external or applied ornament, which in the eyes of some constitutes " Style "; Babbitt, The New Laocoon, p. 23 *et seq.*

without taking into account its genesis and motive. Some

The psycho-logical basis of the Figures

of the Figures of speech were regarded as mere embellishment, while it was recognised in a dim way that others of them, as well as the Figures of thought, have their roots in certain emotions. At times, indeed, an attempt is made to penetrate[1] to the psychological basis of a Figure, and its effect in stirring emotion, without, however, any subtle analysis of it. Aristotle, as we have seen, endeavours to explain the appeal made by a good antithesis, while the author of the treatise *On the Sublime* has the signal merit of seeking to divine the psychological atmosphere in which the Figures he selects[2] for discussion had their origin. It is clear that a Figure like Asyndeton[3] is natural to an orator labouring under violent emotion, and seeking to give speedy release to thoughts straining at the leash. The dropping of the connecting particles gives the effect of impassioned movement and rugged impetuosity. With vehement and overmastering passion was generally associated another[4] Figure, which involved the repetition of the same word. It was a Figure that in itself could add to the external charm of style, but in reality it sprang from a speaker's desire to emphasise a particular concept, and leave it firmly implanted in the minds of his hearers by delivering, as it were, a swift succession of blows. The treatise *On the Sublime* seeks[5] a psychological basis also for Hyperbaton, while it touches

---

[1] This holds of the Auctor ad Herennium and Quintilian, rarely of Cicero, who is generally satisfied with an enumeration of the Figures.

[2] C. 16 *et seq.*; cf. also Demetr. 52 *et seq.*, 108, 263 *et seq.*

[3] περὶ ὕψους, c. 20, *ib.* 21, where the author contrasts the effect when the connecting particles are restored; Arist. Rhet. III. 6. 6, *ib.* 12. 3, where he considered the bearing of Asyndeton on delivery; Demetr. 194; Hermog. περὶ μεθ. δειν. (Sp. II. 435); cf. Ad Her. IV. 30. 41; Q. IX. 3. 50, 54.

[4] The Figure took various forms; cf. Ad Her. IV. 13. 19 (Repetitio); *ib.* 28. 38, on the allied Figure "Conduplicatio"; Cic. De Or. III. 206, Or. 85, where it is excluded from the Plain style; *ib.* 135; Q. IX. 3. 29 *et seq.*; Fronto, II. 158, calls it "commotissima figura"; Aq. Rom. 30; Arist. Rhet. III. 12. 2, where its bearing on delivery is noted (cf. Poet. c. 19); Demetr. 61, 268; περὶ ὕψους, 20. 2, on ἐπαναφορά.

[5] C. 22; Q. VIII. 6. 62 *et seq.*, considers it from the point of view of artistic structure and euphony.

briefly on the emotional effect of Climax,[1] and its power of contributing to passion and sublimity.   Hyperbole[2] was a Figure that was grounded in the common human tendency to exaggerate, and, if skilfully used, could be a powerful weapon in the hands of the orator who wished to exalt his own cause, and discredit that of his opponent.   It had, however to be kept within reasonable limits.[3]   Figures like Pleonasm[4] and Periphrasis[5] were primarily designed to enhance the beauty of normal expression, especially in a writer who is labouring to set forth adequately an elevated thought, but in an author who lacks the touch of genius, such Figures might easily degenerate into empty bombast.

The Ancients at times speak of achieving the effect of " vividness," and of the power exhibited both by poets and orators of placing events, as it were, before the eyes of their readers or hearers.   This element of vividness could be imparted by a brilliant image,[6] or an apt and powerful metaphor.[7]   The Ancients evidently regarded this quality[8] as such an important factor in style, that they raised it to the dignity of a special Figure, variously named[9] by different Roman authors. It is difficult, however, to say how far the ancient theorists regarded it as emanating from a writer's creative power, and as the product[10] of his own vital processes of thought. Quintilian evidently thought it could be achieved by a minute

The quality of vividness

---

[1] C. 23 ; Ad Her. IV. 25. 34, points out its affinity with " Repetitio " ; De Or. III. 207 ; Q. IX. 3. 54 *et seq.*

[2] Ad Her. IV. 33. 44 ; De Or. III. 203, Top. 45 ; Q. VIII. 6. 67 *et seq.*

[3] περὶ ὕψους, c. 38. 2, criticises Isocr's tendency to use it to excess ; Ar. Rhet. III. 11. 16, says it has a " juvenile " character ; *vide infra*, p. 119.

[4] Q. IX. 3. 46–47.

[5] *Ib.* VIII. 6. 60–61 ; περὶ ὕψους, 28–29.

[6] Ad Her. IV. 45. 59 ; περὶ ὕψους, 15. 2 *et seq.*

[7] Q. VIII. 6. 19.

[8] *Ib.* VIII. 3. 61 *et seq.*, for an interesting discussion of ἐνάργεια ; IV. 2. 63 *et seq.*

[9] Ad Her. IV. 55. 68, calls it " demonstratio " ; cf. Cic. De Or. III. 202, Or. 139, Part. Or. 20 ; Q. VI. 2. 32 (illustratio, evidentia) ; Halm, op. cit., I. 62, II. 517, 521 (enargia) ; on ἐνέργεια cf. Ar. Rhet. III. 10. 6 (with Cope's note) ; *ib.* 11. 2 ; Q. VIII. 3. 89.

[10] Cf. Middleton Murry, op. cit., c. 4–5, for a discussion of what he styles " crystallization," and kindred problems.

description of a scene, but such a description might issue in nothing more than a mere mechanical reproduction of details. But, in one passage[1] at least, he seems to suggest that the quality was derived not merely from an author's power of visualising a scene, but of reproducing sensuous details to which he had emotionally reacted in a very special way.

I have touched only on some salient points in connection with the Figures, but even this brief discussion may serve to show that their treatment by the ancient theorists was often mechanical and inadequate. The Figures, if they were the outcome of genuine feeling, could[2] do much to heighten the beauty of style both in prose and poetry, and lend it colour and emotional suggestiveness. The temptation, however, was strong to regard them as mere external ornament that could be applied indiscriminately according to a writer's fancy. They continued[3] to hold an important place in rhetorical theory, and the battles that raged around them, form an interesting episode in the history of criticism.

The Figures in later theory

The precepts we have dealt with under the head of "ornatus" concern the formal elements of style, and, as I have said, are capable of being applied mechanically, unless they are vitalised by the driving force of a great personality. The Ancients insisted on another virtue of style, that of Decorum, which looked beyond the merely formal elements, and considered style in relation to the subject matter. Particularly in the case of oratorical prose, this virtue took into account other considerations, some of them accidental and external, it is true, but still such as might serve as a check against an empty and indiscriminate parade of rhetorical embellishment.

The virtue of Decorum

[1] Cf. his analysis of the passage from the Verrines, VIII. 3. 64–65 ; cf. VI. 2. 34 *et seq.*

[2] Cf. Brunetière, Essays in French Literature, p. 247 *et seq. ;* the chapter is entitled "An Apology for Rhetoric."

[3] Cf. Saintsbury, op. cit., I. p. 374, II. 150 ; Gayley and Scott, Methods and Materials of Literary Criticism, pp. 208–209, 235 *et seq. ;* Spingarn, Critical Essays, Vol. I. p. 37 *et seq.*

The concept of Decorum was primarily an aesthetic one,[1] rooted in man's sense of the order and harmony that con-
The import- ance of Decorum stitute the beauty of the visible Universe, but the concept soon came to be applied to the sphere of human conduct,[2] and, particu-
larly by the Stoics, was made the norm to guide men in the various duties of their lives. In the realm of Art, Decorum, which Milton calls " the grand masterpiece to observe," was regarded[3] as a principle to be respected above all others. As applied to literature, it was considered by many[4] to be the supreme virtue of style. A style that was to be success-ful in making its appeal, and in carrying conviction,[5] must scrupulously fulfil the precept of propriety. Aristotle, as one would expect from a critic of his temperament, lays chief stress on clearness as the essential element in style, but he is careful[6] to assign a place of almost equal importance to Decorum. Dionysius declares[7] that this virtue is one of the sources of beauty and charm in composition. Hence it is not surprising that the principle of Decorum, in its many aspects, was invoked in the criticism of poets and prose writers,[8] and often made the touchstone of their success or failure. Amongst the Greek orators, Lysias[9] was held up as the great exemplar of propriety, while it was felt that Isocrates,[10] with his tendency to swelling pomp and over-ornateness, often failed to attain it.

[1] Cf. Cic. De Off. I. 14, De Fin. II. 47.

[2] Cicero is constantly appealing to the principle of Decorum in the " De Officiis "; cf. Or. 70 *et seq.* ; Plato, Laws, 669–670, where both the ethical and aesthetic nuances of the concept enter in ; Kroll, Die historische Stellung von Horazens Ars poetica, p. 91, finds the origin of the concept in Damon's theory of Music.

[3] Cic. De Or. I. 132 : " caput esse artis decere "; cf. Q. XI. 3. 177.

[4] Cic. Or. 123 ; Q. I. 5. 1 ; Dionys. Lys. 9 : κρατίστην ἁπασῶν ἀρετὴν καὶ τελειοτάτην; Ad Pomp. c. 3.

[5] De Or. III. 91, Part. Or. 19 ; Q. VIII. 3. 42 ; Ar. Rhet. III. 7. 4, *b.* 12. 6.

[6] Rhet. III. 2. 1, cf. Poet. 22. 1.

[7] De C. V. c. 11–13, *ib.* c. 20.

[8] Cic. Or. 70, 72 ; Q. X. 1. 27, *ib.* 46, on Homer's pre-eminence in this quality (cf., however, περὶ ὕψους, 9. 7) ; *ib.* 62, 71.

[9] Dionys. Lys. 9, 13 ; cf. περὶ ὕψους, 34. 2, on Hyperides.

[10] Dionys. De Isocr. 3.

The concept of Decorum, as understood and applied by the Ancients, is almost bewildering in its complexity. Plato was familiar with it, but Aristotle seems to have been the first to apply the concept extensively to literature. For him the law of Decorum was closely bound up with the principle of the Golden Mean that played so vital a part in his philosophy. In the use of the various ornaments of style, a writer should above all aim at observing the Mean.[1]   Consequently, excess[2] was to be avoided as violating the principle of propriety, and as constituting one of the most flagrant faults of style. Proportion should always be maintained[3] between the style and the subject matter, between expression and the emotion experienced by the writer, while in addition the orator has to take into account various aspects of ἦθος, and consider the seasonableness or unseasonableness[4] of employing the rhetorical embellishments at his command.

Analysis of the concept

Aristotle comprises in a single chapter all the essentials of the doctrine of Decorum, but it remained for others to refine upon his teaching. In the Roman writers[5] on style we find indeed the concept of Decorum resolving itself in its fundamentals into avoidance of excess, and observation of the Mean. Wherever there is excess,[6] there is faultiness of style. A good style then should as a first essential be proportionate to the subject, and exhibit a perfect adaptation of means to end. The principle of Decorum was no less valid for poetry[7] than for prose, but it found its widest application in oratory. Here it could range in all its

The Roman theorists

---

[1] Rhet. III. 2. 15, *ib.* 3. 3 : ἀλλὰ δεῖ στοχάζεσθαι τοῦ μετρίου ; *ib.* 12. 6.

[2] *Ib.* III. 2. 1, 10.

[3] Cf. Rhet. III. 7, for various aspects of Decorum, *ib.* III. 2. 3, 9.

[4] *Ib.* III. 7. 8 : τὸ δ' εὐκαίρως ἤ μὴ εὐκαίρως χρῆσθαι κοινὸν ἁπάντων τῶν εἰδῶν ἐστίν.

[5] Cic. Or. 73, Part. Or. 19 ; cf. De Off. I. 14 ; Q. VI. 3. 26 (on wit) VIII. 6. 41, XI. 3. 181 (on delivery) : " regnare maxime modum ; " XI 10. 80 : " tutissima fere per medium via."

[6] Q. VIII. 3. 42, XI. 1. 91.

[7] *Vide infra*, p. 423 *et seq.*

complexity,[1] as the orator had to consider not merely the necessity of adapting his style and delivery to his subject, but had to take into account[2] the occasion of his speech, his own character, the character of his client in a forensic case, and the character of the audience which he was addressing.   In fact, the law of Decorum dogged[3] his footsteps at every turn.   Even in the various portions of his speech, an orator had to make his style conform to the object he had in view ; he had to subject it to modifications, to a heightening[4] or lowering of the key, to contraction or expansion, as the case demanded.

As I have said, the first essential was that style should be in harmony with the subject,[5] which in the case of the orator **Style to be in** is equivalent to saying that it should be pro-
harmony with portionate to the issue at stake.   The ancient
the subject theorists, when in this connexion they speak of proportion, excess, or defect, generally had in mind the varying degrees of rhetorical embellishment comprised under the head of " ornatus."   The orator had to attend to his choice of words, and ensure[6] that no word was more dignified than the idea he wished to express.   It was left to his judgment to determine how far[7] he would employ artistic structure in his prose, and seek for rhythmical effects.   Lastly, as the use of the Figures served[8] to set up a dividing line between the various styles, an orator who

---

[1] Cic. De Or. II. 20, III. 53, 210 *et seq.*, Or. 71 ; Q. XI. 1. 14, XII. 10. 69 *et seq. ;* cf. Dionys. De Lys. 9, for a good summary of the doctrine of Decorum as applied to oratory.

[2] The Stoics demanded only that the style should be proportionate to the subject ; Diog. Laert. VII. 59.

[3] Q. III. 8. 60 *et seq.*, VIII. 3. 14 ; cf. Ar. Rhet. III. 12. 5 *et seq.*, on changes necessitated according as a speech was forensic or deliberative, etc.

[4] Cic. De Or. II. 183, Or. 110 *et seq.*, 124–125.

[5] De Or. II. 320, Or. 71, 100 *et seq.*, 123 ; Q. IV. 2. 61–62, VIII. 3. 14, X. 4. 128, X. 1. 101 (on Livy's speeches) : " omnia cum rebus tum personis accomodata " ; XI. 1. 2, XII. 10. 44, 69 ; Demetr. 237 ; Theon, Progym. Sp. II. 116. 15.

[6] Q. I. 5. 3 : " laudamus enim verba rebus bene accomodata " ; Demetr. 114 ; Dionys. De C. V. c. 3, *ib.* c. 20.

[7] Or. 196 *et seq.*, 209 *et seq.*

[8] Cf. Cic. Or. 75–99, for the characteristics of the various styles ; Q. XII. 10. 60 *et seq. ;* Demetr. 59 *et seq.*

wished to observe propriety, had to decide to what extent his subject would admit the adornment they afforded. Such stylistic devices, as I have said, served to raise the tone of prose, to lend it vivacity and colour, and to invest it with impressiveness, if the subject so demanded. But, in oratory particularly, a speaker has at times to reef his sails, and be restrained both in style and delivery, when dealing with a case that is comparatively trivial and unimportant. There were some who either from incapacity, or lack of judgment, were never able to satisfy these demands, and who insisted[1] on using the Grand style on all occasions. They were always ornate and highly coloured, unmeasured in their vehemence, throbbing with passion,[2] even when they were dealing with the most commonplace theme. This defect reminds us of the description which a modern critic[3] gives of William Cobbett's style:—" he bludgeons all he touches, and spends the same monotonous emphasis on his dislike of tea and on his hatred of the government." Such writers fail to see that it was one of the most serious breaches of Decorum to be guilty of what Cicero well describes[4] as " tragoedias agere in nugis." It was like[5] putting the mask and buskins of Hercules on an infant boy, or the head[6] of the Colossus of Rhodes on the body of a dwarf. The early Sophists relied on their skill in the manipulation of language to make " small things great,"[7] but their efforts ended too often in a style wholly out of proportion to their theme. Aristotle dealt[8] in his own incisive way with the

[1] Cf. Or. 99 ; Q. VIII. 3. 21 ; ib. X. 2. 23, on those who are capable of only one style.

[2] Cf. περὶ ὕψους, III. 5, on the fault of " Parenthyrsus," which may be defined as " unseasonable and empty emotion."

[3] Raleigh, Style, p. 106.

[4] De Or. II. 205 ; cf. ib. 17, for his definition of " ineptus " ; Q. XI. 1. 3 ; cf. ib. VIII. 3. 56 et seq., on κακόζηλον, which, in some at least of its manifestations, connoted such a breach of Decorum ; Ar. Rhet. III. 7. 1 Demetr. 119 et seq.

[5] Q. VI. 1. 36 ; cf. περὶ ὕψους, 30. 2, on the impropriety of putting a large tragic mask on an infant.

[6] Lucian, Quomodo conscribenda sit historia ? c. 23.

[7] Cf. Plato, Phaedrus, 267. A ; Isocr. Panegyr. 8 ; Demetr. 120 et seq. cf. Apul. De Platone et ejus dogmate, II. 231, on Sophistic rhetoric.

[8] Rhet. III. c. 2–3 ; cf. Dionys. De Lys. 14 ; Rohde, Der griech. Roman p. 358 et seq.

faults of Sophistic prose, mostly faults of excess, due to the use of words or ornament out of place in prose, or above the dignity of the subject.   But such violations of Decorum were common in every sphere of literature, in poetry[1] as well as in prose.   They were frequently found in oratory, and were manifested in their most repugnant form in the schools of declamation.   Many indeed show a tendency to employ diction too elevated[2] for their subject, and in their efforts to be impressive reject[3] a large part of current speech. Many like Isocrates[4] give way to the temptation of describing everything with a touch of hyperbole, the most frigid of Figures, as Demetrius calls[5] it.   It was noted that the Hellenistic historians[6] were prone to the latter fault. Demetrius speaks[7] of Cleitarchus as describing a wasp in terms that would be more appropriate to the Erymanthian boar.

At times a grandiose style might be adopted for a trivial subject for the purposes[8] of parody or burlesque, but such a proceeding was a serious fault in sober prose, and was especially condemned in oratory.   We often find contrasted[9] the unimportant case of some private suit involving for the most part a prosaic discussion of legal formulae, and the trial for a capital offence, when a man's civil status was at stake, and when the pleader had to bring into play all the resources of his eloquence in his defence.   Any but a plain style would be out of harmony with the former case, where a clear state-

The trivial subject

---

[1] Cf. Aristoph. Frogs, 1330 *et seq.*, where Eur's tendency to this fault is satirised ; Babbitt, The New Laocoon, p. 246, illustrates the fault in another sphere, in criticising Strauss's Domestic Symphony as " showing a disproportion between expression and what is expressed."

[2] Ad Her. IV. 10. 15, on " oratio sufflata," " cum verbis . . . gravioribus quam res postulat aliquid dicitur " ; cf. Q. VIII. 3. 30.

[3] Q. VIII. 3. 23 ; cf. Babbitt, Rousseau and Romanticism, p. 57, on the " fear of the trivial word, that might destroy the illusion of the grand manner."

[4] περὶ ὕψους, 38. 2.   [5] 124.

[6] Cf. Lucian, op. cit., c. 27, on the historians of his own day.

[7] 304 ; *vide infra*, p. 497.

[8] Q. VIII. 3. 48 : " cum ex industria risus inde captatur " ; cf. Aristoph. Frogs, loc. cit.

[9] Cic. Or. 72, 102, Ad Fam. IX. 21. 1, De opt. gen. 10 ; Pliny, Ep. VI. 33. 9 ; Tac. Dial. 37 ; Q. XI. 1. 44, XII. 10. 39, 70.

ment[1] of facts and logical acumen are the great essentials. Best adapted to such a case is a style[2] that is lucid and easy, betraying no trace of elaboration, but exhibiting something of the casual quality of ordinary conversation. The orator in such circumstances[3] will draw his diction mostly from the speech of everyday life. Again, in trivial cases he must not strive after rhythmical effects,[4] nor aim at elaborate periodic structure.[5] In such cases restraint in the use of Figures[6] was especially demanded, while the orator had to renounce altogether the Gorgianic Figures, the artifice of which is so easily detected.

In striking contrast to all this is the case of great moment, where big issues are at stake, where there is involved a question of public policy,[7] or the trial of a distinguished citizen on a capital charge. Here elevation[8] of style is essential, and commonplace or vulgar language out of place. It was as flagrant a breach of Decorum to handle a great subject in a mean way,[9] as to deal with a trivial one in a grandiose manner. However, even in such circumstances, the orator has to conceal his art, but in many passages of his speech he may[10] deploy all the forces of his eloquence, and indulge in digressions,[11] amplification,[12] bold Figures,[13] and artisti-

When great issues are involved

[1] Cf. Q. VIII. 3. 14–15.

[2] Or. 76 *et seq.*, on the characteristics of the Plain style ; *ib.* 124 ; Q. IV. 2. 61–62, XI. 1. 93.

[3] Cf. Q. IV. 2. 116–118, on the style of the " narratio " in trivial cases ; V. 14. 33 (on the " probatio "), VIII. 3. 18 ; however, something more is at times demanded in the " narratio " ; *vide infra*, p. 121 n. 7.

[4] Cf. Or. 77 ; Q. IX. 4. 21, demands a simplicity that does not altogether eschew rhythm, but conceals its use.

[5] Cf. Q. IX. 4. 134, where long " cola " and short periods are recommended for the " narratio " ; cf. Demetr. 5–6.

[6] Or. 81, 83–84.

[7] Cf. Cic. De Or. II. 337 *et seq. ; vide infra*, p. 122.

[8] Cf. Q. III. 8. 61 *et seq.*, for various views on deliberative oratory ; περὶ ὕψους, 43. 5.

[9] Cf. Demetr. 237, on the fault which he styles τὸ ξηρόν.

[10] Or. 125, Ad Att. I. 14. 3–4 ; Q. V. 14. 34.

[11] De Or. II. 311–312.

[12] Or. 125–127.

[13] Cf. Ad Her. IV. 15. 22, on the use of " exclamatio," " cum rei magnitudo postulare videbitur " ; περὶ ὕψους, 23. 4 ; Demetr. 59 *et seq.*

cally constructed periods.[1] The great aim of the orator on such occasions was to move his audience, and play upon their emotions, and, in his peroration especially, he was granted full licence to employ every weapon in his armoury.

Rhetorical theory applied the principle of Decorum, not only by insisting that an orator's style should conform to

Decorum in the different parts of a speech

the general character of the case which he pleaded, but also by enjoining[2] that it should conform to the character[3] of the different parts of his speech such as the exordium, statement of facts, and peroration. The principle, as thus conceived, was often meticulously applied[4] by those who accepted a three-fold division of style, and who brought the various styles into relation with the " officia oratoris." It was in general agreed that the aim and duty of the orator were different in the different parts of his speech. His chief purpose in the exordium was to impress favourably judge or audience, so that on most occasions an orator's language at the opening of his speech should be designed to give pleasure,[5] and should attract by its finish and its concilia-tory tone, while at the same time it should avoid palpable artifices of style that might prejudice his hearers rather than win their favour. An orator's aim in the " narratio " was to expound the facts of his case. The Plain style was con-sidered[6] best adapted for such a purpose, as clearness and brevity were the great essentials, though other qualities[7] were at times demanded in this portion of a speech. In the

[1] Or. 210; Q. IX. 4. 128.

[2] Or. 71, 123–124; Q. XI. 1. 6, XII. 10. 71.

[3] In practice this would depend mainly on the nature of the " officium oratoris " in the various parts.

[4] There is evidence at times of a reaction against such rigid formulism; f. Q. V. 14. 33; *vide infra*, pp. 149, 472.

[5] Cic. De Inv. I. 15. 20; De Or. II. 311, 315, 317–318, 322, Part. Or. 5, Top. 97; Q. II. 5. 7, IV. 1. 58; cf. Ar. Rhet. III. 14. 7; Dionys. De Lys. 17; Süss, Ethos, p. 119 *et seq.*, on the bearing of " ethos " on the " ex-rdium."

[6] Ad Her. I. 9. 14; Cic. De Inv. I. 28, De Or. II. 80, 326 *et seq.*, Or. 22; Q. IV. 2. 31 *et seq.*, XII. 10. 59.

[7] Cic. Or. 210; Part. Or. 31–32, Top. 97 (reading " moratae cum dig-itate "); Q. IV. 2. 61 *et seq.*, IX. 4. 134; cf. Ar. Rhet. III. 16; Dionys. De Lys. 18, 25, on Lysias as a model in the " narratio."

peroration[1] an orator's chief aim[2] was to move his audience by a powerful emotional appeal, and for that the Grand style was considered the most effective weapon, as enabling him by its force, brilliance, attractiveness, and its impetuous march, to mould his hearers into sympathy with his own feelings.   The logical outcome of this aspect of Decorum was to assign the position of pre-eminence[3] to the orator who could wield each style in turn according to his purpose.

According to another aspect of the doctrine of Decorum it was prescribed[4] that an orator's style should be in harmony with the dignity of the occasion,[5] and the nature of the place in which his speech was delivered.   The various strands of the doctrine were in fact subtly interwoven, and regard for the circumstances of time and place in practice generally signified regard for the importance of the issues at stake, as well as for the audience to whom the orator was primarily making his appeal ;   for a speaker was expected[6] to take account of the character of the latter, if he wished to make his appeal effective, and avoid striking a false note.   In deliberative oratory much would depend on whether an orator was championing a cause before the august assembly of the Senate,[7] or before the popular assembly,[8] where a less finished style was needed, and where a speaker could employ cruder devices, and apply his colours with a less delicate touch.   In forensic cases, an orator will naturally

The occasion and the audience

---

[1] De Or. II. 311, Or. 127, 130–131, Part. Or. 15 ; Q. IX. 4. 128.

[2] The Roman orator in particular.

[3] *Vide infra*, pp. 221–222.

[4] De Or. II. 17, III. 210, Or. 71, 123 ; Q. IX. 3. 102 (in connection with the use of Figures), X. 3. 15, XI. 1. 7, 14, 46, XII. 10. 2, 70.

[5] Cf. Ar. Rhet. III. 7. 8 ; on καιρός *vide* Theon, Progym. Sp. II. 115 Süss, op. cit. p. 18 *et seq.*, on καιρός in the Rhetoric of Gorgias ; Dionys De C. V. c. 12, uses the word in the sense of good taste, or due measur (cf. Rhys Roberts, Glossary) ; De Lysia, 11, 13 ;   Hesiod, W. and D., 694 cf. Sheppard, The Oedipus Tyrannus, Introd. p. 60 *et seq.*, for some interes ing remarks on its use in the " Oedipus."

[6] De Or. II. 20 ; Q. III. 8. 35 *et seq.*, VIII. 3. 14, XI. 1. 45 ; cf. Ci Pro Sestio, 119, for a practical application of the doctrine.

[7] Cf. Fronto, II. 38, on M. Aurelius' use of the image of the " utriculus in a speech before the Senate.

[8] Cf. Ar. III. 12. 5, on δημηγορικὴ λέξις.

have to take into account the character of the judge.   It
makes a vast difference whether he is pleading a private case
before a single judge,[1] who is primarily concerned with its
legal aspect, and little likely[2] to be swayed by florid eloquence
and the artifices of rhetoric, or whether he is defending the
cause of a man on trial for a capital offence before a number
of judges, and a court that awaits the issue in eager suspense.
In such a case, and before such an audience, an orator may
unmask all his batteries, use every device known to rhetoric,
and, especially when he has dominated[3] his hearers, may
employ in safety glowing language that goes to the extreme
verge of daring, even though such language may seem
extravagant, when what Cicero calls the " animorum incen-
dia " have died down.   An orator who pleads a similar case
before one in supreme authority[4] like the Emperor, will
have to alter the tone and style of his speech to suit the
altered conditions, as Cicero did in his " Caesarian " speeches,
delivered before Julius Caesar " intra domesticos parietes."[5]

In many subtle ways the character of the audience reacted
on the orator's style, as Cicero saw[6] in the case of the
Asianist orators.   Both in his emotional

The need of adaptation

appeals, and in the nature of his arguments,
a speaker had to adapt his style to suit[7] it,
and take into account not merely the common instincts of

[1] De Or. III. 211, Or. 72, De opt. gen., 10.
[2] Aper evidently had a different opinion of the judges in his day ; cf.
Tac. Dial. 20 ; Q. IV. 1. 57.
[3] De Or. II. 205, Or. 27, 210 ; Q. IX. 4. 129 ; Ar. Rhet. III. 7. 11 ;
an audience thus transported is less critical.
[4] Q. V. 13. 6, in such circumstances recommends a deliberative rather
than a judicial style of oratory ; ib. XI. 3. 150.
[5] Cf. Pro Rege Deiotaro, c. 2 ; to explain the style of these speeches
there is no need to have recourse to the hypothesis that Cicero was influenced
by the theories of the Atticists ; we have to remember, moreover, that
Caesar was a soldier ; cf. Q. XI. 1. 32, on the simple style suited to a soldier ;
Fronto, II. 144 ; cf. Plut. Caes. c. 3, on Caesar's estimate of his own style.
[6] Or. 24 : " semper oratorum eloquentiae moderatrix fuit auditorum
prudentia " ; cf. Kellett, The Whirligig of Taste, p. 74 et seq., for an
interesting discussion of the reactions of the public on the author ; vide
infra, p. 196.
[7] De Or. II. 337 ; cf. ib. 186, for the need of studying the tastes and
prejudices of the judges ; Q. III. 7. 23 ; Ar. Rhet. II. 21. 15–16, III. 7. 6.

human nature, but also the particular tastes and prejudices[1] of those whom he was addressing. The orator who wished to reach the heart of his audience, had to study its psychology.[2] He had to observe men at the various stages[3] of their existence, and discover what were their salient characteristics as they reached or passed certain milestones on the road of life. He had, moreover, to take into consideration the occupations and rank of those who listened to him, and introduce subtle changes of tone according as he was addressing an audience of young or old, rich people or poor, soldiers or civilians, Greeks or Romans.

The question of character had other aspects that had a bearing upon the law of Decorum. An orator who undertook to plead a cause, had to have regard for

The factor of character

the character[4] both of his client and his opponent,[5] and temper his speech according to their rank or moral worth. It was still more important that the style and tone of his speech should be in harmony with his own character,[6] as different styles suit different persons. A phrase or sentiment suitable in one speaker, might be completely out of place as coming from the lips of another. From this point of view, an orator's style should be the reflection[7] of the man. A speaker had to consider his own dignity,[8] and his record in public life, in framing his speech, and insure that there was nothing in it that jarred upon his audience. Thus, as one of the surest means

---

[1] National tastes and prejudices would be an important factor ; cf. Sen. Ep. 40. 11 ; Q. III. 7. 24, V. 10. 24 ; Cicero exploited Roman prejudice against the Greek character in the " Pro Flacco," while in the Verrines, in deference to Roman prejudice, he affects ignorance of the works of the Greek artists ; *vide infra*, p. 151.

[2] Ar. Rhet. II. c. 2 *et seq.*

[3] Ar. Rhet. II. c. 12 *et seq. ;* cf. Cic. De Off. I. 122–123.

[4] De Or. II. 183, Or. 123 ; Q. XI. 1. 42, 57.

[5] Whether the opposing counsel, or the accused, if he was conducting a prosecution.

[6] De Or. III. 210, Or. 71 ; Q. III. 8. 35, IX. 3. 102, XI. 1. 4, 31, 37 ; Ar. Rhet. III. 7. 6 (with Cope's notes) ; Theon, Progym. Sp. II. 115.

[7] De Or. II. 184 : " ut quasi mores oratoris effingat oratio " ; Sen Controv. VII. 4 (19). 6 ; Q. XI. 1. 30 : " nec sine causa Graeci prodiderunt ut vivat quemque etiam dicere."

[8] De Or. III. 53, 211 ; Q. XI. 1. 29.

of winning the favour of his hearers, an orator was enjoined to give his speech an " ethical " cast,[1] that would reflect his sincerity, his integrity of purpose, his high sense of honour, and his love of virtue.

The principle of Decorum further prescribed that the style of a speech should be in keeping with the speaker's age.[2] Certain faults of style may be condoned in the young, but they merit less indulgence in those of maturer years, and may be intolerable in the old. Youth, exulting in its newly-found power of wielding words, loves brilliance[3] and exuberance, and in general affects a style glowing with gaudy colours, but lacking in discipline and reserve. Age, bringing the discrimination and restraint that are the fruit of a ripened judgment, begins[4] to realise that its earlier essays were wanting in the moderation essential to true art. A style marked by a certain austerity, and mellowed by the years, suits the character of older men.[5] Hence the Romans remarked the incongruity in the style of Hortensius,[6] who carried into his old age the florid exuberance of his youthful manner. Cicero declared[7] that his own style was growing grey with the years.

The factor of age

We have still to examine another aspect of Decorum that might be styled dramatic,[8] as it is seen in its finest manifestation in the apt delineation of character achieved by the poets. The dramatic poets in particular must make a study of human life in all its complexity, and must insure that they attri-

Dramatic decorum

[1] On the importance of ἦθος τοῦ λέγοντος, cf. Ar. Rhet. I. 2. 3, II. 1. 4, III. 16. 8 ; Cope, Introduction, p. 108 et seq. ; cf. Q. VI. 2. 13, 18 et seq., XI. 1. 14 ; Süss, op. cit., p. 116 et seq., 126 et seq.

[2] Pro Caelio, c. 3 ; Q. III. 8. 48 ; Ar. Rhet. III. 7. 6, where the factor of age seems to concern the speaker as well as the audience.

[3] De Or. II. 88, Or. 107 et seq. ; Q. II. 4. 4 et seq., XI. 1. 32, XII. 6. 3–4 ; cf. Ar. Rhet. II. 12. 14, on the tendency to excess in youth.

[4] De Or. II. 74, Br. 316, De Leg. I. 11 ; cf. Isocr. Panath. 1–3, Letter to Philip, 27.

[5] Cic. Cato Major, 28 ; Sen. Ep. 40. 2 ; cf. Plato, Laws, 670 D, on the musical rhythms suited to older men.

[6] *Vide infra*, p. 240.

[7] Br. 8.

[8] *Vide infra*, p. 481.

bute to the " dramatis personae " no action, word, or sentiment out of keeping with their character. The dramatist
who wishes to give a faithful picture of life, must have
sounded all the depths and shoals of human nature, and
must have probed the subtle differences[1] of character
that spring from such factors as age, sex, rank, occupation,
and nationality. The poets are held up as the great
exemplars[2] of Decorum in the sense I have explained,
though they sometimes failed[3] to observe it, owing perhaps
to their neglect of the dramatic situation, but more frequently through their not having realised their characters
in the first instance with anything approaching definiteness
of outline. Euripides,[4] with his love of rhetorical debate,
and his tendency to speculate on the problems of religion
and philosophy, often makes his " dramatis personae " the
mouthpiece of ideas that are out of harmony with their
characters. As thus studied, character tended, it is true,
to crystallise into conventional types,[5] but here, as elsewhere, the Ancients were bent on concentrating on what
was essential and permanent in human nature. In their
studies of the various stages of human life, they took little
account of the idiosyncrasies of individuals, but fixed their
attention rather on the characteristics which human beings
usually display in youth, in manhood, and in old age.

Dramatic Decorum had its place, too in oratory.[6] Its
most obvious application is seen in the case of those who
wrote speeches for others to deliver, and who aimed to make
the style conform to the character of the speaker. Lysias,[7]

[1] *Vide infra*, pp. 405, 424 *et seq.*
[2] Cic. De Off. I. 97 ; Q. X. 1. 27, *ib.* 70–71, on Menander ; Legrand,
op. cit., p. 257 ; Plut. Comp. of Aristophanes and Menander, I. 6, II. 12 (there
quoted) ; Evanthius, De Fab. III. 4 ; Donatus, Ad Andr. 447 (on Terence).
[3] Cf. Cic. Or. 70, 74 ; Don. Ad Eun. 507 ; sometimes, of course,
Decorum was deliberately violated for purposes of parody.
[4] Ar. Poet. 15. 5 ; cf. Troades, 884 *et seq.*, Iphig. in Tauris, 380 *et seq.*
[5] *Vide infra*, p. 426.
[6] And, of course, in other prose genres as well ; cf. Dionys. περὶ μιμ
II. 2 (Usener), p. 24, where Xenophon is censured for putting philosophic
discussions into the mouths of private individuals and barbarians ; cf. Cic
Ad Att. XIII. 16. 1.
[7] Dionys. De Lys. c. 8, for his skill in ἠθοποιΐα; *ib.* c. 9, 13, 19
Q. III. 8. 51.

remarkable in all things for the observance of Decorum,
Its place in
oratory was supreme in the art of framing speeches,
the style of which was in perfect harmony
with the character of those who were
to deliver them. But, apart from the profession of the
" logographer," the orator at times introduced character
sketches into his speeches, and regaled his audience with
transcripts from life, whether by way of the portrayal of
individuals,[1] or of types. In this sense he could impart an
" ethical " tone[2] to his speech that might serve him well in
the course of his argument. An orator who possessed a
talent for true and vivid portraiture,[3] and for those subtle
touches that evinced a profound acquaintance with human
life and human character, could do much to invest his
speech with a wonderful charm[4] and persuasiveness. The
introduction of the human element would serve to relieve
the strain of the argumentative passages, and lend to the
narrative portions[5] greater variety and animation. Hence
it is that Aristotle insists on the study of character as part
of a training in rhetoric, primarily, it is true, that the orator
who is acquainted with the psychology of his audience,
may be able to make his appeal more effective, but also
that, if he has to portray character, he may do so without
marring his portrait by incongruous and inappropriate
elements. Amongst the Greek orators Hyperides, as well
as Lysias, was noted for his power of happy characterisation,
but that gift was denied[6] to the greatest orator of them all.

---

[1] Ar. Rhet. III. 16. 9 ; note the safeguards A. thinks it necessary to suggest
in such circumstances.

[2] Cf. *Ib.* 8, on giving an ethical cast to the " narratio," though he there
dwells chiefly on the character of the speaker ; cf. Q. VI. 2. 8 *et seq.*, for
various aspects of " ethos ; " *ib.* 15, 19.

[3] For ἠθοποιΐα as a Figure, cf. De Or. III. 204 (" morum ac vitae
imitatio "), Or. 138 ; Q. IX. 2. 58 ; *ib.* VI. 2. 17, on scholastic exercises
in character drawing ; Rut. Lupus, I. 21 ; Aq. Rom. 4.

[4] The element of ἠθικόν in its various aspects was thus connected with
the orator's duty of giving pleasure (delectare), and in this way was brought
into relation with the Middle style ; cf. De Or. II. 182, 212–213, Or. 128 ;
Süss, op. cit., p. 204 *et seq. ; vide supra*, p. 73.

[5] Cic. Part. Or. 32 ; Volkmann, op. cit., p. 163.

[6] περὶ ὕψους, 34. 2–3.

Dramatic Decorum had to be observed also in the expression of emotion.[1] A speaker's words were supposed to reflect faithfully the emotions under which he was labouring. It was, of course, always regarded as a prime essential that these should not be merely counterfeited,[2] but genuinely felt by the orator who, if he were a man of delicate sensibility and ready sympathy, might easily be stirred to the depths of his soul.

Another department of oratory in which the principle of Decorum held sway, was the province of the " Laughable."

Decorum in laughter

The orator who aims at exciting laughter,[3] must take into account the character of his audience, of his subject, the circumstances of time and place, the character of his opponent, and finally his own personal character and dignity.

Lastly, the rhetorical theorists made subject to the rule of Decorum the orator's delivery,[4] his " sermo corporis,"[5]

Decorum in delivery

which, especially among Southern peoples, could exhibit an eloquence of its own. In this sphere, too, the principle of the Golden Mean[6] was operative, and forbade extravagance in the use of voice and gesture, and in fact, the whole carriage of the orator. It was prescribed[7] that his delivery should be in harmony with his theme and the general style of his speech, and that, within its limitations, it should, by means of the

---

[1] Sen. Ep. 114. 20 : " iracundi hominis iracunda oratio " ; cf. Hor. A.P. 104 *et seq.*; Ar. Rhet. III. 7. 1 *et seq.*, 16. 10, Poet. c. 17. 1445 a ; Dionys. De Lys. 19.

[2] De Or. II. 189 *et seq.*, Or. 132 ; Q. VI. 2. 26 *et seq.* ; on this question in relation to the poets, cf. Hor. A.P. 102 ; περὶ ὕψους, 9. 11 ; cf. Sen. De Ira, II. 17, on the possibility of counterfeiting emotion so successfully as to produce it in others ; *vide infra*, p. 482.

[3] *Vide infra*, p. 363 ; cf. Sen. Controv. IX. 4 (27). 17 ; Tac. Dial. 22. 10, on " foeda et insulsa scurrilitas."

[4] De Or. I. 132, Or. 74 ; cf. De Off. I. 126, where the question of gesture is touched on from a more general point of view ; Q. X. 1. 17, XI. 3. 30 *et seq.*, 61.

[5] De Or. III. 222, Or. 55 : " est enim actio quasi quaedam eloquentia corporis " ; Q. XI. 3. 65 *et seq.*

[6] Cic. Or. 60 ; Q. VI. 3. 26, XI. 3. 181 ; *ib.* 88 *et seq.*, 117.

[7] Or. 56, *ib.* 86, on " actio " in the Plain style ; Q. XI. 3. 61, 67 ; cf. IX. 4. 138–139, on rhythm in relation to delivery.

delicate modulations of the voice and the accompanying gestures, be expressive of the speaker's thoughts and emotions.[1] In fact, the law of Decorum governed delivery as strictly, and with the same minuteness of detail,[2] as it governed style. Delivery should conform[3] not merely to the general character of the case as a whole, but to the character of its several parts. Just as style differed in the exordium, statement of facts, and peroration, so was delivery subject to similar variations. To render the sway of Decorum complete even in this province, the theorists demanded that the orator should take into account his own character and that of his audience, as well as his aim and duty in pleading.

These latter aspects of Decorum have, it is true, only an indirect bearing upon style, but I thought it not wholly irrelevant to deal with them, if only as an illustration of how formalism can run riot. We must remember also that Decorum was perhaps the dominant[4] note in the Classical theory of style, and in fact in the Classical theory of Art in general. It was a principle that later held a foremost place in Neo-Classical theory,[5] and there can be little doubt that such formalism as we have witnessed, led to some at least of the extravagances[6] associated with the concept of Decorum among those who in after centuries posed as the heirs of the Classical tradition.

There are two other requisites for style met with in Classical theory, sincerity and variety. Both of these are in a measure bound up with the law of Decorum,
Other requisites for style the observance of which could insure variety, and impart also the quality of sincerity.[7] The style that respected propriety in its manifold aspect,

---

[1] De Or. III. 215 *et seq.*   [2] Q. XI. 3, will supply abundant illustrations.

[3] Q. XI. 3. 92 *et seq.*, 150 *et seq.*, 161 *et seq.*, 170, on delivery in the peroration.

[4] Saintsbury, op. cit., Vol. I. p. 46 ; Menéndez Y. Pelayo, Historia de las Ideas Estéticas, Vol. I. p. 49 ; Bénard, L'Esthétique d'Aristote, pp. 262–265.

[5] Cf. Laokoon, ed. Howard, Introd. p. 86 *et seq. ;* Robertson, Essays towards a Critical Method, p. 18.

[6] Babbitt, Rousseau, p. 124 *et seq.*, 144–145.

[7] The " persuasiveness " of style would in part depend on this ; on the element of τὸ πιθανόν, cf. Ar. Rhet. III. 7. 4, 10, *ib.* 12. 6 ; Cic. Part. Or. 19 ; Q. VIII. 3. 42.

would according to ancient theory inevitably carry conviction, and create the impression of the author's sincerity, whereas one that was guilty of excess, and exhibited the faults classed under the head of " frigidity," would quickly raise the suspicion that a writer was less concerned to treat his subject adequately than to produce telling effects. Where the emotions were concerned,[1] personal sincerity, as we saw, was demanded of the orator as the first essential, but the law of Decorum insisted also that in the expression of emotion the language employed should be proportioned to the emotion experienced. A passion that was hollow[2] and unreal, that expended itself without a commensurate object, was condemned, but genuine and inspired emotion was permitted almost every boldness[3] of speech, because it carries with it the ring of sincerity, and in its sublimity[4] can disregard meticulous and hampering rules.

The note of sincerity[5], though allied with the virtue of Decorum, might be considered apart in certain of its aspects.

The note of sincerity   It was generally felt that a style, the art of which became obtrusive, betokened a lack of sincerity. Genuine passion, as Demetrius[6] says, needs no art. Too great solicitude for the niceties of style indicates[7] rather the dilettante who trifles with his subject, and has more regard for his manner than his matter, than one who is in earnest and swayed by deep emotion. A style that is pretentious[8] and decked out with all the trappings of rhetoric, will create a similar impression. Any suggestion of artificiality was felt to be fatal especially to the forensic[9] orator, who thereby impairs his prestige, and

---

[1] Cf. Cic. De Div. I. 80.

[2] *Vide supra*, p. 118.

[3] *Vide supra*, p. 123 ; cf. περὶ ὕψους, 20. 2, 32. 1, 38. 5.

[4] *Ib.* c. 8, on vehement and inspired passion as a source of the Sublime.

[5] We might call it in this connection objective sincerity.

[6] 27.

[7] *Ib.* 300; cf. *ib.* 53 ; μικροπρεπὲς γὰρ ἡ ἀκριβεία ; Dionys. De Lys. 14 ; Sen. Ep. 75. 6, 115. 1–2 ; Q. IX. 4. 112–113.

[8] περὶ ὕψους, 23. 4 ; cf. Ar. Rhet. III. 3. 4 (on excessive ornament) : ἅπαντα γὰρ ταῦτα ἀπίθανα ; Dionys. De Isocr. 14.

[9] Cic. De Or. III. 100, Pro Caecina, 65 ; Q. IV. 2. 126, IX. 4. 143 ; *vide supra*, p. 104.

awakens rather the hostility than the sympathy of judge and audience. One who is supposed to be labouring under a deep sense of wrong, will present an absurd spectacle, if he endeavours to speak in a style that rigidly[1] adheres to all the technical rules of rhetoric. The appearance of natural-ness[2] and spontaneity is of the first importance to the orator. Hence, there were some[3] who, in their reaction against an over-studied style, would condemn all effort at elaboration, and hold up as the exemplars of eloquence the earliest orators who spoke according to the dictates of nature.

The ancient theorists generally, as we have seen, held that in epideictic[4] oratory a speaker might employ all the embellishments of rhetoric with impunity, as his aim was to produce pleasure rather than conviction in his audience. No Figure[5] was held to be too bold, no ornament too gaudy for the oratory of display. But the orator who pleaded a case in the law courts, had above all to avoid the appearance of over-niceness, or of straining after effects of style.

The epideic-tic and fo-rensic styles

Artificiality might spring from many sources, one of them being a too great fastidiousness in the choice of words. It is out of place, says Quintilian,[6] to be over-scrupulous about words, when the highest interests are at stake. Any manifestation of preciosity in a speaker, or indication[7] that he is in pursuit of the rare word, or is indulging[8] in language that is highly coloured and inflated, will diminish his reputation for sincerity. Composition, too, could open up the way to artificiality, parti-cularly in the employment of rhythm. Rhythmical effects should seem to come spontaneously,[9] and the writer or

Artificiality

---

[1] Q. XI. 1. 53–54.   [2] Ar. Rhet. III. 2. 4.

[3] *Vide infra*, p. 326; cf. Jensen, op. cit., p. 157; Raleigh, op. cit., p. 104, for some interesting remarks that have a bearing here; *vide supra*, p. 96.

[4] Dionys. De C. V. c. 23, περὶ μιμ. V; *vide supra*, pp. 71, 104.

[5] Cf. Ad Her. IV. 22. 32 (on the Gorgianic Figures): " ejusmodi autem studia ad delectationem quam ad veritatem videntur adcommoda-tiora."

[6] VIII. 3. 13; cf. Dionys. De Lys. 14.

[7] Q. XI. 1. 49 *et seq.*, 53.

[8] Demetr. 221.   [9] Q. IX. 4. 147.

speaker who sought them, should endeavour to conceal[1] his
art. The continuous use of elaborate periods was another
feature that produced an unfavourable[2] impression. Such a
feature might suit the character of epideictic oratory, but in
the other oratorical genres it would impress the hearers as
affected and unreal, and quickly produce satiety. In this
connection, Cicero in one luminous sentence[3] sums up the
case that might be urged against any writer who allows his
style to be marred by the excessive use of a particular device,
or by mannerisms that are soon detected : " si enim semper
utare,[4] cum satietatem adfert tum quale sit etiam ab im-
peritis agnoscitur ; detrahit praeterea actionis dolorem,
aufert humanum sensum auditoris, tollit funditus veritatem
et fidem."

There was, however, no element of style that lent itself
so easily to the suspicion of artificiality as the Figures, and
no ornament that called so much for restraint. Figures are
most effective[5] when they seem to be used unwillingly, or
at any rate inspired by the occasion, and infused by the
spirit of some over-powering emotion. They exercise their
greatest charm, when the fact that they are Figures escapes
detection, for their studied use creates the impression of
a stratagem.[6] Abnormal Figures may possess the stimulus
of novelty, but they quickly pall upon an audience. The
Auctor ad Herennium in a passage[7] that shows a fine
critical acumen, emphasises the need of the strictest economy
in the use of the Gorgianic Figures (" cum in veritate
dicimus "), if they are to be a real ornament of style, and
not to lead to puerile[8] display. Figures so obtrusive and so
full of allurement would, if multiplied, be unsuited especi-

---

[1] *Vide supra*, p. 104.

[2] Demetr. 15 ; speakers who accumulate periods, become as giddy-
headed as drunken men.

[3] Or. 209 ; cf. *ib.* 215 (on rhythm) ; Aq. Rom. 19 ; Q. IX. 4.
42–43.

[4] i.e. the periodic style.

[5] *Vide supra*, p. 110 ; cf. περὶ ὕψους, 17. 1, 18. 2, 38. 3.

[6] Cf. Cic. Or. 170 (on rhythm).

[7] IV. 23. 32 ; cf. Cic. Or. 38 : " quae in veritate causarum et rarius
multo facimus et certe occultius."

[8] *Vide supra*, p. 110.

ally to the style[1] of forensic oratory. "When terror,[2] hatred, and pity are the weapons called for in the fray, who will endure the orator who expresses his anger, his sorrow, or his entreaties in neat antitheses, balanced cadences, and exact correspondences ? " Vehement and over-powering[3] passion, as we saw, is sufficient to condone almost every audacity of speech, but a writer or speaker is not always touched by the divine fire, and in general has to guard against seeming to strive after studied effects. The many ornaments that help to raise the tone of prose, should seem to be part of the warp and woof of a writer's thought, and never flaunt themselves in wanton fashion.

The Ancients realised[4] that in style as elsewhere art wins its greatest triumphs, when it is concealed, and produces the effect of nature. Hence the Plain[5] style

Ars est celare artem proved so attractive to many, because it appears to be unstudied and careless of its effects, and carries with it an air of spontaneous ease and simplicity. Those who were most successful in this style, contrived to conceal their art so effectively that many considered[6] the Plain style of oratory easy of imitation, just as many believed they could vie with the writers of Satire and Comedy, because of their apparent lack of elaboration. Lysias was considered the greatest master of the Plain style, as by his skill in composition he achieved[7]

[1] And to other styles with a serious purpose in view ; Cic. Or. 84, rules them out of the Plain style : " ne elaborata concinnitas et quoddam aucupium delectationis manifesto deprehensum appareat " ; Demetr. 26 *et seq.* : οὔτε γὰρ δεινῶς λέγοντι ἐπιτήδεια ; Dionys. De Lys. 3.

[2] Q. IX. 3. 102 (Butler's translation) ; cf. *ib.* XI. 1. 49–53.

[3] Cf. Raleigh, op. cit., p. 98 (dealing, however, with the use of Figures in poetry) : " imagination working at white heat, can fairly subdue the matter of the poem to them, or fuse them with others of the like temper, striking unity out of the composite mass."

[4] Cf. Cic. Or. 38, 150 ; Q. IV. 1. 56–57, *ib.* 2. 127 (on the orators of his day): " perire artem putamus nisi appareat; " *ib.* XII. 9. 5–6 ; Sen. Controv. X. pr. 14 : " partem esse eloquentiae putabat (i.e., Augustus) eloquentiam abscondere " ; Ar. Rhet. III. 7. 10 ; Dionys. De Isaeo, 16 ; περὶ ὕψους, 22. 1.

[5] Cf. Cic. Or. 76 *et seq. ;* Sen. Controv. I. pr. 21, on " dissimulata subtilitas " ; Sen. Ep. 100. 4–5 ; Q. VIII. 3. 14.

[6] Cic. Or. 76 ; *vide infra,* p. 375.

[7] Dionys. De Lys. 4 ; cf. Q. IX. 4. 17.

with the commonest words the effects of charm, elegance, and even grandeur at times, without recourse to the elaborate Figures and the poetical ornament beloved by many of his contemporaries. His style was the fruit of the most perfect artistry, though it seemed to be natural and unstudied.[1] Aristotle[2] had already noted how a writer may conceal his art by selecting his words from the speech of every-day life, as was proved by the signal success of Euripides among the dramatists, but in such a case it is the author's skill in composition that helps to create a thing of beauty out of the commonest materials. Others adopted different contrivances to conceal their art, either assuming an appearance of negligence,[3] or deliberately aiming at clumsy and unpleasing effects, such as the admission of hiatus, the introduction of harsh rhythms, and a seeming disregard for the demands of euphony. Such devices were desirable especially in a style[4] that was in danger of being too florid, elaborate, and over-rhythmical, or in a style of cloying sweetness, or in one that was enervated by excessive smoothness and polish.

In all this we see the value of the principle of variety[5] that serves to impart the necessary contrast, and relieve style of a sameness that would quickly become insipid to readers or to hearers. The ancient theorists give constant warnings[6] of the satiety that springs from the unvarying use of one parti-

The law of variety

---

[1] Dionys. op. cit., 8 : δοκεῖ μὲν γὰρ ἀποίητός τις εἶναι καὶ ἀτεχνίτευτος ὁ τῆς ἁρμονίας αὐτοῦ χαρακτήρ; cf. De Isaeo, c. 16, 18, De Dem. c. 2, 13, περὶ μιμ. V, VIII (Usener, pp. 27, 31–33).

[2] Rhet. III. 2. 5.

[3] Cic. Or. 77–78 : " quaedam etiam negligentia est diligens;" *ib.* 20 : " impoliti et consulto rudium similes "; cf. Q. IX. 4. 31 ; Demetr. 53 ; cf. Sen. Ep. 114, 15, where such effects become a form of affectation.

[4] Cf. Cic. De Or. III. 100 ; Pliny, Ep. I. 16. 5 ; Q. IX. 4. 144, *ib.* XI. 2. 47 (on the use of delivery to gain such effects) ; Gellius, XII. 2. 9, where the Younger Seneca charges Cicero with occasional imitations of Ennius in his prose " ad effugiendam infamiam nimis lascivae orationis et nitidae "; cf. Dionys. De C. V. c. 19.

[5] Cf. Cic. De Or. II. 177 : " tractatio autem varia esse debet, ne aut cognoscat artem qui audiat, aut defatigetur similitudinis satietate "; cf Pliny, Ep. III. 13. 4, on the law of contrast.

[6] Ad Her. IV. 23. 32, 31. 42 ; De Or. III. 97–103 (a passage of particular importance) ; Q. V. 14. 30, VIII. 3. 52 ; Aq. Rom. 19, 21.

cular style, or of certain stylistic devices. There are some who can employ only the Grand style, which, even, when it is appropriate, is likely to prove too dazzling in its splendour, and too fraught with emotion to be endured[1] for any lengthy period. These do not realise that variety[2] has a charm of its own, that, through the operation of the law of contrast, it can enhance the beauty of style, while at the same time it obviates the suspicion of artificiality and insincerity. The principle of Decorum, by its insistence on the adaptation of style to subject-matter and the other factors already considered, logically involved the need of variety. There is thus a certain interrelation between this principle and what we might call the laws of variety and sincerity.

It will have been noticed that the Roman theorists in particular busied themselves primarily with oratorical style. **The Greek theorists on style** Of the Greek theorists, Aristotle's main concern was with oratory, though he made a distinction between the λέξις γραφικὴ and ἀγωνιστική that might have been fruitful, if he had given us a more extended treatment of the point. As it is, he works out his theory of the first-named style largely by way of contrast with the style of actual pleading. Our knowledge of Theophrastus' treatise on Style is in reality very limited,[3] but with his insistence on the Peripatetic Mean, and his doctrine of the virtues of style, he was in a position to treat the problem apart from the oratorical genres. Demetrius was catholic enough in his tastes, and furnishes us with a great wealth of illustration both from poetry and prose, but yet in many vital questions he was inclined to be dominated by the exigencies of oratorical theory. Dionysius of Halicarnassus, in his studies of the ancient orators, naturally thought much in terms of the stereotyped styles of oratory, but, even when he goes on to deal with writers such as Herodotus, Thucydides, and Plato, his views were still largely coloured by the formalism of the rhetorical text-

[1] Cf. De Or. II. 183, 200, on the need of varying it.
[2] Ad Her. IV. 11. 16; De Or. III. 102; Pliny, Ep. V. 17. 2; Q. IX. 3. 4; Dionys. De C. V. 11, 19; περὶ ὕψους, 34. 2.
[3] Though Mayer, op. cit., can find traces of the treatise in the most unlikely places.

books, though at times he gets clear of its influence, and takes a wider view of the problem of style. Particularly in his treatise on " Literary Composition," he was handling a subject that could find its application in every sphere of literature, and range outside the narrow round of rhetorical teaching. The author of the treatise *On the Sublime* was dealing with a special aspect of style, which he considered to be a distinguishing mark of either the great poet or the great prose writer. His luminous vision was able to penetrate into the very essence and soul of style. Even when he wanders into the sphere of oratory, it is evident that he is chafing against the restraints of hide-bound theory, and seeking to rise to a consideration of larger issues.

The Roman writers keep as a rule to the straight path of the rhetorical tradition, and give us little that could be applied to style in general, though in point of fact the doctrine of the " Virtues," which Cicero applies so rigidly to the various kinds of oratory, was capable of a much wider application. Happily, I suppose, for their own reputations, they attempted no definition of Style, though Cicero gives us something approximating to one, when he says[1] : " omne quod de re dilucide dicitur mihi praeclare dici videtur." Quintilian[2] has a dictum that reminds us of Coleridge's definition of Poetry as " the best words in the best order "; " nam cum Latina, significantia, ornata, cum apte sunt collocata, quid amplius laboremus " ? Petronius[3] attempts a description of Style, excellent as far as it goes, but largely negative owing to its preoccupation with the faults of the schools of declamation.

Both Cicero and Quintilian have some valuable comments (welcome in view of the tendency to emphasise merely external ornament) on the intimate union that should exist between matter and form. Cicero likens[4] it to the union of soul and body, or conceives[5] the form as springing from the matter as child

Some Roman views

Some general considerations

---

[1] De Fin. III. 19.   [2] VIII. pr. 31.
[3] Satyr. 2 : " grandis et ut ita dicam pudica oratio non est maculosa nec turgida, sed naturali pulchritudine exsurgit."
[4] De Or. III. 24 ; cf. *ib.* 19.
[5] *Ib.* II. 146 ; cf. III. 125 ; Q. VIII. pr. 21.

from parent. He naturally deprecates[1] anything like a mere empty parade of high-sounding words that seem to have no relation[2] to a writer's thought. Here we have a condemnation of the attempt[3] at " fine " writing that is so justly censured by all who have regard for true style. À propos of this, we sometimes[4] meet with the consideration that a grand or imposing style is impossible when one has to enter on minute calculation, or exact analysis, or close argumentation. This consideration was in part at the bottom of the aversion displayed by many historians[5] to the giving of exact figures, or the reproduction of details of treaties and historical documents, though in such suppressions they were actuated also by a desire to maintain the uniformity of their style. In his own sphere, the orator felt that the wings of his rhetoric would quickly droop, if he had to expound and discuss numerous microscopic details. Cicero speaks[6] of the plain style that he employed in conducting his case " *Pro Caecina*," which turned wholly on the interpretation of a legal formula. The law of Decorum demanded the Plain style in such circumstances, but, even if he had so wished, the orator would have found it difficult to raise the tone of his speech in the midst of exact definition and analysis, unless he decided to digress from the issue before the court. " Ornatissimae sunt igitur orationes eae, quae latissime vagantur."[7] An orator who had to deal at length with particulars, felt himself cabined and confined ; hence his anxiety to divert his speech to more general[8] considerations, to employ

---

[1] De Or. I. 51, *ib.* 17 ; Q. VIII. pr. 18.

[2] Cf. Dionys. De Lys. 4 : οὐ τοῖς ὀνόμασι δουλεύει τὰ πράγματα, τοῖς δὲ πράγμασι ἀκολουθεῖ τὰ ὀνόματα ; cf. De Isocr. 12.

[3] " Un esprit médiocre croit écrire divinement, un bon esprit croit écrire raisonnablement " (La Bruyère) ; cf. Q. X. 3. 14–15 : " numquid melius dicere vis quam potes ? " cf. the fault of " écrire trop bien " (Anatole France).

[4] Cf. Or. 124–125 ; Pliny, Ep. VI. 33. 9 ; Q. IV. 5. 6 ; cf. V. 14. 30–31.

[5] Cf. Peter, Die gesch. Lit. II. p. 282 ; Pliny, Ep. IX. 16. ; cf.1 Jensen, op. cit., p. 157, on the difficulty of treating particulars in poetry.

[6] Or. 102.

[7] De Or. III. 120.

[8] *Vide infra*, p. 157, on the use of θέσις ; the orator, like the poet, in this way became more " philosophical."

commonplaces,[1] and thus open up the way to a grander and more impressive form of eloquence.

We might next turn to a brief consideration of some of the faults of style analysed for us by the Roman writers.

Defects of style Though in such analysis they are concerned mainly with oratorical style, they at times enunciate principles that can be applied in other spheres. The *Auctor ad Herennium* describes[2] for us the defective styles in oratory. As is clear from his analysis, these styles exhibit many defects which are akin[3] to virtues, and arise because through lack of judgment[4] the virtues of the legitimate styles are carried to excess. Cicero's analysis of the faults of the Asianists and Roman Atticists, as we shall see, suggests that their defects were due to the fact that they carried to extremes the respective qualities of the Grand and the Plain styles. The faults of the Declaimers, too, lay as a rule in their perversion of the Grand style, and were mostly faults of excess. Their defects could in part be traced to the themes chosen, which might seem to lack distinction unless arrayed in gaudy rhetoric, but in part they were due to their desire to appear striking and novel at all costs. The younger Seneca, in his diagnosis[5] of the literary maladies of his contemporaries, traces them to the moral decadence of the age which, having exhausted customary pleasures, became oppressed with a restless boredom manifesting itself in literature as well as in domestic life. Maecenas[6] was in many respects typical of the period, with his affected and effeminate style, and his quest after the unfamiliar and bizarre both in choice of words and in construction. The desire for novelty led some to affect a studied compression resulting in obscurity ; it led others to excessive archaism, others again to a hankering after new coinages, or splendid and poetical diction, in their efforts to avoid the

---

[1] Cic. De Inv. I. 106, De Or. III. 106 ; περὶ ὕψους, 11. 2, 12. 5.

[2] IV. 10. 15 *et seq.*

[3] Cf. Q. X. 2. 16, on " proxima virtutibus vitia " ; *vide infra*, p. 481.

[4] Cf. Ad Her. loc. cit. (on the defective counterpart of the Grand style) : " specie gravitatis falluntur " ; *vide supra*, p. 74.

[5] Ep. 114 ; *vide infra*, p. 334.

[6] *Vide infra*, p. 327.

commonplace. We find, indeed, that there are certain faults that run counter to each of the virtues of style ; while in the employment of the specific embellishments that come under the head of " ornatus," most defects are due to lack of variety, or to an excess[1] that could be obviated by a due regard for Decorum.

We find at times an attempt made to define styles outside the sphere of oratory. The Younger Seneca formulated a

Styles other than oratorical theory of the philosophical style as one of studied[2] brevity and plainness. The theory owes much to Stoic influence, but much also to the doctrine of Decorum ; for Seneca professed[3] it unbecoming in a philosopher who dealt with serious problems, and had a high moral aim, to trouble overmuch about the niceties of style. In face of the grave issues of life, and in a subject where truth[4] is paramount, solicitude about words[5] might well be regarded as mere trifling. Cicero in the *De Finibus*[6] puts forward a similar view of the philosophical style, and Quintilian[7] evidently regards anything in the nature of striking embellishment, such as rare words or rhythmical phrases, as at variance with the profession of the philosopher. It is evident that such views are strongly coloured by Stoic theory.[8] Philosophers, however, were not always so rigidly restricted, and both the Academy and the Peripatetic school had shown[9] that philosophy could deck itself out in splendid raiment, and speak in tones of grandeur and sublimity. Yet philosophical style, for all the glory

---

[1] This is also true of many of the faults which Quintilian embraces under the head of κακόζηλον, VIII. 3. 56–58.

[2] Ep. 40. 14 ; cf. Smiley, op. cit., p. 50 *et seq.*

[3] Ep. 100. 2, 4 ; cf. Ep. 52. 13, 59. 5, 75. 3 ; *vide infra*, p. 332.

[4] Ep. 40. 4 : " quae veritati operam dat oratio, incomposita debet esse et simplex."

[5] Ep. 100. 10.

[6] III. 19 : " istius modi autem res dicere ornate velle puerile est ; " cf. Or. 51 : " philosophia . . . ubi res spectatur, non verba penduntur."

[7] XI. 1. 33–34 ; cf., however, IX. 4. 19, on raising the tone of the Dialogue, when it treats of a philosophical subject.

[8] Cf. also Cic. Or. 46 ; *vide supra*, p. 70.

[9] Cic. De Or. III. 67 *et seq.*, Br. 120 *et seq.*, Or. 62 ; cf. De Fin. I. 15 : " ego a philosopho, si afferat eloquentiam, non asperner " ; Pliny, Ep. I. 10. 5 ; Hirzel, Der Dialog, I. p. 177 *et seq.*

conferred on it by Plato, or the rhetorical colouring given it by certain members[1] of the New Academy, was carefully marked off from that of the orator. For one thing, it was felt[2] that philosophy, as compared with oratory, dealt with abstruse subjects in a language too technical to make its appeal a popular one. Cicero[3] is fond, too, of contrasting the gentle, reserved, unimpassioned utterance of the philosopher with the vehemence and emotional power especially of the forensic orator. In one passage[4] at least, he makes it evident that he was influenced by the theory of the " sermo " in thus endeavouring to formulate a style suited to the needs of philosophy. It is clear that in his eyes the note of " lenitas "[5] was the dominant one in the philosophical style. It was evidently this, too, that influenced him to bring the Middle style into relation with the philosophical schools, and to suggest[6] that the orators who were successful in it drew their inspiration mostly from that source.

I will deal in another context[7] with some of the attempts made to define the style of historical writing. It is worthy of note that the Ancients, in endeavouring to formulate styles other than the oratorical, frequently had recourse to the standards prevailing in the sphere of rhetoric, either by way of comparison or contrast.

[1] Notably Carneades.

[2] Cf. Or. 64, De Fin. III. 4.

[3] Br. 121, Or. 62, 127 ; cf. Br. 31 ; Q. X. 1. 36.

[4] Or. 64 ; *vide supra*, p. 36.

[5] De Leg. I. 11 ; cf. De Off. I. 3, on the " quietum disputandi genus " of the philosophers.

[6] Or. 95 : " e philosophorum scholis tales fere evadunt " ; one of the characteristics of the Middle style was " loci communes sine contentione " ; on Demetrius of Phalerum, *vide infra*, p. 209.

[7] *Vide infra*, p. 512 *et seq.*

CHAPTER III

CICERO AS CRITIC

CICERO'S MULTIFARIOUS occupations would seem to have left him small opportunity for carrying out the function of the critic, yet his efforts at criticism are deserving of recognition, even though they run mostly on conventional lines. In fact Cicero, especially in his judgments on the Roman orators, will well serve to illustrate how stereotyped criticism could become. He, however, deserves praise for having studied the secrets of the art of oratory, and endeavoured to formulate its procedure, even though he was in this following closely in the wake of Greek rhetorical theory. He made a striking contribution to historical criticism, when in the *Brutus* he sought to describe the various stages in the development of oratory at Rome, which culminated in his own age and person, while his quarrel with the Atticists reveals a divergence of ideals that has some value for the history of Roman criticism.

He was naturally most at home when dealing with the art of which he was so perfect an exponent, but here and **Cicero as** there throughout his works we find judg-**critic of the** ments on poets and poetry that deserve at **poets** least a passing treatment. He proclaims his enthusiasm for literature, and for poetry[1] in particular, though it is the enthusiasm of the dilettante who finds in the works of the poets a relaxation from the strain of more serious pursuits. When defending Archias, he, in fact, apologises for such enthusiasm on the grounds of its utility for his profession, thus endeavouring to placate Roman[2] prejudice.

If one may judge by the frequency and aptness of his

[1] Cf. Pro Archia, 12 *et seq., ib.* 16 ; Pro Sestio, 123 ; cf. Hortensius, fr. 6, Usener, Dionysii Halicarnassensis, etc., p. 118.
[2] *Vide supra,* p. 124.

quotations,[1] Cicero had a very intimate knowledge of the

His many
quotations
from them

older poets of Rome. On their behalf he sounds[2] the national note in his complaint of those ultra-Hellenists who, either from excessive sloth, or an over-refined fastidiousness, refuse to read the Latin versions of Greek plays when they can have access to the originals. Some of his quotations must have been hackneyed, as the "oderint dum metuant"[3] of Accius, or the "hinc illae lacrimae"[4] of Terence, as well as several from the *Annales* of Ennius, but many of them must have been unfamiliar to the ordinary public, and the fruit of Cicero's own untiring study of the older Roman poets. These quotations are interspersed throughout almost all his works,[5] and serve to drive home some lesson in Ethics, or to illustrate a point in Rhetorical theory, while, following the example of the leading actors of his day, he was able to adapt[6] lines from the drama to questions of contemporary politics.

The dramatic poets, indeed, seem to have made a very special appeal to him. The serious and lofty tone of

The appeal of
the Drama

Tragedy[7] would be in harmony with his own temperament. We owe to him the definition of Comedy preserved by Donatus. The definition is not original, but it shows that Comedy had an attraction for him as a transcript of life,[8] though he may

---

[1] Cf. Q. I. 8. 11 ; Zillinger, Cicero und die alt-römischen Dichter, p. 89 *et seq.*, has tabulated Cicero's quotations in convenient form ; *ib.* p. 68 *et seq.*, for some interesting remarks on Cicero's method of quotation ; *vide infra*, p. 284.

[2] De Fin. I. 2. 5 ; cf. Tusc. Disp. II. 26 : "studiose equidem utor nostris poetis."

[3] Pro Sestio, 102, De Off. I. 97, Phil. I. 34.

[4] Pro Caelio, 61 ; cf. De Off. I. 30, De Leg. I. 33, for another favourite quotation from Terence.

[5] Zillinger, op. cit., p. 58, remarks that such quotations are especially frequent in the years when Cicero was composing his works on Rhetoric and Philosophy.

[6] Pro Sestio, 118 *et seq.*, Phil. I. 36, Ad Att. XVI. 2. 3.

[7] Cf. Ad Fam. XVI. 8. 2 (on Euripides) : " singulos ejus versus singula testimonia puto."

[8] Cf. Pro Roscio Am. 46–47, Tusc. Disp. IV. 45, Cato Major, 65, Phil. II. 15 ; *vide infra*, p. 374.

deny[1] the title of poet to the Comic dramatist. It was probably their qualities of realism no less than their racy wit, that also made him so keen a student of the *Satires* of Lucilius, to whom he pays[2] generous homage.

His translations[3] from Homer and the Greek Tragedians show that he had studied these also to some purpose, though **Cicero's knowledge of the Greek poets** his versions[4] rarely attain to anything approaching the precision and delicacy of the originals. He notes[5] the different treatment of the character of Ulysses in Homer, and in the Tragedians.

From all this it is clear that he had a knowledge of Greek poetry, and was especially well versed in the early Roman **The formal side of poetry** poets, but one is struck by a certain instability in his judgments in these matters. To exalt the poet in the person of Archias, he recognizes[6] that inspiration is needed for the true poet, though he enunciates the doctrine of poetic frenzy with great caution. Elsewhere, however, he is inclined to insist on the art of the poet and the formal side of poetry. From this standpoint he proclaims[7] that prose is more difficult than poetry, because the latter follows a definite metrical scheme, while the prose-writer has no fixed pattern to guide him. He recognizes[8] in a general way the difference between the poet and the orator, and realizes[9] something of the essential nature of poetry in the grand impassioned sweep which characterised the prose of Plato and Democritus, but with this concession he proceeds to dwell on the formal affinities[10] between the orator and the poet. In most of his criticisms[11] of the Latin poets he concentrates on defects of form.

[1] Or. 67.   [2] *Vide supra*, p. 55.
[3] De Off. III. 82, De Fin. V. 49, Tusc. Disp. II. 20 *et seq.*, III. 29, 71 ; cf. Farrington, Primum Graius Homo, p. 41 *et seq.*
[4] It is, however, clear from his criticism of Atilius' version of the Electra of Sophocles (De Fin. I. 5) that Cicero had ideas of his own on translation.
[5] De Off. III. 97.
[6] Pro Archia, 18 ; however, *vide infra*, p. 474.
[7] Or. 198 ; *vide supra*, p. 101.
[8] Or. 66 *et seq.*
[9] Though he is merely quoting the opinion of other critics.
[10] *Vide infra*, p. 443.
[11] Ad Att. VII. 3. 10, Br. 258, Tusc. Disp. III. 20 ; *vide supra*, p. 50.

Pacuvius, Caecilius, Accius, are all censured for faults of style, and mostly from the standpoint of the purist.

Terence is singled out for special praise because of his choice and elegant diction, though he evidently attracted[1] Cicero also by his general charm, and by the restful tone of his comedies. It is interesting to see the latter adopting the new standard of " urbanitas " in his disparaging reference[2] to the poets of Corduba. Arguing as he does in the *De Oratore*, that the orator who uses all the resources of rhetoric will treat a subject more attractively than the expert, he goes[3] on to describe how the poets Aratus and Nicander, each in his own subject, excelled in the brilliancy of their presentation. Again, it is the rhetorician in Cicero that grows[4] enthusiastic over Archias' power as an " improvisatore," and his faculty of dealing frequently with the same subject in different words. Cicero's own poetry was greeted with derision[5] both by his contemporaries[6] and by succeeding ages, but yet it had certain merits on the formal side. In his translations particularly, he showed himself a clever versifier, and rendered no little service to Latin poetry by his advance towards smoothness and regularity in the technique of his verse.

It is all the more remarkable that, being thus engrossed in form, he failed to appreciate what was being done for
Latin poetry by the younger[7] school of
The " poetae novi " Roman poets, and has no word of praise for Catullus, the greatest of the Neoterics. The tradition of Ennius was still too strong for him, while there were other[8] considerations also that would have helped to

---

[1] Note the many quotations from him in one of Cicero's earliest works, the De Inventione ; cf. Suet. Life of Terence, c. 5 ; *vide supra*, p. 24.

[2] Pro Archia, 26.

[3] De Or. I. 69 ; the " poetica facultas " of Nicander evidently refers merely to form ; cf. De Rep. I. 22.

[4] Pro Archia, 18 ; *vide infra*, p. 440.

[5] De Off. I. 77, In Pis. c. 29–30, Phil. II. 20 ; Tac. Dial. c. 21 ; Q. XI. 1. 24 ; Juv. X. 122 ; Mart. II. 89. 3.

[6] Caesar, however, naturally passed a favourable judgment on Cicero's verses in praise of him ; cf. Ad Q. Fr. II. 15a. 2.

[7] The " cantores Euphorionis," as he contemptuously calls them, Tusc. Disp. III. 45.

[8] *Vide infra*, p. 284.

render him hostile to the aspirations of the " new poets."
His failure to appreciate true poetic greatness is nowhere
more apparent than in his perfunctory criticism of Lucretius,
wherein[1] he merely re-echoes the words of his brother,
though the criticism is interesting as being one of the first
that we know of in Latin literature, in which the contrast
of " ars " and " ingenium " is applied to poetry.

In several of his judgments on poetry Cicero adopts a
strictly ethical standard, and appraises the poet by his
capacity as teacher, thus applying a criterion
that was common amongst both the Greeks
and the Romans. Torquatus[2] refuses to
spend his time in perusing poets who teach nothing solid
or useful, but afford only childish amusement. The poets[3]
make men tend towards a cloistered and secluded life, and
lead them into effeminacy. Plato was right in expelling
them from his Ideal Commonwealth. Cicero blames[4] the
poets, especially the Comic poets, for their exaltation of
passion in their love-scenes, though the tragedians and lyric
poets are equally offenders in this respect. He has some
severe strictures[5] on the licentious poetry of Philodemus,
and in general lyric poetry made little appeal to one of his
serious temperament. Though he praises[6] his brother's
translation of Sophocles' Satyric play, the *Banqueters*, yet
there were evidently elements of obscenity in the original
of which he disapproved. For the same reason the coarse
and often obscene humour of the mime[7] was little to his
taste. He was attracted, on the other hand, towards the
didactic poets of Alexandria, as is evidenced by his trans-

The ethical
standpoint

---

[1] Ad Q. Fr. II. 9 (11). 3 ; *vide infra*, p. 474.
[2] De Fin. I. 72 ; cf. Ad Att. II. 22. 7, on Alexander of Ephesus " non
boni poetae, sed tamen non inutilis."
[3] Tusc. Disp. II. 27 : " nervos omnis virtutis elidunt " ; *ib*. III. 3, De
Nat. Deor. III. 91 ; cf. Tusc. Disp. II. 49, where Pacuvius is exalted above
Sophocles from the ethical standpoint.
[4] Tusc. Disp. IV. 68–71 : " de comoedia loquor, quae, si haec flagitia non
probaremus, nulla esset omnino "; cf. S. August. De Civ. Dei, II. 9, for a
similar sentiment from Cicero's " De Republica."
[5] In Pis. 70 ; *vide infra*, p. 160.
[6] Ad Q. Fr. II. 15. 3.
[7] De Or. II. 239, 242, Or. 88.

lations of Aratus.[1] The learning of such poets, as well as their potentialities for instruction, probably formed the basis of their appeal to him. It was, seemingly, similar considerations that evoked his reference[2] to what he styles the brilliant poem of Empedocles, though Aristotle[3] would deny the title of poet to that philosopher.

That he was not devoid of appreciation for the drama, and for dramatic art, is made clear by his letter[4] to Marius on the plays represented when Pompey's theatre was being dedicated. The great actor Aesopus, whose retirement from the stage was overdue, failed piteously in his part. Cicero's humanitarian instincts revolted at many aspects of the games then given, while his aesthetic feelings were outraged by the over-elaborate pageantry that marked the revival of the *Equus Trojanus* of Naevius and Accius' *Clytemnestra*. It looks as if he had here in mind the submerging[5] of the purely dramatic interest of the plays by spectacular effects. Yet, in his *De Republica*,[6] following closely in Plato's footsteps, and adopting a similar ethical standard, he passed some severe censures on the poets, and seems to have condemned the dramatic poets in particular, as well as the whole art of the theatre.

The art of the Drama

As one would expect, he is often inclined to judge poets from their utility for the training of the orator. Seneca has preserved[7] for us a dictum of his, in which he declared that, even if his span of life were doubled, he still would not have time to read the lyric poets. It is clear[8] that he had at least a passing acquaintance with them, but probably lyric poetry, as being

The poets and the training of the orator

---

[1] Cf. De Or. I. 69, De Rep. I. 22, *ib.* 56, De Nat. Deor. II. 104 *et seq.*, Acad. Pr. 66, De Div. I. 13 *et seq.*, Ad Att. II. 1. 11.

[2] De Or. I. 217.

[3] Poet. c. I.

[4] Ad Fam. VII. 1.

[5] *Vide infra*, p. 385.

[6] Cf. S. August. De Civ. Dei, II. c. 13–14.

[7] Ep. 49. 5; Usener, op. cit. p. 120, is probably right in ascribing this dictum to the " Hortensius "; on this dialogue, cf. Reid, The Academica of Cicero, Introd. p. 39 *et seq.*

[8] Cf. Tusc. Disp. I. 101, *ib.* IV. 71, Ad Att. IX. 13. 1, Or. 183.

too subjective and erotic[1] in character, would be regarded by him as affording[2] no assistance towards perfecting himself in his profession. He shows[3] especial interest in the dramatic effect of certain passages from the older dramatists. He had the advantage of seeing two of the greatest actors[4] that Rome had produced, Roscius and Aesopus, and is said[5] to have been taught elocution by Roscius himself. He tells us of the effect produced when some tragic passage full of dramatic import was delivered in a crowded theatre, as when one heard the moving verses from the *Andromache Aechmalotis*,[6] which he is so fond of quoting. Here evidently was something that made a direct appeal to the orator who wished to master the art of delivery,[7] and become a Roscius in his own domain. Cicero in his young days[8] found paraphrasing from the poets a useful exercise, while he realised[9] that poetry can contribute to that wide culture which he regarded as essential for the perfect orator. Thus, on the utilitarian side, it had its attractions for him.

I have already referred to the vacillation that marks Cicero's judgments, where poets and poetry are concerned.

Cicero's vacillating judgments   For instance, he sharply criticises from the stylistic point of view the poets Caecilius and Pacuvius, but again, though with some hesitation, he awards the palm[10] to Pacuvius for Tragedy, and to Caecilius for Comedy. He wavers on the relation of the old Roman poets to their Greek originals, representing them in one passage[11] as translating word for word from the Greek

[1] Seneca's " illi ex professo lasciviunt," in the context quoted above, may be an echo of Cicero.

[2] Simonides of Ceos had an interest for him owing to the " art of memory " that he had invented ; cf. De Or. II. 351 *et seq.*, De Fin. II. 104.

[3] Cf. De Fin. V. 63, on the Dulorestes of Pacuvius ; cf. Laelius, 24, Acad. Pr. 88, Tusc. Disp. I. 106, Pro Sestio, 120 *et seq.*

[4] Cf. De Div. I. 79–80, Pro Archia, 17, De Off. I. 114.

[5] Plut. Cic. 5.

[6] De Or. III. 102, 183, 217, Tusc. Disp. I. 85, III. 44.

[7] De Or. I. 127 ; the orator must have " vox tragoedorum "; cf. *ib*. III. 213 *et seq.*, Or. 55 *et seq.*

[8] De Or. I. 154.

[9] *Ib*. 158.

[10] De opt. gen. I. 2 ; cf. Tusc. Disp. II. 49, De Or. I. 246.

[11] De Fin. I. 4.

and in another[1] as reproducing not the words but the sense of the original. He pays a tribute[2] to the wider appeal that Greek poetry makes as compared with Latin, while he condemns the ill-placed enthusiasm of those Hellenists who neglect the national literature. His judgments[3] on Lucilius show a similar inconsistency.

Such vacillation is in part to be explained by the different standards of judgment which Cicero adopted, and is in part due to the fact that, even in this domain, he **Reasons for his** retained the temperament of the advocate **vacillation** who will sacrifice consistency to make a telling point. Again, for the sake of dramatic decorum,[4] he may attribute views at variance with each other to the characters of his Dialogues. Moreover, we must remember that he was not always independent in his criticisms. His judgment[5] on Atilius as a " ferreus scriptor " goes back to Porcius Licinus, while his characterisation of him as " poeta durissimus " is probably an echo from the same source. When, with a certain hesitation, he assigns the palm in Comedy to Caecilius, in spite of his own manifest enthusiasm for Terence, he is probably dependent[6] on the judgment of Volcacius Sedigitus. That he was influenced by the literary studies of Varro seems clear from the fine tribute he pays[7] to his work on the Roman poets. Though Cicero has several reminiscences of Plautus, he shows no special predilection for him, and that odd judgment[8] of his which took Plautus as a type of the refined and liberal jest, may well be derived from Aelius Stilo, or his pupil Varro, both of whom were enthusiastic[9] students of the poet. Apart from his own

[1] Acad. Post. 10 ; cf. De opt. gen. 14, De Fin. III. 15, where Cicero touches on the question of free translation.

[2] Pro Archia, 23.

[3] He calls Lucilius " homo doctus et perurbanus," while in De Fin. I. 7, he attributes to him " doctrina mediocris."

[4] Cf. Q. II. 17. 6.

[5] De Fin. I. 5 ; *vide supra*, p. 64.

[6] *Vide* Leo, Gesch. der röm. Lit., p. 225 ; Zillinger, op. cit., p. 38 ; *vide supra*, p. 66.

[7] Acad. Post. 9.

[8] De Off. I. 104.

[9] *Vide infra*, pp. 295–296 ; for Servius, the brother of Paetus, and another ardent worker on Plautus, cf. Ad Fam. IX. 16. 4.

bias towards historical studies, it is evident that the interest[1] which he evinces in the chronology of the early Roman poets, may be traced directly to the labours of Varro. It is difficult to decide from what source he derives his judgment on the styles of Ennius and Pacuvius in the *Orator*,[2] though his reference to the " ornati elaboratique versus " of the latter may be an echo of Lucilius' criticism of the high-flown diction of that poet. Rarely do we get from himself anything that might be regarded as aesthetic[3] criticism, or as showing insight into the essential nature of poetry. For the most part, he remained insensible to the real secret of the poet's charm.

We turn now from Cicero as critic of the poets to Cicero the critic of oratory. Here he was in the domain where he won his greatest glory. Whatever his failure

The domain of oratory

as a poet, whatever his instability in the sphere of politics may have been, even his bitterest enemies were ready to pay homage[4] to the over-mastering power of his eloquence. He may be said to have begun his career as a critic in the *De Oratore*, though in that work he was concerned chiefly with the theory of rhetoric. His name as an orator was already securely established, and he could embody in the treatise the results garnered from his practical experience. He was conscious of his superiority over all his rivals at the bar or in the assembly. With the years his vision had widened. He was dissatisfied[5] with his first essay on rhetorical theory as too narrow and immature, and was no longer content with the mere technical precepts of the rhetoricians.

The *De Oratore* was designed[6] to be more than a mere

Reaction against the Rules

handbook of rhetorical precepts, and was to open up a wider vista to aspiring orators. Even before this period,[7] Cicero had realised the necessity of a liberal education for the orator. In the

---

[1] Br. 60 ; *vide supra*, p. 51.   [2] 36.   [3] Cf. Tusc. Disp. III. 45.

[4] Cf. Br. 253 ; Sen. Suas. VI, VII ; Vell. I. 17 ; Pliny, N. H. VII. 30 ; Q. VIII. 3. 64, 66, XII. 1. 20, *ib.* 11. 28 ; Plut. Cic. 4.

[5] De Or. I. 5, on the " De Inventione " ; cf. Q. III. 5. 15, 6. 59.

[6] Ad Fam. I. 9. 23 ; cf. Or. 43, on the " Orator."

[7] Pro Archia, 12, Div. in Q. Caec. c. XII ; cf. Laurand, De Ciceronis Studiis Rhetoricis, p. 1 *et seq.*, 103.

De Oratore he is in fact in revolt[1] against the Rules, and against the narrowness of the conventional rhetorical training, though he makes it clear that he does not altogether despise the doctrines handed down by the Greek authors of technical treatises. Those who composed arts of oratory were, for the most part, men devoid of wide culture,[2] who delivered a series of minute precepts calculated to evoke the ridicule[3] of the practised orator. They laid down rigid rules[4] to govern the various parts of a speech, and falsely[5] imagined that such rules constituted the whole art of oratory. School[6] rhetoric with its narrow routine and lack of vision can never by itself create a perfect orator, and the practised speaker, though he may often follow the guidance of the Rules, will never allow[7] himself to become enslaved to their tyranny.

Cicero was thus in reaction against the narrow outlook of the text books, and wished to draw rather on the experi-

Programme
for the ora-
tor

ence[8] of real life for the training of the orator. Hence he selected as his chief spokesmen in the *De Oratore* Crassus and Antonius, the two most distinguished orators in the Rome of their day.[9] The schools might turn out glib[10] speakers or clever pleaders, but not genuine orators. Cicero's great aim was to show that the orator must be a man of the widest[11] culture and most extensive knowledge, and must be versed in all the liberal arts. He must be instructed in almost all the branches of Philosophy,[12] especially Logic, Psychology, and Ethics ; he must[13] have read the poets, have studied history and Civil

---

[1] De Or. I. 23, *ib.* 146, II. 75, on " pervulgata precepta," III. 70, 81, 92, 121 ; *vide supra*, p. 121 n. 4.

[2] De Or. II. 133 : " hebes et impolitum genus "; cf. *ib.* II. 10.

[3] De Or. III. 54, *ib.* 75.   [4] *Ib.* II. 79–80, III. 76.

[5] *Ib.* I. 52, 203 ; cf. Br. 263, 271, on " Hermagorae disciplina."

[6] De Or. I. 105, 157, II. 64.   [7] *Ib.* II. 322, 323, 326.

[8] De Or. I. 208, II. 87, 298 ; cf. III. 74, where Crassus appeals to his practical training.

[9] The dramatic date of the Dialogue is 91 B.C.

[10] De Or. I. 73, 83, 263 ; cf. Or. 47.

[11] De Or. I. 17 *et seq.*, 72, 159, 264, *ib.* II. 5 ; cf. Br. 322 : "litteris quibus fons perfectae eloquentiae continetur "; Or. 113–120.

[12] De Or. I. 60 *et seq.*, 87 ; cf. Or. 15.

[13] De Or. I. 158–159, 193, 201, II. 68, on the study of poetry and history.

Law, and must be trained in delivery in a way equal to the greatest actors. The real orator will thus be able to lift his case above the exigencies of the moment, and survey it in aspects that touch humanity at large. His oratory will not be mere empty sound, but the rich eloquence, full of colour, life, and variety,[1] that wells up from the abundant knowledge of a well-stored mind.[2]

Such is the varied programme that Cicero in the person of Crassus outlines for the training of the orator. Antonius,[3] Discussion of who finds such a programme too heavy a the burden for ordinary mortals, takes a nar- programme rower[4] view of the culture necessary for the orator. He would be satisfied if he had a smattering[5] of certain subjects, and applied to the expert for instruction, as the need arose. Antonius is here making concessions to Roman[6] prejudice against anything like a parade of what it considered useless knowledge. It is evident,[7] however, that he champions his view partly for debating purposes, for he subsequently comes round to Crassus' standpoint.

Cicero's programme is interesting from many points of view, and is, of course, of particular importance for the Importance history of Roman[8] education. My excuse of the for dealing with it here is that it will help us programme to understand more fully his ideal of what the orator should be, and give us a better insight into some of his criticisms in the *Brutus*. In the *De Oratore* Cicero is in fact making a plea for the advantages of a liberal education

[1] De Or. III. 80.
[2] Cf. Petron. 118 (though in a different context) on " mens ingenti flumine litterarum inundata."
[3] Probably Cicero attributes the narrower view to Antonius, as one who had written a technical treatise on Rhetoric ; cf. De Or. I. 94, 206, III. 189, Br. 163 ; Q. III. 1. 19 ; the narrower view is also attributed to Q. Cicero (De Or. I. 5) and Sulpicius (*ib*. III. 147).
[4] De Or. I. 213 *et seq*., 235 *et seq*., *ib*. 260 ; Ant. will be content with " quae sunt in usu civitatum vulgari ac forensi, remotis ceteris studiis."
[5] De Or. I. 218.
[6] Cf. *ib*. II. 4, 153, 156 ; Q. XII. 9. 5 ; cf. Pliny, N. H., 29.7.14 ; Plut. Cic. 5 ; Schneidewin, Die antike Humanität, p. 328 ; for other evidence of Roman prejudices, *vide supra*, p. 124.
[7] De Or. I. 263, II. 37, 40, 60, 68.
[8] Cf. Gwynn, Roman Education, c. 6.

against the narrow training of the specialist. With such an ideal before him, he naturally condemns the restricted programme of the " Latini Rhetores,"[1] who trained men to be ready speakers without imparting to them any of the refinement of general culture. The culture that he himself wished to have imparted, was in most essentials Hellenic,[2] but this was despised by the Latin teachers of Rhetoric, who were national and democratic[3] in their outlook, and in reaction against the Greek culture so intimately associated with the aristocracy.

In later days we find an echo of Cicero's programme in the *Dialogus*[4] of Tacitus, who in the person of Messalla

Later echoes of it   pleads for the necessity of a broad culture in the orator against the narrower views of Aper. Cicero's ideal is interesting, also, in view of the fact that he was charged by his opponents with being an Asianist in disguise. The Asiatic orators generally were content with the routine training of the schools, and were noted[5] for their lack of polite learning. Augustus characterised[6] their oratory as " inanis sententiis verborum volubilitas." We find Cicero himself frequently[7] condemning mere high-sounding rhetoric that is barren of ideas, and has no learning to support it.

[1] They were suppressed by Crassus 92 B.C.; cf. Cic. De Or. III. 93 ; Tac. Dial. 35 ; Gellius, XV. 11. 2 ; Q. II. 4. 42 ; Norden, Die antike Kunstprosa, I. p. 222 *et seq.* takes the " De Oratore " as directed primarily against the " Latini Rhetores," but it seems to me that Cicero's main object is to set his programme of wide culture for the orator over against the narrowness of mere technical training ; cf. Curcio, Le Opere Rhetoriche di M. Tullio Cicerone, p. 133 *et seq.*, for various views on the scope of the " De Oratore."

[2] De Or. III. 93–95, 137, *ib.* I. 14 ; *vide infra*, p. 178.

[3] Plotius Gallus, the chief of them, was a friend of Marius (Pro Archia 20); for the political aspect of the movement, cf. Marx, Ad Herennium, Introd. p. 141 *et seq.*; cf. Suet. De Rhet. c. 1–2, where it is recorded that Cicero in his youth was deterred from attending the instruction of Plotius, probably by Crassus, or others of his aristocratic friends ; cf. De Or. II. 2.

[4] Cf. especially c. 30–32 ; *vide infra*, p. 344.

[5] *Vide infra*, p. 238.

[6] Suet. Aug. 86.

[7] De Or. I. 51, III. 136, *ib.* 142 : " malim equidem indesertam prudentiam quam stultitiam loquacem "; Or. 236, Part. Or. 81 : " inanis quaedam profluentia loquendi."

The scheme of education outlined in the *De Oratore* is interesting from another point of view, inasmuch as it embodies an ideal which Cicero in the *Brutus* claims[1] to have realised in his own person.

Cicero's own training

He there gives us a detailed and striking picture of his training as an orator, including his philosophical[2] studies under such masters as Philo and Antiochus, his relations with the Stoic Diodotus,[3] his study of Law under Scaevola,[4] his travels[5] in pursuit of the higher culture, his rhetorical training under Molon and Demetrius Syrus, his associations with some of the leading orators of Asia, and his assiduous practice in writing and in declaiming[6] both in Greek and Latin, so different from the method of declamation in vogue under the Empire. He thus aimed at being learned[7] before he entered the Forum, and began his profession as pleader. He describes[8] for us in vivid fashion the power he derived in his orations from all this laborious training, and from the extensive learning which he had acquired. It is little wonder that he characterises[9] his speeches as " refertae philosophorum sententiis," and that he claims to have attracted men's gaze by a new style[10] marked by a depth and solidity that had their roots in a rich and varied erudition.

Perhaps the chief interest of the programme which Cicero outlines in the *De Oratore* (though it only concerns us

---

[1] Br. 305 *et seq.*; cf. Tac. Dial. c. 30.

[2] Cf. De Fin. I. 16 (for Zeno and Phaedrus), De Nat. Deor. I. 6 ; Reid, Academica, Introd. p. 1 *et seq.*

[3] Cf. Ad Att. II. 20. 6, Ad Fam. XIII. 16. 4, Acad. Pr. 115, Tusc. Disp. V. 113.

[4] The Augur ; he studied also under Scaevola, the Pontifex ; cf. Laelius, I.

[5] Cf. Or. 146.

[6] Br. 310; cf. De Or. I. 149 ; there, two methods of declamation are contrasted ; the defective method, resembling the later form of declamation in its unreality, may have been practised by the Latini Rhetores ; cf. Norden. op. cit. I. p. 248 ; Ad Fam. VII. 33. 1 ; Suet. De Rhet., I ; Sen. Controv. I. pr. 12 ; cf. Q. X. 1. 23, on speeches written as rhetorical exercises.

[7] Br. 311.

[8] *Ib.* 322.

[9] De Nat. Deor. I. 6.

[10] Br. 321 ; the " dicendi novitas " I take to be the style of oratory which bore the mark of wide culture ; cf. Or. 106.

indirectly here), is that in it we find re-echoed an old dispute,[1]
which had with varying fortune raged in
Revival of an Greece since the days of Plato. That
old dispute philosopher, as we know, was at war with the
pretensions of the Sophists, and their claims to be the chief
teachers of wisdom. To their form of instruction he opposed
his own genuine philosophy, which rested on scientific
principles, and aimed at the discovery of truth. He held
that the formal training given by the Sophists in Rhetoric,
the " art of persuasion," was useless and even harmful
without scientific knowledge. He maintained that Rhetoric
was not an art, and in his own system he subordinated it to
Dialectic, and insisted moreover on the need of a training
in Psychology for the orator, if he were to succeed in stirring
men's emotions. Rhetoric and Philosophy were thus placed
in opposition, and the stage was set for a quarrel which
developed with varying degrees of bitterness as the years
went on, the philosophers claiming certain privileged
spheres as their own, and denying the orator the right of
entrance to them. The quarrel, too, in part developed into
a struggle for the control of education. Cicero in many
passages[2] deplores the injurious effects of the estrangement
thus effected. This quarrel is one that mainly concerns the
history of education, but I think it necessary to deal briefly
with it, if we are to understand Cicero's attitude to the
various philosophical schools, and the contribution they
could make towards the training of the orator.

Isocrates aimed at uniting both Philosophy and Rhetoric
into a philosophic rhetoric, but his " Philosophy "[3] was
very different from that of Plato. It was a
Relations of combination of rhetoric and political science,
Philosophy approximating to our idea of general culture.
and Rhetoric
Aristotle's attitude to Rhetoric was in most respects similar

[1] Cf. De Orat. I. 36 ; Von Arnim, Leben und Werke des Dio von Prusa,
p. 20 *et seq.* ; Prümm, Quaestionum Tullianarum Specimen, p. 5 *et seq.*

[2] De Or. III. 56–58, 60, 72, 122, Or. 13, 17 ; Von Arnim, op. cit.,
p. 63 *et seq.*, 96 *et seq.*

[3] Cf. Plato, Phaedrus, 279 B ; Thompson, Phaedrus, p. 170 *et seq.*; De
Or. III. 59, 139 ; for Isocrates' programme, cf. Peter, Wahrheit und Kunst,
p. 20 *et seq.*; Burk, Die Pädagogik des Isokrates, p. 65 *et seq.*

to that of his master Plato. For him, also, it was a pendant
to Dialectic. He excluded it from the sphere of ethico-
political science which it claimed for its domain. For all
that, Aristotle's practical mind laid much greater stress[1]
than his master on the value of Rhetoric, and he considered
it important enough to find a place in the curriculum of his
school. Amongst the later philosophers, Epicurus, whose
aim was pre-eminently practical, was decidedly hostile[2] to
Rhetoric. He was averse to the philosopher's participation
in political life, and could find no use for Rhetoric even in
the law courts. Still he regards it as an independent branch
of instruction, and both he and later Epicureans spoke
favourably of the epideictic genre in oratory. The Stoics[3]
brought Rhetoric once more into close relation with Philosophy, and considered it together with Dialectic as part of
the λογικὸν μέρος. For them Rhetoric was a science and
a virtue. However, they tended to identify it so closely with
Dialectic, and so neglected the stylistic side of oratory, that
their system could not contribute much towards the perfection of the orator, or towards imparting a wide culture.
With the Scholastic system of Hermagoras, Rhetoric got
a fresh lease of life at the beginning of the second century,
B.C., and began to assert its claims anew. The philosophers
naturally opposed its pretensions. With Rome now more
amenable to the influences of Greek civilization, the problem arose whether Philosophy or Rhetoric would play the
leading part in dispensing culture to the Romans, and in
the training of their statesmen. The old quarrel broke out
with renewed bitterness. Of the three philosophers who
came to Rome in 155 B.C., Critolaus[4] and Diogenes[5] were

[1] De Or. III. 141 ; cf. Tusc. Disp. I. 7, where, however, Cicero exaggerates the influence of Isocrates on Aristotle ; cf. Hubbell, The Rhetorica
of Philodemus, p. 366 et seq.

[2] De Or. III. 63–64 ; cf. Acad. Post. 5 ; Q. XII. 2. 24.

[3] De Or. III. 65 et seq.; Von Arnim, op. cit. p. 77 et seq.; Striller, op.
cit. p. 8.

[4] Cf. Philodemus, Rhet. II. 98, 102 et seq., 220 ; cf. Sudhaus, Supplementum, Preface ; Cicero however, De Or. II. 160, speaks in not unfriendly
terms of Critolaus.

[5] Cf. Philodemus, II. 99, 208, 216, 227 ; cf. Hubbell, op. cit., p. 332
et seq., 346 et seq.; cf. Cic. De Or. II. 157 et seq.

especially hostile to the pretensions of Rhetoric. We find echoes of such hostility in Philodemus, Cicero,[1] and Quintilian.

Plato had furnished the Philosophers with their most formidable weapon, when he denied that Rhetoric was an

Campaign against Rhetoric

art.[2] The so-called orators, as Mnesarchus said,[3] are merely glib speakers, " operarii lingua celeri et exercitata." Oratory, as some contended, was the product[4] merely of a natural gift aided by experience. It existed long before the " art " of rhetoric came into being, as is proved by the successful orators[5] who had no technical training. It was maintained[6] that Rhetoric was useless for practical life, while in the hands of designing men it could be employed to the detriment of society, of which Philosophy was the only true benefactor. Philosophy alone could lay the proper foundation for oratory. In particular, the philosophers sought to curb the pretensions of their opponents by limiting the scope of Rhetoric, and by denying[7] it the right to treat certain questions which they claimed as their own preserve. As Cicero complains, they strove to drive the orator from the guidance of States, and confine him to petty speeches, and to pleading in the law-courts.

The teachers of Rhetoric put forward their case with equal vehemence. They declared[8] that the orator was

The claims of Rhetoric

capable of speaking on any subject " ornate copioseque," and claimed[9] special merit for the part which he had played in ordering and civilizing primitive society, though the philosophers

---

[1] Cf. especially De Or. I. 41–95.

[2] *Ib.* I. 90 *et seq.*, 109, where it is called an " art " in the popular sense ; Philodemus, II. 68, 101 ; Q. II. 17. 2 *et seq.*, *ib.* 42 ; Hubbell, op. cit., p. 368 *et seq.*

[3] De Or. I. 83 ; cf. Schmekel, op. cit., p. 297.

[4] Philod. I. 27, col. VII ; Q. II. 17. 5 *et seq.*

[5] Aeschines and Demades were two stock examples ; cf. Philod. II. 97 ; Q. II. 17. 12 ; Hubbell, op. cit., p. 371.

[6] Philod. I. 250, col. XVII., II. 159, fr. 20.

[7] De Or. I. 41 *et seq.*

[8] Cf. De Inv. I. 7.

[9] De Or. I. 33.

maintained[1] that in this task they had played the more important rôle. The orator had been driven[2] from a kingdom which belonged to him by right, and Cicero wishes to regain it. His scope[3] must be unlimited, and he must have the right to deal with all the great political questions that exercise the minds of men. There must be a return to the old union of oratory and philosophy which was conspicuous in the most eminent Greek[4] statesmen. In fact both Philosophy and Rhetoric, when studied in isolation, are crippled and ineffectual. Above all, Cicero wished to win back for the orator the right to deal with θέσεις,[5] especially those general questions of an ethico-political content from which the philosophers wished to exclude[6] him. These helped to widen his horizon, and lift him above the needs of his particular case. For that reason, the orator's culture must be of the most comprehensive character. Philosophy is to be the handmaid of Rhetoric, and in all its branches, Ethics, Psychology, Physical Science,[7] must minister to its needs. This claim is tantamount to a revival of the old Sophistic[8] ideal, with the difference that the new Sophists (if the term may be allowed) had the advantage of all the philosophical speculation that had been carried on since the days of Plato. They had thus a richer harvest to reap, and could also hope to acquire more accurate and scientific knowledge than their predecessors.

I have treated of this quarrel between Philosophy and

[1] *Vide infra*, p. 438.
[2] De Or. III. 70, 108 : " de nostra possessione depulsi "; *ib.* 123.
[3] *Ib.* II. 68, III. 76, 122, 143.
[4] *Ib.* III. 138–139, Or. 119; cf. Philod. II. 226, *ib.* 299, fr. 7, on Pericles' study of Philosophy ; on Demosthenes' study of Plato, cf. Br. 121, Or. 15 ; Philod. I. 351 ; Plut. Dem. 5.
[5] De Or. I. 56, III. 109, Br. 322, Or. 46, 125, Top. 79, Ad Q. Fr. III. 3. 4 : " nostrum instituendi genus esse paulo eruditius et θετικώτερον "; cf. Q. XII. 2. 25 ; Von Arnim, op. cit, p. 108 *et seq.*
[6] In De Inv. I. 8, Cicero himself excludes " theses " from the scope of the orator ; cf. Q. III. 5. 14 *et seq.*, on Cicero's change of attitude.
[7] *Vide* Von Arnim, p. 43 *et seq.*, on the view of Nausiphanes who held that a knowledge of Ionian Physical Science was necessary for the orator ; cf. Cic. Or. 16, 119 ; Philod. II. 5, 231, combats the view.
[8] Cf. Von Arnim, p. 98; Cicero often shows his sympathy with the ideals of the early Sophists ; cf. De Or. III. 59, 128, 132.

Rhetoric, as it serves to furnish a background to Cicero's
The Philos- ideal of culture in the *De Oratore*, and helps
ophical schools us to realise better its full import. Now
and oratory Cicero is particularly interesting when he
sets out to define his attitude to the various philosophical
schools from the standpoint of their utility to the orator.
From many passages[1] it is clear that he considered himself
most indebted to the Academy for his own success in oratory, though he acknowledges, too, that the Peripatetics
have done much to advance the art. This tribute to the
Academy is all the more remarkable in view of its founder's
pronounced hostility to Rhetoric,[2] and it proves that Rhetoric had by now won an honoured place in the curriculum
of the New Academy. It is probable that, in the ideal which
he puts forward for the training and culture of the orator,
Cicero was especially influenced by his master Philo,[3] who
taught Rhetoric as well as Philosophy.

Sometimes[4] he couples together the Academic and Peripatetic schools as the two most favourable to the development of the orator and statesman. Their practice[5] of arguing
both sides of a question would make a strong appeal to the
forensic orator, though Aristotle was evidently[6] the first to
institute the practice. Still, Cicero regarded the Academy
as pre-eminently the parent[7] of eloquence. Amongst the
teachers of the New Academy, Carneades had a special
attraction for him, not only because of his custom[8] of

[1] De Or. III. 67, 80, 145, Or. 12 ; cf. Tac. Dial. 31 ; Q. XII. 2, 23
et seq.

[2] At any rate to Rhetoric, as taught by the Sophists.

[3] Tusc. Disp. II. 9, De Or. III. 110, Br. 306 ; cf. Von Arnim, p. 97
et seq.; Kroll, Neue Jahrb. 1903, Cicero und die Rhetorik, p. 681 *et seq.*,
argues less convincingly in favour of Antiochus, who had strong leanings
towards Stoicism.

[4] De Or. III. 109, Br. 120, De Fin. V. 7 ; cf. IV. 5–6.

[5] De Or. III. 107, Tusc. Disp. II. 9.

[6] Or. 46, De Fin. V. 10.

[7] Cf. Paradoxa, Pr. 2 (where he has the New Academy especially in mind):
" ea philosophia, quae peperit dicendi copiam;" De Nat. Deor. II. 168,
De Fato, 3 ; Laurand, op. cit., p.57 *et seq.*

[8] De Or. III. 80 ; the principle of the New Academy " modo hoc, modo
illud probabilius videtur," would naturally make a strong appeal to an orator
of Cicero's temperament ; cf. Acad. Pr. 121, De Or. III. 67.

arguing against every thesis proposed, but because of his extraordinary eloquence, to which he pays many tributes.[1] Carneades had much to do with establishing the tradition of eloquence in the Academy, a tradition which was evidently maintained by the later representatives of the school.

As regards the Peripatetic school, Cicero is fond of contrasting[2] the broad character of Aristotelian Dialectic with the hyper-subtleties of the Stoic school.

The Peripatetics Though Aristotle was influenced by Plato in subordinating Rhetoric to more scientific studies, yet the prominent place which he gave it in the curriculum of his school, attracted[3] Cicero to his system. His practice of training his pupils to discuss general questions with arguments for and against,[4] not in the jejune manner of the philosopher, but with the copiousness of the orator, and his thorough treatment of topics,[5] were regarded by Cicero as especially valuable. One thing that will strike a modern student of Aristotle as strange, is the many tributes Cicero pays[6] to his " golden flood of speech," a description that might well suit his successor Theophrastus, but seems singularly inappropriate as applied to the Aristotle that we know. Theophrastus probably[7] did much to make the Peripatetic school acceptable in the eyes of Cicero, who was indebted to him for many features in his theory of style.

The Epicureans, as far as the development of the orator was concerned, were regarded[8] by Cicero as a negligible quantity. Epicurus himself had disparaged

The Epicureans Rhetoric, and, setting before his followers a purely practical end in his philosophy, had in general despised[9] the higher culture. He considered

---

[1] De Or. III. 68, 71, II. 161, De Fin. III. 41, Acad. Post. 46, Acad. Pr. 60 ; cf. Colin, op. cit., p. 572–3, for an interesting criticism of Noumenios on Carneades ; *vide supra*, p. 30.

[2] *Vide infra*, p. 161.   [3] De Inv. II. 6, De Or. II. 160.

[4] Or. 46 ; cf. Q. XII. 2. 25.   [5] De Or. II. 152, Top. 2.

[6] Acad. Pr. 119 (with passages cited by Reid) ; cf. Q. X. 1. 83 ; Plut. Cic. 24.

[7] Cf. De Inv. I. 61, De Fin. I. 14 ; Cicero used to call him his τρυφὴ ἰδία.

[8] De Or. III. 63–64, 78, Br. 131.

[9] De Fin. I. 14, *ib.* 26, II. 27 ; Q. II. 17. 15 ; cf. Philod. I., p. 100.

political life incompatible with the untroubled calm of mind which he regarded as the basis of happiness. In his own style[1] he aimed especially at perspicuity, and made no pretence of elegance or ornateness, though Theon[2] charged him with straining at times after rhythmical effects such as were affected by Hegesias and the Asianist orators. To Phaedrus, his oldest master and life-long friend, Cicero attributes[3] a certain refinement and culture, while Zeno was another Epicurean who evidently[4] aimed at an ornate and impressive style. To the culture of another member of the school, and a pupil of Zeno,[5] that strange bohemian figure Philodemus of Gadara, a " pliant and very charming Greek," Cicero pays a tribute[6] mingled, however, with censure that was designed to lend colour to his indictment of Piso. He credits him with a gift for witty, polished, and elegant verse, but condemns his lascivious tone.[7] Such literary remains of his as have reached us show him to have been a versatile man of letters[8] who, as Cicero says, not only busied himself with philosophy, but with those other studies which the members of his sect generally neglected. Zeno and Philodemus were thus exceptions in their school. Amongst the Roman writers[9] on Epicureanism there generally prevailed a tradition of uncouth style which Cicero visits with severe strictures.

He is particularly interesting when he proceeds to deal with the relation of Stoicism to oratory, and to criticise the orators of the school. He was powerfully attracted to-

[1] De Fin. I. 15 ; Dionys. De Comp. Verb. c. 24 ; Blass, Die griechische Beredsamkeit, p. 52 ; Diog. Laert. X. 13 (there quoted).

[2] Progym. II. 71 (Spengel).

[3] De Nat. Deor. I. 93.

[4] De Nat. Deor. I. 59 ; cf. Acad. Post. 46, on his admiration for Carneades.

[5] Cf. Philod. Rhet. I. 78, 97.

[6] In Pis. 68 et seq. ; in De Fin. II. 119, he is referred to in more serious terms ; cf. Mahaffy, The Silver Age of the Greek World, p. 158 et seq.

[7] The poems attributed to him in the Greek Anthology bear out Cicero's indictment ; cf. also Hor. Sat. II. 121 ; cf. Hubbell, op. cit., p. 251, on his probable relations with the Augustan group, Horace, Virgil, Varius, and Quintilius.

[8] His chief treatises are those on Music, Rhetoric, and Poetics.

[9] Acad. Post. 5, Tusc. Disp. II. 7, IV. 6, Ad Fam. XV. 19. 2 ; Cicero, of course, in these passages is referring to the prose-writers.

wards the ethical system[1] of the Stoics, and is ever ready
to render homage to their highmindedness
and seriousness of purpose. Moreover, the
Stoics had proclaimed[2] Rhetoric to be a virtue, though the
more rigid amongst them maintained[3] that the " Sapiens "
alone was an orator. Cato's famous description[4] of the
orator as " vir bonus dicendi peritus," was probably of
Stoic origin.

The Stoics

Still no matter how favourable in theory the Stoics were
to oratory, in practice all else was dominated[5] by their
system of Dialectic. Cicero is fond of contrasting[6] the dialectical system prevailing in
the Academic and Peripatetic schools with the more subtle[7]
and complicated system of the Stoics. Their habit of minute
division and accurate definition, their system of rigid syllo-
gistic reasoning, their series of rapid interrogations, were
like so many thorns[8] strewn in the paths of their opponents,
or so many snares[9] for the unwary. Zeno used the famous
simile[10] in which he compared Dialectic to the closed fist, and
Rhetoric to the open palm, but in the system of his school
it was almost invariably the closed fist that was brought into
play. Naturally Cicero, though trained himself by Diodotus,

Stoic Dialectic

[1] De Off. III. 20 ; cf. De Nat. Deor. I. 4, on the Stoic view of Providence ;
Sihler, Cicero of Arpinum, pp. 292–293.

[2] De Or. I. 83, III. 65.

[3] Cf. Diogenes, Philod. Rhet. I. p. 346.

[4] Cf. Q. I. pr. 9, II. 15. 34, II. 16. 11, XII. 1. 1, *ib.* 9 ; cf. Sen. Controv. I. pr. 9 ; Philod. II. 127, fr. 13 ; Radermacher, Studien zur Geschichte
der griech. Rhetorik, p. 285 *et seq.*, traces the dictum to Stoic sources ;
Morr, Poseidonios von Rhodos über Dichtung und Redekunst, p. 54 *et seq.*,
who in this connection deals with the cognate dictum of Poseidonius " that
no one can be a good poet, who is not first a good man " ; Colson ad Q. I.
pr. 9, finds the dictum latent in Aristotle's precepts concerning the ἦθος
τοῦ λέγοντος, but it is probable that the Stoics, who held Rhetoric to be a
virtue, first gave explicit expression to it.

[5] De Or. II. 157 *et seq.*, Br. 119.

[6] De Fin. IV. 6, Tusc. Disp. IV. 33, Or. 114–115.

[7] Br. 114 ; cf. Tusc. Disp. III. 13.

[8] De Fin. III. 3, IV. 6, Acad. Pr. 112 ; Tusc. Disp. IV. 9 : " spinas
partiendi et definiendi."

[9] De Or. I. 43, Tusc. Disp. V. 76.

[10] Or. 113, De Fin. II. 17 ; Q. II. 20. 7 ; cf. Br. 309.

considered all the subtle minutiae[1] of Stoic Dialectic as
incompatible with the copiousness and expansiveness of the[2]
genuine orator. Moreover, the Paradoxes to which the
earlier Stoics in particular attached so much importance,
were a stumbling-block[3] to the ordinary man, to whom the
orator had to direct his chief appeal. Again, the Stoics,
though strong in argumentative power, were deficient in the
important element of " inventio." In addition, the Stoic
doctrine of ἀπαθεία inevitably tended to produce a type of
oratory that was distasteful to one of Cicero's temperament,
and opposed to his conception[4] of the scope of eloquence.
The Stoics concerned themselves almost wholly with a plain
statement of facts,[5] and relied for victory[6] on the inherent
justice of their case. Their doctrine of ἀπαθεία[7] forbade
them to appeal to the emotions. For them to speak the
truth was to speak well.[8] They cultivated thought more than
diction, and whether they were engaged in a dialectical discussion, or pleading a case, their language was colourless
and without emotional content. Of set purpose they
eschewed[9] all beauty and charm of expression, and cultivated a plain style of speaking which often bordered on
uncouthness.[10] Cleanthes and Chrysippus both wrote treatises on Rhetoric, but of such a character[11] that one whose

[1] Cicero is fond of using diminutives to describe them ; cf. interrogatiunculae, ratiunculae, conclusiunculae.

[2] In Paradoxa, Pr. 2, Cato's " minutae interrogatiunculae " are contrasted
with " dilatare argumentum " ; Br. 118–120 ; cf. the contrast between
δημηγορεῖν and Socrates' method of question and answer, Plato, Rep. I.
350 E.

[3] De Or. I. 83, III. 66 ; cf. Pro Murena, 61 et seq.

[4] *Vide infra*, p. 222 et seq.

[5] On those who aim at " docere " alone, cf., Q. IV. 5. 6, V. pr. 1 ;
Fronto, II. p. 66, denies that Chrysippus confined himself to " docere."

[6] De Or. I. 229 ; *vide supra*, p. 69.

[7] De Or. I. 220, 225 et seq., 230, De Fin. IV. 7 ; Q. VI. 1. 7.

[8] Cf. Smiley, op. cit., p. 50 et seq.

[9] Cic. Paradoxa, Pr. 2 : " in ea haeresi quae nullum sequitur florem
orationis" ; cf. Q. X. 1. 84, XII. 2. 25 ; cf. Egger, L'Histoire de la Critique
chez les Grecs, pp. 356–359, on Stoic hostility to Art ; Menéndez Y
Pelayo, op. cit., Vol. I. p. 309 et seq.

[10] Cf. De Fin. IV. 78, on their philosophical style ; *vide supra*, p. 139.

[11] De Fin. IV. 7 ; cf. Dionys. De Comp. V. c. 4 ; Cleanthes, however,
was not contemptible as a stylist.

ambition it was to be dumb, should make them his sole study. The Stoic Diogenes of Babylon, when enumerating[1] the virtues of style, added a fifth virtue, συντομία, to the four usually associated with the name of Theophrastus. This virtue of brevity is a significant element in Stoic theory, and is one that was evidently cultivated carefully in practice. Diogenes also numbers κατασκευή amongst the virtues of style, but for the Stoics this must necessarily have been ornament of the most meagre kind. If it connoted positive[2] embellishment at all, it must have added little to purity of idiom, and to clearness and precision of language, on which the later Stoics in particular strongly insisted.

In view of this, and considering Cicero's own standpoint on the duties of the orator, it is hardly surprising that he

Character of Stoic oratory finds[3] Stoic oratory too subtle and restricted in scope, too lacking in fulness and body, too plain and unadorned, to make a strong appeal to a popular audience. It is interesting to note that many of the epithets which Cicero employs to describe the Plain style, are often[4] employed by him to characterise the style of the Stoics. This would seem to show that his description of the " genus tenue " owed much to his study of the Stoic orators, though under the stress of his polemic with the Atticists he was obliged to formulate that style more fully and more precisely than he had hitherto done.

We have already seen[5] something of the influence of Stoicism in the Scipionic circle, and have considered some

Some Stoic orators of its orators. We now turn to a considera- tion of other Stoic speakers[6] whom Cicero criticises, and we shall see how strong was the impress of the Stoic tradition upon their oratory. One

[1] *Vide supra*, p. 36.

[2] Stroux, op. cit., p. 35 *et seq.*, holds against Hendrickson that it connoted positive ornament.

[3] Br. 120, *ib.* 309, De Fin. III. 40, on the " limata tenuitas " of Stoic style ; cf. Tac. Dial. 31. 8.

[4] De Or. I. 50, II. 159, III. 66, Tusc. Disp. IV. 9 ; cf. Or. 20 : tenues, acuti, omnia docentes, et dilucidiora non ampliora facientes; *vide supra*, p. 69.   [5] *Vide supra*, p. 29 *et seq.*

[6] Two of these, Tubero and Rutilius, were also members of the Scipionic circle.

of the most prominent of these was Q. Mucius Scaevola, the Pontifex Maximus, who became Cicero's instructor in Law, on the death of his distinguished namesake, the Augur. He was the most celebrated lawyer of his day, but though Cicero styles him " juris peritorum eloquentissimus,"[1] his limitations as an orator were apparent both in the famous " causa Curiana,"[2] and in his defence of Rutilius Rufus. In the former case the character[3] of his oratory was wholly ineffective, when matched against the wit of Crassus and the force and range of his eloquence.

His limitations were seen to an even greater degree in his defence of Rutilius, who after his term of office in Asia was accused of extortion. It was an occasion

The defence of Rutilius

of supreme importance, when, in defence of a man standing his trial on a capital charge, all the resources of the orator should have been brought into play, and no effort spared to appeal to the emotions of those who were to decide the issue. Mucius' speech[4] was clear, elegant, and refined in diction, but his eloquence lacked the richness and passionate vigour that so critical an occasion demanded. The speech was indeed appropriate for the defence of such a man as Rutilius, who was a pupil[5] of Panaetius, almost a perfect embodiment of the " Sapiens," and one of the noblest products of the Stoic school. It was characteristic of his Stoic outlook that he condemned[6] as degrading the theatrical, though successful, appeal made by Galba[7] who, to excite compassion, had introduced his ward and children into Court, and commended them to the protection of the people. In his own

[1] Br. 145 ; cf. De Or. I. 180 ; Vell. II. 9. 1.
[2] De Or. I. 242–243, II. 24, 140 et seq., Br. 145–146, 195 et seq., Pro Caecina, 53, Top. 44 ; vide infra, p. 174.
[3] Cf. " breviter et presse," " verbis enim ad rem cum summa brevitate mirabiliter aptus."
[4] De Or. I. 229 : " Q. Mucius, more suo, nullo apparatu, pure et dilucide."
[5] Vide supra, pp. 30–31 ; cf. De Or. I. 227 ; on his Autobiography, cf. Tac. Agr. I ; Peter, Hist. Rom. Rel. Vol. I. p. 254 et seq. ; frs. pp. 189–190.
[6] De Or. I. 228 ; Q. II. 15. 8 ; cf. Br. 86–90, on Galba's power as an orator ; Cima, L'Eloquenza Latina, p. 78 et seq. ; Meyer, Or. Rom. Frag. pp. 58, 106–107.
[7] When brought to trial for his conduct in Lusitania.

case Rutilius would not employ either Crassus or Antonius, the leading advocates of the day, whose style of oratory was at variance with Stoic ideals, but he entrusted his defence to his nephew Cotta, and to Scaevola, and relied for his acquittal on the justice of his cause rather than on the aid[1] of emotional and meretricious eloquence. It was natural for him to seek the assistance of Scaevola, a brother Stoic, but it is significant, too, that he selected Cotta, an orator of the plain style. There were thus no appeals to the emotions, not even a foot was stamped, says Cicero, lest it be reported to the Stoics ; so a man of noble character was condemned[2] because of a defence which would have been successful only in Plato's Ideal Commonwealth.[3] Both Cicero[4] and Quintilian draw a parallel between the defence of Socrates and that of Rutilius, who faced his judges strong in the consciousness of his own integrity. Rutilius, like so many of the Stoics, was a distinguished lawyer,[5] but he had no natural gifts as an orator, and his speeches[6] exhibited the dryness, severity, and lack of charm that were so characteristic of his sect.

One of the most uncompromising of the Stoics was Tubero,[7] who, though he was connected[8] with the Scipionic
Aelius Tubero circle, yet showed little of its softening and refining influence. He was the nephew of the younger Scipio, and the pupil[9] of Panaetius, but his Stoicism tended to degenerate into the hardness of the Cynic. He pronounced the[10] funeral oration on the occasion

---

[1] Cf. De Or. I. 229 : " ne ornatius quidem aut liberius causam dici suam quam simplex ratio verit .tis ferebat."

[2] For his exile, cf. Br. 85 ; Livy, Epit. 70 ; Val. Max. II. 10. 5 ; Suet. De Gr. 6.

[3] De Or. I. 230 ; it is interesting to note that Aristotle (Rhet. III. c. 1.) regards μοχθηρία τῶν πολιτειῶν as one of the causes that gave rise to ornate and emotional oratory ; vide supra, p. 69.

[4] De Or. I. 231 ; Q. XI. 1. 12.

[5] He was trained by P. Mucius Scaevola, De Off. II. 47.

[6] Br. 110, 113–114, ib. 116, where Cicero classes him with the " oratores statarii " ; cf. Suet. Aug. 89, for his speech " De Modo Aedificiorum."

[7] Br. 117 et seq.

[8] De Rep. I. 14–15 ; cf. Lael. 101.

[9] Vide supra, p. 31 ; cf. De Or. III. 87.

[10] Vide supra, p. 37.

of his uncle's death, the speech having been composed by
Laelius, but the funeral banquet[1] which he gave, was more
worthy of Diogenes the Cynic than of the illustrious
Africanus.   His oratory was harsh and uncouth, a reflex
of his life and training.   He was one of the bitterest
opponents[2] of the Gracchi, a good lawyer,[3] but a poor
speaker, whose strength lay altogether in his dialectical
skill.[4]   Tubero is thus a standing memorial of a Stoicism
which was untempered by humanity, and moulded its
adherents into something intractable and forbidding.

Of the style of oratory of other Stoics, Cicero tells[5] us
little.   Aelius Stilo in his grammatical studies came strongly

Other Stoics   under the influence of the Stoic school, but,
although he combined the teaching of
rhetoric with his grammatical studies, and even wrote[6]
speeches for others, he had no pretensions to be an orator.
Cato Uticensis, who was later to undergo a kind of apotheosis for his fidelity to the Stoic creed, is in fact the only
Stoic to whom the gift of real eloquence is attributed.   This
compliment is paid[7] to him by his nephew Brutus.   Cicero
himself joins in the tribute, but declares that Cato, while
deriving from Stoicism all that it could give him, owed his
eloquence above all to his training by the masters of Rhetoric.
In the *Pro Murena*,[8] with the instinct of the skilled
advocate he had emphasised the harsh and unattractive
features of Cato's Stoicism, but it is clear[9] that, notwithstanding the latter's philosophical tenets, there was in his oratory
a certain grace and charm combined with vehement earnestness.

We have seen Cicero's views on the culture of the orator,

[1] Pro Murena, 76 ; Sen. Ep. 95. 72 ; cf. Sen. Controv. II. 1 (9). 8.
[2] Lael. 37.
[3] Gellius, I. 22. 7.
[4] Br. 117 : " doctissimus in disputando."
[5] Cf. Br. 175, on Sextus Pompeius.
[6] Br. 206–207 : " leves oratiunculas."
[7] Br. 118.
[8] 61–66, *ib.* 74 ; cf. De Fin. IV. 74 ; Q. XI. 1. 70.
[9] Cic. Paradoxa, Proem ; Q. XI. 1. 36 ; Plut. Cato M. 5 ; Cato's speech
in Sallust's Catiline (52) can give little idea of his style, but it evidently made
a deep impression on the occasion.

and on the utility of the various philosophical schools for
his training. We turn now to consider some
other aspects of his criticism, especially as
it is revealed to us in the *Brutus*, which is
one of the most important documents of formal criticism
that has come down to us from Roman times. In this work
he treats of many insignificant orators,[1] who should hardly
have figured at all in a critical survey of Roman eloquence.
He carried this practice so far that Atticus protests[2] against
his draining out the dregs. Part of Cicero's aim in the
treatise was to show how difficult[3] a thing oratory really was,
how slow and toilsome was the ascent towards perfection,
and how comparatively few orators[4] worthy of the name
existed in the various epochs of Roman history. The easier
method would have been to have dealt only with orators of
outstanding merit, but his own achievement in reaching
perfection could be set in a still fairer light, if it could be
contrasted with the shortcomings of a host of predecessors.
He was urged, too, by patriotic[5] motives to show what Rome
could accomplish, and desired to have as many orators as
possible to pit against the Greeks. He endeavours to make
the history of Latin oratory run as far as possible on lines
parallel with the development[6] of oratory in Greece, though
the task was no easy one.

The scope of the " Brutus "

In his account of the orators before Cato, he has at times
to have recourse to mere conjecture,[7] or to depend on
vague tradition. He is forced to appeal[8] to
Ennius as a witness for the eloquence of
Cethegus, while he apologises[9] for his omis-
sion of certain of the primitive orators by saying that nothing

The orators before Cato

---

[1] Br. 181 : " de his autem, quos ipsi vidimus, neminem fere praeter-
mittemus " ; cf. Fronto, II. p. 146 : " illos etiam quos in Bruto Cicero eloquentiae civitate gregatim donavit " ; Leo, Die griechisch-röm. Biographie,
pp. 219–220 ; Jahn-Kroll, Ciceros Brutus, Introd. p. 6.

[2] Br. 244 ; cf. *ib.* 176, 269, 297.

[3] *Ib.* 137 ; cf. De Or. I. 16.

[4] Br. 182, 270, 333.

[5] Cf. Or. 23.

[6] Br. 26 *et seq.* ; cf. De Or. II. 92 *et seq.*

[7] Br. 52, 55, 56 : " tantum modo conjectura ducor ad suspicandum."

[8] *Ib.* 57.   [9] *Ib.* 181.

can be written about those who neither have left anything in the way of personal writings, nor figure in the writings of others.   It is possible[1] that for his account of some of the earliest orators he was dependent on one of the Annalistic historians, and was guided in his judgment of them by the fictitious speeches attributed to them by such authors.   His first judgment[2] on Appius Claudius is based on an inference from the influence he exerted in the Senate, when the question of war with Pyrrhus was still trembling in the balance, though he later speaks[3] of his speech on that occasion as still extant.   In general, Cicero's criticisms of the orators of the Pre-Catonian period are designedly couched in the vaguest terms, and he is careful to concentrate more on their political achievements than on their accomplishments in the sphere of eloquence.

He reaches more solid ground in Cato, whose speeches he had studied.   Even after Cato, orators figure in his list, none of whose speeches had survived, and at

Cato and after

times, owing to the scantiness of the records, he was probably forced to add details suggested by his own fancy.[4]   In that period he had naturally to rely on written or oral[5] tradition to eke out the characteristics of many orators.   Later, in the case of the orators whom he himself had heard, the question of delivery came to be an important element in his criticism.

When we consider the vast number of orators that are reviewed in the pages of the *Brutus*, it is not surprising that many of the criticisms are perfunctory in

Perfunctory criticisms

character.   Different orators are criticised in practically identical terms, while occasionally the criticism is reduced almost to the proportion of a

[1] Cf. H. Jordan, Die Einleitung des Ciceronischen Brutus, Hermes, VI. 1872, p. 196 *et seq.*

[2] Br. 55.

[3] *Ib.* 61 ; cf. Cato Major 16 ; Livy, X. 19. 6 ; Plut. Pyrr. 19.

[4] Cf. De Or. II. 9 : "non de Ser. Galbae aut C. Carbonis eloquentia scribo aliquid, in quo liceat mihi fingere, si quid velim."

[5] Cf. Br. 79, "dicunt," "aiunt," *ib.* 105, 108, 109 ; Hendrickson, Literary Sources in Cicero's " Brutus," A.J. Phil. 1906, p. 184 *et seq. ;* Hendrickson conjectures that sometimes what Cicero attributes to an oral source is really derived from a literary one.

mere label.[1] At times the criticisms are couched in purely negative terms,[2] while in other cases Cicero lays emphasis rather on external characteristics[3] than on qualities essential to the orator. He groups together demagogues such as Saturninus and Servilius Glaucia, who rose to prominence in the democratic movement under Marius. His character-isation[4] of Saturninus, whom he compared to Hyperbolus, is particularly interesting, showing as it does that the demagogue struck the popular imagination chiefly by his personal appearance, the vigour of his gestures, and the peculiarities of his dress.

In the *De Oratore*, as we have seen, Cicero reacted against the tyranny of the Rules, and the minute and elaborate precepts delivered by the writers on Rhet-

The conven-
tional scheme
of Rhetoric

oric. Many of the authors of Rhetorical handbooks indulged to excess in refined division and sub-division of their subject, and such technical minutiae were often the only field in which their scholastic subtlety[5] could hope to display originality. Cicero himself often endeavours to leave the impression that he is not tied down to the rigid precepts of the schools. Hence, his attempt to vary[6] the usual divisions of the subject-matter of Rhetorical theory, and to diversify the terminology, though in a measure due to the diversity of his sources, was due also to his desire to impart an air of casualness and freedom to his own treatment of such questions. For all that, we find that in the *Brutus* many of Cicero's criticisms

[1] Cf. Br. 94, on the Mummii; *ib.* 108, on Ap. Claudius; cf. De Or. III. 28.

[2] Cf. Br. 221, on Q. Varius: " et verbis nec inops nec abjectus "; *ib.* 238 (C. Macer); *ib.* 247 (Lentulus Marcellinus).

[3] Cf. Br. 97, on the Caepiones.

[4] *Ib.* 224; Aristotle's characterisation of Cleon's oratory might be compared ('Aθ. πολ. 28. 3); cf. also, Aristoph. Achar., 380 *et seq.*

[5] In the " De Inventione " Cicero shows how strongly he himself was under the influence of scholastic Rhetoric; cf. *ib.* I. 20, where the exordium is divided into " principium " and " insinuatio "; *ib.* 27. on the kinds of narratio; *ib.* 12, where Hermagoras adds " negotialis " to the usual divisions of Rhetoric; cf. Q. III. 9. 1; Plato, Phaedrus, 266–267, on τὰ κομψὰ τῆς τέχνης; Arist. Rhet. III. 13. 3, *ib.* 5.

[6] Cf. Or. 43, where we have three parts of oratory set out " aliquanto secus atque in tradenda arte "; contrast De Or. I. 142, II. 79, 307.

are cast into the mould of the traditional schemata of the Rhetorical treatises. This form of criticism (dogmatic, if we care to style it so) constituted the line of least resistance for Cicero. The Rhetorical framework[1] was ready to hand, and it was easy for him to select one or more of its parts, and to make success or failure in them the touchstone for his judgments on various orators. It is mostly due to this method that there is often an air of routine and perfunctoriness about his criticisms. Let us consider how he applies the method.

Three pre-requisites were considered essential, if an orator was to achieve success. These are set forth in different places[2] by Cicero in terms that **Pre-requisites** slightly vary, but they figure in his criticism **for the orator** of many orators. P. Crassus is judged[3] under the heads of ingenium, studium, domesticae disciplinae, while to Brutus are attributed[4] natura admirabilis, exquisita doctrina, singularis industria. Cicero's method is especially well illustrated in the case[5] of Scaurus and Rutilius. He deals not merely with the qualities of these two orators in the concrete, but considers in the abstract also certain aspects of rhetorical theory, that are designed to help him ultimately in his appraisement of their merits. Many other orators are in part judged[6] by the presence or absence in them of the above-mentioned pre-requisites.

Next Cicero keeps before him the well-established[7] division of oratory into the judicial, deliberative, and demonstrative kinds. Naturally, with the needs of **The kinds of** practical life in view, he was mostly inter-**oratory** ested in the first two divisions. Many orators, who were not distinguished as pleaders in the courts, made

---

[1] Cf. Piderit-Harnecker, Introd. to " De Oratore," p. 51 *et seq.*, for a good summary of it.

[2] De Or. II. 147 : acumen, ratio (ars), diligentia ; cf. *ib.* I. 113 (ingenium), *ib.* 148 (exercitatio), De Inv. I. 2 (ars, studium, facultas a natura profecta) ; *vide infra*, p. 472.

[3] Br. 98.   [4] *Ib.* 22 ; cf. 125, on C. Gracchus.

[5] Br. 110 *et seq.*, where ingenium, industria, doctrina, inventio, etc., are considered.

[6] Cf. Br. 233, 236 (M. Piso), 245 (T. Torquatus), 267, 282.

[7] De Inv. I. 5. 7, De Or. I. 22, 141, Part. Or. 10, Top. 91.

their mark when a question of public policy had to be debated in the Senate, or before the Popular Assembly. Scaurus was particularly successful[1] in Senatorial debates, while many others are enumerated[2] who showed an aptitude for deliberative eloquence. The mob orators are grouped[3] together, as they were a special feature of the turbulent days of the Marian revolution. On the other hand, Cicero remarks[4] that the genius of Antonius was more suited to forensic than to deliberative oratory. Amongst forensic orators, some[5] were noted rather for their skill in prosecution than in defence.

Again, Cicero sets forth,[6] but with a certain diversity in different treatises, the parts of oratory that were usually treated in the Rhetorical scheme. He **The parts of** makes use of this stereotyped scheme in **rhetoric** many of his criticisms. His method is particularly illuminating when he deals with Antonius,[7] whose strength lay in his powers of invention, his capacity for the orderly arrangement of his speeches, and his retentive memory,[8] precisely the parts of oratory which were assigned to him for treatment in the *De Oratore*. He is credited, too, with a forceful and impressive delivery.[9] As regards style (elocutio), however, while Cicero concedes[10] to him the virtue of " Latinitas," he suggests that, though he could produce telling effects in his prose, he never reached the highest point of artistic expression.

Following closely in the footsteps of Theophrastus, Cicero had already in the *De Oratore*[11] dealt with the virtues

---

[1] Br. 112.

[2] Br. 135, *ib.* 136 : " Sp. Thorius satis valuit in populari genere dicendi ; " 178, 222 (Drusus and Q. Catulus), 268 (Lentulus).

[3] *Ib.* 223–224.

[4] *Ib.* 165.

[5] *Ib.* 131, on Caesulenus.

[6] De Inv. I. 9 : Inventio, Dispositio, Elocutio, Memoria, Pronuntiatio ; cf. De Or. I. 18, 113, 142, 187, II. 79 ; cf. Or. 43, Part. Or. 3.

[7] Br. 139 *et seq.* (on Inventio, Dispositio, Memoria in A.), *ib.* 215.

[8] Cf. Pro Cluentio, 140.

[9] Cf. De Or. III. 32, In Verrem, V. 3, Tusc. Disp. II. 57 ; *vide infra*, p. 180.

[10] Br. 140.

[11] I. 144, III. 37 *et seq.*

of style under the heads *Latine, plane, ornate, apte.*
He found the virtue of correctness in its
The "virtues" highest manifestation in the orators of
of style the Scipionic circle, though other orators
also are commended[1] for the purity of their Latin. While
every Roman was expected[2] to display this quality, yet to
refer to its presence in an orator was not wholly irrelevant,
as there were influences at work which tended[3] to impair
the purity and elegance of the language. Cicero devotes
little attention to the virtue of clearness, which was regarded
by some as the fundamental virtue of style. The virtue to
which he refers under the heading of " ornate," was more
complex, as it demanded[4] attention to the choice of words,
to composition, and to the use of Figures. Cicero finds in
Antonius a certain shortcoming as regards his choice of
words, which he selected rather for their expressiveness
than for their beauty, though in most of the other elements[5]
that constituted " ornatus," he is worthy of commendation.

Curio[6] formed a striking contrast to Antonius. He
lacked that wide culture which Cicero considered to be the
Curio and greatest ornament of the orator. He was
others a conspicuous failure in almost every depart-
appraised ment[7] in which the orator should shine, but
he succeeded in masking all these serious defects by the
wealth and brilliancy of his diction. To Antistius are
attributed[8] skill in Invention, the careful arrangement of
his speech, and a good memory, but there was no distinction about his style,[9] and he was a failure in delivery. Sometimes orators are credited with a capacity for Invention
alone, particularly those that were trained in the system of
Hermagoras.[10]

---

[1] *Vide infra*, p. 246.   [2] *Vide supra*, p. 78.   [3] *Vide infra*, p. 244.
[4] De Or. III. 96 *et seq.*, *ib.* 149 *et seq.*, 171 *et seq.*, 200 *et seq.* ; *vide supra*,
p. 85.
[5] Cf. Br. 140, where Cicero deals with his composition, and his power
in employing Figures of thought.
[6] *Ib.* 213 *et seq.* ; *vide infra*, p. 187.
[7] Such as Inventio, etc.
[8] Br. 227.
[9] It is considered under the head of ἐκλογὴ ὀνομάτων.
[10] Br. 263, 271 ; cf. Tac. Dial. XIX. 13 ; Q. III. 11. 22.

It is interesting to see how Cicero judges his great rival Hortensius, in the light of these traditional divisions of

Hortensius oratory. He deals[1] with him under the heads of memory, style, capacity for skilful arrangement, a characteristic which in him was remarkable owing to the manner in which he set forth the divisions of his speech, and at certain intervals summarised the points of his argument. Finally he treats of his delivery which was marked by certain mannerisms, and was suited[2] rather to the actor than to the forensic pleader. As we shall see, Cicero gives a more detailed examination of the style of Hortensius in another context,[3] and his criticism of it helped to make an effective point for him in his quarrel with the Atticists. With regard to the orators that he himself had known, he is naturally inclined to dwell on their delivery. In certain orators,[4] delivery was practically their only virtue.

It should be noted that Cicero at times endeavours to vary his formulae by changing the order usually observed in

C.'s attempts to vary his formulæ the scheme of Rhetoric. A pertinent example[5] is his criticism of his son-in-law C. Piso, who is considered first under the head of " exercitatio," then is dealt with from the point of view of style,[6] while lastly his powers in Invention and delivery are examined.

Cicero, as one might expect from the prominence which he gives them in his controversy with the Atticists, considers

The " officia oratoris " certain orators from the standpoint of the " officia oratoris." In the practical issues of an orator's career, these constituted the real test of success or failure. The strength of the Stoic orators, as we have seen, lay in their capacity for making a clear exposition of their case, and arguing it with logical acumen, but Cicero insists on the limitations of the plain

[1] Br. 301 *et seq.*; cf. Pro Quinctio, 35, Div. in Caec. 45 (quoted by Kroll, *ad loc.*
[2] Cf. Gellius, I. 5. 2.
[3] *Vide infra*, p. 239.
[4] Br. 234–235; cf. Or. 56.
[5] Br. 272.
[6] Under the aspects of choice of words and composition.

style of oratory adopted by the Stoic school. In this connection he makes[1] an interesting contrast between the eloquence of Scaevola and Crassus in the famous " causa Curiana," following out his comparison in a series of antitheses so elaborately balanced, that he begins[2] to fear they may seem too artificial to be founded on fact. Scaevola distinguished himself by his legal knowledge, his clear and elegant style, and his capacity for subtle argumentation. Crassus, however, proved the better pleader, inasmuch as he delighted[3] all present by the grace and charm of his style, and by his wit and cleverness in repartee, while at the same time he gave a convincing exposition[4] of the legal points in question, and lastly through his power of moving[5] the feelings of his audience, succeeded in bringing the court into sympathy with his own point of view. The standard of the " officia oratoris " is again pressed into service in the contrast[6] between Cotta and Sulpicius, while the same criterion is applied to Calidius,[7] who showed ability in expounding and arguing his case, could give pleasure to his hearers by a graceful delivery and a style of elaborate polish and symmetry, but yet failed in what Cicero regarded as the orator's highest duty, that of rousing the emotions. I have dealt with these points in almost wearisome detail, as I wished to show how much Cicero was indebted to the traditional scheme of Rhetoric in his judgments on various orators.

In his criticism of Roman orators, Cicero was accustomed to look also to the degree of culture which they possessed. Many of them had great natural ability,[8] but they lacked that comprehensive education which helps to broaden men's vision, impart a certain grandeur and impressiveness to their eloquence.

Orators judged by their culture

---

[1] Br. 144 *et seq.*, *ib.* 195 *et seq.*; *vide supra*, p. 164.

[2] Br. 149 : " licet omnia hoc modo ; sed vereor ne fingi videantur haec ut dicantur a me quodam modo."

[3] Br. 197 : " *delectavit* animosque omnium . . . quod est unum tribus, quae dixi ab oratore effici debere."

[4] *Ib.* : " quod est ex tribus oratoris officiis alterum."

[5] *Ib.* 198 : " hoc erat oratoris officium partitione tertium, genere maximum."

[6] *Ib.* 202–203.   [7] *Ib.* 274 *et seq.*   [8] Cf. Or. 143.

and raise it in its finer moments beyond mere transitory interests into sympathy with humanity at large. Cato, natural genius though he showed himself to be, was devoid of what Cicero calls " politissima doctrina transmarina atque adventicia."[1] The culture that Cicero looked for, was essentially Hellenic in character, and, like Horace when guiding the footsteps of aspiring poets, he considered the study of the " exemplaria Graeca " of the highest importance. Aemilius Lepidus is selected[2] for special commendation as one who had evidently studied Greek models with profit. He comments[3] on others, too, who were proficient in Greek studies, some of them to a degree remarkable for the period in which they lived. Q. Catulus, who, as we have seen,[4] was one of the most distinguished Hellenists of his time, is looked[5] upon as a typical product of the " modern " culture, as contrasted with the crudity of an earlier age, while special homage is paid[6] to the Greek learning of M. Piso. Titius,[7] tragic dramatist as well as orator, was to Cicero something of a mystery, as, though he lacked Greek culture,[8] his speeches showed a quality akin to Attic elegance and refinement. In striking contrast with Titius was the attitude of Memmius,[9] the patron of Lucretius, who, deeply versed in Greek literature, despised the products of native genius, and thus continued the tradition of Graecomania so vividly depicted for us by Lucilius in the person of Albucius.

The standpoint of Memmius was one that could evoke little sympathy from Cicero, whose ideal was the ideal of Cicero's ideals all sane Hellenists, the fusion of Greek and and Roman culture into an amalgam that would achievements retain the massive solidity of Roman civilisation, while acquiring something of the suppleness and

---

[1] De Or. III. 135 ; *vide infra*, p. 200.   [2] Br. 95–96.

[3] *Ib.* 104, 169, 173, 175.   [4] *Vide supra*, p. 59 *et seq.*

[5] Br. 132.   [6] *Ib.* 236 ; *vide infra*, p. 188.

[7] *Ib.* 167 ; cf. Fronto, I. p. 166 ; Macrob. Sat. III. 16. 14, for a rather vivid specimen of T's style.

[8] Cicero must mean here the culture of Greek Rhetoric, as T. shows a knowledge of Greek literature in his plays ; cf. Ribbeck, Die röm. Tragödie, p. 612 *et seq.*

[9] Br. 247.

charm of the Greek. Many had worked for the realisation
of that ideal, but Cicero felt that he himself had contributed
to bring it nearer to fulfilment than any of his predecessors.
He was proud of his achievements, and it is little wonder
that, often in his rhetorical treatises, his own age, his own
culture, and all that it stood for, are set up as a standard in
judging others. It is part of the rôle of Brutus and Atticus
in the *Brutus* to give prominence[1] to what Cicero had
accomplished for Latin prose literature. The multiplicity[2]
of his writings, the grander and more ornate style of oratory
he had introduced, had helped to throw his predecessors
into the shade. Cicero had done more[3] than any other
Roman orator to make his own era supreme in eloquence,
to add[4] to the richness of his native tongue, and make it
the rival of Greek in expressiveness. Hence it was neither
trivial nor empty praise to describe Catulus as educated
according to the standards of Cicero's times.

From this point of view, Cicero's criticism of Crassus is
worthy of notice. In him[5] might first be discerned the
maturity and almost perfection of Latin
oratory. The added touch of perfection
could be given only by one who was possessed
of a more extensive culture, and[6] was better equipped in
History, Law, and Philosophy. In the circumstances,
Brutus draws[7] the natural inference that such a one has
now appeared in the person of Cicero himself, while to the
mind of Atticus the very perfection of Cicero's oratory
makes his praise[8] of the early Roman orators with all their
crudity seem the merest irony. But Cicero himself was
never slow to manifest his pride in his own achievements.
In the *Orator*, into which he claims[9] to have put what-

*Cicero in re-
lation to
Crassus*

---

[1] Cf. Br. 123.   [2] Cf. Or. 108.

[3] Cf. Caesar's tribute Br. 253–254; *vide supra*, p. 149.

[4] *Vide infra*, p. 203 *et seq.*

[5] Br. 161.

[6] So Cicero would have us conclude that the ideal of culture described
by Crassus in the " De Oratore " was not reached by Crassus himself; cf.
De Or. I. 77, II. 1.

[7] Br. 162.

[8] *Ib.* 293 *et seq.*; *vide infra*, p. 264.

[9] Ad Fam. VI. 18. 4, *ib.* XV. 20. 1.

ever critical powers he possessed, we see how constantly his own achievements were before his mind, and how frequently he recurs to his speeches for illustrations. Holding, as he did, that the perfect orator should be master of all three styles, he is able to point[1] to his *Pro Caecina*, *Pro Lege Manilia*, and *Pro Rabirio*, as exemplifying, if not in perfection, at least in adumbration, the diversity of style which should distinguish every great orator. Against his predecessors[2] who failed in variety, and showed mastery over only a single style, he can set the diverse tones[3] of his own " multiplex et in omnia genera fusa oratio." The orator's greatest power lay in his capacity to stir the emotions, and Cicero again recurs[4] to his speeches as proofs of his skill in wielding so potent a weapon. There is no kind of impassioned appeal that he did not essay, and nothing in the whole gamut of emotion that cannot be exemplified from his orations. He has recourse to them, moreover, to illustrate certain aspects of style,[5] such as the rhythmical effect of the Gorgianic figures, or the appropriate use[6] of an elaborate rhythmical period in forensic oratory, where it had to be employed with artistic restraint, if it were to avoid creating a prejudice against an orator's pleading. In passages where an advocate is pressing home his proofs, or refuting the arguments of the opposing counsel, the use of shorter clauses (membra et incisa) is more effective, but even in these shorter clauses rhythm is not neglected, as Cicero shows[7] by examples from his speech in defence of Scaurus.

It is clear, then, that Cicero was conscious of great

---

[1] Or. 102 *et seq.*

[2] Crassus and Antonius, however, were near to his ideal ; cf. Or. 106.

[3] Or. 108 : " eaque (i.e., Cicero's oratorical writings) hanc ipsam habent quam probo varietatem."

[4] *Ib.* 129 *et seq. ;* cf. Br. 190.

[5] Or. 165, where he appeals to the Pro Milone ; *ib.* 167 ; cf. in Verrem, IV. 115.

[6] Or. 210, where the Verrines are again quoted ; cf. *ib.* 232, where the Pro Cornelio is adduced to illustrate the rhythmical effect of a particular clausula.

[7] Or. 223, *ib.* 225, where the Pro Cornelio is invoked ; cf. 222–223, for Crassus' use of " membra " and " incisa " ; *vide supra*, p. 104.

achievements, so that he would naturally be inclined to emphasise them in face of the disparaging criticisms of his Atticist opponents. He felt that he had brought Roman oratory to a height never reached by his predecessors, and that he had moulded Latin prose into an instrument of artistic expression. He may then be pardoned, if at times he sets up what he himself had accomplished as a standard in judging others.

Brutus makes a reasonable demand[1] when he asks Cicero to trace the steps by which he had reached his present pre-eminence as an orator. The answer is given later,[2] when Cicero proceeds to set forth at length the various stages of his training, and to tell of his endeavours to overcome certain constitutional defects which hampered his earliest efforts in oratory. It is a story of laborious days and unremitting toil, invaluable for its autobiographical details, and it has not unjustly been described[3] as the most perfect attempt at self-analysis in Latin literature previous to St. Augustine. It is valuable, too, as showing how essentially Hellenic was Cicero's training. He came, it is true, under the influence of some of the great orators of Rome in his early days, but of men who themselves for the most part were nurtured in the Hellenic tradition. He studied, of course, Roman History and Roman Law, and could act[4] as a champion of the old Roman poets, but his culture and training were fundamentally Hellenic. There was a time when he seemed likely to come under the influence of the " Latini Rhetores," who were endeavouring to give a national bias to rhetorical studies in Rome, but he was diverted[5] into other paths by some Philhellenist friends. He is willing[6] to acknowledge his debt to Greece, but occasionally, as we shall see, conscious of what he has accomplished for Latin letters, he shows a tendency to disparage the achievements of the Greeks.

The story of Cicero's training

[1] Br. 232.
[2] *Ib.* 305 *et seq.* ; *vide supra*, p. 153.
[3] *Vide* Schanz, op. cit., I. 2. p. 306 ; cf. Norden, A.K. I. p. 221.
[4] De Fin. I. 4.   [5] *Vide supra*, p. 152.
[6] Ad Q. Fr. I. 1. 28, De Fin. II. 68, Tusc. Disp. II. 27 ; *vide infra*, p. 203.

Another value attaching to Cicero's account of his training, and of the difficulties which he had to contend with, is
Value of his self-revela-tion the introduction of the personal note. He
gives us a glimpse, as it were, into his work-
shop, though we could wish for more than
a glimpse. On the other hand, in his criticisms of other
orators we miss the personal element, and feel that he is
rarely in touch with the individual. Most of the orators
who appear in the pages of the *Brutus*, seem mere dummy
figures, who are subjected to a perfunctory criticism from
which the individuality of the orator never emerges. Though
Cicero was not insensible[1] to the element of individuality,
and its effect in producing diversity of style, and though
he had many opportunities of giving prominence to individual character, yet such occasions for tracing the
relation between the man and the orator are rarely seized.
Excuse is sometimes made for such a shortcoming on the
ground that in Rome the Individual was wholly over-
shadowed by the State, and aroused little interest, but the
' Memoirs' of such men as Catulus, Scaurus, and Rutilius,
show that the Individual had begun to count, while the last
century of the Republic witnessed a riot of individualism
that finally issued in the disasters of the Civil Wars. Considering the plan of Cicero's work, we could not expect him
in every case to recreate the individual for us with the
laboured analysis of a Sainte-Beuve, but in a genre such as
oratory, and particularly as regards the orators whom he
himself had known, we could in fairness demand from him
a more complete revelation of their personalities than he
has given us.

He does not, of course, wholly fail us here, and especially
as regards the group of orators who figure as speakers in
Personal ele-ments in his criticism the *De Oratore*, we feel that we are brought
into touch with the living men. Though
Cicero was a mere stripling in the later years
of the older men of this group, yet he came into close contact with most, if not all of them, and, though the most

---

[1] Cf. De Or. III. 34 : " ut, quot oratores, totidem paene reperiantur
genera dicendi;" Br. 204, Or. 52 ; Haenni, Die litterarische Kritik in
Ciceros " Brutus," p. 42 *et seq.*

prominent amongst them left little[1] or no written remains, yet the tradition of the achievements of such men as Crassus and Antonius must[2] have always been steadily maintained at Rome. His criticism of Antonius in the *Brutus* is done on regulation lines, but even in this case, and still more in that of Crassus, our interest in the man is awakened. He fails, it is true, to give a complete portrait of these two men, the greatest orators that Rome had so far produced, but from the rôles which he assigns them in the *De Oratore*, and from his many references to them in others of his works, their ideals and personalities stand defined with comparative clearness.

Antonius was in many respects a child of nature, or certainly wished to appear so. In comparison with Crassus he was careless in his choice of diction, and though he **Antonius** was well acquainted[3] with Greek literature and philosophy, and interested in the theory of Rhetoric,[4] he, partly from a desire to pander to Roman popular prejudice, wished to avoid the appearance of such erudition. We have already seen the elements of Antonius' strength and weakness. His genius was best suited to forensic pleading, though his knowledge of Law was imperfect, but his capacity for emotional appeal, and his forceful delivery, compensated for this deficiency. These qualities were never better displayed than in his defence[5] of Aquilius, when, to excite pity, he tore open his client's tunic, and exhibited the wounds he had received in his country's service during the Servile War. Again, his successful defence of Norbanus[6] showed his ability for overcoming the inherent weakness of his case by masterly pleading. On occasions,[7] also, he proved that he was not devoid of biting wit

---

[1] De Or. II. 8, Or. 132, Pro Cluentio, 140.

[2] Cf., however, De Or. II. 7.

[3] De Or. I. 82, II. 3, *ib.* 59 *et seq.*, 156.

[4] *Vide supra*, p. 151.

[5] De Or. II. 124, 194, In Verrem, V. 3; Livy, Ep. 70; cf. Tusc. Disp V. 55 : " M. Antonii omnium eloquentissimi, quos ego audierim."

[6] De Or. II. 107, 167, 197 *et seq.*, De Off. II. 50; cf. Br. 304, Tus Disp. II. 57, for his speech in his own defence, when arraigned under th Lex Varia ; cf. Meyer, Or. Rom. p. 145.

[7] De Or. II. 265, 274.

Cicero seems to have been especially attracted to Crassus. He made him the mouthpiece of his own views in the *De Oratore*, and his many references to him help us to realise the extraordinary versatility of that orator. When quite a young man, he earned a reputation for eloquence by his prosecution[1] of C. Carbo. He was deeply versed in Greek literature, though he affected[2] to despise it, and set the wisdom of his own countrymen above that of the Greeks. His suppression of the school of " Latini Rhetores," apart from political considerations, would suggest that he cherished ideals[3] similar to those of Cicero himself, and wished to effect as complete a fusion as possible of Greek and Roman culture. He aimed at rendering[4] Latin a polished and flexible medium of expression, and one that could discuss intellectual problems as adequately as Greek. Through his efforts and those of Antonius, Roman eloquence, says Cicero, was first put on a level with that of the Greeks. In contrast with Antonius, Crassus, who seems to have studied Greek models with more profit, was noted[5] for his refined and well-chosen diction. He avoided obsolete expressions, and, though his style was ornate,[6] it was free from studied affectation and meretricious ornament. Cicero appropriately assigns to him the task of dealing with Style in the *De Oratore*. It may have been from his study of the Greeks that Crassus learnt restraint[7] in his delivery. He was remarkable[8] not only for his caustic wit and his power of invective, but also for his gift of humour, that was all the more effective because it was accompanied by a grave and even stern appearance.

[1] De Or. I. 40, 121, II. 170, III. 74, Br. 159, De Off. II. 47, In Verrem, II, 3, Ad Fam. IX. 21. 3.
[2] De Or. II. 4.
[3] *Ib.* III. 95 ; at any rate, we may assume that Crassus would be in sympathy with the main outlines of the programme attributed to him in the De Oratore," though not fully realised in his own person ; *vide supra*, p. 176.
[4] Cf. Br. 138, 161, 296 ; Tac. Dial. 26 : " Crassi maturitatem."
[5] De Or. III. 171, Br. 143, 215.
[6] Cf. De Or. III. 96 *et seq.*, for his ideal
[7] *Ib.* III. 33, Br. 158 ; cf., however, De Or. III. 220 ; *ib.* 31, on Sulpicius, who took Crassus as his model.
[8] *Ib.* I. 27, II. 220, 222 *et seq.*, 240, 242, 259, 267, 289, De Off. I. 133

His wit was seen to advantage in his speech supporting the
Lex Servilia, when its deadliest shafts were directed against
the tribune Memmius, while his faculty for invective was
revealed especially in his speech[1] against the Consul
Philippus, delivered shortly before his death. His delicate
play of humour[2] was employed with striking effect in the
" causa Curiana " against his opponent Mucius Scaevola,
who exhibited much of the pedantic accuracy, narrowness,
and over-seriousness of the Stoic school. Crassus was unrivalled in altercation, a faculty that won for him much
applause when he was defending[3] himself from the charges[4]
of luxury brought against him by Domitius Ahenobarbus,
his colleague in the Censorship. It is clear,[5] moreover,
that Cicero regarded Crassus as master of every emotion,
as one that could mingle grave and gay, and alter at will
the tone and colour of his speech. He vividly depicts[6] for
us the hushed expectancy that prevailed amongst the audience, when Crassus was about to speak. Unlike Antonius,
he was successful both in forensic and deliberative oratory.
When still young, and probably influenced[7] by the political
ideals of C. Gracchus, he won admiration for his speech in
favour of founding a colony at Narbo, though the Senate
was opposed to the scheme. A speech[8] of his later years
in support of the Lex Servilia was considered by Cicero as
a model to be studied, and above all as evidence that in
Crassus, Latin oratorical prose had reached its maturity.
He quotes[9] from the speech an example of natural rhythm
that follows on antithetical arrangement of clauses, while

[1] De Or. III. 2 et seq.
[2] It is interesting to note that Crassus refrained from caustic wit and
invective against a man of Scaevola's character ; cf. De Or. II. 221.
[3] Ib. II. 45, 227 et seq., Br. 162, 164.
[4] Cf. Pliny, N.H. XVII. 1. 2 et seq. ; Val. Max. IX. 1. 4 ; Suet. Nero
2, for some details of the case.
[5] De Or. III. 4 et seq.
[6] Br. 158.
[7] Vide Leo, Gesch der röm. Lit. p. 310.
[8] De Or. I. 225, Br. 161, 164, ib. 296, where Atticus declares that Cicero's
praise of the speech is ironical ; cf. De Or. II. 223, Pro Cluentio, 140,
Q. VI. 3. 44, for the difference in Crassus' standpoint in the two speeches
just mentioned.
[9] Or. 219 ; cf. Q's criticism, IX. 4. 109.

he reproduces[1] an interesting passage from his speech against Carbo that illustrates the figures of antithesis and homoeoteleuton. Norden[2] considers Crassus to have been an Asianist. There are certain considerations that lend colour to this view, amongst them being the fact that he was a pupil of Coelius Antipater.[3] Moreover, we are faced with the exaggeration and unrestraint of a passage[4] from his speech on the Servilian Law, with his striving[5] after the effects of the Gorgianic figures, and his general tendency[6] to use shorter clauses instead of elaborate periods, a practice that might easily degenerate into the mannerism of a Hegesias. However, this latter feature was in part due to the love of altercation, in which his greatest power lay. Though Crassus exhibits certain Asianist characteristics,[7] his literary remains are too scanty to enable us to decide if he was a thorough-going Asianist. Cicero's references to his regard for the purity of his Latin, the general refinement and elegance of his style, and the restraint of his delivery, would lead one to conclude that he never indulged in the worst excesses of Asianism.

In Antonius and Crassus, then, as they are portrayed for us by Cicero, we feel that we are in contact with two vibrant and original personalities. It is interesting to note that in his treatment of these two orators Cicero often has recourse to the method of σύγκρισις, so beloved[8] by ancient critics and biographers. It was under certain conditions a legitimate

The method of σύγκρισις

[1] De Or. II. 170; cf. ib. 220 et seq.; Q. VI. 3. 44, for his speech in defence of Cn. Plancius; Cima, op. cit., p. 158 et seq.; Meyer, Or. Rom. p. 148.

[2] A.K. I. p. 174.

[3] Vide infra, p. 514 et seq.

[4] De Or. I. 225; ib. 227, where Rutilius condemns the passage; cf. Blass, Die griechische Beredsamkeit, p. 120.

[5] De Or. II. 170.

[6] Ib. III. 190, Br. 162, Or. 223.

[7] The reference to him in Lucilius may contain a hint of Asianist leanings; vide supra, p. 46.

[8] Cf. Leo, Die griech-röm. Biographie, p. 149 et seq.; Butcher, Harvard Lectures, p. 258; Vaughan, English Literary Criticism, Introd. p. 49 et seq., on the use and abuse of the comparative method; Saintsbury, op. cit., Vol. I. p. 186, 434, Vol. III. p. 535.

device, and effective when properly used, and when an attempt was made to contrast, and by contrast to bring into greater relief, the salient characteristics of two men. In criticism, however, it was a device that was too often mechanically employed, and that resulted in a comparison or contrast of merely superficial qualities, or in an attempt to establish degrees of merit. Cicero is particularly fond[1] of coupling the names of Antonius and Crassus. He compares them from the standpoint of style, delivery, their attitude to Greek culture, and the general character of their pleading. He thus brings out many points of contrast between these two, though we feel that he might have made more effective use of the method in their case, especially in view of his manifest desire to treat them with greater thoroughness and sympathy than any of the other orators who figure in his pages. He employs[2] the method of σύγκρισις again in the case of Crassus and Scaevola. Though he had here an easier task, as the characters of the men and of their oratory stood at almost opposite poles, yet his comparison of them strikes one as too artificial and mechanical.

He is constantly contrasting[3] another pair of orators, Sulpicius and Cotta, to whom he assigned rôles in the *De Oratore*. Neither of them left[4] any literary

Cotta and Sulpicius

remains. They were very different in temperament, and significantly enough Sulpicius took Crassus as his chief model,[5] though he lacked the charm of his wit, while Cotta[6] aimed at imitating Antonius. Though Cicero could have little sympathy with the later political development[7] of Sulpicius, he pays[8] many

---

[1] De Or. I. 93, II. 4 *et seq.*, III. 32 *et seq.*, Br. 143–144, 207, 215, In Verrem, II. 2. 191.

[2] In dealing with the " causa Curiana "; *vide supra*, pp. 164, 174.

[3] De Or. I. 30, III. 31, Br. 201 *et seq.*

[4] Or. 132 ; cf. Br. 205 ; the speeches that went under the name of Sulpicius, were believed to have been written by P. Canutius.

[5] De Or. I. 97, II. 12, 89, III. 47, Br. 203.

[6] Cicero says that he never exhibited the forcefulness of Antonius ; there seems, in fact, little affinity between these two orators.

[7] De Har. Resp. 41, 43, De Or. III. 11 ; Vell. II. 18.

[8] De Or. I. 132, Br. 203, 306.

generous tributes to the eloquence of one who was richly
endowed by nature with the qualities that go to make a
great orator, a splendid presence, a clear rich voice, a
dignity and grace of gesture that seemed more fitted to the
stage than to the law-courts. Yet he notes[1] in him some
defects of pronunciation, something of the broad, rustic
accent affected by Aurelius Cotta. Sulpicius displayed,[2] too,
a certain contempt for that wide culture advocated by
Crassus as essential for the orator, and relied on his natural
ability for success both as a forensic and popular speaker.
He was a forcible character whose fiery nature found its
most adequate expression in a swift and vehement rush[3] of
highly emotional eloquence, so that Cicero regarded him
as the most impressive, and (so to speak) tragic orator he
had known. It was his ardent and impetuous temperament
that led, especially in his early years, to a certain exuberance and redundancy[4] in his oratory, qualities which
experience and assiduous practice in writing would naturally tone down. He first won his spurs by his prosecution[5]
of Norbanus, who was, however, successfully defended by
Antonius. In his later years, particularly in the course of
his tribunate, his fiery eloquence was often displayed in the
stormy arena of party politics.

Cotta was an orator of quite a different calibre. From
Cicero's characterisation of him, one might style him as

Cotta's plain style Atticist in pre-Atticist[6] days at Rome, which
makes Cicero's evident admiration for him
all the more remarkable. He took Antonius
as his model, and, as in the case of that orator, one of his
strongest points was Invention. He lacked,[7] however, the

[1] De Or. III. 46 ; possibly Sulpicius hoped by such a mannerism to be
more effective as a popular speaker.
[2] De Or. III. 147, Br. 214.
[3] Or. 106 : " nihil leniter Sulpicius."
[4] *Vide infra*, p. 225.
[5] De Or. II. 124, 197 *et seq.*, De Off. II. 49.
[6] In the " Brutus " (202), Cicero applies to him epithets that had become
the watchwords of the Atticists : " nihil erat in ejus oratione nisi sincerum,
nihil nisi siccum atque sanum ; " possibly Cicero wished to suggest in this
passage that the boasted qualities of the Atticists were nothing new in Rome ;
vide infra., pp. 219, 223.   [7] Br. 203.

vigour of Antonius' eloquence. His style was of the plainest,[1] his language correct and carefully chosen. Like the Stoic orators, he made no appeals to the emotions, and depended for success on the careful marshalling of his arguments, and the elimination of all that was irrelevant to his case. We may take it that his style of oratory was the result of deliberate choice, though it was in part conditioned by the weakness of his constitution, and in part by a bias towards philosophical studies which made him an adherent[2] of the New Academy. Cicero, who pleaded with Cotta on the latter's return from exile, shows his admiration for him throughout his rhetorical treatises, though he is probably exaggerating, when he declares[3] that he was once tempted to take him as his model, were it not that the glamour of Hortensius turned him into other paths. Like Antonius and Sulpicius, Cotta left no written speeches. The speech[4] which he delivered, when tried under the Lex Varia, was written for him by Aelius Stilo. Cicero wonders that so accomplished an orator as Cotta should claim as his own other trivial speeches composed by the same author. Thus in Sulpicius and Cotta we have two interesting personalities, and two important figures in the history of Roman oratory, whose characteristics Cicero has helped us to realise the better by the strong contrast of divergent temperaments.

Cicero treats with evident sympathy the remaining speakers of the *De Oratore*, Catulus and his half-brother Gaius Julius Caesar Strabo, but, as I have dealt[5] with these in another context, they need not detain us here. It is clear that in Cicero's criticism of all the orators just mentioned, we can detect something of the personal note something that distinguishes them from the many others

Remaining speakers in the " De Oratore "

---

[1] De Or. II. 98 : " acutissimum et subtilissimum dicendi genus " ; *ib* III. 31, Or. 106 : " nihil amplius Cotta " ; *vide supra*, p. 165, on his par in the defence of Rutilius.

[2] De Or. III. 145 ; he defends his point of view in the " De Natur Deorum."

[3] Br. 317.

[4] *Ib.* 205–206.

[5] *Vide supra*, pp. 62–63.

who flit across his pages, and are dealt with in a brief perfunctory notice. He lets us see how their characters and ideals reacted upon their oratory.

On some other occasions, too, he treats us to personal touches, as when he describes[1] the mannerisms and affectations of the demagogues, while he introduces us[2] to a particularly interesting personality in Curio, who, though deficient in all other departments of oratory, yet stood high amongst the orators of his day by reason of his fluency, and his choice and impressive diction. Curio, in fact, seems to have neglected of set purpose the study of Law and History, and to have despised the training and education that went to the making of the perfect orator. His memory[3] was so defective that, even in the Dialogue which he wrote attacking[4] Julius Caesar, he was guilty of serious anachronisms, while his delivery[5] was so uncouth and lacking in grace as to excite the laughter of his audience. He is an interesting example of an orator in whom high literary qualities compensated for very serious defects.

Other personal touches

Again, in Cicero's treatment of Servius Sulpicius we can perceive[6] something of the personal note. He was a fellow-student[7] of Cicero's in his youth, but preferred to win eminence as a lawyer rather than as an orator, though he was gifted with an elegant style, and was one of the most cultured men of his time. His fame as a lawyer was due to the fact that he

Servius Sulpicius

---

[1] Br. 224–225, 233.

[2] Br. 210–220, 234; cf. De Or. II. 98, Br. 122, on his father who was also an orator.

[3] Br. 217 *et seq.*, Or. 129.

[4] Cf. Suet. J. Caes. 9, 49, 50, 52, for his hostility to Caesar; his son, the " venali Curio lingua " (Lucan, I. 269), was an ardent Caesarian.

[5] Br. 216; cf. Pliny, N.H. VII. 55, for the nickname " Burbuleius " given to him; Val. Max. IX. 14. 5; Westermann, Gesch. der Beredtsamkeit, II. p. 104 *et seq.*

[6] Br. 150 *et seq.*; cf. Q. X. 1. 116, *ib.* 7. 30, XII. 10. 11 : " acumen Sulpicii," in reference probably to his ability as a lawyer.

[7] Cicero's admiration for him is evident from Phil. IX, De Off. II. 65; cf. Ad Fam. IV. 1–6; S's letter to Cicero on the death of his daughter Tullia, is well known.

had studied Law on scientific[1] lines, and, by his application
to it of the principles of Stoic Dialectic, had clarified and
systematised it. With Cicero the critic, whose admiration
for Sulpicius is so manifest, it is interesting to compare
Cicero the advocate, who, when defending Murena against
Sulpicius, disparages[2] the subtleties of the lawyer, and contrasts him unfavourably with the soldier and man of action.

We find some personal touches, also, in Cicero's brief
sketch[3] of another fellow-student,[4] M. Piso, whom he con-

M. Piso sidered to have been more deeply imbued
with Greek learning than any Roman who
had gone before him. He was a profound[5] student of
Philosophy, and was selected by Cicero to defend in the
closing book of the *De Finibus* the ethical system of Antiochus, who was endeavouring to reconcile the doctrines of
opposing schools. Piso was endowed with a keen critical
faculty and a caustic wit, but his hasty temper, and probably, too, his great devotion to philosophical studies made
him incapable of tolerating for long the ineptitude that
often characterised the law-courts, and the drudgery[6] entailed by them. He does not seem to have been endowed
with much natural talent for oratory, but in any case his
scholar's temperament led him into other paths of study,
and hindered the development of such talent as he possessed.

With the orators I have mentioned Cicero had come into
close personal contact, whether as friends of his youth who
had helped to guide and inspire his studies, or as com-
panions in the various stages of his own training, or as contemporaries and sometimes rivals in his forensic and political
career. He did most of them the honour of introducing

1 Cf. De Or. I. 190, where such an ideal is foreshadowed.
2 Pro Mur. especially 19–30 ; cf. Q. XI. 1. 69.
3 Br. 236.
4 Br. 240, 310, De Fin. V. 1 *et seq.* ; he is said by Asconius to have given
Cicero instruction in oratory in his youth ; cf. Marx, Ad Herennium, Introd.
pp. 79–80.
5 Cf. De Or. I. 104, for his association with the Peripatetic Staseas ;
De Fin. V. 8, *ib.* 75.
6 Cic. Ad Att. I. 13. 3, passes rather an unfavourable judgment on him
owing to his inactivity, when consul, in the case of Clodius ; cf. *ib.* I. 14, 16.

them as speakers in one or other of his Dialogues. That circumstance alone required an intimate knowledge of their personalities and ideas, and rendered easier his task of appraising their oratory in the *Brutus*, though he does not always use to the full the opportunity thus afforded of revealing the relation between the man and the orator. There are other orators such as Hortensius, Calvus, and Calidius, who receive more than a perfunctory treatment, but these can best be dealt with in connection with Cicero's polemic against the Atticists.

One could wish that Cicero, in support of his criticisms, had made a more extensive appeal to individual speeches

Individual speeches than he does, though the plan he adopts in the *Brutus* practically precludes such an appeal. There were evidently many speeches that stood out conspicuously from the common crowd, though their merit often lay in the political circumstances in which they were delivered, rather than in any literary distinction. Cicero had studied[1] Cato's speeches, though they were neglected in his day. The main lines at least of the speech of Q. Metellus against Tib. Gracchus were reproduced[2] in Fannius' History. Galba was an orator who had studied Greek models with profit, and was endowed with emotional qualities in a marked degree, but his written speeches seemed[3] to be notably archaic in style and to lack body, as compared with his spoken utterances. He, like Hortensius in later days, was an orator that spoke[4] better than he wrote, and relied for success on his passionate delivery, and the emotional appeal of the moment. Cicero[5] had before him, too, the speeches of Gaius Carbo and Tib. Gracchus, both of them orators of great distinction according to the testimony of their own generation, but their speeches, though marked by acumen, showed no brilliancy of diction, and hardly corresponded with the high reputation which these two orators enjoyed. A passing reference is

[1] Br. 65.
[2] *Ib.* 81.
[3] *Ib.* 82.
[4] *Ib.* 91–94.
[5] *Ib.* 104.

made[1] to speeches delivered against each other by two bitter opponents, C. Gracchus and Aelius Tubero. The speech of Curio[2] in defence of Servius Fulvius, when charged with incest, was considered of surpassing merit in Cicero's boyhood, but was cast into the shade by the achievements of later orators. The peroration of a speech by C. Galba in his own defence against a charge of complicity in the Jugurthine conspiracy, enjoyed[3] such a reputation, when Cicero was young, that it was customary to learn it by heart. The speeches of C. Fimbria were also studied[4] by Cicero as a boy, but fell into almost complete oblivion. A few at least of Crassus' speeches were preserved[5] entire, while others survived in part only, but they are referred to in the most general terms by Cicero, at times to cast light on his political opinions, or again to illustrate the charm of his wit, or his cleverness in altercation. Cicero on occasion quotes from his speeches to exemplify the efficacy of a particular line of argument, or some point in the theory of style, but he makes no attempt to appraise an individual speech and give a detailed criticism of it. Though he describes[6] Curio's speeches as "languidiores," he considers them worthy of attention if only for their literary qualities. He shows[7] critical acumen in an interesting judgment which he passes on a speech (" de sociis et nomine Latino ") delivered by Fannius against C. Gracchus. It was considered to have merits beyond the capacity of Fannius, and was said by some[8] to have been composed by Persius, by others to have been the fruit of collaboration on the part of a number of nobles. Cicero argues that if the speech were known to have been written by Persius, Gracchus would have taunted Fannius with accepting his aid. The second hypothesis he excludes by an appeal to internal evidence. A speech so uniform in tone and style

[1] Br. 117.
[2] *Ib.* 122.
[3] *Ib.* 127 ; cf. Sallust, Jug. 40, on popular feeling at the time.
[4] Br. 129.
[5] *Ib.* 160–161.
[6] Br. 220.
[7] *Ib.* 99–100.
[8] Probably adherents of Gracchus.

could not, in his view, have been the result of collaboration.

We come now to consider what is perhaps Cicero's most valuable contribution to Roman criticism, his use of the **The historical** historical method. Historical criticism is the **method** best corrective of dogmatic criticism, though Cicero did not always view it in that light, or avoid the pitfalls to which dogmatic criticism must inevitably lead. It is in the *Brutus* particularly that we find the historical method most fully applied, and it is this characteristic of the work, and not its gallery of miscellaneous orators, that makes it such an important document in Roman criticism. It was no small achievement on Cicero's part to take a single genre, and attempt to trace[1] its development in the different epochs from comparatively early times down to his own day. In this task he was considerably helped by the labours of Atticus, to whose *Liber Annalis* he often professes indebtedness.[2] It is evident,[3] too, that he made use of the historical work of Fannius.

He enunciates[4] the dictum, which at first sight seems a truism, but yet is a cardinal principle in historical criticism :

Principles of " nihil est enim simul et inventum et per-
historical fectum." It is the principle of slow develop-
criticism ment and progress in the Arts. Quintilian,
approaching the problem from a different angle, lays down[5] a similar principle, especially in his efforts to combat those who sought to exalt what they styled the natural oratory of primitive times, or those who tended to bar progress by a lifeless[6] imitation of their predecessors which would give us nothing higher than Livius Andronicus in poetry, and the *Annales Pontificum* in history. Nature in her choicest

---

[1] Cf. Br. 15, 20 ; " quando esse coepissent, qui etiam et quales fuissent " ; *ib.* 74 : " oratorum genera distinguere aetatibus."

[2] Br. 13 *et seq.*, 42, 44, 72, 74 ; cf. De Fin. II. 67, Ad Att. XII. 23. 2, XVI. 13b. 2 ; Atticus' strong point was the establishment of chronology ; cf. Or. 120 ; Nepos, Att. 18 ; Peter, Wahrheit und Kunst, pp. 312–314.

[3] Br. 82, 299 ; Brutus had made an epitome of this work ; cf. Ad Att. XII. 5. 3.

[4] Br. 71.

[5] Q. IX. 4. 5 : " quae porro ars statim fuit ? quid non cultu mitescit ? " ; *ib.* X. 2. 8.

[6] *Ib.* X. 2. 7, XII. 11. 27–28.

works prescribes a gradual[1] development, but she is always steady and deliberate in her onward march towards perfection. Under the guidance of this principle of Progress, Cicero traces[2] the development of Greek sculpture from the unnatural stiffness of Canachus to the almost complete perfection of Polyclitus. Similarly, the development of Painting is traced to its highest achievement in Apelles. It is clear[3] that the method of historical criticism had already been applied to the Arts. Greek oratory[4] may have been similarly treated. It was, moreover, a favourite practice[5] with ancient critics to draw analogies between the plastic arts and literature. All this would pave the way for the application of the historical method to Roman oratory. In the *Brutus* also, Cicero briefly touches[6] on the development of early Roman poetry, and, allowing for the age in which they lived, he pays appropriate tributes to the first poets of Rome. À propos of poetry, he draws from the principle quoted above the important deduction that poets existed before Homer. Evidently the perfection of the Homeric poems could in Cicero's view have been reached only after a long and painful period of striving. Turning to oratory, he gives[7] us a rapid and imperfect sketch of the origins and development of oratory amongst the Greeks, but he is careful to note the rise of artistic prose (polita atque facta quodam modo oratio),[8] and especially the achievement of Isocrates in attaining to periodic structure, and in applying the laws of rhythm to his own genre.

When Cicero turned to treat of Roman oratory, he was naturally tempted to make its history amongst his own

---

[1] Q. X. 3. 4, XII. 11. 25.

[2] Br. 70.

[3] Cf. Blass, op. cit., p. 226, on Pasiteles' History of Art; Pliny, N. H. XXXVI, 5 (4). (there quoted); *vide*, Gayley and Scott, op. cit., p. 196, on the application of the method to the Fine Arts by the Moderns.

[4] Cicero's sketch of it was probably drawn from some such study of the Greek orators.

[5] Dionys. De Isocr. 3; De Din. 7; Q. XII. 10. 3 *et seq.*; Brzoska, op. cit., p. 81 *et seq.*

[6] Br. 71 *et seq.*

[7] *Ib.* 26 *et seq.*; cf. De Or. II. 92 *et seq.*

[8] *Ib.* III. 184; *vide infra*, p. 249.

countrymen run on lines parallel to those of oratory
Development of Roman oratory amongst the Greeks. In this he was but following a tendency common amongst Roman
critics, who sought to equate as far as
possible the literatures of the two peoples. It was in such
cases that the comparative method ran the risk of being
seriously abused. In the primitive period of Roman
oratory the basis of comparison was almost entirely lacking,
and Cicero is compelled to eke out his criticisms on very
scanty material. The earliest Roman orators were wholly
ignorant[1] of the art of Rhetoric, which for Cicero meant
Greek Rhetoric. Having little material[2] at his disposal, he
is designedly vague in his references to their characteristics.
His position is more secure when he deals with Cato, whose
speeches he had studied, but for reasons of polemic against
the Atticists he purposely exalts him, and attributes[3] to
him all the virtues of the orator. It is not always easy to
apply the notion of Progress[4] to literature, but Cicero, who
had particularly in view the standard of Greek culture, the
requirements of Greek Rhetoric, and the perfection of
technique, is able to point to several landmarks in the
advance of Roman oratory. With Sulpicius Gallus,[5] who
was a profound student of Greek literature, a definite step
forward is recorded, and a richer and more brilliant style
of oratory becomes prevalent. An advance was also marked
in the person of Servius Galba,[6] who, according to Cicero,
was the first Roman to essay the appropriate functions of
the orator. He appealed to Cicero as an orator who, even
in that age, could employ with effect most of the resources
of the trained rhetorician. Progress is again evident in
the case[7] of Aemilius Lepidus, who reproduced in his oratory
something of the smoothness of the Greeks, and exhibited

[1] De Or. I. 14 : " totius rationis ignari " ; cf. Tusc. Disp. I. 5 ; Q. IX.
4. 4.
[2] *Vide supra*, p. 167.
[3] Br. 65.
[4] *Vide* Babbitt, Rousseau and Romanticism, p. 298 n. ; *vide infra*, p. 266.
[5] Br. 78.
[6] Br. 82 ; cf. *ib.* 295, 333, Tusc. Disp. I. 3 ; Poiret, L'Éloquence
judiciaire à Rome, pp. 245–246.
[7] Br. 96 ; *vide supra*, p. 175.

a certain artistry in his style. C. Gracchus,[1] both by reason of his training and his splendid natural ability, would have been one of the greatest of Roman orators, and an ornament to Latin literature, if he had lived long enough for his powers to attain their full development, but, as it was, his early promise remained unfulfilled, and his speeches lacked the final touch of perfection. Again, a most important landmark is noted when Cicero declares[2] that the maturity of Latin oratorical prose was reached in the person of Crassus, though something still remained to be added. It was a subtle and almost indefinable something, emanating from the culture[3] imparted by a more liberal education.

Cicero thus traces for us the various stages in the progress of Roman oratory. It is true that the stages are not always too clearly defined, nor is it always easy to see in what the progress consisted. An orator's culture, the range of his emotional power, his ability to give pleasure to his hearers by variety of tones, would all count with Cicero, while he naturally lays stress on the literary qualities of oratorical prose, and the strivings after greater finish and perfection of style.[4] As we have already seen, he often sets up his own achievements as a standard in judging others. His training in rhetorical theory, his acquaintance with Greek philosophy, the general range of his learning, the perfection of his style, and his mastery over every mood in oratory, all combined to raise him to an eminence[5] from which he could survey what had been accomplished by his predecessors. As far as artistic prose was concerned, Cicero probably conceived himself to be in a position analogous[6] to that of Isocrates amongst the Greeks. The early Roman

In what did progress consist ?

[1] Br. 125–126, 296, 333, Pro Fonteio, 39, De Har. Resp. 41 ; Vell II. 6 ; Plut., Tib. Gr. 2 ; there were some who preferred him to Cicero : cf. Gellius, X. 3 ; Norden, A.K. pp. 171–172.

[2] *Vide supra*, p. 176 ; cf. De Or. II. 121, where Crassus is credited with being the first to perform all the " officia oratoris."

[3] *Vide supra*, p. 150.

[4] It is interesting to note that he emphasises the power of employing periodic structure ; cf. Br. 96 (on Lepidus), *ib.* 162 (on Crassus).

[5] Br. 322 is especially important in this connection ; cf. Tac. Dial. c. 30

[6] *Vide infra*, p. 249.

orators did not know how[1] to employ periodic structure, and were ignorant[2] of the laws of prose-rhythm, the application of which to Latin prose Cicero claims to have treated more fully than any who had gone before him. Though he is inclined to make the perfection of his own oratory a criterion in appraising others, yet he never applies the criterion too rigidly. He was saved from the temptation by another principle of historical criticism which recognises that men are children of their age, and are generally subject to its limitations. Except in rare cases, they will rise no higher than the level of contemporary culture and contemporary taste.

The principle that men are the products of their age and environment is almost a commonplace of historical criticism. It is a principle that has been stoutly championed by many modern critics, though it must be accepted with certain reservations. One of its earliest applications is found in Eratosthenes,[3] who protested against the belief in Homer's omniscience and infallibility, and laid it down that the critic in studying him should remember that the poet's knowledge was circumscribed by the limitations of his time. In dealing with environment, it was customary[4] with the Ancients to relate literature to certain aspects of the national life, and to emphasise its dependence on moral, social, and political conditions. Eloquence in particular was supposed to respond to the rise and fall of the social[5] and political barometer. But in general, the decline of liberty, the increase of luxury, and the consequent decay of the robust virtues of an earlier age, were believed to lead to perverted standards of taste that rendered impossible the continuance of great literature. It is interesting to find Shelley maintaining[6] that "in periods of the decay of social life, the drama

The influence of environment

---

[1] De Or. III. 198 ; cf. *ib*. 39.
[2] Or. 169–170, *ib*. 185 ; cf. Q. IX. 4. 16 ; *vide infra*, p. 248.
[3] Cf. Bury, The Ancient Greek Historians, p. 189 ; Strabo, VIII. 3. 3 *et seq.* (Loeb. ed.) C. 337.
[4] Sen. Ep. 114. 1 *et seq., ib*. 9–12 ; Petr. Satyr. 2, 88 ; Pliny, Ep. VIII. 14. 2 ; Περὶ ὕψους, c. 44.
[5] Tac. Dial. c. 12.
[6] A Defence of Poetry ; cf. Vaughan, op. cit., pp. 176–177.

sympathises with that decay," and that " the corruption and extinction of the drama in a nation where it has once flourished, is a mark of a corruption of manners, and an extinction of the energies which sustain the soul of social life." Contemporary taste seems often fickle[1] and arbitrary, but it has its reactions upon literature, and may bring about changes almost imperceptible to the men of the time. National character, social and political conditions, not to mention other factors,[2] will all contribute to the formation of contemporary taste, but it is difficult to define the extent of their influence. In all this we are dealing with considerations which are often nebulous and intangible. It may be admitted that a relation " exists between literature and the general social condition of a nation," but, as Leslie Stephen remarks,[3] literature " occupies far too small a part in the whole activity of a nation, even of its intellectual activity, to serve as a complete indication of the many forces which are at work, or as an adequate moral barometer of the general moral state." Oratory in particular, it was said,[4] was designed to make a popular appeal, and tended to adapt itself to its environment and to the requirements of each succeeding age, and was thus conditioned by the standard of prevailing taste. As Cicero puts[5] it, " semper oratorum eloquentiae moderatrix fuit auditorum prudentia." In support of his statement he points[6] to the contrast

---

[1] Cf. Sen. Ep. 114. 13 : " oratio certam regulam non habet ; consuetudo illam civitatis, quae nunquam in eodem diu stetit, versat " ; cf. Tac. Ann. XIII. 3, on Seneca himself as " ingenium amoenum et temporis ejus auribus accomodatum."

[2] Cf. Q. II. 10. 3, on the connection between the rise of the schools of Declamation, and the decline of oratory ; here, of course, one has to go further back, and trace the connection between the rise of the Declaimers and the change in political conditions.

[3] English Literature and Society, pp. 21–22 ; cf. Hennequin, La Critique Scientifique, pp. 14–15, on Taine's theory of environment ; Saintsbury, op. cit., Vol. III. pp. 160, 441–442.

[4] Tusc. Disp. II. 3 ; Sen. Ep. 102. 16 ; Tac. Dial. c. 18 : " mutari cum temporibus formas quoque et genera dicendi " ; ib. c. 19. 2, 8 ; Q. XII. 10. 2, 10, 45 ; cf. Cic. De Or. II. 337, where, however, Cicero is thinking rather of the argumentative side of oratory ; vide infra, p. 341.

[5] Or. 24 ; cf. Part. Or. 15 ; vide supra, p. 123.

[6] Or. 25 et seq. ; vide infra, p. 210.

between the type of eloquence that prevailed amongst the Asiatic peoples, who lacked elegance and refinement, and the purity and sanity of the eloquence of the Athenians, who were always remarkable[1] for their sound critical judgment. Here, of course, the factor of national character[2] would also have to be considered in estimating the difference between the two types.

Now, in the case of the Roman orators generally, it is not easy to estimate what factors of environment Cicero

Factors of environment in Rome

considered to have exercised the most potent influence. Here one would have to take into account the many aspects of the orator's art. Cicero naturally regards[3] purity of speech as one of the great essentials for the orator. In other connections he sets[4] great value on the influence exercised by the environment of the family circle, and he regards[5] it, too, as a powerful factor in fostering purity of speech. An intellectual coterie like the Scipionic[6] circle would, even outside its own sphere, have had a profound influence in the same direction. We find, again, that the Roman orators proper,[7] responding to the intellectual milieu of the Capital, generally maintained the tradition of correct and elegant Latinity, though in this respect Cicero, under the influence of the now prevailing conception of " urbanitas," is probably inclined to idealise them. Of other effects of intellectual environment we have seen something already, when considering the influence of the various philosophical[8] schools upon oratory, an in-

---

[1] Aristophanes in another sphere pays many tributes to the keen critical sense of the Athenians; cf. Clouds, 521, Frogs, 809.

[2] Cf. Q. XII. 10. 17 *et seq.*; Cic. Pro Archia, 26, evidently has this factor in mind in his reference to the poets of Corduba; cf. Sen. Ep. 40. 11.

[3] Br. 254, 258; he emphasises this particularly in the " Brutus," at a time when the Purist movement was strong in Rome; *vide supra*, p. 172.

[4] De Off. I. 118, De Rep. I. 36, De Leg. I. 47, In Verrem, V. 30, Pro Lig. 20; for environment as a topic, cf. De Inv. II. 29.

[5] De Or. III. 45, 48, Br. 210, 213, 252, on the influence of " domestica consuetudo " on Caesar; Q. I. 1. 4, Tac. Dial. c. 28 *et seq.*, on the home training of the Gracchi; cf. Br. 104; Q. I. 1. 6; Plut. Tib. Gr. 8.

[6] Cf. Br. 258; *vide supra*, p. 34.

[7] *Vide infra*, p. 244.

[8] Cf. also Br. 37, on the influence of Theophrastus on Demetrius of Phalerum; Or. 12, 95; Q. XII. 1. 28; cf. Haenni, op. cit., p. 29 *et seq.*

fluence which left the deepest impression in the case of Stoicism, and issued in the plain, unemotional style of speaking that was characteristic of the adherents of that school. An enthusiasm for Greek philosophy and literature, but an enthusiasm that was tempered with sanity, was since the days of Scipio typical of the intellectual circles in Rome, which thus would have fostered the culture which Cicero regarded as so essential for the orator aiming at perfection.

Of the influence of political environment we get occasional glimpses in Cicero. He expressed the opinion[1] that oratory finds its fairest field in a well-estab-

Political environment lished, tranquil, and flourishing State. This opinion is especially interesting, seeing that Tacitus put forward[2] a different view, and held that oratory shows its greatest development amidst the burning passions of party conflicts. Cicero himself lived through the worst horrors of the Civil Wars, in which some[3] of the most distinguished of Roman orators had been sacrificed to the vengeance of their enemies, and he would be little likely to pay party strife[4] a tribute that would connect it with the development of his own favourite pursuit. In Rome eloquence had always been fostered[5] and encouraged, and had held a position of the highest honour.[6] We find in Cicero a foreshadowing[7] of the effect upon oratory likely to ensue, as the result of Caesar's growing domination. In later days under the Imperial regime, Tacitus can speak[8] of the pacification of eloquence as well as of all things else. Cicero clearly suggests[9] that it was political environment that pre-

[1] De Or. I. 14, 30, II. 33, Br. 45, Or. 141.

[2] Dial. c. 36–37 ; cf. c. 40–41, on some of the disadvantages of such conditions ; *vide infra*, p. 345.

[3] De Or. III. 1 *et seq.*, Br. 303–304, 307.

[4] Cf. Br. 324 : " perterritum armis hoc studium nostrum conticuit subito et obmutuit " ; *ib*. 6, 22, 332, De Off. II. 67.

[5] Tusc. Disp. I. 5.   [6] Or. 141.

[7] On the actual effect, cf. De Off. II. 2, III. 2.

[8] Dial. c. 38.

[9] Br. 45 : " nec in impeditis ac regum dominatione devinctis nasci cupiditas dicendi solet," words probably written with the growing menace of Caesar's power in view ; *ib*. 46, on the rise of oratory in Siciliy on the expulsion of the tyrants ; cf. Περὶ ὕψους, 44. 2, on democracy as the nursing mother of genius.

vented oratory from being intensively cultivated in certain of the Greek states outside Athens. Sparta in particular was noted[1] for its lack of orators, though here the result was due to more than the political factor. Oratory required the breath of freedom for its development, but even in Republican Rome itself, where encouragement for it always existed, individual political events might help to foster it still further, just as the establishment of the " quaestiones perpetuae "[2] provided a stimulus for forensic eloquence.

Some accounts must then be taken of the subtle and manifold influence of environment. It was not unnatural for Cicero to regard men as in the main conditioned by their age, and with such a principle in view to be indulgent to their shortcomings.

Application of the historical method

One must distinguish between the " inventa necessitatis "[3] and the " inventa voluptatis." Ancient orators who were content with the bare essentials, are to be honoured[4] for what they achieved, not condemned for what they lacked. It is interesting to note the contrast between Horace's rigid application of the standard of Augustan correctness in his judgments on the Ancients, and the wide sympathy that Cicero exhibits in dealing with the earlier orators, who were crude in comparison with the perfection of his own age. As we shall see, Cicero in the *Brutus*, for purposes of polemic against the Atticists, is inclined[5] to exalt unduly the oratory of Cato, though elsewhere[6] he is not so complimentary to him. For all that, even in the *Brutus*[7] he recognises his defects, his archaic colouring, his uncouth language at times, his crudeness in composition, his ignorance of the laws of

[1] Br. 50 ; Vell. I. 18 ; Tac. Dial. 40 ; cf. Philodemus, Rhet. II. 216.

[2] Br. 106 ; cf. Tac. Dial. 38–39, where the effect on oratory of the court procedure of his day is contrasted with Republican times.

[3] Cf. also Tac. Dial. c. 22. 16.

[4] Or. 169 : " nec ego id quod deest antiquitati flagito potius quam laudo quod est."

[5] Br. 61, 65 *et seq.*, 68 ; cf. De Rep. II. 1, Pro Archia, 16.

[6] Or. 152 : " orationes illae ipsae horridulae Catonis " ; cf. Q. XII. 10. 10 ; cf. De Or. II. 53, De Leg. I. 6, on Cato as historian ; Peter, Hist. Rom. Reliquiae, Vol. I. p. 127 *et seq.*, *ib.* frs. p. 55 *et seq.*

[7] Br. 68 ; cf. Gellius, VII. 3. 53 (on a passage from Cato) : " eaque omnia distinctius, numerosiusque ac comptius fortasse dici potuerint."

prose-rhythm. These shortcomings, however, he attributes[1]
to the age rather than to the man. Cato is said[2] by Cicero
to have lacked the " politissima doctrina transmarina,"
though for all his anti-Hellenism[3] he was not wholly deficient in Greek culture. We know nothing of his treatise[4]
upon Rhetoric addressed to his son, beyond two well-
known dicta, but it is probable that Cato, before he set
himself to the task, made himself acquainted with Greek
rhetorical theory. His speeches at any rate, though lacking
in finish, show that he could make effective use of many of
the rhetorical devices[5] common in Greek oratory. Still,
several generations had to elapse before perfection could be
attained.

In many other passages,[6] Cicero brings into prominence
the notion that the orator is the product of his age and
environment, and must be judged by its standards. Men
as a rule do not advance beyond the level[7] of contemporary
taste. Atticus is prepared to approve of Cicero's commendation of Lepidus' speeches, provided he praises[8] them as
products of antiquity. If Thucydides, Cicero declares,[9]
had lived in a later age, his style would have been more
mellow and mature.

The theory, however, must be applied with certain
reservations. " No man of genius is the creature of his

---

[1] Br. 68 : " ita enim tum loquebantur " ; *ib.* 294 : " orationes autem
ejus ut illis temporibus valde laudo " (Atticus) ; *ib.* 298, De Or. I. 171.

[2] *Vide supra*, p. 175.

[3] *Vide supra*, p. 30 *et seq.*

[4] Sen. Controv. I. pr. 9 ; Pliny, Ep. IV. 7. 5 ; Q. III. 1. 19, XII. 1. 1.

[5] Cf. Br. 69, on his use of Figures ; Gellius, VII. 3. 52 : " in tota ista
Catonis oratione omnia disciplinarum rhetoricarum arma et subsidia mota
esse " ; Norden, A.K. I. p. 166 *et seq. ;* Leo, Gesch. der röm. Lit., p. 283
et seq.

[6] Br. 96 : " Pompeius non contemptus orator temporibus illis " (a
common formula) ; *ib.* 102 (on Caelius Antipater), *ib.* 173.

[7] Br. 124 : " loci sane inanes (i.e., the topics in Curio's speeches), verum-
tamen nondum tritis nostrorum hominum auribus, nec erudita civitate
tolerabiles " ; *ib.* 333, on the eloquence of the Gracchi ; *ib.* 104 ; cf.
De Fin. I. 7 (on the age of Lucilius) : " neque tam docti tum erant ad
quorum judicium elaboraret " ; cf. De Rep. II. 18.

[8] Br. 295 : " modo ita laudes ut antiquas."

[9] *Ib.* 288 ; cf. Horace on Lucilius, Sat. I. 10. 67.

time or his surroundings."[1] The man of genius will rise
Reservations in applying it above the petty conventions and perverted tastes of his contemporaries ; he will fashion anew traditional material, and, gifted as he is with a rarer vision, will be the pioneer in leading others into strange and hitherto uncharted regions. Cicero says[2] of Herodotus and Thucydides that, though they coincided with the age of the Sophists, " longissime tamen ipsi a talibus deliciis vel potius ineptiis afuerunt." Gellius passes[3] an encomium on Cato for endeavouring to surpass the standard of eloquence prevailing amongst his contemporaries, while he pays[4] a tribute to a passage from a speech of C. Gracchus as showing a finer and more harmonious composition than was customary in his day. But as a rule ancient critics, dominated by rule and convention, gave little consideration to the play of individual genius in our sense of the word. When they spoke[5] of a style being a mirror of the man or of his life, they had chiefly in view a man's moral character. They took little account of the intellectual element, or of the subtle and elusive activities of genius. Hence in literature they were inclined to ignore the reactions of a strong individuality against the shackles of contemporary standards.

Ancient critics took account not only of the gradual development of a genre, but also of its decline. As we
The decline of genres have seen, various reasons were advanced to explain the decay of great literature, and these in a measure could be brought forward to account for the decline of a particular genre. We sometimes meet with the conception[6] of recurring cycles, originally applied as a cosmical theory, according to which

---

[1] *Vide* Vaughan, op. cit., p. 92.

[2] Or. 39 ; this is not altogether true of Thucydides, who shows traces of the influence of Sophistic Rhetoric ; *vide infra*, p. 492.

[3] X. 3. 16.

[4] XI. 13. 2.

[5] Cf. Cic. Tusc. Disp. V. 47 ; Sen. Ep. 75. 4 : " concordet sermo cum vita " ; *ib*. 115. 2 ; *vide supra*, p. 124.

[6] The idea was used by Virgil in the Fourth Eclogue ; cf. Bury, op. cit., pp. 205–206 ; Dionys. Hal. on Ancient Orators (there quoted) ; Saintsbury, op. cit., Vol. III. p. 156, on Vico's theory of cyclical progression.

' the world's great age began anew " after a period of exhaustion, but capable, too, of being applied to the history
of literary genres with their birth, decay, and revival.   At
other times we meet with the idea of the simple and natural
decline of a genre.   It was considered[1] an inexorable law of
nature that things from a humble beginning reached the
highest point of perfection only to pass therefrom into
senility and decay.   When Attic oratory had reached the
summit of its greatest glory in Demosthenes and his contemporaries, a deterioration set in, which was especially
noticeable in Demetrius of Phalerum.[2]   Cicero, who was
concerned with the rise of Roman oratory, till it came to
full maturity in his own age and person, would naturally not
be seriously preoccupied with its decline, but still he can
envisage[3] the possibility of its decay, and even its complete
extinction.

Cicero's endeavour to trace, however imperfectly, the
history of a single genre,[4] and his extensive application of
The value of   the historical method, were no small achieve-
Cicero's con-   ment for a Roman critic at the time.   We
tribution   have come to look upon the historical method
as almost a necessary part of the equipment of every critic,
but its rise to importance is a comparatively recent phenomenon.   Dryden was the first English critic[5] to make a
systematic use of it.   In appraising Chaucer, he recognised[6]
that " he lived in the infancy of our poetry, and that nothing[7] is brought to perfection at first."   His succeeding
remark on the development of Roman poetry from Ennius,
Lucilius, and Lucretius, to Virgil and Horace, would sug-

[1] Sallust, Jug. 2 ; Sen. Controv. I. pr. 7 ; Vell. II. 11 ; cf. Thucyd.
II. 64 : πάντα γὰρ πέφυκε καὶ ἐλλασσοῦσθαι ; *vide infra*, pp. 269, 401.
[2] *Vide infra*, p. 209.
[3] Tusc. Disp. II. 5.
[4] Cf. Vaughan, op. cit., Introd. p. 54, on Daniel's " Defence of Ryme " :
" perhaps the first instance, in which English criticism can be said to have
attempted tracing a literary form through the various stages of its growth " ;
cf. Gayley and Scott, op. cit., c. 5 ; Saintsbury, op. cit., Vol. III. p. 294, on
Hallam.
[5] Vaughan, op. cit., introd. p. 80, text p. 78 *et seq.*
[6] Preface to the Fables.
[7] *Vide supra*, p. 191, on Cicero's dictum.

gest that Dryden was indebted to some Roman source for his application of the method. It is probable that both Tacitus and Quintilian learned the use of the historical method from Cicero. We shall see[1] in another chapter how important a true historical perspective was in the quarrel of the Ancients versus the Moderns, and how it conduced to a sane attitude in the dispute. Though Cicero deserves credit for employing the historical method so extensively, yet we cannot but recognise his shortcomings in the use of it. The divisions of the various epochs of Roman oratory seem often arbitrary and ill-defined, while he does little to set forth their distinguishing characteristics. It is the rise of some prominent orator that often serves to mark for Cicero the dividing line between the different periods. He reveals, as we have seen, certain advances in the development of oratory amongst his countrymen, but he is not always explicit or precise in declaring what it was that constituted their progress at the different stages to which he refers.

Another achievement for which Cicero deserves credit, was his enrichment of the critical vocabulary of Latin. On many occasions the reproach of poverty was levelled[2] at the Latin language, and in this respect it was contrasted unfavourably with Greek. Cicero did more than any other Roman to rescue it from that reproach, and to make Latin a copious language, capable[3] of dealing with any scientific subject. Caesar himself paid[4] a glowing tribute to him for his enrichment of his native tongue. Cicero was indeed conscious of his achievements in that sphere, and was fully alive[5] to the wealth of language at his command. He was so conscious[6] of having

Cicero's enrichment of Latin

---

[1] *Vide infra*, pp. 292, 307.

[2] Pro Caecina, 51, De Fin. III. 51 ; Lucr. I. 139, 832, III. 260 ; Sen. Ep. 58. 1 ; Pliny, Ep. IV. 18 ; Q. III. 6. 97 ; Gellius, II. 26. 5, *ib.* 7.

[3] Cf. De Or. III. 95.

[4] Br. 254, where Cicero is styled " princeps atque inventor copiae ; " *ib.* 255 ; cf. De Fin. V. 96 ; Sen. Suas. VI. 26 ; Goelzer, La Latinité de S. Jérome, Introd. p. 16 *et seq. ; vide supra*, p. 176 *et seq.*

[5] Ad Fam. IV. 4. 1, Ad Att. XII. 52. 3 : " verba tantum adfero quibus abundo."   [6] Cf. Phil. II. 20.

helped to make Latin prose a pliant and copious medium of expression, that he represents[1] it as not only equalling, but surpassing Greek in its resources and expressiveness. With a touch of national vanity, he declares[2] that if the Romans have hitherto failed to equal the Greeks, it is because they did not wish to do so. He felt[3] that the task of naturalising Greek philosophy at Rome had not been adequately accomplished before his day, even though Lucretius in his own sphere had struggled valiantly to overcome the difficulties caused by the " patrii sermonis egestas." In attempting such a task, Cicero had to contend against the strong prejudices[4] of his countrymen who regarded philosophical studies as impractical for a serious-minded Roman. He had to struggle against the indifference, if not the opposition, of the ultra-Hellenists,[5] as well as discouragement from those who despaired[6] of such subjects being adequately treated in Latin. Difficulties, too, would have arisen from the Purists, but, in spite of all obstacles, he persevered manfully with his task of creating a philosophical terminology[7] in Latin, of teaching[8] philosophy to speak Latin, as he himself phrases it, and of opening up to his countrymen the rich and varied treasures of Greek speculation.

Cicero must have done much, also, to extend the critical vocabulary of the Romans. He shows himself richest in
Extension of   terms of literary criticism in the *Brutus* and
the vocabulary *Orator*. His studies, for example, of such
of criticism   orators as Crassus and Antonius, Calidius and Hortensius, and his characterisation of the three types of style, show a wealth of critical vocabulary that must in large measure have been a new phenomenon at Rome. It would be interesting to speculate how far this critical vocabulary was developed in the stress of his quarrel with

---

[1] De Fin. I. 10, III. 5, Tusc. Disp. II. 35, III. 10, De Leg. I. 27, Br. 138 ; Sen. Controv. X. 4 (33). 23, VII. pr. 3.

[2] Tusc. Disp. I. 1, IV. 5.

[3] Tusc. Disp. IV. 6 ; cf. *ib.* I. 5, Acad. Post. 5.

[4] De Off. I. 19, II. 2, Acad. pr. 5, De Div. II. 7.

[5] De Fin. c. I–III, Acad. Post. 4, 10.

[6] De Nat. Deor. I. 7–8, Acad. Post. 14, 18.

[7] De Fin. III. 3, Acad. Post. 5 ; cf. Plut. Cic. 40, on Cicero's method ; *vide supra*, p. 82.   [8] De Fin. III. 40 ; cf. Tusc. Disp. I. 6, II. 5.

the Atticists, but there can be little doubt that, for the purposes of that dispute, Cicero exercised all his ingenuity to set forth his point of view in language that was at once elegant and technical. The critical vocabulary of the Romans was for the most part based on that of the Greeks, but Cicero must have done much to naturalise many Latin equivalents for the Greek terms. Certain critical terms had, of course, been in vogue before Cicero's day,[1] and in his own age Varro's literary studies must have contributed not a little towards stabilising the vocabulary of criticism, but we can to some extent measure Cicero's achievement, if we compare him with the *Auctor ad Herennium*.

This latter work gives us for the most part the bare skeleton of Rhetoric, and a jejune enumeration of rhetorical rules, but in the fourth book the author attempts to deal with the problem of Style. Mommsen, with his invincible prejudice against Cicero, will have it[2] that " the rhetorical writings of Cicero are far from coming up to the didactic chasteness of form and precision of thought of the Rhetoric dedicated to Herennius." Prejudice must be blind indeed to utter such a judgment on reading especially Cicero's great trilogy of rhetorical works, with their breadth of view, their abundant and varied critical vocabulary, not to speak of the ease with which Cicero deals with a difficult subject, and his many happy, if at times conventional, judgments on the orators of Rome. The *Auctor ad Herennium*, though he endeavours to impart a distinctively national[3] colouring to his work, still follows closely in the footsteps of the Greeks as regards the technical terms[4] which he employs. Many passages indicate that he was not at home amidst such terms, which for the most part had not yet been stabilised. He hesitates[5] to adopt a particular term, while

The "Auctor ad Herennium"

[1] Even from the time of Terence and Lucilius.
[2] The History of Rome, Vol. V. p. 508.
[3] Cf. IV. c. 7 ; Marx, Introd. pp. 115, 121 ; Wilkins, Ciceronis De Oratore, Introd. p. 51 *et seq.*
[4] IV. 7. 10 : " nomina rerum Graeca convertimus."
[5] Cf. IV. 10. 15, on " sufflata ;" *ib.* 11. 16, on " dissolutum "; *ib.* on " exile," which is evidently in process of being evolved as a term in literary criticism.

at times his terms are so vague,[1] that they would be unintelligible without the appended definition.   The difficulty[2] of translating the technical terms of Greek Rhetoric
and literary criticism appears to have been always a formidable one for the Romans, so much so that several Latin
words were in vogue for the same Greek term, none of which
seemed to express its meaning quite fully.   Cicero himself
often felt[3] the difficulty, and as Latin lacked[4] the precision
of the Greek, he had recourse to various devices to compensate for the deficiencies of his native tongue.   He frequently uses more than one term to translate a single Greek
word, or employs[5] a paraphrase to insure his rendering of
the Greek.   At times,[6] too, if he is doubtful about the ade-
quacy of his translation, he will append the Greek term.

The terms used in Greek Rhetoric and literary criticism
are often based on metaphor,[7] and the same is true of their
Cicero's rich-   Latin equivalents.   Metaphors derived from
ness in critical agriculture, bodily health, dress, from various
terms   crafts and from the plastic arts, from warfare
and the conflicts of the arena, are pressed into service to

[1] Cf. IV. 20. 27, " compar " = ἰσόκωλον; ib. 53. 66, on " conformatio ";
he was evidently in difficulties when attempting to find Latin terms for many
of the Figures.

[2] Cf. Q. V. 10. 1, on the Greek term ἐνθύμημα, which he prefers to
the Latin " commentum " or " commentatio "; ib. VI. 2. 32, on ἐνάργεια;
ib. VIII. 6. 44, where " allegoria " is rendered by the vague Latin term
" inversio "; different terms such as " reticentia," " obticentia," " inter-
ruptio," were used to express ἀποσιώπησις; cf. Q. IX. 2. 54; vide supra,
p. 109.

[3] In De Or. III. 186, for the Greek περίοδος he uses " quasi ambitus
verborum," ib. 190, " quasi conversio verborum, ib. 198, " quasi orbis
verborum "; cf. Br. 162, Or. 208; cf. Or. 211, on the use of " incisa "
and " membra " (cf. Ad Her. IV. 19. 26) for κόμματα and κῶλα; Or.
79, where " quasi supellex " is used for κατασκευή; cf. Curcio, Le Opere
Rhetoriche, p. 215 et seq., for some terms used by Cicero in the " Partitiones
Oratoriae," and not found elsewhere.

[4] Vide Causeret, op. cit., p. 17; cf. Geigenmueller, Quaestiones Dionysianae, for a comparison of the Greek and Latin terms; also the Glossaries
in Rhys Roberts' editions of Demetrius, Dionysius, and the Περὶ ὕψους.

[5] Cf. his attempts to express ἀλληγορία and προσωποποιΐα, De Or. III.
166. 205, Or. 94. ib. 85. 138; Top. 35, for his rendering of ἐτυμολογία.

[6] Br. 162, Or. 36, 83, 93–94, Top. 34.

[7] Cf. Van Hook, The Metaphorical Terminology of Greek Rhetoric and
Literary Criticism.

enlarge the critical vocabulary of Latin. Considering the difficulties of the task, Cicero's hesitation about his terms is comparatively rare, while in copiousness[1] of critical vocabulary he surpasses any of his predecessors whose works have survived. He ranges with ease over the subjects he discusses, and his language, though vague at times, has an elegance and appropriateness that make his rhetorical treatises one of his greatest glories. To take but one instance, in his characterisation[2] of the oratory of Calidius, he shows a comprehensiveness, a delicacy of appreciation, and high literary qualities, that were something new in Roman criticism, and an immense advance on anything so far accomplished by his countrymen. Cicero must have done much not merely to extend, but to stabilise the vocabulary of criticism amongst the Romans, and thus must have rendered easier the task of subsequent critics, such as Tacitus[3] and Quintilian.

[1] Several important critical terms in Cicero are missing in Ernesti's Lexicon.

[2] Br. 274 *et seq.*

[3] Cf. Gudeman, Tacitus, Dialogus, Introd., pp. 21–22, and his notes, especially to chapters 18–25.

CHAPTER IV

CICERO AND THE ATTICISTS

CICERO'S QUARREL with the Atticists was in many respects the most important episode of his career as a critic. The influence of the quarrel permeates his two great treatises, the *Brutus* and *Orator*, as well as the brief tractate *De Optimo Genere Oratorum*. Modern students of Cicero may at times be tempted to see traces of the quarrel where they do not exist, but in the works referred to, the controversy was always in the foreground of Cicero's thoughts. The Atticist movement challenged his supremacy as an orator by setting up a particular ideal as the only true representative of the Attic tradition, and, not content with this, it sought to brand Cicero with the stigma of Asianism, which in the eyes of many was a synonym for oratory that was faulty and corrupt.

The term " Asianism " has, however, been taken by some to embrace a much wider field[1] than Asiatic oratory, and has been considered as a symbol of
" Asianism " almost everything that is tasteless and depraved in style, without reference to geographical[2] considerations. Many of the faults of Asiatic oratory can be traced back to the early Sophists,[3] who earned the condemnation of Plato and Aristotle[4] not only for the general spirit of their rhetoric, but for the affectations and extravagances of their style.

[1] Cf. Wilamowitz-Moellendorff, Asianismus und Attikismus, Hermes, Vol. 35, p. 1 *et seq.*

[2] In De Or. III. 43, Cicero has geographical considerations in mind.

[3] *Vide* Norden, A.K., Vol. I. p. 379 *et seq.*, 408–410; *ib.* p. 351 *et seq.*, on the Second Sophistic movement; Schmid, Griechische Renaissance in der Römerzeit, p. 23 *et seq.*

[4] Aristotle's chapter on " frigidity," Rhet. III. 3, is important in this connection; *vide supra*, p. 87.

Gorgias[1] in particular with his love of antithesis, balance of clause, and jingle of sounds, his fondness for paradox and conceits, his poetical diction, and his constant straining after rhythmical effects, is the parent of some of the most striking defects in what is styled Asianism. Such faults, however, were not confined to oratory, but made their appearance also in the historians, who in their love of the fanciful and marvellous,[2] and their anxiety to lend colour to their style, were guilty of many of the worst excesses of the rhetoricians. Cicero, who in this instance ignores geographical considerations, classes Timaeus[3] as a representative of the first of the two types of Asianism which he describes.

In oratory, especially epideictic oratory, the seeds of many of the most glaring faults were thus undoubtedly sown
Decline of ora- by the early Sophists, but, though Isocrates[4]
tory in Greece and his followers were deeply influenced by the Sophistic movement, the Attic orators in general with their sense of restraint and decorum avoided the extravagances and puerilities of Sophistic rhetoric. With the passing of the great Attic orators a decline set in. The loss of freedom[5] in Greece, and the changed position of the Greek States, had their inevitable reactions upon oratory; for the surest incentive to great oratory had disappeared. Cicero, as we have seen, associates the decline with the name of Demetrius[6] of Phalerum, who was a pupil of Theophrastus, and who aimed in his speeches at the quiet and restrained style of the philosophical school rather than at fiery and vigorous eloquence. There was, it was said, a certain enervating charm about his speeches, but he cannot be made responsible for the serious faults that were soon to disfigure the art of oratory. It is, however, not without

---

[1] *Vide supra*, pp. 99, 110.
[2] Cf. Strabo, I. 2. 35 ; Diodorus, I. 37.
[3] Br. 325 ; *vide infra*, p. 499 *et seq.*
[4] Isocrates, especially in his later years, showed a more restrained style ; *vide supra*, p. 100.
[5] *Vide supra*, p. 198.
[6] De Or. II. 95, Br. 38, Or. 92, where he is set down as a representative of the Middle style ; De Off. I. 3 ; Q. X. 1. 33, *ib.* 80 ; Q. styles him " almost the last of the Attic Orators " ; cf. Br. 285.

significance that some credit[1] him with being the inventor of the fictitious declamation, an exercise that was destined to generate some of the wildest excesses of rhetoric.

The real decline must have begun, when oratory migrated[2] to the Greek States of Asia Minor, and began to reflect there the salient traits of the national[3] character. The luxurious and undisciplined character of the Oriental would find its natural expression in a style that was bombastic and excessively ornate,[4] in a copiousness that always bordered on redundancy,[5] in a love of far-fetched metaphors and poetical diction, in plays upon words and puerile efforts after novelty[6] of thought and expression, and in the general lack of restraint that critics associated with Asianist oratory. All this was the direct antithesis[7] of the best Attic tradition, with its love of sanity and propriety, its distrust of startling novelty, and its aversion to insipidity. Asianism also showed its affinity with the first Sophistic movement in its neglect of the theory[8] of rhetoric. It felt itself bound by no tradition, and could substitute arbitrary caprice for the strict rules of the art of oratory. The champions[9] of Atticism looked on the Asianists as lacking in culture. The Asiatic orators, moreover, like the Sophists of old, were strong in improvisation,[10] a characteristic that became prominent also in the schools of Declamation. Even the poets from Asia Minor, such as Archias and Antipater of Sidon, were remarkable for their gift of improvising verse.

Oratory in Asia Minor

[1] Q. II. 4. 41–42.   [2] Br. 51, Or. 25 *et seq.*

[3] Cf. Cic. Pro Flacco, 64 *et seq.* ; Q. XII. 10. 17.

[4] Cf. the second species of Asianism described by Cicero, Br. 325.

[5] *Vide infra*, p. 236.

[6] The " conceit," which the author of the περὶ ὕψους (IV. 1) condemns in Timaeus.

[7] Cf. Br. 284.

[8] For the Sophists oratory was an ἄτεχνος τριβή ; cf. Phaedrus, 260 E.

[9] Dionys. " On the Ancient Orators," c. 1 ; Egger, Denys d' Halicarnasse, p. 39 *et seq.*

[10] Cf. Pliny, Ep. II. 3. 1, on Isaeus ; Juv. III. 74 ; Sen. Controv. VII. pr. 2, *ib.* IV. pr. 7 ; Philost. Vitae Soph. 583, 617 ; Rohde, Der griechische Roman, p. 336 *et seq.* ; Schmid, Der Atticismus, Vol. I. p. 27 *et seq.*, on improvisation amongst the later Sophists.

It is, however, to the schools of Declamation that we must go, if we wish to discover the qualities of "Asianism"[1] at its worst. The declamations there practised were divorced from real life. In Cicero's day the aim[2] was to keep the subjects declaimed as close as possible to reality, but, when political freedom had declined, Rhetoric tended to withdraw almost entirely into the schools, and expend itself on subjects that were out of touch with ordinary life. With the scope of oratory restricted, both master and pupil had often to exercise a perverted ingenuity to impress[3] their hearers, and each declaimer endeavoured to surpass the other in striking effects. The pursuit of novelty[4] at all costs was perhaps the dominant characteristic of the schools. Seneca gives us many vivid descriptions of the puerilities of these declaimers, whose affectations had degenerated into a disease.[5] Many of them were conscious of their faults, but persisted in cherishing[6] them with an unreasonable affection. Unnatural, corrupt, extravagant, unrestrained, are some of the epithets that Seneca applies[7] to them. It is little wonder that he regarded their frenzied rhetoric as a species of insanity.[8] Men seemed[9] deserted by their reason, when they indulged in the exercise of declamation. Their lack of critical taste most frequently issued in a style that was florid and bombastic,[10] with a tendency to empty volu-

The schools of Declamation

---

[1] Cf. Verg. Cat. V : " Ite hunc inanes, ite, rhetorum ampullae, inflata rore non Achaico verba."   [2] *Vide supra*, p. 153.

[3] Sen. Controv. IX. pr. 5 : " ille inter fremitum consonantis turbae intendendus animus est."

[4] Sen. Controv. IX. 6 (29). 16 (ed. Kiessling, which is quoted throughout).

[5] *Ib*. Contr. II. 4 (12). 11 : " hunc novitium morbum "; *ib*. VII. 5 (20). 12 : " gravis scholasticos morbus invasit " ; Suas. II. 17.

[6] Cf. his remark on Ovid, Contr. II. 2 (10). 12.

[7] Suas. I. 13, Contr. I. 4. 10, *ib*. II. pr. 1, on Arellius Fuscus; X. 5 (34). 21.

[8] Suas. I. 12, Controv. II. 1 (9). 25, X. pr. 9, *ib*. 4 (33). 22 : " nostri quoque bene insanierunt " ; cf. Petron. c. 3 : " qui necesse habent cum insanientibus furere."

[9] Cf. Seneca's contrast of Asinius Pollio as declaimer and in the law-courts, Controv. IV. pr. 3.

[10] Controv. IX. 2. 27, X. 1 (30). 14 ; Petron. 1 ; cf. Q. XII. 10. 16, on the bombast of Asianism.

bility,[1] and vain repetition[2] and redundancy. It was characteristic of the declaimers that, when they lighted on a happy phrase, they frequently[3] marred it in their efforts to make it more pointed and impressive. They were fond also of indulging[4] in plays on words, and in witticisms that were often tasteless and out of place. It is clear from many passages[5] that Seneca, while condemning the extravagance and absurdity of their thoughts, censures the declaimers also for their love of gaudy and excessive ornament.[6] They frequently sacrificed[7] sense to sound, and, in their search for the embellishments of rhetoric, were ready[8] to omit the essential, in order to achieve some startling effect. Their thoughts were often pretty and effeminate, and the rhythm of their prose was designed to be in harmony with them. As one would expect, they made extensive use of the Gorgianic[9] figures, which evidently appealed to them by their very obtrusiveness. But of all devices, the epigram was the most favoured[10] in the schools. A well-pointed epigram was the surest means of gaining the applause for which the declaimers craved. It was passed[11] from mouth to mouth, and secured a reputation for its author. The epigram was a favourite device in the prose of the Silver Age, and, though, as Quintilian says, there is no sin in a

[1] Cf. Pliny, Ep. V. 20. 4, on Fonteius Magnus, a Bithynian orator ; Suet. Aug. 86.

[2] Suas. I. 16.

[3] Controv. IX. 5 (28). 17, on Montanus ; like Ovid, " nescit quod bene cessit relinquere."

[4] Suas. II. 4 : " electi sumus non relicti " ; Controv. IX. 4 (27). 17 : " multa in re severa temptavit salse dicere."

[5] Suas. I. 12, Controv. VII. 5 (20). 9 : " quidam bellas res dixerunt, quidam ineptas, immo multo ineptas " ; ib. 15, Controv. IX. 6 (29). 11.

[6] Suas. II. 23, Controv. IV. pr. 10.

[7] Controv. VII. 4 (19). 10 ; cf. IX. 2. 27.

[8] Ib. IX. pr. 2 : " sequitur hoc usque in forum declamatores vitium ut necessaria deserant, dum speciosa sectantur " ; Philostr. V. S. 586, might be compared ; Philostr. naturally furnishes many parallels with Seneca.

[9] Suas. II. 16 ; " nos sine deliciis educamur, sine muris vivimus, sine vita vincimus " ; Controv. II. 4 (12). 12 : " Maximus dixit quasi tricolum tale qualia sunt quae basilicam infectant " ; Controv. X. pr. 9.

[10] Controv. I. pr. 22, VII. 3 (18). 8, IX. pr. 1.

[11] Controv. X. 1 (30). 14 : " sententias ... <quae> summa hominum admiratione circumferebantur " ; cf. Tac. Dial. c. 20.

good epigram, still many vitiated their style by an immoderate use of it. The declaimers, too, exhibited many faults of delivery,[1] prominent amongst them being a singsong intonation, which became prevalent in the courts as well as the schools, and was condemned[2] by many writers. It is little wonder that Seneca, appalled by the trivialities of the schools, exclaims :[3] " in scolastica quid non supervacuum est, cum ipsa supervacua sit."

Seneca's picture of the excesses of scholastic rhetoric is supplemented for us by Petronius who, with his fine critical sense, was the relentless foe of the " ventosa et enormis loquacitas "[4] which he styles a modern importation from Asia into Athens.

Petronius on the Declaimers

In many passages[5] he shows his repugnance to the eloquence of the schools with its " honey-balls of phrases." His ideal was the Attic restraint of a style that was neither blotchy nor inflated, but characterised by a natural beauty of its own. Though, to the mind of Petronius,[6] Asianism and the worst extravagances of the schools were identical, not all[7] the declaimers were Asianists. Seneca makes[8] special mention of some professed Asianists. Many of these, like Nicetes,[9] must have had considerable influence at Rome, and must have done much to engender a taste for turgid and flamboyant rhetoric, with the result that, in the eyes of many, Asianism became synonymous with every form of affecta-

[1] Cf. Q. XI. 3, who touches on some of them.

[2] Suas. II. 10; Sen. Ep. 114. 1; Tac. Dial. 26; Pliny, Ep. II. 14. 12–13; Q. I. 8. 2, XI. 1. 56, ib. 3. 57 et seq.; Philost. V. Soph. 492, 513; Dio, Or. XXXII. 65; cf. Schmid, Der Atticismus, Vol. I. p. 41; Norden, op. cit., Vol. I. p. 424 (quotation from Emperius); vide infra, p. 237.

[3] Controv. III. pr. 12.

[4] Satyr. 2; cf. Suet. Aug. 86.

[5] Cf. 1, 4, 6.

[6] Cf. ib. 2, 44.

[7] Rohde, Die asianische Rhetorik und die zweite Sophistik, Rhein. Mus. 41 (1886), p. 170, allows a too great preponderance to Asianism in the schools.

[8] Vide infra, p. 330.

[9] Cf. Sen. Suas. III. 5, 7, Controv. IX. 2. 23, X. 2 (31). 18; for Nicetes Sacerdos, who was prominent at a later date, vide infra, p. 339.

tion in style (cacozelia).[1]   These did not take account of the fact that other styles[2] could have their own form of affectation.   They should have considered that Asianism had abundance of its own sins to answer for, without being made identical with " cacozelia."

Cicero did not live to see Asianism develop its most obnoxious defects in the schools of declamation under the Empire.   He was, however, well acquainted **Two kinds of** with the general qualities of Asiatic oratory, **Asianism** two kinds of which are characterised by him in the *Brutus*,[3] the one aiming at epigrammatic effects, at prettiness of diction, at symmetry and balance of clause, the other copious and florid, with a tendency to bombast. He marks out for special condemnation Hegesias,[4] who may be taken as a representative of the first type of Asianism ; for he made at times puerile efforts after symmetry. Though Cicero was not fated to see the riot of epigram engendered by the declamations under the Empire, yet it is evident that, in the first type of Asianism described by him, the striving after epigrammatic effect was before his mind.   It is, indeed, one of his great merits as a critic that, before he could witness Asianism in its most perverted form, he was able to put his finger on many of its corrupt[5] tendencies.

Hitherto we have been concerned with the **Impurity of** stylistic faults of Asianism.   Besides faults **speech** of style, it exhibited another serious defect in the impurity of its speech.   With the spread[6] of the

---

[1] Diomede (Keil, Vol. I. 451) defines " cacozelia " as " per affectationem decoris corrupta sententia . . . haec fit aut nimio cultu aut nimio tumore," a definition that would perfectly suit Asianist oratory ; Q. VIII. 3. 56, more correctly defines it as a fault in every kind of style.

[2] Cf. Sen. Controv. IX. 2. 28, for " cacozelia " in the plain style ; Wilamowitz-M., op. cit., Hermes (35), p. 28 *et seq.* ; Brzoska, op. cit., p. 31 is wrong in making Asianism identical with " cacozelia."

[3] 325 *et seq.* ; cf. Norden, op. cit., Vol. I. p. 133 *et seq.*, for illustrations.

[4] Br. 286–287 ; Or. 226–230 ; cf. Strabo, XIV. 1. 41 (C. 648), who credits Hegesias with being the real founder of Asianism ; Blass, Die Rhythmen der asianischen und römischen Kunstprosa, p. 18 *et seq.* ; *vide infra* p. 498, on Hegesias as historian.   [5] *Vide infra*, p. 236.

[6] Cf. Q. XII. 10. 16, where Santra finds the origin of Asianism in defective knowledge of Greek amongst the peoples of Asia Minor ; cf. Wilamowitz-M., op. cit., p. 4.

Κοινή, violations of correctness, as judged by Attic standards, would naturally be rife. Such lapses were severely criticised in the Asianist orators by champions of Atticism such as Dionysius and Caecilius of Caleacte. Cicero has little to say on this aspect of Asianism, though he was sensible[1] of the contrast between the perfect purity of Attic speech, the "urbanitas," that according to him was the mark of the humblest Athenian citizen, and the defects of foreigners, especially when they haled from Asia.

Reaction against Asianism, with all its works and pomps, was bound to set in amongst those who cherished the purity and restraint of the best Attic tradition. It seems not improbable that the reaction was two-fold, according as the rhetorician or the grammarian, each impelled by his own interests, directed his attention to the defects of Asianism from the standpoint of style or purism, though later critics like Dionysius, possessed of wider sympathies, criticised it from both standpoints.

The Atticist reaction

Various views[2] have been expressed with regard to the centre in which the reaction first set in, some favouring Alexandria, others Pergamum, while others again make the claim for Athens or for Rhodes. Though, as Norden says,[3] the problem as to where the reaction against Asianism began, should be kept distinct from the problem of the formation of the Canon of Attic orators, still it is evident that the Canon was drawn up at some centre,[4] where opposition to Asianism was strong, and where the study of the Attic orators was intensively cultivated. We must not forget, however, that there were centres such as Athens and Rhodes, in which the Attic tradition, though obscured at times, was never obliterated. At Athens the sense of restraint,[5] and a rever-

The centre of reaction ?

---

[1] De Or. III. 42–43, Br. 51, 172, 258, Or. 25, De opt. gen. 7; cf. Rohde, Der griechische Roman, p. 351 et seq.

[2] Vide Heck, Zur Entstehung des rhetorischen Attizismus, p. 5 et seq.; Schmid, Die griechische Renaissance, pp. 10–11.

[3] A.K., I. p. 149 et seq.

[4] Brzoska, op. cit., p. 56, makes a good case for Pergamum; Hartmann, op. cit., makes a less convincing case for attributing the authorship of the Canon to Caecilius.   [5] Vide supra, p. 197.

ence for purity of diction innate in its people, must always have formed a strong barrier[1] against the flagrant extravagances of Asianism. The study of Demosthenes,[2] who was a favourite author with many, would have helped to keep intact there the highest ideals of Atticism.

At Rhodes, where the study of Rhetoric flourished[3] from an early date, there was, according to Cicero,[4] always in evidence a finer sense of moderation than on the continent of Asia. Hyperides was a favourite model[5] with the Rhodians. It is probable,[6] however, that Cicero exaggerates the importance of the Rhodian school, seeing that he himself came so strongly under its influence. But, for all that, there were certain factors operative at Rhodes that would have resisted the incursion of Asianism. Stoic influence[7] was felt there, especially through the agency of the two great philosophers, Panaetius and Poseidonius, and this in itself would have acted as a deterrent against the exaggerated pomp of Asiatic oratory. Again, the authority of a teacher such as Molon[8] would have had no little effect in inculcating respect for a style of oratory that was marked by temperateness and precision.

The Scholastic Rhetoric[9] of Hermagoras, in turning

Rhodes

[1] Rohde, Die asianische Rhetorik, etc., p. 175 *et seq.*, goes so far as to make Athens responsible for the reaction against Asianism about 60 B.C., but there were other influences working in that direction before that date.

[2] De Or. I. 88, Or. 105.

[3] Cf. Q. XII. 10. 19, on Aeschines' connection with it; Philost. V. S. 481, makes him the founder of fictitious declamations, when in exile there; cf. also Q. III. 1. 17.

[4] Br. 51, Or. 25; cf. Q. XII. 10. 18–19; Q., however, notes the inferiority of Rhodian as compared with Attic Oratory.

[5] Dionys. De Din. 8.

[6] *Vide* Blass, Griech. Bered. p. 3; Sandys, Cic. Orator, Introd. p. 37; cf. Marx, Ad Herennium, Introd. p. 157 *et seq.*

[7] Cf. Susemihl, Gesch. der griech. Lit. II. p. 493 *et seq.*; Aelius Stilo studied there, when he accompanied Metellus Numidicus into exile; cf. Suet. De Gr. 3; Marx, op. cit., Introd. p. 139.

[8] Br. 245, 312, 316, Ad Att. II. 1. 9, Pro Plancio, 84; Plut. Cic. 4; Q. III. 1. 16, who styles him Apollonius Molon; *ib.* XII. 6. 7; cf. Laurand, De Ciceronis Studiis Rhetoricis, p. 49 *et seq.*; Suet. J. C. 4; Susemihl, loc. cit., p. 489 *et seq.*

[9] Cic. De Inv. I. 8, II. 8; Q. III. 1. 16, *ib.* 11. 22.

men's attention to the " art " of Rhetoric as practised in
former times, may have contributed its
The Rhetoric share to the Atticist reaction, even though
of Hermagoras Hermagoras busied[1] himself primarily with
" Inventio." The Asianists, as a rule, neglected the theory
of Rhetoric, though even amongst them there were some
exceptions.

Clearly, then, in many quarters there were influences
operating in favour of the old ideals of Atticism against
The rise of the tastelessness and flamboyancy of Asianist
Roman oratory, but it is not easy to determine what
Atticism were the precise influences that helped to
give shape to the theories of the Roman Atticists, as they
are called. The leader[2] of the band was Calvus, but another
name prominently associated with the movement was that
of Calidius. According to St. Jerome,[3] the master of the
latter was Apollodorus of Pergamum, who had many Roman
pupils including Octavian, the future Emperor. Augustus
may have imbibed his dislike[4] of Asianism from Apollodorus. The glimpses[5] that we get in the Elder Seneca of
this master, and of his influence on his pupils, lead one to
the conclusion that he inculcated a plain style, if he was not
a professed Atticist.

Another factor which may have contributed to the
development of the theories of the Roman Atticists, was
Stoic influ- the Stoic concept of style which I have already
ence ? discussed. Stoic influence was strong at
Pergamum,[6] and the pupils of Apollodorus
may have come under its sway through the medium of
their Pergamene master. Moreover, since the days of the
Scipionic circle, the Stoic theory of the Plain style was
revealed to the Romans by the teaching of Panaetius and
Diogenes of Babylon, and was exemplified by the practice

[1] Br. 263, 271.
[2] Br. 284 : " sed et ipse errabat et alios etiam errare cogebat."
[3] Blass, op. cit., p. 155 ; Hieronym. Chron. s.a. 690–691 (there quoted).
[4] *Vide infra*, p. 262 ; cf. Strabo, XIII. 4. 3 (C. 625).
[5] Controv. II. 5 (13). 11, *ib.* 13, X. pr. 15 ; cf. Q. II. 11. 2, III. 1.
17–18, IV. 1. 50 ; Tac. Dial. 19.
[6] *Vide* Susemihl, op. cit., II. p. 483 *et seq. ;* Volkmann, op. cit., pp. 9, 458.

of the many orators who were adherents of the school.
Though the Roman Atticists were not professed Stoics,
they may still[1] have been influenced by the ideals of the
Stoic orators.

One wonders, too, whether in the case of Calvus, his
study[2] of Alexandrian literature did not react on his theory
of prose style. Its poetry could teach him

Calvus   the lesson of polish[3] and restraint and delicate
artistry in language, while, if he was a student of Alexandrian prose literature, he could have become acquainted
with Agatharchides' polemic against the extravagances of
the Asianists. Calvus, according to Cicero, showed exquisite refinement of style, but through an over-scrupulous
fear of tainting its purity, through an excess of morbid self-
criticism, and a painful striving after finish and precision,
he never attained[4] the true vigour of the orator. This
chastened, but attenuated style might, says Cicero, appeal
to a circle of the select,[5] but it was too subtle and elegant
for the common herd. Calvus, too, exhibited recondite
learning, which was in harmony with his character as a
" doctus poeta."[6] The qualities then, that Cicero attributes
to him, lead one to believe that his pre-occupation with the
technique of Alexandrian verse, and the exquisite sense
of form he had thereby acquired, influenced his views on
oratorical prose. He was gifted, moreover, with a refined
critical taste, and loathing all that was insipid and bizarre,

[1] Cf. Fiske, op. cit., p. 340, who, however, is inclined to exaggerate Stoic
influence on the Atticists.

[2] I find that Schanz, op. cit., I. 2. p. 217, has some such idea in
his mind.

[3] Cf. Br. 283–285, for Calvus' ideals ; portion of Cicero's criticism of
Calidius (Br. 274 *et seq.*) might well serve to characterise the artistry of the
Alexandrian poets.

[4] Cf. Q. X. 1. 115 : " sancta et gravis oratio et castigata " ; *ib.* X. 2. 25,
XII. 10. 11 ; Tac. Dial. 25 : " adstrictior Calvus."

[5] " Doctis et attente audientibus " ; were the " docti " his brother
Atticists, or his brother poets ?

[6] Cf. Prop. II. 34. 89 ; Tenney Frank, " Cicero and the poetae novi,"
A.J. Phil. XL. p. 396 *et seq. ;* with the " reconditae litterae " attributed to
Calvus (Ep. Ad Fam. XV. 21. 4) cf. Br. 191, on " poema reconditum,"
which only a select few can appreciate ; on Calvus' poetry, cf. Pliny, Ep.
I. 16. 5, V. 3. 5 ; Plessis and Poirot, Calvus, p. 1 *et seq.*, for fragments.

cultivated especially sanity[1] and purity of speech. Such
sanity and feeling for correctness were set up as a counterpoise to the frenzied rhetoric of the Asianist orators.
Calvus might have witnessed for himself, even in Rome,[2]
something of the lack of taste that characterised the Asianist
manner. He might have heard, too, from his friend
Catullus, on his return[3] from Bithynia, an account of the
puerilities and excesses of Asianist oratory, as practised on
its native soil.[4] Such various influences, apart from his
own critical acumen, would have inclined him to believe
in the superiority of a style of oratory that was faultless in
its diction, elegant, and restrained, and would have gradually
produced in him the conviction that such a style represented
the true Attic ideal.

Calidius was active in the Roman Courts from the year
64 B.C., Calvus from 58 B.C., and it seems natural to suppose

Calidius that these two orators (to mention only the
two foremost Atticists) were already speculating as to the most perfect type of style in their own
sphere. It is not easy, however, to determine how they
first came into conflict with Cicero. Calvus is considered
by Cicero the standard-bearer of the Atticists. Whether
his opposition[5] to Cicero was influenced by political motives, and by the condemnation of his father,[6] it is difficult
to say, though without doubt these factors were of some
weight. Calidius, like Calvus, had formed his own theory
of style, and regarded[7] the exponents of the Grand style as
indulging in a kind of frenzy or drunken revelry. Cicero
gives us a fine characterisation of Calidius' style,[8] which

[1] Br. 284; "sanitas" became the great watchword of the Atticists;
cf. *ib.* 278, on Calidius; Tac. Dial. 23 : "illam ipsam quam jactant
sanitatem"; Q. X. 1. 44, XII. 10. 15; cf. Petron. 2 : "ne carmen quidem
sani coloris enituit."

[2] In such an orator as Hortensius.

[3] Cf. Catullus, 10; *ib.* 53, 96, for his friendship with Calvus.

[4] Cf. Pliny, Ep. V. 20. 4.

[5] Cicero and Calvus were joined in the defence of Sestius in 56 B.C.

[6] On Licinius Macer, cf. Ad Att. I. 4. 2, Br. 238; Plut. Cic. 9; on
Macer as historian, *vide infra*, p. 516.

[7] Br. 276, 278.

[8] It is interesting to note that C.'s style, as described by Cicero, is more
akin to the Middle style than to the Plain style of the extreme Atticists.

charmed by its clearness, its purity of diction, its flexibility and variety, the artistry of its composition, and its skilful and unobtrusive use of ornaments such as figures and prose-rhythm. Yet, in spite of all these excellencies on the literary side, he seemed to Cicero to lack the fire which is essential to the orator, if he is to be successful in the greatest of his tasks—the moving of his audience. Quintilian[1] attributes to Calidius the quality of plainness, while Caelius Rufus says[2] that he was very eloquent in his own defence, but ineffective as an accuser, though this criticism of Caelius may to some extent be influenced by the fact that accusation was his own strong point. Cicero's picture of Calidius is marked by much sympathy and insight, even though it reveals ideals divergent from his own. There is, on the other hand, a definite note of polemic in his references to Calvus, who was a more aggressive champion of the Atticist point of view.

Now Cicero published the *De Oratore* in 54 B.C., when he was in the full maturity of his powers. It is important **Publication** to get a clear conception of his ideal of **of the** eloquence in that work, and to see if it con- **" De Oratore "** tained anything that might have occasioned the breach with the Atticists which looms so large in his later rhetorical treatises. It is important, also, to discover how far he had then formed ideas on the scope and nature of oratory which he afterwards brought prominently into play in his controversy with his opponents.

We find that he had already formed the conception of the " officia oratoris," though he does not define them with the clear precision of his later works. At **The " officia** times he enumerates in full the three duties[3] **oratoris "** of the orator, while again he stresses[4] the necessity of conciliating the audience in cases where impassioned eloquence would be out of place. It is clear,

---

[1] XII. 10. 11 : " subtilitatem Calidii " ; *ib.* 39 ; cf. XI. 3. 123, 155 ; the speech of C. " De domo Ciceronis," referred to in Q. X. 1. 23, seems to have been merely a rhetorical exercise.

[2] Ad Fam. VIII. 9. 5.

[3] Docere, conciliare, movere ; *vide supra*, pp. 74, 121.

[4] De Or. II. 182.

however, that he considered[1] as supreme the orator's duty of exciting in his hearers whatever emotion he desired. Men, he declares, decide more often under the influence of passion than of reason.

Moreover, he had already[2] formed the conception of the three styles appropriate to the three " officia oratoris." At
The Three Styles times he differentiates the styles on the ground of delivery,[3] while on other occasions he distinguishes[4] them chiefly on the score of diction and composition, though naturally, where spoken speech was in question, there would be an intimate association between style and delivery. He is fond[5] of contrasting the Grand style with the Plain, or again[6] with a style of a quieter character, whose aim was to please and conciliate the audience. This latter was grounded in an appeal to the moral sense,[7] by which the speaker sought to convey a favourable impression both of his own character and that of his client. This was a task especially associated with the Middle style, but, though Cicero already possessed the idea of the three styles corresponding to the " officia oratoris," he makes no very serious attempt to differentiate clearly[8] the characteristics of the Middle and the Plain styles, or to define their relations. At this period evidently, the vital difference for him lay between the Plain and the Grand styles. Later, when in open controversy with the Atticists, it was essential for him to characterise in greater detail the qualities of the various styles, and to determine their provinces. It was then, too, that he brought into prominence the idea that the perfect orator should be

---

[1] *Ib.* I. 60 : " quod unum in oratore dominatur " ; cf. II. 178, 185 *et seq.*, Br. 322, Or. 97.

[2] De Or. II. 121, *ib.* 128–129 : lenitas orationis, acumen, vis, correspond to delectare, docere, movere ; *ib.* 215 ; *vide supra,* pp. 69, 74.

[3] *Ib.* I. 255.

[4] *Ib.* III. 199 (on " habitus orationis et quasi color ") : " plena, tenuis, particeps utriusque " ; *ib.* 212 ; cf. *ib.* 177.

[5] *Ib.* II. 97–98 (contrast of Cotta and Sulpicius), *ib.* 215, III. 31.

[6] De Or. II. 182–183, 211–213 ; cf. *ib.* 72–74.

[7] *Vide supra,* p. 124.

[8] Cf., however, De Or. II. 200–201, where the relation of the various styles to each other is glanced at.

master of all three styles. It was the mark of a great orator to be able to introduce rapid changes of light and shade, to pass from a plain unadorned style to one of heightened grandeur, as the subject[1] or occasion demanded.

In the *De Oratore* Cicero clearly indicates his preference for the Grand style, which by its richness and variety,[2] its
Preference for the Grand style wide range, its use[3] of commonplaces and amplification, its vehement and forceful delivery, was especially designed to move the emotions of an audience. Herein was seen in all its plenitude the effect of the " flexanima atque omnium regina rerum oratio."[4] It is the Grand style that distinguishes the genuine orator from the clever speaker. The former, according to Antonius,[5] had not yet appeared above the Roman horizon, though the ideal may be reached by Crassus, or some future orator who (as Cicero himself did) will surpass him in industry and a greater range of learning. It is clear[6] that Crassus himself was the embodiment of Cicero's own ideal of oratory, in so far (Cicero would have us understand) as it could be realised before his own genius and achievements brought it into the region of actuality.

One effect of Cicero's predilection for the Grand style is that, when he proceeds to discuss the virtues[7] of style
Cicero's discussion of the virtues of style in general, he deals in a merely perfunctory[8] way with the two virtues of correctness and clearness. No orator, says Antonius,[9] was ever admired for speaking correct Latin, and little praise

[1] In accordance with Decorum the orator frequently had to change his tone, cf. De. Or. II. 205 : " neque parvis in rebus adhibendae sunt hae dicendi faces " ; III. 210 *et seq. ;* cf. Ep. ad Fam. IX. 21. 1 ; *vide infra,* p. 232.

[2] De Or. I. 59 ; a perfect orator is he who " de omnibus rebus possit copiose varieque dicere " ; *ib.* II. 120, 214.

[3] De Or. II. 324, III. 104 ; cf. De Inv. I. 106, II. 108.

[4] De Or. II. 187.

[5] De Or. I. 94, III. 54, 189, Or. 18, 106 ; Q. XII. 1. 21 ; this opinion was expressed in the treatise on Rhetoric written by Antonius ; *vide supra,* p. 151.

[6] Cf. De Or. I. 230, II. 188 *et seq. ; vide supra,* p. 176.

[7] Cf. De Or. III. 37 *et seq.,* 49.

[8] *Vide infra,* p. 255.

[9] *Ib.* III. 52 ; *vide infra,* p. 245.

is merited by clearness of style. These two virtues, however, were claimed especially by the adherents of the
Plain style, whose great function it was to instruct. Cicero
had larger ambitions, and concentrated[1] his attention
mainly on the two remaining virtues of ornateness and
decorum which were calculated to delight and move an
audience. He devotes a large space to setting out all the
means that could adorn speech, and convert it from a merely
colourless medium for conveying ideas into an instrument
of imaginative and emotional power. Moreover, the compliment which he pays[2] to Hortensius gives some indication
as to where in those days lay his predilection. Cicero could
afford to be generous to his rival, as he had by now wrested
from him the supremacy of the Forum, but, though he
always felt a certain affinity between himself and Hortensius
in the grandeur and impassioned sweep of their oratory,
still he would be careful to draw a distinction between his
own style and the Asiatic manner of his rival.

However, though showing a clear preference for the
Grand style, and though conscious of the limitations of the
Plain style, yet he did not emphasise these
limitations as strongly as he afterwards did.
In the *De Oratore* he speaks without hostility of the Stoic ideal of style, though he recognises
how circumscribed were the Stoic orators, and how power-
less when great issues were at stake. He speaks[3] with
respect, and even with a certain enthusiasm of Cotta, whose
style was of the plainest. Different orators, though following
diverse styles,[4] may all win renown, just as painters, sculp-
tors, and poets have gained distinction, though they did not
in their several spheres adhere to a uniform style. Each
should follow the bent of his own genius, and give free scope
to his individuality.

The Plain
style in the
" De Oratore "

---

[1] *Ib.* 53–54, 96 *et seq.*, 210 *et seq.*

[2] De Or. III. 228 *et seq.*; it is easy, however, to exaggerate the sigifi-
cance of the compliment, as Heck, op. cit., p. 45, seems to me to do; Cicero
evidently had before his mind the compliment paid to Isocrates in the
Phaedrus; cf. Or. 41; *vide infra*, p. 239.

[3] *Vide supra*, p. 185 *et seq.*

[4] De Or. III. 25 *et seq.*, 34–35; cf. Br. 204, Or. 52 *et seq.*

With Cicero's ideal of those days before us, the interesting question arises whether traces can be found in the

**Polemic in
the " De
Oratore "**

De Oratore of the quarrel that was soon
to engage so much of the orator's attention.
Certainly no traces of open polemic can be
found there, though there are certain passages that seem
to have a veiled polemical purpose. We have seen that
Calvus and Calidius were prominent[1] as orators before the
publication of the treatise, and, as I have said, presumably
had already formed their ideas as to what a perfect style of
oratory should be. In that work Cicero glorifies the grand
ornate style of eloquence, and proclaims the task of rousing
emotion as the supreme duty of the orator. His natural
leanings[2] were towards a rich and highly embellished style,
and, like[3] so many amongst the peoples of the South, his
temperament found its fullest expression in strongly emotional oratory. It was in appeals to the emotions[4] that his
greatest power as an orator lay, as is evidenced by the
perorations[5] of his own speeches, and by the fact[6] that, when
he pleaded in conjunction with others, the concluding
speech was assigned to him owing to his capacity for playing
with effect upon the feelings of his audience. All Cicero's
glorification of embellished and impassioned oratory, and
above all Antonius' expressed opinion[7] that the ideal orator,
the master of the Grand style, was yet to seek in Rome,
would be something in the nature of a challenge to those
who preferred a plainer and less impassioned style of eloquence. It is possible that critics had already begun to
murmur against Cicero's own style as too highly coloured
and redundant. It may have been some such critic who

[1] *Vide* Heck, op. cit., p. 31 *et seq.*

[2] In addition to the " De Oratore," cf. Ad Att. I. 14. 3 (61 B.C.), De Div.
I. 80.

[3] Cf. De Or. I. 228, II. 124, 195, Or. 131 ; cf. In Verrem, V. 1. 3.

[4] Q. XI. 1. 85; " summus ille tractandorum amimorum artifex " ;
Gellius, X. 3. 7 *et seq.*

[5] Cf. Pro Cluentio, 197 *et seq.*, Pro Plancio 83 : " ut miserabiliores epi-
logos possem dicere " ; *ib.* 101 *et seq. ;* cf. Or. 131.

[6] Br. 190, Or. 130.

[7] Men would incline to ignore the dramatic date of the Dialogue, and
apply Antonius' opinion to contemporary conditions.

held[1] that (to strengthen his own position) he had depicted Antonius[2] as more florid and copious in his oratory than was actually the case. The apologetic remark[3] with which Crassus begins his discussion of rhythm may be a concession on Cicero's part to those who were antagonistic to rhythmical prose. Again, Cicero has a tilt[4] at those who are unable to adopt periodic structure, though he may really have in mind certain orators who deliberately abstained from it through their fidelity to the ideal of the Plain style. Moreover, his reference[5] to the redundancy of Sulpicius, and his palliation of it as a defect incidental to youth, may be a virtual defence against criticisms of his own excessive copiousness. Whether or not these indications can be taken as evidence of a veiled polemic in the *De Oratore*, it is certain that the issues in the Atticist quarrel were not yet definitely knit, but it is more than probable that the treatise was accepted as a challenge by those whose ideal of style differed from that of Cicero, and who felt themselves aggrieved by his exaltation of a style which some of them at least would regard as extravagant and bombastic. We may then regard it as likely[6] that the first skirmishes in the Atticist campaign took place soon after the publication of the *De Oratore*. It is important to note that Cicero had already to hand in that treatise most of the weapons that he was to employ later against the Atticist position, though in the course of the conflict he had to subject his views to certain modifications.

It has[7] been held that Calvus, on the publication of

[1] De Or. III. 16.

[2] Poiret, L'Éloquence Judiciaire, p. 253, notes that Cicero (De Or. III. 32) applies certain epithets to Antonius that suggest Atticism, but Cicero also attributes to him " summa varietas," which he would deny to the Atticists.

[3] *Ib.* 173 : " quod jam vereor ne huic Catulo videatur esse puerile " ; the question of prose rhythm, as we shall see, was a crucial one between Cicero and the Atticists.

[4] De Or. III. 198.

[5] *Ib.* II. 96, *ib.* 88 : " volo enim se efferat in adulescente fecunditas " ; " item volo esse in adulescente, unde aliquid amputem " ; *vide infra*, p. 239.

[6] In a letter to Atticus, 54 B.C. (IV. 19. 1), Cicero uses the phrase " Latinus Ἀττικισμός," referring to Atticus by way of a joke, but considering the date of the letter, the phrase may have a deeper significance.

[7] Heck, op. cit., p. 52.

the *De Oratore*, regarded Cicero's ideal as Asianist. Of course, only an extreme Atticist could hold such a view, but though the *De Oratore* helped to knit the issues, I am inclined to think that Cicero's critics directed their attack quite as much against his practice as against his theory. At any rate, they took[1] up the position that the Plain style characterised by elegance, restraint, and purity of diction, was the genuine Attic style, and that they alone were the true representatives of the Attic tradition.

The issues knit

It is difficult to decide how many adherents Calvus gathered to his standard. Quintilian describes[2] the Atticists as a select circle of the initiated, who, true to the psychology of a coterie, considered all as aliens who refused to conform to their own rigorous code. The view[3] has been put forward that the Atticists were all nobles or aristocrats, and all Romans, who had the motto " urbanitas "[4] emblazoned on their ensigns, but this explanation of the origin of Neo-Atticism will not suffice. Calvus belonged to the plebeian " gens Licinia," while it is probable,[5] too, that Calidius was a plebeian. Moreover, Cicero himself, whom they branded as an Asianist, had shown as much solicitude as the Atticists for the ideal of " urbanitas," even before[6] the Neo-Atticist movement had taken definite shape.

Who were the Atticists ?

Whatever explanation of the origin of Neo-Atticism and of its quarrel with Cicero we may put forward, and even when we give due weight to the factors of education and environment, we must return in the end to the fundamental consideration of differences of character and temperament. Quintilian[7] has

Decisive factors

[1] Br. 285, 287, Or. 28, 75, 83, De opt. gen. 11–13 ; Q. X. 1. 44, XII. 10. 21.

[2] XII. 10. 14 ; cf. Br. 283 ; Calvus' style appealed especially to such a circle ; Fronto, I. p. 30 : " multo placentes illos sibi et provocantes Atticos."

[3] *Vide* Plessis and Poirot, op. cit., p. 79 *et seq.* ; Curcio, De Ciceronis et Calvi arte dicendi quaestiones, p. 16 *et seq.*

[4] Cf. Fiske, op. cit., p. 124.

[5] For his Caesarian sympathies, cf. Caesar, B.C., 1. 2.

[6] Cf. De Or. III. 42–44 ; *vide infra*, p. 244.

[7] XII. 10. 17.

got hold of much of the truth, when he traces the rise of Asianism to the peculiarities of national character. As regards individuals, Cicero could never be an " Atticist " in the sense in which his opponents used the word. He who was not always satisfied[1] with the grandeur of Demosthenes, was too imaginative and emotional to be thus cabined and confined. A rich, ornate,[2] and rhythmical prose[3] was necessary for the full play of his feelings. Cicero had not the keen penetrating gaze into the heart of a subject that will concentrate on essentials, and despise the trappings and the accessories. It was in the Asianist style that the passionate temperament and somewhat theatrical[4] character of Hortensius found their most adequate expression. So, too, the luxurious and emotional nature of Antony[5] led him towards the Asiatic style. In these cases, as well as in Cicero's predilection for the Grand style, the choice was largely a matter of temperament. Those whom their natural inclinations, or the influences of education, urged towards the Plain style, might readily enough see in Cicero's oratory evidence of Asianist leanings. Their standpoint would become more offensive in Cicero's eyes, when they began to theorise about the best style, and to put forward their own as the true Attic ideal.

Charges against Cicero It is evident that it was Calvus who propounded the Neo-Atticist theories with greatest vigour. It has been said that he wrote technical treatises on oratory, though there is little evidence to support this view.[6] As Tacitus tells us, correspond-

[1] Or. 104 : " tamen non semper implet aures meas ; ita sunt avidae et capaces."

[2] Cf. some interesting remarks of Shairp, Aspects of Poetry, p. 130 *et seq.*, on the pure and ornate styles in Poetry.

[3] *Vide supra*, p. 224.

[4] Cf. Br. 303, on his delivery ; Div. in Caec. 46 ; Gellius I. 5. 2 ; Mart. Capella (Dick), Bk. V. 543 ; Norden, A.K. I. p. 221 ; Macrob. Sat. III. 13 (there quoted) ; Hortensius relied a good deal on his delivery, and spoke better than he wrote ; Q. XI. 3. 8 ; Cic. Or. 132.

[5] Plut. Ant. 2 ; cf. Cic. Phil. II. 42–43 ; Suet. Aug. 86 ; as in the case of Maecenas (Sen. Ep. 114. 4), the style was the reflex of the man ; *vide infra*, p. 327.

[6] This view is based on the " commentarii " mentioned by Tacitus, Dial. 23 ; cf. Plessis and Poirot, op. cit., p. 83 ; Schanz, op. cit., I. 2,

ence[1] passed between him and Cicero, in which the style of
the latter was branded as nerveless and flabby, while Calvus
in turn was considered by Cicero to be bloodless and
attenuated. Quintilian,[2] in terms that are reminiscent of
Tacitus, gives us a summary of the various charges brought
against Cicero by the Atticists. Therein he is characterised
as an Asianist, bombastic, redundant,[3] pointless in his
witticisms, too florid and unrestrained, and (an accusation
which shocks Quintilian) almost effeminate in his rhythms.
We cannot determine exactly the date of the correspondence
between Calvus and Cicero, but it is probable that an inter-
change of views passed between them soon after the publication[4] of the *De Oratore*. With the departure of Cicero
for his province, the Atticists for a time had the field to
themselves, and we may take it that they did not lose the
opportunity of advancing their own peculiar views. It may
seem strange that Cicero makes no mention of the quarrel
in the letters which he wrote from his province, but with
his many problems of administration, with the threat of a
Parthian invasion hanging over him, and the clouds of
Civil war gathering at home, his mind was too preoccupied
to concern itself with literary problems. It may not, how-

p. 218 ; Sen. Controv. I. pr. 12, where Calvus defines " declamare," shows,
however, his interest in such matters.

[1] Dial. 18 ; cf. Q. XII. 1. 22 ; Cicero is styled by Calvus " solutus et
enervis " ; by Brutus, who is mentioned also in connection with the controversy, Cicero is considered " fractus atque elumbis " ; Calvus is styled
by Cicero " exsanguis et attritus " (v. l. " aridus," though " attritus " suits
better the morbid self-criticism of Calvus) ; cf. Br. 283 : " verum sanguinem
deperdebat " ; Ad Fam. XV. 21. 4 ; cf. Heck, op. cit., pp. 60–61, on the
correspondence ; Priscian, II. 490. 12 (there quoted).

[2] XII. 10. 12 *et seq.* ; cf. IX. 4. 1, *ib.* 53.

[3] Cf. Q. IX. 3. 46, where Caecilius brands as pleonastic Cicero's " ex-
cessit, evasit, erupit."

[4] Harnecker, Cic. und die Attiker, Neue Jahrb. für Phil., 1882, p. 60,
seems to me to put the correspondence altogether too late (i.e. in 48–47 B.C.) ;
Calvus died in 47 B.C., and it is probable that the quarrel had continued for
some years before his death ; Seneca's phrase (Controv. VII. 4 (19). 6) :
" Calvus, qui diu cum Cicerone iniquissimam litem de principatu eloquentiae habuit," if it can be taken to refer not merely to a rivalry for supremacy in the Forum, but to a rivalry of ideas as to the best form of eloquence,
seems to favour an earlier date.

ever, be fanciful to see in his longing[1] for Rome evidence of
his anxiety to be once again in the arena of the Forum,
especially if there was any serious assault on his supremacy
as an orator.

There is one piece of evidence that gives some support
to those who assign a late date to the correspondence
Correspond- referred to above. We first hear of such a
ence with correspondence[2] in a letter written by Cicero
Calvus (46 B.C.) in answer to Trebonius, who had
evidently taken him to task for having, in writing to Calvus,
lavished too high praise upon his oratory. As Cicero says
in his defence, that letter was not intended for general
publication. Though it was written before Calvus' death,
it appears to have come only recently into the hands of
Trebonius. There is then in question a definite letter in
which Calvus was lauded by Cicero, but it is possible that
this letter may have been the last of a series,[3] and designed
partly to influence[4] one whom Cicero was endeavouring to
convert to his own views, partly, perhaps, as a lenitive for
the asperity that had hitherto marked their controversy.

Cicero had enjoyed supremacy in the Forum for a number
of years, and it must have been particularly galling to him
The choice to find his position threatened, serious charges
of models made against his style of oratory, and the
Atticists uncompromisingly maintaining that
their own plain style represented the genuine Attic ideal.
Holding such a theory, it was natural for them to select
Lysias[5] as their great model, though some were found to
follow Thucydides, some even Xenophon. In fact, the
question of the choice and imitation of models formed one
of the chief grounds of controversy between Cicero and his

[1] Ad Fam. II. 11. 1 : " mirum me desiderium tenet urbis " ; *Ib.* 12. 2 :
" urbem, urbem, mi Rufe, cole et in ista luce vive."

[2] Ad Fam. XV. 21. 4 ; there, however, the reference is to one particular
letter.

[3] Tacitus, at any rate, evidently had a series of letters in mind ; cf. Dial.
18 ; *ib.* 25 ; Heck, op. cit., pp. 60–61.

[4] Cf. Ad Fam. XV. 21. 4 : " multae erant et reconditae litterae, vis non
erat (i.e. in Calvus) ; ad eam igitur adhortabar ; in excitando autem et in
acuendo plurimum valet si laudes eum quem cohortere."

[5] Br. 63, 64, De opt. gen. 9 ; cf. Or. 28 *et seq.*

opponents. Cicero endeavoured to show that not only were the Atticists in part wrong[1] in their choice of models, but that they were defective in their imitation of them, and generally succeeded only in reproducing their faults. In the *De Oratore* he[2] had briefly traced, not indeed with any degree of accuracy or historical insight, the development of Greek prose through its various stages, viz., the early period in which Pericles, Alcibiades, and Thucydides were characterised by a compressed brevity and plainness of style, the period of Lysias,[3] Critias, and Theramenes, marked by a richer vein, the perfection of Greek oratorical prose in Isocrates and Demosthenes, and its decline in Demochares and Demetrius of Phalerum. The Roman Atticists took[4] their models from the two opening periods. Those, says, Cicero,[5] who elect to follow Thucydides, take as their model one whose style[6] is more suited to history than to forensic oratory, and moreover fail to reproduce his finest qualities. Xenophon also was an author unsuitable[7] to the forensic orator.

As I have said, the Atticists considered Lysias their great prototype. Cicero could not here quarrel with their choice, as he had done in the case of Thucydides and

Lysias as model

Xenophon. To impugn the Atticist position he had to show that Lysias was not the only Attic model possible, that there were several species[8] of Attic oratory, and that the Atticist contention that the Plain style was the only Attic style, was based on ignorance[9] and

[1] e.g. in their selection of Thucydides and Xenophon.

[2] De Or. II. 92–95 ; it is interesting to note his insistence on the influence of models in this development (cf. *ib.* 91, 96) ; the account of the development in Br. 27 *et seq.*, is fuller, and differs in some details ; cf. Or. 29, for a different view of Pericles' oratory.

[3] Cicero is not so generous to Lysias in his later treatises, reacting probably against the Atticists' admiration for him.   [4] Cf. Heck, op. cit., p. 62.

[5] Br. 287–288, Or. 30–32, *ib.* 234, on his lack of periodic structure ; De opt. gen. 15–16 ; cf. De Or. II. 56, where Cicero pays him a very generous tribute ; *vide infra*, pp. 259, 513.

[6] This, in spite of Demosthenes' admiration for him.

[7] Or. 32 ; cf. De Or. II. 58 ; Q. X. 1. 33.

[8] Br. 285, 291, Or. 28 ; cf. Tac. Dial. 25.

[9] De opt. gen. 11, Ad Fam. XV. 21. 4 (on Calvus) : " genus quoddam sequebatur, in quo judicio lapsus," etc.

defective judgment. Lysias was an Atticist, but an Atticist of narrow range, whom one can praise[1] only within certain limits. He confined himself for the most part to private[2] and trivial cases, and probably, even if he had tried, could never have risen to the sublime heights of Demosthenes' oratory. Each one will, of course, praise what he himself can successfully imitate. But even the Atticists' imitation of Lysias is defective,[3] as they aim at reproducing merely his plainness. Cicero in irony suggests[4] that for their purpose they might find the elder Cato as promising a model as Lysias.

It was part of Cicero's answer to his opponents to point out the limitations of Lysias. He, moreover, was able to

Limitations of the Plain style

counter their position by dealing[5] at great length with the Plain style in general, and by showing how restricted was its range. He sets forth its characteristics in a detailed way, emphasising its kinship with the language of ordinary life, its avoidance of rhythm, elaborate periodic structure, or striking ornament, its moderate use of metaphor, and its insistence on clearness and correctness. It will exhibit restraint in delivery, and in general will concentrate on matter rather than on form, suggesting a certain air of negligence that is really designed to conceal[6] its art. This style should have its seasoning of wit and humour, qualities which, though essentially Attic, find little place in the writings of the Neo-Atticists. The Plain style, in fact, seems easy of imitation until one essays the task of writing in it. It is then[7] that its

[1] Br. 35 : " egregie subtilis scriptor atque elegans, quem *jam prope* audeas oratorem perfectum dicere " (*Ib.* Demosthenes is styled " plane perfectus ") ; Or. 226 : " alterum paene Demosthenem " ; cf. Q. X. 1. 78, nothing more perfect than Lysias " si oratori satis est docere."

[2] De opt. gen. 10–11 ; cf. Dionys. De Lysia, 16.

[3] Br. 64 : " studiosos, qui non tam habitus corporis opimos quam gracilitates consectentur," Or. 29 ; even Hegesias took Lysias as his model, but with strange results ; cf. Or. 171, on defective imitation.

[4] Br. 68 ; cf. *ib.* 293.

[5] Or. 75 *et seq.* ; cf. Dionys. De Lysia, 4, 13, on the style of Lysias ; several points of resemblance may be noted in Cicero and Dionysius.

[6] *Ib.* 3, 8.

[7] This, of course, is intended as a warning to the Atticists, and a suggestion that they have not been able to avoid the pitfalls ; cf. Tusc. Disp. II. 3 ; *vide supra*, p. 133.

pitfalls become apparent. There are certain defects[1] akin to virtues, and the danger was always present that the Atticists in endeavouring to reproduce the plainness of Lysias would carry the Plain style to excess, and end by becoming arid,[2] spiritless, and attenuated. The danger was all the more real for a Roman, as the genius of his language made it well nigh impossible[3] for him to reproduce the delicate charm and elegance of the Greek.

The Atticists, of course, in championing the Plain style put forward no new theory of style. Before they ever

The Plain style no novelty

appeared on the scene, the Plain style had been cultivated by many Romans, while in Cotta[4] was to be seen a distinguished exponent of it. In the *De Oratore*, as we saw, there was no note of hostility to those who adopted such a style, even though Cicero realised its shortcomings. He allowed,[5] too, for the personal element in the formation of one's style. He even stresses[6] the fact that he himself can employ the Plain style, when the occasion demands it, but in face of the Atticist contention he was forced to emphasise its limitations. Against his opponents he had a formidable weapon to wield in the theory[7] of the " officia oratoris." Moreover, the law of Decorum[8] demanded that style should be altered in accordance with the orator's aim. Herein lay the signal

---

[1] Br. 202 : " cavenda est presso illi oratori inopia et jejunitas " ; *ib.* 283, 285 (on Calvus), De opt. gen. 8 ; cf. Sen. Controv. I, pr. 21 ; " nihil est iniquius his, qui nusquam putant esse subtilitatem, nisi ubi nihil est praeter subtilitatem " ; *vide supra*, p. 74.

[2] Cf. Q. XII. 10. 14, on the " Atticists " of his day : " unde nunc quoque aridi et exsuci et exsangues."

[3] Q. IX. 4. 145, XII. 10. 27, 35 *et seq.*, X. 1. 100, *ib.* 5. 2 ; cf. Cic. De Or. II. 28, where the Greeks concede to Catulus " suae linguae subtilitatem elegantiamque," showing how they prided themselves on these qualities.

[4] *Vide supra*, p. 185.

[5] *Vide supra*, p. 223.

[6] Or. 101–102, on the " Pro Caecina " ; *vide supra*, p. 123, on his " Caesarian " speeches.

[7] On its place in the " De Oratore," *vide supra*, p. 220 ; cf. Br. 185, 276, Or. 69, De opt. gen. 3, 5, 16.

[8] Or. 70 *et seq.*, 104 : " at quid sequi deceat videmus " ; cf. Schlittenbauer, Die Tendenz von Ciceros Orator, p. 221.

failure of the Atticists, who were restricted to one style, and here, too, Cicero by his mastery[1] over all styles enjoyed the advantage over them. He is able to give illustrations of how his speeches varied in style according to the subject and the occasion, and how variations of style are to be found even within the limits of a single speech.

It is interesting to note that in this portion of his polemic Cicero relies much on the magic name of Demosthenes, the supreme orator,[2] who was Protean[3] in char-

The range of Demosthenes acter, but excelled particularly in sublime and impassioned eloquence, so that later theorists could formulate a fourth style based on his predominant[4] qualities of force and vehemence. The Atticists should measure oratory by the power of Demosthenes, and not by their own weakness. Cicero, who was in reality an eclectic,[5] tries to create the impression that Demosthenes was ever before him as an ideal,[6] even though he might never attain to his greatness, and that whoever selected him for imitation could never[7] be accounted an Asianist. Demosthenes was master of the Grand style, and for all that a genuine Attic orator.

Though the perfect orator should have a mastery over all three styles, Cicero, as he had already done in the *De Oratore*, awards the palm to the Grand

The Grand style supreme style, the great medium of emotional[8] eloquence. He is at pains to contrast[9] its effects with those of the Plain style, the chief function of which is

---

[1] Or. 102 *et seq.*; cf. De opt. gen. 10; such a mastery is the mark of the perfect orator, Or. 100 *et seq.*, 123 *et seq.*; *vide supra*, pp. 221–222.

[2] Br. 141, Or. 104, De opt. gen. 13; cf. Dionys. De Isaeo, 20.

[3] Br. 35, Or. 23, 110 *et seq.*; cf. Dionys. De Dem. 8, *ib.* 21-22; Nassal, Aesthetisch-Rhetorische Beziehungen, p. 141, on ancient judgments on Demosthenes.

[4] *Vide supra*, p. 76.

[5] Cf. Q. X. 1. 108.

[6] Br. 288; he credits even Brutus with an admiration for Demosthenes, Or. 105.

[7] Ad Att. XV. 1a. 2; cf. Or. 234; Q. XII. 10. 23–24; Jahn-Kroll, Brutus, Introd., p. 9.

[8] Br. 276, Or. 20, 128, De opt. gen. 5; cf. Br. 200.

[9] Br. 201 *et seq.*, 278, Or. 97–98; for the purposes of his polemic at this point, Cicero can ignore the Middle style.

to instruct.[1]   In the *Brutus*[2] he harps once more on the
" causa Curiana," with the evident purpose of showing how
impotent was the oratory of a Scaevola, when ranged against
the eloquence of Crassus who was master of every style.   He
exhibits[3] the failure of the Plain style of Laelius, when
pleading the cause of the publicani, as contrasted with the
subsequent success of Galba's impassioned oratory.   He
draws[4] the moral of all this in the case of Calidius, who, for
all the artistry of his style, lacked the vigour and the fire
essential to move his audience.   To make the contrast
between himself and the Atticists more pointed, he insists[5]
on his own achievements in emotional eloquence, which he
employed with telling effect, especially in the perorations of
his speeches.   He was master of every mood of emotion, and,
being moved[6] himself, could stir others into harmony with
his own feelings.

It was this impressive and impassioned style of oratory
that enabled the orator to make his strongest appeal to the
multitude.   Here again, Cicero points the
contrast between the Atticists and himself,
though he was not always[7] inclined to pay so
much homage to popular judgment, which tended to be
capricious and unstable.   Now, Stoic theory not only precluded an appeal to the emotions of the crowd, but was often
at variance[8] with popular opinion and popular taste.   Philosophy of its very nature will find favour[9] only with a few
intellectuals, while poetry, especially learned[10] poetry, will
be appreciated only by a select coterie.   But it was in every

The appeal
of the Grand
style

---

[1] Br. 89, Or. 20 : " tenues, acuti, omnia *docentes* " ; *ib*. 69.

[2] 144 *et seq*., 194 *et seq*. ; *ib*. 256 ; *vide supra*, p. 164.

[3] Br. 85 *et seq*. ; *vide supra*, p. 38.

[4] Br. 276.

[5] *Vide supra*, p. 224.

[6] Cf. De Or. II. 189.

[7] Br. 193, 196, Or. 237, De Fin. II. 81, Paradoxa, III. 2 ; cf. Tac.
Dial. 34 : " populi diversissimarum aurium," etc.

[8] De Or. III. 66 ; cf. Br. 120 : " Stoicorum astrictior est oratio aliquan-
toque contractior quam aures populi requirunt " ; *vide supra*, p. 162.

[9] Tusc. Disp. II. 4.

[10] Br. 191, on " poema reconditum " ; *vide infra*, p. 385.

way essential[1] for oratory, if it was to ensure its existence, to be popular in its appeal, and win the approval of the multitude. The great orator, then, will excite the admiration not only of the cultured few, but of the general public,[2] which if it does not understand the cause, will at any rate appreciate the effect of sublime eloquence. Cicero, with his own achievements still in mind, paints[3] for us a vivid picture of what should be in store for a distinguished orator, of the crowd that throngs to hear him, of the rapt attention with which his opening words are awaited, of the applause which punctuates his speech, and above all, of his masterly skill in moulding the feelings of his audience into perfect sympathy with his own. It is not the orator of the Plain style who can accomplish this miracle, but the orator whose eloquence[4] exhibits the characteristics of fire and vigour, of fervid imagination, of grand and sonorous diction. Cicero once more draws the moral of all this to the detriment of the Atticists. He issues a challenge to them to try the effect of their oratory on a popular audience. He wishes to leave the impression that they are a select and exclusive circle, whose oratory can never[5] have a wide appeal. When he feels that his victory over them is complete, he even goes so far as to proclaim[6] that they are either ignored or, if ever employed, are driven in derision from the Forum.

So far we have been occupied principally with Cicero's assault, or rather counter-attack on the general position of the Atticists. We have now to consider **Cicero's method of refutation** another side of the quarrel, the charges brought by the Atticists against his own style, and the orator's method of parrying them. Cicero, as we

---

[1] De Or. I. 12, II. 159, 338, Br. 183 *et seq.*, 191 : " oratio popularis adsensum vulgi debet movere "; cf. Q. VIII. 3, 6 (quoting a letter from Cicero to Brutus) : " nam eloquentiam, quae admirationem non habet, nullam judico."

[2] cf. Saintsbury, op. cit. II., p. 539, on Gravina's dictum " ne con solo popolo, ne senza il popolo." [3] Br. 290 ; cf. 289, on Demosthenes.

[4] *Ib.* : " subsellia grandiorem et pleniorem vocem desiderant "; *ib.* 317, Or. 29, 168, on the popular appeal of a rhythmical period ; *ib.* 236.

[5] Br. 283 ; *ib.* 278, on Calidius.

[6] De opt. gen. 11 : " cum aut non adhibeantur ad causas, aut adhibiti derideantur "; cf. Tusc. Disp. II. 3.

have seen,[1] was accused of being an Asianist, and his oratory was characterised as redundant and bombastic, loose and flabby, too florid and unrestrained, effeminate in its rhythms, and pointless in its witticisms. This was truly a formidable indictment.

Now Cicero seeks to rebut the general charge of Asianism, and to outflank his opponents, first by showing that he is thoroughly acquainted with the general[2] characteristics of the Asianist orators, and then by a searching criticism of their defects. Sometimes his criticism is indirect, as when he catalogues[3] the faults which the genuine Attic orators would avoid, faults against good taste, propriety, and purity of diction. Most often, however, his criticisms are direct, as when he condemns[4] the Asianists for their redundancy, the very defect that was attributed to himself. He comments,[5] too, on the excessive exuberance and immaturity of the Asianist style, which resembled wine that had not properly fermented, and needed the mellowing influence of time. He also criticises the Asianists' use of rhythm; for, as we shall see, the question of rhythm was a crucial one in the dispute between himself and the Atticists. He notes how the Asianists in their enslavement[6] to rhythm were ready to sacrifice sense to sound. In their efforts to gain rhythmical effects they inserted unnecessary words, and for the same reason often had recourse to unnatural transpositions[7] of the word order. Some of them, too, like Hegesias,[8] showed a tendency to cut up their sentences into a series of short clauses of a markedly rhythmical character. In this con-

Criticism of Asianist defects

---

[1] *Vide supra*, p. 227.

[2] *Vide supra*, p. 214.

[3] Br. 284, De opt. gen. 7.

[4] Br. 51 : " parum pressi et nimis redundantes " ; De opt. gen. 8, on their " vitiosa abundantia " ; cf. Q. XII. 10. 17.

[5] Br. 288 (a passage which I believe to apply to the Asianist style) : " e novam istam quasi de musto ac lacu fervidam orationem " ; cf. Or. 107 " quae nequaquam satis *defervisse* post aliquanto sentire coepimus."

[6] Or. 230 : " Asiaticos maxime numero servientes."

[7] Or. 229–230 ; the fault is exemplified from Coelius Antipater ; *vide infra*, p. 514 *et seq.*

[8] *Vide supra*, p. 214 ; cf. Ad Att. XII. 6. 1, for a parody of H.'s style

nection, their most serious defect was a fondness[1] for the employment of the dichoreus, which soon produced monotony. These latter, indeed, were fatal defects, as the art of prose-rhythm had to be concealed, if it was to add to the beauty and charm of style. Cicero evidently, too, had the Asianists in mind, when he condemns[2] the bombast and the hollow and unreal pathos displayed by orators who carry the Grand style to excess, and indulge in highflown speech when the occasion least demands it. In common with other critics, he censures[3] the sing-song intonation, which was so marked a feature in the delivery of many Asianists.

Though a similar reproach could hardly be cast against his oratory, especially in his later days, Cicero to make his indictment of the Asianists complete, touches[4] on the impurity and lack of refinement in their diction. When eloquence migrated to Asia, it lost the healthy glow of Attic speech. Cicero remarks,[5] also, on a certain heaviness and richness of language which characterised the orators of Caria, Phrygia,[6] and Mysia, though such qualities were in harmony with the national taste. The failure[7] of the Asianists in correctness, and their fondness for new coinages, were even more vehemently attacked by later critics. It is interesting to note that Cicero condemns[8] a tendency to new coinages in Sisenna, who[9] had probably come under Asianist influence.

Their lack of culture, and their failure to study the tech-

Failure in correctness

---

[1] *Vide* Blass, Die Rhythmen, p. 28 ; *vide supra*, p. 106.

[2] Or. 99 ; *vide supra*, p. 118.

[3] Or. 27, 57 ; *vide supra*, p. 213.

[4] *Vide supra*, p. 215.

[5] Or. 25 ; cf. his reference (Pro Archia, 26) to the poets of Corduba ; Sen. Suas. VI. 27.

[6] Caecilius, from his rigid Atticist standpoint, wrote a treatise κατὰ φρυγῶν ; Nassal, op. cit., pp. 155–156, positing an earlier date than is usually assigned to Caecilius, thinks Cicero may here be influenced by this treatise, but all this must remain in the region of conjecture until the problem of Caecilius' date is definitely settled.

[7] *Vide* Norden, A.K. I, p. 189 ; Schmid, Der Atticismus, Vol. I, p. 44.

[8] Br. 259–260, *ib.* 228, where he is strangely referred to as " bene Latine loquens " ; *vide supra*, p. 82.

[9] *Vide infra*, p. 516.

nical rules of their art, were sometimes[1] cast as a reproach
against the Asianist orators. We have seen
the elaborate programme that Cicero prescribed in the *De Oratore*[2] for the education
of the orator. His insistence on his own laborious training,
and the wide culture he had acquired in the course of it,
may have been designed, not merely to prove that his
eloquence in its finish, its flexibility, and its breadth of view,
was superior to that of even the greatest of his predecessors,
but also to distinguish him from the uncultured orators of
Asia, who were often more remarkable for a glib readiness
of speech than for any depth and solidity in their oratory.
It is not without significance that he connects[3] Hortensius'
ultimate failure to please discerning judges with the relaxation of his study and his industry.

The Asianists' lack of culture

Now all this censure of Asianist oratory would constitute
an admirable defence of Cicero's own ideals. For all that,
Cicero must have felt a certain weakness in
his position, where it was a question of his
early speeches, in which some Asianist features were apparent. In these speeches Cicero was guilty
of serious faults[4] of style, such as the excessive use of the
Gorgianic figures, and a tendency to employ neologisms,
archaisms, and words from vulgar Latin. He had evidently
a feeling of admiration for certain orators[5] whom he met in
his travels through Asia. These influenced him for a time,
but they eventually failed to satisfy him, so that he drifted
to Rhodes, where he found other ideals prevailing. Feeling
that his early speeches were the weak point in his armour,

Weaknesses in Cicero's position

---

[1] *Vide supra*, p. 210.

[2] Cf. also Or. 113 *et seq.*

[3] Br. 327 ; Hortensius, as we have seen, spoke better than he wrote ;
contrast Cicero's own incessant use of " stilus," Br. 321 ; *vide infra*, p. 240.

[4] Cf. Landgraf, Kommentar zu Ciceros Rede Pro Sex. Roscio Amerino,
p. 3 *et seq. ;* Norden, op. cit., I, p. 225 *et seq.*

[5] De Or. II. 95, on the brothers Menecles and Hierocles, who in Cicero's
boyhood were the model orators of Asia, Br. 325, Or. 231 ; cf. Br. 315, or
Menippus of Stratonicea : " si nihil habere molestiarum nec ineptiarum
Atticorum est, hic orator in illis numerari potest " ; Strabo, XIV. 2. 2
(C. 660) ; Br. 51 : " Asiatici oratores non contemmendi quidem nec celeri
tate nec copia " ; Plut. Cic. 4.

he seeks to justify them on the plea of " juvenilis redundantia,"[1] which soon, he declares, was moderated[2] under the restraining influence of Molon, though he is frank enough to suggest[3] that his master's task was no easy one. He goes out of his way to apologise for the lack of reserve shown in one[4] of his juvenile efforts, though he claims[5] that even in those days he had the capacity, too, for an oratory that was plain and unadorned. Moreover, he is careful to create[6] the impression that time has had a refining and mellowing influence upon his style.

In those early days, the example of Hortensius and the Hortensian[7] style of oratory must have counted much with

Significance of his criticism of Hortensius Cicero. When he returned from his travels, there were two orators supreme[8] in Rome, Cotta an orator of the Plain style, and Hortensius, vehement, ornate, and passionate in his eloquence. Cicero, by his age and temperament, felt himself drawn into rivalry with the latter. All through life he never failed to pay many generous tributes[9] to his most formidable opponent in forensic oratory. For all that, he was evidently afraid lest he should be considered to have come too strongly under the spell of the Hortensian manner, and for that reason his criticism of the orator seems to me to be designed as a subtle defence especially of his own early achievements.

[1] Br. 316; cf. De Or. II. 88, where he defends the exuberance of Sulpicius' style on a similar plea ; Q. XII. 1. 20 ; *vide supra*, p. 225.

[2] Br. 316 : " nam et contentio nimia vocis resederat, et quasi deferverat oratio."

[3] Loc. cit. : " is dedit operam, si id modo consequi potuit," etc.

[4] Or. 107, on Pro Sexto Roscio Amerino, 72 ; the passage with its elaborately balanced tetracolon, its antithesis, and its general tone of bombast, can best be paralleled in the pages of the Elder Seneca ; cf. Landgraf's notes ad loc.

[5] Or. 108 : " ipsa enim illa juvenilis redundantia multa habet attenuata."

[6] Br. 8, De Leg. I. 11.

[7] Br. 301 *et seq.* ; *vide supra*, p. 223.

[8] Br. 317.

[9] Pro Quinctio 8, Pro Sulla, 3–4, Pro Sestio, 14, Pro Milone, 37, De Or. II. 228–230, Br. 1 *et seq.* ; the role Cicero assigned H. in the " Academica " and in the lost dialogue " Hortensius," are additional proofs of his regard for him ; cf. Reid, Acad. Introd., p. 44 *et seq.*

In this criticism,[1] he is led to give a careful analysis of the two styles of Asianism, both of which were exemplified in Hortensius. His Asianist manner did not seem so much out of harmony with his character in his youth, and it always appealed to young men and to the common crowd, but, as the years went by,[2] his impetuous and impassioned oratory, with its glitter and its epigrams, its excessive embellishment and striving for effect, seemed strangely out of place, and earned the condemnation of men of mature judgment. Cicero would not, of course, admit a complete parallel between Hortensius and himself, even with regard to his early years, and, though he felt himself on unsafe ground, would repudiate the suggestion that his youthful speeches were tinged with Asianism. By a laborious training, including incessant exercise in writing, and by association[3] with some of the master minds of Greece and Rome, he had got rid of his youthful defects. If Hortensius had shown a similar zeal, and had submitted his talents to a rigid discipline, he might have modified his youthful manner, and purged his oratory of its worst extravagances.

The general character of Cicero's style being one of the questions at issue between him and the Atticists, he seems to me to make another point in his defence, when he suggests[4] that " Asianism " was in reality an excess of the Grand style. Just as the orator of the Plain style had to beware of becoming bald and jejune (a tendency marked among the Atticists, according to Cicero), so the orator of the Grand style had to guard against passing into tasteless bombast. Moreover, the

The excess of the Grand style

---

[1] *Vide supra*, p. 214; cf. Br. 326: " haec autem genera dicendi aptiora sunt adulescentibus, in senibus gravitatem non habent " ; 327 : " remaneba idem nec decebat idem " ; Or. 106.

[2] An old man cannot afford to wear a scarlet coat; cf. Arist. Rhet. III 2. 9; *vide supra*, p. 125.

[3] Cf. Or. 146.

[4] I thus interpret Br. 202 : " cavenda est presso illi oratori inopia e jejunitas, amplo autem inflatum et corruptum orationis genus " ; cf. Ad Her IV. 10. 15 ; Q. X. 2. 16 : " pro grandibus tumidi " ; Pliny, Ep. IX. 26 5 ; a correspondent (apparently with " Atticist " tendencies) criticise certain phrases of P. as " tumida," which he himself regards as " sublimia " *vide supra*, pp. 74, 138.

orator who employs[1] the Grand style on all occasions, even
when the subject does not demand it, or when the minds
of the audience have not been attuned to it, seems like a
madman or drunken reveller in the midst of sane and sober
people. To an Atticist like Calidius, the ornate, emotional
style of oratory seemed to be a species of frenzy, but
Demosthenes proved[2] that it was possible to speak in the
Grand style and still remain a perfect Atticist. Yet, even
Demosthenes was criticised[3] by Aeschines for the unrestraint
of certain of his phrases, but, as Cicero says, it is easy when
a speech is over, and the ardour of the audience has cooled,
to criticise a venturesome word or phrase uttered in the full
glow of an orator's inspiration. Thus, for Cicero's defence,
the distinction between the Grand style and the excesses to
which it might easily lead, is a point of cardinal importance.
The danger of transgressing the due limits is apparent in
an orator of Cicero's temperament. It was probably with
such a danger in mind that he practically excluded[4] from
the *Orator* the subject of epideictic oratory, though he is
careful to show that it was associated with some of the most
flagrant faults of the early Sophists.

The tendency to indulge in excessive and over-florid
ornament would be a serious temptation for the orator of
the Grand style. Cicero himself was[5] evidently charged with violating the canons of
good taste in this respect, and probably for
that reason thought it prudent to give a briefer[6] treatment
of the Figures in the *Orator*[7] than in the *De Oratore*, and

**Over-florid
ornament**

[1] *Vide supra*, p. 237.
[2] Ad Att. XV. 1a. 2.
[3] Or. 26–27 ; cf. Aesch. In Ctesiph. 166 ; Philodemus, Rhet. I. p. 197,
for criticisms of D.'s delivery on the part of Aeschines and Demetrius of
Phalerum ; Dionys. De Dem. 55.
[4] Or. 37 *et seq.*, *ib.* 42, 65–66 ; cf. Kroll, Orator, Introd., p. 10 ; Schlittenbauer, op. cit., pp. 214–215.
[5] Cf. Or. 142 : "nam si vitiosum est dicere ornate, pellatur omnino e
civitate eloquentia " ; cf. Q. XII. 10. 12–13.
[6] Cf. Or. 134 *et seq.* with De Or. III. 200 *et seq.* ; Q. IX. 3. 90, notices
the difference in the two works ; cf. Bauerschmidt, Ergebnisse einer Vergleichung, etc., p. 39.
[7] When he was in conflict with the Atticists, and was in danger of having
his position misconstrued.

to define carefully the limits to which the representatives of the three styles of oratory might go in the employment of such embellishments. Serious defects might arise from the abuse of them, and especially from the abuse of the Figures associated with the name of Gorgias. Epideictic oratory, as we have seen, might employ[1] these latter openly, and to an almost unlimited extent, but in forensic eloquence the orator of the Plain style should scrupulously avoid[2] them, while in the other styles orators should employ such devices with an economy that would allow their art to remain concealed. On this score, too, Cicero must have had misgivings about his earliest speeches, in which he succumbed[3] to the lure of the Gorgianic figures. He never,[4] of course, relinquished the ornament afforded by them, and came to value them especially for their rhythmical qualities, but he learned to realise that they might easily disfigure rather than enhance style. His maturer[5] judgment thus enabled him to use them with discrimination, and to temper his earlier excesses.

The really fundamental difference, however, between Cicero and the Atticists was concerned with the principles of Composition. It is for that reason that **Fundamental issues** Cicero gives an analysis of these principles so elaborate and minute, that he feels called[6] upon to make some apology for devoting so much attention to the subject. He feels justified especially by the consideration[7] that very many of his countrymen have been more conspicuous for their natural talent as speakers than for knowledge of the rules of artistic prose. Let us, however, first see how he deals with the choice of words and particular forms[8] from the point of view of euphony. In the

---

[1] Or. 38 et seq., ib. 65 ; vide supra, pp. 104, 131.

[2] Or. 84.

[3] Vide Landgraf, op. cit., p. 4.

[4] Or. 164–167 ; cf. his much-admired passage, Pro Archia, 16.

[5] As happened in the case of Isocrates, Or. 175–176, ib. 40 et seq. ; cf Isocr. Panathen. 1–2, Letter to Philip, 27 ; vide supra, p. 100.

[6] Or. 141 et seq. ; cf. ib. 140, where " de artificio dicendi (litteris) tam multa mandare," was reprobated by certain of his critics.

[7] Or. 143.

[8] Ib. 153 et seq.

choice of certain forms he champions the cause of Anomaly, ranges himself on the side of custom,[1] and sets a high value on the appeal to the ear which, in matters of euphony, is a better guide than the pedantic rules of the Analogist. All this is interesting in view of the fact that in the *Brutus* Cicero favours Analogy, but only in a passage[2] in which he wishes to pay a special compliment to Julius Caesar for his work *De Analogia*. Whether the Atticists as a body were Analogists,[3] or whether Cicero had them in mind, when he thus so strongly supports the claims of Anomaly in the *Orator*, it is difficult to decide, though there were certain forms[4] used by Calvus which seem to indicate that he was on the side of the Analogists. Cicero, however, contends that, in the selection of his words generally, the orator, regardless of meticulous precepts, should show a preference for those that were sonorous, though he should not imitate[5] the poet in choosing words mainly for their sound values.

The Atticists,[6] as one might expect, were uncompromising advocates of Purism. The two greatest of the Roman Atticists, Calidius and Calvus, are represented[7] by Cicero as scrupulous in their adherence to correct usage. Then we have Caesar's dictum[8] about the avoidance of the " inauditum

Purist movement

---

[1] *Ib.*: " consuetudo elegans Latini sermonis " ; *ib.* 155, 157 : " impetratum est a consuetudine ut peccare suavitatis causa liceret " ; *ib.* 159 : voluptati autem aurium morigerari debet oratio " ; *ib.* 161 : " quod si docta consuetudo tam est artifex suavitatis " ; cf. Tusc. Disp. III. 20 ; . I. 6. 18 ; *vide supra*, p. 79 *et seq.*

[2] 258, 261 ; cf. 253.

[3] Norden, op. cit., I. p. 184, favours the identification ; Kroll, Orator, introd., p. 12, seems to me more correct in denying any essential connection between the two ; in practice, however, the Atticists were purists, if not analogists.

[4] Q. I. 6. 42 ; cf. Plessis and Poirot, op. cit., pp. 23–24, on the forms delita " and " triclinarius " used by him.

[5] Or. 163 ; cf. Or. 80, De Or. III. 150.

[6] On Atticists such as Caecilius and Dionysius, cf. Blass, Die griech. ered., pp. 206, 220.

[7] Br. 274 (on Calidius) : " nec vero ullum (verbum) aut durum aut solens " ; *ib.* 283 (Calvus) : " metuensque ne vitiosum colligeret," *ib.* 4 ; cf. Or. 25 (on the Athenian ideal) : " eorum religioni cum serviret ator, nullum verbum insolens, nullum odiosum ponere audebat " ; cf. Q. . 1. 58.

[8] *Vide supra*, p. 79.

244 ROMAN LITERARY THEORY AND CRITICISM

atque insolens verbum." Both Asinius Pollio and Messalla
ranged themselves with the Purists. Moreover, as part of
the Purist movement, we have gradually emerging the
concept of " urbanitas,"[1] in which the correctness of the
Latin in use in Rome is contrasted with the impurities of
provincial Latin. " Urbanitas " is a word with many shades
of meaning, but, in as far as it applied to language, it
denoted the purity, precision, and refinement[2] of the spoken
speech, and the elegance of expression that were the distinguishing mark of the cultured inhabitant of Rome. With
the extension of the franchise, the contrast between the
speech of the city man and the peculiarities[3] of the provincial
dialects would be more strongly emphasised. The distinction between Roman and provincial Latin was, as we
have seen, already familiar to Lucilius,[4] but the term
" urbanus," with its peculiar associations, was of comparatively recent[5] origin, though Cicero, forgetting for the
moment the dramatic date of the De Oratore, makes Crassus
discourse on " urbanitas."[6] Whether or not the word was
invested with its peculiar associations by the Atticists, it is
difficult[7] to say, though their purist tendencies make this
probable.

Cicero and
" Latinitas "

Though Cicero, as far as Latin usage was
concerned, would doubtless rank himself
among the " urbani," yet he would hardly
adopt the rigorous standards of the Atticists. They, on their

---

[1] Cic. De. Or. III. 42–44, Br. 170–172, ib. 242, on the Caepasii
" oppidano quodam et incondito genere dicendi " ; Q. I. 5. 12, VIII.
2–3.

[2] The question of pronunciation would also be involved ; cf. Cic. on
Cotta, De Or. III. 42, Br. 259.

[3] There was always the fear that the purity of Roman Latin would be
infected with " peregrina insolentia " ; cf. De Or. III. 44, Br. 258, Ad Fam.
IX. 15. 2 ; Cicero evidently would include provincialisms under " peregrina
insolentia," though Q. I. 5. 56, decides to regard Tuscan, Sabine, and
Praenestine words, as of native origin.

[4] Vide supra, p. 41.

[5] Cic. Ad Fam. III. 8. 3 : " hominem non solum sapientem, verum etiam,
ut nunc loquimur, urbanum " (51 B.C.) ; Varro, R.R., I. 2. 1 ; Q. VI.
3. 34–35.

[6] De Or. III. 43 : " ex istis, quos nostis, urbanis."

[7] However, vide supra, p. 226.

own theory[1] of the Plain style, were bound to avoid the
unusual word, though they might employ it on rare occasions. Cicero, in the *De Oratore*, as we have seen, had given
merely a brief treatment of " Latinitas,"[2] with all that it
implied as regards correctness of forms and construction,
and choice of words. As became one who believed in the
superior efficacy of the Grand style, he was more interested
in all that could enhance the beauty of oratorical prose, or
increase its emotional power. The unusual[3] word could add
on occasion an element of distinction to style, but Cicero
was careful to define the limits to which one might go in
its employment. The orator[4] will use the rare word with
restraint and discrimination, and must always consider how
far the canons of correct usage will allow him to go. A real
difficulty, however, might arise when it became necessary
to determine what was the " consuetudo bene loquendi."[5]
Cicero would have permitted[6] for the sake of euphony
certain forms condemned by the Analogists. The more
rigid Purists among the Atticists would probably have
objected even to the restricted licence which he grants to
the orator in the use of rare words and new coinages. As
regards his own practice, his earliest speeches[7] might well
have offended the susceptibilities of the Purist, though even
the most uncompromising champions of correctness would
find little material for offence in his later[8] orations. His
perfunctory and somewhat cavalier treatment of " Latinitas "
in the *De Oratore* would hardly, of course, have satisfied
those who were out to purge their native tongue of its
defects. The Purist movement was particularly vigorous in
the years[9] following the appearance of the *De Oratore*, as

[1] As expounded, however, by Cicero; cf. Or. 76: " summissus est et
humilis, consuetudinem imitans "; *ib.* 81, 85.
[2] De Or. III. 38–40; *vide supra*, p. 222. [3] *Vide supra*, p. 90.
[4] De Or. I. 155, III. 39, 150, 153, 170; Or. 80.
[5] *Vide supra*, p. 79.
[6] Thus taking account of the influence of popular usage, and the natural
development of the language.
[7] *Vide* Landgraf, op. cit., p. 6 *et seq.*; *vide supra*, p. 238.
[8] His own sensitiveness to correct usage is seen in Pro Plancio, 30, Phil.
II. 22.
[9] It probably was in existence even before this, though Cicero did not
take it too seriously.

is evident from the publication[1] of Caesar's *De Analogia*. Cicero probably felt[2] that some concession had to be made to a movement that had associated with it the name of Caesar, with the result that " Latinitas " comes into greater prominence in the *Brutus*. His adoption for the moment of the standpoint of the Analogist, his many tributes[3] to those Roman orators who were distinguished for correctness in the use of their mother tongue, his acknowledgment[4] that pure Latinity is the very foundation of eloquence, are evidence that he wished to make some compensation for his meagre treatment of " Latinitas " in his earlier work. As far, however, as one can gather, the Atticists did not charge Cicero with impurity or impropriety of speech. It remained for the malignity[5] of Asinius Gallus to find fault with him on that score.

As I have said, one of the main causes of Cicero's contention with the Atticists centred in the question of composition,[6] and it is for this reason that he devotes so much attention to the subject in the *Orator*. He deals[7] with the collocation of words from the point of view of euphony, touching on such matters as the avoidance of hiatus[8] and harsh combinations of sounds. He did not, however, approve of a smoothness that would rob his oratory of its vigour, and wished above all to avoid the suspicion of over-niceness and artificiality.

The problem of Composition

[1] *Vide infra*, p. 255.

[2] He can still, however, declare : " non enim tam praeclarum est scire Latine quam turpe nescire," Br. 140.

[3] Br. 108—109, 132—133, 135, 143, 210, 233, 252 (on the influence " domestica consuetudo " on Caesar), 258, 259, 267.

[4] Br. 253, 258 ; Cicero himself had, however, enunciated a similar principle in the " De Oratore," III. 151.

[5] Pliny, Ep. VII. 4. 3 ; Q. XII. 1. 22 (where it is said that both Asinius Pollio and Asinius Gallus attacked Cicero for " vitia orationis " ; it is difficult to say if Q. has here in mind faults of Latinity) ; Gellius, XVII. i. et seq. ; Suet. Claud. 41 ; cf. Q. I. 7. 34 ; Gellius, X. 21, on Cicero's solicitude for correctness ; *ib.* XIII. 20. 22.

[6] Cf. Q. IX. 4. 1, XII. 1. 22.

[7] Or. 149 *et seq.*

[8] *Vide supra*, p. 96.

[9] Or. 150.

An even more important element in the Atticist quarrel was the question of periodic structure and prose rhythm.[1]

Prose Rhythm
Cicero had thus good reason for entering on such an elaborate discussion of the origin and nature of rhythm, and its employment in prose, and claims[2] that he has dealt with these problems more fully than any Roman before his day. According to Quintilian, Cicero was accused[3] of being sensuous, extravagant, and almost effeminate in his composition. It is clear that his opponents wished to convey the impression that the over-elaborateness of his periods, and especially his striving after rhythmical effects,[4] rendered his prose lacking in vigour. In several passages of the *Orator*, he brings us near to the heart of the dispute, as when he protests,[5] in terms that recall his adversaries, against the idea that oratorical prose is enervated by the introduction of rhythm, though he takes[6] occasion to warn orators against the marring of their style by a series of short clauses that are markedly rhythmical. We have an echo of the quarrel also in a passage in which he contrasts the curt, broken, and jerky sentences of those who make Thucydides[7] their model, with the full, rounded periods adopted by others. There were evidently many who disliked[8] the rhythmical qualities of Cicero's own oratory. The Atticists' hostility to rhythmical prose was in part based on the principles of the Plain[9] style. This kept close to the "sermo cotidianus," and,

[1] Q. IX. 4. 53, *ib.* 64.
[2] Or. 226; cf. Q. IX. 4. 1.
[3] Q. XII. 10. 12 : " in compositione fractum, exultantem, ac paene viro molliorem " ; in Tac. Dial. 18, he is called among other things solutus, *enervis, fractus, elumbis ; vide supra*, p. 227.
[4] Cf. the criticism of Isocrates' style, Dionys. De Isocr. 2–3.
[5] Or. 229 : " tantumque abest . . . ut *enervetur* oratio compositione verborum, ut aliter in ea nec impetus ullus nec vis esse possit."
[6] Or. 231 : " nec minutos numeros sequens concidat *delumbetque* sententias " ; cf. Br. 287 (on the style of Hegesias) : " at quid est tam *fractum, tam minutum* " ? cf. περὶ ὕψους, 41, on the effect of an over-rhythmical style.
[7] *Vide infra*, p. 259.
[8] Cf. Or. 170, on " invidiosus numerus."
[9] Or. 77 : " eum (the orator of the Plain style) tamquam e vinculis numerorum eximamus " ; *vide supra*, p. 120.

while aiming at clearness and correctness, affected a certain negligence[1] in composition in order to avoid any suggestion of elaborate symmetry, or suspicion of, thereby endeavouring to exert upon its audience the fascinations[2] of style. It was especially necessary to guard against such a suspicion in forensic[3] oratory. But other grounds of opposition to prose rhythm were discovered. Cicero introduces[4] an Atticist objector to it who appeals both to his own personal taste, and to the practice of the Ancients of not employing rounded periods. Brutus was evidently one of those whose temperament led them to disapprove strongly of a prose that was strikingly rhythmical. This is the secret of his demurring[5] to Cicero's praise of Isocrates. Quintilian tells[6] us that he stood almost alone in his disapprobation of the rhythm in a passage from Demosthenes' Third Philippic, and that, in his passion for simplicity and severity of style, he was partial[7] to iambic endings which would make his language akin to that of ordinary life.

Cicero devoted a large section[8] of his *Orator* to answering such objectors. He endeavours to show the beauty of

Defence of Prose Rhythm

rhythm and of periodic structure, and to point out how strong is their appeal to those who have ears[9] for such harmonies, by contrasting the effect of a compact, well-rounded period with sentences that are loose and ill-constructed. The Ancients who are invoked by his opponents, would have employed such devices, if they had known them, and even they at times stumbled by chance[10] on rhythmical effects. If his

[1] Or. 20 : " impoliti et consulto rudium similes " ; *vide supra*, p. 134.
[2] *Vide supra*, p. 132.
[3] Or. 170 : " nimis enim insidiarum ad capiendas aures adhiberi videtur " ; cf. περὶ ὕψους, 41. 2 ; *vide supra*, pp. 104, 131.
[4] Or. 168–169.
[5] *Ib.* 40.
[6] IX. 4. 63.
[7] Q. IX. 4. 76 ; cf. *ib.* 3. 95 ; Q., however, notes a hexameter ending in one of his letters (IX. 4. 75) ; In Tac. Dial. 18, B. is styled " dijunctus," which seems to indicate a lack of periodic structure ; cf. Peterson, ad. loc.
[8] 168–236.
[9] The ear will naturally be the great arbiter where rhythm is concerned ; cf. Or. 168, 177–178, 227, 232 *et seq.* ; Q. IX. 4. 116.
[10] Cf. De Or. III. 198, Br. 33, Or. 177.

opponents are not sensitive to the inherent beauty of rhythm, and to its necessity for the perfection of oratorical style, they may perhaps be convinced by the authority[1] of Greek theorists such as Isocrates, Aristotle, and Theophrastus. Cicero then proceeds to set forth in detail the cause and the nature of rhythm, and to define strictly the limits to which it may be employed by the orator. While laying a certain stress on the euphonious arrangement of words, he concerns[2] himself principally with two species of rhythm, a certain natural rhythm that springs from balanced and symmetrical clauses such as are found in the Gorgianic[3] figures, and the rhythm that comes from the employment of specific feet such as are met with in the poets. His own leanings towards the Gorgianic figures, especially in his earliest speeches, had helped to cast suspicion on him as an Asianist, and it is for that reason that in the *Orator* he is careful to criticise[4] the dangerous tendencies in the prose of Gorgias and Thrasymachus.

Isocrates corrected many of the faults of his predecessors. Cicero has a special purpose in view in tracing the part played by him in the development of Greek prose, because, allowing for the difference between the epideictic and other styles of oratory, his debt[5] to him in matters of style and composition was no small one. In defending Isocrates then against such a critic as Brutus, he was in a measure defending his own position. He pays many tributes to the Greek orator, even ascribing to him in the *De Oratore*[6] the invention of prose-rhythm. Isocrates was undoubtedly influenced[7] by

The position of Isocrates

[1] *Ib.* 172.
[2] Or. 181, 219–220, *ib.* 149.
[3] It is interesting to note that in the " Orator " Cicero seems to value the Gorgianic figures particularly for their rhythmical effects ; in the " De Oratore " they are classified rather with the Figures in general, De Or. III. 06 ; cf., however, *ib.* 198.
[4] *Vide supra*, p. 100 ; cf. Q. IX. 3. 74.
[5] On the theoretical side of oratory, cf. De Inv. II. 7, Ad Fam. I. 9. 23 ; . De Or. II. 10, where Isocr. is styled " pater eloquentiae " ; Hubbell, The Influence of Isocrates on Cicero, p. 16 *et seq.*
[6] III. 173 ; Br. 33 ; cf. Or. 175, for his revised opinion.
[7] Arist. Rhet. III. 9. 7 ; Dionys. De C. V. c. 23, De Isocr. 1, 13 ; Cic. r. 176, Cato Major, 13 ; Q. III. 1. 13, IX. 3. 74 ; Blass, Die attische

his predecessors, but Cicero aims at showing that he understood[1] better than they the beauty of periodic structure, and the laws that should govern rhythm in prose. If the " Art " of Rhetoric attributed to Isocrates is authentic,[2] he laid down the important principle that in prose rhythm there should be an admixture[3] of all kinds of feet, while the suggestion of verse should be carefully avoided. Thus the art of rhythm would be more effectively concealed. Moreover, instead of the short rhythmical clauses affected by certain of the Sophists, he introduced an ampler and more rounded period, and rhythms that were less harsh and obtrusive. As time went on, he favoured a less highly rhythmical prose. Like Cicero himself, he felt called upon to make some apology[4] for the extravagances of his youthful manner. But, though Isocrates marked a distinct advance upon his predecessors, his style was never wholly free from serious defects.[5] There was in him a tendency to luxuriance and redundancy, at times even an inclination to bombast, and a fondness for effects that were often puerile. There was a monotonous smoothness in his periods that made his style seem languid and nerveless. He could never wholly escape from the lure of the Gorgianic figures, and was always in danger of becoming a slave to the beauty of rhythm. Cicero passes[6] over in silence the defects of his prose, but indirectly defends him by making him the greatest exponent of epideictic[7] oratory, which enjoyed[8] a larger freedom in the use of rhetorical ornament than the forensic and deliberative styles.

Beredsamkeit, II. p. 176 et seq. ; Philod. Rhet. II. 97, reckons him among the Sophists ; vide supra, p. 100.

[1] Or. 40–41, 172, 174–176.

[2] Vide Sheehan, De Fide Artis Rhetoricae Isocrati Tributae, who defends its authenticity.

[3] Vide supra, p. 101 ; cf. Or. 190, where Hieronymus claims to have discovered many verses in Isocrates' own writings.

[4] Vide supra, p. 242 ; cf. De Or. III. 36, on his attitude to Theopompus

[5] Cf. Dionys. D. C. V. c. 19, 23, De Isocr. 3, 12 et seq. ; Demetr. 12 περὶ ὕψους, 38. 2.

[6] Cf., however, Or. 151, on his avoidance of hiatus.

[7] De Or. III. 141, Or. 37, 42, 207, De opt. gen. 17 ; Q. X. 1. 79 Dionys. De Isocr. 2 ; Blass, Die att. Bered. II, p. 205 et seq.

[8] Vide supra, pp. 71, 131.

In this connection, he seeks to guard further against the attacks of his Atticist opponents on the subject of rhythm,

The limits of Rhythm in prose by clearly defining the limits to which it may be employed. Isocrates was his master in many things, but he wishes to avoid the suspicion that he was unduly subservient to his influence. Hence he once more stresses the distinction between epideictic and forensic oratory with which we have already dealt. Here it will be sufficient to note how insistent Cicero is that, especially in forensic oratory, rhythm should not be obtrusive, and should seem to come spontaneously.[1] There are certain rhythms suited[2] to certain styles, while even within the limits of a single speech subtle changes[3] of rhythm are essential. If an orator's thoughts and language are impressive, the rhythm of his speech, while giving pleasure, will not attract attention, but, if rhythm is absent, his style will be felt to lack a certain charm. Cicero, however, feels bound to protest against the orator[4] who aims at little else than rhythmical effects. His criticisms of the Asianist orators make it clear that herein lay one of their greatest faults. He was careful, too, to point out[5] that the grand periodic style was an instrument that was not always to be used in forensic oratory, where it was suited especially for passages of heightened emotion, and for narrative passages of more than ordinary dignity. All this is an ingenious defence of his own practice. His insistence on the beauty of rhythm when properly employed, and at the same time his rigorous limitations of its use, constitute a sufficient answer to those who might maintain that, like the Asianists, he was enslaved to it. When he speaks[6] with indignation of the possibility of Demosthenes being accounted a native of Tralles (i.e., an Asianist) by the rigid

[1] Or. 219.

[2] Ib. 196.

[3] Ib. 212 : " cursum contentiones magis requirunt, expositiones rerum tarditatem " ; vide supra, p. 102.

[4] Or. 170, ib. 236 : " composite et apte sine sententiis dicere insania est."

[5] Or 209 et seq., ib. 221 : " haec (i.e. ' incisa ' and ' membra ') enim in veris causis maximam partem orationis obtinent."

[6] Or. 234.

Atticists, we feel that in Cicero's mind his own name could have been substituted for that of the Greek orator. He issues a final challenge[1] to the Atticists to write something in the style of Isocrates, Aeschines, or Demosthenes, if they wish to prove that it was by deliberate choice, and not through despair that they avoided rhythmical prose.

Cicero had dealt[2] at great length with the theory of the Laughable as applied to oratory, and had insisted on the importance of a due measure of wit in the orator. Many tributes[3] were paid to him both in his own and succeeding ages in respect of this gift, in which he was considered the superior of Demosthenes. In spite of this, the Atticists had accused him of being at times pointless[4] in his witticisms. There was a measure of truth in the accusation, but Cicero retorted by pointing out how completely they themselves failed in wit, the most Attic of endowments. Both wit and humour have a place in the Plain[5] style which they so ardently championed. To neither could Cicero's opponents lay claim. Even if Cicero were to admit his own failure in wit, he can still point[6] to the fact that some of the greatest of the Attic orators were not conspicuous for this quality.

Indictment of Cicero's wit

As I have already said,[7] difficulties arise when we try to determine what other members besides Calvus and Calidius constitued the Atticist circle. It will not do, as some advocate, to give the title " Atticist " to every follower[8] of the Plain style. It is clear, I think, that when Cicero speaks of Atticists, he has

The Atticist circle

---

[1] *Ib.* 235.

[2] *Vide infra*, p. 362 *et seq.*; cf. Br. 322, on his own power of using this weapon effectively.

[3] Ad Fam. IX. 16. 4, XV. 21. 2; Q. VI. 3. 3, X. 1. 107; cf., however Q. VI. 3. 2, on the lack of discrimination in Cicero's wit; Plut. Comp of Cic. and Dem. I.

[4] Q. XII. 10. 12: " in salibus aliquando frigidum "; cf. Cicero himself on witticisms " domo adlata, quae plerumque sunt frigida " (Or. 89).

[5] Or. 87 *et seq.*; *vide supra*, p. 36.

[6] Or. 90; Dem. " non tam dicax fuit quam facetus "; cf. Q. VI. 3. 2 21; Dionys. De Dem. 54; περὶ ὕψους, XXXIV. 2, where he is contrasted with Hyperides.

[7] *Vide supra*, p. 226.

[8] All the Stoic orators would thus share in the title.

in mind, not all those who had adopted the Plain style, but those who theorised about style, and maintained that the Plain style was the only Attic style.

Cornificius belonged to the circle of the " poetae novi,"[1] and seems, moreover, to have been infected by the theories **Cornificius** of the Atticists. It is evident[2] that he held views on the best style at variance with those of Cicero, who sent him a copy of his *Orator* in the hope of getting his approval for the work, but yet with some misgiving that it might not altogether find favour with him.

The younger Cato is sometimes classed with the Atticists, but it is doubtful[3] if he belonged to their number. His style **Cato and** possessed a certain charm acquired from his **Caelius Rufus** teachers of Rhetoric, but it is clear that his greatest strength lay in the dialectical quali- ties which he had acquired from his Stoic masters. Again, there seems little reason for classing Caelius Rufus as an Atticist. He is often mentioned[4] by ancient authors in company with professed Atticists, but rather as a contem- porary than as one who shared their views. Cicero's refer- ence[5] to him in the *Brutus* almost certainly concerns his political activities. The qualities of style (splendida et grandis oratio), which Cicero attributes[6] to Caelius, an old pupil[7] of his own, and the absence of any note of literary polemic in the correspondence that passed between them, make it improbable that he took the Atticist side. It is at any rate unlikely that he would have been friendly disposed to Calvus, the bosom friend of Catullus,[8] or would

[1] Cf. Macrob. Sat. VI. 5. 13, on his " Glaucus "; Ovid, Tristia, II. 436; Schanz, op. cit., I. 2, p. 87; Tenney Frank, Vergil, p. 116 *et seq.*

[2] Ad Fam. XII. 17. 2.

[3] In spite of the tribute to him, which Cicero puts into Brutus' mouth, Br. 118; *ib.* 119; cf. Paradoxa, Proem; Plut. Cato Min. 5.

[4] Vell. II. 36. 2; Pliny, N.H. VII. 49. 165; Tac. Dial. 38; Columella, De Re Rust. I. pr. 30.

[5] Br. 273 : " nescio quo modo discessu meo discessit a sese ceciditque, postea quam eos imitari coepit quos ipse perverterat."

[6] Br. loc. cit., Pro Caelio, 45.

[7] *Ib.* 9; Q. XII. 11. 6.

[8] For the relations of Caelius and Catullus, cf. Cat. 69, 77, with Ellis's notes.

have shown sympathy with his literary theories. Caelius was remarkable for his natural talent,[1] his wit,[2] and his gift of invective,[3] which made him especially formidable as a prosecutor, but his faulty composition,[4] his love of vulgarisms, and the archaic colouring of his style, would hardly have satisfied the fastidious taste of Calvus and his circle.

It is difficult to determine how far Julius Caesar embraced the views of the Atticists. It was generally acknowledged[5] that, if he could have devoted time to the development of his talents, he would have risen to the greatest heights as an orator. He is praised[6] especially for the purity, elegance, and refinement of his language, qualities which he acquired partly through the influence of domestic tradition,[7] and partly by his own careful study of correct usage. His treatise[8] on Analogy was dedicated to Cicero, and aimed at putting the Latin language on an orderly and rational basis, thus rendering it safe from the capriciousness of custom. It is clear that he had devoted long and earnest study to the question. His book seems to have dealt primarily with problems of grammar, with the forms,[9] inflexions, and classification of words, but it dealt, too, with the purity of Latin as the

The views of Julius Caesar

---

[1] Q. XII. 10. 11 : " indolem Caelii."

[2] Br. 273 : " faceta et perurbana . . . oratio " ; Q. VI. 3. 25, *Ib.* 39, 41.

[3] Q. IV. 2. 123–124, gives us a good specimen of his powers in this direction ; *ib.* IX. 3. 58, X. 1. 115, X. 2. 25 ; Sen. De Ira, III. 8. 6, calls him " iracundissimum " ; Suet. De Rhet. 2.

[4] Cf. Tac. Dial. 21, *ib.* 25, where he is called " amarior," probably in reference to the immaturity of his style, and not to his powers of invective ; cf. Q. I. 6. 29, on his use of " frugi " ; *ib.* 42 ; Westermann, op. cit., II, pp. 206, 209 ; Meyer, Or. Rom., p. 193 *et seq.*, with quotation from Diomede on Caelius' use of " hietare."

[5] Suet. J.C. 55 (quoting a letter from Cicero to Nepos) ; cf. Br. 261, where Cicero says : " in communibus (not quoted by Suet.) non video cui debeat cedere " ; Tac. Dial. 21, Annals, XIII. 3 ; Q. X. 1. 114.

[6] Br. 252, 261 ; Gellius, XIX. 8. 3 ; cf. Caesar's own criticism o Terence as a " puri sermonis amator."

[7] Tac. Dial. 28.

[8] Br. 253 *et seq.* ; Q. I. 7. 34 ; Fronto, II. 28 : " De Analogia libro scrupulosissimos scripsisse " ; Suet. J.C. 56.

[9] Fronto, loc. cit. ; Gellius, XIX. 8. 3 *et seq.*

foundation[1] of eloquence (and presumably of good style in general), and counselled[2] the avoidance of unusual words.

Hendrickson has put forward[3] the view that the *De Analogia* was written as a protest against Cicero's meagre and perfunctory treatment of " Latinitas "

His " De Analogia "

in the *De Oratore*, where the orator with his predilection for the Grand style had concentrated chiefly on the qualities that could heighten the emotional effect of eloquence. He defends his view with great acumen, but still it is difficult to believe that Caesar would have dedicated the work to Cicero, if it had been intended as a protest against his shortcomings. Moreover, Caesar's tribute to the orator as " paene princeps copiae atque inventor," and his praise of the service which Cicero had rendered to Rome by the enrichment of his native tongue, seem hard to reconcile with such a theory. Some support, however, may be found for it in the note of warning contained in the same tribute against the neglect of the " sermo cotidianus." It seems, indeed, certain that Cicero in the *Brutus* was influenced by the strong Purist movement then prevailing, of which the *De Analogia* was but one expression. We cannot, of course, minimise the influence[4] of this latter work, but apart altogether from the treatise, and the peculiar position of its author in Roman political life, Cicero would probably have felt himself bound to pay some homage to the ideals of the Purists.

Caesar's " Atticist " leanings seem to have been chiefly on the side of the purist and grammarian. We do not hear of his having sponsored any theory of com-

The character of his oratory

position. Though he laid special emphasis on purity of diction, he did not altogether neglect the ornaments[5] of rhetoric in his own oratory, and

---

[1] Br. 253 : "verborum dilectum originem esse eloquentiae "; Kroll, ad loc., is inclined to lay too little stress on this aspect of Caesar's treatise ; cf. Br. 261.

[2] *Vide supra*, p. 243 ; cf. Cic. Ad Att. XII. 6a. 2, on Caesar's smile at Atticus' use of " quaeso."

[3] The " De Analogia " of Julius Caesar, Classical Phil. I. p. 97 *et seq*.

[4] That is evident in the whole discussion, Br. 252 *et seq*.

[5] Br. 261 ; Suet. J.C., 55.

was remarkable for the passionate character of his delivery.[1] Suetonius mentions the interesting fact that in his youth he took as his model Caesar Strabo, whose style[2] was elegant indeed, but almost conversational in tone. Caesar would have supported the Atticists' stand for purity of diction, but when we consider the bitter attacks[3] made by Calvus on him and his friends, it is difficult to believe that, in spite of their subsequent reconciliation, he could have shown complete sympathy with the band of rigid Atticists who were so vehemently striving to impose their views on the Roman public. However, in the domain of history, his *Commentaries*, written[4] in clear, direct, and graceful language, without effort at embellishment, would have satisfied the requirements of the most uncompromising Atticist.

It is evident from what has been already said, that in the matter of style Brutus was ranged with the opponents of Cicero. The question[5] of prose rhythm and elaborate periodic structure was one of the chief points at issue between them. The character of Cicero's appeal in the *Orator* affords evidence enough that Brutus did not favour highly ornate and emotional oratory. Cicero considered[6] Brutus' own style as lacking in vigour and spirit. He describes[7] his Capitoline speech as refined both in thought and diction, but declares that he himself would have treated the subject with greater fire. Aper in the *Dialogus* characterises[8] Brutus' speech for

The position of Brutus

---

[1] Suet. loc. cit. ; Q. X. I. 114 (on his " vis " and " concitatio ") ; Apul. Apol. 95, attributes " calor " to him.

[2] *Vide supra*, p. 62 ; Caesar's forcible and passionate delivery seems difficult to reconcile with Suet.'s statement, unless his oratory underwent a change in his later years.

[3] Cic. Ad Fam. VII. 24. 1 ; Suet. J.C., 49, 73 ; Plessis and Poirot, op. cit., p. 3, fr. 3.

[4] Br. 262 ; cf. Hirtius, B. Gall. VII. pr. (quoted by Kroll *ad loc.*) ; Suet. J.C., 56, where an adverse criticism from A. Pollio is quoted ; *vide infra*, pp. 513, 518.

[5] *Vide supra*, p. 248.

[6] Tac. Dial. 18, where Cicero styles him " otiosus " ; Statius' reference (Silvae, IV. 9. 20) to " Bruti senis oscitationes " is obscure.

[7] Ad Att. XV. 1a. 2 ; cf. *ib*. XIII. 46. 1, on the effect of Brutus' " Cato," as compared with Cicero's.

[8] Dial. 21 ; cf. Plut. Brutus, 6.

Deiotarus as dull and tedious. Cicero's verdict[1] on the speech is more favourable, though, possibly out of a desire to pay a special compliment to his friend, he attributes qualities to it which are not usually associated with his oratory. Brutus was essentially of the philosophic temperament, given to introspection, and incapable of the ardour and enthusiasm which one looks for from a great orator. His writings[2] on philosophy, as well as the dedication of philosophical treatises to him by Cicero, make it probable that philosophy[3] was his main intellectual interest. His outlook was pre-eminently that of the student,[4] which accounts for his fondness for mere academic[5] exercises even in oratory. Cicero ascribes[6] to him the statement that he was more interested in the theoretical side of rhetoric than in its practical values. Apart from the reactions of the Atticist quarrel, it is hard to imagine a man of such a character as Brutus being attracted to the glowing and passionate eloquence which was Cicero's ideal for the supreme orator. Cicero possibly had hopes that, after his elaborate defence of his own theory of style in the *Orator*, he might wean Brutus from his Atticist allegiance, though he concludes[7] that treatise with a foreboding[8] (afterwards realised) that his arguments may have fallen upon deaf ears.

The enmity of Asinius Pollio towards Cicero is well known,[9] and caused him to attack most bitterly both the **Asinius Pollio** man and the orator. It is not, however, easy to decide how far Pollio shared the views of Calvus and his followers. To judge from his character in

---

[1] Br. 21 ; Brutus pleaded " ornatissime et copiosissime " ; Ad Att. XIV. 1. 2 : " valde vehementer eum visum et libere dicere."

[2] Tusc. Disp. V. 1. 2, De Fin. I. 8 ; Sen. Ep. 95. 45.

[3] Cf. Br. 120, 149 ; Tac. Dial. 21 : " Brutum philosophiae suae relinquamus " ; Q. X. 1. 123 ; Q. XII. 10. 11, attributes " gravitas " to his oratory, which may in part be the outcome of his philosophic training ; cf. Tac. Dial. 25 ; Plut. Br. 2.

[4] Cic. Br. 22, 331–332, Or. 34 ; Q. X. 7. 27 ; for his historical studies, cf. Ad Att. XII. 5. 6, XIII. 8 ; Plut. Br. 4 ; for his poetry, cf. Tac. Dial. 21 ; Pliny, Ep. V. 3. 5.

[5] Q. III. 6. 93, X. 1. 23, X. 5. 20.

[6] Br. 23.   [7] Or. 237.

[8] Ad Att. XIV. 20. 3, XV. 1a. 2.

[9] Sen. Suas. VI. 14, 24, 27 ; Tac. Dial, 25 ; Q. XII. 1. 22.

other matters, it is not improbable that he took an independent line in his opposition to Cicero. He was a keen and forceful critic,[1] who evidently set a high value on purity[2] of language, so that he condemned Livy for his provincialisms, and Sallust because of his excessive fondness for archaisms. His own style, however, seemed to Aper so archaic in colouring that, with characteristic exaggeration, he described[3] him as reproducing not only in his tragedies,[4] but in his speeches, the qualities of Accius and Pacuvius. Quintilian considers[5] that, as regards his oratorical style, he might have belonged to an earlier generation, so little did he exhibit of the brilliancy and charm of Ciceronian prose. The archaic, or what we might more correctly call the old-fashioned[6] character of his style, was evidently due, not to any love of archaism,[7] but to the fact that he lacked the grace and distinction of modern prose. He developed a style[8] that aimed at precision, but one that was harsh, jejune, and unadorned. As happened in the case of Calvus, the peculiarities of his style seem to have been in part the outcome of a morbid self-criticism,[9] though he allowed himself to indulge more freely in rhetorical embellishments

[1] Sen. Suas. II. 10, Controv. II. 3 (11). 13, IV. pr. 11 ; Q. VIII. 1. 3, IX. 3. 13 ; Gellius, X. 26. 1 ; Suet. De Gr. 10 ; Gudeman's suggestion (Dial. 21. 12) that Livy's condemnation (Controv. IX. 2. 26) of those " qui verba antiqua et sordida consectantur," has reference to Pollio, is hard to reconcile with the latter's criticism of Sallust, and his general regard for purity of speech.

[2] Q., however, criticises his use of " hos lodices," I. 6. 42.

[3] Dial. 21 ; *vide infra*, p. 325.

[4] To which Virgil pays so high a tribute, Eclog. VIII. 10, *ib*. III. 86 ; cf. Hor. Sat. I. 10. 42 ; Odes, II. 1. 9 ; cf. Pliny, Ep. V. 3. 5, for his lighter poems.

[5] X. 1. 113.

[6] Q. was judging him by the standard of Ciceronian prose, Aper by that of his own " Moderns."

[7] Q. I. 8. 11, notes, however, his fondness for quotations from the older poets, but that was a characteristic of the oratory of the period.

[8] Tac. Dial. 21 : " adeo durus et siccus est " ; Q. X. 2. 17 : " tristes ac jejuni Pollionem aemulantur" ; Q. harps on his " diligentia," in reference probably to the careful precision of his language, X. 1. 113, X. 2. 25, XII. 10. 11.

[9] Sen. Controv. IV. pr. 3 : " illud strictum ejus et asperum et nimis iratum ingenio suo judicium."

when declaiming than in his ordinary pleadings. He seems to have eschewed deliberately anything in the nature of a highly rhythmical prose. He had no love for the rounded periods and harmonious cadences of Ciceronian prose,[1] but affected[2] rugged and jerky sentences with abrupt and unexpected endings. Quintilian mentions[3] his partiality for iambic endings, which, as we saw in the case of Brutus, were designed to impart a certain simplicity and severity to his style.

The suggestion[4] has been made, though there is no direct evidence for it, that Pollio was one of those who took Thucydides as model. Cicero is especially severe[5] on the Atticists who imitated Thucydides. The historian's style[6] was immature and archaic in character, while the speeches which he interspersed throughout his history were often, through his desire for compression, so obscure as to be unintelligible. With the contrast of Isocratean style in mind, Cicero misses in him the rounded period, though at times his prose was rhythmical not from design, but from a chance collocation[7] of words. Dionysius, who devoted[8] so much attention to the style of Thucydides, though he recognises some impressive rhythms in the Funeral speech, regards the historian as a representative of the αὐστηρὰ ἁρμονία, which, in its striving after the appearance of freedom and naturalness, affects a certain ruggedness and irregularity. Cicero expressly condemns[9] the followers of Thucydides for failing

A follower of Thucydides ?

[1] Sen. Ep. 100. 6–7, contrasts the two types of composition.

[2] Hence the difficulty of the reading " numerosior," Tac. Dial. 25 ; " nervosior " has been proposed ; cf. Gudeman *ad loc.* ; Val. Max. VIII. 13. 4, styles P. " nervosae vivacitatis haud parvum exemplum."

[3] IX. 4. 76.

[4] Kroll, Orator, Introd. p. 11 ; Groebe, Art. A. Pollio in Pauly-Wissowa.

[5] *Vide supra*, p. 230.

[6] Br. 287–288, *ib.* 29 ; cf. De Or. II. 93 ; Dionys. Ep. ad Pomp. c. 3, Ad Amm. II. c. 2, De Thucyd. 24 *et seq.*

[7] Or. 219 ; Cicero here seems to have in mind the rhythmical effect of the Gorgianic figures, though he elsewhere (Or. 39) denies that Th. came under the influence of Gorgias ; cf. Dionys. Ad Amm. loc. cit. ; Demetr. 39–40, 44–45, for rhythmical effects in Th. ; *vide infra*, p. 492.

[8] De C. V. c. 10, 18, 22 ; cf. Demetr. 48, 181.

[9] Or. 32, *ib.* 170 (where he seems to have in mind especially the followers

to attain the grandeur of his thought and diction, and for reproducing solely the discordant and unpleasing elements in his composition. Such imitators regard themselves as perfect Thucydideans, if they string together some curt and disjointed phrases. They, too, would be amongst the most vehement opponents of the rhythmical periods beloved by Cicero. Quintilian speaks[1] of those who obscure their meaning by the abrupt closing of their sentences in their efforts to surpass Sallust and Thucydides. Sallust had probably done much to make the imitation[2] of Thucydides popular at Rome. He endeavoured to reproduce in his own writings[3] something of the archaic colouring, the abruptness, and compressed brevity of the Greek historian. In his own day he set the fashion,[4] which his followers usually carried to excess, of truncated and unrhythmical sentences, and a conciseness that often resulted in obscurity. In the qualities here set forth we can see the affinity between Sallust and those imitators of Thucydides whom Cicero has described. When we consider the characteristics of Pollio's style, especially as depicted for us by Seneca, and take into account his historical[5] studies, it is not unwarranted to assume that, even in his oratory,[6] he took the Greek historian as his model, and imitated some of the least attractive elements of his style.

Messalla, too, has been reckoned among the Atticists. Like Pollio he was a poet[7] and historian. He was interested[8]

---

of Th.) : " hoc freti isti et ipsi infracta et amputata loquuntur, et eos vituperant qui apta et finita pronuntiant " ; *ib.* 234–235 ; on followers of Thucydides, cf. Virg. Catal. 2 ; Q. VIII. 3. 28 ; Dionys. De Thucyd. 52 *et seq.*, 55, περὶ μιμ. Usener, p. 24 ; De Din. 8 ; Philod. Rhet. I. p. 151 ; Nassal, op. cit., p. 101 *et seq.*

[1] X. 2. 17.

[2] Q. X. 1. 101, matches him with Thucydides ; cf. Vell. II. 36. 2.

[3] Q. IV. 2. 45, VIII. 3. 29, IX. 3. 12, X. 1. 32 ; *vide infra*, p. 273.

[4] Sen. Ep. 114. 17 : " sic Sallustio vigente amputatae sententiae, et verba ante expectatum cadentia et obscura brevitas fuere pro cultu."

[5] Hor. Odes, II. 1. 1 *et seq.; Peter, Hist. Rom. Rel. II. p. 83 *et seq.*, *ib.* p. 67 *et seq.*

[6] For fragments, cf. Curcio, De Ciceronis et Calvi, etc., p. 84 *et seq.*

[7] Pliny, Ep. V. 3. 5.

[8] Q. I. 5. 15, I. 7. 23 (on his treatise on the letter " s ") ; *ib.*, 35.

particularly in grammatical questions and in the history
of the Latin language, and was evidently
Messalla. strongly on the side of the Purists.[1]
Quintilian praises[2] the transparency and polish of his
diction, but considers that he did not do full justice
to his powers. Tacitus, though he finds[3] the exordia
of his speeches tedious, pays a tribute[4] to him for the ripe-
ness and charm of his style, and the careful precision of his
language. He was fond of translating from the Greek as a
rhetorical exercise, and succeeded[5] in the very difficult task
of reproducing in Latin the delicacy (subtilitas) of Hyperides'
speech for Phryne. Though we hear[6] of certain Atticists
who took Hyperides as their model, and though Messalla
exhibits many of the qualities associated with Roman
Atticism, he seems to have been too young to have shared
directly in the ideals of Calvus and his circle. Quintilian,
however, speaks[7] of him as having begun to plead when
Cicero " held the citadel of eloquence." Still, between his
return from Athens[8] and Cicero's death, he was probably
too deeply involved[9] in the designs of Brutus and his fellow-
revolutionaries to have done much pleading, though he had
already gained a reputation as an orator. The elder Seneca
gives us[10] some glimpses of him in the schools of declamation,
where he evidently had little sympathy with the extravagances of many of the declaimers. But the fine tribute that
Cicero pays[11] to his personal character[12] and to his talents as

---

[1] Schol. to Hor. Sat. I. 10. 28, on his objection to the Greek word
" schoenobates " ; Sen. Controv. II. 4 (12). 8, Suas. II. 17 ; Q. I. 5. 61 ;
however, Q. I. 6. 42, notes his use of the plural " gladiola " ; *ib.* VIII.
3. 34, on his coinage of " reatus."   [2] X. 1. 113.
[3] Dial. 20 ; contrast Q. IV. 1. 8, who finds his exordia effective.
[4] Dial. 18.   [5] *Vide infra*, p. 429.
[6] Br. 67 ; cf. Acad. Post. 11.   [7] Q. XII. 11. 28.
[8] He studied there with young Cicero ; cf. Ad Att. XII. 32. 3, XV.
17. 2.
[9] Cic. Ad Brut. I. 12. 1 ; Vell. II. 71 ; Plut. Br. 40, 42.
[10] Suas. III. 6, Controv. III. pr. 14.
[11] Ad Br. I. 15. 1 (if the latter can be regarded as genuine) : " ita gravi
judicio multaque arte se exercuit in verissimo genere dicendi " (a strange
tribute, if Messalla was then a pronounced Atticist) ; cf. Sen. Suas. VI. 27,
on Ena's panegyric on Cicero in Messalla's house.
[12] Cf. Q. X. 1. 113, XII. 10. 11.

an orator, makes it improbable that he joined in the Atticists' polemic against Cicero's style.

As far as Cicero is concerned, we need not follow further the fortunes of Roman Atticism. Octavian, the future Emperor, is generally counted among the Atticists inasmuch as he was an adherent[1] of the Plain style, advocating restraint, and condemning the empty volubility of the Asianist orators and affectation of every kind. Dionysius in an interesting passage[2] speaks of the part which Rome played in bringing about a revolution in taste, and a revival of reverence for the old Attic models. He pays a special tribute to the ruling classes (οἱ δυναστεύοντες) as the chief agents in effecting such a revolution. It is not unlikely that Dionysius had here in mind among other factors the powerful influence of Augustus in setting the standard of taste. Dionysius speaks as if the victory of Atticism was assured, though under Augustus the most glaring faults of Asianism were to appear in their most exaggerated form in the schools of declamation.

We are largely dependent upon Cicero himself for the account of his quarrel with the Atticists. He would naturally be tempted to stress the aspects of the discussion which told most in his own favour, and would be inclined to exaggerate the weakness of his opponents' position. The picture that he draws[3] of Calvus' oratory, would lead one to believe that it could only be appreciated by a select few, that it lacked vigour, and that Calvus in common with his brother Atticists failed to appeal to the masses. There are, however, indications from other sources[4] that Calvus by the vehemence of

The attitude of Augustus

Exaggerations in Cicero's advocacy ?

[1] Sen. Controv. IV. pr. 7, X. pr. 14 ; Suet. Aug. 86, *ib.* 89 ; cf. Fronto, II. p. 136 ; Gellius, X. 24. 2, XV. 7. 3 ; Macrob. Sat. II. 4. 12 ; *vide supra*, p. 217.

[2] De Antiq. Or. c. 3.

[3] Br. 283 *et seq.*, Ad Fam. XV. 21. 4 ; Tac. Dial. 21, in the main agrees with Cicero ; Calvus never rose to the height of his Vatinian orations through lack of " ingenium ac vires " ; *ib.* 34.

[4] Catullus, 53 ; Sen. Controv. VII. 4 (19). 6 *et seq.;* Tac. Dial. 39 (note his reference to " frigidissimos quoque oratores ") ; Pliny, Ep. I. 2. 2 ; Q. X. 1. 115 : " et frequenter vehemens quoque " ; Fronto, II. 48 : " in judiciis ... Calvus rixatur " ; Apul. Apol. 95, attributes " argutiae " to him

his delivery was able to impress the crowd. His speeches, like his poems, gave evidence of a fervid imagination, and his style of composition was often[1] the reflex of his own impetuous temperament. There is evidence,[2] too, that, in spite of the severe standards of judgment that Cicero attributes to him, he was wont to employ figurative language in his speeches. We may in part explain the enigma by supposing that he was a more rigorous Atticist in theory than in practice. It is possible also that he rose to sublimer heights of eloquence in his Vatinian[3] orations than he ever reached again, and that in his later speeches, caught in the meshes of his own theories, he aimed at a more delicate and attenuated style of oratory. We must, of course, take also into account the possibility of exaggeration on Cicero's part. When the Atticists championed the Plain style, it was to Cicero's interest to depict their ideal as resulting in a barren and lifeless eloquence, incapable of stirring the emotions of an audience, or of making a strong popular appeal.

How Cicero could colour facts to his own advantage is seen in the rôle which he assigned to Brutus in the dialogue

The rôle assigned to Brutus

that bears his name. Brutus is there made[4] to pay homage to Cicero for the many new speeches he had composed, and to approve[5] warmly of Caesar's tribute to him for having enriched his native tongue. Again, he is made to note the likeness between the oratory of Cicero and that of Marcellus, and to lavish[6] high praise upon the latter, as if he set the seal of his approval on Cicero's own style. When we hear Brutus, with his strong Stoic leanings, declare[7] that it is the orator's greatest glory to inflame the feelings of his audience, and find[8] him giving unqualified praise to the Asianist Horten-

---

[1] Seneca, loc. cit., notes his power of altering the rhythm of his speeches.

[2] Q. IX. 2. 25, 3. 56; Pliny, Ep. I. 2. 2; Aquila Rom. Halm, I. p. 35; Curcio, De Ciceronis et Calvi, etc., p. 74 et seq., for his fragments.

[3] Most of the authorities besides Cicero, who refer to him, evidently regard these as his greatest glory.   [4] Br. 123.

[5] Ib. 254; cf. Ad Br. I. 17. 5 (Brutus to Atticus, if the letter is genuine).

[6] Br. 249–250: " omniaque sic suppetunt ut ei nullam deesse virtutem oratoris putem."

[7] Br. 279; cf. 192, on the influence of a crowd on the orator.

[8] Ib. 328: " et Hortensium magnum oratorem semper putavi,"

sius, our incredulity is still further awakened. Brutus may have been inspired with a love of Demosthenes by his teacher Pammenes,[1] but it is more than doubtful if he would be willing to join in Cicero's extravagant admiration for the Greek orator. We can imagine Brutus protesting against some of the views he is made to express. In the *Orator*, Cicero seems to keep closer to reality in the rôle which he assigns to his friend. He is probably stating the truth when he speaks[2] of Brutus' interest in the theory of prose rhythm. Brutus' protest[3] against Cicero's praise of Isocrates seems natural, and in harmony with the general character of his own oratory. But, when we remember his difficult temperament, his hauteur and reserve, of which Cicero often complains, and recall how vehement[4] and decided he was in the opinions he embraced, we feel it is not easy to accept without qualification many of the views attributed to him.

Atticus, too, is said to have professed Atticist[5] sentiments, though we may conclude from his general character that they were never strongly voiced. However,

Atticus Cicero appropriately enough selects him to deal with the characteristics of Caesar's oratory, to emphasise the purity of his Latin, and the work he had done to purge his native language of its defects. He protests[6] against Cicero's stooping to deal with the very dregs of Roman oratory, but his most important rôle in the *Brutus* is to correct[7] the false impression that may be made by what he considers Cicero's exaggerations. Irony, he declares, may be in place in philosophical discussions, but not in sober history. He sets down to mere irony Cicero's comparison of Cato and Lysias, his praise of many of the older orators, and above all, his extravagant laudation of Crassus' speech in support of the Lex Servilia. Though, in taking up this

---

[1] Br. 332; Or. 105.

[2] Or. 174.

[3] *Vide supra*, p. 248.

[4] Ad Att. XIV. 1. 2 : " quidquid vult, valde vult " ; Plut. Br. 6.

[5] The most relevant passages are Ad Att. XV. 1a. 2, *ib.* II. 1. 1, where his fondness for a plain unadorned style is evident ; his purist tendencies are seen in his doubts about Cicero's translation of καθῆκον by " officium."

[6] Br. 244, 251, 297.

[7] *Ib.* 292 *et seq.*

position, Atticus aimed at setting Cicero's own achievements in a more favourable light by contrast, yet he was actuated, too, by a desire to tone down what many might regard as overstatement on Cicero's part. All this goes to show that the latter had misgivings about the reception that would be accorded to some of the views he had expressed. Hence, though we may allow that Cicero has reproduced with comparative fidelity the main outlines of the Atticist quarrel, yet it is evident that some at least of the details will have to be accepted with reservations.

CHAPTER V

ANCIENTS V. MODERNS

THE QUARREL as to the relative merits of the Ancients and the Moderns is one that we are not unfamiliar with even in comparatively recent times. It seems to be one of the phenomena of literary history that tend to recur at certain intervals. In France and England towards the end of the seventeenth century the battle[1] was fought with extraordinary vehemence by the champions of the respective sides. It developed into a veritable " Battle of the Books," in which opponents sought to overwhelm each other by a vast parade of erudition. In France, in particular, the atmosphere of the Academy was favourable to such learned warfare. Perrault first raised the standard of revolt against the long-established supremacy of the Ancients, and his extravagant praise of the " siècle de Louis " was a challenge to all who believed in the pre-eminence of Ancient literature. In England, where such men as Wotton and Sir W. Temple were associated with the struggle, the battle was waged with equal vehemence, and characterised by a no less vast display of learning. One of the motive forces in the conflict was a conviction in the minds of the Moderns that excessive admiration for the Ancients was laying, as it were, the dead hand of tradition on contemporary literature, and hindering its advance. Brunetière has briefly and lucidly summed up for us the value of the quarrel from the critic's point of view. It served to introduce the idea of Progress,[2] though it is not always easy to apply such a conception to literature. It ended the belief that rules, especially those drawn from

---

[1] On the quarrel in France and England, *vide* Saintsbury, op. cit. Vol. II, pp. 320, 412, 503 ; Brunetière, L'Évolution des Genres, p. 111 *et seq. ;* Sandys, A History of Classical Scholarship, Vol. II, p. 403.

[2] *Vide supra*, p. 193.

Classical models, were inflexible and infallible, and it pointed to the possibility of drawing upon other models than the Ancients. It, moreover, familiarised men's minds with the idea of a certain relativity in literature.

When we turn to Roman literature we find many traces of a conflict on the relative merits of the Ancients and Moderns,[1] though from the nature[2] of things the issues were different from those of modern times, when two literatures could be placed in direct opposition. In Rome the stage was not so elaborately set for the combat as in France or England, nor was the conflict waged with such an array of learning, but none the less, the champions on both sides often showed conspicuous ardour and animosity in defence of their positions.

The quarrel in Rome

It is not always easy to estimate the mentality of those who took sides in the quarrel. There are some[3] who are ever inclined to cast a halo of romance around everything ancient, and to worship Antiquity for its own sake. Volcacius Sedigitus, in his Canon of the Comic Poets,[4] finds a place, even though it is the last, for Ennius " causa antiquitatis." Quintilian pays homage[5] to the same poet as to a grove that has been rendered sacred by its age. Juvenal tells us[6] of the patron who insists on reciting his own verses, and in the pride of his achievements will yield to Homer alone, because he lived a thousand years ago. There was a certain massive robustness about Antiquity that possessed a charm for many people. Cicero takes painting[7] as an illustration, and remarks that though the garish colours of modern artists may delight

Mentality of the combatants

---

[1] These terms have, of course, to be here used relatively, but they will serve to indicate certain divergences of ideals that appear at different stages in Roman literature.

[2] Seeing that we are now dealing with a single literature.

[3] Macrob. Sat. III. 14. 2 : " vetustas quidem nobis semper, si sapimus, adoranda est " ; Gellius, X. 3. 15 ; cf. Scott, The Architecture of Humanism, p. 56 *et seq.*, on the Romantic fallacy.

[4] Gellius, XV. 24.

[5] X. 1. 88 ; cf. *ib.* XII. 10. 3 (on the Greek painters) : " primi, quorum quidem opera non vetustatis modo gratia visenda sunt," etc.

[6] VII. 38.

[7] De Or. III. 98.

us for a time, we soon grow tired of them, while the rough-
ness and uncouthness of the Ancients still retain a fascination
for us. Quintilian speaks[1] of those who, evidently in
reaction against the affectations and extravagances of contemporary eloquence, declared that only the ancient orators
should be read, because in them alone was to be found the
natural eloquence that was free from elaboration, and that
most resembled the speech of living men.

For many the Past is a Golden Age[2] which has become
idealised in their imaginations. In the domain of morals,
some, disillusioned and disgusted with the
depravity of their own times, turn a wistful
gaze towards it as an age of primeval inno-
cence and unalloyed happiness. They raise the cry of
" Back to Nature " in their wish to escape from the artificiality and complexity of modern civilisation. Men of simple
tastes, like Varro and the elder Seneca,[3] turned for consolation from the luxury and depravity of the life they saw
around them to the contemplation of the robuster virtues of
an earlier Rome, the " mores antiqui," on which, as Ennius
had proclaimed, the greatness[4] of Rome was founded. Even
those like the younger Seneca[5] who were on the side of the
Moderns in literature, yet revolted against the vices of their
age, and tended to look to the Ancients for their ideals in
morality.[6] Under the Empire votaries[7] of Stoicism, such as

Idealising the Past

[1] *Vide infra*, p. 326 *et seq.*
[2] Ovid, Met. I. 89 ; Sen. Ep. 90. 5 ; Tac. Dial. 12, Ann. III. 26 ; Juv.
III. 312, VI. 1 *et seq.; the author's Horace and his Age, p. 102 ; cf.
Schmekel, op. cit., p. 450 *et seq.*, on the influence of Poseidonius in diffusing
the idea of the Golden Age ; Babbitt, Rousseau and Romanticism, p. 77
et seq., on Primitivism.
[3] Controv. I. pr. 6 *et seq. ;* Livy's Preface, 5 *et seq. ;* Pliny, N.H. IX.
104, XIII. 20 *et seq.;* Tac. Ann. III. 26, XIV. 20 ; even Propertius
condemns the luxury and decadence of his time, III. 13. 4, *ib.* 60 : " fran-
gitur ipsa suis Roma superba bonis."
[4] Tac. Ann. IV. 32–33, contrasts the glories which the Ancient historians
had to relate with the trivialities he himself has to chronicle : " nobis in arto
et inglorius labor."
[5] Ep. 86. 6 *et seq.*, 87. 9, N.Q. VII. 31–32.
[6] Cf. Macrob. I. 5. 2 : " vivamus ergo moribus praeteritis, praesentibus
verbis loquamur."
[7] Tac. Ann. XIV. 57, XVI. 22 ; cf. Pliny, Ep. I. 17. 3 ; Juv. V. 36 ;
Boissier, L'Opposition sous les Césars, p. 97 *et seq.*

Thrasea and Helvidius Priscus, idealised the Past in their own way, moved partly by political, partly by moral motives. They yearned for Republican Rome, and worshipped the memories of Brutus and Cassius who fulfilled their ideal of patriotism.

Some found[1] their age intellectually decadent, and naturally set themselves to inquire into the causes of the decline.

Complaints of decadence Various solutions of the problem were advanced. Specific causes could at times be cited, and we often see a tendency in such speculations to pass from the conception of decadence in the moral order to decadence in literature. It is not, however, easy to apply the notion of decadence to literature. In the eyes of some, difference spells decadence, a position against which, as we shall see,[2] Aper protests in the *Dialogus*, when he claims that the oratory of his own day is not necessarily inferior, because it is different from the oratory of the past. The elder Seneca looked on the Rome of his day as intellectually decadent, especially in the sphere of oratory. Here it was a decline not so much in perfection of form[3] as in ideas, which in the rhetoricians of the schools were too often puerile and bizarre. In them especially there was evident a disproportion between the triviality of the ideas, and the language in which they were clothed. Velleius has[4] his own ideas of decadence, and regards it as an inevitable law of nature[5] that each genre should reach perfection for a brief period, and then decay. But out of this death new genres may spring to life. Men, having despaired of surpassing or equalling their predecessors, seek for untilled fields to cultivate, though to the mind of Velleius this incessant search for novelty is a hindrance to perfection in any line.

[1] Cf. Sen. Controv. I. pr. 6 *et seq.* on the causes of the decline of eloquence ; *vide supra,* p. 195 *et seq.*

[2] *Vide infra,* p. 342 ; cf. De Gourmont's defence of Mallarmé, Decadence, p. 139 *et seq.*

[3] Cf. Scott, op. cit., p. 184 (in reference to architecture) : " the period of so-called decadence is often marked by a superabundance of technical resources, which stifle the conception."

[4] *Vide infra,* p. 401.

[5] Scott, op. cit., c. VI, on the Biological Fallacy.

Many of the Roman authors themselves have endeavoured to analyse the motives of those who despise the achievements of their contemporaries in literature, and reserve their praise for writers who have passed away. Men, they say,[1] are inclined to hate living worth, and envy of contemporary merit is set down as one of the great motive forces that impel them to neglect the Present for the Past. It is, moreover, as the author of the treatise *On the Sublime* says,[2] characteristic of human nature to find fault with the age in which one lives. Envy or indifference[3] often makes men blind to contemporary excellence.[4] This is a characteristic that is not confined to any period. Tacitus tells us[5] that, probably even in Cato's day, there were some to be found who placed Appius Claudius above him, for the reason apparently that he belonged to an earlier generation.

Analysis of motives

Naturally there were protests raised against the tendency to idealise the Past. Ovid proclaims[6] that his own age is the Golden Age ; others may find pleasure in the Past, but the age in which he lives is the one best suited to his temperament. He is prepared[7] to treat the writings of the Ancients with due reverence, but he will not set contemporary poets below them. Seneca, as we have seen, has many strictures on the luxury and depravity of his own times, but, for all that, he is ready to defend[8] his age as no more corrupt than past centuries. Tacitus also raises[9] his voice against extravagant

Progress v. Tradition

---

[1] Hor. Ep. II. 1. 21 ; Prop. III. 1. 21, *ib.* 35 ; Ovid, Am. I. 15. 39, Trist. IV. 10. 123, Ex Ponto, III. 4. 73, IV. 16. 3 ; Vell. II. 92 : " praesentia invidia, praeterita veneratione prosequimur"; Sen. Ep. 79. 17 ; Tac. Dial. 18 : " vitio autem malignitatis humanae vetera semper in laude, praesentia in fastidio esse " ; Pliny, Ep. I. 16. 8 ; Mart. V. 10. 3, VIII. 69 ; Fronto, II. p. 204 : " faveri praeteritis, invideri praesentibus."

[2] C. 44.

[3] Tac. Ann. II. 88 : " dum vetera extollimus recentium incuriosi."

[4] On the other hand, " antiquis scriptoribus rarus obtrectator," Tac. Ann. IV. 33.   [5] Dial. 18.

[6] Ars Am. II. 277, III. 113, 122 : " haec aetas moribus apta meis."

[7] Trist. V. 3. 55 ; *vide infra*, p. 290.

[8] Ep. 97. 1 *et seq. ;* Seneca is not consistent here ; for, as we have seen above, he often turns to the Past for his ideals of morality.

[9] Ann. III. 55 : " nec omnia apud priores meliora."

laudations of the Ancients. Many writers went further still, and proclaimed[1] the superiority of their works over the crude efforts of the Past, and their conviction that in artistic finish they will be able to surpass their predecessors. Here we have the doctrine of Progress applied to literature, a doctrine[2] that unfortunately, in the minds of some, issues in the belief that the latest novelty is the best, whatever be its intrinsic merit. We can, indeed, often discern in the quarrel the conflict[3] of the two opposing principles of Progress and Tradition, impelling men in turn to exalt the achievements of their own age, or those of by-gone times.

Among the influences that tended to turn men's minds towards the Past, not the least potent was the Antiquarian movement. Antiquarianism[4] was at all times in vogue at Rome, and naturally busied itself with everything that could throw light on the origins and early history of the Eternal City. There were, of course, professed historians, like Cato and Aelius Tubero,[5] who dealt with the beginnings of Rome, but scholars like Julius Congus,[6] the friend of Lucilius, rose to prominence as enthusiastic students of antiquity. Crassus in the De Oratore[7] recommends a study of Roman Law, and of such monuments of antiquity as the Libri Pontificum and the Twelve Tables,[8] as affording a picture of ancient life and custom, as well as of the character of the language in use in former ages. The tradition of antiquarian studies was maintained at different periods by Aelius Stilo and his pupil

The Antiquarian movement

[1] Livy, Pr.: " dum novi semper scriptores aut in rebus certius aliquid allaturos se aut scribendi arte rudem vetustatem superaturos credunt."
[2] Cf. Babbitt, Rousseau, etc., p. 64.
[3] Cf. Rigault, Histoire de la Querelle des Anciens et des Modernes, c. I.
[4] Cf. Peter, Die geschichtliche Lit., Vol. I. p. 108 *et seq.*
[5] Tubero traced the history of Rome from the destruction of Troy ; cf. Peter, op. cit., Vol. I. p. 366 *et seq.*
[6] Cic. De Or. I. 256 ; in Schol. Bobb. (quoted by Wilkins ad loc.) he is called " homo curiosus et diligens eruendae vetustatis " ; Cic. Pro Plancio, 58 ; Lucil. frs. 592–596 (cf. Marx ad loc.) ; Peter, Hist. Rom. Reliq., Vol. I. p. 169 *et seq.*
[7] I. 193 *et seq.*
[8] Cf. Cic. De Leg. II. 59 ; Cicero had learnt them as a boy.

Varro, by Atticus[1] and Cicero's freedman Tiro,[2] by Julius
Hyginus,[3] the friend of Ovid, by Fronto, and the many
enthusiastic votaries of the Past that figure in the pages of
Gellius. In contrast with these we have Virgil, who was not
a professed antiquarian, but whose study[4] of Roman origins
set the fashion among contemporary poets. Propertius in
particular, though he is essentially modern in spirit, is
stirred by memories awakened by the *Aeneid*, and will now
sing of " cognomina prisca locorum."[5] The legends of
far-off days began to be regarded with a new reverence.
Sites such as the Forum and the Palatine, in which early
Rome was cradled, were surrounded with a halo of romance.
The primitive festivals[6] that were so much interwoven with
the life of the Romans, and reflected their earliest civilization, began to have a new fascination for the writers of the
Augustan age. Such antiquarianism might easily lead to an
unbalanced enthusiasm and an excessive admiration for the
achievements of the Past. Virgil's genius, however, and his
desire to sing the glories of the new regime, enabled him to
hold the balance evenly between the claims of early Rome
and the Rome of his own day.

Language was another sphere in which the rival claims
of Past and Present were sometimes manifested. Many
writers in practice inclined to excess in their
use of either neologisms or archaisms.[7] The
use of archaic words cannot, of course, always
be taken as evidence that a writer had definitely taken sides

The sphere of language

---

[1] Nepos, Att. 18 : " moris etiam majorum summus imitator fuit antiqui-
tatisque amator " ; I have referred elsewhere to his " Liber Annalis."

[2] Gellius, VII. 3. 8 : " haudquaquam rerum litterarumque veterum
indoctus."

[3] Suet. De Gr. 20 ; Peter, Hist. Rom., Vol. II. p. 101 *et seq.*, *ib.* frs.,
p. 72 *et seq.*

[4] Cf. Q. I. 7. 18 : " Vergilius amantissimus vetustatis "; *ib.* IX. 3. 14 ;
Gellius, V. 12. 13 ; Norden, Aen. VI. p. 368, 432 *et seq.*; cf. Macrob.
Sat. I. 24. 19, III. 2. 10.

[5] IV. 1. 69, 2. 6 *et seq.*, IV. 4, IV. 9, IV. 10 ; cf. Tib. II. 5. 19 *et seq.*;
Ovid, Ars Am. I. 99 *et seq.*

[6] *Vide* Horace and his Age, pp. 48–49, for the importance of the antiquarian movement in the Augustan Revival of religion.

[7] Gellius, XV. 25, XVI. 7, XVIII. 11, XX. 9, on the faults of poets
such as Laevius, Laberius, Cn. Matius, Furius Antias.

as a champion of the Ancients. In the case of some, such a peculiarity had degenerated into a mere mannerism,[1] and was a token of their desire for the piquancy of the unfamiliar.[2] However, in others it had a deeper significance. Long communing with the authors of the Past begot in them, if not actually dissatisfaction with the style of their contemporaries, at least a desire to reproduce the archaic colouring of an earlier period. In his review of Roman oratory in the *Brutus*, Cicero speaks[3] of the speeches of Galba as more redolent of antiquity than those of Laelius, Scipio, or even Cato. Laelius himself was more archaic in style[4] than Scipio, and seems to have taken express pleasure in using words that had about them the flavour of a by-gone generation. L. Cotta[5] expressly set out to imitate the language of ancient writers, and his very affectation of the rustic brogue was due in part to his belief that he was thus imitating the accents of the earlier orators of Rome. According to Aper,[6] his choice of words, and the faulty and shapeless structure of his sentences, made the style of Caelius Rufus so archaic that even the most devoted lover of antiquity would refrain from praising this characteristic of his oratory. Amongst prose writers in general, Sallust was regarded as one of the most pronounced of archaists. Quintilian quotes an epigram[7] in which he is pilloried as having stolen much of the language of the elder Cato. He was attacked[8] for this tendency by Asinius Pollio, who went so far as to declare that Ateius Philologus was accustomed to collect obsolete words and expressions for his use. This

---

[1] Cf. Schmid, Der Atticismus, I. p. 44, for this form of affectation in the Second Sophistic movement; Rohde, Der griech. Roman, p. 355.

[2] Sen. Controv. IV. pr. 1: "ad nova homines concurrunt, ad nota non veniunt"; Sen. Ep. 114. 10: "cum adsuevit animus fastidire quae ex more sunt."

[3] Br. 82; cf. Tac. Dial. 18.

[4] Br. 83; cf. 97, on S. Pompeius.

[5] Cic. De Or. III. 42 *et seq.*, Br. 137; Q. XI. 3. 10.

[6] Tac. Dial. 21, *ib.* 18.

[7] VIII. 3. 29; cf. Suet. De Gr. 15, *ib.* Aug. 86; Fronto, I, p. 4, on Sallust as an imitator of Cato; *ib.* II, p. 114.

[8] Suet. De Gr. 10; cf. Gellius, X. 26. 1, where Pollio criticises Sallust's use of " transgressus."

defect in Sallust was probably aggravated by his imitation of Thucydides, and by his natural desire to reproduce something of the old-world colouring of his model. As we shall see, Sallust was one of the authors who enjoyed a great vogue among later archaists.

Virgil has left us a record[1] of his own abhorrence of the excessive affectation of archaism in his denunciation of

Virgil and archaism

Britain's Thucydides, Annius Cimber, " Corinthiorum amator iste verborum." Although he himself might have availed more fully of the licence of the poet, he is commended by Quintilian[2] for the perfect restraint that he exhibits in his use of antiquated diction.[3] The " obtrectatores Vergilii," however, were fond of dilating on his thefts[4] from the old Roman poets, while Seneca sees in certain harsh and uncouth verses of his, evidence of his desire to impart to his poetry the tones of an earlier age. The same critic comments[5] on certain words in Cicero as evidence that even in his prose he had profited by his study of Ennius. This is indeed a carping criticism, as Cicero himself lays down rigid rules to govern the use[6] of archaisms, and, except in some of his earlier speeches, his own practice was generally beyond reproach.[7]

However, in every period some were found who were inclined to use archaic words to excess. Augustus reproves[8] Tiberius for hunting after obsolete and pedantic ex-

[1] Catalepton II ; cf. Q. VIII. 3. 28 ; Suet. Aug. 86 ; Cic. Phil. XI. 14 ; cf. De Witt, Virgil's Biographia Litteraria, pp. 93–94 ; *vide infra*, p. 328.

[2] *Vide supra*, p. 90.

[3] *Vide* Sikes, Roman Poetry, p. 245 *et seq.*, for some excellent remarks on V.'s use of archaisms ; cf. Norden, Aen. VI, p. 365 *et seq.*

[4] *Vide infra*, p. 289 ; these " thefts," however, did not always involve archaism ; V. was able to modernise his borrowings, or invest them with a new significance.

[5] Gellius, XII. 2. 6 ; the words, as recorded by Gellius, are the compounds " suaviloquens " and " breviloquentia," used by Cicero in the " De Republica " ; Cicero was here evidently trying to suggest the usage of Scipio's day ; cf. his use of " solivagum," De Rep. I. 39 ; cf. Sen. Ep. 108. 33 *et seq. ;* Landgraf., op. cit., p. 6.

[6] He deals, of course, especially with their use in oratorical prose.

[7] *Vide supra*, p. 245.

[8] Suet. Aug. 86 ; *vide infra*, p. 327.

pressions. That gloomy and morose figure showed[1]
extreme solicitude about his choice of words,

The love of archaism and probably, in his anxiety to find native terms to the exclusion of the Greek, was led to adopt diction that had long passed out of use. Livy censures[2] those orators who pursue mean and antiquated words, and believe that the resultant obscurity is a token of severity of style. Seneca remarks[3] that disgust of the commonplace leads to a love of archaism, and he derides those who draw on earlier centuries for their language, and speak in the style of the Twelve Tables. According to Quintilian,[4] there are some who, even when they have discovered words best suited to their purpose, will look out for others that are older and less obvious. It is just as if an author,[5] to display his erudition, should search the records of the Pontiffs and the works of forgotten writers for a collection of words which his fellowmen are incapable of understanding. Archaisms have a charm of their own[6] when properly used, but we must not drag words[7] from " the dark backward and abysm of time," and try to speak the language of the Salian hymns. Favorinus tells a youth[8] who is " veterum verborum cupidissimus," that he speaks as if he were conversing with the mother of Evander. Gellius, who was himself devoted to early literature, and who loves to discuss obsolete and uncommon expressions, yet criticises[9] the tastelessness of those who employ language too antiquated to be understood by their contemporaries. From all this it is evident that the affectation of archaism was prevalent in

[1] Suet. Tib. 70–71 ; cf. De Gr. 22 ; Tac. Ann. I. 11, on some of the peculiarities of his style.

[2] Sen. Controv. IX. 2. 26 ; he used to quote the remark of Miltiades the rhetorician : ἐπὶ τὸ λεξικὸν μαίνονται; cf. ib. 25, Controv. X. pr. 2.

[3] Ep. 114. 9–10, 13, 122. 18, on the " vitae communis fastidium " ; cf. Ep. 108. 35, where he tells us to read the philosophers " non ut verba prisca aut ficta captemus."

[4] VIII. pr. 31.

[5] Ib. VIII. 2. 12.

[6] Pliny, Ep. I. 16. 2, evidently found pleasure in the " sonantia verba et antiqua " of Saturninus' speeches.

[7] *Vide supra*, p. 81.

[8] Gellius, I. 10. 1–2 ; cf. Macrob. Sat. I. 5. 1.

[9] XI. 7. 1 *et seq.*

almost every period at Rome. Sometimes, as I have said, such affectation became a mere mannerism, or was due to a desire for the uncommon, but at times it was grounded in a genuine enthusiasm for the literature of the Past, and a romantic attachment to the vestiges of an earlier civilisation.

In Classicism generally, the theory of Imitation and respect for Tradition were two factors that helped to concentrate men's thoughts on the glories of the Past. The theory of Imitation[1] naturally led them back to the great models that had stood the test of time. Certain authors in a genre were raised to a position of canonical authority. This was the case not only with the Greek models that had cast so potent a spell over their Roman imitators, but many of the Roman writers themselves became a law unto succeeding generations, with the result that the rules of the genre[2] in which they worked, tended to become traditional and binding on all who wished to labour in the same field. There was always the danger that men would be content with a mere slavish imitation of such models, with what Sainte-Beuve happily describes[3] as " s'endormir dans la tradition," though it was in a measure obviated by the instinct of rivalry, and the ambition to improve on one's predecessors.

Another characteristic of Classicism as a whole was its attachment to traditional material. The subject matter of an earlier master in a genre was regarded as the common property of posterity. A new stylistic presentation of old themes was considered a sufficient hall-mark of originality. Literary echoing[4] was thus a characteristic feature, especially of Classical poetry. To many of the Greek and Roman writers could fitly be applied the aphorism of Goethe that " in this world there are so few voices and so many echoes." Attachment

The principle of Imitation

Traditional themes

---

[1] *Vide infra*, p. 426 *et seq.*

[2] Cf. Pliny, Ep. IV. 14. 5, VI. 15. 1, IX. 22. 1 ; Friedländer, Roman Life and Manners, Vol. III, pp. 69–70, on " Virgilian " and " Ovidian " writers ; cf. Statius, Silvae, IV. 7. 25–26 ; *vide infra*, p. 411 *et seq.*

[3] Causeries de Lundi, XV.

[4] Cf. Moulton, The Modern Study of Literature, c. 25, *ib.* p. 304, 307 ; World Literature, p. 110 ; Murray, The Classical Tradition in Poetry, p. 7 *et seq.*

to traditional material was particularly characteristic of the
Tragic drama. Antiphanes declared[1] that Tragedy was
altogether happy as compared with Comedy, as it had not to
invent its subjects, though repetition[2] of the same characters,
motifs, and situations, became a feature of the New Comedy.
Aristotle remarks[3] that Tragedy confines itself to the stories
of a few families, as in them was found the fairest field for
the play of the tragic emotions. Phrynichus and Aeschylus,
however, had shown what success could be achieved in the
sphere of the historical drama,[4] while Agathon, who in one
play at least broke with tradition, won the commendation[5]
of Aristotle himself. A poet, however, who decides to
employ the traditional material, must not break up the
framework of the old legend. Horace advises[6] Piso to go to
the Iliad for the subject of a drama[7] rather than rely on his
own inventiveness to create a new plot. Moreover, he lays
down the rule that, if the poet elects to treat the character
of Medea or Achilles, he must deal with it on traditional
lines. Still, even while handling the old legends, a poet could
always find room for originality[8] in detail. Modifications[9]
could be introduced, new motifs brought into prominence,
or a new standpoint adopted. Sophocles, taking less account
than Aeschylus of the darker agencies of Fate, had shown
what could be accomplished by a study of human character
as an instrument in shaping man's destiny, while Euripides

[1] C. A. F. II. 90 (Kock).

[2] *Vide supra*, p. 19.

[3] Poet. c. 14. 1454a ; here he is dealing with the *practice* of the Greek
dramatists ; *ib*. c. 9, where he advocates greater freedom for the dramatist.

[4] Cf. Moschion at a later date ; Norwood, Greek Tragedy, p. 38.

[5] Poet., c. 9 ; cf. Bywater's note 1451b. 21.

[6] *Vide infra*, p. 432 ; cf. Cic. De Or. II. 194, on " heroum veteres casus "
as the subjects of Tragedy ; cf. Lessing, Hamburgische Dramaturgie, p. 344,
on Maffei's advice to young poets to search in the disused quarry of the
fables of Hyginus for Tragic plots, rather than invent new ones.

[7] He praises, however, those who have chosen Roman subjects for their
dramas, A.P. 287.

[8] Cf. Arist. Poet. 14. 1453b.

[9] Cf. Spring, A Study of Exposition in Greek Tragedy (Harvard Studies,
XXVIII), pp. 167 *et seq*., 186, 210, with special reference to the practice
of Euripides.

could treat the same theme[1] with striking success on a plane of realism.

In spite of the scope thus given for novelty of treatment, many must have felt that the traditional material was exhausted, and must have grown tired of the constant rehandling of ancient legends. Choerilus was one of the first to give expression to such feelings, when he remarked on the happiness of him who had served the Muses in the days when the meadow of poetry was still unharvested. In Alexandria, in particular, there was a reaction against the Cyclic[2] poets, who had sought to forge afresh the out-worn material of the old tales, and add lustre to it by decking it out in Epic phrase. The reaction was not merely against the mythological content of these poets, but against the form which they adopted. Callimachus and his followers wished in the Epyllion to produce something that would better suit the taste and needs of their own generation, and they endeavoured to satisfy their desire for originality by wandering into the unfamiliar by-paths of mythology. Horace, too, feels[3] that the way of the Cyclic poets has become trite and commonplace, and that it is no longer easy to give a touch of individuality to " publica materies." Virgil, convinced[4] that the old heroic legends have been worn threadbare, decides to seek fame in other spheres. Manilius, seeing that the paths of poetry have been already too-well trodden, determines to break with tradition, and seek " fresh fields and pastures new."[5] He will not[6] be in the debt of any previous poet, but will set out on a voyage of his own. Both

Reaction against traditional themes

1 *Vide* Dion Chrysos. Or. 52, on the " Philoctetes " story as handled by the three dramatists ; cf. Egger, L'Histoire de la Critique, p. 440 *et seq.* a comparison of the Choephoroi, the Electra of Sophocles, and the Electra o Euripides, is thus instructive.

2 Callimachus, Epigr. : ἐχθαίρω τὸ ποίημα τὸ κυκλικόν ; cf. Sten plinger, op. cit., p. 132 *et seq.*, to whom I am indebted for some of m references here.

3 A.P. 131–132.

4 Georg. III. 3 *et seq.*

5 II. 50 *et seq.* : " *integra* quaeramus rorantis *prata* per herbas " (cf. t ἀκήρατος λειμών of Choerilus).

6 *Ib.* 57 : " nulli vatum debebimus orsa " ; " propria rate pellimus u das " ; Manilius, in vulgar parlance, decides to paddle his own canoe.

in Propertius[1] and Ovid[2] we find at times a strong contrast between their own love-poetry, and the legendary subjects of the Past, which cannot fill them with the glow of inspiration. If Propertius is to treat at all of an Epic theme, he would rather sing the glories of Caesar[3] than the " tale of Troy divine." In Persius,[4] we find derided the poets who recite their mawkish trash about Phyllises and Hypsipyles, or the other pathetic heroines of ancient legend.

One of the most interesting protests against the attachment to traditional themes is to be found in the *Aetna*.[5]

The " Aetna " Every one, the author tells us,[6] has heard of the Golden Age, the tale of the Argonauts, and the destruction of Troy. Men will brave the perils of the sea to visit the sites of ancient glory, and are happy[7] in communing with an age other than their own. They greedily unearth[8] the lying fables of old. He appeals to them not to be deceived by the figments[9] of the poets, but to turn from them, and contemplate[10] the mighty work of the artificer Nature. His own theme is a true one,[11] and hitherto untried. The author is dominated by the spirit of Lucretius, of whom he has many imitations, and preaches with enthusiasm a new gospel of scientific knowledge in his eagerness to dispel old superstitions, and to open up before

[1] I. 7. 1. *et seq.*, II. 1. 4 : " ingenium nobis ipsa puella facit " ; III. 9. 37 *et seq.* ; *vide infra*, p. 415, for another aspect of this contrast.

[2] Am. II. 18. 1, III. 12. 15 : " ingenium movit sola Corinna meum " ; cf., however, Trist. II. 317 *et seq.*

[3] He rejects even subjects from early Roman history.

[4] Sat. I. 33 ; cf. V. 8, *ib.* 17–18, where he contrasts Mycenean banquets with " plebeia prandia."

[5] By some attributed to Virgil ; cf. Suet. Life, 19 : " scripsit etiam de qua ambigitur ' Aetnam ' " ; Favorinus, Gellius XVII. 10, compares Virgil's and Pindar's description of an eruption of Etna, without any reference to this poem ; cf. Ellis, Aetna, Introd., p. 21 *et seq.*

[6] 9 *et seq.*

[7] 567 *et seq.* : " felicesque alieno intersumus aevo."

[8] 570 : " avidi veteris mendacia famae eruimus."

[9] Especially as regards Etna ; cf. 29, 74 *et seq.*, 510.

[10] *Ib.* 599.

[11] 24, 91–92 ; Sen. Ep. 79. 5–6, urges Lucilius to write a poem on Etna, and tells him not to be dismayed by the fact that the subject has often been treated before, for " inventuris inventa non obstant."

the gaze of men an alluring vision of the marvels of the physical Universe.

In a similar spirit of reaction, Seneca declares[1] that he is not interested in antiquarian questions such as the priority in time of Homer or Hesiod, or the ages of Achilles and Patroclus. He derides what he regards as the misplaced labours of Didymus, who wrote innumerable volumes, and investigated such problems as the birth-place of Homer, and the real mother of Aeneas. Such investigations serve only to distract men from the serious study of philosophy. He tells us that he has no inclination to trace out the wanderings of Ulysses, though in true Stoic fashion he turns the story of his wanderings into an allegory of the voyage of the soul through life, and the dangers that beset its course. In the *Dialogus* of Tacitus, Aper, a realist and an uncompromising champion of the Moderns, probably represents the stand-point of many of his contemporaries, when he counsels[2] Maternus not to waste his time on subjects such as Medea and Thyestes, but to engage in the more profitable occupation of pleading in the Forum. Statius, who was himself so deeply immersed in mythological lore, contrasts[3] such out-worn subjects as the Sack of Troy and the wanderings of Ulysses, with the national theme sung by Lucan, the " darling of Latium," in his *Pharsalia*. It is often said by those in search of a formula[4] that it was the tendency of Classicism to treat the familiar, and of Romanticism to strike out on new paths, and seek for novel effects. Martial may have been impelled to react[5] as strongly as he did against traditional themes by the restlessness of a romantic temperament, or at any rate by his desire to bring men into closer touch with the realities[6] of life, and away from the

Other signs of revolt

---

[1] Ep. 88. 6 *et seq.*, *ib.* 37 *et seq.* ; the whole letter is interesting as showing his attitude to the " liberalia studia."

[2] C. 2, *ib.* 9. 2 : " cui bono est, si apud te Agamemnon aut Jason diserte loquitur ? "

[3] Silvae, II. 7. 48 *et seq.;* cf. " trita vatibus orbita " ; Lucan, however, treated such subjects in his boyhood.

[4] Pater, Appreciations, pp. 257–258.

[5] Cf. IV. 49. 3 *et seq.*, V. 53, IX. 50. 3 *et seq.*, X. 4, *ib.* 35. 5 *et seq.*

[6] Cf. X. 4. 8 *et seq.* : " hoc lege, quod possit dicere vita ' Meum est ' " ;

dimness of a legendary Past. The stories of ancient heroes had no attraction for him, when in the life around him he could find a theme of stark realism. The effort of Statius to revive the long mythological Epic must have seemed to him peculiarly inane, and it is little wonder that we find in him traces[1] of a polemic against what he considers the poet's misguided energies. The accents of Statius sounded unreal, and Martial felt that the *Thebaid* could have no message for the men of his generation. We find in Juvenal, also, evidence[2] of a revolt against the legends of the Past, especially as they figured so prominently in the recitations given by the poets of his day. Naturally, such subjects would make little appeal to the Satirist, except in so far as they could be used as a cloak[3] under which he might lash the vices of his time. It was the complex of the life around him, the vanities, the meannesses, the depraved ambitions, and the darker crimes of his contemporaries, that Juvenal determined[4] to make the chief theme of his Satires.

Yet, in spite of the tendency, manifested especially under the Empire, to react against the traditional subjects of mythology, the old legends were still frequently selected for treatment[5] by the writers of Epic[6] and of Tragedy.[7] We cannot say for certain from what source Asinius Pollio[8] drew material

The old legends still selected

"sed non vis, Mamurra, tuos cognoscere mores nec te scire : legas Aetia Callimachi."

[1] XIV. 1. 11, with Friedländer's note.

[2] Sat. I. 2 *et seq.*, *ib.* 52, 162 *et seq.*, VII. 12.

[3] Sat. I. 170–171 ; here, of course, he is thinking chiefly of how the characters of earlier Roman history can be turned to such a use.

[4] Sat. I. 85 *et seq.*

[5] There are plenty of passing mythological references in the lyric and elegiac poets.

[6] Cf. Prop. I. 7. 1 *et seq.* ; Ovid, Am. II. 18. 1 *et seq.*, Ex Ponto, IV. 16 ; the " poetae novi," like their Alexandrian models, showed a preference for the lesser-known legends.

[7] Cf. Ribbeck, Die röm. Tragödie, p. 616 *et seq.*, on the later Republican Tragedy.

[8] Horace's reference, Sat. I. 10. 42, is vague ; V.'s praise of his tragedies in the words " sola Sophocleo tua carmina digna cothurno " (Eclog. VIII. 10), seems to concern chiefly his style, and do not necessarily imply that his subjects were taken from Greek mythology.

for his dramas. It is significant, however, that the two most successful tragedies[1] of the Augustan Age, the *Thyestes* of Varius and the *Medea* of Ovid, derived their subjects from ancient mythology. Even a traditional theme could be made the vehicle for political allusions,[2] though the ardent admirers of the old Republican regime often preferred to voice their feelings more directly by singing the praises of a Cato,[3] or a Domitius.

We may turn now from mere general considerations to more particular aspects of the quarrel. One of the diffi-

"Ancient" and "Modern" relative terms

culties in the controversy is that the terms "Ancient" and "Modern" are relative terms, as many of the protagonists in the dispute were not slow to point out. In the Prologue to Plautus' *Casina*, written probably[4] about the middle of the second century, B.C., on the occasion of the revival of the piece, the writer contrasts[5] the excellence of the old plays with the worthless modern comedies. Plautus is thus already counted among the Ancients. Cato, naturally enough is regarded[6] as an Ancient, when judged by the standard of Cicero's age, though Catulus, because of his culture, would deserve to be ranked among the Moderns. Horace asks[7] how many years it takes to invest a writer with the dignity of an Ancient, and tries to confound his opponents by the fallacy of the "sorites." In the *Dialogus*, Aper begins[8] his defence of the Moderns by bidding his adversaries define whom they mean by the Ancients, and he seeks to show at some length that the term is a relative one. Quintilian, in answering an opponent[9] who objected to the use of "sen-

---

[1] Sen. Suas. III. 7 ; Ovid, Am. II. 18. 13, Tristia, II. 553 ; Tac. Dial. c. 12 ; Q. III. 8. 45, X. 1. 98.

[2] Tac. Dial. c. 3.   [3] *Ib.* c. 2.

[4] Cf. Leo, Gesch. der röm. Lit., pp. 212–216.

[5] Prol. 5 *et seq.* : " qui utuntur vino vetere sapientes puto et qui libenter veteres spectant fabulas."

[6] Br. 69 : " quippe cum ita sit ad nostrorum temporum rationem vetus," etc. ; cf. *ib.* 41 : " Themistocles insecutus est, ut apud nos perantiquus, ut apud Athenienses, non ita sane vetus."

[7] Ep. II. 1. 35.   [8] Dial. c. 16 ; *vide infra*, p. 340.

[9] VIII. 5. 33 : " ad quam usque nos vocatis vetustatem ? " ; cf. *ib.* IX. 3. 1, where Cicero is classed with the " veteres."

tentiae " on the ground that they were not employed by the Ancients, asks him what period he would include in the term " antiquity." Pliny classes[1] Propertius amongst the Ancients. Martial expresses[2] a wish to his friend Macer that in his eyes he may rank inferior to Catullus alone of the ancient poets, while Gellius, who was devoted above all to early Roman literature, does Cicero[3] the honour of numbering him among the Ancients.

We can trace the beginning of the quarrel back to Ennius[4] who, as we saw, might well be considered an important figure in early Roman criticism.

The beginning of the quarrel He exhibits a conscious pride in his own achievement in helping to create a poetic vocabulary, and in introducing the hexameter into Latin to replace the " horridus numerus Saturnius "[5] of former days. He " who had unlocked the secret of the Muses," may well be pardoned, if he felt a certain measure of contempt for his predecessors, none of whom he considered " dicti studiosus."

While Ennius may thus be said to have inaugurated the quarrel, he himself, the greatest of the early poets, often

The importance of Ennius became in after days a touchstone by which a man's attitude to the Ancients or Moderns could be judged. Lucretius, who had little sympathy with the Alexandrian tendencies of the " poetae novi," was remarkable for his admiration for Ennius, and evidently regarded him as the father[6] of Roman poetry. He shows[7] in his own verse how strongly he came under the influence of the older poets. In striking contrast with his attitude was that of the younger school of poets, whose

[1] Ep. IX. 22. 1.

[2] X. 78. 14 et seq. ; vide infra, p. 308.

[3] I. 4. 1 et seq.

[4] Cic. Or. 171 : " ergo Ennio licuit vetera contemnenti dicere ' versibus quos olim,' " etc. ; vide supra, p. 3.

[5] Hor. Ep. II. 1. 157 ; cf. V. Georg. II. 386, on the " versus incompti " of the primitive festivals at Rome.

[6] I. 117 ; Ennius was the first, at any rate, who was successful in transplanting the Greek muses to Latin soil ; for the view of Porcius Licinus, vide supra, p. 63.

[7] Munro, Lucretius, Vol. II, Introd., p. 8 et seq.

contempt for Ennius drew on them the condemnation[1] of Cicero. The latter, though he laboured so hard to achieve an advance in prose, showed himself antagonistic to the ideals of the νεώτεροι in poetry. His opposition to them may have been due partly to political[2] reasons, and in part to the fact that some[3] of the new poets were Atticists in oratory, and thus in conflict with his own ideals. It is possible, too, that the erotic character of their poetry would be little to Cicero's liking, but probably the chief reason for his antagonism lay in his own great reverence for the older[4] poets of Rome. For Ennius[5] in particular, Cicero had the highest admiration, and paid[6] many glowing tributes to his genius. To judge by the frequency and variety of his quotations,[7] he evidently had an intimate acquaintance with all his works, but the *Annales*, especially its earliest books, seem to have appealed most strongly to him. Personally he had a decided leaning towards historical studies, and there he found set forth in majestic language the pageant of Rome's earliest history. In the days before Virgil's genius had opened up a still more splendid vision, the Epic of Ennius was naturally beloved by a patriotic Roman, as breathing to the full the spirit of Roman greatness. We owe to Cicero[8] the preservation of two of the largest fragments of the *Annales*. How trippingly quotations from that poem came off his tongue, is evident from Quintilian's story[9] of the quickness he displayed in retorting with the opening line of the Sixth book to a troublesome witness, Sextus Annalis, who kept pressing him with the question " num-

---

[1] Tusc. Disp. III. 45 : " o poetam egregium ! quamquam ab his cantoribus Euphorionis contemnitur."

[2] cf. Tenney Frank, Cicero and the "poetae novi," p. 396 *et seq.;* Frank can hardly be right in taking Pro Sestio, 123, as a compliment to the new school of poets; in the context Cicero has the dramatic poets chiefly in mind

[3] e.g. Calvus and Cornificius.

[4] *Vide supra*, p. 142 ; cf. Tusc. Disp. I. 3, where he comments on the fact that poetry began to flourish at Rome at a comparatively late period.

[5] *Vide supra*, p. 274.

[6] De Or. I. 198, Pro Mur. 30, Pro Balbo, 51.

[7] Cf. Zillinger, op. cit., p. 100 *et seq.*

[8] De Div. I. 40, 107.

[9] VI. 3. 86.

quid potes de Sexto Annali ?" His ready knowledge of the poem may be seen from his effective paraphrase of a passage from it in his speech[1] for Muraena. However, with all his admiration for Ennius, he censures[2] him for including a poet of such promise as Naevius in his disparaging reference to his predecessors. He avows[3] his own reverence for antiquity, but for all that he was no blind admirer of the Ancients. In his eyes, Livius' Latin *Odyssey* resembles[4] a work of Daedalus in its primitive crudeness, while his plays do not merit a second reading. Naevius' *Punic War* gives[5] the same pleasure as a statue by Myron, which has about it a certain archaic stiffness, but holds the promise of greater things. Pacuvius, Caecilius, Atilius, are all[6] sharply censured for faults of diction or style, while Accius, who was evidently a favourite[7] of Cicero, is reproved also for his failure in correctness. It is clear from this that Cicero's affection for the early poets did not blind him to their defects, but his enthusiasm for them may in part account for his antagonism to the " poetae novi."

The new school of poets had ideals of its own. Strongly influenced by certain of the Alexandrians, they reacted[8] against the long Epic, and cultivated the Epyllion, an example of which has come down to us in Catullus' poem on the Marriage of Peleus and Thetis. The *Io* of Calvus, the *Zmyrna*[9] of Cinna, the *Glaucus* of Cornificius, the *Lydia* and *Dictynna* of Valerius Cato, were memorials of their predilection for this form of poetry. The poets of the new school were " docti." They made their appeal[10] not so much

The new school of poets

---

[1] 30. [2] Br. 76.

[3] Or. 169 : " antiquitas, quae quidem apud me ipsum valet plurimum."

[4] Br. 71. [5] Br. 75.

[6] *Vide supra*, p. 144.

[7] Pro Plancio, 59, Pro Sestio, 120, 122.

[8] Cf. Catullus, 36. 1, *Ib.* 95. 6, on the " Annales " of Volusius, with whose work is contrasted the Zmyrna, small in comparison, but perfect in its finish.

[9] *Vide infra*, p. 381.

[10] Cat. 95. 10, seems to suggest as much : " at populus tumido gaudeat Antimacho," in contrast with the Zmyrna ; cf. Suet. De Gr. 18, on the difficulties of the Zmyrna.

to the people at large as to a circle of the initiated. They aimed at reproducing in Latin the metrical dexterity of the Alexandrians, and of importing into Roman poetry something of their artistic grace and perfection of form. Catullus and his confrères were fond of experimenting[1] with various metres, and the former had the distinction of introducing the Galliambic[2] metre to the Roman public. The Alexandrians, moreover, were given to minute, psychological study of the emotions, and, in their treatment of particular episodes, were inclined to indulge[3] to excess in such analysis. They sought for a form that would be in harmony with such an aim ; one that would possess a clear-cut symmetry, and exhibit precision and perfection of detail. Their Roman imitators learned many of these lessons. It was probably[4] under the influence of the Alexandrian movement that the contrast between " ars " and " ingenium " became so strongly pointed in Roman criticism about this period. It is significant, at least, that Cicero makes use of the contrast in his criticism of Lucretius, at a time when the new school of poets had begun to be active in Rome. The " poetae novi " concentrated especially on the technique of verse. They were dissatisfied with the metrical irregularities and crudities of the older poets, and evidently regarded a poet such as Ennius as lacking in elegance and refinement. They sought for a more elaborate symmetry and more artistic finish in their own verse, and established more rigid rules especially for the hexameter. Catullus carried this latter tendency so far, that his hexameters were marked by a certain monotony.[5] The capacity of the new school for patient elaboration of detail is well illustrated by the years which Cinna spent in polishing a short poem like the *Zmyrna*.

[1] Cf. Cat. 50. 4 *et seq.* ; Lafaye, Catulle et ses Modèles, p. 26.

[2] Martial (II. 86. 5), evidently had no liking for the " mollem debilitate galliambon."

[3] Cf. Lucian, Quomodo Historia sit conscrib. 57, on this characteristic in Parthenius, Euphorion, and Callimachus.

[4] I find that Munro, op. cit., II. Introd., p. 18, has a similar suggestion, but he makes the contrast refer particularly to Ennius as compared with the Neoterics.

[5] Cf. his tendency to end together thought and line ; *vide* Norden, Aen. VI. p. 387.

In his *Orator* Cicero throws some further light on the ideals of the Neoterics. The dropping of a final " s " was

The ideals of the Neoterics

customary with the older poets, especially when two successive words ended with this letter, but this practice was banned[1] by the poets of the modern school. Cicero again has the latter probably in mind, when he glances[2] at the taste of certain of his contemporaries who prefer high-sounding Greek words to words from their own tongue. It is possible that he is also tilting at the νεώτεροι, when he speaks[3] of the poets who, in their efforts to attain euphony, are prepared to sacrifice sense to sound. In a letter[4] to Atticus he refers to the partiality of the new school for hexameters with a spondee in the fifth foot, a type of verse beloved by the Alexandrians. Catullus affected such hexameters, especially in his Epyllion, though he frequently did so for the purpose of gaining some special emotional effect. Cicero, in his antagonism to the " poetae novi," rather contemptuously bands them all together under the title " cantores Euphorionis,"[5] although the description might be applied with greatest aptness to Gallus,[6] who seems to have taken Euphorion as his chief model. Elsewhere Cicero touches[7] on the obscurity of Euphorion, who seems to have been more recondite than most of the Alexandrians, and to have delighted in rare and antiquated diction.

For all the antagonism of the new school to Ennius, some

[1] Or. 161.

[2] *Ib.* 164 ; cf. Kroll's note.

[3] *Ib.* 68.

[4] VII. 2. 1 ; cf. Norden op. cit., p. 441 *et seq.*, on the restrained use of such hexameters both by the earlier poets and the Augustans ; Lafaye, op. cit., p. 189 *et seq. ;* Munro, op. cit., Introd., p. 14, suggests that Lucr. in his latest book avoids spondaic hexameters in reaction against the younger school of poets.

[5] Cicero in this phrase may have meant to refer especially to the younger poets of the school ; Catullus had been dead for about ten years when the Tusc. Disp. was written ; cf. Ellis, Commentary, Introd., p. 33.

[6] Cf. V. Eclog. X. 50 ; Q. X. 1. 56 ; on G.'s love poetry, cf. Prop. II. 34. 91 ; Ovid, Am. I. 15. 29, Trist. II. 445.

[7] De Div. II. 133 ; Euphorion's very obscurity may in part account for his appeal to Tiberius, Suet. Tib. 70 ; cf. Susemihl, op. cit., Vol. I, p. 393 *et seq.*

of its members at least could not wholly escape his influence.

The influence of the older poets He, in common with most of the earlier poets,[1] was addicted to the excessive use of figures such as paronomasia, assonance, and alliteration. Catullus, both in the *Attis* and in his " Epyllion," allows himself some licence in the employment of such devices, though he uses them with restraint, just as he employs compounds[2] that remind us of the early poets, probably with the aim of imparting an archaic[3] colouring to his verse. Though Catullus belonged to the " poetae novi," probably no other of them was as little enslaved as he to the influence of the Alexandrians. The native strength of his genius, his passionate temperament, and a certain breadth of sympathy, must have left him at times dissatisfied with their excessive precision and their prettinesses, and caused him to seek for other models. In such a mood even the crude vigour of early Roman poetry would not be distasteful to him.

There is abundant evidence that Virgil in his earliest years fell under the influence of the new school. The *Culex* alone, with its wealth of mythological **Virgil and the new school** and learned allusion,[4] would satisfy the most pronounced " doctus " amongst the νεώτεροι, while the *Ciris*,[5] though its Virgilian authorship has been denied, is a romantic tale typical of the Alexandrians. Virgil was the friend of Cornelius Gallus, one of the most prominent of the Neoterics, and has left striking memorials of that friendship in his poetry.[6] He pays a tribute[7] to Cinna, and

---

[1] *Vide supra*, p. 5.

[2] Cf. LXIV. 52, 125, 263 ; Attis, 23, 41, 72.

[3] Cf. Pliny, Ep. I. 16. 5, on the use of " duriusculos quosdam " <versus> by Calvus and Catullus, probably for the same purpose.

[4] Drew, Culex, traces the sources of the poem in great detail ; cf. Frank, Vergil, c. 3.

[5] The poem shows the strong influence of Catullus ; cf. Frank, op. cit., c. 4 ; Skutsch (who attributes the poem to Gallus), Gallus und Vergil, p. 19 *et seq. ;* De Witt, op. cit., p. 47 *et seq.*

[6] Eclog. X, VI. 64 *et seq.*, and the original conclusion of the Fourth Georgic (according to the tradition of Servius).

[7] Eclog. IX. 35.

is credited by Macrobius[1] with an imitation of Cornificius.[2] He might have learned from Parthenius[3] also, much of the newer craft of verse.

As time went on, and as Virgil's vision widened, he became amenable to other influences. Preparation for his great Epic compelled him to make a deep **Virgil's vision widens** study of Roman origins, and to wander in imagination through the earliest period of Roman history. He thus became imbued with a profound veneration for antiquity, and for every vestige of the Past. In the development of Latin poetry he occupied a unique position. He was the heir of all the ages of literary achievement amongst the Romans. He had the advantage of being preceded by a school of poets that busied itself with the technique of verse, and that sought to naturalise on Roman soil the polish and elegance of the Alexandrians. Virgil could avoid their artificiality, and yet build upon their experience. The hexameter in his hands became an instrument from which richer and more varied harmonies could be evoked. He embodied in himself all that was best in the culture and refinement of the Augustan age, but so wide and generous were his sympathies that, implicitly at least, he gave ample recognition to the greatest of his predecessors in Roman Epic. He must have realised that Ennius, though the accents of his poetry might be rough and uncouth, had given fuller expression than any other poet to the spirit of Roman greatness. Whether the phrase about " the dungheap of Ennius," attributed to him, be authentic or not, he at any rate paid him the sincerest tribute of imitation.[4] He borrowed[5] freely from his diction,

---

[1] Sat. VI. 5. 13 ; cf. *ib.* 4. 12, though in this case Virgil may have borrowed from other sources.

[2] Frank's (op. cit., p. 116) identification of Cornificius with the Daphnis of the Fifth Eclogue raises more difficulties than it solves.

[3] Cf. Gellius, XIII. 26, for a Virgilian imitation of Parthenius ; cf. Georg. I. 437 ; Macrob. V. 17. 18 ; on P. as supplying the original of the Moretum, cf. Schanz, op. cit., II. 1, p. 107 ; Gaselee, Parthenius (Loeb), p. 254.

[4] While rivalling and improving upon him ; *vide infra,* p. 431.

[5] Macrob. Sat. Bk. VI ; Gellius, XVIII. 5. 7 ; among modern authors, cf. Norden, Ennius und Vergilius, Aen. VI. p. 365 *et seq.;* Regel, De

and in the *Aeneid* especially he was indebted to Ennius in many a line and phrase. Seneca sneers[1] at him for his complaisance towards the " Ennianus populus " in inserting into his Epic some harsh and irregular verses, in order to give to his poem the flavour of antiquity. Incidentally, one might interpret Seneca's phrase " Ennianus populus " as an unconscious tribute to the place[2] of esteem held by Ennius in the hearts of the Roman people. Seneca, however, takes the standpoint of the Moderns, and taxes[3] Cicero, too, with his admiration for certain verses of Ennius, which he himself derides. With his love for the pointed sayings, the tinsel, and the embellishments of contemporary literature, he could find nothing to admire in the grandeur of Ennius' rough-hewn poetry. His was an age when at Rome the memory[4] of ancient authors had for the most part fallen on evil days, though it was held in greater honour in the provinces.

It is clear from what has been said that Ennius was a figure of supreme importance in the controversy regarding the Ancients and Moderns. To return for a moment to the Augustan age, we find that Propertius, though he pays[5] a passing tribute to his power as an Epic poet, yet, as might be expected from so ardent a votary of the Alexandrians, speaks[6] of him as crowning his songs with shaggy wreath. Ovid, nurtured upon similar traditions, and trained amidst the artificialities of contemporary rhetoric, would naturally make much of the contrast between " ars " and " ingenium." He is willing[7] to concede genius to Ennius, though he finds him

More verdicts on Ennius

Vergilio Poetarum Imitatore, p. 52 *et seq.* ; Connington, Vergilii Opera, Vol. I. p. 45 *et seq.* ; *vide infra*, p. 305 *et seq.*

[1] Gellius, XII. 2. 10 ; cf. Sen. Ep. 58. 4–5, 108. 34.
[2] Cf. Mart. V. 10. 7.   [3] Gellius, XII. 2. 4 *et seq.* ; *vide supra*, p. 274.
[4] Cf. Suet. De Gr. 24, on V. Probus' study of some early writers at Berytus " durante adhuc ibi antiquorum memoria, necdum omnino abolita sicut Romae."
[5] III. 3. 6.   [6] IV. 1. 61.
[7] Trist. II. 424 : " Ennius ingenio maximus, arte rudis " ; cf. *ib*. 259, on the Annales : " nihil est hirsutius illis " ; Am. I. 15. 19 : " Ennius arte carens " ; cf. his criticism of Callimachus, *ib*. 14 : " quamvis ingenio non valet, arte valet."

lacking in art. He regarded[1] himself as the successor of
Gallus, Tibullus, and Propertius, and pays many tributes
to the poets of the former generation as well as to con-
tempory poets, who in his youthful eyes[2] had ranked as gods.
We have already[3] seen something of his general attitude on
the relative merits of the Ancients and Moderns. He will
treat with respect the writings of the Ancients, but will not
set the writers of his own day below them. It is interesting,
however, to find that one of the most glowing tributes to
Ennius was paid by another writer of the Augustan age,
Vitruvius, who declares[4] that all who find pleasure in literature, cannot help having the image of Ennius (as of the
gods) enshrined in their hearts.

We shall see that Ennius bulks large in the eyes of the
archaists of a later period. For the moment we need follow
his fortunes no further than to note how he
**Ennius under
the Empire** fares at the hands of some of the poets of the
Empire. Persius speaks[5] in irony of his
Pythagorean dreams. Considering the subject of his Epic,
one would expect Silius Italicus to have come under his
influence, though its precise degree has been disputed.[6]
However, Silius pays[7] a fine tribute to the older poet, as if
he recognised in him a spiritual progenitor, and one of the
greatest figures among the Epic writers of Rome. Statius
was enthusiastic for the poets of his own day, especially
Lucan, to whom must yield[8] the " unpolished Muse of
bold Ennius." In the *Silvae* in particular, his spirit was
akin to that of the Alexandrians[9] and their Roman imitators,
so that he naturally judges Ennius with the contrast of
" ars " and " ingenium " in mind.

[1] Trist. II. 467, IV. 10. 53–54, V. 1. 17.

[2] *Ib.* IV. 10. 41.

[3] *Vide supra*, p. 270.

[4] Bk. IX. praef. 16.

[5] Sat. VI. 10 ; cf. Pr. 2 : " nec in bicipiti somniasse Parnaso memini, ut
repente sic poeta prodirem " ; *vide supra*, p. 4.

[6] Cf. Woodruff, Reminiscences of Ennius in Silius Italicus, p. 356 *et seq.* ;
W. makes a judicious study of the problem.

[7] XII. 408 *et seq.*

[8] Silvae, II. 7. 75 ; Statius' statement makes it clear that Ennius still
continued to be in vogue.

[9] *Ib.* I. 2. 252 *et seq.*

We must now return to consider the position of Horace, who was one of the protagonists in this literary quarrel, and

Horace and the quarrel

who, above all in his later years, stood forth as a redoubtable champion of the Moderns. Even in his *Satires* we find already marked a tendency to set up his own age, with its superior polish and refinement, as a standard in judging the works of the early poets. He lacked the historical perspective that was one of Cicero's greatest assets as a critic. He does, indeed, in one passage give[1] an indication of possessing the historical sense, when he declares that, if Lucilius had lived in the Augustan age, he would have pruned away his redundancies, and have been more polished and compact. He here implicitly recognises that his defects were, in part at least, due to the period in which he lived, a concession that may have been wrung from him by the admirers of the older poet, who resented his strictures on their favourite. It is clear that about this time there was a revival of interest in Lucilius. We know from Suetonius[2] that he attracted the attentions of the grammarians, and that Valerius Cato, poet and " litterator,"[3] had studied his *Satires* under Philocomus. This Lucilian revival evidently led the admirers of the poet to make extravagant claims for him, which may have been given greater prominence as a counterblast to Horace, who had begun to labour in the same genre. The latter reacted strongly against such excessive admiration of his predecessor.

I shall deal with this matter in detail in the oncoming chapter. It will suffice to point out here that, even at this

" Augustan " correctness

early period, Horace had begun to form his ideal of " Augustan "[4] correctness. This ideal was in part[5] the outcome of his own temperament, and in part due to the influence of the literary

[1] Sat. I. 10. 68 ; cf. Cic. Br. 288, on Thucydides : " ipse enim Thucydides, si posterius fuisset, multo maturior fuisset et mitior " ; *vide supra*, p. 200.

[2] De Gr. 2, *ib.* 14, on Curtius Nicias' book on Lucilius, which won the approval of Santra.

[3] He is thus styled by Messalla, Suet. De Gr. 4 ; *vide infra*, pp. 357, 368.

[4] If the term is not premature.

[5] *Vide infra*, p. 377.

circles with which he was associated. Though he praises Lucilius for his sincerity and singleness of purpose, and pays a tribute to his power of invective, yet he found his laughter lacking in the urbanity and restraint which the refinement of his own age demanded. Moreover, the style of the older satirist is weighed and found wanting. In his eagerness for self-expression, he was unwilling to submit to the discipline of careful composition, so that there was much in his verses that seemed to Horace uncouth, inharmonious, and redundant. The latter, setting so high a value on elegance and polish, was inclined to demand too much from Lucilius, and to overlook some of his real merits. But there is no doubt, too, that his severe criticism of his defects was in part a reaction against the immoderate enthusiasm of the poet's admirers.

It is interesting to note that in one passage of the *Satires*, Horace shows a certain reverence for Ennius, and quotes[1]

Horace and Ennius
some lines from his *Annales* as an example of true poetry which survives even when the metrical structure has been disturbed. It is probable, notwithstanding, that he included him amongst the " poetarum seniorum turba "[2] to whom he refers somewhat contemptuously, and we shall see that at a later period he speaks of him in slighting terms.

On the other hand in this early period, though he criticises sharply some of the poetasters of his day as well as a

Horace and the " Moderns "
turgid writer like Furius,[3] and though he shows little respect for the professional guild of poets,[4] he manifests[5] his enthusiasm for certain of his contemporaries, especially those who belonged to his own circle, and who evidently embodied in their writings the ideals towards which he himself was striving. He selects for special commendation representatives of various genres, as if he wished to show how versatile

---

[1] Sat. I. 4. 60.

[2] *Ib*. X. 67, *ib*. 66 : " rudis et Graecis intacti carminis auctor " is by some taken as referring to Ennius, but it may well apply to the earliest efforts in Italian poetry, before Greek influence began to be operative.

[3] *Vide infra*, p. 302.

[4] *Vide infra*, p. 303.

[5] Sat. I. 10. 40 *et seq*., *ib*. 81 *et seq*.

was his age. Fundanius, though alone of his generation, was successful in upholding the tradition[1] of Comedy (Palliata). Pollio[2] was the great name in contemporary Tragedy. In his *Eclogues* Virgil, by his tender grace and delicate humour, had done honour to the Pastoral Muses. In the days before Virgil had revealed to the Roman world his genius as an Epic poet, Varius, a " bird of Homeric song,"[3] by the bold vigour of his style was showing his power of dealing with an Epic theme.

Even in this early period then, it is clear that Horace showed a bias in favour of the writers of his own age, but it was only at a later stage that he stood out as the uncompromising champion of the Moderns. In the meantime the supporters of the Ancients seem to have been particularly active. They set[4] an inordinate value on every line of ancient literature, and, in Horace's view, judged the achievements of the older poets with an admiration that was blind to their defects. They were ready to criticise adversely the works of contemporary writers,[5] while they cast a halo of reverence round every vestige of antiquity, and regarded with a kind of sacred awe such documents as the Twelve Tables and the Salian hymn.

An uncompromising champion

Such enthusiasm was in all probability greatly fostered by the antiquarian studies of Varro.[6] Interest in ancient authors had been manifested[7] even before this in the commentary of Lampadio on the *Bellum Punicum* of Naevius, the lectures of Vargunteius on the *Annales* of Ennius, and the attention

Antiquarian studies

---

[1] It looks as if Horace wished to represent him as a modern Terence ; cf. the characters mentioned, and " comis garrire libellos," with Cicero's description of Terence as " quiddam come loquens " ; cf. Sat. II. 8. 19, on Fundanius as a friend of Maecenas.

[2] Cf. Odes, II. 1. 9 ; the " Thyestes " of Varius had evidently not yet been published.

[3] Odes, I. 6. 2 ; cf. Ep. I. 16. 27, for some lines from his panegyric of Augustus ; V. Eclog. IX. 35 ; cf. Macrob. Sat. VI. 1. 39, *ib*. 2. 19–20, for some remains of his poem " De Morte."

[4] Hor. Ep. II. 1. 20 *et seq*., *ib*. 54, 78, 86 ; *vide infra*, p. 378 *et seq*.

[5] Ep. II. 1. 77.   [6] Varro lived until 27 B.C.

[7] Suet. De Gr. 2, *ib*. 8, on Andronicus' " Criticisms of the Annals of Ennius," *ib*. 14 ; cf. Fronto, I. 166.

devoted to Lucilius by such scholars as Laelius Archelaus and Vettius Philocomus. Varro himself was but carrying on the tradition of Aelius Stilo,[1] one of the most distinguished antiquarian scholars that Rome had produced. Aelius had worked[2] on the Twelve Tables, and had written a commentary on the Carmen Saliare. He had laboured[3] upon Plautus, and had declared that only twenty-five of the plays that passed under his name, were genuine. His interest in Ennius is evidenced by his judgment[4] that the poet had himself in mind, when he described the duties of a client in the seventh book of the *Annales*.

Varro, " diligentissimus investigator antiquitatis,"[5] was a worthy successor of his master, and during his own life

Varro and in after days many tributes[6] were paid to his antiquarian studies, and to the wide range of his learning. His labours were indeed immense, and seem to have covered the whole field of early Latin literature. Naturally, through his grammatical studies, and his preoccupation with metrical questions[7] and the history of the Latin language, he would be attracted to the works of the early poets. The list[8] of his writings is a formidable one, and shows how comprehensive were his interests. Of particular importance, from the point of view of literary history, was his work *De Poetis*,[9] which shows that he was

---

[1] Cf. Cic. Br. 169, 205–207, Acad. Post. 8 ; Gellius, I. 18, X. 21. 2, XVI. 8. 2 ; Suet. De Gr. 3 ; Marx, Ad Herennium, Introd., p. 138 *et seq.* ; Funaioli, Grammaticae Romanae Fragmenta, p. 51 *et seq.*

[2] Cic. De Or. I. 193, De Leg. II. 59 ; cf. Varro, De L.L. VII. 2, on his interpretation of the Carmen Saliare ; Funaioli, op. cit., p. 57 *et seq.* ; *ib.* p. 73.

[3] Gellius, III. 3. 1, *ib.* 12 ; cf. Q. X. 1. 99.

[4] Gellius, XII. 4. 5 ; cf. Valmaggi, fr. 158, who assigns the fragment to Bk. VIII ; *vide supra*, p. 3.

[5] Cic. Br. 60.

[6] Cic. Acad. Post. 9, sums up his studies : " plurimumque idem poetis nostris omninoque Latinis et litteris luminis et verbis attulisti " ; Q. X. 1. 95, XII. 11. 24 ; Apul. Apol. 42 ; Aug. De Civ. Dei. VI. 2 ; Funaioli, op. cit., p. 179 *et seq.* ; *vide infra*, p. 348.

[7] Funaioli, p. 306 *et seq.*

[8] *Ib.* p. 182 ; the list is derived from St. Jerome.

[9] He also wrote a work " De Poematis " ; cf. Funaioli, pp. 213, 319 *et seq.*

engaged in investigating the origins of Roman poetry and
problems of chronology,[1] regarding which he corrected the
erroneous views of Accius.   His special studies of Plautus
were embodied in the *Quaestiones Plautinae*, and *De Comoediis Plautinis*.   Like his master, he devoted[2] attention to
the genuineness of Plautus' plays.   His appeal to internal
evidence to establish the authenticity of certain of the plays
would go to show how deeply he had studied the language
and usage of Plautus.   It is a debatable question how far
Suetonius was indebted to him for his Life of Terence, but
the commentaries of Donatus provide evidence of his
interest in that dramatist.   It is especially important to note
that neither Varro, nor Aelius Stilo, confined himself to
mere grammatical and antiquarian studies, but indulged
in literary criticism[3] as well.   We find[4] the former quoting
Aelius as declaring that the Muses would have spoken in
the language of Plautus, if they had chosen to speak Latin.
Varro apparently accepted[5] as genuine the Epigram attributed to Plautus.   His interest in Ennius is seen in one[6]
of his *Satires*, where he introduces a certain Pompilius as
saying that he himself is proclaimed a disciple of Pacuvius,
Pacuvius of Ennius, Ennius of the Muses.   He praised[7]
the beginning of Terence's *Adelphi* as superior to the
original.   He moreover has left us a number of brief
criticisms[8] of the ancient dramatists, which remind us of
the labels[9] attached by the admirers of the Ancients to their

[1] *Vide supra*, p. 51.

[2] Gellius, III. 3. 2 *et seq.* ; Leo, Plautinische Forschungen, p. 23 *et seq.*,
65 *et seq.*

[3] On the critical marks (based on Aristarchus) used by Aelius, Varro, and
others, cf. Funaioli, pp. 54–56 ; Cic. Ad Fam. IX. 10. 1 ; Suet. De Gr. 14.

[4] Q. X. 1. 99 ; note Hor. Ep. II. 1. 23 *et seq.*, where an enthusiast for the
Ancients proclaims that documents such as the Twelve Tables were uttered
by the Muses on the Alban Mount.

[5] Quoted in the " De Poetis " (Gellius, I. 24. 3) : " Postquam morte
datu'st Plautus, Comoedia luget," etc.

[6] Riese, Varronis Satirae, p. 183 ; cf. Vahlen, Conjectanea, p. 6.

[7] *Vide supra*, p. 16.

[8] " ἤθη nullis aliis servare convenit quam Titinio, Terentio, Attae " ;
" πάθη vero Trabea, Atilius, Caecilius facile moverunt " ; cf. Funaioli,
p. 203.

[9] Cf. Hor. Ep. II. 1. 56 *et seq.*

favourite authors. He assigns[1] the palm to Caecilius for
his plots, to Terence for his character-drawing, to Plautus
for his dialogue. One criticism[2] of his on a contemporary
author might be taken as evidence of his bias in favour of
the Ancients. From all this it is evident that the labours
of such men as Aelius Stilo, Varro, and the Grammarians[3]
generally, helped to keep alive the interest of many in the
ancient writers. Aelius had been dead since 70 B.C., but
the tradition he had established was nobly upheld by Varro,
whose studies must have in turn influenced others. The
enthusiasm of such men for the early writers, and their
favourable criticisms of them, may have directly inspired
the often extravagant encomiums which Horace in his
Epistle to Augustus attributes to the admirers of the
Ancients.

In one passage[4] Horace himself shows some interest in
native literary origins, but in general such questions made
Horace and the little appeal to him. As the years went on,
" exemplaria he evidently looked with increasing admira-
Graeca " tion on the " exemplaria Graeca," and such
admiration, combined with his own natural refinement and
fastidiousness, made him turn in disgust[5] from every trace
of ancient rusticity. He had other ideals than those of the
antiquarians. He regarded himself as the apostle of the
new era, and looked to the creation of a poetic literature that,
in form at least,[6] would draw its inspiration from the un-

---

[1] Parmeno, fr. 15, Riese, p. 191 ; *vide supra*, p. 17.

[2] " Cum Quintipor Clodius tot comoedias sine ulla fecerit Musa," Riese,
p. 105 ; cf. Nonius, Vol. I. p. 165 (Mueller) for another contemptuous
reference to Clodius in Varro's " epistula ad Fufium " ; Clodius, however,
may have deserved all the contempt that V. pours on him.

[3] The Grammarians had certainly much to do with bringing about a
revival of Lucilius ; it was a Grammarian, Orbilius, that administered his
dose of Livius Andronicus to Horace in characteristic fashion ; cf. Suet.
De Gr. 9.

[4] Ep. II. 1. 145 *et seq.*, on the Fescennine verses and their development ;
he was naturally interested, too, in the rise and progress of Satire, when it
became established as a literary genre, Sat. I. 10. 46 *et seq.*, *ib.* 64 *et seq.*,
II. 1. 62.

[5] Cf. Ep. II. 1. 157, *ib.* 160 : " vestigia ruris."

[6] And at times in matter, as is evident from the subjects for tragedy which
he favours.

dying works of the Greeks in the Golden Age of their creative faculty, and that would be itself a model of elegance
and correctness. Enthusiastic judgments on the merits of
the Ancients provoked a violent reaction[1] in him, and often
made him unjust in his estimate of the early poets.

Plautus seems to have been at all times a favourite poet
with the archaists.[2]   Horace, with the discernment of the
true critic, has touched[3] on some of his
His judgment most serious defects, such as the looseness
on Plautus of his plots, the crudeness of his character-
drawing,[4] and the irregularity of his metres, but he seemed
incapable of appreciating his finer qualities as a Comic
writer.   Plautus seemed to him to be indifferent to the
success of his plays as a whole, and to fail in that rigid unity
which he himself prescribes[5] for the poet.   Possibly, as
Leo suggests,[6] he was thinking most of all of the plays in
which Plautus had practised contamination, but with small
success.   The latter, as is clear both from his own Prologues
and from those of Terence, had an uncouth and unlettered
audience to appeal to, and he endeavoured to hold their
attention by a succession of comic scenes often issuing into
broad farce, and strung together with little regard for
symmetry or unity.   It is surprising, however, that Horace
can find no word of commendation for his humour and
comic power.   He himself had laid down[7] stringent rules
to govern the laughter of the Satirist, and possibly he
judged the writers of Comedy by similar standards, so
that Plautus seemed to him wanting in elegance and
urbanity.[8]   Moreover, he failed to recognise the vigour, the
vivaciousness, the wealth of colour in Plautus' dialogue, and

---

[1] Ep. II. 1. 64 *et seq.*   [2] *Vide infra*, p. 315.

[3] Ep. II. 1. 170 *et seq.* ;   A.P. 270 *et seq.*

[4] Even his parasites, in Horace's eyes, recall the Atellan plays rather than
the Greek originals.

[5] A.P. 23, where Horace probably had before his mind especially the unity
of the drama.

[6] Gesch. der röm. Lit., p. 136.

[7] Sat. I. 10. 6 *et seq.*

[8] A.P. 270 *et seq.* ;   note his contrast of the " inurbanum " and " lepidum
dictum " ;   Cicero on the other hand takes Plautus as a type of refined and
elegant wit ;   *vide supra*, p. 148.

the copiousness and original force of his language. He
was probably incensed, too, at the extravagance of the
poet's admirers in comparing him to Epicharmus, though
they seem to have based their comparison justly enough on
the lively march of his dialogue.

Horace clearly shows his predilection for Terence, whom
he nowhere censures, though he quotes[1] in irony a dictum
of his admirers. He takes[2] many illustra-
The mantle of Menander tions from his plays and evidently regarded
him as the ideal writer of Comedy in the
early period[3] of Roman literature. Terence's elegance of
diction, his refinement and restraint as an artist, his care
for the unity and compactness of his plays, would make a
strong appeal to the fastidiousness of the Augustan poet.
Like Horace himself, he had much of the coterie spirit, and
valued the commendation of the cultured few. Horace
would probably consider that, if on any Roman poet, the
mantle of Menander had fallen on him, and not on Afranius,[4]
whom his votaries regarded as the Roman counterpart of
the Greek dramatist.

With a certain lack of historical knowledge, Horace
criticises Accius as a metrist,[5] and waxes ironical over the
epithet " altus " applied to him by his
His criticism of Accius admirers. It is not easy to divine the
meaning of the epithet, though it probably
connotes[6] a certain sublimity in style, which in the minds
of some may have been associated with the distinctively

[1] Ep. II. 1. 59

[2] Sat. I. 2. 20, I. 10. 40, II. 3. 259 *et seq.*, A.P. 94 ; cf. Fairclough,
Horace's view of the relations of Satire and Comedy, A.J. Ph. 1913, p. 183
et seq.

[3] Or possibly in any period ; we have suggested that Horace regarded
Fundanius as a modern Terence ; *vide supra*, p. 294.

[4] Cf. the Prologue to the Compitalia where Afranius acknowledges his
debt to Menander among others ; cf. Cic. De Fin. I. 7.

[5] A.P. 258, where his treatment of the Iambic trimeter is criticised.

[6] Cf. Leo, Gesch. der röm. Lit., p. 399, with the references there given ;
cf. Q. X. 1. 97, who ascribes to him as well as to Pacuvius " gravitas sententiarum, verborum pondus, auctoritas personarum " ; Gellius, XIII. 2. 3,
quotes Pacuvius as saying of his style : " sonora quidem esse quae scripsisset
et grandia, sed videri ea tamen sibi duriora paulum et acerbiora ", *vide supra*,
p. 52.

rhetorical character of the poet's works.   Cicero had a
high opinion[1] of Accius' talent as a dramatist, while Ovid
was impressed[2] with the spirited accents of his poetry.
According to Quintilian, he was generally considered as
exhibiting more vigour than Pacuvius, so that the enthusiasm of his admirers cannot have been altogether misplaced.

In his later works Horace is critical of the faults of Ennius,
even though he indirectly pays a tribute[3] to the perennial
Later verdict
on Ennius
glory of his Epic, and speaks[4] of him as
having enriched the Latin language.   He
criticises the heaviness[5] of his iambic tri-
meters, a fault which in Horace's eyes was due either to
hasty workmanship, or to ignorance[6] of verse technique.
As an Epic poet, his votaries were fond of proclaiming him
as a second Homer, but Horace suggests that he had done
little to justify such claims, and seemed indifferent to the
fulfilment of his Pythagorean dreams.[7]

Enough has been said to show that Horace, especially in
his later years, was an inflexible champion of the Moderns,
Low standard
of public
taste
or at any rate the Moderns of his own
school.   Several influences were at work to
make him as intransigeant as he was.   He
was in reaction against the excessive admiration shown by
those who favoured the Ancients.   The Roman public for
the most part was marked by an absence[8] of critical discernment, which became more apparent when it endeavoured
to formulate its judgments on early Roman literature.   It
could grow enthusiastic over Livius and Naevius with all
their shortcomings, while in its eyes a graceful expression,

[1] *Vide supra*, p. 285.
[2] Am. I. 15. 19 : "animosique Accius oris."
[3] Odes, IV. 8. 19–20.
[4] A.P. 56.
[5] A.P. 259 *et seq. ;* such an effect was due to the too frequent introduction
of spondees ; Mueller, Q. Ennius, p. 242, notes that the number of spondees
in Ennius is lessened by dropping the final " s."
[6] Horace's own knowledge of the history of the Iambic trimeter is here
at fault.
[7] Cf. Fronto, II. 66 : " magister Ennii Homerus et Somnus " ; Ennius'
dream provided congenial matter for the satirist ; *vide supra*, p. 291.
[8] Ep. II. 1. 60 *et seq.*, *ib.* 182 *et seq.*, A.P. 263 *et seq.*

or one or two well turned verses were sufficient to commend a poem as a whole. Horace had already formed his own ideals of elegance and correctness, of the polish that results from patient labour, of delicacy and precision in verse technique. Such ideals were probably the common heritage of the circle to which he belonged, but in his case they were strengthened by his careful study of the best Greek models.[1] It is evident that at the time when he was pleading so vigorously the cause of the Moderns, his mind was much preoccupied with the " exemplaria Graeca." He was thus impatient of the immoderate praise given to the early poets, especially when he set their crude[2] and careless workmanship side by side with the technical finish of the Greek writers.

It is sometimes said[3] that the quarrel of Horace and his opponents on the merits of the Ancients and Moderns might in large measure be reduced to a conflict of Hellenism and Nationalism. Such **Horace's motives analysed** a factor may have entered into it, but the quarrel cannot always be resolved into such simple elements. The Ancients, too, as a rule drew their inspiration from Greek sources. On Horace's side, I believe, the dominant[4] consideration was the greater or less degree in which a Roman poet approximated to the symmetry and faultlessness of the Greeks. Horace's ardour in the conflict is an index of his desire to remove the obstacles which hindered the progress of Roman poetry in its advance towards perfection of form, and to set forth a programme which the poets of his own and succeeding generations might follow with advantage. He foresaw the danger that unmeasured admiration of the Ancients might lead to the neglect of severer standards of taste. To his mind such admiration could only result in setting the seal of approbation on faults

[1] In this respect Horace himself might be considered a champion of the Ancients ; his position would thus find a parallel in that of the Roman Atticists ; *vide infra*, p. 324.
[2] Ep. II. 1. 66 *et seq.*, A.P. 261 *et seq.*
[3] Cf. Pascal, La Critica dei Poeti Romani in Orazio, p. 135.
[4] The admirers of the Ancients took other factors into account, but throughout the debate Horace was primarily concerned w th Form.

which he,[1] and those who shared his views, wished to see eliminated. In his judgments on the Ancients he lacked a proper historical perspective, and, engrossed with his own ideals, he failed to do justice to the achievements of the poets who had to sail on uncharted seas, and who helped to create a poetic language out of crude and imperfect material. He did not always realise that his own age enjoyed the advantage of the long struggle to refine and perfect the Latin tongue.

Yet withal, Horace was no blind admirer of all the poets of his own and the previous generation. His passion for

No blind admirer of the "Moderns" classical restraint and severity would naturally make him intolerant of the bombast of Furius'[2] Epic style. However we interpret his reference to Calvus and Catullus, he certainly showed little appreciation for the genius of these two poets, especially Catullus, who was such an original force in Roman literature. His lack of appreciation has been set down to political motives, or to a divergence of ideals as to the models to be followed. Horace was primarily attracted towards the poets of the Golden Age of Greek literature, while the Alexandrians who inspired the νεώτεροι, made less appeal to him. The question of models may in part account for his coldness towards the poets of the new school, though he has praise[3] for Virgil, who at the opening of his career came under their influence. It is possible that, as the years went on, Horace became more catholic in his tastes, while the illustration he derives[4] from the labour spent on Cinna's *Zmyrna*, would indicate that he had begun to realise that the Alexandrians could impart an exquisite sense of form, and teach the lesson of technical perfection which he himself was striving to inculcate.

[1] *Vide infra*, p. 378.

[2] Sat. I. 10. 36, II. 5. 41; cf. Q. VIII. 6. 17; the identification of Furius with Furius Bibaculus is not without its difficulty, as the latter belonged to the anti-Caesarian party (Tac. Ann. IV. 34), and would hardly have written a poem on Caesar's Gallic wars; *vide infra*, p. 368.

[3] Sat. I. 10. 45; Virgil, of course, had befriended him, when he most needed a friend; cf. Sat. I. 6. 54.

[4] *Vide infra*, p. 381.

Apart from the natural opposition of rival coteries, Horace's own sense of humour would incline him to laugh

The guild of poets

at the pretensions[1] of the professional guild of poets, who were chiefly occupied with mutual admiration, and an eternal parade of their talents. If, as is likely, he is glancing[2] at Propertius, the "Roman Callimachus," in his criticism of contemporary writers, his hostility might be explained not merely by a natural opposition to a rival poet,[3] but by Propertius' proclaimed adherence to a particular model. Horace was concerned not merely with the choice of models, but also with the manner of their imitation. Propertius' claim[4] to be the Roman counterpart of Callimachus might in his eyes savour of that servile[5] imitation which he regarded as a fundamental defect. He looked above all for a vital imitation.[6] He himself might imitate the metre and the spirit of Archilochus, but he would probably regard it as a poor compliment to be considered merely the Roman counterpart of the Greek poet.

One would imagine that the achievements of poets such as Horace and Virgil, would have made their place in the

Tributes to Virgil and Horace

affections of their countrymen secure for all time. Virgil's glory as an Epic poet, the splendid harmonies of his verse, his imaginative sweep over the origins of Rome, his embodiment of the spirit of Roman power and greatness, would seem to have entitled him at least to that recompense. Propertius paid[7]

[1] Sat. I. 10. 38, Ep. I. 19. 39 *et seq.*, II. 2. 91 *et seq. ;* poetry was becoming " scholastic " in their hands ; cf. Ep. I. 19. 40 : " grammaticas ambire tribus " ; cf. Suet. De Gr. 11, on Bibaculus and V. Cato.

[2] Cf. Ep. II. 2. 90, *ib.* 100.

[3] Propertius, to judge by his eulogy of the Aeneid, was also a friend of Virgil's ; cf. Pascal, op. cit., p. 130, quoting Asconius on the friends of Virgil : " cum inter se plurimum invidia arderent."

[4] III. 9. 43. IV. 1. 64 ; cf. II. 34. 31, where he advises Lynceus to imitate Philetas and Callimachus ; Propertius' appreciation of Calvus and Catullus (II. 25. 4, *ib.* 34. 87–89) would not help to endear him to Horace ; *vide infra*, p. 412.

[5] *Vide infra*, p. 430.   [6] Ep. I. 19. 23 *et seq.*

[7] II. 34. 61 *et seq. ;* cf. Ovid, Ars Am. III. 337–338, Rem. Am. 396, Am. I. 15. 25 ; Ex Ponto, III. 4. 84 ; Dom. Marsus, Epigr. on Tibullus ; *vide infra*, p. 419.

a glowing tribute to the *Aeneid*, declaring it to be greater than the *Iliad*, and sang the praises, too, of the poet of the *Georgics* and the *Eclogues*. Possibly in Virgil's own lifetime, or certainly soon after his death, Quintus Caecilius Epirota gave public readings[1] of the poet's works. Petronius learnt well the lessons of the Augustans. The chapter[2] in which he refers to " Roman Virgil," and pays Horace the tribute of " curiosa felicitas," might well stand as an expression of Augustan ideals. He emphasises the difficulties and exclusiveness[3] of the poet's calling, the need for refinement of diction and that unerring taste that will ensure an even texture of style free from manifest protuberances.[4] Virgil would satisfy one of his requirements for the poet, possessing, as he did, a mind " ingenti flumine litterarum inundata." Moreover, he had chosen a theme in which he could skilfully mingle legend and history. The free play[5] of his genius, his deft treatment of the marvellous and of the interposition of the gods, are evidence that he conceived his task in the spirit of the inspired poet, as Petronius demands from those who essay an Epic subject. In the same period Seneca criticised Virgil for the archaic colouring of the *Aeneid*, but for all that he proclaimed[6] him " maximus vates." The poets[7] of the next generation cherished the memory of the great Augustan, and rendered striking homage to his genius.

Virgil's position, however, was challenged even in his lifetime,[8] and some of the bitterest criticisms were directed

---

[1] Suet. De Gr. 16 : " primusque (dicitur) Vergilium et alios *poetas novos* perlegere coepisse."

[2] Satyr. 118.

[3] He quotes Horace's " odi profanum vulgus et arceo."

[4] " Ne sententiae emineant extra corpus orationis expressae " ; Petronius' insistence on " sententiae " throughout the chapter shows the influence of his own age.

[5] Cf. " praecipitandus est liber spiritus."

[6] Dial. X. 9. 2 : " maximus vates et velut divino ore instinctus " ; cf. Ad Polyb. 8. 2.

[7] On Silius Italicus, cf. Pliny, Ep. III. 7. 8 ; Statius, Theb. XII. 816 : " divinam Aeneida " ; Juv. XI. 180 *et seq. ;* Mart. V. 5. 8, VII. 63. 5, VIII. 18. 5 *et seq.*, XI. 52. 18, XII. 4. 1, XIV. 185.

[8] Suet. Life of Virgil, 43 *et seq.*

against him by the "obtrectatores Vergilii," from whose

The "obtrec-tatores Vergilii" malevolence Asconius Pedianus endeavoured to defend him. Want of propriety in his language, defects of style, plagiarism, weakness in historical and antiquarian knowledge, lack of skill in the management of his story, constituted the chief charges levelled against him. We have in the pages of Gellius and Macrobius[1] echoes of the polemic, to which scholars such as Julius Hyginus and Annaeus Cornutus contributed with their adverse criticisms of the poet. Agrippa had called[2] him a suppositious child of Maecenas, the inventor of a new form of affectation in style, which employed familiar words in an unusual way. The Purists challenged[3] his right to the coinage of new words. Virgilian criticism frequently took the form of a comparison[4] of the Roman poet with Homer, often[5] to his disadvantage, though at times his admirers held[6] him to have equalled, or even surpassed his Greek prototype. Such critics were generally content to weigh parallel passages,[7] with little consideration of the genius, the aim, and the historical setting of the two poets.

Though Virgil was defended by Asconius, and treated sympathetically by Probus, and though he gradually won

The "Mo-derns" in Persius his way to a position of complete supremacy in Roman poetry, yet such adverse criticisms tended to obscure his fame with a section of his countrymen, especially for part of the century after his death. In this connection, the first Satire

[1] Cf. N.A. I. 21 (for Hyginus' interest in the text of V.), II. 6, *ib.* 16, V. 8, VI. 6. IX. 10, X. 16 ; cf. Connington, Vol. I. Introd. p. 29 *et seq.* ; Georgii, Die antike Äneiskritik, p. 560 *et seq.*, for a summary of the criticisms passed on the Aeneid ; Sikes, op. cit., p. 67 *et seq.*, on the general character of Virgilian criticism ; *vide infra*, p. 317.   [2] Suet. Life, 44.

[3] Hor. A.P. 53 ; cf. Connington, op. cit., p. 33 *et seq.*

[4] Q. X. i. 85–86, allows Virgil superiority in art ; cf. Juv. VI. 436.

[5] Even in the case of a critic such as Probus who was generally favourable ; cf. Gellius, IX. 9. 12 *et seq.* ; Servius, Ad Aen. IV. 359, XI. 554, for other unfavourable criticisms of Pr. ; on Pr. as critic, cf. Mart. III. 2. 12 ; Gellius, I. 15. 18 ; *vide infra*, p. 317.

[6] Cf. Juv. XI. 180–181 ; Macrob. especially Book V. c. 11–12.

[7] Cf. Macrob. Bk. V ; Gellius, XVII. 10, where Pindar and Virgil are compared in the same spirit.

of Persius is illuminating. In it we have another echo of
the quarrel of the Ancients and Moderns. The Satire was
written to ridicule[1] the prevailing fashion in the poetry of
the day, but even allowing for the licence of the Satirist,
and his tendency to colour facts for his own purpose, it
may fairly stand as a revelation of the vagaries of contemporary taste. Persius depicts in lively fashion the
extravagances which the practice of Recitation naturally
engendered, and the chorus of praise[2] that greeted the
effusions of aspiring poets, who were afflicted[3] with the
" cacoethes scribendi " as in the days of Horace. We are
not surprised, when the poets' friends and clients exclaim[4] : " are there (in face of the Modern poetry) people
who still linger over a shrivelled volume of Accius, or who
are attracted by the archaic style of Pacuvius ? " We are
startled, however, when the champions of present-day
elegance quote[5] the opening of the *Aeneid*, and characterise
it as puffy and frothy stuff.[6] To such supporters of the
Moderns Virgil already seems old-fashioned. It may not
be fantastic to see in this contemptuous reference to the
Aeneid evidence of the influence of the campaign of
malignant criticism that had been carried on against the
Augustan poet.

However, the battle for the Ancients continued. Tacitus
tells us[7] that there were some in his day who preferred

---

[1] Cf. Suet. Life of Persius : " mox omnibus detrectaturus cum tanta
recentium poetarum et oratorum insectatione, ut etiam Neronem principem
illius temporis inculpaverit."

[2] For the New Poetry, cf. Sat. I. 63 : " Quis populi sermo est ? quis
enim nisi carmina molli *nunc demum* numero fluere " ; *ib*. 92 : " sed numeris decor est et junctura addita crudis " ; *ib*. 99 *et seq*., for a specimen of
the new style ; the large admixture of Greek words is remarkable.

[3] Sat. I. 51 *et seq*.

[4] *Ib*. 76 *et seq*.; cf. Hendrickson, The First Satire of Persius, p. 106
et seq., Class. Phil. Vol. XXIII. 2 ; Hendrickson's interpretation of the Satire
is in several points an improvement on the old interpretations.

[5] Sat. I. 96 *et seq*.

[6] Some difficulty has been felt about " spumosum " ; cf. Hendrickson,
op. cit., p. 112, who favours " spinosum."

[7] Dial. c. 23 ; cf., however, c. 12 : " plures hodie reperies qui Ciceronis
gloriam quam qui Vergilii detrectent " ; Virgil had still his " obtrectatores,"
though they were fewer than Cicero's ; cf. Mart. X. 21. 4, on Sextus, who
rated Cinna higher then Virgil.

Lucretius to Virgil. Their taste was evidently determined

Champions
of the
" Ancients "
active

by the archaic tone of the *De Rerum Natura*. These, too, would rather read Lucilius than Horace. The older Satirist seems to have been always held in honour by those who had a relish for the Ancients. Quintilian tells[1] us of enthusiasts in his own day who set him above not only all other Satirists, but even all other poets.

He himself takes the middle way, and condemns such ill-considered admiration, just as much as he condemns the strictures of Horace on Lucilius. This

The position
of Quintilian

is typical of the position of Quintilian, who, with his sense of historical perspective, usually preserved a sane attitude in the quarrel. He recognises the merits of the Ancients, but is prepared to censure their defects. It is not the beauty[2] of Ennius he admires so much as his sacred and venerable character. With the charm and elegance of Greek Comedy before his mind, he is little disposed[3] to share the enthusiasm of the critics who lavished praise on the early Roman writers in this genre. In Tragedy, the works of Accius and Pacuvius, for all their good qualities, seemed to him to lack polish[4] and the final touches of perfection, but he considered that the age in which they lived rather than they themselves, was responsible for such defects. Quintilian, however, recognised the value of the Ancient poets for rhetorical training, even though their strength lay more in their natural talent than in artistic finish. In his eyes, the Augustans were always supreme, Virgil in Epic, Varius in Tragedy, Horace in Satire and Lyric poetry, but this does not preclude him from paying a generous tribute to the poets[5] of his own generation.

[1] X. 1. 93 ; cf. Mart. XI. 90 ; Marx, Luc. Carm. Reliq. Vol. I. Introd. p. 117 *et seq.*, 125 *et seq.*, on the vogue of Lucilius.

[2] X. 1. 88.

[3] *Ib.* 99–100 ; Terence's plays, however, are styled " in hoc genere elegantissima."

[4] *Ib.* 97 ; " ceterum nitor et summa in excolendis operibus manus magis videri potest temporibus quam ipsis defuisse."

[5] *Ib.* 96, where he includes Caesius Bassus in the list of Lyric poets, " sed eum longe praecedunt ingenia viventium " ; on Bassus cf. Ovid,

The younger Pliny, like Quintilian, endeavours to hold the balance evenly between the claims of the Ancients and the Moderns.   He admires[1] the former, but does not, as some do, despise the genius of his own age.   Pliny's term "Ancient" was evidently an elastic one, as he applies[2] it even to Horace and Propertius.   As regards the Moderns, he showed a fairly just appreciation of his contemporary Silius Italicus, in ascribing[3] to him art rather than genius.   Martial had laid Pliny under a debt by some complimentary verses,[4] in which he declared that his own age and future generations would compare his eloquence with that of Cicero.   He could requite such a flattering tribute only by a generous homage[5] to the poet's talents, though he ends on a note of doubt as to whether Martial's works are destined to immortality.

The Younger Pliny

In Martial himself we find many echoes of the quarrel. We have seen[6] how strongly he reacted against the traditional themes of ancient legend, which he regarded as inane and inappropriate for his generation.   He protests[7] against the taste for the early poets evinced by many in his day, and sets down to envy their neglect of living writers.   He is especially vehement in his attack[8] on Chrestillus, who values a line of Lucilius more than Homer, and who in his ecstasy over the archaic diction of Ennius, Accius, and Pacuvius, has no word of praise for the smooth[9] cadences of modern verse.   It is not, however, always easy to determine what meaning Martial

Martial

Trist. IV. 10. 47 ; Persius, Sat. VI ;   Suet. Life of Persius, for P.'s relations with that poet ; Sandys, A History of Classical Scholarship, Vol. I p. 213, for his work on metre.

[1] Ep. VI. 21. 1 : " sum ego is qui mirer antiquos, non tamen ut quidam temporum nostrorum ingenia despicio " ; the letter was written in praise of Vergilius Romanus, who was so successful in his imitation of ancient models.

[2] *Vide supra,* p. 283.   [3] Ep. III. 7. 5.

[4] X. 19.   [5] Ep. III. 21.

[6] *Vide supra,* p. 280.

[7] V. 10, VIII. 69 ; cf. X. 9. 5.

[8] XI. 90.

[9] " Carmina nulla probas molli quae limite currunt " ;   cf. Persius I. 63 ; *vide supra,* p. 306.

attached to the term " veteres." In one passage,[1] at least, where he looks forward to being read " inter veteres poetas," he numbers Catullus amongst them. His opposition to the old poets was evidently directed against those of the pre-Catullan period, for his admiration for the poet of Verona is manifested in many passages.[2] In writing[3] to Sextus, the keeper of the Palatine Library, he expresses the hope that his works may find a place beside those of Pedo, Marsus,[4] and Catullus. It is evident that he counted the two latter poets especially amongst his models, and that his ambition was to rival their fame. With regard to the Moderns, he revered the memory of Persius amongst the poets of the former generation, while he renders[5] striking homage to Lucan, a Spaniard like himself, to whom some denied the title of poet. He speaks, however, with bitter scorn of the plagiarists and poetasters of his own day. Of the legitimate poets, Statius had then won fame by his Epic, but we have seen reason to believe that its subject made little appeal to Martial. His friendly feelings for Juvenal are evident,[6] though they seem to be a tribute to the man rather than the poet. Of Silius Italicus he was an enthusiastic admirer, and lavished praise[7] upon him which would now be regarded as extravagant, styling[8] him the equal of Virgil. The truth seems to be that the critic in Martial was often merged in the courtier. The man who could[9] call Nerva " the Tibullus of our time," would not be likely to practise restraint, if extravagant praise were calculated to advance his interests.

With the reign of Hadrian and the Antonines we enter on a new and more pronounced phase of the question of Ancients and Moderns. This was an age when the study

---

[1] *Vide supra*, p. 283.

[2] IV. 14. 13, V. 30. 3, VI. 34. 7, VII. 14. 3, VIII. 73. 8, X. 103. 5, IV. 194 ; *vide infra*, p. 412.

[3] V. 5.

[4] Cf. II. 77. 5, VII. 99. 7, VIII. 56. 24.

[5] VII. 21–23, X. 64. 3 : " Heliconis gloria nostri" ; XIV. 194.

[6] VII. 24, *ib.* 91, XII. 18.

[7] IV. 14, VII. 63, VIII. 66, IX. 86.

[8] XI. 49. 4 ; cf. VI. 64. 10, for Silius' appreciation of Martial.

[9] VIII. 70. 7 ; cf. IX. 26 ; Pliny, Ep. V. 3. 5, on Nerva as a poet.

of the early Roman writers was taken up again with renewed ardour. It was essentially a period
**Hadrian and
the Antonines** in which antiquarian[1] interests were supreme,
when men loved to make pilgrimages[2] to
places renowned in ancient story, and linger over the
glories of the Past. There was a new birth of Hellenism,
and a closer intimacy established between Greek and
Roman scholars. It is not unlikely that the Atticist movement, which found such zealous champions in Herodes
Atticus[3] and others, and turned men's minds back to the
old Classical models of Greece, may have had its reaction
in Rome in awakening afresh a keen interest in the earliest
Roman writers. There were, of course, other influences at
work in that direction. This was an age when the inspiration of original genius was exhausted, and when the pedant's
love of the bizarre or the obsolete in literature impelled him
to a study of primitive authors. Such tastes were at times
engendered by the appeal of a certain quaintness[4] in the
language of the earliest writers, but were often the outcome
of a desire for a display of erudition that would establish a
scholar's superiority over the common crowd.

Hadrian himself was a dilettante[5] with an ambition for
literary fame. His lines written for the tomb of Arete, the
wife of Parthenius, may be taken as evidence of his interest

[1] Cf. Peter, Die geschichtliche Litteratur, Vol. I. p. 125 *et seq.*;
Norden, A.K. I. p. 344 *et seq.*; Rohde, Der griechische Roman, p. 32

[2] For Hadrian's passion for such travels, cf. Spartianus, Vita Hadrian
c. 13–14; *ib.* 16, where Florus touches on it in some mocking verse;
such a taste is illustrated also in Gellius, XII. 5.

[3] *Vide* Philostr. V.S. 564; cf. Schmid, Der Atticismus, Vol. I. p. 1
et seq.; *ib.* II. 14, IV. 10; cf. I. p. 212, for the support given to the Attic
movement by the Roman Emperors from Hadrian to Alexander Severus
Philostratus supplies us with some details of Hadrian's interest in t
Sophists.

[4] Cf. Gellius, III. 3. 6 (on Favorinus' hearing a passage from the Ner
laria, attributed to Plautus): " delectatus faceta verborum antiquitate
vide infra, p. 313.

[5] Spartianus, XIV. 8, XVI. 1 *et seq.*; cf. Henderson, The Life a
Principate of the Emperor Hadrian, p. 240 *et seq.*; for the view that Hadri
was the Emperor in whom Juvenal centres his hopes (Sat. VII. 1),
Friedländer, Roman Life and Manners, Vol. IV. p. 314; Wight D
A Literary History of Rome in the Silver Age, p. 605.

in the Greek poet. He would thus share the taste of Tiberius, who like him was also prone to archaism. In his predilection for the Ancients, he must have done much to set the fashion for his time. We are told[1] that he preferred Cato to Cicero, Ennius to Virgil, Coelius to Sallust. His own style was a reflex of his studies. Fronto accused[2] him of affecting a spurious appearance of ancient eloquence. The Emperor's interest in matters of verbal criticism is shown by his calling[3] into question the correctness of " obiter," " quanquam apud Laberium haec vox esse dicatur."

In all this, he well reflects the spirit of the age, a spirit which both as regards his own reign, and more especially[4] that of the Antonines, is most fully disclosed to us in the pages of Gellius. The labours of the grammarian[5] and the antiquarian were then regarded as of supreme importance. The highest compliment which Gellius can pay[6] to a friend is to style him " rerum litterarumque veterum peritus." He himself had studied under men who were deeply versed in ancient literature, such as Antonius Julianus,[7] and Sulpicius Apollinaris,[8] the master of Pertinax. He moved in the circle of Fronto, and was the friend of that picturesque figure Favorinus[9] of Arles,[10] who, philosopher and sophist as he was, enjoyed great popularity in his day, and was

The spirit of the age

[1] Vita, XVI. 6.

[2] II. 138 : " veteris eloquentiae colorem adumbratum ostendit Hadriana oratio " ; the words, however, are from the margin of the Codex ; cf. b. 206 ; Gellius, XVI. 13. 4, on his speech " De Italicensibus."

[3] Charisius, G.L. (Keil), I. p. 209.

[4] On the chronology of Gellius, cf. Friedländer, op. cit., Vol. IV. p. 322 t seq.

[5] Cf. Nettleship, The Noctes Atticae of Aulus Gellius, A. J. Ph. 1883, . 391 et seq.

[6] Cf. VII. 7. 1, XIX. 7. 1.

[7] I. 4. 1, IX. 1. 2, XV. 1. 1 et seq., XVIII. 5. 1, XIX. 9.

[8] VI. 6. 12, XIII. 19. 1 et seq., XVI. 5. 5, XVIII. 4. 1, XIX. 13. 1, XX. 6. 1.

[9] I. 21. 4, II. 22, ib. 26, III. 1, IV. 1, V. 11. 8, IX. 8. 4, ib. 13. 5, . 12. 9 (where he is styled " memoriarum veterum exsequentissimus "), XII. 1. 1, XIII. 24. 2, XIV. 1, XVI. 3, XVII. 10, XIX. 3.

[10] Ib. II. 22. 20 ; Philostr. V.S. 489 ; Lucian, Eunuch, 7 ; Favorinus was a pupil of Dion Chrysostom.

influential enough to quarrel[1] with Hadrian and still retain his patronage. During his stay at Athens, Gellius shared the friendship of Herodes Atticus,[2] who was prominent in the Sophistic movement of the time, and was a distinguished patron of the Arts.

Gellius and his Roman friends were all agreed in their love of antiquity, and their veneration for the early literature of Rome. They delighted to discuss[3] the institution of the Vestal Virgins, the origin of the Fratres Arvales, the character of the Laws of the Twelve Tables, and similar antiquarian problems. It was the day of the bibliophile, who loved[4] to wander through the booksellers' shops, or search the libraries for editions of old authors. Gellius tells[5] us how he and his friend Julius Paulus came across a copy of the *History* of Fabius, which the bookseller declared to be without blemish. He himself discovered[6] in the library at Patrae a copy of the *Odyssey* of Livius Andronicus, which confirmed the correctness of the form " insece." In the convivial gatherings and the ordinary social intercourse of the circles to which he belonged, the earliest poets and prose writers most frequently formed the subject of conversation. He gives[7] us many glimpses of such gatherings, at which some old lyric poet or historian was read, or Sallust's Catiline, or a speech of Gaius Gracchus, or a passage from Quadrigarius, was discussed, and rare forms especially noted. With his friend Celsinus he pays[8] a visit to Julius Paulus, who lived in the Ager Vaticanus, and during their meal listens to a reading of the *Alcestis* of Laevius. On their way back to the city he and his friend occupied themselves

The love of antiquity

[1] Philostr. loc. cit. ; cf. Spartianus, Vita Hadriani, XV. 12, XVI. 11 (with Centerwall's notes).
[2] Gellius, I. 2, IX. 2, XVIII. 10. 1, XIX. 12 ; cf. Philostr. V.S. 545 *et seq.*
[3] N.A. I. 12, VI. 7, XX. 1.
[4] IX. 4. 1 *et seq.*, XVIII. 4.
[5] V. 4.
[6] XVIII. 9. 5 ; cf. IX. 14. 3, on a copy of Claudius Quadrigarius which he discovered in the library at Tibur.
[7] II. 21. 4 *et seq.*, 22. 1 *et seq.*, 23, 26, XI. 13, XVII. 2.
[8] XIX. 7.

with pondering over the figurative language, and the novel and striking expressions in Laevius' work. Particularly interesting is his account[1] of the celebration of the Saturnalia during his stay at Athens. The questions[2] proposed for discussion by the company on that occasion throw a flood of light on the prevailing taste in literature.

Such taste, as I have said, was in part determined by the appeal[3] of a certain charm and quaintness in the archaic language of the earlier authors, which had a flavour of the uncommon, welcome to jaded palates. Gellius tells us[4] how his master Antonius Julianus used to revel in the language, and especially in the daring coinages of the old poet Cn. Matius. He, however, is careful to issue a warning[5] against attachment to words that are extreme in their obsoleteness. Words were sometimes[6] quoted from an early author, which naturally enough seemed doubtful Latin to those who were " imperiti antiquitatis." A scholar who boasted of his unrivalled knowledge of Sallust, sums up the attitude of many at the time, when he says :[7] " priscorum et remotorum go verborum medullas et sanguinem, sicuti dixi, perspicere t elicere soleo."

The charm of the Ancients

Though attracted by the archaic charm of the primitive writers, the interest of Gellius and his friends in their works was often merely that of the grammarian. A supposed solecism is discovered[8] in Cicero, and it is at once defended by the usage of a formidable array of pre-Ciceronian writers. What is believed

The interest of the grammarian

---

[1] XVIII. 2.

[2] Amongst others we find " aut sententia poetae veteris lepide obscura, t historiae antiquioris requisitio, aut inopinati rariorisque verbi indagatio."

[3] Cf. N.A. IX. 13. 4 ; Quadrigarius tells the story of M. Torquatus simplicique et incompta orationis antiquae suavitate " ; X. 3. 15, where me prefer C. Gracchus to Cicero because there is in him " umbra et color uasi opacae vetustatis " ; XII. 4. 3 (on Ennius) : " odor quidam vetustatis his versibus tam reverendus est."

[4] XX. 9 ; Matius wrote Mimiambi ; ib. X. 24. 10, XV. 25 ; he also ade a translation of the Iliad, VI. 6. 5, IX. 14. 14.

[5] XI. 7. 1.

[6] XVII. 2. 3, ib. 5 et seq., on forms such as " inlatebrare " and " fruiscor " m Quadrigarius.

[7] Ib. XVIII. 4. 6 ; vide infra, p. 347.   [8] I. 7.

to be the discovery of an uncommon word or a rare grammatical form, will lead to the quotation of a vast number
of poets and prose writers from the days of Livius Andronicus. We can feel a certain sympathy with the man against
whose opinion the form "pluria" was thus supported,
when he replied :[1] "tibi habeas auctoritates istas ex
Faunorum et Aboriginum saeculo repetitas." Even the
philosophers were caught by the contagion, and devoted
their time to tracing the history and meaning of particular
words. Domitius (nicknamed "Insanus" by his contemporaries) taunted them in the person of Favorinus with being
"mera mortuaria glossaria."[2] Gellius and his associates in
numerous points depend on the grammarians of the pre-
ceding generations, but it is clear that they carried out many
investigations of their own. Fronto,[3] as we shall see, must
have had no small influence in promoting such studies.

As regards particular authors, we find that there is
scarcely a poet from Livius Andronicus to Catullus that is
not quoted by Gellius, though rarely with
any aesthetic appreciation[4] of their works.
They are most often cited to illustrate some
point of verbal criticism, though they are occasionally
appealed to on a matter of historical or antiquarian interest.
As one might expect, Ennius was the favoured poet among
this band of archaists. His Satires, his Tragedies, but above
all his *Annales*, figure prominently in the pages of the
Noctes Atticae. Gellius tells us of[5] a reading of the
Third Book of the *Annales* that took place before a large
company on the occasion of a holiday in Rome. How great
was the vogue of the poem is evident also from the fact
that a public reading of the Seventh Book was given

The vogue of Ennius

[1] N.A. V. 21. 7.
[2] *Ib.* XVIII. 7. 3 ; the phrase is Cato's ; cf. *ib.*: "namque colligit
lexidia, res tetras, et inanes, et frivolas."
[3] Cf. N.A. XIII. 28. 6 : "hoc judicium Frontonis, etiam in parvi
minutisque vocabulis, non praetermittendum putavi, ne nos forte fugere
lateretque subtilior hujuscemodi verborum consideratio."
[4] Gellius, however, treats us to some sound criticism in his comparison o
Caecilius and Menander, II. 23.
[5] XVI. 10.
[6] *Ib.* XVIII. 5.

in the theatre at Puteoli by an " Ennianista "[1] (as he himself wished to be styled). The subsequent discussion as to the superiority of the reading " quadrupes equus " or " quadrupes eques " is illuminating. Gellius, to decide the matter for himself, consulted an edition of the poem emended by Lampadio,[2] which confirmed the correctness of the reading " eques." He waxes[3] enthusiastic over the verses in which Ennius defines the duties of a friend towards one superior to him in birth and station. He was attracted[4] by their unaffected charm, as well as by their old-world colouring. He praises[5] the poet also for his skilful and graceful version in his *Satires* of Aesop's fable of the crested lark. Though Ennius is thus occasionally[6] referred to with something suggestive of aesthetic appreciation, he usually shares the fate of the other early poets, and is most often quoted to illustrate trivial points of grammar or of language.

Next after Ennius, Plautus probably enjoyed most favour in that age, if one can judge by the many tributes[7] paid to his diction. Gellius tells us[8] of some ardent students of the poet, who were prepared to pronounce on the genuineness of a Plautine comedy from internal evidence alone. It is interesting also to note that the old writers[9] of Mimes and Atellan plays are

Other authors favoured

[1] Who evidently wished to occupy a position analogous to that of the rhapsodes in Greece who specialised in Homer.

[2] Cf. Suet. De Gr. 2, where he is mentioned only in connection with the " Bellum Punicum " of Naevius.

[3] XII. 4.

[4] The words " multa tenens antiqua, sepulta vetustas quae facit, et mores veteresque novosque tenentem," etc., naturally made a strong appeal to Gellius.

[5] II. 29. 20.

[6] Cf. II. 26. 21 : " verba illa ex annali quartodecimo Ennii amoenissima " ; cf. XX. 10. 4.

[7] N.A. I. 7. 17 : " Plautus verborum Latinorum elegantissimus " ; VII. 17. 4, XIX. 8. 6, where he is styled by Fronto " linguae Latinae decus."

[8] III. 3. 1 : " non indicibus Aelii ... credituros, sed ipsi Plauto moribusque ingenii atque linguae ejus " ; cf. Cic. Ad Fam. IX. 16. 4.

[9] Cf. N.A. XVII. 14, on Publilius Syrus, many of whose " sententiae " are quoted ; Pomponius, *ib.* X. 24. 5, XII. 10. 7, XVI. 6. 7, XVIII. 6. 6; Novius, XV. 13. 4, XVII. 2. 8.

once again being studied. Laberius is praised[1] for his verses on Democritus, but criticised[2] for his fondness for new coinages, and his use of excessively mean and vulgar words. Generally speaking, the motive force in the study of such writers was the lure of the unfamiliar word, or the rare grammatical construction. In a symposium,[3] at which Antonius Julianus and Gellius were present, the former, when asked by the Greeks of the company for his opinion on the Greek lyric poets, and when challenged to produce anything comparable to them in Latin literature, significantly enough goes back to pre-Catullan times to the erotic pieces[4] of Valerius Aedituus, Porcius Licinus, and Quintus Catulus. The *Satires* of Varro are again in favour They had not a great vogue[5] for the century after thei author's death, though they influenced Seneca and Petronius and at a later stage were sympathetically handled by Quintilian.[6] Gellius frequently quotes them, and tells us of a contemporary who boasted as if he were the only on living capable of interpreting them. With regard to the Neoterics, it is evident that Gellius had a certain affectior for Catullus, whom he styles[8] " elegantissimus poetarum. He had some knowledge, too, of the poems[9] of Calvus anc Cinna, though his tendency was to regard them chiefly a " docti poetae," in accordance with the traditional attitude.

It is to his credit that, for all his attachment to the earl Roman poets, he was still capable of realising the greatnes

[1] X. 17 : " versibus quidem satis munde atque graphice factis " (fron the " Restio ").

[2] XI. 15. 1, XVI. 7, XIX. 13. 3.

[3] XIX. 9 ; note the concessions of the Greeks : " ecquis nostrorur poetarum tam fluentes carminum delicias fecisset ? nisi Catullus, inquiun forte pauca, et Calvus itidem pauca."

[4] " quibus mundius, venustius, limatius, pressius, Graecum Latinumv nihil quidquam reperiri puto."

[5] Cf. Riese, op. cit., Introd. p. 49 *et seq.* ; Norden, In Varronis Satura Menippeas, p. 294 ; Seneca, Apocolocyntosis, 8.

[6] X. I. 95, *ib.* I. 4. 4.

[7] XIII. 30. 1.

[8] VII. 20. 6 ; cf. VI. 16. 2, where he defends the use of deprecor " *do tiuscule* positum in Catulli carmine."

[9] IX. 12. 10, 12, XIX. 9. 7, *ib.* 13. 5 : " Cinnae non ignobilis nequ indocti poetae."

of Virgil. He would naturally be drawn to him as a "mul-

**Virgil in the
" Noctes
Atticae "** tae antiquitatis hominem,"[1] but in many
passages[2] he shows his power of appreciating
his poetic qualities, his mastery of technique,
and the music of Virgilian verse. Virgil, however, is often
involved in the same fate as his predecessors, and is quoted[3]
in illustration of a particular word or grammatical construction. Even in these as well as in other passages, the
author of the *Noctes Atticae* is instructive as showing the
trend of Virgilian criticism from Virgil's day onwards. We
are treated[4] to a comparison of him with the Greek poets
from whom he had borrowed. Though he suffers at times
when set side by side with Homer, in other cases the
comparison is to his advantage, while Gellius himself can
admire at least his power of selection and adaptation, and
his tact in not attempting to reproduce the untranslatable.
He makes[5] one acute criticism in comparing a line of Virgil's
with its prototype in Homer. He praises the simplicity and
sincerity of the Greek poet, while he finds in Virgil's line a
suggestion of the artificiality of the Neoterics. In many of
his references to him there is clear evidence of the influence
of the labours of such commentators as Julius Hyginus,
Annaeus Cornutus, and Valerius Probus, and echoes of
their criticisms[6] of the poet's faults in style, or his failure
in historical or antiquarian knowledge. It is manifest from
the *Noctes Atticae* that textual criticism of the poet had begun
early, and was being continued with appeals to copies[7]
descending from his own time, and even emended by his
own hand. At times Gellius, either in his own words,
or in the words of some admirer, defends[8] him against

---

[1] V. 12. 13.

[2] III. 2. 14, VII. 20. 4, X. 11. 6 *et seq.*, XX. 1. 54, where he is styled
" elegantissimus poeta " (an encomium already passed on Catullus).

[3] IV. 1. 15, 16. 7, 17. 5, VII. 12. 6, VII. 17, VIII. 5, IX. 12. 17, XIII.
20. 3 *et seq.* (where Gellius is borrowing from Valerius Probus), XV. 13. 10.

[4] IX. 9. 3 *et seq.*, *ib.* 12 *et seq.*, XII. 1. 20, XVII. 10 ; *vide supra*, p. 305.

[5] XIII. 26. 3 ; probably the influence of Parthenius on Virgil, referred
to in the same chapter, may have suggested the criticism to Gellius.

[6] *Vide supra*, p. 305.

[7] I. 21. 2, II. 3. 5, IX. 14. 7, XIII. 20. 4.

[8] I. 21. 4 *et seq.*, II. 16 (S. Apollinaris v Caesellius Vindex), V. 8, VI. 6,
IX. 10. 5.

hostile criticism, though on other occasions he is content[1] to acquiesce in a disparaging verdict on the great Augustan. On these occasions he was evidently distrustful of his own judgment in face of the prestige of such critics. However, if nothing else, his vehement indignation[2] at the aspersions cast by Seneca on Virgil gives us a fair measure of his admiration for the poet.

In all this archaistic movement Fronto was a figure of supreme importance, and must have exercised considerable

Fronto's theory of Style

influence[3] on many of his contemporaries. The chapters[4] of Gellius in which he appears, show what deference was paid to his opinions, especially when a question of ancient literature was involved. His Imperial pupil, Marcus Aurelius, speaks[5] of him as one to whom he is likely to be indebted for all the literature he shall ever know. He had pronounced antiquarian[6] tastes, and his theory of style led him inevitably back to a study of the oldest authors. In defending the expression " cum multis mortalibus " in Quadrigarius, he confesses[7] indeed that his love and veneration for that author and for ancient literature in general, may blind his judgment. He was opposed[8] to the coinage of new words, but he rejoices[9] especially that Marcus Aurelius seeks out the best words, and does not snatch at those that first present themselves. He was insistent[10] on the study of synonyms, and holds[11] up for Marcus' imitation those old authors, few in number, who do not shirk the hazard and the toil of hunting out their words. In such writers are to be found those "in-

---

[1] IX. 9. 12 *et seq.*, X. 16, XVII. 10.

[2] XII. 2. 10 *et seq.*; *vide infra*, p. 352.

[3] Cf. Fronto, II. 36, where he speaks of his " secta "; Sid. Apoll. I. 1. 2, speaks of " Frontoniani "; *vide* Brzoska's article in Pauly-Wissowa Hertz, Renaissance und Rococo, p. 26 *et seq.*

[4] II. 26, XIII. 28, XIX. 8, *ib.* 10, *ib.* 13.

[5] Fronto, I. p. 78.

[6] *Vide* Peter, Die gesch. Lit. Vol. I. p. 125 *et seq.*

[7] N.A. XIII. 28. 3.

[8] Fronto, II. 54, 114; cf. I. 218; Brock, Studies in Fronto and his Age p. 108.

[9] II. 42.

[10] II. 76, 82.

[11] I. 4.

sperata atque inopinata verba "[1] which he misses in Cicero's prose. Words are to be tracked[2] to their lair, and are to be distinguished by their place, rank, weight, age, and dignity. He commends Marcus[3] for his care in digging deep for his word, and in adapting it to his meaning. He tells us[4] that he himself employs vulgar and obsolete diction, and it is evident that the old and rare[5] word had a special attraction for him. Follow, he declares,[6] the words from the old mint, and avoid the debased coinage of the Moderns. Fronto evidently meant to make current coin once more words that would be regarded by the rigorous purists as obsolete, while he aimed at pressing into his service vulgar words that had not yet gained citizenship[7] in the literary language. The old words, however, spotted[8] and discoloured as they were, needed careful handling, and almost something of the art[9] of the engraver, to make them current coin. In the first instance, they required to be freed from their rust, and burnished afresh. A similar care was needed to give a touch of refinement[10] to vulgar words. Fronto demanded[11] also that old words be applied with new meanings, as Sallust[12] employed the word " antiquitas " in the sense of " reverend regard." Moreover, much can be done by careful arrangement[13] to add new vigour to familiar words. This striving after an enriched vocabulary, drawn in part from antique

---

[1] " Quae non nisi cum studio atque cura atque vigilia atque *multa veterum carminum memoria* indagantur," I. 6 ; *vide infra*, p. 350.

[2] II. 52, 54.   [3] I. 6.   [4] II. 80.

[5] Cf. Gellius, XIX. 8. 16 ; Fronto, I. 8, for some of the expressions that he favours.

[6] II. 112 ; cf. *ib.* 76 : " ut . . . prisco verbo adornares, colorem vetusculum appingeres " ; *ib.* 78 : " scis colorem sincerum vetustatis appingere."

[7] Cf. Gellius XIX. 13. 3.   [8] Fronto, II. 114.   [9] Cf. *ib.* I. 10.

[10] *Ib.* II. 76 : " ut de volgaribus elegantia, de contaminatis nova redderes."

[11] *Ib.* II. 114 : " sed usurpatum concinnius aut congruentius, aut accomodatius " ; cf. I. 6 : " ut verbum ex alto eruas et ad significandum adcommodes."

[12] *Vide infra*, p. 350.

[13] *Ib.* II. 52, 78 ; Horace's theories in the A.P. (46 *et seq.*, 70 *et seq.*) will naturally suggest themselves, but we have to remember that archaisms were for Horace only an occasional ornament, and not a vital element in his theory of style.

sources, in part from the copiousness of the popular language and the attempt to infuse new life into familiar or obsolete words, constitute in a large measure the secret of Fronto's " elocutio novella,"[1] He was powerfully attracted by the archaic colouring of the earlier authors, and his theory of style represented a reaction against the restrictions of the purists, and more especially against the artificialities of the Silver Age, as embodied in a writer such as Seneca.[2] He was oblivious of the fact that his own precepts for the revival of archaisms, and for the laborious tracking down of synonyms and of unexpected and unlooked-for words, not to mention his use of other kinds[3] of embellishment, would inevitably lead to a new form[4] of artificiality. Certain[5] of his precepts were, indeed, designed as safeguards against the dangerous tendencies of his theory, while he is careful to differentiate[6] from the other kinds the epideictic branch of oratory, in which all the trappings of rhetoric could be employed without restraint. Whatever we may think of Fronto's theories, his attempt to reanimate Latin prose will at least rank as an interesting experiment.

It is not difficult to divine what his choice of authors[7] would be, dominated as he was by such a view of Style. He **Fronto's choice of authors** contributed much to the formation of the literary taste of his pupil Marcus Aurelius, and evidently suggested the writers[8] he should study. " Many-sided "[9] Ennius naturally figures[10] largely in his pupil's reading, while Fronto's own admiration

---

[1] II. 80.

[2] *Ib.* 102 *et seq. ; vide infra*, p. 331 *et seq.*

[3] *Ib.* II. 76, 86.

[4] Cf. Wight Duff, op. cit., p. 651.

[5] Cf. I. 6 : " multo satius est volgaribus et usitatis quam remotis et requisitis uti, si parum significent."

[6] I. 104–106 ; cf. *ib.* 52 (Ad M. Caes. III. 1).

[7] Here I am dealing only with the poets, which for Fronto's purpose were almost more important than the prose writers.

[8] II. 4 : " aut te Plauto expolires, aut Accio expleres, aut Lucretie delenires, aut Ennio incenderes."

[9] " Multiformis," II. 48.

[10] *Ib.* I. 76, 78, 94, 106, 302 (where M. asks for extracts from Lucretius and Ennius).

for the poet is revealed in several[1] passages. With others he
is praised[2] for his zeal in searching out words. Plautus,
" decus linguae Latinae,"[3] also made a strong appeal to
Fronto, who in his writings supplies abundant evidence[4] of
the influence of Plautine diction upon him. Naevius,
Lucilius, Pacuvius, Accius, the writers of Mimes and
Atellan plays, a strange medley indeed, were all[5] called upon
to complete the literary equipment,[6] and form the style of
Marcus Aurelius. Lucretius, too, was a favourite author[7]
with Fronto, and evidently on his advice formed no inconsiderable part of the literary pabulum of his pupil. Terence
is neglected, probably as not supplying the " insperata atque
inopinata verba." Of the later poets, Fronto shows a certain
affection for Horace, of whom he has several reminiscences.[8]
On one occasion he calls him " memorabilis poeta,"[9] which
was high praise from him, considering the trend of his
tastes. His affection for him may in part have been inspired
by sentimental reasons, as he claimed a connection with him
through his possession of the gardens of Maecenas. The
Augustan poet, however, would not be likely to appeal to
the lofty moralist in Marcus, who begs[10] that his name be
not mentioned again, as for him Horace has ceased to exist.
It is strange how little appreciation Fronto shows for Virgil,
to whom he pays but[11] the perfunctory compliment of styling
him " poeta verborum diligentissimus." Of the poets nearer
to his own age he mentions none by name, while he makes

---

[1] I. 10, 166, II. 20 (where the Telamon is quoted), ib. 74.
[2] I. 4.
[3] Gellius, XIX. 8. 3 ; cf. Fronto, II. 4, ib. 114.
[4] Ib. I. 8, 112, 136 (where a passage from the " Colax " is praised),
II. 6, 102 ; cf. ib. 192 for a reference to the " Miles Gloriosus."
[5] Ib. I. 4, II. 4, II. 48, where Fronto sums up the characteristics of the
early poets ; cf. I. 138, on " Novianae Attellaniolae " ; ib. II. 102, on the
" dictobolaria " of Laberius.
[6] Ib. I. 106, on M.'s course of reading ; ib. 138, on his practice of
making excerpts.
[7] Cf. II. 48, where he is styled " sublimis " ; ib. 70, 74 ; cf. I. 302.
[8] I. 44, II. 8.
[9] I. 122.
[10] Ib. I. 138.
[11] Gellius, II. 26. 11 ; cf. ib. 12, 18.

a bitter attack[1] on the prelude to Lucan's *Pharsalia* for its redundancy of expression. Lucan was a Modern, and a relative of Seneca's, and these considerations, together with his political views, must have combined to arouse Fronto's hostility.

We turn now to consider the fortunes of the quarrel in so far as it affected the writers of prose. I need not dwell upon the fact that Cicero notes[2] the archaic style of certain of the Roman orators. This may have no more significance than the indication of personal choice, or the influence of their age upon them.

The writers of prose

For a more definite phase of the quarrel we have to return to the question of Atticism and Asianism. Broadly speaking,[3] we might style Atticism a movement towards the Ancients, inasmuch as it professed to be based on ancient models, while Asianism[4] was more indicative of the modern tendencies in Rhetoric, and was tainted with many of the defects of the living speech. The Atticist movement was essentially Classical, and set up the " auctoritas veterum " as the supreme standard of correctness. In Greece in particular, as the impurities[5] of the Κοινή became more numerous and more obtrusive, for all who were concerned with the problem of Ἑλληνισμός, a return to the Attic authors was inevitable. In oratory, where the influence of the Atticist movement was most felt, such a return was regarded as imperative, if the Attic spirit of elegance and restraint was to be resuscitated as a counterpoise to the tastelessness and gaudiness of modern rhetoric. There was,

Atticism and Asianism

---

[1] II. 104.

[2] Cf. Br. 68, on Cato's style : " antiquior est hujus sermo et quaedam horridiora verba " ; but Cato's style, as here described, was in harmony with his own age ; *vide supra*, p. 273.

[3] For the contrast between the New and Old, cf. Dionys. De Antiq. Or. c. 1, on the ἡ ἀρχαία καὶ φιλόσοφος ῥητορική, as contrasted with modern fashions ; cf. Norden, A.K. I. pp. 149, 263 *et seq.*, 367 *et seq.* ; Blass, Die griechische Bered. p. 37 ; Jebb, The Attic Orators, II. pp. 438–439.

[4] Some of Asianists, however, professed to follow Attic models ; cf. Cic. Br. 286.

[5] *Vide supra*, p. 215.

of course, always a danger[1] that Atticism would be content to reproduce the archaisms and mannerisms of its chosen models, and, caught in the meshes of pedantry and scholasticism, might degenerate into a lifeless imitation of the Ancients. Minute rules could be given for correctness and beauty of expression, but though it might be possible to revive the language of an Isocrates or a Demosthenes, it was not so easy to revive their thoughts and feelings, and the atmosphere in which they lived.

When we turn to Roman " Atticism," we find that most of the Atticists with whom Cicero came into conflict, had

Were the Roman Atticists archaists ? their minds fixed on Greek[2] models. It has been maintained[3] that in general they were archaists, in the sense that they admired the " Ancients " of their own literature, and wished[4] to reproduce the artlessness and simplicity of early Roman eloquence. There seems to me to be need of a distinction, when we are dealing with the Roman Atticists. If we can trust Cicero's picture of them, some at least of those with whom he was in controversy, were not conspicuous for their admiration of old Roman literature. They had not studied[5] Cato as Cicero had. The *Life of Scaurus*[6] was not read by any of Cicero's contemporaries. Curio's speech for Servius Fulvius, which was considered of supreme excellence in Cicero's boyhood, was now almost wholly neglected,[7] while Fimbria's speeches suffered[8] a similar fate. Brutus is ignorant[9] of Catulus' book on his consulship, while he calls on Cicero[10] to explain certain speeches of the olden days. Gaius Gracchus was practically the only early orator studied[11]

---

[1] Cf. Lucian, Ῥητόρων Διδάσκαλος, 16–17; Schmid, Der Atticismus, I. p. 215 *et seq.*, II. pp. 7, 310–311; Stemplinger, op. cit., p. 123, on Atticism as a μίμησις τῶν ἀρχαίων.

[2] Such as Lysias, Thucydides, and Xenophon.

[3] Cf. Norden, A.K. I. p. 259, who believes that the aim of the " Brutus " was to counter the Atticists' excessive admiration for old Roman oratory.

[4] Cf. Plessis and Poirot, Calvus, p. 95 : " cette école prétendait se rapprocher le plus de la primitive éloquence romaine, qui dédaignait les artifices le style."

[5] Br. 65–68.
[6] *Ib.* 112.
[7] *Ib.* 122.
[8] *Ib.* 129.
[9] *Ib.* 133.
[10] *Ib.* 300.
[11] *Ib.* 125.

by Brutus, who gives Cicero the credit[1] for having awakened his interest in the Ancients. If, as Poirot says, the Roman Atticists as a body harked back to the primitive eloquence of their own countrymen, it is difficult to see why Cicero would have urged[2] them to take as their model the elder Cato, the " Roman Lysias," as he calls him, though in irony. It is not easy to imagine that the refined and urbane Atticists, models of elegance, such as were Calvus and his associates,[3] would evince any enthusiasm for the crude, unpolished, though vigorous prose of Cato. The " Atticists " (or at any rate the adherents of the Plain style) of a later period were enthusiastic admirers of Cato, and it is evident[4] that he, along with the orators of the Scipionic circle and the Gracchi, constituted for them the ideal of eloquence. However, the band of Atticists headed by Calvus, with whom Cicero was more immediately in conflict, were pre-occupied[5] especially with the study of Greek models.

Still there are indications that a section of the Atticists, even in Cicero's day, set up the early Latin orators as a **The position of certain Atticists** standard of perfection. Cicero refers[6] to them when defending the introduction of rhythm into oratorical prose. He himself professes[7] the highest veneration for the achievements of the Ancients, who, however, could not in the nature of things have attained to the perfection reached in his own age. Tacitus, indeed, states that Caelius, Calvus, and even Cicero himself, found[8] something to imitate in the old orators. He tells us[9]

[1] *Ib.* 123.

[2] Br. 68.

[3] We should remember, too, in this connection the attitude of the " poetae novi " towards the early Roman poets.

[4] Cf. Q. XII. 10. 39 : " non Scipio, Laelius, Cato in eloquendo velut *Attici Romanorum* fuerunt ? " *vide infra*, p. 327.

[5] Poirot, op. cit., p. 99, thus exaggerates when he says : " on pourrait aussi chercher dans les Gracques les précurseurs de l' Atticisme," i.e., the Atticism of Cicero's day.

[6] Or. 168 : " non erat hoc (i.e., prose rhythm) apud antiquos " ; the objection is brought by an opponent of Cicero ; cf. 169 : " nominibus veterum gloriantur " ; *vide supra*, p. 248.

[7] *Ib.* : " antiquitas quae quidem apud me ipsum valet plurimum."

[8] Dial. 18 ; Aper deplores the fact of such imitation.

[9] *Ib.* 22.

further that part of the issue between Cicero and his opponents was that they admired the Ancients, while he preferred the oratory of his own day. We must, however, allow for a certain exaggeration on the part of Aper in his attempt to parallel his own championship of the Moderns with that of Cicero. In any case, Tacitus' statement is too vague to enable us to determine which opponents of Cicero he had in mind, or to what period belonged the Ancients which they admired. It is not unlikely that Cicero, in speaking of those who under the aegis of the Ancients objected to rhythmical prose, may have been referring to an orator such as Asinius Pollio. We have already suggested[1] that he was possibly one of those who took Thucydides as model, and whose style in consequence was archaic in character ; but Pollio may have also been preoccupied with the old Roman orators, and may have endeavoured to reproduce something of their simplicity and naturalness. Aper finds[2] his style, not only in his tragedies, but even in his speeches, reminiscent of Accius and Pacuvius. What, however, is more relevant to our present point, is Seneca's criticism[3] of him as rugged, jerky, and unrhythmical, qualities that might easily attach to an ardent admirer of primitive Roman oratory.

It seems to me evident that the Atticists of Cicero's day cannot be classed indiscriminately as admirers of the Ancients, though at a later period the older orators were certainly in favour with the advocates[4] of the Plain style. The younger Pliny tells us[5] of a friend who discussed ideals in oratory with him, and who in his own speeches aimed at brevity and plainness, quoting in his support Lysias amongst the Greeks, Cato and the Gracchi[6] amongst the Romans.

---

[1] *Vide supra*, p. 259.

[2] Dial. 21 ; we must here again make allowance for a certain exaggeration on Aper's part ; *vide supra*, p. 258.

[3] Ep. 100. 7–8 ; it is interesting to note the strong contrast that Seneca points between the styles of Pollio and Cicero.

[4] It is, however, not always certain that we can apply the terms " Atticist " to all of these.

[5] Ep. I. 20. 1 *et seq.*, 19 *et seq.;* the letter is important for the contrast of the Plain and the Grand styles, as well as the excesses of these.

[6] It is interesting, however, to note that Leo, Gesch. der röm. Lit.

This champion of the Plain style might well be numbered among those Roman Atticists who took the early orators amongst their own countrymen as their models.

Quintilian raises some interesting questions in this connection. He speaks[1] of certain orators who affected a plain,

Some problems in Quintilian commonplace, effortless style, and who eschewed the ornament of the epigram on the ground that it was not employed by the Ancients.[2] Domitius Afer, possibly with the desire of imparting an archaic character to his style, used to transpose words[3] at the cadence of his sentences for the purpose of making his rhythms harsh. There were some[4] who would exclude every attempt at artistic form in prose, and who contended that language, as it chances to present itself in its uncouth state, is the more natural and the more virile. They looked[5] for a form of eloquence which resembled the speech of everyday life. They, too, were of opinion[6] that the delivery that was unstudied and the outcome of spontaneous impulse, was the only one worthy of a manly orator. In the eyes of such critics, the oldest orators, unadorned and unpolished as they were, spoke[7] most in accordance with the dictates of nature. Whether these " Naturalists " and archaists are also to be accounted Atticists it is difficult to decide, unless we are prepared to give the title to every advocate of a plain style. It is probable, indeed, that some of them were Stoics, as, in harmony with Stoic theory,[8] they question the utility[9] of employing metaphor and periphrasis, when each thing has been assigned a name of its own. There are, however, indications that some at least of those who

---

pp.308–309, finds Asianist features in C. Gracchus, who is described by Cicero (Br. 126) : " grandis est verbis . . . genere toto gravis."

[1] VIII. 5. 32.

[2] Ib. 33, where it is probable that they appealed to the example of Cato and the Gracchi ; cf. II. 5. 21, XII. 10. 10, ib. 45 ; vide supra, p. 131.

[3] IX. 4. 31 ; cf. XI. 3. 10 ; however, vide supra, p. 134.

[4] IX. 4. 3 ; vide Scott-James, The Making of Literature, p. 78.

[5] XII. 10. 40, 42.

[6] XI. 3. 10.

[7] X. 1. 43.

[8] Cic. Ad Fam. IX. 22. 1.

[9] Q. XII. 10. 41.

would exclude the epigram and other forms of embellishment from oratory, and who favoured the imitation of the Ancients, posed as Atticists.[1] It was probably with the idea of deriding their claim that Quintilian with a touch of irony described[2] as the Attic orators of Rome, Scipio, Laelius, and Cato, who would certainly be numbered amongst their models.

Apparently then, Atticism had many facets, and while at times it fixed its attention on the Classical authors of Greece, again it drew its inspiration from the old Roman orators. Asianism on the other hand might be identified with the new style, and in a measure be considered a reflex of living speech with all its imperfections. This is evident from the many occasions on which the new style and the old are set in opposition.[3] I have already referred to a passage in the *Brutus*[4] in which Cicero points a strong contrast between the excessively archaic style of Thucydides, which one section of the Atticists followed, and the new brand of unfermented speech which was equally unsuitable for imitation. He had, in the context[5] that immediately preceded, dealt with Hegesias, a typical Asianist, and evidently had him in mind in his contemptuous reference to the modern style.

We find the contrast further emphasised in an interesting chapter of Suetonius,[6] who tells us that Augustus used to treat with equal contempt the " antiquarii " and " cacozeli." By the first he meant archaists such as Tiberius, who loved to hunt for obsolete and pedantic expressions. In the " cacozeli "[7] he stigmatised such disciples of the modern school as Antony and Maecenas. We have already seen[8] that Antony's

The old style and the new

" Antiquarii " and " cacozeli "

---

[1] Q. X. 2. 17 : " qui carent cultu atque sententiis, Attici scilicet."
[2] XII. 10. 39.
[3] *Vide supra*, p. 322.
[4] 287–288 ; *vide supra*, p. 236.
[5] Br. 286.   [6] Aug. 86.
[7] For Diomede's definition of " cacozelia " as applicable to Asianist oratory, *vide supra*, p. 214.
[8] *Vide supra*, p. 227 ; cf. Virg. Cat. V, where the line " ite hinc inanis, cymbalon juventutis," is referred to Antony by De Witt, op. cit., p. 34 ; cf. Suet. De Rhet. 4–5, for Antony's teachers,

luxurious and theatrical character found its most adequate expression in the gaudy rhetoric of the Asianists. Augustus used to ridicule[1] the " unguent-dripping curls " of Maecenas' style. Messalla could evidently find nothing better to typify the stylistic defects of the moderns than what he describes[2] as the " curling-tongs " of Maecenas and the " jingles " of Gallio.[3] Even the younger Seneca, who in literature at least might be expected to champion his own age, found the style of Maecenas[4] extravagant and effeminate, while as a moralist he saw in it an illustration of the dictum " qualis vita talis oratio." Maecenas used to affect unnatural transpositions of the word-order that, according to Quintilian,[5] were designed to create the impression of riotous freedom. Such transpositions were characteristic also of the Asianist orators.[6]

In the strictures passed by Augustus we find revealed two opposing tendencies, the one looking back to the Ancients, the other following the lead of the **Two opposing** modern fashions in rhetoric, especially as **tendencies** they hailed from Asia, or held sway in the schools of Declamation. In the light of this there is a special significance in the passage in which he sets on one side the ideals of archaists such as Annius Cimber[7] and Veranius Flaccus, and on the other the empty volubility of the Asianist orators, regarding both as equally worthy of reprobation. He himself endeavoured to steer a middle course,

---

[1] Cf. Macrob. Sat. II. 4. 12, for Augustus' parody of Maecenas' style ; Suet. Life of Virgil, 44, where Agrippa calls Maecenas a "novae cacozeliae repertor."

[2] Tac. Dial. 26 ; *vide infra*, p. 343.

[3] A friend of Ovid, and prominent in the schools of Declamation ; cf. Sen. Suas. III. 6–7 ; Controv. III. pr. 2, VII. pr. 6, X. pr. 8, 13 ; his " jingles " evidently came from his excessive use of the Gorgianic figures.

[4] Ep. 19. 9, 114. 4 *et seq.*, *ib.* 7 : " istis orationis portentosissimae deliciis" ; cf. Ep. 101. 11, 120. 19 ; we get side-lights on Maecenas' character in Hor. Ep. I. 1. 94 *et seq. ;* Tac. Ann. I. 54. 3 ; Vell. II. 88 : " otiis ac mollitiis paene ultra feminam fluens " ; Juv. I. 66, XII. 39 ; cf. Lunderstedt, De C. Maecenatis Fragmentis, p. 18 *et seq.*

[5] IX. 4. 28.

[6] Who employed them for the sake of rhythmical effect.

[7] *Vide supra*, p. 274.

and cultivated a restrained[1] and elegant style that avoided both obsolete diction, and the overstudied symmetry and riot of epigram so dear to many of his contemporaries.

We find the contrast between the new and the old styles appearing in a somewhat different form, when we turn to the schools of Declamation, especially as they are described for us by Seneca. There were to be seen in their most luxurious growth many of the worst defects of the modern style. Degeneracy was, indeed, inevitable when declamation became an art[2] in itself, and was practised for its own sake. In the old days it was merely a preparatory exercise to fit a man for his career as a practical orator. Under modern conditions, men on entering the schools soon seemed to be transformed into other beings. The training they underwent there unfitted[3] them as a rule for the task of practical pleading. The subjects proposed for treatment were divorced[4] from reality, and gave free play to the workings of diseased imaginations. The more bizarre their ideas, and the more extravagant the language in which they were clothed, the more certain were the declaimers to win applause. The excesses witnessed in the schools were a novel[5] phenomenon in Rome in the early Empire, and were an abomination in the eyes of men such as Seneca and Quintilian, who found in them a reason for the decline of eloquence. The former has analysed[6] for us with great acumen the corrupt tendencies of the new[7]

Old and new in the Elder Seneca

[1] On Augustus and Atticism, *vide supra*, p. 262.

[2] On the difference between the old and new forms of declamation, *vide supra*, p. 153.

[3] Cf. Controv. VII. pr. 6–7, on Albucius ; Suet. De Rhet. 6 ; on the other hand Cassius Severus explains the causes of his own failure in the schools, Controv. III. pr. 8 *et seq. ;* cf. Bornecque, Sénèque, Le Rhéteur, Introd. p. 19 *et seq.*

[4] Controv. III. pr. 12–13, IX. pr. 4–5 ; Petron. Satyr. 1 ; Tac. Dial. 31 ; *vide infra*, p. 338.

[5] Cf. Controv. II. 4 (12). 11–12, on "novitius morbus" ; Seneca often speaks of "novi declamatores," Controv. I. 1. 14, I. 4. 7, I. 8. 11, 16, II. 5 (13). 13, VII. 1 (16). 20 : "magna novorum rhetorum manus" ; cf. Tac. Dial. 14, where "novi rhetores" and "veteres oratores" are contrasted. [6] *Vide supra*, p. 211 *et seq.*

[7] Controv. I. pr. 12 : "hoc enim genus materiae quo nos exercemur adeo novum est, ut nomen quoque ejus novum sit" ; cf. Prof. Summers' paper "The Declamations under the Empire."

rhetoric. I have already suggested that many of the defects so conspicuous in the schools were identical with those of the Asiatic orators. Some of the declaimers were, indeed, professed Asianists.[1] Not all of them,[2] however, were so, and there must have been some real worth[3] in many of the professors of declamation, and some intrinsic merit in an exercise in which men such as Pollio, Messalla, Agrippa, and Augustus were interested.

For our present purpose Seneca's work is of especial value as marking a period of transition[4] which he himself had lived through. We are still occasionally reminded that the genius of the Republican period has not wholly departed, though it flits but seldom round the schools like a wraith of its former self. There are still some who practise declamation,[5] but refuse to succumb to the prevailing fashion of declaiming in public. There are some who follow a plain style,[6] and others who even in their declamations were inspired by the ideals of a former generation.[7] Labienus was an interesting figure, inasmuch as he typified in himself the period of transition,[8] and exhibited the colouring of the old style and the vigour of the new. Seneca himself was convinced[9] that the highest achievements that Roman eloquence could pit against the claims of arrogant Greece, were to be found in Cicero and his contemporaries. Holding such a conviction,

A period of transition

---

[1] Controv. I. 2. 23, IX. 1 (23). 12, ib. 6 (29). 16, X. 5 (34). 21 : " Craton . . . professus Asianus qui bellum cum omnibus Atticis gerebat."

[2] *Vide supra*, p. 213.

[3] Cf. Controv. IX. 2. 23, X. pr. 13 ; Edward, The Suasoriae of Seneca, Introd. pp. 16–20.

[4] Cf. Controv. I. pr. 6 (Seneca to his sons) : " quod non contenti exemplis saeculi vestri, prioris quoque vultis cognoscere."

[5] Controv. IV. pr. 2 (Pollio), X. pr. 4 (Labienus).

[6] Controv. II. 1 (9). 24, on " aridi declamatores," ib. 5 (13). 15, VII. 5 (20). 15, IX. 3 (26). 11 ; the " Apollodorei " (Controv. X. pr. 15) would probably be also numbered amongst these.

[7] Controv. IX. 2. 25 : " Rufus Vibius erat qui antiquo genere diceret " ; it is not always easy to understand what Seneca means by " antiquus," though here it seems to mean nothing more than the style of Republican eloquence as opposed to the " Modern " style ; cf. ib. X. pr. 2.

[8] *Ib.* 5 : " cultus inter nostrum ac prius saeculum medius."

[9] Controv. I. pr. 6, 11 ; cf. X. pr. 6, Suas. VI.

he was naturally dissatisfied with the general trend of the new age. Genius had declined,[1] the youth of the day had become torpid and enervated by unmanly pursuits, and oratory, which lay so near to his heart, had suffered an eclipse. Men were restlessly hunting[2] for novelties, and neglecting[3] the great examples of other days. Yet Seneca recognised that the new rhetoric, with all its defects, possessed a certain vital energy, and he could at times pay a generous tribute[4] to some of the declaimers.

The new rhetoric was vehemently denounced by Petronius[5] for its floridness, extravagance, and unreality. In **Petronius and the new rhetoric** his reactions against it, he had particularly in mind the contrast between the old Attic restraint, as well as the natural beauty characteristic both of the prose and poetry of Classical Greece, and the windy and immoderate eloquence, which was a modern[6] importation from Asia into Athens. This, as if it were some pestilential planet, had infected the minds of ambitious youths. We have already suggested[7] that in Petronius' view the worst excesses of the schools could be traced to Asianist sources.

In the same period we can trace other phases of the struggle of the Ancients and Moderns. The younger Seneca **The Younger Seneca** was definitely enrolled[8] under the standard of the latter. He had no interest in antiquarian questions,[9] and no appreciation[10] for the literature of early Rome. He shows distinct hostility to[11]

[1] *Vide supra*, p. 269 ; cf. Controv. X. pr. 7.   [2] *Ib.* IV. pr. 1.

[3] *Ib.* III. pr. 15 ; they would even prefer Cestius to Cicero, if they did not fear the consequences ; cf. IV. pr. 9.

[4] *Ib.* 7 *et seq.*, on Haterius ; however, Haterius seems to have retained something of the spirit of a former generation.

[5] Satyr. 1 *et seq.*, 6.

[6] " Nuper ventosa istaec et enormis loquacitas Athenas ex Asia commigravit " ; it is difficult to determine exactly what Petronius had in mind by his " nuper."   [7] *Vide supra*, p. 213.

[8] *Vide supra*, p. 290.   [9] Ep. 88. 6 ; *vide supra*, p. 280.

[10] Ep. 58. 5, 59. 6 : " neminem mihi videtur ex antiquis legisse, apud quos nondum captabatur plausibilis oratio " ; *ib.* 108. 33 ; Gellius, XII. 2. 3 *et seq.*, *ib.* 12 : " qui honorem coloremque veteris orationis Soterici lectis compararit."

[11] Ep. 114. 13 ; cf. 108. 35.

writers with archaistic tendencies, though he deplores the fact[1] that certain words have become obsolete through over-fastidiousness. It is doubtful, however, if we should take seriously the statement of Suetonius[2] that he prevented Nero from reading the ancient orators in order that he might the longer retain the Emperor's admiration for himself. Seneca might perhaps be induced to display some interest in the literature of the Ciceronian period, but in his own prose he showed himself a perfect representative of modern tendencies.

Quintilian, who wished to correct the corrupt and faulty style of his own age, and to recall it to finer ideals,[3] enters an energetic protest[4] against what he conceives to be the degenerate features of Senecan prose. There were many characteristics in Seneca calculated to arouse his hostility. The philosopher had his own theory of style,[5] though his practice was often at variance with his theory. There are few writers in Roman literature who show more evidence of studied artistry ; yet, taking the lofty standpoint of the moralist,[6] he declares that he aims at spontaneous and unstudied utterance, and that he seeks to improve his fellow men, not to tickle their ears. In one passage[7] he condemns a swift rush of copious language as unsuited to the philosopher, whose aim is to instruct, while again he has a word of praise[8] for the impetuous march of the style of Fabianus whom he so much admired. The true Seneca is revealed at other times, when he declares[9] that he does not wish the great problems of philosophy to be treated in a dry and jejune

Quintilian's protest

---

[1] Ep. 58. 1 ; cf. Bourgery, Sénèque Prosateur, p. 214 *et seq.*

[2] Nero, 52.

[3] Ciceronian prose would be for Quintilian the great ideal.

[4] X. 1. 125 *et seq.*

[5] Cf. Merchant, Seneca and his theory of style, p. 44 *et seq. ;* Gercke, Seneca-Studien, p. 133 *et seq.*

[6] Cf. Ep. 24. 15, 40. 4, 52. 14, 75, 1, 4, 100. 2, *ib.* 4 : " oratio sollicita philosophum non decet" ; *ib.* 10 : " vis illum adsidere pusillae rei, verbis ? " 115. 1, *ib.* 2 : " non est ornamentum virile concinnitas " ; *vide supra*, p. 139.

[7] Ep. 40. 3.

[8] Ep. 100. 2-4.

[9] Ep. 75. 3.

manner, or confesses[1] that, once his mind is exalted by the grandeur of its meditations, he forgets his ideals in his effort to reach a more sublime style, and speaks in accents not his own. In truth, this rich and versatile genius was a law unto himself. In harmony with his own practice, he held that Style was not bound by fixed rules,[2] but changed to suit the needs of ever-varying custom.[3] Such a principle would be abhorrent to a Classicist such as Quintilian, who showed such loyalty to Ciceronian standards. Seneca, as might be expected from his father's son, retained a certain reverence for Cicero,[4] but for all that, he abandoned the periodic style favoured by him. He evidently found the march of his prose too slow,[5] and its composition lacking in variety, while he probably missed in him the pointed expressions so dear to his own generation. Seneca, in fact, embodied in his own prose many of the faults of his contemporaries. His love of short phrases, antitheses, balanced clauses, word-play, alliteration, and the jingle of similar syllables, shows how closely allied he was to the traditions of the schools. Ovid, a typical product of the rhetorical school, is for him " poetarum ingeniosissimus,"[6] Seneca was fond, too, of a pregnant brevity[7] dear to certain declaimers. It was, however, above all in his love of paradox and epigram,[8] that he showed himself a characteristic Modern. Many of these faults had been noted by the elder

[1] De Tranq. An. I. 13–14 : " oblitus tum legis pressiorisque judicii, sublimis feror, et ore jam non meo."

[2] Ep. 114. 13 : " oratio certam regulam non habet " ; Marchesi, Seneca, p. 200, rather grandiosely describes Seneca's style as " sciolto da ogni archittetura convenzionale."

[3] Cf. the standpoint of Aper, Dial. 18.

[4] Ep. 40. 11, 118. 1, Dial. II. 17. 3.

[5] " Gradarius fuit " ; cf. Ep. 100. 7–8, 114. 16.

[6] N. Q. III. 27.

[7] Ep. 59. 5 : " loqueris quantum vis et plus significas quam loqueris " ; cf. Sen. Controv. III. pr. 7 : " plus sensuum quam verborum habentes."

[8] In this connection, his appreciation of Publilius Syrus is significant, Ep. 8. 8 et seq., Ep. 108. 9 ; cf. Controv. VII. 3 (18). 8 ; cf. Summers, Seneca, Select Letters, p.15 et seq., The Silver Age of Latin Literature, p. 6 et seq., for a history of the pointed style ; Canter, Rhetorical Elements in the Tragedies of Seneca, p. 85 et seq., for his use of " sententiae " in his dramas ; vide infra, p. 460.

Seneca, especially as making a strong appeal to young men, but neither his father's warnings, nor his own advance in years had rendered them less attractive to his son. As was said of Ovid,[1] " non ignoravit vitia sua, sed amavit." For the strange thing is that Seneca has analysed[2] most of these faults with remarkable acumen, and ruthlessly condemned defects that were prominent in himself. He was thus blind to many of his shortcomings, or loved them too well to abandon them. His genius was suited to his age,[3] and, rendered famous as he was by his studies,[4] his versatility, and a certain moral earnestness, which even Quintilian allows him, it is little wonder that he enjoyed immense popularity with his contemporaries. With its abandonment of the periodic style, its taste for paradox and epigram, its unnatural modes of expression,[5] its allusiveness, its tendency towards obscurity, and at times towards a studied asymmetry, the Senecan " manner " made a powerful appeal[6] to the young men of the day, even though its very defects[7] constituted the basis of the appeal. Seneca's mind was of the histrionic order,[8] and this no less than his sensational end helped to increase his popularity. For a period at least the seductive charm of his prose proved irresistible, though there were murmurs of disapproval,[9] and though his appeal soon began to lose some of its power.[10] Words used by

[1] Controv. II. 2 (10), 12 ; cf. Q. X. 1. 130 (on Seneca) : " si non omnia sua amasset."

[2] Ep. 114. 1, ib. 10, 14 et seq.

[3] Tac. Ann. XIII. 3 : " ut fuit illi viro ingenium amoenum et temporis ejus auribus adcommodatum."

[4] Ib. XII. 8, XIII. 2.

[5] On the syntax of Seneca, cf. Bourgery, op. cit., p. 306 et seq.

[6] Suet. Caligula, 53 : " Senecam tum maxime placentem" ; Suet., Life of Persius, notes that Persius was not impressed by him ; " sero cognovit et Senecam, sed non ut caperetur ejus ingenio " ; cf. Tac. Ann. XIII. 42, on his vogue : " studiis inertibus et juvenum imperitiae suetum " ; Q. X. 1. 126 ; Gellius, XII. 2. 12–14.

[7] Rocheblave, De M. Fabio Quintiliano, p. 60, will have it that Seneca " ex cognitis atque tritis vitiis novas sermonis gratias, novum nitorem, novas quoque praestigias . . . eduxit et exprompsit."

[8] Cf. Tac. Ann. XIII. 11, XV. 61–63.

[9] Caligula (Suet. loc. cit.) used to refer to him as " sand without lime."

[10] Cf. Q. X. 1. 126 : " tum autem solus hic fere in manibus adolescentium fuit " ; Quintilian seems to suggest that his popularity had already waned

Boileau to describe writers who have a passing vogue, might well be applied to Seneca : " de faux brillants, la nouveauté de style, un tour de l'esprit, qui était à la mode, peuvent les avoir fait valoir." Still his influence was such that it proved a serious obstacle to Quintilian, when he set out to win back the youth of his generation to severer standards in prose. Seneca might be read with impunity by men whose taste was moulded on rigorous lines, but in Quintilian's eyes his style was especially dangerous for the young, abounding as it did in attractive vices. Most of the young men who took him as a model, would regard themselves as perfect Senecans, if they succeeded in reproducing his peculiar mannerisms. It would be well, says Quintilian,[1] if Seneca had used his own talent, while allowing himself to be guided by another's judgment. Apart from his defects of style already referred to, there were elements in his language that were bound to rouse the opposition of Quintilian ; for he allowed himself a generous licence[2] in the use of poetical diction, new coinages, and words drawn from the vulgar tongue. Quintilian reserves him for the last place in his gallery of authors, and devotes more than ordinary space to a discussion of his character as a writer, because[3] he regarded him as embodying more completely than any other the corrupt tendencies of the modern style. Besides his express criticism of him, he probably had him in mind also in the strictures contained in many other passages of the " Institutio Oratoria."

We may at this point take the opportunity of dealing

Quintilian's general position

with Quintilian's general attitude in the quarrel, as far as prose was concerned. As a rule it was a sane one.[4] He had no sympathy with the extremists on either side. One party declared[5]

when he was writing, though his elaborate criticism of Seneca's style would seem to indicate that it still possessed some power of attraction.

[1] X. 1. 130.

[2] Cf. Bourgery, op. cit., p. 208 *et seq.*, 223 *et seq.*, 249 *et seq.*, for examples.

[3] There seems no reason to search for any more subtle reason for Quintilian's opposition, or to represent it, as Rocheblave does, as due to the hostility of the Rhetorician to the Philosopher ; *vide* op. cit., pp. 10, 18, 31.

[4] *Vide supra*, p. 307.

[5] Cf. X. 1. 43, 2. 17 ; *vide supra*, p. 326 *et seq.*, on Quintilian and the " Naturalists."

that the Ancients alone were worthy of being read, that in them alone natural eloquence was to be found. When such enthusiasts, says Quintilian, clothe their own thoughts in uncouth and inharmonious language, they regard themselves as the equals of the Ancients. He sounds a note of warning[1] to teachers who may be too ardent admirers of the Ancients, not to allow their pupils' minds to become desiccated by concentrating on the study of Cato, the Gracchi, and other authors of the same period. The eloquence of the ancient orators was excellent in its day, but it is out of keeping with modern requirements, which demand a more finished style. Still, Quintilian realises that it would be well if the pupils of his time could absorb some of the robust and virile qualities that were native to the early orators of Rome.

The opposing party finds pleasure[2] only in the voluptuous ornaments of present-day oratory, where everything is contrived to charm the ears of the unlettered multitude. Quintilian advises his pupils[3] to be on their guard against the allurements of modern style, with its cloying sweetness and its prettinesses, which so strongly appeal to juvenile minds. He has analysed for us with great thoroughness the defects of his contemporaries, especially in oratory,[4] with which he was primarily concerned. He touches[5] on their passion for epigram,[6] which some make the one object of their quest, and regard as the sole merit in every kind of literary achievement. Search for a piquant conclusion for every sentence resulted

His criticism
of the
" Moderns "

---

[1] II. 5. 21 ; cf. XII. 10. 45 ; some would even go beyond Cato and the Gracchi ; *vide supra*, p. 326.

[2] X. 1. 43.

[3] II. 5. 22 : " ne recentis hujus lasciviae flosculis capti voluptate prava deleniantur " ; the passage is in Quintilian's happiest vein as a critic ; he probably had Seneca here in mind.

[4] However, in dealing with the " Modern " style, Quintilian seems to make little distinction between oratorical style proper, and the prose style made fashionable by a writer such as Seneca.

[5] II. 11. 3, 12. 7.

[6] I. 8. 9 ; cf. II. 11. 7, V. 13. 31, 42, VII. 1. 44, VIII. 4. 29, *ib.* 5. 1 *et seq.*, for a discussion of " sententia " as an ornament of style ; *ib.* 25, 31 : " nec multas plerique sententias dicunt, sed omnia tamquam sententias."

in a succession of tiny epigrams, often irrelevant as well as indicative of a depraved taste. In another striking passage,[1] Quintilian censures the general wantonness of style[2] displayed by contemporary orators, their licence of diction, their unrestrained bombast, and their empty commonplaces. These[3] consider that a corrupt style is the one calculated to win applause, and they use all the garish colours of a decadent eloquence that will quickly lose its false brilliance when tested by a critical taste. They remind us of those who believe that art,[4] to produce its effect, must be blatant and obtrusive. Again, we are told that in the hands of certain Moderns eloquence had become effeminate,[5] and had lost every virile quality in its eagerness for smoothness and polish. Some aim at a highly brilliant and ornamental style,[6] which has the effect of emasculating the subject treated. Such people, not being content with direct expression, pile up words in meaningless circumlocutions, while they are often too precious in their choice of diction. Not being ready to adopt the words naturally suggested by their subject, they search out for uncommon ones, and consider it a sign of genius,[7] if it takes a genius to fathom their meaning. Cicero, who regarded it as a serious fault[8] to employ words at variance with the prevailing idiom, is looked upon[9] by the modern rhetoricians as defective both in polish and in learning.

I need not dwell upon other faults such as the use of effeminate rhythms, and the childish quest of synonyms, which, to judge by Quintilian's strictures, were conspicuous in his day. He believed that eloquence had been debauched

[1] XII. 10. 73 *et seq.*

[2] " Lascivia " or " licentia " was a favourite word with Q. to express this idea ; cf. II. 5. 22, VIII. 5. 34, XI. 1. 56.

[3] The whole passage (XII. 10. 73 *et seq.*) might be compared with Seneca's descriptions of the declaimers ; cf. II. 3. 9, 5. 10 *et seq.*, for other characterisations of modern defects ; *vide supra*, p. 111.

[4] *Ib.* IV. 2. 127.

[5] V. 12. 18, *ib.* 20, on " eloquentia libidinosa."

[6] VIII. pr. 20 *et seq.*, 2. 17 *et seq.*, 3. 56 *et seq.*

[7] VIII. 2. 21 ; cf. *ib.* 19, on the obscurity that comes from brevity ; cf. II. 5. 11.

[8] De Or. I. 12.   [9] Q. VIII. pr. 26.

in particular by the excesses of the declaimers.[1]   Like others
of their critics, he emphasised[2] the unreality of the subjects
which they declaimed, while he regarded as a crowning
absurdity the chanting intonation[3] which was a feature both
of the courts and of the schools.

Though Quintilian reflects adversely[4] on the debasement
of contemporary taste, he can still see much virtue in his
own age, and can pay a passing compliment[5]
even to the declaimers.   Being a critic of
wide sympathies, he recognises[6] that the
Moderns have many merits, while he is even enthusiastic[7]
about Trachalus and Julius Secundus amongst the orators
he himself had known, and is generous in his praise of " the
accomplished advocates of the present day who are rivals of
the Ancients."   If the Ancients surpassed the Moderns,[8]
they surpassed them in their ideals rather than in natural
talent.   Adopting a standpoint which would not be approved
by passionate admirers of the Ancients, he contends that
some concession[9] must be made to the changed conditions
of the time, and to an audience that demands something
more refined and moving than in by-gone days.   He
declares[10] that there is no sin in a successful epigram, and
protests merely against the extravagant use of such an
ornament of style.   Men of mature judgment may read with
profit both ancient and modern authors.   However, when
Quintilian sets out to strike a balance, he tells us[11] that, if
a choice were forced upon him, he would prefer the oratory
of the Ancients with its uncouth diction to the licentious
eloquence of the Moderns, that, with its effeminate rhythms,

*Quintilian's
concessions*

---

[1] II. 10. 3, VII. 1. 41–44, VIII. 3. 76, XI. 1. 55–56.
[2] II. 11. 3, VIII. 3. 23 ; *vide supra*, p. 329.
[3] *Vide supra*, p. 213.
[4] II. 5. 10, XII. 10. 74.
[5] II. 11. 2, 7.
[6] II. 5. 23 *et seq.*
[7] X. 1. 119 *et seq.*, XII. 5. 5.
[8] II. 5. 24.
[9] IV. 2. 122, XII. 10. 45–47 ; cf. Aper, Dial. c. 19.
[10] VIII. 5. 32 ; cf. XII. 10. 48.
[11] VIII. 5. 34, IX. 4. 142, where I adopt a portion of Butler's admirable
translation.

" trips along in wanton measures that suggest the accompaniment of castanets."[1]

The efforts of Quintilian to bring about a reform, and a return to Ciceronian standards, evidently met with some

Pliny's tastes success. The younger Pliny, his pupil,[2] confesses that he tried to rival Cicero,[3] and is not satisfied with the eloquence of his own day. On the general question as to the merits of the Ancients and Moderns, we have seen[4] that he is disposed to adopt a compromise, declaring that while he admires the Ancients, he will not disparage the talents of his own age. Still, it is evident[5] that he was not blind to the glaring faults of contemporary oratory. In his own speeches he professes to write[6] so as to satisfy every palate, but he too often succumbed to the prevailing taste for gaudy and ornate oratory.[7] His natural inclination,[8] in fact, seems to have been towards the Grand style, but evidently some of his more ambitious efforts struck critics of discernment[9] as turgid and exaggerated. His *Panegyricus*,[10] with its riot of epigram, antithesis, alliteration, word-play, and its general lack of restraint, makes it clear that at times he forgot the teaching of Quintilian for that of the Asianist Nicetes Sacerdos.[11]

We now turn to consider the *Dialogus* of Tacitus, a work which we have taken somewhat out of its order, but which

---

[1] Cf. Pliny, Ep. II. 14. 13 (in reference however to delivery) : " sola cymbala et tympana illis canticis desunt."

[2] *Ib.* 9, VI. 6. 3.

[3] Ep. I. 5. 12; cf. I. 2. 4, I. 20. 4, where Pliny, however, shows what an eclectic he can be ; IV. 8. 4.

[4] *Vide supra*, p. 308.

[5] Ep. II. 14 ; the whole letter is interesting as showing traces of Quintilian's influence ; cf. V. 20. 4, on the Asiatic volubility of Fonteius Magnus, " unus ex Bithynis, plurimis verbis, paucissimis rebus."

[6] II. 5. 7 *et seq.*

[7] *Ib.* 5 : " sunt enim quaedam adulescentium auribus danda."

[8] Cf. Ep. III. 13. 3, III. 18. 10, IX. 26. 2.

[9] *Ib.* 5 ; cf. II. 5. 6, VII. 12. 4.

[10] Pliny's pride in this achievement is seen in Ep. III. 13, *ib.* 18 ; cf. Norden, A.K. I. p. 320.

[11] Ep. VI. 6. 3 ; Tac. Dial. 15 ; cf. Philost V. S. 511, on his style : ἡ δὲ ἰδέα τῶν λόγων τοῦ μὲν ἀρχαίου καὶ πολιτικοῦ ἀποβέβηκεν, ὑπόβακχος καὶ διθυραμβώδης.

is of cardinal importance in the quarrel of the Ancients

The " Dia-
logus " of
Tacitus

and Moderns. Aper is an unflinching champion of the Moderns, and, in his advocacy
of them, defends[1] those tendencies of
contemporary oratory which, at least in the hands of the
unskilful, constituted its worse defects. He possessed a good
deal of native genius[2] that was vigorous and unspoilt, and
showed a predilection for extempore speaking.[3] Like
Crassus in the De Oratore,[4] he despised literary culture,
though he was not devoid of it. He was essentially utilitarian in his views,[5] showing no enthusiasm for the poet's
calling, and measuring the glory of eloquence by the
emoluments and prestige that it brings. He shows himself
a clever dialectician, and opens his case[6] by making a point
which smacks somewhat of the sophistry of the schools.
When his opponents speak of " Ancients," whom do they
mean ? The term " Ancient " is a relative term, and the
orators of the Ciceronian age, on whom they chiefly rely in
their disparagement of present-day eloquence, might according to Aper's reasoning be accounted Moderns as much
as Ancients. When he proceeds to his defence proper, we
find that he is an evolutionist, if one may use the term, or
at any rate that he believed in a certain relativity in literature.[7] His defence of modern oratory[8] is based on its

[1] Gudeman, Introd., p. 69, rightly styles him an Asianist ; he appeals to
his sharp criticism of the stricter Atticists, but Aper criticised Cicero as well ;
we must remember that Aper's " Asianism " was derived chiefly from the
rhetorical schools.

[2] Dial. c. 2.

[3] Ib. c. 6 ; vide supra, p. 210.

[4] De Or. II. 4 ; it would be interesting to trace the many features, apart
from the question of style, for which Tacitus is indebted to Cicero in the
Dialogus, but that lies outside the scope of the present work.

[5] C. 3–10.

[6] C. 16 ; cf. Messalla's answer, c. 25 : " mihi autem de vocabulo pugna
non est " ; vide supra, p. 282.

[7] Cf. Brunetière, L'Évolution des Genres, pp. 137–138, for some interesting remarks that have a bearing here.

[8] Supposed by the champions of the Ancients to begin with Cassius
Severus, Dial. c. 19, ib. 26 ; cf. Sen. Controv. III. pr. 1 et seq., ib. VII. 3. 8,
where he is styled " summus Publilii (Syri) amator " ; Q. X. 1. 116–117 ;
Tac. Ann. I. 72, IV. 21.

relation to the prevailing taste of society.[1] For one thing, the present-day advocate may not be as discursive as the ancient orator, for the law-courts now insist upon a more matter-of-fact directness. Moreover, the style of oratory like the style of acting has changed. To attempt to restore the old style of eloquence would be comparable[2] to the revival on the stage of the gestures of Roscius, or Ambivius Turpio. In Aper's eyes the present age is the more enlightened, and concessions have to be made to the taste of the Moderns, who look for more piquancy, polish, and ornateness in oratory, and will not endure the jejune and uncouth style of ancient times. The forensic pleader under modern conditions[3] must captivate the judge by a rapid marshalling of his proofs, by the pointed brilliance of his language, by the beauty of his descriptions,[4] and the general sparkle of his style. It is evident[5] that Aper was strongly under the influence of the rhetorical schools, and was dominated by their ideals. To him appealed especially the brilliant epigram, and the striking phrase,[6] apt for quotation, and beloved above all by the young men of the day. A successful epigram,[7] or a more than usually poetic passage, was repeated from mouth to mouth, and even written to friends in the provinces. In an age[8] when the boundary line between prose and poetry had become less well defined, it is little wonder that Aper demands from the orator something of the charm of the poet. Quintilian, too, as we have seen, was willing to make some concessions to his age, but

[1] Dial. c. 18 : " mutari cum temporibus formas quoque et genera dicendi " ; ib. c. 19 : " novis et exquisitis eloquentiae itineribus opus est " ; vide supra, p. 195.

[2] Ib. c. 20.

[3] Cf. c. 38–39, where the drawbacks of the modern system are set forth.

[4] Such descriptions were popular in the schools of declamation ; cf. Sen. Suas. I.

[5] Cf. Dial. c. 14, on his attachment to " scholasticae controversiae " and " novi rhetores " ; ib. c. 42.

[6] Ib. 20 : " aliquid inlustre et dignum memoria."

[7] Vide supra, p. 212.

[8] The invasion of prose by poetry was especially marked in the rhetorical schools ; on the question of the poetic element in Silver Age prose, cf. Wight Duff, op. cit., pp. 19–20 ; Bourgery, op. cit., p. 223 et seq. ; vide infra, p. 444.

he would strenuously oppose certain tendencies in modern oratory to which Aper was ready to give his sanction.

Aper insists[1] that, even though the form of oratory has changed, the change does not necessarily connote inferiority, as some of his opponents would imply. In fact, his defence of contemporary oratory is based on the idea of Progress. The Past was a crude age and could be satisfied with crude achievements, but the Moderns demand an advance on antiquated methods. As I have already remarked,[2] it is not always easy to apply the conceptions of Progress and Decadence to literature, and the champions of the Ancients might well protest that every novelty did not signify an advance, and that the progress so vigorously defended by Aper was in reality a decline.[3]

Aper's conception of progress

Aper, as we have said, shows himself a skilful advocate who can colour facts to his own advantage. While he insists[4] that it is the tendency of envious human nature to praise what is old, and show contempt for present-day achievement, he proceeds himself to disparage unduly the accomplishments of the Ancients. He could show some reason for his characterisation[5] of the earlier orators of Rome, such as Cato, Carbo, and Galba, but he does less than justice to the orators who flourished towards the close of the Republican period. His opponents maintained that there was nothing in modern times comparable to their eloquence. Aper admits[6] that progress has been made since the days of the primitive orators, but he belittles[7] the achievements of so distinguished an orator as Calvus, and emphasises, perhaps unduly, the archaic[8] character of Caelius and Pollio.

A skilful advocate

---

[1] Dial. c. 18 : " nec statim deterius esse quod diversum est."

[2] *Vide supra*, pp. 266, 269.

[3] A decline had taken place both in Greece and Rome ; cf. Messalla, c. 15.

[4] *Ib.* c. 18.

[5] Even Messalla will grant him this point ; cf. c. 25 : " cum fatear quaedam eloquentiae eorum ut nascenti adhuc nec satis adultae defuisse."

[6] C. 18.   [7] C. 21.

[8] Cf. c. 18, where Calvus, Caelius, and even Cicero are said to have imitated the " Primitives."

With characteristic exaggeration he says that the latter seems to have been a fellow-student of Menenius Agrippa and Appius Claudius. To his modern mind, orators such as Caelius and Calvus seemed cold, tedious, and prosaic. He is inclined to be generous in his tribute[1] to Cicero, though he is dissatisfied with his earlier[2] speeches, even from the point of view of their emotional power, in which Cicero specifically excelled. He has a thrust at the " Atticists "[3] of his day with their uncouth and dreary style. He especially shows his skill as a pleader, when he attributes[4] to his opponents in the debate some of the qualities of style for which he himself had a predilection.

Messalla is as uncompromising a champion[5] of the Ancients as Aper is of the Moderns. He was a Classicist, and

Messalla champions the Ancients insisted[6] on the importance of studying the great models of the Past. There was evidently at that time a party who vigorously supported the cause of the Ancients. Aper represents them as preferring Lucilius to Horace, Lucretius to Virgil, and as extolling the style of Sisenna and Varro above that of Aufidius Bassus[7] and Servilius Nonianus.[8] Messalla, however, as represented by Tacitus, was not an indiscriminate admirer of the Ancients. He is willing[9] to admit that the primitive Roman orators had their shortcomings, though if he had to make the choice, he would prefer the unpolished but virile eloquence of the early orators to the false and meretricious style of the Moderns, which for him is symbolised[10] by the extravagances of a Maecenas or a Gallio.

[1] C. 22 ; cf., however, c. 18, 20.

[2] " Nam priores ejus orationes non carent vitiis antiquitatis " ; *vide supra*, p. 238.

[3] Cf. c. 23, on their boasted " sanitas," the great watch-word of the Atticists of Cicero's day ; Tac's characterisation of them owes much to Cicero ; cf. Br. 284–285, De opt. gen. 8.

[4] C. 23.

[5] Cf. c. 15 : " non desinis, Messalla, vetera tantum et antiqua mirari " ; Maternus and Secundus were also on the side of the Ancients ; cf. c. 16, 27.

[6] C. 30.

[7] cf. Q. X. 1. 103 ; Pliny, Ep. III. 5. 6.

[8] Q. X. 1. 102.

[9] Dial. c. 25–26.

[10] *Vide supra*, p. 328.

For Messalla the supreme glory of Roman oratory is centred in Cicero and his contemporaries in the late Republican period. Aper could find no Modern to match their excellence.

Messalla soon passes[1] from the question of the relative merits of the Ancients and Moderns to the more fundamental problem of the causes of the decline in present-day oratory. With all the zeal of a " laudator temporis acti," he proceeds to anatomise the elements of decadence that appear in the life around him. For he regards his age as truly degenerate,[2] inasmuch as all the arts[3] no less than eloquence have suffered an eclipse. The depravity of society, the decay of old institutions, the neglect of the discipline which was the foundation of Roman greatness in the Past, have all contributed to bring about this deterioration. Youths have now to struggle against the disadvantages of a defective home training, lack of parental control, and, worse still, impaired ideals on the part of those who should guide their early education. Reared in a vicious atmosphere, they learn to have more interest in actors, gladiators, and the racecourse, than in the studies that would equip them for their profession. The evil is only accentuated in the rhetorical schools,[4] where neither professor nor pupil has a serious outlook, and where students labour at subjects that have no relation to reality. In chapters[5] that are strongly suggestive of the influence of Cicero, Messalla regrets the absence in his contemporaries of the wide culture essential to the great orator. He traverses much the same ground as Cicero does in the *De Oratore*, when he contrasts the narrow routine training given by the professional rhetoricians with the encyclopaedic culture that enables an orator to rise to something higher than mere technical skill in his profession, or the immediate exigencies of a particular case. No great

De causis corruptae eloquentiae

---

[1] C. 28 *et seq.*
[2] *Vide supra*, p. 269.
[3] Cf. Petron. Satyr. 88 ; *vide supra*, p. 195 *et seq.*
[4] C. 35 ; cf. c. 30 : " expetuntur quos rhetoras vocant " ; *ib.* c. 31.
[5] C. 30–32 ; we have a specific reference to Cicero's own laborious training as described in the " Brutus " ; cf. c. 32, where Or. 12 is referred to.

oratory could flourish under modern conditions, and the progress so much vaunted by Aper is in reality a retrogression. Messalla analyses the most glaring defects of contemporary eloquence, and is especially[1] severe on the meretricious adornment, the trivial thoughts, the disorderly structure, and the generally frivolous and affected style of the Moderns. Orators, moreover, are effeminate and theatrical in their delivery, and adopt the chanting intonation beloved by many Asianists.[2] In the hands of such people the Arts have become interchanged[3] as it were, the orator now being said to speak prettily, and the actor to dance eloquently. Messalla, with that reverence for correctness which was traditional in his family, complains,[4] too, that the outrageous faults incidental to the language of everyday life have begun to invade oratorical prose.

In the eyes of Maternus[5] also, modern oratory has deteriorated, but he finds the origin of the decline in changed political[6] conditions. There is no longer the **A note of compromise** same scope for eloquence as in Republican days, when disorder was rife, when political passions ran high, and the clash of parties offered a fairer field to a brilliant speaker. However, the peace and stability of the Imperial regime provide some compensation. He is probably voicing Tacitus' own views, when he ends[7] on a note of compromise, and urges each one to enjoy the blessings of his own time without disparaging other ages.

We will close our review of the quarrel by returning to Gellius and Fronto, and considering briefly their predilec- **Gellius' choice of prose authors** tions in the matter of prose authors. I have already dealt with the ideals of their age, as they are reflected in the pages of these two writers. It is not difficult to divine what authors would

---

[1] C. 26. [2] *Vide supra*, p. 213.

[3] Cf. some interesting remarks of Babbit, The New Laocoon, pp. 182–185, on the confusion of the Arts as a sign of a decadent Romanticism.

[4] C. 32.

[5] C. 36–41 ; Gudeman, however (Introd. p. 65), argues with a good deal of plausibility that this portion of the Dialogus should be assigned to Julius Secundus.

[6] *Vide supra*, p. 198 *et seq.* ; cf. Pliny, Ep. VIII. 14. 8.

[7] C. 41.

most powerfully attract them, dominated as they were by such ideals. Cato was a favourite with Gellius as well as with the other archaists of his time. He seems[1] to have appealed to him as the embodiment of the stern and unbending type of old Roman. There is scarcely a work of his that is not quoted in the *Noctes Atticae*. His authority[2] is invoked on points of antiquarian and historical interest, but more especially on matters of linguistic usage. Gellius evidently felt a certain pride in refuting[3] the opinion of Verrius Flaccus on the meaning of the phrase " servus recepticius " as employed by Cato. He seems to have made a special study of his speeches, attracted in part by the archaic[4] charm and vigour[5] of their language, in part by their value as exhibiting[6] the first, though faint, beginnings of Roman eloquence. He defends[7] his speech " For the Rhodians " against certain criticisms of Cicero's freedman, Tiro, which he characterises as vapid and inane. In his enthusiasm, he credits[8] Cato with having employed all the resources of rhetoric in the speech. In another passage[9] he sets him above Gaius Gracchus in the vital force and wealth of his language, and declares that he was striving towards something higher than the eloquence of his own age. This is high praise, especially when we consider that the style of Gracchus[10] made a strong appeal to Gellius, though he sometimes was forced to temper his enthusiasm for it when confronted with the penetrating criticism of his master Castricius. The latter, while admiring the rhythmical[11] character of the opening of Gracchus' speech against

[1] Cf. N.A. I. 15. 8 *et seq.*, XI. 2. 2, XIII. 23, XIV. 2. 21.

[2] Cf. II. 28. 5, where he is styled " vir in cognoscendis rebus multi studii."

[3] XVII. 6.

[4] XVI. 1. 3.

[5] XI. 18. 18.

[6] XIII. 24. 12 : " quae quoniam sunt eloquentiae Latinae tunc primum exorientis lumina quaedam sublustria," etc.

[7] VII. 3. 8 *et seq.*, though he calls Tiro " haudquaquam rerum litterarumque veterum indoctus."

[8] *Ib.* 52.

[9] X. 3. 15.

[10] Cf. X. 3. 1.

[11] Gellius, XI. 13. 2, says of it " collocata verba sunt accuratius modulaiusque quam veterum oratorum consuetudo fert."

Popilius, blames[1] him for his redundancy, and for seeking rhythmical effects for their own sake.

As regards history, Gellius evidently had studied all the old writers such as Fabius Pictor, Cincius Alimentus, Sempronius Asellio, Aelius Tubero, and **Amongst the** Tuditanus, while he was especially attracted **historians** towards Claudius Quadrigarius, whose archaic style, with its simple and unadorned charm, he marks[2] out for special commendation. Sallust, archaist himself and imitator[3] of Cato, would naturally have a great fascination for Gellius and his friends. He is praised for the propriety[4] of his language, and for the elegance[5] and conciseness of his style. Gellius may at times criticise his defects, but he is generally prepared to defend[6] him against the adverse criticisms of others. He betrays his standpoint, when he styles[7] the *Jugurtha* " summae fidei et reverendae vetustatis liber," but it is clear, too, that for the members of Gellius' circle, who were so interested in the usage of words, Sallust possessed a powerful attraction as a " novator verborum."[8] How great was his vogue is well illustrated by the story[9] of the meeting of Gellius and Sulpicius among the booksellers' stalls with a man who proclaimed himself the unrivalled interpreter of the historian's language.

Gellius was acquainted with the labours[10] of the learned[11]

---

[1] The standpoint of Castricius (*ib.* 10) is interesting ; if there is any defect in Gracchus, " id omne et auctoritas ejus exhausit, et vetustas consumpsit."

[2] IX. 13. 4 ; Quadrigarius was evidently a writer in vogue among the archaists ; cf. IX. 1, XIII. 28, where his phrase " cum multis mortalibus " is defended by Fronto ; XV. 1. 4 : " optimi et sincerissimi scriptoris."

[3] N.A. II. 17. 7, X. 21. 2 ; *vide supra*, p. 273.

[4] X. 20. 10.

[5] IV. 15. 1 ; cf. III. 1. 6, where he is called " subtilissimus brevitatis artifex."

[6] X. 26 (against the criticism of Pollio) ; cf. XX. 6. 14.

[7] IX. 14. 26.

[8] I. 15. 18, IV. 15. 1.

[9] XVIII. 4.

[10] Cf. I. 18. 1 (where Stilo is corrected by Varro), II. 21. 8, III. 3. 1 (on his " Indices Plautini "), XII. 4. 5, XVI. 8. 2 (on his " De Proloquiis ") ; *vide supra*, p. 295.

[11] X. 21. 2 : " qui doctissimus eorum temporum fuit."

grammarian Aelius Stilo, and appeals to him occasionally on questions of linguistic usage. Of those who worked in the same field subsequently to Aelius, he is particularly fond of quoting Nigidius Figulus and Varro, with whose learning[1] he was deeply impressed. He quotes almost all of Varro's works, and draws much on his studies on the Latin language, and his many researches[2] into ancient literature.

It is to Gellius' credit that with all his bias towards antiquarianism, and his preoccupation with the early Roman prose-writers and orators, he could still regard the glory of Cicero's eloquence as supreme.[3] He is indignant[4] that some critics can discover in Gaius Gracchus a chaster, more vigorous, and more copious orator than Cicero. Cato in his eyes ranks above Gracchus, and Cato was but groping towards ideals which Cicero brought to perfection. Again, he takes[5] up the defence of the latter against the younger Seneca. We get a measure of his admiration for the great orator from a passage[6] in which he puts on the same footing the perverted beings who express false and blasphemous opinions about the gods, and critics such as Asinius Gallus and Licinius Largius, who dared to censure certain expressions of Cicero as lacking in propriety and correctness.

Gellius' admiration for Cicero

We shall find that Fronto's predilections in prose ran on much the same lines as those of Gellius, though in his case they were in the main subservient to his theory of style, and to the rhetorical training of his imperial pupil. Cato was a favourite[7] author with him, and is the object of extravagant encom-

Fronto's predilections

---

[1] Cf. IV. 16. 1, where he styles them " viros Romani generis doctissimos " ; XIX. 14. 1 *et seq.*

[2] III. 3. 2 (for his work on Plautus), III. 11 (on the relative ages of Homer and Hesiod), XVII. 21. 43 *et seq.* (on the chronology of the early Roman poets).

[3] I. 5. 2, XVII. 13. 2 ; cf. the interesting passage, XII. 13. 17, where Cicero is mentioned among " veteres nostri."

[4] X. 3. 1.

[5] *Vide supra*, p. 274 ; cf. XIII. 24. 7 *et seq.*, where he is defended against a charge of redundancy ; *ib.* 20. 22.

[6] XVII. 1. 1.

[7] Fronto (Haines), I. 152 ; cf. Gellius, XIX. 10. 10.

iums.[1]   He is praised[2] for his careful choice of words, while
the chaste and unsullied sweetness of his style is compared[3]
with that of Herodotus.   His powers of invective[4] were
remarkable, while it is said[5] that he and Gracchus alone
amongst the early orators could sound the trumpet note.
Fronto highly prized the Figures as an element in style,
and he pays[6] Cato the great compliment of saying that
none of the Greek or Roman orators he has read, has used
the figure of paraleipsis more elegantly than he did in his
speech " De sumptu suo."   In view of Fronto's devotion
to him, it is not surprising that he was the author most
favoured by Marcus Aurelius, who styles[7] him his patron.
Of the other early orators Fronto seems[8] to have taken a
certain interest in Servius Galba, whose emotional power is
so highly praised by Cicero, but, next after Cato, Gaius
Gracchus most strongly attracted[9] him by the impetuous
force of his eloquence.   Marcus, on his teacher's advice,
had made[10] a special study of the speeches of that orator.

In history, Quadrigarius was one of the authors preferred
by Fronto, who praises his graceful style, and confesses[11]

**His choice in
history**

his love and veneration for him.   But as
one might expect, Cato's imitator, Sallust,[12]
was the historical writer for whom he felt
the greatest admiration.[13]   He, too, is praised[4] for being

[1] II. 150 : " orator idem et imperator summus " ; *ib.* 200 : " fandi
agendique laudibus longe praestantibus omnium Cato Porcius " ; cf.
Schwierczina, Frontoniana, p. 9 *et seq.*

[2] I. 4.

[3] I. 42 ; cf. II. 48, where he is said to write " verbis multijugis."

[4] I. 128.

[5] I. 106 ; cf. II. 74.

[6] II. 44.

[7] I. 152 : " nam uni M. Porcio me dedicavi atque despondi atque dele-
gavi " ; cf. I. 116, 144, 172, 178, 180.

[8] I. 172.

[9] Cf. II. 48, *ib.* 64, where he is coupled with Cato and Cicero as one of
the great exemplars of Roman eloquence.

[10] I. 78, 300.

[11] Gellius, XIII. 28. 3 : " nisi si me scriptoris istius omnisque antiquae
orationis amor atque veneratio caeco esse judicio facit."

[12] I. 4.

[13] I. 152.   [14] II. 74.

able to sound the trumpet note, while he is commended[1] for the symmetry of his style, and his skill in the use of Figures. Sallust's archaism would naturally have attracted Fronto, but the secret of his appeal in part lay in the historian's power[2] of infusing a new meaning into old words, and thus helping to revivify the language. He was evidently one of the models specially recommended to Marcus, whose labours[3] on the historian had their reactions on his own style.

In Fronto's case also it is remarkable that, steeped as he was in the spirit of the earliest Roman writers, he could still retain a profound veneration for Cicero.

His tributes to Cicero He is almost unmeasured in his praise of him " the head and fount of Roman eloquence."[4] He touches on his wealth of language, the rhythmical character of his prose, and his power[5] of using Figures with emotional effect. He glories[6] in a successful imitation of the Ciceronian manner. He has a special word of praise for Cicero's speech on the Manilian law, which he recommends[7] for Marcus' perusal, and says that Pompey earned the title " Magnus " not so much by his own achievements, as by the orator's encomium of him. But, in Cicero, who was opulent in all other kinds of words, Fronto misses[8] the " insperata atque inopinata verba," which were the great object of his own quest. These are words with an element of freshness and surprise, that when discovered seem inevitable[9] in their appropriateness. Fronto may have

---

[1] II. 48, where he is said to write " structe " ; *ib.* 158 *et seq.*

[2] Cf. II. 114, on Sallust's use of " antiquitas," though Fronto does not seem to approve wholly of it.

[3] I. 12–16, where Marcus successfully reproduces the sententious style of Sallust ; cf. *ib.* 300, II. 70.

[4] I. 4 ; cf. II. 142 : " summum supremumque os Romanae linguae " ; II. 48, 64, 100 : " ut aestimes nostrum mediocre ingenium quantum ab illo eximiae eloquentiae viro abludat."

[5] II. 158–160, where Cicero's effective use of ' epanaphora ' is brought to Marcus' notice.

[6] II. 42 : " ecquid agnoscis formam sententiae tullianae " ; cf. I. 68.

[7] II. 30, II. 100 (on the Pro Sulla) ; cf. II. 4, I. 300, for Marcus' interest in Cicero. [8] I. 6.

[9] He seems in a measure to anticipate Flaubert's theory of the " mot juste."

been attracted to Cicero's *Letters* in particular, because[1] they contained more of such words than his other compositions. He was evidently[2] impressed, too, by their easy style, and, in urging Marcus to leave none of the *Letters* unread, his final verdict is that there is nothing more perfect than they.

In striking contrast with such admiration is Fronto's marked hostility to the " Modern " Seneca, though he once **Fronto's** ironically[3] describes himself as " Senecae **hostility to** Annaei sectator." For one thing, Seneca **Seneca** was a free-lance[4] in literary theory, but Fronto's antipathy to him was in great measure the dislike of the archaist for one who made no secret of his contempt[5] for the Ancients. Moreover, Fronto, who had other ideals, and who hoped to infuse new life into Latin prose by a study of the early Roman authors, would have little taste for the artificialities,[6] affectations, and depravities of the Modern school, of which Seneca was the most prominent representative. Moderns such as he, were too often endeavouring to make current a debased coinage. In an important letter[7] to Marcus Aurelius, which unfortunately is in places obscure owing to the condition of the text, Fronto vigorously attacks the hybrid style of eloquence that seeks to engraft together the pine-nuts of Cato and the soft and feverish plums of Seneca. In comparison with it, Sergius[8] may not be so rhythmical, nor sprightly,[9] nor so full of jingling

---

[1] Cf. II. 158 (in reference to the Letters) : " si quid eleganti aut verbo notabili dictum videretur, excerpsi " ; cf. I. 100.

[2] I. 122.

[3] II. p. 6, though some have without reason gone so far as to consider Fronto to belong to Seneca's school ; cf. Brock, op. cit., p. 130.

[4] *Vide supra*, p. 333.

[5] Cf. Gellius, XII. 2. 1 : " nihilque ex veterum scriptis habens neque gratiae neque dignitatis " ; *ib.* 12.

[6] Though Fronto, as we have seen, had his own form of artificiality ; *vide supra*, p. 320.

[7] II. 100 *et seq. ;* it seems clear from the letter that Marcus was in danger of neglecting his master's teaching, of succumbing to the charm of Seneca, and being infected by the debased modern fashions.

[8] Possibly Sergius Flavus ; cf. Q. VIII. 3. 33.

[9] Reading " cordaces " ; " cordatas " has been suggested, but does not suit the context so well.

sounds, but in Fronto's eyes he was evidently more sober and impressive. Seneca is rich[1] in thoughts, but he jogs along in commonplace[2] fashion, and nowhere rises to sublimity. He has about him something of the dexterity of the juggler, whose feats would be loudly applauded by schoolboys.[3] It was a serious fault in the Senecan school to repeat interminably the same thought clothed in a different dress. It may be urged[4] that certain of Seneca's sayings are clever, and not without dignity, but, as Fronto says with biting sarcasm, even little silver coins are sometimes found in sewers. He tells Marcus to cling to the old mintage, as scurf and itch are contracted by thumbing books such as those of Seneca. There are many elements in the Senecan style that might pass as genuine, until they are critically examined. He apparently has Seneca in mind in his reference[5] to the use of mean and slovenly words, and language arranged rhythmically and with an effeminate flow, while he probably glances at him also in his enumeration[6] of the faults which he supposes Marcus to disclaim.

Gellius too, as we have seen,[7] was another who showed a strong antipathy to Seneca. His judgment[8] on the philosopher was probably indebted to Quintilian for some of its features, and to Fronto for others. Some critics, he declares, consider

Gellius' verdict on Seneca

---

[1] II. 102 : " neque ignoro copiosum sententiis et redundantem hominem esse " ; cf. Q. X. 1. 128–129 : " ingenium facile et copiosum " ; Gercke, Seneca-Studien, p. 142 et seq., has an interesting analysis of the similarities and differences in the verdicts of Q., Gellius, and Fronto, on Seneca ; cf. Faider, Études sur Sénèque, p. 64 et seq.

[2] Cf. Gellius, XII. 2. 1 : " quod oratio ejus vulgaris videatur et protrita " ; " eruditio autem vernacula et plebeia."

[3] Possibly an echo of Q. X. 1. 126, where Seneca's attraction for young men is deplored ; cf. Gellius, XII. 2. 12 et seq.

[4] II. 104 ; cf. Gellius, XII. 2. 13.

[5] II. 106 ; the sentence, however, is from the margin of the Codex.

[6] II. 110 : " dicas fortasse quid in orationibus meis novicium, quid crispulum, quid luscum, quid purpurisso litum aut tumidum aut pollutum " ? cf. I. 120, where Fronto has also in view some of the depravities of the Modern style.

[7] Vide supra, pp. 318, 348.

[8] Cf. XII. 2. 1, where he professes to be merely repeating the criticisms of others.

that there is a lack[1] of elegance in Seneca's diction, but they do not deny his learning, and pay a tribute to his zeal in the castigation of vice. When Gellius thus refers to Seneca's erudition and to his high moral purpose, but speaks[2] of him as a dangerous literary model for Roman youths, he is following closely in the wake of Quintilian. Other critics, he tells us, condemn the banality and triteness of Seneca's language, the foolish and empty vigour of his thoughts, while they regard him as displaying a learning that is without distinction, and a cleverness that is witty in its way, but superficial. In all this we can discern some reflection at least of Fronto's indictment of the philosopher. Finally, when Gellius states that Seneca was censured because he derived no charm nor dignity from the writings of the Ancients, we feel that he is echoing the sentiment not merely of Fronto, but of others of his contemporaries who were inspired by similar ideals. The whole discussion is of interest, as revealing to us how prominently Seneca figured in the quarrel of the Ancients versus the Moderns.

[1] Gercke, op. cit., p. 142, suggests that Q. may have thus criticised Seneca in his lost work " De causis corruptae eloquentiae."
[2] XII. 2. 12 *et seq.*

CHAPTER VI.

HORACE AND THE CLASSICAL CREED

HORACE MADE his first essays in criticism soon after he began his career as a poet. He had set himself to revive the Lucilian tradition in Satire, but in a form that would be more palatable to the taste of his own generation. One[1] of the *Satires*, however, that he had published, had been marked by a coarseness and obscenity redolent of the brutal frankness of the Cynic, while in the midst of his moralisings upon life he had directed some rather bitter attacks upon individuals. Others besides the immediate victims felt[2] their position endangered, and challenged the right of the Satirist thus to pillory his neighbour, and set himself up as a " censor morum." In their view the satirist is a being void of humane instincts, who delights to wound[3] by his bitter[4] and malignant wit, who is the slave of laughter, and in his efforts to raise a laugh will not spare even his friends. Moreover, he is a slanderer and takes[5] a pleasure in publishing his attacks broadcast to the city.

Now it is interesting to note that similar charges were

[1] Sat. I. 2.

[2] Sat. I. 3. 19 *et seq.*, I. 4. 24 : " sunt quos genus hoc minime juvat " ; II. 1. 23 : " cum sibi quisque timet " ; II. 3. 321 ; cf. Ep. II. 1. 150–151, on the effect of the bitter invective of the Fescennine verses.

[3] Sat. I. 4. 78 : " laedere (an important word) gaudes " ; cf. *ib.* I. 10. 80, II. 1. 21 : " tristi laedere versu " ; *ib.* 67 ; cf. the use of " nocere," A.P. 284.

[4] In Sat. I. 4. 93, he is styled " lividus et mordax," II. 1. 1, " nimis acer " ; on such qualities in Satire, cf. Ovid, Trist. II. 565 ; Stat. Silvae, I. 3. 103 ; Mart. VII. 72. 13, X. 33. 5.

[5] Sat. I. 4. 36 *et seq.* ; cf. Sat. II. 1. 46, where H. says that whoever attacks him, " insignis tota cantabitur urbe."

brought[1] against Lucilius in his own day. He, too, was
The indict- accused of indulging in bitter[2] and cynical[3]
ment of the wit which sought to wound[4] opponents with
Satirist its barbed arrows, while he was upbraided
also with spreading[5] his calumnies indiscriminately amongst
the public. The parallels[6] in fact between Lucilius and
Horace are quite remarkable. Particularly in the fourth
Satire of his First Book, Horace sums up the general
objections that might be urged against the Satirist. Ultimately, of course, it lay with Horace himself to formulate
the objections, and he would naturally formulate them in
the way that he could most effectively answer.

In reply to the charges made, Horace in the first place
would evidently claim that he was in the line of the tradition
Horace's of the Old Comedy[7] in attacking only those
reply who deserve it, and who are the enemies of
society. If like Lucilius, who was[8] " uni
aequus virtuti atque ejus amicis," he set himself up as a
" censor morum,"[9] it is solely to castigate[10] evil doers, and
perform his duty to society. Those who lead honest lives
need never fear the lash of the Satirist. Horace, moreover,
is careful to distinguish himself from professional[11] informers

---

[1] *Vide supra*, p. 55.

[2] Fr. 1014 (Marx) : " tuis factis saevis et tristibus dictis " ; cf. Horace's
use of " tristis," Sat. I. 10. 11, II. 1. 21.

[3] Frs. 1025, 1095–97 ; cf. Hor. Sat. I. 4. 93, Ep. I. 17. 18 : " mordacem
Cynicum."

[4] Fr. 1035 : " quoniam incilans nos *laedis*."

[5] Frs. 1015–1016 ; cf. 970.

[6] Cf. Marx ad loc. cit. ; Fiske, Lucilius and Horace, though not always
convincing, is valuable as showing the influence of Lucilius on Horace ; cf.
especially his studies of Hor. Sat. I. 4, I. 10, II. 1.

[7] Sat. I. 4. 3 *et seq.*; cf. *ib*. 67 *et seq.*, II. 1. 64, 85 ; cf. Q. X. 1. 65 (on
the Old Comedy) : " in insectandis vitiis praecipua " ; on the social service
rendered by the Old Comedy, cf. Lane Cooper, Aristotelian Theory of
Comedy, p. 86 (quoting Tzetzes) ; Grant, op. cit., pp. 46–47 ; Lejay,
Horace, Satires, Introd. p. 56 ; Kaibel, Comicorum Graecorum Fragmenta,
Vol. I. pp. 14, 18.

[8] Sat. II. 1, 70 ; cf. Luc. frs. 1031–1034.

[9] Cf. Sat. I. 3. 26 ; Luc. frs. 1019–1020.

[10] Cf. Persius, V. 15 : " pallentes radere mores " ; Cic. Ad Fam. XII.
16. 3, for Trebonius' interesting defence of his satiric verses.

[11] Sat. I. 4. 65 *et seq.*, II. 1. 47.

and accusers, and takes special pains to dissociate from his writings the perfidy[1] and malignity of the slanderer and backbiter,[2] who is prepared to wreck the character of an absent friend, or damn it with faint praise. The affectionate regard in which Horace was held by his friends,[3] and the spirit of candid criticism that marked their intercourse, are a sufficient guarantee that the poet had never indulged in such malignity. He declares[4] that he will refrain from aggression in his *Satires*, and will employ them solely as weapons of defence, though this statement seems somewhat disingenuous in view of the indignation of the victims who were castigated in his earliest writings.

The poet has recourse to another line of apology, the object of which is at first sight not obvious. Men, he tells[5] us, who are the slaves of various vices, and who fear to come under the lash of Satire, dread poetry and hate poets. Horace assures them that his humble *Satires* do not[6] lay claim to the title of high poetry. The answer can bring little consolation to his victims, who would not be impressed with any subtle distinctions regarding the medium in which they were ruthlessly held up to ridicule. In this section, in fact, Horace dexterously conceals his real purpose, which was to determine his own place and that of Lucilius in the hierarchy of poetic genres. For his victims much more relevant are his other claims[7] that he writes rarely, and that his works are not meant for the general public, but recited under compulsion[8] to a few chosen friends. However, the sting that was left by offending[9] lines, such as those that cast opprobrium on Rufillus and

The title of poet

---

[1] Cf. his use of " niger," Sat. I. 4. 85, 91, 100, Ep. II. 2. 60.

[2] Sat. I. 3. 21, 4. 81, 10. 79 ; cf. Theophrastus' picture of the κακολόγος (Jebb, p. 110) ; *vide infra*, p. 363.

[3] Sat. I. 3. 69 *et seq.*, I. 4. 80, 135, I. 10. 81 *et seq.*

[4] Sat. II. 1. 39.

[5] Sat. I. 4. 33.

[6] They are not therefore to be rated highly as a literary genre ; *vide infra*, p. 374 *et seq.*

[7] Sat. I. 4. 18, 23, 71 *et seq.*, I. 10. 74 : " contentus paucis lectoribus."

[8] Luc. fr. 1009, seems to suggest a similar compulsion.

[9] Sat. I. 2. 27, 4. 92.

Gargonius, shows that they did not long remain the exclusive possession of a small coterie, but had attained sufficient publicity[1] to wound their victims grievously.

For the moment we are concerning ourselves here with Horace's general defence of his *Satires*, and are not dealing

Horace's censures on Lucilius

with the other problems raised in Satire I. 4. Horace had maintained that in his satirical writings he was, in certain respects, true to the tradition of the Old Comedy and to Lucilius. He had given a measure of praise[2] to the wit of Lucilius, but he had also passed some severe censures on his style. These censures had evidently called forth angry protests from the admirers of Lucilius, and Horace felt called upon to make an extended reply,[3] and to define more closely his attitude to the older poet. In Horace's day and for some time previously, there was a revival[4] of interest in Lucilius, and the poet found ardent champions in Valerius Cato[5] and his followers. It is difficult to say how far the attempt had been made to define the " Lucilianus character "[6] before the publication of Horace's Satire I. 4, but probably Lucilius' admirers had attributed to his work something of the urbane and refined[7] humour, the brilliant and scintillating wit, of the writers of the Old Comedy, as well as their lofty poetic qualities. Horace, therefore, is at pains to deny the attributes of lofty poetry to the genre practised by Lucilius and himself. He paid, as we saw, a tribute to

[1] Cf. Lejay, Sat. I. 4, Introd. pp. 100–101, for some interesting remarks on Horace's method of publication.

[2] Sat. I. 4. 7 ; " facetus, emunctae naris."

[3] In Sat. I. 10.

[4] *Vide supra*, p. 292.

[5] The lines usually prefixed to Hor. Sat. I. 10, if not authentic, at any rate almost certainly enshrine a genuine tradition ; Hendrickson's three articles on " Horace and Valerius Cato " are particularly important on this question ; *vide* Class. Phil. XI (1916). p. 249 *et seq.*, XII (1917). p. 77 *et seq.*, 329 *et seq.* ; cf. Valerii Catonis Carmina, ed. Giles, p. 44.

[6] Varro, R. R. III. 2. 17, uses this expression evidently with reference to the spirit of invective that characterised Lucilius ; for later critics, cf. Apul. Apol. 10 ; Diomede, Keil, I. 485 ;

[7] For this claim they could point to the authority of Cicero ; *vide supra*, p. 55.

Lucilius' wit, but a tribute that must have seemed grudging to the enthusiastic admirers of the older poet, while his strictures on his style evidently evoked from them an indignant protest, and caused them to proclaim anew their admiration of Lucilius' achievements. Now in Satire I. 10, Horace reacts so strongly against the extravagant claims made for the work of Lucilius, as not merely to repeat his former strictures on the poet's style, but to raise the question whether Lucilius' type of wit was in all respects true to the spirit of the Old Comedy, and suited to the Satiric genre.

For the moment we will occupy ourselves with the latter question, leaving aside for the present the question of style. It is important to note that Horace in this discussion is aiming not merely at determining the place of Lucilius in Roman Satire, but is raising a wider issue, the laws that should govern the genre of Satire. Already in Satire I. 4, he had given us some light on the quality of the laughter he would like to see associated with Satire. He would claim for his own work a spirit of playfulness,[1] and of genial humour in his raillery, and would disavow any suggestion of the bitter invective that wounds, or the malignity of the backbiter. He also marks[2] himself off from the buffoon, who indulges in immoderate and unseasonable laughter, and in his bitter sallies will not spare even a friend. In his picture[3] of the " scurra," he brings into prominence a type that had already been studied[4] by the Greeks in their conception of

The true spirit of Satire

---

[1] Sat. I. 1. 24, I. 4. 139, I. 10. 37 ; cf. Persius, I. 116–118, on the quality of Horace's humour : " admissus circum praecordia ludit " ; cf. *ib.* V. 16 : " ingenuo culpam defigere ludo " ; Mart. VII. 12. 9 : " ludimus innocui " ; the whole epigram should be compared ; *vide supra*, p. 53, on Lucilius' use of " ludus " as a term for his Satires ; *vide infra*, p. 373.

[2] Sat. I. 4. 35 (cf. Kiessling-Heinze *ad loc.*), *ib.* 82 *et seq.* ; cf. Luc. fr. 971.

[3] He gives us many glimpses of the " scurra " ; cf. Sat. I. 5. 52, I. 8. 11, II. 1. 21, II. 7. 15, 36, II. 8. 21, 63, Ep. I. 15. 26 *et seq.*, I. 18. 2, 11.

[4] Here I must acknowledge my indebtedness to Hendrickson's articles, Horace, Serm. I. 4, A.J. Phil. XXI. 2, p. 121 *et seq.*, Horace and Lucilius, in " Studies in honour of B. Gildersleeve," p. 151 *et seq.* ; also to Fiske, Grant, and Lejay, op. cit.

the βωμολόχος. The Greeks, as we know, dealt[1] extensively with the subject of the " Ludicrous." When Horace then, in Satire I. 10, endeavours to state more in detail his attitude towards the humour of Lucilius, and to define the quality of the laughter that should inform Satire, he deals with ideas that had long been familiar to the Greek theorists on the subject, but which probably had come to him through the medium of kindred discussions in Latin, especially in the pages of Cicero.

In briefly reviewing the Greek position, we may pass over the pre-Aristotelian[2] period, though from Socrates is

Greek theory preserved a dictum on the sparing use of
of the laughter, while in Plato[3] we find the concep-
"Laughable" tion of the βωμολόχος, the distinction between the good-natured and ill-natured jest, and incidental remarks on the " Ludicrous " as it figures in the writers of Comedy. More important for our purpose is Aristotle's doctrine[4] on the " Laughable." He was interested in defining the qualities of laughter and of the comic spirit, from the different standpoints of ethics or personal conduct, and of the requirements of Drama and of Rhetoric. In the Ethics[5] we have a study of the contrasted types of the βωμολόχος, the εὐτράπελος, the εἴρων and ἀλαζών, each considered with reference to the standard of the Golden Mean, wherein virtue lay. The βωμολόχος[6] or buffoon, is one who indulges in unmeasured[7] laughter, and who, in his efforts to raise a laugh on all occasions, becomes enslaved to laughter. To effect his purpose he will spare neither himself nor others, and is prepared to wound[8] his

[1] Cic. De Or. II. 217, 288 ; Q. VI. 3. 11, 22.
[2] *Vide* Grant, op. cit., p. 13 *et seq.*
[3] Cf. Rep. III. 388 E, on the φιλόγελως; Rep. X. 606 C, Laws, XI. 934 E *et seq.* ; Lane Cooper, op. cit., p. 98 *et seq.* ; cf. Aristoph. Frogs, 358.
[4] Which was evidently discussed at length in portions of the Poetics now lost ; cf. Rhet. I. 11. 29, III. 18. 7.
[5] Nic. Eth. IV. 8. 1128a *et seq.* (cf. E. E. 1234a. 4), *ib.* II. 7. 1108a.
[6] Theophrastus' ' βδελυρός ' bears some resemblance to him without his humour ; cf. Jebb, p. 98.
[7] Cf. Hor. Sat. I. 4. 82 : " solutos qui captat risus hominum."
[8] Cf. μὴ λυπεῖν τὸν σκωπτόμενον, and Horace's use of " laedere."

victims, and utter jests such as a refined person would avoid. In contrast to such a character Aristotle depicts the tact and urbanity that distinguish the man of cultured[1] wit, whose jesting observes due measure, and will leave no bitter memories in the minds of his hearers. Aristotle frequently contrasts[2] the characters of the εἴρων and ἀλαζών, but what is more to our purpose is the contrast he establishes[3] between the wit of the εἴρων, and that of the βωμολόχος. We need not here enter into the complex meaning[4] of the word εἴρων. It will suffice to say that, where wit was concerned, Aristotle considered that irony, with its restraint and refinement, was a much more gentlemanly[5] thing than the vulgar clownishness of the buffoon. He is particularly interesting when he endeavours to define the spirit of laughter that should preside over Comedy. He clearly indicates his preference. Homer, he tells us,[6] pointed out the true way to writers of Comedy, by dramatising the ludicrous instead of composing personal invective. Again, Crates made a distinct step forward when he abandoned the lampooning[7] form, and " universalised[8] his plots and themes." Invective is the proper weapon when one is dealing with great[9] crimes, but Comedy, if true to its spirit, concentrates on the 'ludicrous,' a deformity or ugliness that is neither painful nor destructive. Comedy will above all take as its province the harmless foibles and follies of men. Aristotle pointedly contrasts[10] the method of the Old Comedy with its vulgar personal abuse and obscenity of language (αἰσχρολογία), and the more refined method of

---

[1] On εὐτράπελος, cf. also Rhet. II. 12. 16.

[2] Cf. Ribbeck, Alazon, pp. 4–6.

[3] Rhet. III. 18. 7.

[4] *Vide* Jebb, op. cit., p. 51 *et seq.*; Grant. op. cit., pp. 28–29, 125 *et seq.*

[5] Cf. Eth. Nic. IV. 8. 1128a, on the jests that befit the ἐπιεικὴς καὶ ἐλευθέρος.

[6] Poet. IV. 1448b.

[7] *Ib.* V. 1449b: ἀφέμενος τῆς ἰαμβικῆς ἰδέας; cf. Anon. περὶ κωμ. Kaibel, op. cit., p. 8.

[8] Butcher's translation.

[9] Cf. Rhet. III. 7. 3; Cic. De Or. II. 237–238, Or. 88.

[10] Eth. Nic. IV. 8. 1128a; cf. Grant, op. cit., p. 28; Starkie, Acharnians, Introd. pp. 39, 68.

innuendo[1] (ὑπόνοια) adopted by the Comic writers of his
own age. In another[2] context, with the Old Comedy evidently in mind, he refers to the pain inflicted and the anger
aroused by mockers and comic poets, whom he ranks with
evil speakers and libellers of their neighbours. Aristotle,
indeed, may have been impressed[3] with the genius of the
Old Comedy, but it is evident that the spirit of its laughter
did not appeal to him as the ideal which should reign on
the Comic stage.

Whatever was the origin of the Coislinian Treatise,[4] it is
probable that it incorporates many elements of the Aristotelian tradition on Comedy. What is
relevant to our purpose in the treatise is the
distinction it makes between Comedy proper,
which employs " innuendo,"[5] and the abuse (λοιδορία)
which openly reproves the evil qualities in men. We have,
moreover, references in it to the comic characters of the
βωμολόχος, the εἴρων, and the ἀλαζών, though no effort
is made to define them. Finally, the important dictum is
enunciated that the laughter of Comedy should not be
immoderate, while the significant statement[6] is added that
in the Old Comedy there is a superabundance of the
ludicrous. There is no need to take account for our purpose
of other Greek theorists, though Demetrius[7] draws a
distinction between the man of refined wit (εὐχάριστος)
and the buffoon (γελωτοποιῶν).

Amongst the Greeks, Aristotle remains our great

The Coislinian Tractate

---

[1] Cf. Kaibel, op. cit., p. 15, on the method of the Middle Comedy :
ὥσπερ αἰνιγματωδῶς καὶ οὐ φανερῶς ἠλέγχοντο ὑπὸ τῶν κωμικῶν.
[2] Rhet. II. 6. 20 ; cf. ib. 2. 12.
[3] Lane Cooper, op. cit., p. 18 et seq., endeavours to estimate his attitude
to Aristophanes, but his views are not always convincing.
[4] Vide Kaibel, op. cit., p. 50 et seq., for the text ; Lane Cooper, op. cit.,
p. 224 et seq. ; Starkie, op. cit., Introd. p. 38 et seq.
[5] Ἔμφασις is the word employed in the Tractate, Kaibel, p. 52 ; the
term often signifies hint or suggestion ; cf. Demetr. 57, 171 ; for the Figure
of ἔμφασις, cf. Rhys Roberts, ed. of Demetr. p. 278.
[6] Tract. 10 : παλαιά ἡ πλεονάζουσα τῷ γελοίῳ.
[7] 168 ; cf. ib. 128, 163 et seq., 171 ; Vahlen, Die Rhetorik, p. 284 et seq.,
touches briefly on some relevant points ; cf. Dionys. De Dem. 54, περὶ
ὕψους, 34 (quoted by him).

authority[1] on these problems, and it is clear that he aimed at analysing the quality of the laughter that should form the soul of Comedy, and also the laughter that befitted men in the ordinary intercourse of life, as well as the orator in his profession. He condemns the coarse and brutal jest that sears its victims ; he reprobates the immoderate and ill-timed laughter of the buffoon, while he clearly shows his predilection for the playful and delicate irony of the refined wit. In the light of such ideals he found the Old Comedy wanting, and his adverse verdict on it had its influence on later[2] critics, though it was not universally upheld.

For our purpose Cicero is the most important of the Roman writers who dealt with the problem of the " Ludicrous." It is clear that he followed closely in the wake of the Aristotelian tradition.

The Roman theorists

In the *De Officiis* he examines the problem from the ethical standpoint, and his treatment of it shows evidence of Stoic colouring due to the influence of Panaetius. Men's conduct, he tells us, should above all be governed by the law of Decorum, which is based on the Golden Mean[3] that is the foundation of every virtue, but is seen in its highest manifestation in the virtue of Temperance.[4] Men must exercise restraint, and show considerateness in their dealings[5] with their fellow-men, and must have regard for the standards of human nature as a whole, and the instincts that help to make society what it is. They may indulge in sport and jest, but the manner[6] of jesting should not be extravagant and unrestrained, but refined[7] and witty. Cicero distinguishes[8] between the illiberal jest with its wantonness and obscenity, and the liberal jest that is marked by clever and urbane wit. He is at variance with Aristotle in regarding[9] the Old Comedy as representative

---

[1] Unfortunately Theophrastus' treatise περὶ γελοίου is lost.

[2] Plut. Quaest. Conviv. VII. 8. 3 ; cf. Platonius on Cratinus, Kaibel, p. 6.

[3] Cf. Or. 73 : " in omnibusque rebus videndum est quatenus ; etsi enim suus cuique modus est, tamen magis offendit nimium quam parum."

[4] De Off. I. 100.   [5] *Ib*. 98, 107, 110, 152 *et seq.*; cf. *ib*. III. 26.

[6] *Ib*. I. 103.   [7] Cf. Ad Att. I. 13. 1, on " humanitatis sal."

[8] De Off. I. 104.

[9] Cf. Anon. περὶ κωμ. 3, Kaibel, p. 7, where the same view is put forward.

of the liberal jest. He commends the irony[1] (urbana dissimulatio) which was apparent in the fascinating and
humorous conversation of Socrates,[2] and was also a characteristic of the Younger Scipio, while he rules[3] out everything in the nature of obscenity and cynic frankness of
speech. He reprobates,[4] too, the wit that takes delight in
making malicious and slanderous statements about the
absent. True to the doctrine of Decorum, he enjoins moderation in laughter and consideration for the feelings of others,
while he condemns the coarse, ill-timed,[5] and often bitter
jesting, that was commonly associated with the character
of the buffoon,[6] who is unsparing in his witticisms, and
finds his greatest pleasure in offending the susceptibilities
of his hearers. He expresses[7] regret at the disappearance
of the subtle and refined wit that was once the distinguishing
mark of the Roman.

In the *De Oratore*,[8] he examines the problem from a somewhat different standpoint, but, while recognising that wit
The " Laugh- has its place in oratory, he insists that the
able " in the orator in his jesting must be governed by
" De Oratore " the law of Decorum. A jest, if conceived in
the proper spirit, is often[9] in the hands of the orator a more
effective weapon than serious argument. Cicero, while
dealing here with the subject at length, has in the *Orator*[10]
conveniently summed up his doctrine for us : " illud
admonemus tamen ridiculo sic usurum oratorem ut nec
nimis[11] frequenti ne scurrile[12] sit, nec subobscoeno ne

---

[1] *Vide supra*, p. 36 ; cf. Q. VI. 3. 85, 92, IX. 2. 44 *et seq ;* in De
Off. I. 137, there is a passing reference to the opposite character of the
ἀλαζών.

[2] Cf. Reich, op. cit., I. 1, p. 360 *et seq.*

[3] De Off. I. 127–128, 148 ; cf. Fiske, op. cit., pp. 84–85, 279.

[4] De Off. I. 134.

[5] *Ib.* 144.

[6] De Or. II. 239, 245–247.

[7] Ad Fam. IX. 15. 2 ; cf. VII. 31. 2.

[8] II. 216 *et seq.*

[9] *Ib.* 236 ; *vide infra*, p. 366.

[10] 88.

[11] Cf. De Or. II. 238 : " in jocando moderatio " ; *ib.* 247.

[12] Cf. Q. VI. 3. 8, 82–83.

mimicum, nec petulanti[1] ne improbum, nec in calamitatem[2] ne inhumanum, nec in facinus ne odii locum occupet, neque aut sua persona aut judicum aut tempore alienum." The orator in his jests should spare his friends,[3] and not be like him whom Quintilian describes as prepared to lose a friend rather than miss the occasion for a witticism. Above all, he will avoid the jest full of gall and bitterness that leaves behind it a wound[4] that can never be healed. Regard for the occasion, his own dignity, and his audience, the avoidance of needless offence, and in general, restraint and refinement in his jesting, will distinguish the orator from the buffoon. The orator, moreover, will shun every suggestion of the vulgar mimicry and obscenity[5] of the Mime.[6] We may note that Quintilian is in close agreement with Cicero on the subject of jesting, as it touches the sphere of the orator. In several passages he deals with the character of the buffoon in much the same spirit as Cicero, and notes[7] in addition his tendency to jest against himself.

When Horace then set out to criticise more in detail the quality of Lucilius' laughter, and to lay down rules to guide the Satirist to the true spirit of jesting,

Horace and the tradition he did so in the light of ideas that had long been familiar to the Greeks, and that had been made accessible to the Romans especially in the writings of Cicero. Horace's picture[8] of the buffoon shows in fact many close parallels with Aristotle, and with the Roman writer. Now, Horace had paid a tribute to Lucilius' power of invective,[9] and had given a measure of praise to his wit, but, as a counterblast to his strictures, the admirers of

[1] Cf. Q. VI. 3. 33, XI. 1. 86 *et seq.*
[2] Cf. Q. VI. 3. 31.
[3] Or. 89; cf. De Or. II. 237 : " parcendum est maxime caritati "; Q. VI. 3. 28.
[4] Cf. Q. loc. cit. : " laedere nunquam velimus " ; *vide supra*, p. 354.
[5] Cf. Ovid, Trist. II. 497 : " mimos obscena jocantes "; cf. Q. VI. 3. 47, on the obscenity of the Atellan farces.
[6] Cf. De Or. II. 239, 242, 274 ; *ib.* 251, on the " Sannio," one of the characters in the Mime ; Reich, op. cit., Vol. I. 1, p. 67.
[7] VI. 3. 82.
[8] *Vide supra*, p. 358.
[9] Sat. I. 4. 6 *et seq.*; cf. I. 10. 3, II. 1. 64 *et seq.*

Lucilius had evidently put forward extravagant claims for their favourite poet, so that Horace feels it incumbent on himself to adopt a still more critical attitude, and to hedge around with restrictions his former concessions. If, he declares, he were to give unstinted praise to Lucilius, on the same standard he would be forced to admire the *Mimes*[1] of Laberius as artistic creations. As the context indicates, he is evidently thinking primarily[2] of the character of the humour of Laberius,[3] whose writings, besides being tinged with political bitterness, must have exhibited much of the coarseness and obscenity that usually marked the Mime. According to Horace, the Satirist who strives to be an artist in his genre, must frequently vary his tone,[4] indulging now in invective, now in quiet raillery. Satire as a rule moves on a humble plane, but there are times when the Satirist may exhibit something of either the vehement force of the orator,[5] or the sublimity of the poet. Again, in another change of mood he will have recourse to the restrained[6] and delicate irony[7] of the " urbanus," which was especially suited to the " sermo," a title that Horace[8] more than once

[1] Sat. I. 10. 5.

[2] The expression " pulchra poemata " would at first sight suggest that Horace was thinking primarily of form ; the following lines, however, reveal his real purpose.

[3] Cf. Suet. J.C. 39 ; Gellius, XVII. 14. 2, on his " maledicentia et arrogantia," where Caesar was concerned ; Macrob. Sat. II. 7. 2 ; Reich, op. cit., I. 1, p. 60 *et seq.*

[4] Sat. I. 10. 11 : " et sermone opus est modo tristi, saepe jocoso " ; on Horace's use of " tristis," *vide supra*, p. 355.

[5] The reference here is somewhat obscure, but seems to be to the orator's power of invective, and his capacity for stirring the emotions ; Kiessling-Heinze in connection with this passage refer to the qualities of τὸ δεινόν and τὸ ὑψηλὸν τοῦ λόγου, attributed to the Old Comedy ; cf. Kaibel, p. 18 ; vehement invective will usually issue in the Grand style ; cf. Juv. I. 165 : " quotiens Lucilius ardens infremuit " ; possibly, however, Cicero's distinction between " sermo " and " contentio " may throw some light on the passage ; *vide supra*, p. 53.

[6] It may be for that reason that some of Horace's critics thought his Satires " sine nervis," Sat. II. 1. 2.

[7] *Vide supra*, p. 363, for Cicero's discussion of " urbana dissimulatio " and its association with the " sermo " ; cf. Hor. Ep. I. 9. 9–11 : " dissimulator opis propriae " ; *ib.* on " frons urbana."

[8] Sat. I. 4. 42, 48, Ep. I. 4. 1, II. 1. 250–251, II. 2. 60 ; Lucilius too, as we have seen, employs this term for his Satires ; *vide supra*, p. 53 *et seq.*

applies to his Satires as indicative of their easy and casual nature.

In thus touching on the character of the " urbanus,"[1] he introduces a word which, though of recent origin, had **Urbanitas** already acquired a wealth of meaning ranging from purity and correctness of speech to the elegance and refinement, both in wit[2] and manners, that were the distinguishing characteristic of the educated Roman. Such a one, in Horace's view, will exhibit above all the qualities of reserve and moderation. Horace next contrasts bitter invective (acre) and raillery (ridiculum), which is seen at its best in the subtle humour of the " urbanus," and which is a more effective weapon in the hands of an advocate[3] in serious cases than a violent diatribe. The faculty of " liberal " jesting was characteristic of the writers of the Old Comedy, says Horace, in this opinion agreeing with Cicero and differing from Aristotle.[4] Lucilius' ardent admirers, especially such as Hermogenes and Demetrius,[5] evidently had proclaimed that he exhibited in his *Satires* the spirit of the Old Comedy writers. They had done so, believing that coarse, violent invective represented their whole spirit, and ignorant of the range, variety, and complexity of such authors. Horace implies that in reality Lucilius had missed the finer[6] and subtler elements of his Greek models, and thus lacked the quality of laughter suited to the genre of Satire.

He thus endeavours to formulate a portion of the " lex

---

[1] Cf. Q. VI. 3. 45, 102 *et seq.*, for a discussion of the word ; cf. Hendrickson, Horace and Valerius Cato (Cl. Ph. XII), p. 88 *et seq.* ; Grant, op. cit. p. 119 *et seq.*

[2] Cf. Cic. De Off. I. 104, on the " liberal " jest : " elegans, urbanum, ingeniosum, facetum " ; cf. De Fin. I. 39, II. 103, De Domo Sua, 92, Pr Caelio, 6, 33, 36, Br. 273, De Or. I. 17.

[3] Here evidently Horace was thinking, too, of its effect in oratory ; c Cic. De Or. II. 236 ; Sat. II. 1. 86, on the effect of the " bona carmina " Ar. Rhet. III. 18. 7, on Gorgias' dictum.

[4] *Vide supra*, p. 360.

[5] " Simius iste," Sat. I. 10. 18 ; cf. Schol. ad loc.

[6] His admirers had ignorantly styled him " comis et urbanus," Sa I. 10. 65 ; on " comitas " and its importance, cf. Cic. De Off. II. 48, De O II. 182, Or. 128 ; cf. Hendrickson, Horace and Lucilius, p. 156 *et seq.*

operis " that governed Satire. It will not be here wholly
out of place to consider briefly how his own
**Horace's
practice** practice harmonises with his theory. Lucilius had indulged at times in violent
invective, especially where political[1] opponents were concerned, and had ventured to attack some of the leading men
of the State. In Horace's day, some consideration had to
be shown for the law of libel,[2] certain aspects of which are
discussed by Trebatius. But apart from this, Horace
would hardly consider the time favourable for political
satire. He was living down the indiscretion[3] of Philippi,
and through the influence of Maecenas was becoming more
and more securely attached to the new regime. It would
indeed ill become him to cast opprobrium on the adherents
of his old party. Moreover, the rivalry between Antony
and Octavian had been eased for the moment by the pact
of Brundusium, and Horace would be rendering poor service
to the State by stirring up political animosity. It is sometimes urged that the poet's scornful reference[4] to Calvus
and Catullus, and his attack on Furius Bibaculus, were
inspired by political considerations on account of their
diatribes[5] against Julius Caesar, but even the zeal of the
newly converted, especially in one of such an independent
character as Horace, would hardly go the length of
seeking to avenge insults offered in the past to the house of
Caesar. Horace's animosity can well be accounted for by
the quarrels and differences of ideals that prevailed in the
literary coteries of the day. The intransigeance of the
coterie spirit is nowhere better illustrated, as many of
Horace's bitterest thrusts are directed against his opponents
in the sphere of literature. Still, even when allowance is made
for an element of irony, it must be admitted that Horace

---

[1] Cf. Book I, on Lupus ; Hor. Sat. II. 1. 67 ; Persius, I. 115.
[2] Sat. II. 1. 82–83 ; cf. Ep. II. 1. 152 *et seq.*, A.P. 283 ; Cic. De Rep.
IV. 12.
[3] Ep. II. 2. 47.
[4] Sat. I. 10. 19 ; Sikes, op. cit., p. 59, argues with some plausibility that
Horace's shaft was here directed chiefly against Demetrius, the ape of Catullus;
vide supra, p. 302.
[5] Suet. J.C. 73.

shows a certain respect[1] for Valerius Cato, the head of the school which sought to exalt Lucilius, and was offended by the criticisms passed upon him. Cato was himself a poet[2] who, in the spirit of the Neoterics, followed Alexandrian models, but he also distinguished himself as a student and critic of the poets. Horace, however, is unsparing in his invective against the lesser lights of Cato's school, such as Demetrius,[3] Hermogenes,[4] and Fannius.[5] The first two had angered him by claiming for Lucilius all the merits of the Old Comedy, though they had never read a play of the period. With merciless sarcasm he bids[6] them to go and whine amidst the benches of their lady pupils. His criticisms of the epic style of Furius Bibaculus,[7] though clearly deserved, may have derived their note of hostility from the association of Furius with the school of Cato, and his somewhat extravagant admiration for the Master. It is evident from his contemptuous references that, like his predecessor Lucilius, Horace was at variance also with the guild[8] of professional poets, who had formed into a close corporation, the guiding principle of which seemed to be mutual admiration. In the earlier book of his *Satires* in particular, Horace thus directs his most deadly shafts against the adherents of rival literary schools, and shows how uncompromising the coterie spirit may be. When he

[1] Cf. Sat. I. 10. 52, where " doctus " probably refers to him ; in the lines prefixed to this Satire he is spoken of with respect, and, as we have said, the lines may contain a genuine tradition.

[2] " Summum grammaticum, optimum poetam," as Furius Bibaculus styles him ; cf. Suet. De Gr. II, IV, XI.

[3] Sat. I. 10. 18, 79, 90.

[4] Sat. I. 3. 129, 4. 72, 9. 25, 10. 80.

[5] Sat. I. 4. 21.

[6] Sat. I. 10.91 ; Horace, while having here in mind the Greek phrase κλαίειν κελεύω, seems to me to use " plorare jubeo " in another sense ; Hermogenes and Demetrius probably taught elocution as well as singing, and may have affected the wailing intonation that Cicero notes as characteristic of the Asianist orators ; cf. Or. 27 : " cum vero inclinata ululantique voce more Asiatico canere coepisset," etc., *vide supra*, p. 213.

[7] If it is Bibaculus that is referred to in Sat. I. 10. 36, II. 5. 39–41 ; cf. Suet. De Gr. IV, XI ; Q. X. 1. 96, knows Bibaculus only as a writer of Iambics ; cf. Tac. Ann. IV. 34 ; Diomede, K. I. 485 ; *vide supra*, p. 302.

[8] *Vide supra*, p. 303.

came to write his later book, his position as a poet was more secure, and his reputation was established, above all with the men[1] whose judgment was of value. He could afford to ignore the attacks of those who sought to disparage his talent, and pay a more generous[2] tribute to Lucilius than he had done at an earlier period.

Now, apart from the subject of political life, which Horace avoided, and apart from literary polemic, in which his invective often seems envenomed, Horace had
Literary
influences open to him the still larger field of private life, wherein to display the spirit of his satire. I need not dwell on the various literary[3] influences, especially those of Cynic and Stoic origin, that helped to give his *Satires* their present form, but in trying to appraise the standard which formed the basis of many of Horace's judgments in that work, I believe that we must look to an author nearer home. We shall find that Horace derived from Cicero more than his conception of refined wit.

In the *De Officiis*, Cicero, as we saw, applies the law of Decorum to the regulation of human conduct. As I have
The " De
Officiis " already said, that law is grounded in the concept of the Golden Mean, which is our surest[4] guide in life. Whether in speech or dress, it calls upon us to avoid the extremes[5] of effeminacy and boorishness. In expense or display, it will prevent[6] us from going to a vulgar excess, and in our dealings with our fellow-men will help us to keep our emotions under control. The law of Propriety above all demands[7] a uniform consistency in each single action, and in our life as a whole. Man must be true, not only to his own individual character,

---

[1] Cf. Sat. I. 10. 81 *et seq.*

[2] Sat. II. 1. 29 *et seq.*, *ib.* 62 *et seq.*

[3] *Vide* Fiske, op. cit., c. 3 ; Lejay, op. cit., Introd. p. 7 *et seq.* ; Helm, Lucian und Menipp, p. 204 *et seq.*, 265 *et seq.*, and elsewhere ; Heinze, De Horatio Bionis Imitatore.

[4] De Off. I. 130 : " mediocritas optima est " ; cf. I. 89, II. 59.

[5] *Ib.* I. 129–131.

[6] *Ib.* I. 140–141 : " ut ea quae pertinent ad liberalem speciem et dignitatem, moderata sint " ; cf. *ib.* 136.

[7] *Ib.* I. 111, 125, 144.

but, as the Stoics especially would insist, to the universal[1] laws of human nature. From these a social[2] sense is developed which imposes on man his most solemn duty, and helps to discipline[3] his instincts within proper limits. A community will have its established[4] customs and conventions, to which its members must conform, if its existence is to be ensured.

Even a casual reading of Horace's *Satires* will make it apparent how closely he was treading in the footsteps of Cicero. He lays down[5] the principle of the

Horace and Cicero

Golden Mean as the norm of conduct, as at a later date he proclaimed the value of the " aurea mediocritas " in the well-known Murena Ode,[6] which seems indebted to Cicero for some of its traits. Virtue lies in the middle way ; extremes must be avoided, but many people in endeavouring to avoid one extreme rush[7] to its opposite. Horace is fond[8] of depicting for us in concrete fashion contrasted types of such extremes as the miser and the spendthrift, while at times he deals with their vices in the abstract,[9] noting their aberrations from the Golden Mean. Again, he illustrates[10] a quality that keeps faithfully to the middle way. No one, he declares,[11] can object that the poet himself is infected with the vice of avarice or meanness, which are violations of the law of Propriety. A condition also imposed by that law is to

[1] *Ib.* I. 107 : " communis (persona) . . . a qua omne honestum decorumque trahitur " ; *ib.* 110.

[2] *Ib.* 153 : " necesse est, quod a communitate ducatur officium, id maximum esse " ; cf. 152–160, on the social instinct ; III. 26.

[3] *Ib.* I. 157 : " magnitudo animi, remota communitate conjunctioneque humana, feritas sit quaedam et immanitas."

[4] *Ib.* 148 : " quae vero more agentur institutisque civilibus," etc.

[5] Sat. I. 1. 106 : " est modus in rebus " ; cf. Ep. I. 2. 71, I. 18. 9 ; Horace and his Age, p. 80 *et seq.*, where, however, I did not allow for Cicero's influence.

[6] II. 10 ; cf. Cic. De Off. I. 89–90.

[7] Sat. I. 2. 26 ; cf. I. 1. 103, II. 2. 54, 64, II. 3. 166–167.

[8] Sat. I. 1. 101, 105, II. 3. 175 ; cf. Epode I. 33 ; cf. Ep. II. 2. 193, for a study of various " types."

[9] Cf. Sat. I. 4. 26.

[10] Cf. Sat. II. 2. 65, for his definition of " mundus."

[11] Sat. I. 6. 68, 107 ; cf. Ep. II. 2. 203–204.

maintain consistency in our lives and actions. Tigellius ran counter to it in always oscillating[1] between extremes, though he might be considered constant in his inconstancy. With subtle irony, Horace makes[2] Davus accuse his master of this very defect which he condemns in others. With such examples of vacillation may be contrasted the steadfastness of the Stoic " Sapiens,"[3] who by his courage and self-control can defy all the assaults of Fortune.

As we have already seen, Cicero attaches great importance to the social instinct, and to the established customs and conventions of a community, when

Social conventions considering how the law of Propriety should be observed in practice. Horace, too, has a practical standard (" traditum ab antiquis morem ")[4] to which his father appeals, when castigating the vices of his neighbours, and which is at the basis of the moralisings[5] of Ofellus. Horace's father was distinguished by a bluffness and frankness which did not seek to hide ugly facts by an array[6] of fair words. He was accustomed, when condemning a vice, to point to some living embodiment of it as an example to be avoided by his son. It is interesting to note that Cicero, too, advises[7] us to correct our faults by observing the faults of others, and by harkening to the criticisms of the wise.[8] His father's practice had no little influence upon Horace who, in the midst of a general discussion,

---

[1] Sat. I. 3. 9 : " nil aequale homini fuit illi " ; cf. Sat. II. 7. 10 (on Priscus), *ib.* 20.

[2] Sat. II. 7. 28, *ib.* 112, on his restlessness ; Ep. I. 8. 11 ; cf., however, Ep. I. 14. 16, II. 2. 200.

[3] Sat. II. 7. 83 *et seq. ;* cf. his picture of Lucilius, II. 1. 31 ; we must not, of course, forget that the figure of the " Sapiens " comes in for its share of Horace's irony.

[4] Sat. I. 4. 117 ; cf. II. 7. 23 : " laudas fortunam et mores antiquae plebis."

[5] Sat. II. 2. 10 : " si Romana fatigat militia adsuetum graecari " ; *ib.* 104-105 ; cf. the standpoint of Servius Oppidius, Sat. II. 3. 168 *et seq.*

[6] As in Sat. I. 3. 44 *et seq.*

[7] De Off. I. 146 ; cf. Sat. I. 4. 128 : " sic teneros animos aliena opprobria saepe absterrent vitiis."

[8] De Off. I. 147 : " adhibere doctos homines vel etiam usu peritos " ; cf. Sat. I. 4. 122, where Horace's father " unum ex judicibus selectis objiciebat."

often with surprising suddenness, introduces[1] an individual name to illustrate the vice under consideration. The name of Nomentanus is thus repeated so frequently, that in the end it has come to be in Horace's mind the embodiment[2] and type of prodigality, and a standing monument to warn all who would dissipate their patrimony in folly. Some of the individual names that occur in Horace, are found also in Lucilius,[3] while others[4] belonged to the generation that preceded him. But such names are frequently used by Horace as typical of the vices which they serve to illustrate.

In all this Horace is imbued rather with the spirit of the New Comedy than with that of the Old. Cicero had supplied him with a philosophy of life and conduct which, though coloured by Stoic influence, was grounded in the Peripatetic concept of the Golden Mean. The same concept was at the basis of another work, the *Characters* of Theophrastus, which has strong affinities with the New Comedy.[5] Theophrastus, without employing individual names, studies various types of character that violate the law of Decorum, and are guilty of aberration from the Golden Mean towards excess on the one side or the other. In practical life, one might say that man best fulfils the law of Decorum by being true to the social instinct, and to the conventions of a community. The Comedy of types is founded on the idea[6] that society has a settled norm of conduct, and can laugh at the abnormalities[7] of its members who depart from the conventional standard. Most of the members of society exhibit certain " eccentricities,"[8] but some of these are less

The spirit of the New Comedy

---

[1] Sat. I. 1. 95, 101, 105, I. 4. 28.

[2] Sat. II. 3. 224 : " nunc age, luxuriam et Nomentanum arripe mecum " cf. I. 8. 11, II. 1. 22, 3. 175.

[3] Cf. Naevius, Sat. I. 1. 101, II. 2. 68, Luc. fr. 1212 (Marx) ; Maenius, Sat. I. 3. 21, Ep. I. 15. 26 *et seq*., Luc. fr. 1203 ; Gallonius, Sat. II. 2. 47, Luc. fr. 1238 (with Marx's note).

[4] e.g. Cervius and Turius, Sat. II. 1. 47–49.

[5] Menander, even in the existing fragments, shows some striking affinities with his master, Theophrastus.

[6] *Vide* Horace and his Age, p. 80.

[7] When they are harmless.

[8] The moralist would call them " vitia " ; cf. Sat. I. 3. 68, I. 4. 25 *et seq.*

obtrusive and less harmful than others. The miser and
the spendthrift are, each in his own way, eccentric. The
parvenu Nasidienus is abnormal in his own way, and runs
counter to the principle of Decorum by his extravagant[1]
and vulgar display of his wealth. Horace's standard is
obscured in some of the later[2] *Satires* by being couched more
in the language of Stoic morality, according to which the
passions are diseases and forms of madness, but even there
it remains fundamentally the same. In the spirit of Comedy,
Horace can laugh at such abnormalities, while he is true to
the same spirit[3] in directing his ridicule against many
essentially harmless faults. Such are the foppery and
effeminacy of Rufillus,[4] or Albius'[5] craze for collecting
antiques, while, though our modern conceptions are different, a defect[6] such as he mocks at in Gargonius, was considered to be a fair target for refined wit. The lapses from
the conventional standard with which Horace mostly deals,
would, like his own " vitia mediocria,"[7] deserve to be met
with irony and quiet raillery rather than with bitter invective. Viewed from this standpoint, Horace is fairly
justified in his claims that his *Satires* are conceived in a
spirit of playfulness,[8] and are free from malignity, while
under a sportive[9] demeanour they may be made to serve a
moral end. Such Horace would declare to be his prevailing
characteristic, though at times his pen is dipped in gall,
as when he deals with a public character such as Canidia,
or with the poets and critics of a rival school. It seems,
indeed, strange that the offending line to which he himself
refers,[10] could have aroused much indignation, but, at any
rate, it gave the poet an opportunity of proclaiming and

[1] Cf. Cic. De Off. I. 139–141.
[2] Sat. II. 3, II. 7.
[3] *Vide supra*, p. 360.
[4] Sat. I. 2. 27, I. 4. 92.
[5] Sat. I. 4. 27 ; cf. II. 3. 20 *et seq.*, II. 7. 95, 101.
[6] Cf. Cic. De Or. II. 239 ; Q. VI. 3. 37.
[7] Sat. I. 4. 130, 139 ; cf I. 3. 20, I. 6. 65.
[8] *Vide supra*, p. 358.
[9] Sat. I. 1. 23 *et seq.* ; cf. Fiske, op. cit., pp. 88, 144 *et seq.*, on the concept
f σπουδαιογέλοιον ; Comedy can have its serious aim ; cf. Aristoph.
rogs. 389 ; Plut. Mor. 68 B.
[10] Sat. I. 4. 92.

defending his conception of Satire, and of defining the quality of the laughter that should prevail in the genre.

Horace, to define more fully the " lex operis," sets himself also to the task of analysing the nature of the style of Satire. He tells[1] us that in his *Satires* he **The style of** writes " sermoni propiora " ; he refuses to **Satire** accept the title of poet, and puts his *Satires* on a level with Comedy, by which he means especially the New Comedy. The Alexandrian critics had already raised the question[2] whether Comedy, though in verse, was entitled to be ranked as poetry. Comedy is a " cotidianae vitae speculum "[3] ; it deals with ordinary people and commonplace[4] subjects, and in accordance with the law of Decorum should be written in a style[5] that resembled the language of everyday life. Horace calls his *Satires* " sermones," a title that was designed to suggest their casual, discursive, conversational tone, and their capacity for passing from one topic to another with an ease that at times obscures the binding unity of the Satire. He evidently considered that Satire, which like Comedy dealt with themes of ordinary life, found its most fitting medium of expression in the plain style of the " sermo."[7] Satire, thus couched in plain, prosaic style,[8] could not lay claim to the lofty qualities

---

[1] *Ib.* 42.

[2] Cf. *ib.* 45 *et seq.;* Cic. Or. 67, 184 : " at comicorum senarii propt[er] similitudinem sermonis sic saepe sunt abjecti," etc.

[3] *Vide supra*, p. 55 ; cf. Kaibel, op. cit., pp. 67, 72, *ib.* pp. 11, 2[1] Funaioli, op. cit., p. 320 *et seq.;* Diomede, Keil, I. 488 ; cf. Q. X. 1. [6] (on Menander) : " ita omnem vitae imaginem expressit " ; Cic. Pro Rosc[io] 47 : " imaginem vitae cotidianae " ; he also styled Comedy " imitatione[m] vitae, speculum consuetudinis, imaginem veritatis " (Wessner, Donat[us] Vol. I. p. 22) ; cf. Evanthius, " cotidianae vitae speculum " ; *vide inf[ra]* p. 402.

[4] Cf. Hor. Sat. II. 4. 9, Ep. II. 1. 168 ; cf. H. Rushton Faircloug[h] op. cit., p. 183 *et seq.*

[5] Hor. A.P. 89 ; cf. Anon. περὶ κωμ. 12, Kaibel, p. 8 ; Tract. Coislin. Kaibel, p. 52 ; Strabo, I. 2. 6.

[6] Lucilius, as we saw, called his Satires a " species vitae."

[7] *Vide supra*, p. 36 *et seq.;* for the use of the term, by Lucilius, v[ide] *supra*, p. 53 *et seq.*

[8] Sat. II. 6. 17 : " Musa pedestris " ; cf. Ep. II. 1. 250–251 ; Persi[us] V. 14 : " verba togae sequeris."

that were the mark of high poetic genius. But, as Comedy[1] can at times lift its voice, so Satire can on occasion abandon the path of prosaic plainness, and attain to the impassioned accents of the orator, or the elevation of the poet, either when stirred by some deep emotion, or merely for purposes of parody.[2]

In general, then, Satire should be written in a plain style, but its very plainness and seeming lack of elaboration serve

The qualities of Satiric writing to create the illusion that such a genre is easy[3] of imitation. Horace evidently wished to correct such a mistaken view, as even in Satire an author is not dispensed from the labour of careful composition. He therefore sets forth at some length the qualities or " virtues "[4] of the style that should characterise it, and he does so with the double purpose of defining more closely the law of the genre, and of proclaiming his own ideal of style as a standard by which he can test the merits of Lucilius, and discount some of the claims made for him by his more foolish and extravagant admirers. In Satire I. 4, he had passed certain criticisms on Lucilius' style that were resented[5] by the lovers of the poet. In Satire I. 10, he formulates some positive precepts of his own, but even in these there is an implied criticism of his predecessor. He demands brevity[6] in style, or rather the avoidance of that redundancy which he had set down[7] as one of the defects of Lucilius. This very redundancy was in part responsible for the lack of clearness which Horace reproves in his predecessor. In the Satirist, as we have seen, Horace demands[8] a variety of tones that will inevitably carry with

---

[1] Hor. A.P. 93 ; cf. Donatus ad Adelphi, 790.

[2] Cf. Hor. Sat. I. 5. 9, II. 1. 13, II. 4. 94, 5. 62 et seq., 6. 100, 8. 34, 54.

[3] Sat. II. 1. 3 ; cf. Ep. II. 1. 169, A.P. 240 et seq. (Blakeney, ad loc., gives some apt quotations from Byron, Pope, etc.) ; cf. Cic. Or. 76 (on the Plain style in oratory) ; Dionys. De Lys. 8 ; Isocr. Panegyr. 12 ; Cope, op. cit., p. 285, on Archimelus' epigram regarding Euripides' style.

[4] There is an interesting parallel in Philodemus, περὶ ποιημ. Jensen, p. 13 et seq., 65 et seq., ib. p. 157 ; Philodemus, however, is dealing with poetic style in general ; vide infra, p. 477.

[5] Cf. Sat. I. 10. 1 et seq., ib. 50. [6] Sat. I. 10. 9 ; vide infra, p. 477.

[7] Sat. I. 4. 11, I. 10. 51, 69 ; cf. Q. X. 1. 94.

[8] Sat. I. 10. 11 et seq. ; variety of style will at any rate be indirectly involved, if Horace's demands are satisfied.

it a variety of style.   In a measure, he demands purity of speech, when he reproves the foolish[1] admiration which makes it a merit in Lucilius to have mingled Greek words with Latin.   Here he was evidently influenced by the purist principles of men such as Asinius Pollio and Messalla,[2] who had studied with meticulous care the correctness[3] of Latin usage, and withstood the incursion of foreign[4] words into Latin.   Horace, moreover, is here indirectly condemning the practice of the Roman school of poetry (including Valerius Cato and his disciples), that followed Alexandrian models, and sought the effects of sweetness[5] and sonorousness by the introduction of Graecisms into their verse.   He himself shows remarkable restraint in his use of Greek words, though he is willing[6] to enrich his native tongue by new words formed on the analogy of the Greek.

The virtue of propriety[7] would at least be implied in the doctrine which connects the plain[8] style with the genre of Satire as being a mirror of ordinary life.   In thus setting forth his ideas on the necessary qualities of style, Horace may possibly have

The virtue of propriety

[1] Luc's admirers apparently did not take into account that the poet usually employed such Greek words for purposes of parody or comic effect ; *vide supra*, p. 42.

[2] His mention of Messalla is therefore significant, Sat. I. 10. 29 ; on Messalla's purism, *vide supra*, p. 261.

[3] In this respect Horace could hardly demand a rigid purism in a genre such as Satire, that of its nature would readily admit vulgarisms ; cf. Ruckdeschel, Archaismen und Vulgarismen in der Sprache des Horaz ; Bourciez, Le " Sermo cotidianus " dans les Satires d'Horace.

[4] It is interesting to note that Horace, in dealing with this problem, views it as much from the nationalist as from the purist standpoint.

[5] Cf. Cic. Or. 163–164 (with Kroll's notes) ; cf. Macrob. VI. 4. 17 *et seq.*, *ib.* 22, on Virgil's restraint in the use of such words ; Hendrickson, Horace and Valerius Cato, p. 336 *et seq.*, has some admirable pages on the use of Graecisms in the Latin poets ; *vide supra*, p. 306.

[6] A.P. 52–53 ; cf. Q. IX. 3. 17, on the influence of Greek idiom on Horace ; Waltz, Des Variations de la Langue et de la Métrique d'Horace, c. 4.

[7] Cic. De Off. I. 111, regards the mingling of Greek words in Latin as a breach of propriety.

[8] Cf. Sat. II. 4. 9 : " utpote res tenues tenui sermone peractas " ; I use the term " plain " here without any Rhetorical implication ; *vide infra*, p. 476.

been influenced by the formulation of the Plain[1] style in Stoic circles, but, while admitting this possibility, I would hesitate to refer Horace's treatment of style in the *Satires* to any hide-bound formula of the Rhetorical schools, or to exact from the poet the strict technical meaning of terms[2] that were current there.   There were other influences at work upon Horace, who in formulating his precepts for style is either tacitly or explicitly criticising the defects of Lucilius.   Moreover, he wished to set forth his ideal of what we might call " Augustan " correctness, and therein possess a standard by which the merits and defects of his predecessor, and in fact of the older Roman poets generally, could be measured.   The precepts for style that he thus formulated, were merely an anticipation of his later critical creed, which in some respects grew more definite, but in spirit remained substantially the same as in those early years.

Horace lets us into the secret of his own methods, and thus incidentally throws light on his ideals.   He had no

Horace's ideals

ambition[3] to be styled the author of many verses, but aimed at making whatever he wrote pre-eminent in quality.   In this respect he contrasts himself not only with Lucilius,[4] who seemed to have had almost a gift of improvisation in the ease and copious flow of his verse, but also with worthless versifiers[5] such as Fannius and Crispinus, who boasted of their poetic fertility.   At a later[6] period, he traces the faults of Ennius,

[1] Especially as found in the " sermo " ; Fiske, op. cit., p. 124 *et seq.*, endeavours to work out a close parallel between Horace and the Stoic treatment of the " virtues " of style, but while an analogy may exist between the two, it should not be pressed too closely ; Fiske finds a reference to the virtue of κατασκευή in Sat. I. 4. 54, but this virtue, as formulated by the Stoics, would leave room for little, if any, positive ornament.

[2] Such as " brevitas," " limatus," " tenuis," etc. ; *vide infra*, 476.

[3] Sat. I. 4. 13 : " nam ut multum, nil moror " ; *ib.* 18 ; cf. Sat. II. 3. 1.

[4] *Vide supra*, p. 53 ; contrast Virgil's practice of working at a few verses each day, Q. X. 3. 8.

[5] Sat. I. 1. 120, I. 4. 14 *et seq.* ; cf. I. 9. 23, where the Bore declares : " nam quis me scribere plures aut citius possit versus ? "

[6] A.P. 261 : " aut operae celeris nimium curaque carentis " ; cf. Ep. I. 1. 51 *et seq.*, *ib.* 67, 170 *et seq.*

Plautus, and the older poets generally, to too rapid and careless workmanship, just as he ascribes[1] the defects of Lucilius to the same cause. Such poets will follow their own caprices[2], and do anything rather than submit to the stern discipline of careful composition. Such indolence in the case of Lucilius resulted in harsh and unpolished verse, in lack of clearness and in redundancy, faults which can be obviated only by orderly[3] arrangement and by careful pruning. In all this, Horace is anticipating either his own positive precepts for style, or the criticism of the older poets which he designed as a counterblast to the extravagant praise of their admirers, who claimed[4] that their works were of almost perfect finish and faultless beauty, because they exhibit an occasional apt word or well-turned phrase. On the contrary, in the light of Augustan literary ideals he finds[5] their verse archaic, lifeless, and untuneful.[6]

Horace's critical vocabulary is worthy of some notice, if only as a further revelation of his ideals. Whether he is

Horace's critical vocabulary

issuing a warning to the youthful aspirant to poetic honours, or criticising the Ancients, many of his critical[7] terms indicate an abhorrence of verse that is harsh and untuneful, unpolished, inelegant, void of substance, or wanting in clearness or verve. It is evident that by implication he demands the opposite qualities. He clearly, in fact, indicates[8] his predilection for verse that is tuneful, smooth of flow, well turned, and of fine texture. When he speaks[9] of the elegance that drove out

---

[1] Sat. I. 4. 12 : " piger scribendi ferre laborem."

[2] Cf. A.P. 265 : " idcircone vager scribamque licenter ? "

[3] Cf. A.P. 41, 446 *et seq.*

[4] Ep. II. 1. 71 *et seq.* ; *vide supra*, p. 294 *et seq.*

[5] Ep. II. 1. 66–68.   [6] Cf. also A.P. 263.

[7] Ep. II. 1. 66–67, " dure," " ignave " ; *ib.* 76 : " crasse compositum illepideve " ; *ib.* 233 : " Choerilus incultis qui versibus et male natis," etc. ; *ib.* 266 : " nec prave factis decorari versibus opto " ; *ib.* II. 2. 106 : " mala qui componunt carmina " ; A.P. 231 : " leves ... versus " ; *ib.* 322 : " versus inopes rerum " ; *ib.* 441 : " male tornatos ... versus " ; *ib.* 445–446 : " versus inertes, duri, incompti."

[8] Cf. Sat. I. 10. 58 : " versiculos ... magis factos et euntes mollius " ; Ep. II. 1. 225 : " tenui deducta poemata filo " ; *ib.* II. 2. 76 : " versus . canoros."

[9] Ep. II. 1. 158.

the uncouthness of former days, his attention is evidently focussed on the refined standards of his own age, even though he declares that some traces of ancient rusticity still remain.   If a poem[1] is to be artistic, and constructed so as to satisfy the taste of the discerning, its author must be ready to undergo the most patient labour and unremitting toil in its composition.

Now, not only Horace's precepts, but his practice of unweaving[2] constantly the web of his own verse, to attain a more perfect finish, throw some light on his conception of literary composition.   To analyse in full the " limae labor,"[3] as he conceived it, would, I am afraid, only end in a confusion of metaphor, if one were to follow closely the line of the poet's thought.   He demanded a ceaseless process of[4] filing, excision, and polishing, that would remove all redundant elements, restrain excessive floridness, and smooth out roughnesses, though there was always the danger[5] that a poet's vigour might be sapped by a too great solicitude for smoothness.   His ideal, moreover, involved meticulous care in composition.   The beauty of elevated verse, such as is found in Epic poetry or Tragedy, will in part depend on the choice of splendid[6] and sonorous diction, though a poet who aims at grandeur, must always beware of falling into empty bombast.[7]   Horace, however, more than once drives[8] home the lesson that words taken from the speech of common life derive a new beauty from being deftly

The " limae labor "

[1] Ep. II. 2. 109 : " at qui legitimum cupiet fecisse poema," etc.

[2] Sat. II. 3. 2 : " scriptorum quaeque retexens."

[3] A.P. 291 ; in Sat. I. 10. 64, Horace, I believe, uses " limatior " rather with his own conception of the " limae labor " in mind, than the technical sense of " limatus " as a quality of the Plain style (Cic. De Or. III. 31, Or. 20).

[4] The process is well described in Ep. II. 1. 167, II. 2. 122, A.P. 293–294, 440–441, 447 ; cf. Sat. I. 4. 11, I. 10. 69 et seq. ; note Horace's favourite words for the process :—compescere, coercere, deterere, recidere, praesecare, tollere, delere, levare ; Q. X. 4, might be compared.

[5] Cf. A.P. 26 : " sectantem levia nervi deficiunt " ; cf. Q. X. 4. 4 : " ut opus poliat lima, non exterat."

[6] Ep. II. 2. 111 et seq.

[7] Cf. A.P. 27 ; vide infra, p. 481.

[8] A.P. 47, 240 et seq. ; cf. Persius, V. 14 ; vide infra, p. 389.

joined together, and placed in an unusual setting. He had
shown, particularly in his *Odes*, that he himself could
accomplish this, and part of his " curiosa felicitas " may be
attributed to his happy skill[1] in infusing fresh life into
ordinary words, by placing them in new surroundings.
Dionysius[2] of Halicarnassus notes[3] Homer's power of
transmuting commonplace words into things of beauty by
his skill in composition, while amongst prose writers he
emphasises[4] Lysias' faculty of elevating ordinary speech to
a new dignity and splendour.

Horace's theory, as we have seen, would deny to Satire
the title of poetry. The language of the *Satires* was akin

Consistency
of Horace's
principles

to the speech of everyday life, so that the
poet had not to weary himself in the search
for beautiful and sonorous diction. Horace,
however, would bind even the Satiric poet to the conscientious workmanship that would eliminate from his verse
impurities of speech, obscurity, redundancy, and harsh and
unmusical effects. He thus had high ideals in setting up
the standard of Augustan correctness, though it was a
standard that might work unfairly when used[5] to test the
achievements of the Ancients. It is important to note that
there is a unity and consistency about Horace's critical
principles, and that, in his earliest as well as his latest years,
he never ceased to preach to poets the need of unremitting
toil, if they were to attain perfection. In his own case the
finest fruits of the " limae labor " are to be found in what he
himself styles[6] his " operosa carmina."

This lesson of patient[7] toil that aims at faultless elegance

[1] Cf. his use of " deterere," Car. 1. 6. 12 ; " mordet," Car. 1. 31. 8 ;
" reparavit," Car. 1. 37. 24 ; in this respect he was certainly " verbis felicissime audax."

[2] Who, it is interesting to note, lived in Rome for some years of the reign
of Augustus ; Horace may have been acquainted with his teaching.

[3] De C.V. c. 3, *ib.* c. 12 ; note his phrase καλὴ συζυγία, c. 6 ; cf. περὶ
ὕψους, 40. 2–3 ; Ar. Rhet. III. 2. 5, on Euripides' use of words ἐκ τῆς
εἰωθυίας διαλέκτου.

[4] De Lys. 3.   [5] *Vide supra*, p. 292 *et seq.*

[6] Car. IV. 2. 31 ; there was also an " operositas " that might be carried
to excess ; cf. Q. VIII. 3. 55 ; Sen. Controv. II. pr. 1.

[7] Cf. A.P. 291 : " limae labor et *mora* " ; *ib.* 293 ; cf. Ep. I. 20. 3.

and perfection of detail, Horace may well have learnt from
the Roman school of poets that followed
Alexandrian models, though he himself
usually looked for inspiration to the Greek
writers of an earlier age. It is significant[1] that, when insisting on the need for delay in publication that will afford
the poet an opportunity for further revision, he evidently
had before his mind the example[2] of a Neoteric poet, who
valued faultless art so highly that he spent years in polishing
an Epyllion. This was done in the spirit of his Alexandrian
models, who sought to compensate for greatness and range
of subject by imparting to their short poems the sparkling
brilliance of a jewel. But, looking in another direction,
Horace may have learnt a similar lesson of toilsome revision
and quest after perfection from the Atticist orators. Calvus,
who in his poetry was a disciple of the Alexandrians, is
described[3] for us by Cicero as making such unwearied
efforts to banish all impurities of language, tastelessness,
and imperfection from his speeches, that in the end his
style became lifeless and attenuated. The same exquisite
care in composition, which set every word in its appropriate
place, and reproduced almost the perfect pattern of a
mosaic, is noted as a characteristic of Calidius.[4] Messalla[5]
was remarkable for a meticulous striving[6] after finish and
perfection, that may have impaired[7] the vigour of his
eloquence. That the Atticists were the sworn foes of
redundancy is evident from Cicero's anxiety to claim
indulgence for his own " juvenilis redundantia." Their
passion for polish and elegance might, as Cicero maintains,

The Alexan-
drians and the
Atticists

---

[1] *Vide supra*, p. 302.

[2] A.P. 388 : " nonumque prematur in annum membranis intus positis,"
suggestive of the example of Cinna's Zmyrna ; cf. Cat. 95 (with Ellis's notes) ;
Q. X. 4. 4, Suet. De Gr. 18 ; *vide supra*, p. 285.

[3] Br. 283–284 : " metuensque ne vitiosum colligeret, etiam verum
sanguinem deperdebat " ; there was, of course, always the danger that self-
criticism might become morbid ; cf. Q. VIII. pr. 31, X. 3. 10, 7. 14.

[4] *Vide supra*, p. 219.

[5] Horace was evidently an admirer of his oratory ; cf. Sat. I. 10. 29,
A.P. 371.

[6] Tac. Dial. 18. 4 : " in verbis magis elaboratus."

[7] Q. X. 1. 113 : " viribus minor " ; *vide supra*, p. 261.

be misplaced in a genre such as oratory, whose appeal should be essentially popular, but their ideals would be likely[1] to attract the notice of a poet of Horace's temperament.

Though he lays down such rigid rules to guide the poet in his craft, yet Horace, in a spirit of broad toleration, is

The rôle of honest critic

prepared[2] to grant indulgence to certain faults that are incidental to human nature, if they are outweighed by more numerous excellences, just as he is prepared to pardon defects in works of large compass like those of Homer.[3] When, however, he rules[4] out mediocrity in poets, his mind seems to be fixed primarily on perfection of form. The poet must be willing to play[5] the rôle of honest critic with himself, and not be blind to the imperfections of his own creations. Moreover, though as a rule poets are averse[6] to frank criticism, the poet who is striving after artistic finish, must be ready to submit the results of his labours to a candid[7] critic whose judgment is discerning. He must also distinguish between the true[8] friend and the flatterer who, in the spirit of the sycophant, will acclaim the verses of a wealthy patron without scruple, and with a zeal resembling that of hired mourners at a funeral. It was all the more necessary to sound this warning note, as on the one hand there was an epidemic[9] of verse-making in those days, and on the other, even in those quarters[10] where a critical taste

[1] The attempt, however, to prove Horace an " Atticist," I would regard as so much misdirected energy.

[2] A.P. 351 *et seq.*

[3] Cf. the standpoint of the author of the περὶ ὕψους (33. 4), who also does not look for a faultless genius.

[4] A.P. 372, *ib.* 378.

[5] Ep. II. 2. 110.

[6] Ep. II. 1. 222.

[7] A.P. 387, 438 *et seq.*; cf. Ep. I. 4. 1, I. 3, where Horace himself plays the rôle of candid critic; Ovid, Ex Ponto, IV. 12. 25; Statius, Silvae, IV. 7. 25; cf. Hor. Sat. I. 4. 132, for the "liber amicus" in the moral sphere.

[8] A.P. 420–433, a passage in which Horace has some close imitations of Lucilius; *vide supra*, p. 58.

[9] Ep. I. 18. 40, II. 1. 117, A.P. 240 *et seq.*, 382, 416.

[10] Cf. Horace's picture of the guild of poets, Ep. II. 2. 91 *et seq.*; Ep. II. 1. 187, on the Knights' taste in drama.

should prevail, there was a tendency to lavish indiscriminate praise.

The habit of comparison between Greek and Roman writers, as well as the eagerness to exalt[1] the achievements of the Romans, and claim for them equality

Unenlightened criticism with, if not pre-eminence over their Greek counterparts, led to much undiscerning criticism. While we may pardon Propertius' rapturous[2] outburst on the publication of the *Aeneid*, at other times our natural instinct is to withhold assent, when we read[3] of Homeric qualities being attributed to writers, some at least of whom, were it not for a passing reference in a contemporary author, would have passed into the limbo of oblivion. Virgil praises[4] the tragedies of Asinius Pollio as something worthy of being ranked with those of Sophocles, while other poets are acclaimed[5] as if they were the embodiment of the spirit of Hesiod or of Pindar. Horace's own criticisms[6] as a rule show restraint. If he calls[7] Varius a " bird of Homeric song," and couples[8] his name in many places with that of Virgil, it is probable that the tribute was paid to real genius, which in another genre, according to Quintilian, was able to produce a tragedy that could stand comparison with any of the Greeks. His advice to those on the staff of Tiberius who were aspiring to literary fame, shows that he did not wish to scatter indiscriminate praise, and that he realised the magnitude of the task of a Roman poet who set himself to contend with Greek models, especially a model of the range and power of Pindar.[9]

Now the coterie[10] to which Horace belonged, and the

[1] Cf. Cic. Tusc. Disp. I. 1 ; Vell. II. 9.

[2] II. 34. 65.

[3] Cf. Panegyr. Messallae, 180 ; Prop. I. 7. 3 ; Ovid, Ex Ponto, II. 10. 13, IV. 12. 27, *ib*. 16. 6 ; Stat. Sil. V. 3. 26.

[4] Eclog. VIII. 10.

[5] Ovid, Ex Ponto, IV. 16. 28 ; cf. Pliny, Ep. IV. 3. 3.

[6] Cf. Odes, II. 9, on Valgius' Elegies ; contrast Panegyr. Mess. 180 ; Horace's restraint is seen again in Sat. I. 10. 40 *et seq*., Odes, II. 1. 9 *et seq*., on Pollio's tragedies.

[7] Odes, I. 6. 2 ; cf. Sat. I. 10. 44.

[8] Sat. I. 5. 40, I. 6. 55.

[9] Ep. I. 3. 10 *et seq*., Odes, IV. 2 ; cf. Stat. Sil. I. 3. 101, V. 3. 152.

[10] Sat. I. 10. 81 *et seq*., shows how he valued its opinion.

literary circles in which he moved, must have had no little

influence in raising his standard of criticism, and in helping him to keep before his mind the highest ideals in the craft to which he was devoting himself. Through contact with these circles he must have learned the value of candid criticism, and have been impressed with the need of a stern apprenticeship as one of the great preliminaries to success in the poetic art. He gives us glimpses from time to time of the members of the literary group which Maecenas had gathered round him, chief amongst them being Plotius, Varius, Virgil, and Aristius Fuscus.[1] Outside this circle he had friends such as Pollio[2], Messalla, Tibullus, and others,[3] whose common devotion to literature was not impaired by political differences. Horace praises[4] the charming intimacy that existed between Lucilius and the two chief figures in the Scipionic circle, Laelius and Scipio. We can see that a similar spirit of kindliness and mutual forbearance existed between the Augustan poet and his own friends. Though Horace on many occasions showed the independence of his character, yet he boasted[5] that he had lived with the great, and, like Terence in his own day, could say that he had found favour with the chief men of the State, both in times of peace and of war.

The coterie spirit in one respect may have reacted unfavourably on Horace, in producing in him an attitude of

intolerance towards those who did not share the ideals of his own group, while the fact of his having the support of powerful patrons may have helped to engender in him a contempt for the guild of professional poets. Another effect of the same spirit was that he wished to make his primary[6] appeal to the members of his own coterie, and to the literary friends with

---

[1] On Fuscus, cf. Sat. I. 9. 61, Odes, I. 22, Ep. I. 10.

[2] Sat. I. 10. 42 ; cf. *ib.* 84–85 ; note " ambitione relegata," as if Pollio stood on a different footing from the friends just mentioned.

[3] Cf. Sat. I. 4. 141 : " multa poetarum manus."

[4] Sat. II. 1. 71 *et seq.*

[5] Sat. II. 1. 76, Ep. I. 20. 23 ; cf. Ter. Adelphi, Prol. 18.

[6] Sat. I. 4. 23, 73, I. 10. 73, Ep. I. 20. 4 ; cf. Luc. fr. 588 (with Marx's note).

whom he associated, rather than to the public at large, though at times he is clearly desirous[1] of a wider circle of readers. He distrusted the instability[2] of popular judgment in the literary as well as in the moral sphere. Its lack[3] of appreciation for the drama gives a fair measure of the critical taste of the Roman populace, while even the Knights were more absorbed in elaborate[4] stage setting than in the dramatic values of a play. Poetry, moreover, is a delicate creation, the essence of which is too ethereal to be appraised by the common crowd. The ordinary man is, for the most part, too insensible to its beauties to judge[5] whether a poem reaches or falls short of the ideal. Cicero admits[6] the validity of popular judgment, when it is a question of oratory, which must appeal to the public, if it is to fulfil its function, but he tells us that it is only by the learned few that a poem on an abstruse subject can be appreciated. With such ideas prevailing, there was a danger that poetry might become an esoteric possession, " the affair of a literary coterie, or an intellectual caste."[7] This was a conception of the poet's craft that too often dominated the learned circles of the Alexandrians,[8] whose poetry with its love of uncommon themes, its display of erudition, and its solicitude for perfection of technique, seemed especially designed to appeal to a chosen few. It is interesting to note that in later ages the same conception influenced

[1] Cf. Sat. I. 10. 76, Ep. I. 19. 34 ; cf. Luc. frs. 592–595.

[2] Ep. I. 19. 37 ; cf. ib. I. 1. 71 et seq., ib. 76 : " belua multorum es capitum " ; Ep. II. 1. 108.

[3] Ep. II. 1. 177-207.

[4] Ib. 187 et seq. ; cf. Ep. I. 6. 41 ; vide supra, p. 146.

[5] A.P. 263 : " non quivis videt immodulata poemata judex " ; cf., however, Ep. II. 1. 63, where some concession is made to popular taste.

[6] Vide supra, p. 234 ; cf. Br. 191 : " poema enim reconditum paucorum adprobationem, oratio popularis adsensum vulgi debet movere " ; the " poema reconditum " (in spite of the mention of Antimachus) points to the learned poetry of the Alexandrians ; on the value of popular taste in matters artistic, various views were held in antiquity ; cf. Butcher, Harvard Lectures, pp. 177–178, on the different views held by Plato and Aristotle.

[7] Cf. Bailey, Poetry and Commonplace, p. 22.

[8] Cf. Callimachus, fr. 28 : σικχαίνω πάντα τὰ δημόσια; cf. Hor. Ep. I. 3. 11 ; Stemplinger, op. cit., pp. 133–135 ; Susemihl, op. cit., Vol. I. p. 168.

certain theorists who held that poets should look to Classical models for their inspiration. " Especially do I wish," says Du Bellay,[1] " to admonish him who aspires to a more than vulgar glory, to separate himself from such inept admirers, to flee from the ignorant people—the people who are the enemies of all rare and antique learning—and to content himself with few readers, following the example[2] of him who did not demand for an audience anyone besides Plato himself." The Atticists were blamed for endeavouring to establish, even in oratory, a literature of the initiated.[3] It was a similar spirit that inspired Horace's " Odi profanum vulgus," though he, as the " priest[4] of the Muses," could offer as an excuse that he was dealing with mysteries beyond the range of ordinary mortals. Moreover, the poet, if devoted to his art, has to withdraw[5] from the common throng, and can listen best to the voice of inspiration amidst the solitude of caves and woods.

Horace's associations with the literary circles at Rome may thus have bred in him a spirit of intolerance towards

Horace's natural tendencies

rival poets, while it engendered an aristocratic conception of the poet's vocation, and a contempt for popular judgment. It led him, however, to nobler standards in his art, helped him to form his ideals of restraint and correctness, of polish and symmetry in the technique of his verse, so that he was unsparing in his criticism of the poets who fell short of those ideals. But such association, we may assume, only helped to develop what were natural tendencies in the poet's own genius. Maecenas from his position had in a more marked degree the advantages of such association, but could achieve nothing but an " oratio portentosissima,"[6] with its many extravagances both in prose and verse.

[1] *Vide* Spingarn, Literary Criticism, pp. 190–191, on Du Bellay's " Défense"; *ib.* p. 215.   [2] Cf. Cic. Br. 191.

[3] Q. XII. 10. 14 : " haec manus quasi quibusdam sacris initiata "; *vide supra*, p. 226.

[4] Ode. III. 1. 3 ; *vide infra*, p. 487.

[5] Odes, I. 1. 32, III. 25, Ep. II. 2. 77 *et seq.*; cf. Ovid, Trist. I. 1. 41 ; Tac. Dial. c. 9, 12 ; Pliny, Ep. I. 6. 2.

[6] *Vide supra*, p. 328 ; cf. Lunderstedt, op. cit., p. 35 *et seq.*, for fragments of Maecenas' verse.

Horace in his early years aimed especially at defining the law of the Satiric genre, but he also had the merit of raising **The essential** another interesting problem, when he en-**qualities of** deavoured to analyse the essential qualities **poetry** of true poetry[1] in contrast to the genres of Satire and of Comedy. The genuine poet has more than ordinary gifts ; he is endowed with the power of lofty,[2] impassioned, and forcible utterance, while his work is infused by the breath of a divine inspiration. In him can be seen what Wordsworth styles " the spontaneous over-flow of powerful feelings " (" acer spiritus ac vis ").

But Horace is concerned, too, with the formal side of poetry. He here would disagree with Wordsworth's **The diction** theory[3] " that there neither is nor can be **of poetry** any essential difference between the language of prose and metrical composition," and would watch with a sceptical interest the English poet's experiment of choosing " incidents and situations from common life," and his effort to " relate and describe them as far as was possible in a selection of language really used by men." In this theory Wordsworth, besides indulging in what Babbitt calls[4] " Rousseauistic paradoxes," was in reaction[5] against the false poetic diction which became fashionable in the eighteenth century, and which too often was divorced from genuine emotion, and usurped the place of true poetic feeling. Like all theories born of reaction, Wordsworth's was carried to excess, and suffered from overstatement, so that Hazlitt[6] was able to protest against the attempt to reduce the " language of poetry to the standard of common sense and reason." Wordsworth, indeed, was striving to bring his language near to the real language of men but, as his selective process indicates,

[1] Sat. I. 4. 43–44, *ib.* 46.
[2] Lejay ad Sat. I. 4. 44, takes " os magna sonaturum " as referring to the subjects of Epic, Tragedy, and elevated Lyric poetry, but Horace is viewing the problem rather from the standpoint of the poet's endowments.
[3] Preface to the Lyrical Ballads, ed. George, p. 11.
[4] Rousseau and Romanticism, p. 248.
[5] *Vide* Vaughan, The Romantic Revolt, pp. 26, 51 ; Lowes, Convention and Revolt in Poetry, p. 138 *et seq.*
[6] Vaughan, English Literary Criticism, p. 132.

not on the " dead level of ordinary intercourse,"[1] but in
moments of vivid sensation. The fallacies underlying
Wordsworth's theory were exposed by Coleridge,[2] who
showed that the poet's own practice was not in harmony
with his theory. He was able to point to the fact that in
many passages of the *Lyrical Ballads* the language differs
from the " real " (or as Coleridge would suggest the
" ordinary ") language of men, while he insisted that, even
if it were conceded that it did not differ, the added charm of
metrical language makes an essential change[3] in the situation.

In the light of such speculations there is an additional
interest attached to Dionysius'[4] analysis of a passage from
the *Odyssey*,[5] the diction of which he main-
Dionysius on tains is composed of the " most ordinary
the Odyssey and humblest words, such as might have
been used offhand by a farmer, a seafaring man, or an
artisan, who set no store by beauty of speech." Though
the style of the passage is generally simple, yet Dionysius'
contention is somewhat naive, as Homer uses several words[6]
that would not occur in ordinary speech, and which contributed not a little to the beauty of the lines. But apart from
such words, Dionysius' position is sound, when he emphasises the spell cast upon the ear by such a passage,[7] the
secret of which mainly resides in the metrical arrangement
of common words, out of which a strange and appealing
harmony is woven. In connection with his own theory,
Wordsworth made one important reservation (which would

---

[1] Cf. Pater, Appreciations, Wordsworth, p. 50.

[2] Cf. Biographia Literaria, c. XIV–XXII ; Saintsbury, op. cit., Vol. III.
pp. 203–214 ; F. W. H. Myers, Wordsworth, p. 106 *et seq.*

[3] However, Wordsworth himself would agree that metre made a difference.

[4] De C.V. c. 3 ; cf. Rhys Roberts ad loc.

[5] XVI. 1–16.

[6] e.g. ὑφορβός, ὑλακόμωροι, αἴθοπα ; Homer, of course, was not
afraid of the ordinary word ; cf. Dio Chrys. Or. 55. 10.

[7] The incidents described here by Homer are comparatively ordinary,
but with the genius of the true poet he has succeeded in " discommoning the
common " ; cf. Saintsbury, op. cit. II. p. 511 ; Bailey, op. cit. p. 5 ; as
Virgil puts it : " In tenui labor, at tenuis non gloria."

be strongly endorsed by Dionysius), when he declared that
" if metre be superadded, a dissimilitude will be produced
altogether sufficient for the gratification of the rational
mind."

Now Horace believed that a new beauty and suggestiveness could be imparted to common words by a skilful[1]
setting, but he demanded something more

Selection in language from the poet. Dominated as he was by
the concept of Decorum, he considered
that Satire and Comedy found their natural
medium of expression in the speech of ordinary life. But
it is not enough[2] for the poet to write in the strain of Satire
or Comedy. It is evident, too, that Horace is looking[3] for
something more than the " language of genuine emotion,
as it comes warm from the lips of suffering men and
women."[4] Though skill in composition may do much to
transform common speech, yet for poetry Horace cannot[5]
rest satisfied with ordinary words alone that lack ornateness. Generally speaking, the poet must exercise[6] a
principle of selection, and will reject words that are un-
impressive and wanting in vigour and stateliness, though
at the same time he will be able to conceal the natural
harshness of certain words by an appropriate[7] collocation.
Here we are reminded of the principles that guided Dante,[8]
who evidently did not believe in the theory that there is no
essential difference between the language of prose and
poetry. He demanded of the poet " gravitas sententiae,
superbia carminum, constructionis elatio, excellentia ver-

[1] Cf. Boileau, L'Art Poét : " D'un mot mis en sa place enseigna le
pouvoir."

[2] Sat. I. 4. 54 : " non satis est puris versum perscribere verbis " ; cf.
Arist. Poet. 22. 1.

[3] In Sat. I. 4. 48–53, examples of real emotion are given which Horace
does not consider poetical.

[4] Shairp, Aspects of Poetry, p. 19.

[5] Cf. A.P. 234 (where he is dealing with the style of the Satyric drama) :
" non ego inornata et dominantia nomina solum . . . amabo."

[6] Cf. the important passage, Ep. II. 2. 111–123 ; the poet will reject
words " parum splendoris, sine pondere, virtute carentia."

[7] *Vide infra*, p. 478.

[8] In the " De Vulgari Eloquentia " ; cf. Saintsbury, op. cit. I. p. 436
et seq. ; Warren, Essays of Poets and Poetry, p. 160.

borum." In the choice of a poetic vocabulary Dante expects[1] the poet to be rigid in his selection, and to make use of the sieve to winnow the noblest words in the language. Horace, while in favour of selecting the best words available from existing speech, evidently felt the need also of some extension of the poet's vocabulary, but, as he was nurtured in a purist atmosphere, his precepts for such extension do not concede much freedom to the poet. He urges[2] him to use archaic words, and to reinstate some of the beautiful old words that once were current in Rome, and have now fallen into decay.[3] Though to support his commendation of him who enriches the mother tongue, he invokes[4] the name of Ennius, yet in practice he himself, in common with the poets of his time, rejects almost entirely the compounds[5] which served as one of the great ornaments of Roman verse in its earliest development, and which were not disdained by such poets as Lucretius and Catullus. The poets of the early period, as we have seen, were endeavouring to grapple with the problem of creating a poetical vocabulary, though some[6] of them were unfortunate in the new formations they attempted. Horace will allow[7] the poet to adopt new words, or use words of his own minting, but this is a licence that must be sparingly[8] used, and will be most effective, if the new coinages are modelled on the analogy[9] of the Greek. In the purist

---

[1] De Vulg. Eloq. II. 7 : " sola vocabula nobilissima in cribro tuo residere curabis " ; " ad exacervanda egregia verba te cribriare oportet " ; cf. E. Gardner, Dante as Literary Critic, p. 92.

[2] Ep. II. 2. 115 ; on Horace's own use of archaisms, cf. Waltz, op. cit., p. 41 et seq. ; Ruckdeschel, op. cit., especially p. 37 et seq.

[3] A.P. 61–70 ; on the process of decay in language, vide supra, p. 81.

[4] A.P. 56.

[5] Horace himself uses " centimanus " and " tauriformis " ; cf. Sikes,, op. cit., p. 228 et seq., who, I find, has already touched on some of the points raised in this section ; Norden, ad Aen. VI. 141 ; Hardie, The Culex, Cl. Q. Jan. 1920, p. 25 et seq.

[6] Vide supra, p. 83.

[7] Ep. II. 2. 119, A.P. 50 et seq. ; Cicero would probably allow a larger licence than Horace to the poet ; cf. De Or. I. 70, Or. 202 ; vide infra, p. 446.

[8] Vide supra, p. 91.

[9] Vide Waltz, op. cit., pp. 83–85, for illustrations from Horace's own works.

atmosphere of the Augustan age one might say with Ben Jonson[1] that "a man coynes not a new word without some perill and lesse fruit ; for, if it happen to be received, the praise is but moderate ; if refus'd, the scorne is assured."

Horace, then, recognised that poetry had in a measure a language of its own, but in his efforts to extend the poet's

Horace and "poetic" diction

vocabulary, he was far from wishing to create a stilted and artificial poetic diction, or to break[2] with the spoken[3] language. In his experiments with speech, he looks for guidance to the arbitrament of custom.[4] The spoken language then is to be the foundation for the poet, but, if it is to serve as a fitting medium for the poet's thoughts, it must be refined and sublimated, given a new force and suggestiveness by a skilful setting, while a judicious infusion of the rare word will help to impart to it beauty and distinction.

There was, of course, always the risk that the quest of the uncommon word might lead to artificiality. The poets,

The danger of artificiality

in their efforts to embellish and lend impressiveness to their style, were fond of employing compound words, but the use of long and elaborate compounds was felt to be suited especially to the genius of Dithyrambic[5] poetry, which often developed a language that bordered on the grotesque. The

---

[1] Spingarn, Critical Essays, Vol. I, p. 37 ; Ben evidently had in mind Q. I. 5. 71.

[2] Ronsard, who in his own day wished to enlarge the poetic vocabulary of France, laid it down as a principle that ordinary speech is not to be banished from poetry ; cf. Spingarn, Literary Criticism, p. 226 ; on the problem before the Pléiade, cf. Wyndham, Essays, Ronsard and La Pléiade, p. 65 *et seq. ;* Gosse, Malherbe, pp. 12, 21 ; on Opitz and a similar problem, cf. Perry, From Opitz to Lessing, p. 29.

[3] Cf. Jensen, op. cit., p. 157, on the dictum that " the poet's language should be an imitation of ordinary speech " ; Stoic influence seems evident from the context.

[4] Ep. II. 2. 119, A.P. 71–72 ; " usus " evidently refers primarily to the usage of the spoken language in cultured circles, but Horace would also naturally take into account literary usage ; we have seen that a similar problem arose in connection with Cicero's appeal to " consuetudo " ; *vide supra,* p. 79.

[5] Ar. Poet. c. 22, 1459. a. 9, with Bywater's note ; cf. Philodemus fr. (there quoted) ; *vide supra,* p. 91.

need for idealisation in language was felt particularly in Tragedy,[1] but writers sometimes assumed that the more remote the language of the Tragic drama was from that of ordinary life, the nearer it approached the ideal. Aeschylus[2] had developed a Tragic style which to many seemed swollen and bombastic. The efforts[3] of Pacuvius and Accius to create a diction worthy of the dignity of Tragedy, had resulted in a language that was often contorted and ludicrous, but at least they paid tribute to the necessity for Tragedy of a garb that was neither commonplace nor mean. Horace realised that a drama wholly arrayed in such language must appear artificial and unreal, and taking into account the law of sincerity in style, he declares[4] that Tragedy must not always indulge in high-sounding speech, but must at times express its emotions in the language of ordinary life, if it wishes to touch the hearts of the spectators. Euripides, in harmony with the bent of his genius towards realism, has, especially in his later plays,[5] aimed to bring his language near to the level of current speech.

But, apart even from the drama, there was in other directions a tendency to emphasise the isolated[6] and exclusive character of the poet's language, or at least to hold that there were many words used by the poets which could not be legitimately introduced into sober prose. The theorists on Rhetoric looked at the problem from their own peculiar standpoint. Cicero notes[7] the difference between the writers of prose

The licence of the poet

[1] Cf. Ar. Frogs, 1059; the law of Decorum would demand a stately language for the stately characters of Tragedy; cf. Philod. Poet. Col. XXXII, Jensen, p. 71; Vaughan, English Literary Criticism, Introd. p. 40; *vide infra*, p. 404.

[2] Frogs, 940 *et seq.*, 1004; περὶ ὕψους, III. 1; Hor. A.P. 280: " et docuit (i.e. Tragedy) magnumque loqui." [3] *Vide supra*, p. 49 *et seq.*

[4] A.P. 95 *et seq.;* the " sesquipedalia verba " may well refer to the inflated diction of the earlier Roman dramatists, though Horace may be glancing also at some contemporary efforts in Tragedy; cf. Ep. I. 3. 14.

[5] Frogs, 959 *et seq.;* cf. Ar. Rh. III. 2. 5; Hor. A.P. 96–97, seems to have Euripides especially in mind.

[6] Ar. Rh. III. 1. 9: ἀλλ' ἑτέρα λόγου καὶ ποιήσεως λέξις ἐστίν; cf. Poseidonius' definition of poetry, Diog. Laert. VII. 60.

[7] De Or. II. 61, *ib.* I. 128: " verba prope poetarum "; Or. 163: " sed ea (verba) non ut poetae exquisita ad sonum."

and " poetas omnino quasi alia quadam lingua locutos."
He may proclaim at times the affinity between the poet and
the orator, but he is careful to emphasise the greater licence
in language conceded to the poet.   Many prose writers of
the Silver Age[1] were censured[2] not only for imitating the
poets in their choice of words, but for borrowing from them
their gaudiest ornament, which judicious critics considered
to be altogether alien to the spirit of prose.   All these
criticisms bear evidence of a consciousness that the poets
spoke a language of their own, a language indeed that was
purged of all dross, that was highly coloured and imaginative, and that served as the proper medium for the poet's
thoughts in the idealised world of his own creation.

There was always the danger, however, that some might
carry such tendencies to extremes, and set up too great a
line of cleavage between the poet's diction
The " voces a
plebe semotae" and the spoken language, while others might
regard the employment of such diction as
the distinguishing mark of the poet, regardless of the inner
spirit of his work.   Petronius' dictum[3] on the language of
poetry is well known : " refugiendum est ab omni verborum, ut ita dicam, vilitate,[4] et sumendae voces a plebe
semotae, ut fiat ' odi profanum vulgus et arceo.' "   This,
if rigidly interpreted, sounds like a plea for the language of
a coterie, and seems to favour a stereotyped and artificial
poetic diction, while ignoring the fact that the spoken
speech must serve as the foundation[5] on which the poet
may " build his lofty rhyme."   A poet like Statius could
exhibit in abundance the " voces a plebe semotae," but he
also showed what an exotic structure could be raised, where
such elements predominate.   Amongst certain of the
Alexandrian poets, the taste for artificial diction went so

[1] Though Aper (Tac. Dial. 20. 19) says : " exigitur jam ab oratore
poeticus decor " ; *vide supra*, p. 341.
[2] *Vide infra*, p. 444.
[3] Satyr. 118.
[4] Petronius is evidently aiming especially at excluding vulgarisms from
poetry ; cf. Hor. A.P. 247.
[5] Cf. Lowes, op. cit., p. 118 *et seq.*, for some interesting remarks that
have a bearing here.

far that Philetas[1] compiled a lexicon of unusual poetical
words. Dionysius, though he evidently realised the magic
with which common speech could be invested by the genius
of a great poet, speaks[2] of a " poetical vocabulary of rare,
foreign, figurative, and coined words." Aristotle touches
the heart of the matter, when he declares[3] that a style composed wholly of such language would be either a riddle or
a barbarous jargon, though he himself seems to encourage
artificiality in recommending[4] different classes of words as
suited to different poetic genres. He safeguards himself,
however, by enjoining moderation as the golden rule in the
employment of all such devices. Now, from all this discussion it is clear that Horace and the Ancients generally
recognised a distinction between the language of prose and
that of poetry. Some were even inclined to widen overmuch the breach between the two. Horace, while he
looked for beauty and distinction in the poet's style, would
set his face against artificiality, and against any break with
the spoken language. The poet can best achieve his
effects by exercising a principle of selection in his choice of
diction, and by a skilful setting of ordinary words, while in
his use of the rare word he must above all observe the law
of moderation.

When dealing with the style of Satire, Horace incidentally raised the interesting problem whether verse is necessarily poetry. Citing the example of Comedy,
Is verse neces- which deals with ordinary subjects in every-
sarily poetry ? day language, he concludes[5] that a composition in verse need not necessarily be
poetry. Aristotle, for whom " imitation " and the universal-
ising power of poetry were the essential elements, had
already insisted on the same truth, when he declared[6] that

[1] *Vide* Sandys, A History of Classical Scholarship, I. p. 118.

[2] De C.V. c. 25.

[3] Poet. XXII. 2, 1458a.

[4] *Ib.* 1459a ; compound words are suited to the dithyramb, rare words
to heroic poetry, metaphor to iambic verse.

[5] Sat. I. 4. 54.

[6] Poet. I. 1447b ; cf. IX. 1451b ; Plut. De aud. poet. 16 C. ; cf., however, Ar. Rh. III. 8. 3, where he styles every composition in verse a poem (but
not necessarily poetry).

Empedocles, even though he wrote in verse, was a physicist[1] rather than a poet. Certain of the Roman critics showed their appreciation of the possible distinction between verse and poetry. Cicero remarks[2] that if the compositions of the " Lyric " poets were deprived of their musical accompaniment, they would descend almost to the level of mere prose. It was not uncommon to regard[3] the *Pharsalia* of Lucan as the work of a historian rather than a poet. Quintilian evidently wished to emphasise the distinction between verse and poetry, when he characterised[4] Cornelius Severus as a better versifier than poet.

Horace in his discussion of the problem has the merit of endeavouring to penetrate to the essential nature **The " disjecti** of great poetry, and of recognising the **membra** imaginative power of the true poet, and his **poetae "** capacity for uttering great thoughts. Many ancient critics were too much inclined to fix their attention on the merely formal element in the poet, though they often showed their regard for the inner spirit of poetry when studying the secret of the sublimity that characterised a writer such as Plato.[5] But, though the distinction between verse and poetry was generally appreciated, the further problem arose whether verse was essential, if a poet was to attain to the highest expression of his thoughts. The passage from Ennius, quoted by Horace[6] as an example of true poetry, would strike one as somewhat rhetorical in character. Horace may have been impressed by the metaphor[7] in " belli ferratos postes," or by the personifica-

---

[1] Cf. Coleridge's distinction between Poetry and Science ; Cicero seems to have had some such idea in De Fin. IV. 10.

[2] Or. 183–184 ; the statement, of course, shows little appreciation of the work of such poets.

[3] Mart. XIV. 194 ; Servius ad Aen. I. 382 ; Schol. ad Phars. I. 1 ; cf. Q. X. 1. 90 ; *vide infra*, p. 418.

[4] X. 1. 89.

[5] *Vide infra*, p. 442.

[6] Sat. I. 4. 60.

[7] As Sikes suggests, op. cit., p. 224 ; several of the modern commentators (e.g. Lejay, Mueller) refer to the spondaic effects as the attraction in the lines, but if we are to follow out logically the line of Horace's thought, we should look for elements independent of metre.

tion of Discordia as a Fury of war, but whatever it was in the passage that appealed to him, he declares that, if the metrical form of these lines be dissolved, we still will find the " disjecti membra poetae." One may legitimately stress the phrase, and argue that, if after the dissolution we find only the " disjecti membra poetae," in Horace's eyes metre contributes something towards the beauty and perfection of the poet's work.

Amongst the Greeks, Plato,[1] Isocrates, and Aristotle, all pay ample tribute to the magic power of verse to cast its spell over its hearers, though Aristotle at times seems to waver[2] on the importance of the melody of verse as a factor that enhances the force of the poet's appeal. Isocrates, indeed, declares that even the most famous poems, if robbed of their metrical form, will sink in our estimation. The change thus effected is likened by Plato to the fading of the bloom[3] on a youthful countenance. Dionysius, in dealing with the passage in Homer already referred to, remarks that the poet is employing the humblest and most ordinary words, which are given a new charm by their metrical setting. If, he declares,[4] the metre is broken up, these same lines will appear commonplace and unworthy of admiration. Cicero has an interesting parallel to this discussion, when he points[5] out how the beauty of a period in prose is marred, if one breaks up the periodic structure, and eliminates the rhythmical effects. Incidentally, he pays homage to the charm imparted to words by a metrical arrangement, when he remarks[6] how the raw material of language can be moulded like wax into many shapes both in prose and poetry according to the fancy of the writer, who can make his words subservient

The magic of verse

[1] Rep. X. 601 B.; Isocr. Evag. 10–11; Ar. Rh. III. 4. 3.

[2] *Vide* Butcher, Aristotle's Theory, etc., pp. 134–135; Prickard, Aristotle on the Art of Poetry, pp. 60–63, 98 *et seq.*

[3] Cf. Dionys. De C.V. c. 25.

[4] De C.V. c. 3 : λυθέντος γοῦν τοῦ μέτρου φαῦλα φανήσεται τὰ αὐτά ταῦτα καὶ ἄζηλα; cf. *ib.* c. 4, *ib.* c. 25, where he again stresses the importance of metre.

[5] Or. 232–235; Philod. περὶ ποιημ. fr. 64 (quoted by Kroll ad loc.); cf. Demetr. 46.

[6] De Or. III. 177 ; cf. *ib.* 174, Or. 174.

to the pleasure of the ear, and expressive of every emotion. There were some,[1] indeed, according to Cicero, who were inclined to neglect the content, and consider the musical power of verse the predominant element in poetry. It is interesting to find a similar criticism in Cicero's contemporary, Philodemus. He carried[2] on a polemic against certain theorists who seemed to attach undue importance to the element of εὐφωνία, making the ear the standard of judgment in poetry, and minimising the value of the thought. Ariston[3] and Heracleodorus[4] thus come under the lash of his criticism, as does Andromen ides,[5] who regarded it as the poet's primary duty to acquire " the rhythms and harmony of the Muses." But, apart from the atmosphere of polemic, all this is a recognition of the spell cast on the hearer by the music[6] of verse. We may finally add the testimony of Seneca, who dwells[7] on the power which poetry, as compared with prose, possesses of rendering impressive thoughts still more impressive.

In all this we find the germs of a debate that has been waged hotly in modern times, on the relative importance of verse in poetry. Sidney[8] maintained that it **Is verse essen-** was " but an ornament and no cause to **tial to poetry ?** poetry," while Coleridge in one of his changing[9] moods held that the " highest kind of poetry can exist

---

[1] Or. 68 : " vocibus magis quam rebus inserviunt " ; Philodemus combats the view that οἱ ἀγαθοὶ ποιηταὶ παρ' οὐδέν ἄλλο πρωτεύουσιν ἢ . . . παρὰ τοῦ ἤχους ; here, of course, the choice of sonorous words may be in question, as well as the metrical effects ; cf. Jensen, op. cit., p. 59 ; vide infra, pp. 478–479.

[2] Vide Jensen, op. cit., p. 157, Text, pp. 43, 55–59, where the κριτικοί are censured.

[3] Ib. p. 137 et seq. ; cf. Text, pp. 43, 47.

[4] Ib. 147–148, Text, p. 49 ; cf. Kroll, Die historische Stellung, etc., pp. 85–86.

[5] Jensen, p. 149 et seq.

[6] Of course, as I have said, we would here have also to take into account the choice of beautiful and sonorous words.

[7] Ep. 108. 10 : " sic sensus nostros clariores carminis arta necessitas efficit " ; the whole passage (6–11) should be noted.

[8] Vide Saintsbury, op. cit., II. 172 et seq.

[9] He was of another mind when he declared that " metre is the proper form of poetry " ; cf. Saintsbury, III. 211–212.

without metre." Others, going to the opposite extreme, show comparative indifference to the matter of poetry, while they prize so highly verbal melody, that they will even allow the poet's intellect to relax its keenness, and lose itself in a flood of emotion, that is often sustained only by the more sensuous elements of the verse. By many,[1] however, the saner view was taken that verse, though not *the* essential, might yet be considered *an* essential in the highest kind of poetry ; for, by its musical qualities, its power of imparting colour and suggestiveness, it is capable of giving the poet's words an added beauty and significance.

One of the marked characteristics of Classical criticism is the tendency to criticise by Kinds. A large number of poetic genres were tabulated[2] such as Tragedy, Comedy,[3] Epic, Lyric, Pastoral poetry, Satire, Elegy, Epigram, to mention but the chief kinds that figure in Roman criticism. These kinds were distinguished sometimes by their form, sometimes by their content.[4] It was customary to endeavour to formulate the law of each genre (" lex operis "),[5] which determined the characteristics to be exhibited by all who laboured in the genre. In conformity with the law of Decorum, each genre was marked off from the others as having a special character and rules of its own.

Criticism by Kinds

Now there are certain broad divisions of poetic literature,

---

[1] *Vide* Lewes, The Principles of Success in Literature, pp. 192–193 ; Saintsbury, II. p. 86, on Castelvetro's dictum that " verse is a kind of inseparable accident of poetry " ; *ib.* p. 96, for an interesting analysis of Patrizzi's views ; cf. Dante's definition of poetry as " fictio rhetorica versificata in musicaque composita," De Vulg. Eloq. II. 4.

[2] Cf. Hor. Sat. I. 10. 36 *et seq.*, Ep. II. 2. 59, A.P. 73 *et seq. ;* Tac. Dial. 10 ; Pliny, Ep. VI. 21. 4 (on Mimiambi) ; Stat. Silv. I. 3. 101 *et seq.*, V. 3. 91 *et seq. ;* Mart. III. 20. 5 *et seq.*, XII. 94.

[3] Cic. De opt. gen. I. 3, distinguishes Comedy and Tragedy generically.

[4] Tac. loc. cit. is thinking primarily of the content ; cf. " elegorum lascivias, iamborum amaritudinem, epigrammatum lusus " ; cf. Mart. VII. 25. 1 *et seq.*

[5] Hor. Sat. II. 1. 2 ; cf. A.P. 86 : " descriptas servare vices operumque colores " ; *ib.* 135 ; Cic. De opt. gen. I. 1 (after the enumeration of various genres) : " suum cujusque est, diversum a reliquis " ; Q. X. 2. 22 : " sua cuique proposita lex, suus cuique decor est " ; Pliny, Ep. IV. 14. 5 ; Juv. VII. 102 ; Mart. Proem. Bk. I, I. 35. 10.

such as those that distinguish it into Epic, Lyric, and
Dramatic poetry. These divisions are a

The division of genres reflex of the poet's attitude to life, and an
indication as to whether his impulse in his
work comes predominantly from the external world, or from
the world of his own emotions. Plato in the *Ion*[1] brings the
genres into relation with his doctrine of inspiration. Each
one is able to compose that to which the Muse has inspired
him, whether it be a Dithyramb, a laudatory Ode, a Dance-
song, an Epic or Iambic poem. But at other times, when[2]
he is concerned with the effect of imitative poetry on the
citizens of his Ideal State, he classifies the genres according
to the extent to which dramatic imitation enters into each.
Aristotle, too, proposes[3] to treat of the several kinds of
poetry on the basis of "Imitation," though he uses[4] the
word in a wider sense than Plato. As in the case of the
imitative arts generally, he distinguishes the genres according as they differ in the means, the objects, and the manner
of imitation.

Aristotle, however, cannot be accused of holding the
doctrine of Kinds rigidly. He recognises the development

Aristotle and the doctrine of Kinds of one genre from another—Comedy from
the Phallic songs, Tragedy from the Dithy-
ramb. He leaves open the question whether
Tragedy has yet perfected its proper "types,"[5] though he
realises its slow development, and seems to suggest that
after many changes it has arrived at its natural form.
Within the sphere of Tragedy itself, he notes without surprise how Euripides broke away from the pomp of Aeschylus towards a more realistic treatment of the drama, while
he records Agathon's success in abandoning the traditional
themes of tragedy, and treating a plot of his own invention.
He, however, condemns Agathon's practice of making his

[1] 533–534.

[2] Rep. 392 D *et seq.*

[3] Poet. c. I–III.

[4] Aristotle is not always consistent in his use of the word ; cf. Bywater
ad Poet. I. 1447a. 16.

[5] Poet. 4. 1449a ; there is some doubt about the meaning Aristotle attaches
to εἴδη in this passage ; I follow Butcher rather than Bywater, who takes
εἴδη in the unusual sense of "constitutive elements."

Choral odes mere interludes instead of an integral portion of the drama, as he wished to uphold above all the fundamental rule of the Unity of Action. Aristotle was in fact endeavouring to draw up, especially for the two genres of Epic and Tragedy, working rules that were based largely on the practice of Homer and the great Greek dramatists. Though Scaliger[1] grandiloquently styles him " imperator noster, omnium bonarum artium perpetuus dictator," Aristotle had no wish to become a literary dictator, or to make the " law of the genre " fixed and irrevocable, as it became in the interpretation of so many of the Neo-Classical critics, for whom the " Rules " were sacrosanct, and to be disregarded by the poet only at the peril of complete failure. Aristotle, indeed, would have marvelled at Lessing's verdict on the *Poetics* as a " work, which I do not hesitate to avow that I consider as infallible as the elements of Euclid." Dryden was nearer the mark when he declared[2] that " if Aristotle had seen ours (i.e. plays), he might have changed his mind." The Greek critic in fact, in distinguishing the genres, and in endeavouring to formulate rules for them, was considering the normal ways in which man's emotional experience finds expression, and was at the same time keeping his attention fixed on the practice of the foremost writers of Greece. He would thus hardly endorse the statement of a modern[3] student of the problem that " for each genre or εἶδος, there exists a distinct law of perfect form," nor again, with his continual reference to the practice of the Greek poets, would he accept the view[4] that the " laws of the genres are nothing but the expression in the sphere of literature of the Platonic doctrine of ideal forms." It is clear that in Aristotle's view the genres were evolved by a process of slow development, which is best exemplified in the case of Tragedy, where new experiments[5] were tried, and successive writers contributed

[1] Poet. Epin. I. 357.

[2] In " Heads of an answer to Rymer " ; cf. Saintsbury, II. p. 397.

[3] Hack, The Doctrine of Literary Forms, Harvard Studies, XXVII, p. 22 ; Hack is, of course, expounding what he regards as the dominant view in ancient criticism.

[4] *Ib.* p. 43.

[5] Cf. Rhet. III. 1. 9, on the change from the Trochaic tetrameter to

their quota to bring it to perfection. In face of this it cannot, I think, be said that Aristotle would be likely to insist on a rigorous interpretation of the " law of the genre." The real evil arose when later critics erected into inflexible laws, often mechanically applied, what in him were primarily meant to be rules for guidance drawn from experience, and from the practice of the foremost writers.

Velleius has an interesting chapter[1] in which he touches on the rise of genres to maturity and perfection, and their subsequent decline. When under the in-

The rise of new genres fluence of great masters a genre is brought to perfection, succeeding writers are fired to emulation, but in despair of surpassing or even equalling their predecessors, they seek out new[2] fields in which to labour. New genres are thus developed both in prose and poetry, while often a prose[3] genre is evolved as a counterpart to a poetic one that is similar in character. The Alexandrians[4] in particular developed a number of new genres in poetry. As it was their lot to be cast into rivalry with the great masterpieces of Classical Greece, they aimed at novelty[5] by experimenting with new metrical forms, and by searching for unworked material in the by-paths of learning, though even the Alexandrians felt the binding force of tradition.[6] One would imagine that, having modified the old genres and invented new ones, they would have been slow to enact uncompromising laws for the government of the various genres. The custom, however,

Iambic verse; Poet. IV. 1449a (on Tragedy): κατὰ μικρὸν ηὐξήθη προαγόντων ὅσον ἐγίγνετο φανερὸν αὐτῆς, κ.τ.λ.

[1] I. 17; the chapter in some of its aspects might be compared with Brunetière, L'Evolution des Genres, pp. 11–26; vide supra. pp. 201, 269.

[2] " Velut occupatam reliquens materiam quaerit novam "; Velleius here seems to lay stress chiefly on " materia."

[3] Cf. Norden, A.K. I. pp. 78, 91 et seq., on the interrelation of θρῆνος and λόγος ἐπιτάφιος, of Epic and History; ib. pp. 132–133, on the development of new genres in Asia Minor; à propos of the development of genres, cf. Leo, Die griechisch–röm. Biographie, p. 90 et seq., on the relation of Encomium and Biography; vide infra, p. 494.

[4] Vide Stemplinger, op. cit., pp. 271–272.

[5] Hor. Ep. II. 1. 90 et seq., bears witness to the general love of novelty amongst the Greeks.

[6] Cf. Callimachus, fr. 442: ἀμάρτυρον οὐδέν ἀείδω.

amongst Alexandrian critics of drawing up Canons of the great Classical writers of Greece, and thus of helping to invest their works and methods with regulative authority in each genre, must have contributed not a little towards a rigid interpretation of the " lex operis." It was felt that the practice of writers who had attained to such pre-eminence, could not be safely ignored by succeeding generations.

Now, Alexandrian influence in turn reacted upon Roman criticism. Accius in the *Didascalica*[1] treated of the various

The influence of Alexandrian criticism

poetic genres, and emphasised their complete distinctness, but the few fragments of the work that remain, fail to reveal how he dealt with the laws that governed the different kinds of poetry. It is clear even from the scanty remains of Lucilius that, in the spirit of Alexandrian criticism, he was endeavouring to formulate the law of the Satiric genre, and to define the character of its style and humour within certain limits. Horace sought to formulate the law of Satire with still greater precision, or rather to reinterpret the " lex operis "[2] in the light of Augustan conditions. It is evident that both Lucilius and Horace, especially in endeavouring to define the style of Satire, had before their minds the conception of Comedy that was commonly propounded in literary theory.

This conception is in itself worthy of attention, as in it we can see the gradual development and hardening of the

Comedy and Tragedy

law of a genre. The definition of Comedy as a " species vitae "[3] was based above all on a study of the New Comedy, which arose when, after the decay of political life in Greece, interest had shifted from the State to the individual. In harmony with this fundamental conception, the style of Comedy was to be akin to the language of everyday life, and avoid anything

---

[1] Fr. 8, Funaioli, op. cit., p. 27 : " nam quam varia sint genera poematorum, Baebi, quamque longe distincta alia ab aliis, nosce " ; *vide supra*, p. 51.

[2] The phrase, as we saw, is his own ; cf. A.P. 135, Sat. II. 1. 2.

[3] *Vide* Kaibel, op. cit., p. 11 : ἡ δὲ κωμῳδία πλάσματα περιέχει βιωτικῶν πραγμάτων; *ib.* pp. 17, 21, 57, for other definitions ; *vide supra*, p. 374 ; Alcidamas, Ar. Rh. III. 3. 4, called the Odyssey καλὸν ἀνθρωπίνου βίου κάτοπτρον, but seems to have used the phrase rather in the allegorical sense, as in the Middle Ages the Aeneid was called a mirror of human life.

approaching " tragica celsitudo."[1]   From the same fundamental conception sprang the prescriptions for the characters[2] of Comedy, wherein humble persons of private
station should figure in contradistinction to the heroes,
leaders, and kings, that are depicted by the writers of
Tragedy.   It is clear that Horace in several[3] passages had
before his mind the conception of Comedy as thus expounded, though he recognises that Comedy may at times
rise above the dull level of ordinary speech.   The conditions
for Comedy, as thus laid down, are an advance on Aristotle's[4]
simple dicta on the genre.   Influenced especially by their
study of the New Comedy, critics had begun to make the
" laws " of Comedy at once more complex and more rigid
as regards matter, style, and the characters portrayed.
Plato had already[5] set Comedy and Tragedy in strong
antithesis, when he declared that the same person could
not be successful in both.   The irreconcilable nature of
the two genres, and the impassable barrier that separated
them, were proclaimed more emphatically by later critics,[6]
who would have agreed with Addison in styling the " Gothic
invention of Tragi-Comedy[7] one of the most monstrous[8]
inventions that ever entered a poet's thought," or with

[1] Cf. Evanthius on Terence, Wessner, Donatus, Vol. I. p. 20 ; *vide
supra*, p. 25.

[2] Kaibel, op. cit., p. 10, *ib*. p. 58 : " in tragoedia introducuntur heroes,
duces, reges, in comoedia humiles atque privatae <personae> " ; *ib*. pp. 64,
66, 72 ; cf. Q. XI. 3. 74 ; Funaioli, op. cit., p. 321.

[3] Sat. I. 4. 45 *et seq*., I. 10. 40–41, Ep. II. 1. 168 *et seq*., A.P. 89 *et seq*.,
237 *et seq*.

[4] Poet. II. 1448a. 15, V. 1449a. 1.

[5] Rep. 395 A ; cf. Laws, 816 D–E, on the nature of Comedy ; however,
in the Symposium (223 D) Socrates argues that a man could be skilled in
both, on the principle that one should have a knowledge not only of a thing,
but of its opposite.

[6] Cf. Hor. A.P. 89–92 ; Cic. De opt. gen. I. 1 : " itaque et in tragoedia
comicum vitiosum est et in comoedia turpe tragicum " ; Mart. VIII. 3. 13.

[7] Plautus seems to have been the first Roman to use the term, thus describing his Amphitruo (Prol. 59), on account of its mingling of persons
proper both to Tragedy and Comedy ; cf. Lessing, H. Dram. p. 395 ; *vide
supra*, p. 26 ; Moulton, The Ancient Classical Drama, pp. 434–435.

[8] Cf. Ovid, Trist. II. 409 : " est et in obscoenos commixta tragoedia
risus " ; however, *vide infra*, p. 407, n. 5.

Lessing in calling it " no less a monster[1] than Pasiphae's Minotaur." The principle of Decorum arose to forbid the banns on any contemplated union of Tragedy and Comedy. The laws of the two genres were worked out so as to stand in direct opposition. As to the characters that should figure in Tragedy, Aristotle[2] had already given the cue, especially when he put the personages of Tragedy and Epic on a footing of equality. Amongst other characteristics, he required that the ideal Tragic hero be a person of great renown and prosperity like Oedipus or Thyestes, or the illustrious men from such families. As usual, later critics set out to give greater definiteness to Aristotle's somewhat vague prescription, and to apply it with all the rigour of an established law. In Comedy, we are told,[3] " humilium domuum fortunae comprehendebantur, non ut in tragoedia publicarum regiarumque." " In tragoedia," says Diomede,[4] " introducuntur heroes, duces, reges."

Horace had such traditions in mind when he spoke[5] of gods, heroes, and kings as the characters of Tragedy. As

Horace on Tragedy

a fitting medium of expression for such characters, the law of Decorum demanded that the style[6] of Tragedy be splendid and elevated, though at times there should be a lowering of the key, as a concession to popular understanding. It is interesting to see in all this the germs of Neo-Classical theory, which laid down stringent rules for the characters and style of Tragedy, limiting the characters to " gods and goddesses, kings, queens, and men of high estate,"[7] while

---

[1] Some of the Neo-Classical critics took Horace's phrase (A.P. 12) : " sed non ut placidis coeant immitia," to refer to Tragi-Comedy ; cf. Menéndez Y. Pelayo, op. cit., p. 183.

[2] Poet. II. 1448a, ib. III. 2, V. 1449b, XIII. 1453a.

[3] Varro, De poematis, fr. 305, Funaioli, op. cit., p. 321 ; cf. Dante, De V.E. II. 4 : " per tragoediam superiorem statum inducimus, per comoediam inferiorem " (an echo of Aristotle).

[4] Keil, I. p. 488 ; vide supra, p. 403 n. 2.

[5] Sat. I. 10. 42 : " Pollio regum facta canit " ; cf. A.P. 114, ib. 227 (on the characters of the Satyric drama that have just appeared in Tragedy).

[6] Hor. A.P. 231, 236 ; cf. Ovid, Trist. II. 553 ; vide supra, p. 392.

[7] Webbe ; cf. Babbitt, Rousseau and Romanticism, pp. 124–125.

as regards style many theorists maintained that verse[1] was the only proper instrument of speech for the characters of the tragic drama.

We have seen that a theory of Comedy had been evolved, largely reflecting the conditions of the New Comedy, stand-

Development of Aristotelian doctrine

ing in certain of its aspects in direct anti-thesis to that of Tragedy, and marking a development that went beyond Aristotle's scanty[2] references to the genre. As regards the elements of Tragedy we have just considered, we have noted an inclination to give greater precision to Aristotle's doctrine, and to apply it with greater rigour than the Master. A brief comparison of Horace and Aristotle on the " laws " of Tragedy will make still clearer how critical theory had hardened, and how marked was the tendency to stereotype such laws, and to endow them with all the authority of an established code. While Horace agrees with Aristotle in many points, in others he re-echoes Hellenistic teaching, and enunciates precepts that at the most can be regarded as by-products of Aristotelian doctrine. He mentions[3] the adoption of the Iambic metre for the dialogue of drama, assigning the same reasons as Aristotle for its adoption, and giving as an additional reason (significant for our know-ledge of Roman playgoers) that it could be heard above the clamour of the audience. Aristotle had insisted especially on unity of action in the drama, and had given[4] rules for character-drawing that will be always valid, such as those that demanded propriety, consistency, and truth to life in the characters portrayed. Horace likewise emphasised[5] the

[1] Cf. Lucas, Tragedy, p. 133 et seq., on some modern attempts to find in rhythmical prose a substitute for verse in Tragedy.

[2] It is a vexed question, as we have seen, how far Aristotelian tradition is embodied in the Coislinian Tractate.

[3] A.P. 80 et seq., ib. 251 et seq.; cf. Ar. Poet. IV. 1449 a. 14, XXII. 1459a. 11, XXIV. 1459b. 5, Rhet. III. 8. 4, on the affinity of the Iambic rhythm with ordinary conversation; cf. Demetr. 43; Cic. De Or. III. 182, Or. 189, 191.

[4] Poet. c. XV.

[5] A.P. 23; in the context he lays down the precept for unity in poetry generally, though he may have been thinking primarily of the drama; cf. Ep. II. 1. 174, where his criticism of Plautus seems to be directed chiefly against his failure in unity; vide infra, p. 482.

need for unity as a fundamental condition. He prescribed[1] that the Chorus in Tragedy should form an integral part of the drama, and refrain from singing odes that were mere ἐμβόλιμα. His rules[2] for character-drawing correspond largely with those of Aristotle. The employment of the " Deus ex machina " to unravel the complications of the plot, was regarded[3] by Aristotle as an inartistic[4] device. Horace's rule[5] for its employment is somewhat vague, but he evidently saw nothing incongruous in using it as a means of rescuing the plot from the hopeless entanglement into which it had been driven by an unskilful dramatist. Though he realised[6] that there had been development in Tragedy, yet he lays[7] down rigid rules limiting the number of actors to three, and the acts of a play to five. These rules are evidence of how the drama had become beset by a rigorous formalism since the days of Aristotle, who merely recounts the advance made by Sophocles in raising the number of actors to three, and refers[8] to certain natural divisions in Tragedy. The law of the Five Acts[9] had no basis in the Classical Tragedy of Greece, but was evidently devised by Hellenistic theorists, who may have wished to find a formula that would cover the practice of contemporary[10]

---

[1] A.P. 193 et seq. ; cf. Ar. Poet. XVIII. 1456a.

[2] A.P. 105 et seq., 112, 316, on the law of propriety ; ib. 126–127, on consistency ; ib. 156 et seq., on truth to life, in connection with the various ages of man ; Ar's rule that the characters should be χρηστά has no parallel in Horace.

[3] Poet. XV. 1454b.

[4] The " Deus ex machina " had, however, its legitimate use in Tragedy.

[5] A.P. 191.   [6] Ib. 275 et seq.

[7] Ib. 189, 192 ; in the context Horace is dealing with Tragedy ; in defining the number of actors he had, of course, in mind those actually taking part in the dialogue.

[8] Poet. IV. 1449a ; he merely notes here the increase in the compass of the plot and the number of ἐπεισόδια, as compared with the drama in its original form.

[9] Varro and Cicero were both familiar with the division into acts, though we find in them no mention of five acts ; V. R. Rust. II. 5. 2 ; Cic. Ad Fam. V. 12. 6, Ad Q. fr. I. 1. 46, Cato Maj. 5, 64, 70, Phil. II. 34 ; cf. Donatus, Praef. to Hecyra, III. 6, Wessner, Vol. II. p. 192.

[10] Who may have limited themselves to three ἐπεισόδια ; cf. Leo, Plaut. Forsch. pp. 230–231, who notes the significance of the term μέρος in the ὑπόθεσις to the Andromache.

dramatists. The attempt[1] to apply the law to Roman Comedy led theorists into many difficulties, so that it is little wonder that the " parum docti," as Donatus confesses, found it difficult to follow the division into acts which certain critics sought to make valid for Comedy.

In his treatment of the Satyric drama Horace seems to me not to be so hidebound by tradition, and in laying down rules for it he evidently desires to take Roman conditions into account. The ingredients of the Satyric drama were simple, and the way of the dramatist comparatively smooth, so that it is possible that literary theory, though it recognised certain conditions as fundamental for the genre, did not subject it to the same rigid formalism as it applied to Tragedy and Comedy. Horace evidently regarded the Satyric play as invented[2] to follow Tragedy, its chief function being to afford relief after the tension of the serious drama. In face of the strong Roman sense of decorum[3] it was a difficult genre to handle, as it was not merely sportive[4] in character, but in it was established a tradition of crude obscenity.[5] The writer of Satyric plays who wishes to avoid offending the Roman[6] instinct for propriety, must not allow himself to be dominated by such a tradition, nor make his verse redolent of the effeminacy or vulgar coarseness characteristic of certain strata of the Roman populace. In the Satyric play the stately[7] personages of Tragedy

The Satyric drama

---

[1] Cf. Evanthius, III. 1, Wessner, Vol. I. p. 18 ; Donatus ad Hecyra. Prol. II. 39 : " primo actu placeo " ; Eun. Praef. I. 5, Adelphi, Praef. I. 4,

[2] Cf. Ar. Poet. IV. 1449a, on the Satyric stage through which Tragedy passed ; *Ib.* on the use of the tripping measure of the Trochaic tetrameter in that early stage.

[3] Cicero (Ad Q. Fr. II. 15. 3) was evidently shocked by the Σύνδειπνοι of Sophocles, translated by his brother ; *vide supra*, p. 145.

[4] Demetr. 169, calls it " Tragedy at play."

[5] Hor. A.P. 233, speaks of " Satyri protervi " ; Ovid, Trist. II. 409 : " est et in obscoenos commixta tragoedia risus ", may well be referring to the Satyric drama ; Ridgeway, The Origin of Tragedy, p. 50 *et seq.*, following his own peculiar view of the origin of Tragedy, finds in the Satyric drama the true Dionysiac element.

[6] As embodied in the Knights, etc., A.P. 248.

[7] *Vide* Walker, Sophocles' Ichneutae, p. 567 *et seq.*, for a discussion of this view of Horace.

appear now in new surroundings, and the problem for the
dramatist is to steer a middle[1] course between the pomp of
the Tragic drama and the familiar[2] tone of Comedy.
Horace had already proclaimed that common speech could
be invested with a new beauty by a poet's skill in composition, and by the nice dovetailing of his words, and he
evidently[3] thought that the style of the Satyric drama
afforded splendid scope for such an experiment. It is
difficult, indeed, to estimate how far Horace's precepts for
the Satyric play were meant to be practical[4] in the literary
conditions of the time. The Satyric drama had been
practised at Rome, at any rate by Pomponius,[5] who however
was best known as a writer of "fabulae Atellanae." Pomponius may have infused into the genre something of the
spirit of the Atellan play, while the note of warning[6] sounded
by Horace seems to suggest that at times the Satyric drama
had been brought down to the level of low comedy (fabula
tabernaria). He evidently wished that any dramatists who
might attempt a Satyric play, would, while keeping true to
the essentials of the genre, at the same time show regard
for Roman prejudices and Roman sense of decency.

In Epic, Homer is for Horace the supreme model. Here
we have an interesting example of how a great poet could
dominate a genre, and impose his methods on all who

---

[1] Cf. Tzetzes, Kaibel, op. cit., p. 36 : καὶ σατυρικὴν τῶνδε τὴν
μεσαιτάτην; Grant and Fiske, Cicero's "Orator" and Horace's "Ars
Poetica," pp. 44–45, with an eye always on the triad of Rhetorical styles,
relate Horace's description of the Satyric style to the Middle style, even as
regards its humour ; vide infra, p. 477.

[2] A.P. 234–235 : "non ego inornata et dominantia nomina solum . . .
Satyrorum scriptor amabo."

[3] A.P. 46 et seq., and 240 et seq., should be compared.

[4] It is interesting to note that Vitruvius (V. 8. 1) sets out the features
peculiar to the Satyric stage ; Birt in his Appendix to Dieterich's Pulcinella,
p. 297 et seq., has no doubt that Horace's aim was a practical one.

[5] So Porphyrio tells us ; Atlante, Sisyphus, Ariadne, were some of the
titles of his Satyric plays ; cf. Dieterich, op. cit., p. 126 et seq.; we may
take it that Q. Cicero's adaptation of Sophocles' above-mentioned play was
intended as a mere literary exercise.

[6] A.P. 227–229 : "ne . . . migret in obscuras humili sermone tabernas" ;
cf. Evanthius, IV. 1, Wessner, Vol. I. p. 21 ; "tabernarias ab humilitate
argumenti ac stili" ; cf. Donatus, ib. p. 25.

laboured in the same field. Homer had been criticised[1] ad-
Homer's au-
thority in
Epic versely from the ethical standpoint, but on
the score of technique, and the general excell-
ence of his achievements, Aristotle had already
advanced his apotheosis by proclaiming his immeasurable
superiority over all other Epic poets. The few faults
which he detects in him, are obliterated by his enthusiastic
praise of his Epic genius. In the serious[2] style, Homer is
peerless amongst poets. Whether he derived it from art
or genius, he showed his marvellous superiority[3] over all
other writers both in selecting his subject, and in conceiving
and maintaining the unity proper to the Epic, wherein many
had been conspicuous failures. Moreover, the *Iliad* and
the *Odyssey* serve to illustrate[4] the various species of Epic,
the simple and the complex, the Epic of emotion and that
of character. Homer was pre-eminent[5] in thought and
diction, and was the only writer of Epic who realised that
the personality of the poet should for the most part be
kept in the background. He, too, it was that first taught
the true art of fiction,[6] so that, even when dealing with
irrational incidents, he could create that "willing suspension
of disbelief" which only the genius of a great poet can
encompass.

Aristotle had thus exalted the merits of Homer in terms
of almost extravagant praise. The Stoics especially, by
The apotheosis
of Homer their allegorical method sought to save the
poet's reputation as a moralist, while many
critics discovered in him the germ of all the
sciences. The tradition of Homer-worship[7] was thus well
established, so that it is little wonder that Horace finds[8] in
him the almost perfect model whose example can suffice

---

[1] Plato, Ion, 530 B, should be noted as an offset to his criticisms of the
poet elsewhere from the ethical point of view.

[2] Poet. IV. 1448b.

[3] *Ib*. VIII. 1, XXIII. 3, XXVI, 6.

[4] *Ib*. XXIV. 2.

[5] *Ib*. 7 ; cf. IV. 9.

[6] *Ib*. XXIV. 9.

[7] Cf. Philod. περὶ ποιημ. Bk. V. Col. 30–31, Jensen, p. 67 *et seq.*

[8] A.P. 140 : " quanto rectius hic, qui nil molitur inepte " ; *ib*. 401 :
"insignis Homerus " ; cf. Vell. I. 5.

to dictate the laws of Epic poetry. Homer may[1] have faults, but they are such as are pardonable in a work of such vast compass, and are more than counterbalanced by the poet's general excellence. Horace contrasts[2] the modest opening of the *Odyssey* and Homer's subsequent achievements, with the blatant profession of the Cyclic poet, whose labour will bring forth only a " ridiculus mus." Homer was too great an artist to attempt to treat the whole story of the Trojan War from its earliest origins. Following Aristotle, Horace commends him for the limitation of his subject in the *Iliad*, for his economy in its treatment, and for the unity[3] that is so distinguishing a characteristic of the poem. He is again probably echoing Aristotle when he praises[4] the poet's skill in fiction. Indirectly we can see the working of Homer's influence in Petronius'[5] precept regarding the need for employing the machinery of the " deorum ministeria " in the Epic. One at least of Petronius' contemporaries had discarded it at his peril. Homer's influence, too, finally established[6] the hexameter as the fitting metre for an Epic poem. This metre, removed[7] as it is from any suggestion of ordinary speech, is the stateliest and most impressive of all metres, and by the test of experience proved its fitness for singing an Epic theme. To employ any other metre for a narrative poem would seem to be a breach of propriety. Nature itself may teach the choice of the proper measure, but it was Homer's example above all that ratified the rule making the hexameter essential[8] for Epic poetry. Ennius, the " alter

---

[1] A.P. 359. [2] *Ib.* 136 *et seq.*

[3] A looser unity, however, than was required in Tragedy ; A.P. 148–152, touches on the unity of the Iliad, though Horace's phrase " semper ad eventum festinat " seems to postulate an almost too rigid and compact unity.

[4] A.P. 151, *ib.* 144, on his " speciosa miracula " ; Horace, A.P. 338, gives a rule for fiction that seems to limit the poet's powers ; *vide infra*, p. 436.

[5] Satyr, 118. [6] A.P. 73–74.

[7] Ar. Poet. 24. 1459b, Rhet. III. 8. 4 ; Demetr. 42 ; Cic. Or. 191–192 ; Q. IX. 4. 88.

[8] Dionys. De C.V. c. 19, says that Epic writers may not depart from this metre ; Horace, loc. cit., is less peremptory : " Res gestae . . . quo scribi *possent* numero, monstravit Homerus."

Homerus," true to the Homeric tradition, abandoned the old Saturnian metre, and adopted the hexameter in the first great Roman Epic.

All this is particularly interesting in view of the fact that Classical criticism inclined to associate[1] certain metres with certain subjects. Nature, as Aristotle says, taught the use of these metres, but Nature's lessons were not imparted by way of revelation, but had to be learned by laborious effort. The Iambic metre was originally adopted for purposes of invective[2], but its fitness for the dialogue of drama was soon discovered, while the Trochaic metre, with its dancing[3] rhythms, was abandoned as unsuitable for that purpose. Ovid declares[4] that the Elegiac metre, usually employed[5] for lighter subjects, cannot bear the weight of an Epic theme, while on the other hand a reader of Martial expresses surprise[6] at an epigram written in hexameters. The Ancients thus recognised the primary fitness of certain metres for certain genres, though that did not prevent[7] them from adapting the old metres to new genres and new material. In this conception of the primary fitness of metres we can discover the key to the tendency to distinguish certain genres by their external form.

Metres and subjects

Now Horace's discussion of Epic poetry is valuable, as I have said, as showing how the influence of a great master could impose laws on succeeding generations of poets. The Classical theory of Imitation especially helped to stabilise such influence. Virgil in his turn was to act as law-giver for many of his successors, and particularly in the Middle Ages[8] was to

A master poet's influence

[1] We have an anticipation of this doctrine in Plato, Rep. III. 398 D; cf. *ib*. 400 D.

[2] Ar. Poet. IV. 1448b; Catullus, 36. 5, 40. 2, 54. 6; Hor. Ep. I. 19. 25, A.P. 79.

[3] Ar. Poet. 24. 1460a, Rhet. III. 8. 4; cf. περὶ ὕψους, 41. 1; Cic. Or. 193; Q. IX. 4. 88.

[4] Ex Ponto, III. 4. 85.   [5] Cf. Hor. AP. 75.

[6] Mart. VI. 65. 1.   [7] *Vide infra*, p. 420.

[8] *Vide* Saintsbury, op. cit., II. p. 77 *et seq*., p. 123 *et seq*.; Babbitt, The New Laocoon, pp. 12–13; Cook, The Art of Poetry, Introd. p. 36, on Virgil's place in Vida's "Poetics."

enjoy much of the idolatry that formerly fell to the lot of
Homer. We find, indeed, other examples where a poet of
genius could in a measure dominate those who followed in
the same genre. Ennius, the first distinguished writer of
Epic in Rome, did something to stereotype Epic diction
amongst the Romans, so that even Virgil[1] could not escape
his influence. In Elegy we can witness the spell of a great
name like that of Callimachus at work upon the Roman[2]
poets who professed allegiance to the Alexandrian master.
We can see a poet of genius exerting his influence in a
humbler way in that verse of varied[3] content known as
Hendecasyllables. This was essentially what Lafaye[4] calls
" poésie de circonstance." Pliny,[5] in sending a volume of
such verse to a friend, was afraid that he might seem to have
passed at times beyond the limits of decency. The tradition
of the genre, he declares, was towards " lascivia rerum "[6]
and " nuda verba," but from these latter he himself abstained. He appeals in his defence to the example of those
who had worked in the same field, but he evidently had
Catullus chiefly in mind as the one who, for the Romans at
least, had best interpreted the law[7] of the genre. Catullus,
too, had provided an excuse for all who wished to indulge
in similar licentious verse, by declaring[8] that, though the
poet himself should be chaste, his verses need not be so.
He has thus left on this type of casual verse a certain
impress that pointed the way to his successors, though he

[1] Norden, Aen. VI. p. 365 et seq.

[2] Prop. II. 1. 40, ib. 34. 32, III. 1. 1, ib. 9. 43, IV. 1. 64 ; cf. Hor. Ep.
II. 2. 100 ; Ovid, Ex Ponto, IV. 16. 32 ; Stat. Silvae, I. 2. 253 ; vide
supra, p. 303.

[3] Hence the many names that might be applied to it ; cf. Pliny, Ep.
IV. 14. 9.

[4] Op. cit., c. III.

[5] Ep. IV. 14. 4 ; cf. V. 3. 2, VII. 4. 1.

[6] Cf. Mart. Bk. I. Proem : " lascivam verborum veritatem, id est epigrammaton linguam," etc., where the poet appeals to the example of Catullus
among others ; ib. X. 78. 16 ; vide supra, p. 309.

[7] Ep. IV. 14. 5 : " hujus opusculi illam esse verissimam legem, quam
Catullus expressit " ; cf. Mart. X. 9. 1 et seq. ; Prop. II. 34. 87 ; Ovid,
Trist. II. 427, where the epithet " lascivus " is applied to Catullus.

[8] XVI. 5 ; cf. Ovid, Trist. II. 353 ; Pliny, loc. cit. ; ib. V. 3. 2 ; Mart.
I. 4, 8, XI. 15. 13, Ausonius, Bk. XVII. VIII. ; Apul. Apol. 9–11.

himself could employ the Hendecasyllabic metre for other purposes, and either make it the vehicle of invective,[1] or use it to voice plaints that were proper to the Elegy.

Horace in his criticism not only took account of various genres, each bound by fairly definite laws, but had in mind also a hierarchy of genres. This was

A hierarchy of genres a characteristic of ancient criticism from the days of Aristotle, who ranked[2] Tragedy as the highest form of art, higher even than Epic, because it better fulfils the artistic function peculiar to itself. The criterion by which the rank of a genre was determined, was at times the form,[3] but more frequently the content,[4] which was believed to have a greater intrinsic value in one genre than in another. This is well illustrated by the attitude of the Elegiac poets to their own genre. The playful[5] elegy, employed above all to voice the joys and sorrows and plaints[6] of love, was described by epithets[7] which were often designed to contrast it with the stately Epic, and show that it occupied a lower place in the scale of genres. Such epithets may be at times employed as nothing more than literary conventions, but, particularly in the Augustan age, they served to express also a sense of the insignificance of mere personal[8] emotions in face of the mighty events that had brought the blessings of Augustan peace, and moulded the Roman Empire into a reality of almost immeasurable power and grandeur. It was only the fervid imagination and lofty[9] tones of the Epic poet that could deal adequately with such pregnant events. Hence we are not surprised

---

[1] Cat. 12. 10, 42. 1.

[2] Poet. c. 26 ; cf. Prop. II. 34. 41 *et seq.*, where Tragedy is ranked above Elegy ; Ovid, Trist. II. 381 : " omne genus scripti gravitate tragoedia vincit."

[3] Cf. Ovid, Ex Ponto, III. 4. 85.

[4] *Ib.* II. 5. 25, Am. III. 1. 11, *ib.* 24.

[5] Tac. Dial. 10 ; Stat. Silvae, I. 2. 7 ; Mart. III. 20. 6.

[6] Hor. Odes, I. 33. 2, A.P. 75.

[7] " Levis," Ovid, Am. II. 1. 21, Ex Ponto, IV. 5. 1 ; cf. Mart. XII. 94. 8 ; Prop. IV. 1. 59 ; Hor. A.P. 77 : " exiguos elegos."

[8] Cf. Prop. II. 34. 44–45.

[9] Tac. Dial. 10 : " heroici carminis sonum " ; Q. I. 8. 5 : " et sublimitate heroi carminis animus adsurgat."

to find Horace[1] in his turn putting the prosaic genre of Satire on a lower plane than the noble and inspired utterance of the Epic.   But we shall have more to say anon about the attitude of Horace and the other Augustans as regards the subject of Epic poetry.

Horace then is in harmony with the general trend of Classical criticism in holding a hierarchy of genres.   He probably had such a conception in his mind, when he laid[2] it down as a guiding rule that a poet should always undertake a task commensurate with his powers.   Here we have, indeed, a dictate of the law of Decorum, which Cicero[3] in another sphere had already emphasised as one of the golden precepts for human conduct.   The tastes[4] and talents of men are varied, and each one as a rule will follow[5] the bent of his own genius.   Propertius, however, saw the need of inculcating[6] the same lesson as Horace, since he warns poets against endeavouring to bear too heavy[7] a burden in their work, and urges them to labour where their skill is greatest. Quintilian, at a later date, enunciates[8] a similar precept for all who wish for success in oratory.

Horace is in practice a living embodiment of his own precepts.   He knows the limits of his powers, and will not strain[9] his genius overmuch.   Even as regards lyric poetry, he can contrast the humble efforts of the Matine bee with the imaginative flights and torrential sweep of Pindaric verse.

The burden to be shouldered

Horace and his own precepts

---

[1] Ep. II. 1. 250 *et seq.* ; cf. Sat. I. 4. 40 *et seq.*, where he has clearly the contrast of the Epic in mind.

[2] A.P. 38–40 ; cf. Sat. II. 1. 12, Ep. II. 1. 259.

[3] De Off. I. 114 : " suum quisque igitur noscat ingenium " ; *vide supra*, p. 58.   [4] Cf. Lucil. frs. 628–630 ; Prop. III. 9. 7.

[5] *Ib.* 20 : " naturae sequitur semina quisque suae " ; cf. Hor. Ep. II. 2. 187, on Genius.

[6] III. 9. 5 : " turpe est, quod nequeas, capiti committere pondus " ; II. 1. 46 ; cf. Ovid, Ex Ponto, II. 5. 26.

[7] It is interesting to compare Dante, De V.E. II. 4 : " unumquemque debere materiae pondus propriis humeris coaequare " ; Boileau and Pope, both imbued with the sense of Decorum, give similar precepts ; cf. Blakeney, op. cit., p. 62.

[8] X. 2. 19 : " tum in suscipiendo onere consulat suas vires."

[9] Ode, I. 6. 8 : " nec saevam Pelopis domum conamur, tenues grandia."

While cultivating as he did the pedestrian Muse in a genre such as Satire, he proclaimed[1] that he had no talent for Epic poetry, and that, however much he might be tempted to essay it from a sense of loyalty to powerful patrons, he will leave[2] to poets of greater competence the task of singing the glories of Augustus or Agrippa. In his *Odes*[3] he declares that his genius is suited for the lighter strains of love poetry, and not for the singing of grim wars[4] or the clash of arms, nor dealing with Epic subjects[5] that could not be fitted to the measures of the lyre.

This awe, or professed awe, of Epic poetry was characteristic of the age. Virgil in his early days tells[6] us how, when he was tempted to sing of " kings and battles," Apollo gave warning that he was to confine himself to the more homely subjects of the Pastoral. The author of the *Panegyricus Messallae* declares[7] that he will leave to Valgius the task of dealing with Epic themes. As we have already noted, the contrast between love-poetry and Epic became a commonplace with many of the Augustan poets. We meet it frequently in Propertius,[8] who will seek all his glory from Elegy, and who confesses[9] his inability to launch out into the formidable undertaking of an epic theme. Apollo rebuked[10] him also for his rashness, when he was moved to emulate the example

Professed awe of Epic poetry

[1] Sat. II. 1. 12 ; Lucilius, too, in his own day had proclaimed his incapacity for Epic ; *vide supra*, p. 57.

[2] Odes, I. 6, IV. 2. 33 *et seq.*; cf. Ep. I. 3. 7, II. 1. 245 *et seq.*; cf. Ep. I. 16. 25 (with Kiessling's note).

[3] Odes, I. 19. 9 *et seq.*, II. 12, IV. 15. 1.

[4] Especially marked out as the province of the Epic poet ; cf. Ep. I. 19. 7, A.P. 73 ; Dom. Marsus, Epigram on Tibullus.

[5] Though, out of compliment to the house of Caesar, he says he will sing of Troy, Anchises, " et almae progeniem Veneris," Odes, IV. 15. 31.

[6] Eclog. VI. 3 *et seq.*

[7] 177–180.

[8] I. 7. 1 *et seq.*, I. 9. 9 *et seq.*, II. 34. 59 *et seq.*, III. 1. 15 *et seq.*, IV. 6. 69 ; cf. his great model Callimachus, fr. 165 : μηδ' ἀπ' ἐμοῦ διφᾶτε μέγα ψοφέουσαν ἀοιδήν τίκτεσθαι.

[9] III. 9. 4 : " non sunt apta meae grandia vela rati " ; cf. II. 10, where he essays Epic themes, but with misgiving ; *vide infra*, p. 421.

[10] III. 3. 15 : " quis te carminis heroi tangere jussit opus ? " cf. Hor. Odes, IV. 15. 1.

of Ennius, and thought he possessed the power to sing of the story of the Alban kings. If indeed he had the genius, he would celebrate[1] the fame of Caesar's exploits, and mingle Maecenas' praises with those of his master, but it is for such as Virgil[2] to sing of the Trojan Aeneas, and proclaim the glories of the victory at Actium. Again, we find in Ovid[3] a similar contrast drawn between Epic and love poetry. He considers[4] that his own endowments fit him for the lighter labour of erotic verse, while it requires a poet of rich and varied powers to sing of Caesar's mighty achievements. Envious Nature bestowed[5] on him but little strength, and this was overwhelmed by the grandeur and brilliance of Caesar's triumph, which he once attempted to celebrate in his verse.

Here then we have many of the Augustan poets voicing their awe of an Epic theme. When Horace refused to sing **Difficulties of** the exploits of Augustus or Agrippa, he was **the historical** in part giving expression to what was a **Epic** literary commonplace amongst his contemporaries. But there were other considerations that would have deterred him from the task, even if his respect for the hierarchy of genres, and his sense of the propriety of not assuming too heavy a burden, had not stood in his way. Whether it was at all possible to revive the great Epic with success had been hotly debated at Alexandria. Callimachus[6] had pronounced that its day was over, and had himself taken refuge in the Epyllion. But what must have weighed

---

[1] II. 1. 25 *et seq.*, III. 9. 33 *et seq.*; cf., however, IV. 6. 13 : " Caesaris in nomen ducuntur carmina."

[2] II. 34. 61 *et seq.*; cf. III. 11. 29 *et seq.*, where Propertius, from another standpoint, celebrates the victory of Augustus.

[3] Am. II. 1. 11 *et seq.*, *ib.* 18. 1 *et seq.*, III. 12. 15 : " quum Thebae, quum Troja forent, quum Caesaris acta, ingenium movit sola Corinna meum " ; Ex Ponto, III. 3. 31 *et seq.*; *ib.* 4. 83 *et seq.*; cf. Stat. Silvae, I. 2. 96 *et seq.*, 5. 5 *et seq.*

[4] Trist. II. 331 *et seq.*, Ex Ponto, II. 5. 26 *et seq.*

[5] Trist. II. 532.

[6] He was, of course, also in reaction against the constant use of traditional material, and preferred to wander himself in the bye-paths of literature ; cf. his sayings ἐχθαίρω τὸ ποίημα τὸ κυκλικὸν, and σικχαίνω πάντα τὰ δημόσια.

chiefly with Horace and his contemporaries, was the difficulty of undertaking an historical[1] Epic in the full light of
the Augustan age. Ennius, indeed, had achieved a conspicuous success in his *Annales*, though he had some advantage in that portion of his Epic dealt with a remote and
legendary period of Roman history. However, the failure
of the historical Epic in after days is evidenced, not only by
the opprobrium which Catullus cast on the *Annales Volusii*,
but by the oblivion that enshrouds such works[2] as the
Bellum Istricum of Hostius, the *Annales* of Furius of Antium,
and the *Bellum Sequanicum* of Varro of Atax. We have,
moreover, the interesting fact that Virgil[3] began an Epic in
his early years before the publication of his *Eclogues*.
Virgil's phrase " cum canerem reges et proelia " is interpreted by Servius[4] to mean either an Aeneid, or the story
of the Alban kings. Donatus' comment is more significant :
" mox cum res Romanas incohasset, offensus materia ad
Bucolica transit." One might argue from this that Virgil's
attempted Epic was a work in which the historical element
predominated. The most formidable problem that would
confront the poet was how, in a sophisticated age such as
the Augustan, he could employ the supernatural machinery
which Homer's example had made almost an essential for
Epic poetry. When Virgil resumed the task of writing an
Epic, he made his path easier by concentrating on the story
of Rome's legendary founder, though with supreme skill he
linked together the Present and the Past, wove into the
texture of his poem some of the chief events of Roman
history, and celebrated the glories of the Julian line and the
rebirth of the Golden Age under Augustus. But the story
of Aeneas, which was his main theme, left ample scope for
the play of the poet's imagination, and allowed him to

[1] Lucilius, in his own day, evidently realised the difficulty of writing an
Epic on the Numantine war.

[2] *Vide* Schanz, op. cit., I. 2. 97–98.

[3] Eclog. VI. 3 ; Tenney Frank, Vergil, p. 67 *et seq.*, argues in favour of
" an Aeneid with Julius Caesar in the background."

[4] If we had not the comments of the Scholiasts, backed by certain passages
in the " Catalepta," we might be tempted to interpret the passage as a mere
literary convention, in view of what we have seen of the other Augustan
poets ; cf. Legendre, Études Tironiennes, p. 2.

employ the conventional machinery of the Epic in a way that could not offend the most sophisticated mind of the age.   At a later date, Lucan was to attempt an historical Epic, and on a subject from Roman history that was comparatively recent.   He evidently felt himself compelled to abandon the recognised Epic[1] machinery, and though he substituted for it other devices, and indulged at times in a somewhat riotous rhetoric, it was his fate, in spite of some generous tributes paid to him, to be branded as a historian rather than a poet.   Petronius clearly perceived[2] the difficulties of the historical Epic.   While a poet might successfully carry out his prescription for the Epic in a semi-legendary subject, the real problem would arise when, in a subject[3] of contemporary history, he sought to give his genius free rein " per ambages deorumque ministeria et fabulosum sententiarum tormentum."

It was, of course, a subtle compliment on Horace's part to avow that his powers were unequal to the task of celebrating the exploits of Augustus, but behind

Virgil's achievement

the avowal lay the consciousness of what a formidable undertaking was the writing of an historical Epic.   He did not wish to play the rôle of Choerilus[4] to the Roman Alexander.   It is clear from Ovid[5] that the Epic was cultivated by many writers in the Augustan age, but it is significant that the subjects they selected for treatment were mostly mythological.   Occasionally an historical subject[6] was attempted, but Ovid's gallery[7] of

---

[1] The introduction of supernatural machinery into the Epic was in after days naturally a serious problem for Christian poets ; cf. Saintsbury, op. cit., II. pp. 56, 270.

[2] Satyr. 118 ; the task, he tells us, before the poet is not merely the recording of real events in verse, for historians can accomplish that far better.

[3] e.g. the exploits of Augustus ; cf. Ovid, Trist. II. 335 : " divitis ingenii est inmania Caesaris acta condere."

[4] Ep. II. 1. 233 ; cf. A.P. 357.

[5] Ex Ponto, IV. 16. 5 et seq.

[6] Ib. 23 ; Pedo's poem on the expedition of Germanicus was one of the best known ; cf. Sen. Suas. I. 15.

[7] Even " magni Rabirius oris " ; cf. Teuffel-Schwabe, I. p. 511, for a supposed fragment of his poem on the battle of Actium and the death of Cleopatra.

Epic writers did little to add to the glory of Roman literature. [All these efforts would naturally be eclipsed by the
splendour of Virgil's fame. He had at once raised the
noblest monument of Roman poetry, and solved the problem of celebrating the lustre of the Augustan regime in the
way that it could be most effectively and artistically solved
by an Epic poet. Contemporary poets could pay the tribute
of open and generous homage[1] to the greatness of the
Aeneid, or the more subtle tribute of echoing[2] its themes.
Moreover, when they avowed that they were unfitted
for the task of singing of the exploits of their Imperial master,
such avowals, at any rate after the publication of the *Aeneid*,
might be interpreted not only as a recognition of the difficulties of the historical Epic, but also as a recognition of
the fact that no poet could hope to surpass Virgil's masterly
skill in dealing with events of recent Roman history.]

Our treatment of Horatian criticism so far, has, I hope,
helped to make clear how much Horace was pre-occupied

Primary dis- with the law of the genre. As in the
tinctions be- case of his rules for Tragedy, he was in-
tween genres clined to interpret it at times too rigidly and
too mechanically. Both the Greeks and the Romans, as
we saw,[3] recognised certain primary and fundamental distinctions which kept divided such genres as Epic, Lyric,
and Drama, distinctions based partly on content, partly on
the method of expression employed by the poet. In this
sense was realised the dictum of Chénier[4]: " nul genre,
s'echappant de ses bornes prescrites, n'aurait osé d'un autre
envahir les limites."[5] Experience had shown[6] the fitness
of particular metres for certain genres and certain subjects.
The metre alone did not constitute a special " Kind," but
the subject and the poet's treatment of it, had also to be
taken into account in the delimitation of the various genres.

[1] Cf. Hor. Ep. II. 1. 246, where Horace seems to have Virgil's Epic
poetry chiefly in mind ; *vide supra*, p. 303.
[2] Cf. Hor. Odes, IV. 15. 31 ; Prop. III. 11. 41 (cf. Aen. VIII. 698),
IV. 6. 15 *et seq.*
[3] *Vide supra*, p. 399.
[4] Cf. Babbitt, The New Laocoon, p. 198.
[5] Cf. Hor. A.P. 92 : " singula quaeque locum teneant sortita decentem."
[6] *Vide supra*, p. 411.

The metre that was found to be naturally suited to a particular genre, as the hexameter to Epic, could be adapted to another genre differing in subject and spirit, as Lucilius and Horace adapted the hexameter to the homely themes of Satire, Lucretius to his didactic treatise *On the Nature of Things*, or Theocritus and Virgil to the Pastoral. The Iambic trimeter was employed in the dialogue both of Tragedy and Comedy, but with different results as it was informed by the spirit of Sophocles, or that of Menander.

Horace, as we saw, associated certain metres with certain genres, but he never wished to lay down the law that a

Horace and the law of the genre

particular metre was indissolubly wedded to a particular genre, exclusive of all others. Without offence against the law of Decorum, a metre, associated intimately with one genre, could be adapted to the spirit of a new genre and take on its " colour." Again, it seems to me, that Horace's prescription[1] to the poet " descriptas servare vices operumque colores," refers to what I have called primary distinctions between genres ; it did not preclude the possibility that one genre might suggest or echo another. For Moderns, especially if they be Romantics, the primary and, in fact, the only function of lyric poetry, is to embody the personal emotions of the poet, as they spring spontaneously from some momentary mood. For the Classical poet, the Lyric could be that and something more. It could express emotion chastened by reflection, that had its roots in events of deep significance for mankind. The lyric poet may sing his lays of love and wine, but he is privileged too, as Pindar was, to " chant the gods and all their godlike race, the conquering champion, the prime horse in course."[2] Much of the poetry of Alcaeus was coloured by the political events of his time. Horace would consider himself to be following the Alcaic tradition, when, in his patriotic[3] Odes, he exalts the achievements of Augustus, proclaims the glory of civic virtue, and summons his countrymen to repentance and reform. The changing and

[1] A.P. 86.
[2] Ben Jonson's translation of A.P. 83–84 ; cf. Blakeney's edition ; cf. Hor. Odes, I. 12. 1 *et seq.*
[3] Cf. Odes, III. 1–6, written in the Alcaic metre.

wayward metres of the Lyric could be made the vehicle
for the expression of the whole gamut of emotion, and
range from playful sally to high seriousness. Horace, indeed, remembering the natural spirit of the Lyric, may
declare[1] that to sing of great deeds, or treat serious subjects,
is unsuited to the " jocosa lyra," as such things are better
reserved for the genius of the Epic poet, but he would
hardly consider himself as guilty of a violation of the law of
the genre, if he were to suggest in his *Odes* the subjects of
another genre, or even treat such subjects within modest
limits in a passing way. He would, however, regard himself
as guilty of a breach of Decorum, if he sought to reproduce
in the measures of lyric verse, and within the narrow[2] compass of an Ode, something of the dignity and grandeur of
the Epic. Hence we often find both lyric and elegiac poets,
warned as they tell us by Apollo, admonishing themselves
not to embark on the dangerous waters of an Epic theme.
Though they may adumbrate such themes, they seem to
have realised as a rule how far the limitations of their genre
will allow them to go. Propertius, though he prescribes[3]
the path along which his Muse must travel, yet at times
broaches Epic subjects, but with a misgiving[4] which implies that he is introducing unwonted strains into Elegy, and
placing too heavy a burden upon it. It is in the light of
all this that we must interpret Quintilian's reference to
Stesichorus, when he describes[5] him as singing of the greatest wars and the most renowned chieftains, and as sustaining
with his lyre the weight of Epic subjects.

As regards Horace's practice, if we conceive the law of
Formalism   the genre as "a distinct law of perfect form,"
and some   and especially if we interpret it with the un-
correctives   bending rigour of the Neo-Classical critics,
then we must condemn the poet as " a desperate mixer of

---

[1] Odes, III. 3. 69 ; cf. II. 12, 13 *et seq.*

[2] Though the cultivation of the Epyllion made it easier to deal, in a way,
with Epic subjects within a comparatively small compass.

[3] III. 2. 1, *ib.* 3. 21 : " cur tua praescripto sevecta est pagina gyro ? "

[4] Of course, we have to remember that the expression of such misgiving
was often only a literary convention.

[5] X. 1. 62 ; cf. Hor. Odes, IV. 9. 8 : " Stesichorique graves Camenae."

genres."[1]   One cannot deny that there is a tendency towards formalism[2] in Horatian criticism, but, as we shall see, Horace himself supplied certain correctives of its worst evils.   He recognised and respected the primary distinctions between certain genres, but that he was not at all times disposed to regard the law of the genre as something final and everlasting, is clear from the fact that he set out to give a new interpretation to the " lex operis " for Satire, though, of course, one might argue that Satire was a new genre amongst the Romans, the laws[3] of which were not as yet fully established.   The Greeks of the Classical era reverenced those primary distinctions of which I have spoken, but they allowed the free interplay of certain genres, and could unite Dramatic, Lyric, and Epic elements into a harmonious whole in Tragedy.   The tendency towards formalism became marked especially in the Alexandrian period, when there was a disposition to elevate the practice of the great Classical writers into a code of laws binding upon future generations.   But, even in that period, there were many engaged in experimenting with new genres, and in modifying the old, and such as they, were little likely to interpret the law of the genre too rigorously.   Much of the formalism in Horace is derived from the Alexandrian[4] age, but its evils were intensified a hundred-fold by the Neo-Classical[5] critics, who followed in his wake.   These, indeed, as Cowper[6] said of Pope : " Made poetry a mere mechanic art, when every warbler had his tune by heart." They erected the Rules into a supreme code, and regarded the law of the genre as a law that was sacred and unalterable, to which every poet was expected to render whole-

---

[1] Hack, op. cit., p. 30.

[2] This, as we have seen, is evident especially in his rules for Tragedy.

[3] In this connection it is interesting to note Juvenal, VI. 634–635 : " Fingimus haec, altum Satira sumente cothurnum, scilicet, et finem egressi legemque priorum " ; Juvenal is introducing a new note into Satire, though he feels he cannot ignore the " lex operis."

[4] Neoptolemos of Parium being, according to Porphyrio, his chief source in the Ars Poetica ; *vide infra*, p. 469.

[5] *Vide* Saintsbury, op. cit., II. p. 230 *et seq.*, pp. 287–289, III. pp. 409–410 ; Moulton, The Modern Study of Literature, p. 312 *et seq.*

[6] *Vide* Bascom, Philosophy of English Literature, p. 218.

hearted obedience.   But it is probably no exaggeration to say that the opprobrium which attached to such Neo-Classical critics as paid Horace the tribute of imitation, reacted adversely on the Roman poet, and was, in a measure at least, responsible for some of the harsh judgments passed on the *Ars Poetica*.

We have already seen evidence of the importance attached to the principle of Decorum in the Classical theory of art in

The doctrine of Decorum

general.   We have seen the operation of the principle in the ethical sphere, and how closely it was bound up with the principle of the Golden Mean.   Its operation, however, was no less potent in the sphere of Aesthetics.   Horace is thus in line with Classical tradition in giving the principle a prominent place in his literary theory, though some modern writers are inclined[1] to exaggerate its importance in his writings, and to see evidence of its operation in almost every one of his critical dicta.   In a measure, of course, their position is unassailable.   Cicero bears[2] witness to the universality of the law of Decorum both in literature and life, while Horace agrees with him in regarding the observation of the law as the foundation of all success in the art of letters.   Horace surely had the principle in mind, when he declared:[3] " scribendi recte sapere est et principium et fons."   In the ensuing verses he appeals to the " Socraticae chartae,"[4] and gives[5] us in effect what is a miniature treatise " De

---

[1] *Vide infra*, p. 480.

[2] Or. 70–73 : " hujus (i.e. the principle of Decorum) ignoratione non modo in vita, sed saepissime et in poematis et in oratione peccatur " ; cf. Philodemus, περὶ ποιημ. Col. VII, Jensen, p. 21.

[3] A.P. 309 ; cf. Cic. Or. 70 : " sed est eloquentiae sicut reliquarum rerum fundamentum sapientia " ; in the context evidently the " sapientia " consisted in observing the law of Decorum which Cicero is discussing ; cf. *ib.* 123, De Or. III. 212, Br. 23, De Leg. I. 58, where " sapientia " is called " mater omnium bonarum artium " ; on the other hand, in De Or. I. 83, III. 65, Cicero is rather expressing the sentiments of rigid Stoicism.

[4] Horace evidently uses the expression for Ethical philosophy generally, Socrates being regarded as the founder of Ethics ; in this branch of philosophy, as is clear from Cicero's " De Officiis," the law of Decorum found its widest application, governing, as it did, human conduct in its many phases ; we have seen already how Horace applied the law in his Satires.

[5] Cic. De Off. Bk. I, will furnish many parallels.

Officiis," touching on our various duties to our country, friends,[1] parents, and on the duties of a judge in his office, or a general in war. The study of the "Socraticae chartae " will lead to one practical result for the poet—" reddere personae convenientia cuique." If the poet is to draw his characters[2] appropriately and true to life, he must be acquainted with the characteristics[3] commonly associated with persons in different walks of life, as well as the duties incumbent on them. He will study varieties of national traits, and will attend to the characteristics which men display in the various periods[4] of their lives from childhood to old age. He will thus avoid the error of representing youth[5] as talking in the accents of the old and imitating their actions, or of making a Satyr speak the smart, but often licentious language of city folk. A play[6] that has brilliant passages, and is firm in its character-drawing, will often be a success, though void of elegance and technical finish. The law of Decorum was applied also to the realm of emotion,[7] and insisted that the various emotions be expressed in language that was in harmony with their nature.

But the principle of Decorum found other applications in Horace. As I have said, it was a principle bound up with that of the Golden Mean. Horace

The Golden Mean   probably had it in mind when he urged[8] the poet not to select a subject beyond his powers. Again, he applies[9] it in connection with the law

---

[1] Cf. Ar. Nic. Eth. VIII. 12–14.

[2] Horace deals with various aspects of character-drawing in A.P. 114 et seq., 156–178, 312 et seq. ; cf. Steinmann, De artis poeticae veteris parte, etc., p. 55 et seq., on some aspects of the problem; ib. pp. 77–78, on τὸ πρέπον ; vide supra, p. 406, on Horace's rules for character-drawing as compared with Aristotle's ; cf. De J. C. Scaligeri Poetice, Lintilhac, p. 20.

[3] It is interesting to note that Cic. De Off. I. 122, deals in a measure with the characteristics as well as with the duties of youth ; the psychological and ethical elements are thus interrelated.

[4] A.P. 114 et seq. ; Ar. Rhet. II. 12–14 ; Cic. Cato Major, 35, 65.

[5] A.P. 176 ; cf. ib. 115.

[6] Ib. 319 : " speciosa locis moprataque recte fabula " ; the passage is interesting, as showing how the value of character-drawing had risen since Aristotle's day.   [7] A.P. 105 et seq. ; vide supra, p. 128.

[8] A.P. 38 ; cf. ib. 385 ; vide supra, p. 414.

[9] A.P. 86, 92 ; vide supra, p. 420.

of the genre. With the reservations I have discussed above, the poet was bound to preserve the appropriate characteristics of each genre, and keep the style in harmony with the subject, both as regards choice of diction and metrical[1] arrangement. Horace invokes[2] the principle of the Golden Mean especially as a safeguard against faults of style. There was always the danger that a writer, in endeavouring to avoid a particular fault, might fall into its opposite, or, in aiming at a particular virtue of style, might be guilty of the fault[3] that was akin to it.

I shall have something further to say in another context on the place of Decorum in Horace's system, but what I have said, will suffice to show the importance he attached to the principle. Aristotle seems to have been the first to give the concept of Decorum a prominent place in Rhetorical[4] theory, but in Hellenistic times it became a dominant factor in " Poetic " and Rhetoric, and in the theory of art in general. It is interesting to note that the doctrine was discussed by Philodemus in connection with the views of Neoptolemus and Crates. We find reference[5] to the importance of having one's style appropriate to the subject and to the characters introduced. Decorum was declared[6] essential in every poetic genre, and the principle was made to govern even the practice of imitation. Philodemus, however, was evidently[7] dissatisfied, as, to his mind, the theorists did not[8] always explain clearly how the principle is to be applied in poetry. Twice he remarks[9] that the doctrine is equally valid for prose. He himself distinguishes[10] τὸ πρέπον τὸ κατὰ

Decorum in literary theory

---

[1] Hence Horace's discussion of the metres suited to particular genres.

[2] A.P. 25 *et seq.*, 31 : " in vitium ducit culpae fuga, si caret arte."

[3] *Vide infra*, p. 481.

[4] Though Plato had made use of it in his criticism of the poets, and his general theory of Aesthetics.

[5] Jensen, op. cit., pp. 21, 69–71 ; *ib.* p. 61, on the " virtues " of Style.

[6] *Ib.* p. 77.

[7] It is not always easy to follow the sequence of his thought owing to the defective condition of the text.

[8] Jensen, p. 79.

[9] *Ib.* pp. 21, 65.

[10] *Ib.* p. 77 ; cf. Kroll's notes ad Cic. Or. 70 *et seq.*

σοφίαν, an ideal that to his thinking is unattainable, and τὸ πρέπον τὸ καθ' ἕκαστον πρόσωπον καὶ πρᾶγμα, that in practice[1] is only sometimes observed.

Now, the domination of the principle of Decorum might be said to account for much of the formalism that we find in Horace. Its demands, if fully respected, would inevitably lead to a certain rigidity in all who were loyal to the poet's precepts. This perhaps is best illustrated in the case of his prescription for character drawing. His desire to have tabulated and studied the characteristics and duties of men in the different periods of their lives, and in their various callings and conditions, primarily aimed at satisfying the requisites of Decorum. But Horace's precepts, if carried out to the letter by the poet, would result in nothing better than the creation of formalised and conventional types. Unfortunately for Horace's reputation, here again the Neo-Classical[2] critics carried his doctrine to extremes, and helped to increase the prejudice that might naturally attach to it, as expounded in the poet's own pages.

The idea of the imitation of models was a cardinal one, especially in the literary theory of Hellenistic and Roman times. Roman literature, particularly in its early stages, was essentially imitative, and though as time went on it asserted its independence, and breathed more of the Roman spirit, yet it never entirely lost its imitative character. The attitude towards the problem[3] of originality in literature, and the converse problem of dependence upon others, was different amongst the Ancients from what it is in modern times. The study and imitation of the great masterpieces of literature were recommended[4] as something laudable. The " efflu-

The Neo-Classical critics

The doctrine of Imitation

---

[1] In the context he has the practice of the poets in mind.

[2] *Vide* Spingarn, Literary Criticism in the Renaissánce, p. 86 *et seq.*, Critical Essays, Vol. I. p. 15 (on the conception of Humours in Jonson and Horatian Decorum); *ib.* p. 59; cf. Simpson, Introd. to Jonson's " Everyman in his Humour," p. 38; Babbitt, Rousseau and Romanticism, p. 173.

[3] Many aspects of this problem are dealt with by Stemplinger, op. cit.; Peter, Wahrheit und Kunst; Fiske, Lucilius and Horace, c. I.

[4] περὶ ὕψους, c. 13; cf. Cic. De Fin. I. 10; Q. I. 11. 3, says (though in another context) : " frequens imitatio transit in mores "; cf. Dionys. Ad Pomp. c. 3.

ences " from the spirit of a great poet or prose-writer could descend upon others, and help[1] them to remould and exalt their own souls. The study of models was urged, particularly in the sphere of oratory, and was a regular[2] part of the training imposed on the student of rhetoric. In the rhetorical schools, as is well illustrated in Dionysius[3] and Quintilian, it was customary to propose the authors, both amongst poets and prose-writers, whom the student might find most useful in equipping himself for his profession of public speaker. By his study of such writers, the future orator will be enabled to enrich his vocabulary, and become acquainted with the niceties and subtle nuances of language. He may thus derive benefit from his reading of poets and historians,[4] but naturally it is to the orators that the student of rhetoric will devote particular attention. Here the question would arise whether a student should confine himself to the study of a single model, or select more than one. Quintilian issues[5] a warning against the dangers that beset the path of one who selects a single model for imitation.

After the rise of Asianist oratory, and with the setting in of the Atticist reaction, the question of the choice[6] of the best Attic models became one of paramount

The choice of models

importance for those who wished to oppose the extravagances of the Asianists, and looked for a return to the purity and restraint of Attic ideals. Though Cicero quarrels[7] with the Roman Atticists both on their choice of models, and the manner of their imitation, he takes the principle of imitation for granted, and urges[8] all who aspire to success in oratory, to select the best

---

[1] Cf. Bacchylides, fr. 14 : ἕτερος ἐξ ἑτέρου σοφὸς.

[2] Ad Her. I. 2. 3 ; Q. X. 2. 1 : " neque enim dubitari potest, quin artis pars magna contineatur imitatione " ; cf. Petron. 4 ; Fronto, I. p. 106, had his own uses for imitation.

[3] *Vide infra*, p. 445.

[4] Cic. De Or. II. 60.

[5] Cf. X. 2, where he lays down rules for imitation ; Sen. Controv. I. pr. 6.

[6] Dionys. De Vet. Or. Censura, c. 4.

[7] *Vide supra*, pp. 229, 259.

[8] De Or. I. 156, II. 90 *et seq.*, III. 39, 47, 125, De opt. gen. 6 *et seq.*

models, and imitate their finest qualities. He ascribes[1] the fact that different styles have prevailed in different periods of Greek oratory, to the preponderating influence of some model selected for imitation. Still, as he says,[2] " in omni re vincit imitationem veritas," and the theorists in rhetoric were fond[3] of emphasising the limited results that, at the best, could be expected from imitation.

The principle of imitation was thus an integral part of literary theory amongst the Ancients, who, however, were wont to scrutinise carefully the manner of the imitation. Plagiarism was severely condemned.[4] By it the Ancients primarily meant the secret[5] and unacknowledged appropriation of another's thoughts and words. On the other hand, not many would have displayed the boldness of Afranius, who confessed[6] that he borrowed not only from Menander, but from Roman authors, whatever he found suitable for his purpose. Horace has made[7] us familiar with the plagiarist under the image of the crow decked out in borrowed plumes. Virgil's enemies endeavoured[8] to make capital out of the " furta Vergiliana," and condemned him for his many borrowings from Homer, and from his predecessors in Roman poetry, but his defenders pointed out that his borrowings were a species of rivalry[9] which, especially in the case of his own countrymen, served to add a new beauty to the original. Virgil accomplished what Ben Jonson describes[10] as converting " the substance or riches of another poet to one's own use." He was pre-eminently successful in his

Imitation and Plagiarism

---

[1] De Or. II. 93.

[2] De Or. III. 215.

[3] Q. X. 2. 9 : " nihil autem crescit sola imitatione."

[4] *Vide supra*, p. 18 *et seq.* ; cf. Vitruv. VII. praef. 7 ; Sen. Controv. IX. 1 (24). 13, X. 5 (34). 20 ; Mart. I. 52. 9, 53, 12, 66. 1.

[5] Cf. Cic. Br. 76.

[6] Preface to the Compitalia, Macrob. Sat. VI. 1. 4 ; cf. Cic. De Fin. I. 3. 7.

[7] Ep. I. 3. 17 *et seq.*

[8] *Vide supra*, p. 305.

[9] Cf. Pliny, N.H. praef. 22.

[10] Spingarn, Critical Essays, I. p. 53 ; cf. Macrob. Sat. VI. 1. 2 : " quae maxime inter aliorum dicta mireris in aliquem usum tuum opportuna derivatione convertere."

imitations, while his borrowings were done in no covert[1] fashion. By the beauty and musical qualities of his language, by the aptness of his setting, he was able to transmute the crude,[2] though vigorous, phrases of Ennius into Virgilian gold.

Now legitimate imitation could take many forms, and exhibit varying degrees of talent. In the early period of Roman poetry, when the poet did little more **Translation** than translate his Greek original, translation[3] was considered a creative act. The poet might exercise a certain freedom in the act, but the polemic[4] waged between Terence and his opponents shows that there was a party at the time, that considered rigorous adherence to the Greek original as a merit rather than the reverse. But, even in such a task, the Roman poet had to struggle, in a language that was undeveloped, to express the thoughts of the Greek writer, who had at his command a language that was rich, elegant,[5] and plastic. The " patrii sermonis egestas," which Lucretius found a stumbling block in his own domain, must have been often apparent to the early Roman poet, when confronted with the copiousness of his Greek prototype. It is interesting to note that the exercise of translation seems to have been always a favourite one with students of rhetoric. Cicero regarded[6] it not merely as an instrument for acquiring a command of Latin, but as a means of enriching the native tongue, in the endeavour to reproduce the thoughts of the Greek orators. He, as a rule, was not satisfied with a literal translation, and frequently[7]

---

[1] Cf. Sen. Suas. III. 7 (in reference to Ovid's borrowings) : " non subripiendi causa sed palam mutuandi, hoc animo ut vellet agnosci."

[2] *Vide supra*, p. 289.

[3] Even when literal ; *vide supra*, p. 20.

[4] Cf. Spingarn, op. cit., Vol. I. Introd. p. 48 *et seq.*, for an interesting discussion of theories of direct translation and imitation advanced by critics of the seventeenth century.

[5] Q. X. V. 2, commends Messalla for reproducing in his translation something of the delicacy of Hyperides' speech for Phryne, no easy task for a Roman ; *vide supra*, p. 232.

[6] De Or. I. 155 ; cf. Q. II. 14. 1 *et seq.*, X. 5. 2 *et seq.* ; Pliny, Ep. VII. 9. 2.

[7] De Off. I. 6, II. 60, De Fin. I. 4, *ib.* 6, III. 15, De Leg. II. 17, De opt. gen. 14.

makes a distinction between the achievement of the mere translator and a more vital[1] and creative kind of imitation, wherein there was room for different degrees of originality. The practice of paraphrase[2] was also common in the Rhetorical schools. In the higher realm of poetry, Catullus, while keeping close to Sappho in his version[3] of her famous ode, could yet go beyond the office of the mere translator,[4] and take liberties with the original.

But, apart from the question of translation, it was recognised as possible for a Roman writer to range from mere servile[5] imitation, which was little better

Vital and servile imitation than plagiarism, to the most vital form of it, which is made familiar to us under the image[6] of the bees that flit from flower to flower, and thence draw material which they transmute into a new creation. Some are satisfied with a lifeless[7] reproduction of their original, while others are content with copying the surface[8] qualities, or the mannerisms of an author. In the age of Sallust, many[9] were found to ape the peculiarities of his style, while Quintilian tells[10] us of those who considered themselves perfect Ciceronians, if they concluded their

---

[1] Acad. Post. 8 : " Menippum imitati non interpretati " ; *ib.* 10 : " non verba sed vim Graecorum expresserunt " ; cf. Q. X. 1. 108, on Cicero himself.

[2] Cf. Cic. De Or. I. 154 ; Q. X. 5. 4.

[3] Cat. 51.

[4] However, the latest fragment of the " Coma Berenices " of Callimachus supplies evidence of a rather close translation on the part of Catullus ; cf. Prescott, The New Fragment of Callimachus' Coma Berenices, Class. Phil. Vol. XXIV (July, 1929), p. 290 *et seq. ;* Kroll, Catull, Appendix, p. 298.

[5] Hor. Ep. I. 19. 19 : " O imitatores, servum pecus " ; cf. Pliny, Ep. I. 16. 5 ; Sen. Controv. IX. 3 (26). 12.

[6] Sen. Ep. 84. 3 *et seq.*, elaborates the image ; Macrob. Sat. I. praef. 5 (following Seneca) ; cf. Lucr. III. 10 ; Hor. Odes, IV. 2. 27 *et seq.*, where the image is used without, apparently, any reference to the specific problem of imitation.

[7] Cf. Sen. Ep. 84. 8, who says in this connection " imago res mortua est."

[8] Cic. De Or. II. 91 ; cf. Middleton Murry, op. cit., p. 20 : " the coterie is formed of those who mistake the accidents for the essentials of true individuality in style."

[9] Sen. Ep. 114. 17 *et seq. ; vide supra*, p. 260.

[10] X. 2. 18.

periods with " esse videatur." Others again were unfortunately attracted by the worst faults[1] of the models which
they studied, and missed their finer traits.

In the Classical theory of imitation we often meet with
the conception of rivalry[2] between a writer and his chosen
model. Authors sometimes set out to deal
The conception with subjects[3] already treated by previous
of rivalry poets or prose-writers, and made it their aim,
not so much to introduce novel[4] ideas into the subject, as to
surpass[5] those with whom they were contending, in grace
and beauty of language. They were indifferent to the
discovery of new material, but they might always hope to
deal with the old[6] from a novel standpoint. Rhetoric, with
its employment[7] of commonplaces, its practice of free
translation, modernisation, and contamination, and its
striving after perfection of form, aided in handing down
many a well-worn theme in a slightly novel[8] guise. In
many genres there was ready to hand material that was
traditional, and that had become public[9] property, but, on
the principle[10] that a thing could be well expressed in more
than one way, a poet could set himself to his task in the
expectation of being able to invest an already familiar theme
with a new charm[11] of style. This indifference to novelty of
subject-matter was a characteristic of Classical literature

---

[1] Hor. Ep. I. 19. 17 : " decipit exemplar vitiis imitabile " ; Cic. Or.
30, 171 ; Q. X. 1. 25, *ib.* 127 (on Seneca's imitators), X. 2. 16 ; Dionys.
De Din. 8.

[2] Pliny, N.H. praef. 22 ; Pliny, Ep. VII. 30. 5, IX. 22. 1–2 ; Q. X.
5. 5 : " circa eosdem sensus certamen atque aemulationem " ; Macrob.
Sat. VI. 1. 2 ; Isocr. Panegyr. 7–10 ; περὶ ὕψους, 13. 4, 15. 5.

[3] *Vide* Stemplinger, op. cit., p. 272, on the treatment of the " Aetna "
theme by Pindar and Aeschylus ; cf. Sen. Ep. 79. 5.

[4] Isocrates (Helen. 13), comments on the difficulty of doing this in themes
already famous.

[5] Cf. the interesting fragment quoted by Jensen, op. cit. p. 49.

[6] Provided it was not what Seneca calls " consumpta," Ep. 79. 6.

[7] *Vide* Fiske, op. cit., p. 47 *et seq.*

[8] *Vide infra*, p. 439.

[9] Cf. Hor. A.P. 131, on " publica materies."

[10] Q. X. 5. 5, *ib.* 7 ; cf. Isocr. Panegyr. loc. cit.

[11] Cf. Sen. loc. cit. : " parata verba invenit, quae aliter instructa novam
faciem habent."

generally, and stands in strong contrast to the free invention favoured by the Romantic school. Though the Greek Tragic dramatists had at their disposal a vast wealth of legendary material from which to draw their plots, yet the three greatest of them had on occasion dealt with the same subject, and had each shown how it was possible to give a new turn[1] to an old legend, and leave on it the impress of his own personality. It required[2] genius to accomplish such a task, but it was precisely in such a task that genius could display its greatest brilliance.

Horace leaves[3] it open to the poet to embark upon an original theme, but again he shows himself faithful to his **Traditional themes or free invention** Classical heritage by favouring the treatment of traditional subjects, on which the dramatist can put the stamp of his own individuality. In representing the characters of ancient story the dramatist must, however, take care not to mar the traditional portrait of them. It is in connection with these problems that Horace lays[4] down some important rules for imitation. The poet who essays a traditional theme, need not always keep to the beaten path trodden by others in the same genre. It is open to him to re-adapt an old *motif*, even though the established[5] usages of the genre are there to bind him with the force of a law. Moreover, the prestige of existing models will naturally act as a lure to him, but he must beware of presenting a mere literal transcript or slavish[6] imitation of them. As we have already seen, Horace condemned plagiarism, and mocked at those of his contemporaries who were servile[7] imitators of himself. He

---

[1] *Vide supra*, p. 277.

[2] Cf. Hor. A.P. 128 : " difficile est proprie communia dicere " ; it is evident from the fragments quoted by Jensen, op. cit., Introd. p. 6, that Philodemus had a similar problem before his mind.

[3] A.P. 119–130; cf. Ar. Poet. IX. 1451b; Ar. was evidently impressed with the success of Agathon's experiment.   [4] A.P. 131–135.

[5] Horace seems to have some such meaning in mind in his use of the phrase " operis lex " in the passage.

[6] Cf. Philod. op. cit., col. XXI (Jensen, p. 69): τό τε μιμεῖσθαι [τὸ] ν Ὅμηρον ἐμ πᾶσι καὶ τὸν Εὐριπίδην . . . οὐκ ἐπιεικὲς εἶναι δόξει ; cf. *ib.* p. 67.

[7] Who evidently were especially prone to imitate external or accidental qualities in him.

sheds further light upon his conception of true imitation, when he deals[1] with his own procedure and his indebtedness to Archilochus. He reproduces, he tells us, the spirit and metre of the Greek poet, not his words nor his subjects. He evidently regarded such imitation as vital in character, and was so proud of his achievement that he boasts of having been the first[2] to introduce the Parian Iambics into Latium. Such[3] imitation, he suggests, should not detract from his glory, as even original poets like Sappho and Alcaeus had borrowed something from the metrical art of Archilochus. He boasts,[4] too, of having been the first to make Alcaeus known to his countrymen. Here again, though he may have borrowed the metre of the Greek poet, and be imbued with something of his spirit, he would claim that the song and the singer[5] were fundamentally Roman. It was considered no ignoble achievement to have adapted the Greek metres to a language with a different genius and a different modulation. The Romans, moreover, even when they were imitative, asserted their title to originality[6], in having introduced to the knowledge of their countrymen a form of literature with which they were hitherto unacquainted. It was regarded as no mean title of honour to be styled the " Roman Homer " or the " Roman Callimachus,"[7] though the poets themselves, or their ardent admirers might bring such titles into contempt.[8] Horace,

[1] Ep. I. 19. 23 *et seq. ;* the whole epistle is important for Horace's views on imitation.

[2] He ignores what Catullus had accomplished ; cf. Hardie, Res Metrica, p. 238, on Horace's claim.

[3] *Vide* Pasquali, Orazio Lirico, p. 107 *et seq.*

[4] Ep. I. 19. 32 *et seq.*; cf. Odes, I. 26. 10, III. 30. 13, IV. 9. 3, where his claims to originality are urged.

[5] In Ep. I. 19. 32, he evidently wishes to stress " Latinus fidicen " ; cf. Odes, I. 32. 3 *et seq.*, IV. 3. 23 : " Romanae fidicen lyrae."

[6] It would be interesting in this connection to analyse the value of the claims made in Lucr. I. 926, Verg. Georg. III. 40, Prop. III. 1. 3, 18 ; *vide supra*, p. 278.

[7] *Vide supra*, p. 303.

[8] Thus in the circumstances (Ep. II. 2. 99), Horace shows no enthusiasm for the title of the " Roman Alcaeus " ; in any case, the title to his mind may have suggested more dependence on the Greek model than he would be prepared to admit.

above all, claims to have drawn his inspiration from the great Classical poets of Greece, whom he regarded[1] as the most perfect models, but who, for all that, are not to be followed too literally. When he enjoins[2] constant and unwearying study of the " exemplaria Graeca," he does so, particularly because they are a standing reproof of the slovenly workmanship of his own contrymen, and can impart the lessons of elegance, refinement, and restraint, the " spiritum Graiae tenuem Camenae."[3]

As an effect[4] of this theory of imitation, there was always the danger that poets might be tempted to desert Nature for the literary model. Amongst Alexandrian critics, in particular, the cult of the written model was developed, and the worship of great masterpieces, and literary[5] echoing from the Past, became a feature of Hellenistic, and later of Roman literature. Though Horace is thus in line with the Classical tradition in recommending the study of models, he is careful to suggest certain safeguards against its abuse, and would never have been prepared to go so far as the Neo-Classical critics who found in the literary model a second[6] Nature, as Scaliger found in Virgil.

Nature v. the literary model

The Ancients[7] in their theory of Aesthetics laid stress especially on unity, symmetry,[8] and measure, as the great constituents of beauty. Horace is again in conformity with ancient[9] theory in demanding rigid unity in a poem. He insists on unity of style, and condemns the purple patch that has no organic[10] connection with the composition as a whole, and

The question of unity

[1] Ep. II. 1. 28 ; cf. Odes, IV. 9. 5 *et seq.*

[2] A.P. 268 ; the context should be noted.

[3] Odes, II. 16. 38.   [4] *Vide* Sikes, op. cit., p. 71 *et seq.*

[5] *Vide supra*, p. 276.

[6] *Vide* Saintsbury, op. cit., I. p. 37 ; Babbitt, The New Laocoon, pp. 12–13.

[7] *Vide* Bosanquet, A History of Aesthetic, p. 4 *et seq.*, 30 *et seq.* ; Babbitt, op. cit., p. 218 *et seq.*, who contrasts the modern demand for what is vital, characteristic, and expressive, as the first essentials in art.

[8] Plato, Philebus, 64 D–E.

[9] *Vide infra*, p. 482.

[10] Note " adsuitur," A.P. 16 ; such descriptions and digressions will also violate the unity of theme ; cf. *ib.* 152 on Homer as a model of unity.

is employed solely as an outlet for the poet's descriptive power. In the drama there must be unity and consistency in character-drawing. The Chorus, too, must submit to the law of unity, and form an integral part of the play. As regards the structure of a play as a whole, the Classical poets and critics favoured a much less complex[1] unity than the Romantic dramatists. Thus the *Merchant of Venice*,[2] with its underplots, and its many interests subordinate to the main theme, offers in its complexity a striking contrast to the almost statuesque simplicity of a Greek tragedy. The ancient conception of unity did not, however, exclude variety[3], but the poet in his quest of variety was bound not to introduce elements that were irrational,[4] or that clashed with the harmony of the whole.

Horace was not one of these who believe that the caprice of the poet suffers no law above itself. In modern times,

The poet's world

Young[5] sounded the tocsin of Pseudo-Romanticism, when he declared that "in the fairy-land of fancy genius may wander wild; there it has a creative power, and may reign arbitrarily over its own empire of chimeras." The poet, indeed, can create a world[6] of his own, and, if he is endowed with the true genius of the poet, can insure our belief in his creation. But, even the poet must not offend our sense of congruity[7] by endeavouring to unite things that are essentially incompatible. Horace would have no sympathy with the false Romanticism which could bring into being a world of chimeras having no conceivable relation with existing experience. Such things he would regard as the fevered dreams[8] of a diseased imagination. He would thus

---

[1] Hor. A.P. 23 emphasises the "simplex" as well as the "unum"; Plato's plea for simplicity in art generally (Rep. III. 397 A *et seq.*) is of interest here.

[2] In this connection Moulton's study in "Shakespeare as a Dramatic Artist," c. 3, is illuminating.

[3] Cf. Dionys. De C.V. c. XI, XIX.

[4] A.P. 29.

[5] *Vide* Babbitt, Rousseau and Romanticism, p. 40.

[6] Cf. Plautus, Pseudolus, 401 *et seq.*; *vide supra*, p. 2.

[7] A.P. 29–30; cf. Claudian, In Eutrop. I. 355, for an interesting parallel.

[8] A.P. 7: "velut aegri somnia."

look askance at the riot of imagination, and the unfettered play of emotion, which many regard as the divine prerogative of poets. He would not allow either imagination or emotion to pass from under the sway of Reason. However, the real difficulty arises when one sets out to determine how far the controlling hand of Reason is to be felt in the fictions of the poets.

Neither Horace,[1] nor the critics who preceded him, were yet in a position to realise adequately the functions of the creative imagination. Horace, only to reject the picture as ludicrous, opens the *Ars*

The creative imagination

Poetica with a description of a strange monster,[2] which a painter might put on canvas. He forgets that figures[3] almost as fantastic appeared in ancient legend, or that they could be made credible by the genius of the poet, who, if he creates the proper atmosphere, can, without offending our sense of congruity, people his world with strange creatures. Though he may have felt it necessary to sound a warning note, yet he is inclined to curb too strongly the poet's imagination with the reins of reason and of logic. In a later passage[4] of the *Ars Poetica*, he seems to go still further, when he insists that the poet's fictions be " proxima veris." The words, if taken literally,[5] would compel the poet to work within narrow and prosaic limits. Horace is here probably endeavouring to give a suitable equivalent for the Greek concept of τὸ πιθανόν, but everything depends on whether he demands an inherent probability in the poet's creations, or whether he is pre-

[1] Nor for that matter many of the modern critics ; cf. Saintsbury's discussion of Addison's views on Imagination, op. cit., II. p. 444 *et seq.*

[2] For similar monsters on Persian tapestry, cf. Aristoph. Frogs, 938 ; note Euripides' criticism of Aeschylus' monsters ; cf. Lewes, Principles of Success in Literature, p. 55 *et seq.*, for a discussion of Imagination that has a bearing here.

[3] Though the scientific temperament of Lucretius rejects them as impossible, V. 878 *et seq.*

[4] 338 ; Horace may here again have been under the influence of Hellenistic theory ; cf. Jensen, op. cit., p. 112.

[5] The French Neo-Classical critics took the narrower view in their insistence on " vraisemblance "; on Aristotle's conception of " Poetic truth," cf Butcher, Aristotle's Theory, c. 3.

pared to admit that the genius of the poet may invest things with a probability of its own fashioning. If we are not attributing too much to Horace, we might[1] on the latter supposition interpret " proxima veris " as things which are made so life-like by the poet, as to create the illusion of reality. Significantly enough, he praises[2] Homer's power of fiction, above all the " speciosa miracula " which sprang from the poet's fertile imagination in the *Odyssey*, and which, with their " plesance and half wonder,"[3] embody the true spirit of poetry. Still, in spite of such momentary enthusiasms, we may as a rule discern Reason and Good Sense sitting enthroned in the background of Horatian criticism. Horace would discipline the poet in the workings of his imagination, just as he would discipline him in the technique of his art. But here again, as in his demand for measure, unity, and symmetry, he displays his loyalty to the tenets of the Classical creed.

[1] Though, I am afraid, lines 339–340 rather tell against this view.
[2] *Vide supra*, p. 410.
[3] *Vide* Ker, The Art of Poetry, p. 19.

CHAPTER VII

THE SUPREMACY OF RHETORIC

ONE OF the remarkable characteristics of Roman criticism
is its tendency to criticise from the rhetorical standpoint, not only the productions of the orator, but the
The predomi- productions of the poet and the historian.
nant position Such a characteristic will appear strange in
of Rhetoric modern times, when the artistic creations of
the poet, and the results of the historian's labours, are
judged by other standards, but it will appear less surprising,
if we consider the predominant position held by Rhetoric
in Roman education from very early times. The teaching
of Rhetoric was, it is true, forbidden[1] at Rome in 161 B.C.,
while the school of the " Latini Rhetores "[2] was closed in
92 B.C., ostensibly because its conception of education was
too narrow. Yet, at all times, the Roman was willing to wield
the weapons which Rhetoric could furnish, and pay his
tribute to the power of the spoken word, and to the spell
which emotional oratory could cast upon its hearers. When
the orator realised how his words could sway the multitude
he might well exclaim with Pacuvius " O flexanima atque
omnium regina rerum oratio."[3] In opposition to the claims
of the poet and the philosopher, oratory had its champions
who urged[5] its right to be regarded as the power which had
brought men together into organised society, and as the

---

[1] Suet. De Rhet. I ; *vide supra*, p. 29.

[2] *Vide supra*, p. 152.

[3] Cf. Cic. De Or. II. 187, *ib*. 33–34, I. 30 *et seq*., De Inv. I. 2. 3, Br. 59
Or. 141, De Nat. Deor. II. 148, Pro Mur. 30 ; Tac. Dial. 32 : " olin
omnium artium domina " ; *ib*. 36 ; Q. I. 10. 7, VI. 2. 4 ; Fronto, II, p
136 : " eloquentia mentibus dominatur."

[4] Cic. Tusc. Disp. I. 62, V. 5 ; Hor. A.P. 391 *et seq*. ; Sen. Ep. 90
Tac. Dial. 12 ; Aristoph. Frogs, 1030 *et seq*.

[5] Cic. De Inv. I. 2. 2, De Or. I. 33, 36 ; Isocr. περὶ ἀντιδ. 253 *et se.*

greatest of civilising influences. According to this view, oratory might establish its claim to be " the first school-mistress of man, the chief agency which leads him from barbarism to civilisation, from the bondage of the senses to the freedom of the spirit."[1] In the eyes of many Romans other accomplishments were " leviores artes,"[2] as contrasted with eloquence. Oratory was the sovereign accomplishment which could unlock[3] the door to all the other arts. Hence the Romans could apply the word " eloquentia "[4] to literature in general, to poetry as well as to prose. The philosopher and the scientist, if they wish to set forth their thoughts in clear and attractive form,[5] must have recourse to Rhetoric, and borrow its trappings. Thus equipped, even the layman, according to Cicero, will treat a subject more convincingly than the expert who lacks the graces of style.

It is little wonder then, that the Romans were willing to undergo a severe course of rhetorical training, and were not repelled even by a multitude of technical minutiae in their eagerness to master such an art. Many of the Ancients were naturally inclined to direct their attention particularly to the formal side of Rhetoric, which taught men the magic power of words,[6] enabled them to invest a trivial subject with dignity, and make new things old and old things new.[7] One who had learned the potentialities of language, and had become endowed with some of its riches, could boast[8] of being able

The formal side of Rhetoric

---

[1] *Vide* Vaughan, The Romantic Revolt, p. 337, on Kant's view of Art.

[2] Cic. De Or. I. 212, Br. 3.

[3] De Or. II. 5 ; Sen. Controv. II. pr. 3 : " eloquentiæ tantum studeas ; facilis ab hac in omnes artes discursus est " ; cf. Aristides, Or. 45 : ἅπαντα διὰ τῆς ῥητορικῆς πεποίηται.

[4] Cic. De Or. II. 55 ; Tac. Dial. 10 ; Pliny, Ep. V. 8. 4 : " orationi enim et carmini parva gratia, nisi eloquentia est summa " ; Q. X. 1. 61, 2. 22.

[5] De Or. I. 49, 62 *et seq.*

[6] cf. Plato, Phaedrus, 267 A–B, on the Sophistic ideal ; Isocr. Panegyr. 8, Helen, 11 *et seq. ;* Spengel, Rh. Gr. I. p. 328 ; *vide supra*, p. 431.

[7] Though Pliny, N.H. Praef. says : " res ardua vetustis novitatem dare."

[8] Cf. Sen. Controv. IV. pr. 7 (on Q. Haterius) ; Ovid, Ars Am. II. 130, Ex Ponto, III. 9. 41 ; Don. ad Terent. Eunuch, Prol. I ; Philostr. V.S. 572, 619.

to treat[1] the same theme in many different ways. Such a one might be tempted to make experiments in various spheres of literature, and with his dangerous gift of fluency, and his skill in the manipulation of words, might, unbidden by the Muses, be led to make incursions even into the realm of the poet. He would certainly be encouraged thereto by the stress that many laid on the formal side of poetry, and the affinity that some endeavoured to establish between the work of the orator and that of the poet.

There were, indeed, many influences at work which tended to emphasise the external elements in the poet's creations. Poetry may be said to have a "rhetoric"[2] of its own, if the expression be used with due safeguards. In examining the art of the poet, one might dwell on his qualities of clearness and orderly arrangement, the character of his rhythms, and his power of creating a subtle harmony by his selection of euphonious diction, or by the skilful setting of his words. Moreover, the poet may contribute to the melody of his verse by the use of alliteration and assonance, and may add a new suggestiveness to his lines by playing with the repetition of some single letter. Figurative speech, splendour and elevation of language, are natural to the poet of vision, of great imaginative range, and emotional power. There was, however, always the danger that the ancient critic, in endeavouring to disengage the "art" of poetry, might regard the elements I have described as so much applied ornament,[3] having little or no vital connection[4] with the poet's thoughts and feelings. The evil was accentuated, if the critic had pursued the traditional course of rhetoric, and sought to fit the poet's technique in many of its aspects into the rigid categories consecrated in the schools. As we

(marginal note:) External elements in poetry emphasised

---

[1] Mostly a fatal gift, as Fronto discerned in the case of Seneca ; *vide supra*, p. 352.

[2] The "art of the word", as one might call it, which touches at certain points the "rhetoric" of artistic prose ; cf. Warren, op. cit., p. 128 *et seq.*

[3] The danger was especially great, when critics dealt with the use of Figures in poetry ; *vide infra.*, p. 448.

[4] In this connection, some of the criticisms passed by Philodemus, Jensen pp. 25–29, are important.

shall see, some of the Ancients thought they could discover a complete system of rhetoric in Homer, but the discovery was due more to the ingenuity of the critics than to the characteristics of the poet.

There were many factors that helped to establish the rhetorical point of view in judging the achievements of the poets. From early times[1], prose-writers had set themselves to study the secret of their appeal, and the Sophistic rhetoricians in particular had tried to win for their own domain some of the pleasure which they afforded. Aristotle[2] notes in this connection that the poets were the first to excite a feeling for style. The Sophists, indeed, indulged to excess in poetical ornament,[3] borrowing freely the diction of the poets,[4] and imitating their figurative language, heedless of the fact that it was unsuited to the genius of prose. They thus developed a style that savoured[5] of the dithyramb. Moreover, they had discovered[6] that the rhythmical element in poetry constituted one of the great sources of its charm, and they were eager to impart a kindred charm to their own writings. Isocrates made[7] a similar discovery, but he realised better than his predecessors that poetry and prose were governed by different laws. Gorgias, in fact, had marred his prose by seeking for rhythmical effects that were suggestive of verse.[8] Such tendencies as I have mentioned,

The rhetorical point of view ; its genesis

---

[1] I am not, of course, here entering into the vexed question of the forms of early Greek prose ; Aly, Die Formprobleme, and Lamb, op. cit., might be consulted.

[2] Rhet. III. 1. 8.

[3] Agathon's speech, Sympos. 194 E *et seq.*, might be compared, cf. Lamb, op. cit., p. 136, n. 3 ; *vide supra*, p. 99.

[4] *Vide supra*, p. 87 ; on the Second Sophistic movement, cf. Rohde, Der. griech. Roman, p. 355 *et seq.*, 358 ; cf. Philost. V. Soph. 620, where tragedy is styled μήτηρ σοφιστῶν, owing to their imitation of its stately manner ; *ib.* 539, for Polemo's dictum ; cf. *ib.* 500, 518 (on Scopelian).

[5] Cf. Plato, Phaedrus, 238 D, where he is evidently glancing at Sophistic prose ; Dionys. De Lys. 3 ; περὶ ὕψους, III. 2.

[6] *Vide supra*, p. 99 *et seq.*

[7] περὶ ἀντιδ. 47, Evag. 9–11 ; Cic. De Or. III. 173–174, Or. 174, where Cicero notes the lessons drawn by Isocrates from his study of the poets.

[8] Cic. Or. 39 : " versiculorum similia quaedam nimiumque depicta " ; cf. Dionys. De Lys. 14 ; though balanced antitheses were in use before

would naturally have helped to turn the attention of the rhetoricians to the formal side of poetry, and have inclined them to treat it in the same spirit as their own peculiar pursuit. Hence the disposition to stress the affinity[1] between poetry and elevated prose. We thus find Isocrates[2] setting up a comparison between compositions in verse and epideictic exercises in oratory, which, being designed chiefly to give pleasure,[3] enjoyed greater licence than was accorded to the more staid and sober eloquence of the law-courts.

A later writer, Dionysius,[4] raises the question how prose can resemble a beautiful poem. He declares that choice of diction may do much to create such a re-

Problems raised by Dionysius

semblance, though he remarks incidentally that many prose-writers are inclined to employ poetical diction to excess. In his eyes, the points of contact between the two are to be found mainly in euphonious arrangement of words and in rhythmical effects.[5] When he sets out to compare the great orations of Demosthenes with the finest poems and lyrics, his mind is fixed chiefly on the formal elements in his prose. Plato's style[6] evidently created a problem for the ancient critics, as it was felt to possess qualities that raised[7] it above the level of ordinary prose. Dionysius pays a tribute to his casual style, but he finds[8] many defects in him in his elevated passages. Plato's

Gorgias' time, it was probably his study of the rhythms of verse that led him to employ such a device to the extent he did.

[1] Cf. Strabo, I. 2. 6 : ὁ πεζὸς λόγος, ὁ γε κατασκευασμένος μίμημα τοῦ ποιητικοῦ ἐστι.

[2] περὶ ἀντιδ. 46 et seq. ; cf. Q. X. 1. 28.   [3] Vide supra, p. 71.

[4] De C.V. c. 25 ; Dionysius has here elevated prose in mind.

[5] In respect of these, he is inclined to overstate his case at times in his eagerness to establish an affinity between the two ; cf. his analysis of a passage from the "Aristocrates" of Demosthenes ; vide Rhys Roberts, ad loc.

[6] Walsdorff, Die antike Urteile über Platons Stil, deals interestingly with the judgments passed on Plato's style from different standpoints.

[7] Aristotle considered it midway between prose and poetry, Diog. Laer. III. 37.

[8] Ep. ad Pomp. c. 2, De Dem. 5, 23 et seq. ; Dionysius does not seem to make allowance for the element of irony in Plato, or for his love of parody (Ar. Rhet. III. 7. 11) ; he may have been influenced, too, by the attitude of Caecilius ; cf. περὶ ὕψους, 32. 7–8.

prose was on such occasions poetical, but in Dionysius' view its poetical character consisted mainly in its use of " figurative and dithyrambic diction." The Roman[1] critics may have been influenced by similar considerations in their judgments on Plato, but they have the merit of directing attention also to the essential elements of poetry in him, his sublimity, the glowing fervour of his imagination, and the other characteristics that mark him as an inspired writer.[2] In general, however, though the ancient critics recognised at times the play of true poetic genius, yet when they spoke of prose being " poetical," they had in mind rather its formal features than its inner soul.

When we turn specifically to the Roman critics, we find that Cicero in particular[3] was fond of emphasising the affinity between the poet and the orator. In

The Roman critics seeking to establish such a kinship, he was probably following in the wake of Isocrates, and had in mind especially emotional and epideictic oratory. Such a view would be even easier of adoption at a later date,[4] when the declaimers were ready to borrow freely the trappings of the poets, in their efforts to rise above the commonplace. Such a tendency would be fostered all the more, when the poets themselves began to take part in the declamations, and set the example of importing into them some of the qualities of their own verse. The elder Seneca gives us occasional glimpses of Ovid in the schools. His declamatory style for the most part showed restraint, but at times[5] his declamation presented the characteristics of a

[1] Cic. De Or. I. 49, Or. 67 ; Tac. Dial. 31 ; Pliny, Ep. I. 10. 5 ; Q. X. 1. 81 ; cf. περὶ ὕψους, c. 12–13.

[2] Democritus was looked on as endowed with similar qualities ; cf., however, De Or. I. 49 : " materies illa fuit physici, de qua dixit, ornatus ipse verborum oratoris putandus est " ; for Democritus' fragments, cf. Diels, Die Fragmente der Vorsokratiker, Vol. I. p. 350 *et seq. ;* Norden, A.K. I. p. 22 ; Lamb, op. cit., p. 119 *et seq.*

[3] De Or. I. 70 : " est enim finitimus oratori poeta . . . multis vero ornandi generibus socius ac paene par " ; *ib.* III. 27, Or. 188, 201, 227.

[4] Cf. Ovid, Ex Ponto, II. 5. 65 *et seq.* (on oratory and poetry) : " distat opus nostrum, sed fontibus exit ab isdem " ; Sen. Controv. IX. 5 (28). 17, where Montanus is styled " inter oratores Ovidius."

[5] Controv. II. 2 (10). 8 : " oratio ejus jam tum nihil aliud poterat videri quam solutum carmen " ; cf. *ib.* 12.

prose poem. It is clear that he exercised[1] no little influence on some of his fellow-declaimers, who were ready to embody in their own utterances a striking phrase, or a thought however tasteless and extravagant, from the poet's works. The declaimers profited,[2] too, by their study of Virgil, to win some new embellishment for their rhetorical exercises. There was indeed[3] a marked tendency in many of the prose writers of the period to employ poetical diction and ornament. The fashion was in the air, if we are to believe Aper, who tells[4] us that something of the beauty and polish of the poet was then demanded of the orator. Many were not satisfied with indulging in poetic diction, but adopted[5] bold metaphors and other figures, even from poets who were remarkable for the perverse extravagance of their own style. Poetical descriptions[6] were favoured in prose, while many[7] affected the inversion of the usual order of words, as if to simulate the manner of poetry.

The rhetoricians thus considered that they could win many new embellishments from poetry. Such a view was **The poets in** also naturally fostered by the fact that the **the curriculum** poets had their place in the curriculum of **of Rhetoric** the rhetorical schools, where there was a tendency to favour such poets, and to consider such aspects of poetry, as were likely to aid in the training of the future orator. We have seen that Cicero[8] adopted this utilitarian

[1] Controv. I. 2. 22, III. 7, X. 4 (33). 25.

[2] Suas. III. 4–5, Controv. VII. 1 (16). 27.

[3] Sen. Ep. 114. 14 ; cf. Q. VIII. pr. 18 *et seq.*, on some of the vicious tendencies in the oratory of his day ; Norden, A.K. I. 331, on poetical word in Tacitus ; Fronto and later writers were acting on principles of their own in rifling the works of the older poets ; cf. Butler and Owen, Apulei Apologia Introd., p. 48 *et seq.*, *ib.* 63 ; *vide supra*, p. 341.

[4] Tac. Dial. 20 ; Aper takes care to emphasise the fact that it is the modern poets that are to be drawn upon ; cf. Ovid, Ex Ponto, II. 5. 70 " sic venit a nobis in tua verba nitor " ; cf. Seneca's quotation from Latro Controv. II. 2 (10). 8.

[5] Q. VIII. pr. 25 : " a corruptissimo quoque poetarum figuras seu translationes mutuamur " ; *ib.* 3. 76 ; Sen. Ep. 114. 10.

[6] Pliny, Ep. VII. 9. 8 ; Q. II. 4. 3 ; *vide infra*, p. 507.

[7] Sen. Ep. 100. 5 : " nec hujus saeculi more contra naturam suam posita et inversa (verba)."

[8] *Vide supra*, p. 146.

standpoint in certain of his judgments on poetry, and that his refusal to study the lyric poets was, in part at least, due to his conviction that they[1] could contribute little to the perfection of the orator. In the *De Oratore*[2] he proclaims the usefulness of a knowledge of the poets for one who aims at elegance of style. Though he realised that they could render other services, yet he was often inclined to view their achievements from the standpoint of formal rhetoric.[3]

Quintilian in his Tenth Book affords us the best example of the course of reading recommended to the student of **Quintilian's Tenth Book** rhetoric. The similarity of his programme with that of Dionysius,[4] and of Dion Chrysostom,[5] shows that he was following on the lines already marked out in the rhetorical schools of Greece.[6] Theophrastus seems to have been one of the first to recommend the reading of the poets to the future orator. Quintilian, in quoting his opinion,[7] declares that the orator may benefit from such reading by being imbued with something of the inspired qualities of poetry, as well as by acquiring sublimity in his language, power to rouse every kind of emotion, and a capacity for appropriate character-drawing. In common with Cicero, he dwells on the fact that such studies by their charm bring balm to minds that are jaded by the labours of the law-courts, while through them the orator is enabled to add piquancy to his speeches[8] by illustrations and reflexions drawn from the poets. With students of rhetoric paraphrase of poetry was a favourite

---

[1] Cf. Dio Chrys. Or. 18. 8 (Arnim, Vol. II, p. 253) : τῷ δὲ πράττειν τὲ καὶ ἅμα τοὺς λόγους αὔξειν διανοουμένῳ οὐκ ἄν εἴη πρὸς αὐτὰ (i.e. lyric, elegiac, etc., poetry) σχολή.

[2] III. 39, *ib.* 48, where " lectio veterum oratorum atque poetarum " is said to help towards correctness.

[3] *Vide supra*, p. 144.

[4] In the περὶ μιμήσεως ; cf. Ad Pomp. c. 3 ; *vide* Usener, op. cit., p. 110 *et seq.* ; Peterson, Quintilian, Book X, Introd., p. 30 *et seq.*

[5] Especially in Or. 18 ; Dionysius was an early contemporary of Quintilian's, but would be evidence for the Greek rhetorical tradition.

[6] *Vide* Stemplinger, op. cit., pp. 109, 111–112 ; Schmid, Der Atticismus I. p. 107.

[7] Q. X. 1. 27 ; cf. Jul. Severianus, Halm, op. cit. II. p. 355.

[8] Q. XII. 4. 1 ; cf. V. 11. 17.

exercise,[1] which continued in vogue for many centuries.[2] It is clear, however, that Quintilian did not wish his pupils to concentrate on the mere formal element in poetry,[3] while he was careful to point out[4] the different aims that should guide the orator and the poet. The former, moving as he was on a lower plane, was not to attempt to follow the poet in his grander flights, nor was he to endeavour to emulate him in the licence of his language and the boldness of his figures. We shall see that even Quintilian himself, pre-occupied with his own art, is at times inclined to be oblivious of this doctrine, and strives to bring the poets and their work into conformity with the formulas of the schools. The danger would be all the more real in the case of teachers not gifted with his discretion.

We have seen that it was customary to stress the affinity between poetry and elevated prose. However, theorists,[5] **Formal differ-** conscious of the fact that the same laws did **ences between** not prevail in both,[6] were accustomed also to **poetry and** **prose** indicate certain points of difference between them. But it is to be noted that the differences discussed were almost exclusively concerned with the externals of style.[7] Some critics[8] declared that, because the poets aimed solely at giving pleasure, they were less fettered in their language than the writer of oratorical prose. They were therefore granted a greater licence[9] in the coinage of new words, and in the use of rare and obsolete ones. Theirs, too, was the privilege of searching out words remarkable for their beauty and musical qualities. It was recognised, as

---

[1] Q. X. 5. 4.

[2] St. Augustine, Conf. I. 17.

[3] The dramatic poets in particular could teach other lessons; cf. Q. I. 8. 5 *et seq.*, I. 11. 1.

[4] X. 1. 28.

[5] Q. X. 2. 21.

[6] The poets themselves, in the face of such theorising, were evidently compelled to raise the question how they differed from the orator; cf. Cic. Or. 66.

[7] Especially the elements that in rhetorical theory were comprised under the head of " ornatus."

[8] Q. X. 1. 28 ; cf. *ib*. VIII. 6. 17.

[9] *Vide supra*, pp. 90–91.

we have seen,[1] that in a measure the poets spoke a language of their own, so that certain words permitted to them were excluded[2] from prose. They were, moreover, conceded a larger freedom in the use of figurative speech.[3] They could indulge without restriction in the figures of thought and diction, be lavish in similes and ornamental epithets, and employ metaphors however daring.

The introduction of rhythm into prose was another development that helped to direct attention[4] to the affinity between poetry and oratorical prose, though critics were also careful to note the points in which they diverged in respect of this element of style. The poet is bound to a definite metrical scheme of recurring pattern. He is forced to take licences[5] with language to suit the exigencies of his metre. His metrical art is thus obvious[6] in its broadest features, though he enjoys the advantage that the music of his verse may serve to beguile the ear, and distract attention from his shortcomings. Artistic prose could show cadences of its own, governed by no rigid laws, but wandering freely, and lending their charm according to the fancy of the writer. The prose-writer, however, in his use of rhythm was bound never to allow his art to become obvious,[7] nor to admit even the suggestion of metre into his composition.

Now, all this study of the art of the poet, especially if directed by teachers who were insensible to his inner spirit,

Poetry drawn into the sphere of Rhetoric would inevitably tend to draw poetry more and more within the ambit of formal rhetoric. It would tend, also, to engender the idea that many of the ornaments of verse[8] were merely applied

---

[1] *Vide supra*, p. 393. [2] Q. VIII. 3. 26.

[3] *Ib.* IV. 1. 58, VIII. 6. 17–18, 20, 24, 40, 66.

[4] Cf. Cic. Or. 188, 201, 227.

[5] To indulge in what Q. (X. 1. 29) calls " eloquendi quaedam deverticula."

[6] The modern " vers libre " would present a problem to the ancient critics ; Pindar's metres were a difficulty for some of them ; cf. Hor. Odes, IV. 2. 11–12.

[7] *Vide supra*, p. 101 ; Tempest, The Rhythm of English Prose, p. 14 *et seq.*, might be compared.

[8] Note Cicero's reference (De Or. I. 70) to the " multa ornandi genera " common to the poet and the orator ; cf. Q. I. 8. 16 : " tropos omnes quibus praecipue non poema modo sed oratio ornatur."

ornament[1], to be used or discarded at will. That was especially true of the Figures, which many were inclined to consider as different colours[2] to be laid on according to a writer's caprice. Dionysius, as we have seen, pays a tribute[3] to certain lines in the *Odyssey*, and argues that their appeal springs mainly from the poet's skill in composition. It is interesting, however, to find him noting the absence in them of noble metaphors and other figurative language, though in reality these would have been out of place in what is essentially a plain narrative passage. The rhetoricians had the Figures[4] carefully tabulated, and in the exercise of a somewhat perverted ingenuity were continually adding to the list. Many of the Figures recognised by them must have been drawn originally from the poets,[5] who struck them out in the glow of an inspired moment, and under the influence of some powerful passing emotion. The rhetoricians in turn, moving in a kind of vicious circle, brought their formidable array of Figures to bear on their judgment of a poet's beauty and impressiveness, but too often considered such ornaments apart from the inmost core of feeling in which they had originated. Quintilian was probably moved[6] by the spirit of the rhetorician in paying[7] homage to Homer's transcendent power in the use of Figures. In his general treatment of the Figures,[8] he is as ready to take his illustrations from the poets[9] as from the prose-writers. The later commentators on Virgil loved to note his use of figurative

---

[1] *Vide supra*, p. 111.

[2] Dryden in " A Parallel of Poetry and Painting " speaks of " Cromatic," with special reference to tropes and figures ; cf. Ker, Essays of John Dryden, Vol. II. p. 147.

[3] De C.V. c. 3.

[4] *Vide supra*, p. 106 *et seq.*

[5] The study of Homer in particular must have contributed not a little to this department of rhetoric ; *vide infra*, p. 462, on Telephus ; cf. Dionys. Ars. Rhet. περὶ ἐσχηματισμένων, C. VIII. 11 *et seq.* ; on the work entitled περὶ Ὁμήρου, *vide* Jensen, op. cit., p. 172–174.

[6] We shall, at any rate, see that Quintilian's general treatment of Homer was much influenced by the conventional scheme of rhetoric.

[7] X. 1. 50 ; cf. *ib.* 96, where Horace is styled " varius figuris."

[8] Bks. VIII–IX.

[9] Especially from Virgil ; cf. Julius Rufinianus, Halm, op. cit., Vol. I, p. 38 *et seq.* ; cf. *ib.* p. 71 *et seq.*

language.[1] The same tendency is apparent[2] in the commentaries on Terence written by Donatus and Eugraphius. The practice of noting the figures employed by a poet is not in itself to be condemned. Everything depends on the spirit in which it is done. There is, however, always a certain presumption that critics, who in other respects read their poet in the light of the stereotyped scheme of rhetoric, regard such elements in his verse not as springing from the body of his thought, but as so much rhetorical embellishment employed to enhance his style.

The attention paid to the art of the poet in the rhetorical schools might also have the effect of creating the illusion

The effect of rhetorical training

that the difference between the poet and the orator was largely formal, a difference of degree rather than of kind. The rhetoricians would probably claim that they had the right to judge the poet in all that pertained to " elocutio." Hence they often classify together poetry and prose genres with reference to style. In the *Brutus*, where he sets out to trace the history of Roman oratory from its remotest origins, Cicero appeals[3] to the writings of Naevius to illustrate the style that prevailed in the early period, when as yet oratory was obscure and undeveloped. On the score of purity of speech he contrasts[4] Caecilius and Pacuvius with Scipio and Laelius. In the *Orator*,[5] having illustrated the law of variety in style from his own speeches, he passes on to show that a similar law was operative in Homer, Ennius, and the writers of tragedy, but he uses terms[6] that are clearly reminiscent of rhetorical theory. We have no remains by which to judge of the tragedies of Julius Caesar Strabo,[7] but it is interesting to note that Cicero finds[8] the same qualities of style pre-

---

[1] Cf. Macrob. Sat. VI. 6. 20, where Servius says : " dies me deficiet si omnia persequi a Vergilio figurata velim"; cf. Moore, Servius on the Tropes and Figures of Vergil, A. J. Phil. XII, p. 157 *et seq.*, 267 *et seq.*

[2] Cf. ad Andria, 149, 285, Eun. 243, Adelphi, 241.

[3] Br. 60 : " illius autem aetatis qui sermo fuerit ex Naevianis scriptis intellegi potest."

[4] *Ib.* 258.   [5] 109.

[6] Note his contrast of " sermo " and " contentio."

[7] *Vide supra*, p. 62.

[8] Br. 177 ; cf. 167, on Titius.

vailing in them as in his speeches. Possibly, in his case the effect of his rhetorical training was apparent even in his dramas.

In the conditions under which it was studied in the schools, poetry might well come to be considered an art as **Poetry regar-** formal as the art of rhetoric, and one that **ed as a formal** with experience could be practised with a **art** similar ease. Such an idea would be strengthened by the tendency to subject each poetic genre to definite laws. Suetonius describes Valerius Cato[1] as a competent teacher, particularly for those who had a turn for poetry, while there must have been many, besides Horace's friends the Pisos, who sought instruction in the art.

It is evident that such an atmosphere as I have described, was congenial to the growth of the poetic dilettantism which **Growth of** became rife in Imperial times. If we can **poetic** trust Horace's testimony,[2] men of every con- **dilettantism** dition were then turning their hand to verse. The educated Roman who had completed a course of rhetoric, had acquired skill in the manipulation of words,[3] and whose ear was attuned to rhythm,[4] might easily be lured by a false ambition to seek entry into the ranks of the poets. Every age will produce its crop of poetasters[5] of the tribe of Bavius and Maevius,[6] who cumber the ground for a time, till they are cast into oblivion amidst the scorn of genuine poets and candid critics. On a somewhat higher plane stand the minor poets, who to us are often nothing more than mere names preserved by chance in the pages of a contemporary.[7] All these would, in a sense, aim at making

---

[1] De Gr. XI : " qui solus legit ac facit poetas."

[2] Ep. II. 1. 117 ; cf. A.P. 382 *et seq.* ; Persius, I. 13, 51 *et seq.* ; Pliny, Ep. I. 13. 1 ; Juv. VII. 51–52.

[3] Had become what Cicero would style " operarius lingua celeri et exercitata," De Or. I. 83.

[4] Cf. Q. IX. 4. 114.

[5] Catullus, XIV. 5, XXII. 3 *et seq.*, XXXVI ; Cic. Pro Archia, 25, Ad Att. II. 20. 6 ; V. Eclog. IX. 33 *et seq.* ; Prop. II. 34. 84 ; Mart. VI. 60, VII. 25, *ib.* 46.

[6] V. Eclog. III. 90 ; Hor. Epod. X. 2.

[7] Cf. Ovid, Ex Ponto, IV. 16, where among well-known names many obscure poets are enumerated.

poetry a profession, but side by side with them was a host of amateurs, notably from amongst the orators, who strove to win the laurels of the poet. If for no other reason, the orator, trained rhetorician that he was, sought relaxation from his forensic labours, or tried to beguile his leisure moments, by the delights of verse-making,[1] in the belief, as Petronius tells us,[2] that a poem was easier to construct than a declamation embellished with quivering epigrams. We find the younger Pliny[3] appealing to the example of many orators, as well as statesmen and Emperors, in defence of some *risqué* verses which he had composed. The elder Catulus, who as we saw was an ardent Hellenist, seems to have been one of the first of the orators to devote himself seriously to the poet's calling. There is, in fact, about the verses preserved from his pen,[4] a grace which shows that he was not devoid of poetic talent. Hortensius was an inveterate verse-maker, if we can trust the testimony of Catullus, who contrasts[5] his abnormal output with the single poem on which Cinna had spent years of patient labour. Hortensius' verse was often in lascivious vein, and in the conditions under which it was produced, could have little merit.[6] Cicero was particularly unfortunate in his incursions into the realms of poetry, though his feeling for rhythm, and his faculty for nice discrimination in words, enabled him to contribute something towards the perfecting of the technique of Latin verse. Quintus Cicero was even more prolific as a verse-maker than his brother. He accomplished the amazing feat of composing four tragedies in sixteen days.[7] These could only have been translations from the Greek, but even as such, especially if he endeavoured to

---

[1] Cf. Nepos, Atticus, 18 : " attigit quoque poeticen ; credimus ne ejus expers esset suavitatis " ; cf. Pliny, Ep. VII. 4. 4.

[2] Satyr. 118 ; Petronius was, of course, thinking especially of the conditions of his own day ; cf. Pliny, Ep. IV. 27. 4.

[3] Ep. V. 3. 5, VII. 9. 12.

[4] *Vide supra*, p. 59.

[5] 95.

[6] Cf. Gellius, XIX. 9, 7, where it is styled " invenusta " ; cf. Varro, De L.L. VIII. 14, X. 78 ; Ovid, Trist. II. 441 ; Pliny, Ep. V. 3. 5.

[7] Ad Q. Fr. III. 5–6. 7 ; on his version of Sophocles' " Banqueters," *vide supra*, p. 145.

reproduce the metres of the originals, they stand as evidence of his marvellous skill as a versifier. Both Cato[1] and Brutus[2] at times abandoned the more serious pursuit of oratory and philosophy for the delights of poetry.

With Julius Caesar,[3] we might say, begins the long line of Imperial poets. Augustus forbade the publication of his youthful productions in verse, evidently

The Imperial poets

regarding them as unworthy of his reputation. Tacitus, with a characteristic touch of irony, says that Brutus and Julius Caesar were more fortunate than Cicero in their poetry, in that fewer people were aware of its existence. Suetonius mentions[4] a hexameter poem on Sicily, and a volume of *Epigrams*, as extant from the pen of Augustus. The Emperor, who gave indications of literary taste, began a tragedy on Ajax, but, dissatisfied with his efforts, he destroyed what he had written, wittily remarking that his *Ajax* had fallen on his sponge. Of the other[5] Imperial poets little need be said, though Quintilian[6] found occasion to indulge in fulsome flattery of Domitian's undeveloped powers, and Martial, with the instincts of the courtier, styled[7] Nerva the Tibullus of his time. Nero's pride[8] in his talents as a poet made it difficult for him to brook known or suspected rivals. Suetonius comments[9] on the ready skill in verse-making which he exhibited in his youth, so that like Ovid he might[10] claim to have " lisped in numbers," even as a boy. The Emperor Titus possessed[11] a similar talent, which reached even to the point of improvisation, both in poetry and oratory.

[1] Plut. Cato Min. 7.   [2] Tac. Dial. 21.
[3] Suet. J.C. 56 ; Tac. loc. cit. ; Pliny, Ep. V. 3. 5.
[4] Aug. 85 ; cf. Pliny, loc. cit. ; Mart. XI. 20, gives an example of what he styles his " Romana simplicitas," evidently from the Epigrams.
[5] cf. Suet. Tib. 70.
[6] X. 1. 91–92 ; cf. Suet. Dom. 2, *ib.* 20, where he says that Domitian neglected liberal studies at the opening of his reign.
[7] VIII. 70. 7, *ib.* IX. 26. 1.
[8] Tac. Ann. XIV. 16, *ib.* 52, XV. 49 ; Suet. Nero, 12, 38, Vitellius, 11.
[9] Nero, 52 : " carmina libenter ac sine labore composuit."
[10] Trist. IV. 10. 25 : " sponte sua carmen numeros veniebat ad aptos."
[11] Suet. Tit. 3 : " vel in orando vel in fingendis poematibus promptus et facilis ad extemporalitatem usque."

This latter gift seems to have been natural[1] in the case of Titus, but a long training in rhetoric, and an acquaintance with the technique of verse, might confer

Facility in verse-making a similar power on any ardent versifier, or give him at least a remarkable facility in his craft. The Younger Pliny like so many in his day was given to verse-making, and tells[2] us that he was lured on by the very ease with which the verses formed under his pen. There must have been many, too, who like Maecenas[3] endeavoured to show their ingenuity by essaying difficult metres such as the Galliambic, or such *tours de force*[4] as the " versus echoici " and the " carmen supinum." It is evident from this survey that, amongst the amateurs at least, the orators, or those who were deeply versed in the art of rhetoric, were responsible for much of the mechanical and uninspired verse that was thus produced. In spite of Martial,[5] it is difficult to believe that in such artificial surroundings the light of inspiration would come to illumine some bard, even with the advent of a generous patron, or better economic[6] conditions.

Now, we have moreover to recognise the fact that even the genuine poets themselves came at times under the

Influence of Rhetoric even on genuine poets influence of rhetoric in the narrow sense of the word, and thus may have provided a justification for the critics who regarded their works from the rhetorical point of view.
However, in dealing with this aspect of our problem we are confronted with some difficulties. At times, certain ornaments of verse are termed rhetorical, which are not specifically so. They may have naturally grown together with

---

[1] Q. X. 7. 19, seems to have regarded such a power as largely acquired, even in the case of Archias and Antipater of Sidon ; on Palaemon, cf. Suet. De Gr. 23 ; Mart. II. 86. 11.

[2] Ep. VII. 4. 7 : " transii ad elegos ; hos quoque non minus celeriter explicui ; addidi alios facilitate corruptus."

[3] Diomede, Keil, Gr. Lat. I. p. 514.

[4] Cf. Mart. II. 86, on such " difficiles nugae " ; Friedländer, ad loc. ; Sid. Ap. Ep. IX. 14 (there quoted) ; Sikes, op. cit., p. 275 *et seq.*

[5] VIII. 56. 5 : " sint Maecenates, non deerunt, Flacce, Marones."

[6] *Vide* Middleton Murry, op. cit., pp. 69–70, for some interesting remarks on the effect of economic conditions on literature.

the poet's thoughts, but they have come to be styled rhetorical, because they have been appropriated, as it were, by the rhetoricians, and included[1] in categories consecrated in the schools. Again, a poet might conceivably derive some benefit from a study of formal rhetoric in seeking to give an added touch of perfection to his work ; but while the inferior poet will but too often allow himself to fall under the spell of rhetoric, the great poet will be content to borrow from it such elements as may enhance the beauty of his art. One must recognise, too, that certain poets, either on the stylistic, or what we might term the dialectical[2] side, are prone to come under the influence of the rhetorical[3] movements of their time. Euripides learnt some lessons from the Sophists, and seems to have studied carefully the method of forensic[4] pleading. He loved[5] to set the stage for a full dress debate on forensic lines, and was prone to employ[6] devices such as verbal antithesis and jingle of phrase, which show that he had imbibed something of the spirit of contemporary rhetoric.

When we turn to the early Roman poets, we find them employing certain ornaments in their verse, the origin of which is not easy to determine. Alliteration[7] and assonance were a marked characteristic of the old Italian " carmina." Antithesis and balance of phrase are found in the primitive legal formulae of Rome, but whether such devices were native[8]

The Roman poets

---

[1] The fate suffered by many of the Figures will serve as an illustration.

[2] It is interesting in this connection to note that Ar. (Poet. c. 19) refers διάνοια to the province of rhetoric.

[3] Cf. Aly, op. cit., p. 34 *et seq.*, for an interesting study of the trial of Orestes in the Eumenides, and the influence upon it of forensic procedure ; cf. *ib.* p. 82.

[4] Aristoph. Pax, 534, calls him ποιητὴς ῥηματίων δικανικῶν, and has many thrusts at his Sophistic quibbling ; Ar. Poet. c. 15, refers to the incongruity of the ῥῆσις of Melanippe ; cf. Haigh, The Tragic Drama of the Greeks, p. 260.

[5] Troades, 906 *et seq.*, furnishes a good example in the debate between Hecuba and Helen ; cf. Ar. Rh. III. 17. 15.

[6] *Vide* Norden, A.K. I. pp. 28–29, on some passages from the Medea.

[7] There seems good reason for considering that these two features were developed independently on Italian soil ; *vide supra*, p. 5.

[8] Lejay, Histoire de la Litt. Latine, p. 155, considers that antithesis was a natural feature of Roman legal formulae.

to the soil, or whether they can be traced to the influence of Greek rhetoric, it is difficult to decide. Again, were the poets in their use of such figures availing themselves of indigenous products, or can their craft be traced to some source in Greek[1] rhetoric ? With the advent of Hellenistic rhetoric, some of the later poets might conceivably yield to its fascinations. Terence, who like his great prototype Menander was sparing of merely rhetorical devices in his comedies, did not disdain[2] them in his Prologues, which were constructed on the lines of a forensic speech. There the poet, or rather his representative, plays the rôle of advocate,[3] and seeks to refute the accusations of malignant enemies, and win the favour of the audience. He shows,[4] both in the marshalling of his arguments, and in his use of certain figures, that he owed something to the theories of the rhetoricians. Terence's contemporary, Accius, stands in a similar position. The story told by Quintilian[5] of his being asked why he did not turn advocate, in view of his wonderful aptitude for making effective[6] replies, shows that like Euripides he could turn to account in his tragedies the art of the forensic pleader. The style of Accius was lofty, vigorous, and at times highly coloured. Like so many of the older poets, he made extensive[7] use of assonance and alliteration, and employed moreover a variety[8] of figures and turns of speech which, whatever their origin, had come to be regarded as the hallmark of rhetoric.

I can here aim at nothing more than to indicate certain

[1] Leo, Gesch. der röm. Lit., p. 36, declares that " die plautinischen Figuren sind die gorgianischen," and postulates the influence of the Sicilian school (coming via Magna Graecia) rather than Hellenistic rhetoric ; cf. Lejay, Plaute, on such features in Plautus' style.

[2] *Vide supra*, p. 25 ; we have seen in our first chapter something of the influence of Greek rhetorical theory in the Scipionic circle ; it is to be noted, however, that rhetorical influences in Terence's Prologues are chiefly on the dialectical side.

[3] Heaut. Prol. 11 : " oratorem esse voluit me, non prologum."

[4] *Vide* Fabia, op. cit., p. 283 *et seq.*

[5] V. 13. 43.

[6] Skill in " altercatio " was highly prized in the orator.

[7] The passage from his Medea, preserved by Cicero (De N. Deor. II. 89), will furnish illustrations.

[8] *Vide* Leo. op. cit., pp. 399–402.

tendencies in Roman poetry in the different periods. Virgil was one of those that suffered in later times at the hands of critics who were obsessed by their interest in rhetoric. In his youth he had frequented the rhetorical schools, but he reacted[1] strongly against their inanities, and against the tastelessness and bombast that characterised some of the orators of his day. For all that, he may have learnt some useful lessons from a sane system of rhetoric. It was probably from the rhetorical schools that he acquired his skill in periodic[2] structure, and the division of his periods into clauses carefully balanced, and at times arranged in antithetical form. However, he was too great a poet to allow rhetoric to dominate him. He concealed his art so effectively that we are rarely conscious of rhetorical colouring in his verse. His themes[3] were at times such as were familiar in the schools of declamation, and beloved by the rhetorical[4] historians. A passage such as the great speech of Anchises in the Sixth Aeneid, might in the hands of a lesser artist degenerate into a display of vapid rhetoric, but even there, Virgil, though he employs[5] a variety of figures, keeps his instrument under control, and creates the impression of restraint in the use of what many would regard as specifically rhetorical ornament.

Virgil and Rhetoric

Virgil's achievement was all the more remarkable, as even towards the end of the Augustan age the decline had definitely begun, and rhetoric, in its most debased and repugnant form, invaded poetry. Such a result was almost inevitable,

The period of decadence

---

[1] Catal. II, *ib.* V : " ite hinc, inanes, ite rhetorum ampullae."

[2] *Vide* Norden, Aen. VI., p. 376 *et seq. ;* cf. the discussion in Dionys. De C. V. c. 26.

[3] Cf. Aen. VI. 509 *et seq.*, the speech of Deiphobus on the taking of Troy and his own fate ; *ib.* II. 298 *et seq., ib.* VI. 847 *et seq.*, styled by Servius " rhetoricus locus."

[4] *Vide* Dionys. Ep. ad Pomp. c. 6, on the topics treated by Theopompus ; *vide infra*, pp. 506–507.

[5] Norden analyses the speech on the lines of formal rhetoric ; Heinze, Virgils epische Technik, p. 424, rightly sounds a warning against the danger of trying to fit Virgil's speeches too closely into the rhetorical schemata ; *ib.* p. 431 *et seq.*

when so many orators had turned poets,[1] and the passage from oratory to poetry seemed easy of accomplishment.[2] The view[3] that rhetoric could lend its aid to the poet in his labours was accepted without qualification, though at times a warning voice[4] was raised against the serious incursion of rhetoric into poetry. The evil effects of its domination were intensified, when the poets themselves began to practise declamation in the schools, and became infected with their spirit. Ovid stands out as a typical example of how baneful such influence could be. His verse in many passages exhibits all the unrestraint and extravagance of the declaimers, their love of glitter and polish and pointed phrase, and their desire[5] to improve what was already good, by a needless exercise of ingenuity. He even incorporated[6] in his verses some of the thoughts of the declaimer Latro, whom he especially admired. Quintilian calls attention[7] to another legacy from the schools apparent in his *Metamorphoses*, the tendency to employ an epigram in order to mark a transition.

There were other factors at work which helped to strengthen the influence of the schools, and impress on Post-Augustan poetry a strongly rhetorical character. The practice of public recitation was prominent amongst such factors, but, as this is a subject that has been often dealt with, it calls for only a passing mention here. Many of the Emperors[8]

The practice of recitation

---

[1] Cf. Tac. Dial. c. 3 ; Stat. Silv. II. 7. 21, on the twin arts in Lucan ; Mart. VII. 63. 5–6, on Silius Italicus.

[2] Stat. op. cit. I. 4. 29 ; Pliny, Ep. IV. 27. 4.

[3] Ovid, Ex Ponto, II. 5. 69 : " utque meis numeris tua dat facundia nervos " ; Fronto, I. 106 : " plerumque enim ad orationem faciendam versus, ad versificandum oratio magis adjuvat " ; cf. Theon, Progym. Sp. II. 70. 25, on the need of a training in rhetoric for orators, poets, and historians.

[4] Q. X. 2. 21 : " id quoque vitandum, in quo magna pars errat, ne . . . in illis operibus (poetry and history) oratores aut declamatores imitandos putemus."

[5] Cf. Sen. Controv. IX. 5 (28). 17 : " nam et Ovidius nescit quod bene cessit relinquere " ; *ib.* II. 2. 12 ; Q. X. 1. 98 ; *vide supra*, p. 443.

[6] Sen. Controv. II. 2. 8.   [7] IV. 1. 77.

[8] Suet. Aug. 89, Claud. 41, Nero, 10, Dom. 2 ; *vide* Butler, Post-Augustan Poetry, p. 2 *et seq.*, for a good account of the literary activities of

extended their patronage to the practice, while some of them gave recitations of their own works. Even so great a poet as Virgil[1] could not ignore the fashion, though his genius enabled him to escape from its most pernicious consequences. Moreover, his aim was not display, but to secure the benefit of criticism. It is important to remember that under the Empire it was the custom to recite every species[2] of literary work, from epic, lyric, and dramatic poetry, to oratory and history. The practice might have been admirable in the case of oratory, though even here Pliny notes[3] certain disadvantages inherent in it, or it might have produced fruitful results even in the case of poetry recited to a few friends of taste and discernment, who were prepared to play the rôle of candid critics, but recitation, as it developed in Rome, could have nothing but injurious results. Even a great poem like the *Aeneid* could have its beauty enhanced by the living voice[4] and dramatic power of the poet, but at Rome many of those who recited, were mere poetasters, who read to an audience mostly depraved in its tastes, and too often distinguished by its lethargy[5] and indifference. Even the poet of talent felt himself constrained to pander to the tastes of such an audience, in order to break down its lethargy, and he considered that the surest means of accomplishing this was by the employment of devices already found effective in the schools of declamation—the forced conceit, the balanced antithesis, the flashing epigram, and the lavish use of the gaudiest rhetorical figures. Such pernicious tendencies would

the Emperors from Tiberius onward, and their influence on contemporary literature.

[1] Vita, 33 : " recitavit et pluribus, sed neque frequenter, et ea fere de quibus ambigebat, quo magis judicium hominum experiretur " ; Sen. Ep. 101. 13 ; Gellius, VII. 20. 1.

[2] Hor. Ep. I. 19. 42 ; Sen. Controv. X. pr. 8 ; Persius, I. 15 *et seq. ;* Tac. Dial. 2, 11 ; Pliny, Ep. I. 13, V. 17. 2 *et seq.*, VI. 15, VII. 17. 3, VIII. 12 ; Juv. I. 1 *et seq.*, VII. 40, 83.

[3] Ep. II. 19; cf. V. 3. 8, where he sets forth some of the general advantages of the practice ; *ib.* 12. 1.

[4] *Vide* Life of Virgil, 29, on the tribute paid to Virgil's voice and delivery by Julius Montanus.

[5] Pliny, Ep. I. 13. 1 ; cf. Tac. Dial. c. 9, where Aper from his own point of view describes the atmosphere of the " recitation."

naturally be fostered also by the public contests in poetry instituted by some of the Emperors.[1]

Thus there were several influences[2] conspiring to promote a riot of false rhetoric in Post-Augustan poetry. There are many modern studies which help us to **Some poets of** realise how far the chief poets of the period **the decadence** succumbed to the lure of declamatory rhetoric. We can see how the influence of his early training[3] and environment led Lucan into what has well[4] been styled " l'abondance stérile," the tendency to wear an idea threadbare by excessive[5] repetition, and by an accumulation of details that add little or nothing to the main conception. Similar influences caused Juvenal to abandon the easy and casual tone of the " sermo," and the genial play of its humour, for the declamatory manner, though in his case his vigorous, if overstrained rhetoric, often serves as a powerful instrument to express his " saeva indignatio " against the darker vices of his age.

In many respects the Tragedies of Seneca are typical of the worst features of the decline. That writer, like the **The Younger** young men of the day, had[6] in his youth **Seneca** frequented the schools of declamation, though it is evident[7] that the Elder Seneca wished to save his sons from their most flagrant extravagances. We may take it for granted that the Younger Seneca did not intend his Tragedies to be acted,[8] and thus he could indulge his most serious faults freed from the discipline imposed by the demands of dramatic technique, and the realities of the stage. He was thus prepared to sacrifice to the exigencies of a spurious rhetoric the dramatic interest

---

[1] Suet. Nero, 12, Dom. 4 ; Tac. Ann. XIV. 21.

[2] There were, of course, other factors than those I mentioned, which helped the decline of poetry in this period, but on these I need not dwell.

[3] The " Life of Lucan," attributed to Vacca, speaks of his declaiming in Greek and Latin " cum magna admiratione audientiae."

[4] By Nisard (employing a phrase of Boileau), Les Poètes Latins de la Décadence, Vol. II, p. 329.

[5] For Fronto's criticism of the opening of the Pharsalia, *vide supra*, p. 322.

[6] Sen. Controv. X, pr. 9 ; *vide supra*, p. 333.

[7] Suas. VI. 16, Controv. I. pr. 6 *et seq.*, *ib.* 10.

[8] He probably, however, intended them to be recited.

of a play, as well as the portrayal of character, which in his hands often developed into a mere pathological study. He chose subjects[1] already treated by the Greek dramatists, but he preferred to dwell on their more morbid aspects, and to exhibit in language of studied extravagance the effect on his characters of some ignoble and ungovernable passion. He showed a preference for the lurid and the terrible, and loved to pile horror upon horror, as when he sets[2] forth in wearisome detail the many forms of witchcraft practised by Medea. His preoccupations with rhetoric are everywhere apparent, even in his choral odes,[3] while he constantly betrays his kinship with the schools by his tendency to unreal emotion, exaggeration, violent paradox, a profusion of epigram,[4] and a ceaseless striving after novel and striking forms of expression. The most blatant of the rhetorical[5] figures crowd thick and fast upon his pages. In his elaboration, too, of the character[6] of the tyrant—a theme beloved by the declaimers—he is reminiscent of the schools. We are not surprised to find the author of the *Quaestiones Naturales* betraying his interest in natural science even in his dramas, though such interest is subordinated to his main purpose of giving long rhetorical[7] descriptions[8] of the heavenly bodies, and of other marvels of nature. Moreover, Seneca, the Stoic moralist, is continually flitting across the

---

[1] The " Octavia," of course, stands apart, if it can be said to be Seneca's.

[2] Medea, 670 *et seq.* ; cf. Lucan, VI. 437 *et seq.*, where Thessalian magic is similarly described in lurid detail.

[3] cf. Her. Fur. 523 *et seq.*

[4] Oed. 699 *et seq.* ; cf. Godley, Senecan Tragedy, p. 231 *et seq.*

[5] Canter, Rhetorical Elements in the Tragedies of Seneca, gives profuse illustrations of the figures used by Seneca, some of which were intimately associated with poetry, while many of them were claimed by the rhetoricians as their own special property.

[6] Cf. Lycus in the Her. Fur. 397 *et seq.*, Thyestes, 176 *et seq.*, Agam, 988 *et seq.* ; Lucan also harps upon the theme ; cf. Boissier, L'Opposition sous les Césars, p. 83 *et seq.*, for political references in Seneca's tragedies ; Lucas, Seneca and Elizabethan Tragedy, pp. 11–12, 61 *et seq.*, on Seneca's tyrants ; *vide infra*, p. 522.

[7] Cf. Her. Oet. 1519 *et seq.*

[8] The ἔκφρασις could be made the vehicle of lofty poetry, or be made to serve merely for rhetorical display ; cf. Nisard, op. cit., II. p. 209 *et seq.* ; Stemplinger, op. cit., p. 232 *et seq.*

plays, and his power[1] of embodying a moral maxim in a terse epigrammatic phrase is as striking in his Tragedies as in his Letters. Thus in the former, we have dramas in which the dramatic values were submerged, and where everything was made subservient to a rhetoric that, even in dealing with commonplace themes, was characterised by unrestraint, artificiality, and a tawdry brilliance.

There may be some justification, as I have said, for regarding from the standpoint of formal rhetoric the poets who in any degree had fallen under its influence, but so strong was the rhetorical tradition, that the majority of the ancient critics endeavoured to make the poets generally, fit into the rigid formulas they had learnt in the schools. They inclined to deal thus even with aspects of the poet's work that were least amenable to such formulas. In Greece, Homer was one of the first to fall a victim to this system. The Sophists busied themselves with his works, and a reference to the poet in the *Clouds*[2] of Aristophanes, suggests that he was even then being studied for the types of oratory that his poems were supposed to exhibit. Protagoras, who boasted of his power of analysing Homer, found[3] fault with the opening of the *Iliad* on the score that the poet was mistaken in the turn of speech which he employed, and had given a command under the impression that he was uttering a prayer. But, as times went on, Homer's admirers tended to discover in him the germ[4] of every art, and particularly of the arts of Rhetoric and Philosophy,[5] while those who interpreted him allegorically,[6]

Rhetorical formulas applied to the poets

[1] Troades, 613, Agam. 242.

[2] 1056 *et seq.*; cf. Xenophon, Mem. IV. 6. 15, on the characteristics of Odysseus' oratory.

[3] Cf. Ar. Poet. c. 19, 1456 b, who evidently was thinking of P's. criticism in connection with the σχήματα λέξεως (in Aristotle's own sense of the term); cf. Q. III. 4. 10 (quoted by Bywater), who relates Protagoras' division of the modes of speech to oratory.

[4] We see foreshadowings of this view in the Ion, 537, 541; cf. Philod. Rhet. II. 110–111, Supplementum (Sudhaus), p. 7, 33, περὶ ποιημ. Jensen, pp. 33, 35; Strabo, I. 2. 3 *et seq.*

[5] Cf. Strabo, I. 2. 17; Sen. Ep. 88. 5 *et seq.*; cf. Jensen, op. cit., pp. 166, 173.

[6] *Vide infra*, p. 485.

could at will read into him their own fancies. At Pergamum,[1] where Stoic influence was predominant, and where grammatical and rhetorical studies were united, scholars tried to discover a whole system of rhetoric in Homer. Such a tendency culminated at a later time in the work of Telephus,[2] who wrote περὶ τῶν παρ᾽ Ὁμήρῳ σχημάτων, and περὶ τῆς καθ᾽ Ὅμηρον ῥητορικῆς, and sought to find in the poet examples of the various kinds[3] of oratory, and in fact the beginnings of the whole art of rhetoric. Even critics[4] who showed a high appreciation of the poet's beauties, and a capacity for penetrating to the secret of his charm, are at times inclined to regard him from the rhetorical standpoint.

Roman criticism of Homer travelled along much the same road as that of the Greeks. Ulysses, Menelaus, and

Rhetorical tendencies in Roman criticism

Nestor were looked upon as illustrating the three contrasted types of eloquence, and as affording proof of the poet's oratorical[5] skill. Quintilian is particularly[6] illuminating on this point, and probably sums up the prevailing tendencies of Homeric criticism, especially among those[7] who were interested in the art of oratory. In Homer, he says,[8] we

---

[1] *Vide* Brzoska, op. cit., p. 59 *et seq.*

[2] *Vide* Egger, Histoire de la Critique, p. 3 ; Schrader, Telephos der Pergamener, Hermes, Vol. 37, p. 530 *et seq.*, who also traces the influence of Telephus on the Homeric Scholiasts.

[3] Judicial, deliberative, etc.; cf. Hermogenes, Sp. Rh. Gr. II, p. 370, *ib.* 406: ἄριστος οὖν κατὰ πάντα λόγων εἴδη . . . Ὅμηρος; *ib.* III. p. 152.

[4] Cf. περὶ ὕψους, IX. 13, where πολιτικόν suggests the qualities of civil oratory ; Dio Chrys. 18. 8, regards the poet from the standpoint of his utility to the future orator ; *vide infra*, p. 464.

[5] Cic. Br. 40 : " neque ipse poeta hic tam ornatus in dicendo ac plane orator fuisset " ; *ib.* 50 ; cf. Gellius, VII. 14. 7 ; Columella, I, pr. 30, styles Homer " parens eloquentiae."

[6] II. 3. 12, X. 1. 46 *et seq.* : " omnibus eloquentiae partibus exemplum et ortum dedit " ; " nec poetica modo, sed oratoria virtute eminentissimus " ; *ib.* 65, XII. 10. 64 ; cf. Sen. Ep. 40. 2.

[7] Q. X. 1. 49 : " ut etiam qui de artibus scripserunt plurimi harum rerum testimonium ab hoc poeta petant " ; cf. XI. 3. 158, on the delivery of Odysseus.

[8] XII. 11. 21.

may discover every art in perfection, or at least adumbrated in no uncertain manner. He finds in the poet material for illustrating the various oratorical styles, and in fact every department of oratory. He proceeds to test him according to the formal scheme of rhetoric, almost as rigidly as Cicero would test the achievements of an orator. Homer in his eyes illustrates the art both of forensic[1] and deliberative eloquence. He exhibits the perfect pattern of exordium, narration, and peroration, and shows his pre-eminence even in the methods of proof and refutation.

In time, Virgil was dealt with on similar lines. Like Homer, he was regarded as a master[2] of every art, and was
Virgilian criticism transformed[3] by his admirers in the Middle Ages into a wizard, and even endowed with the gift of prophecy. Almost in his own day, as we have seen,[4] he was a favourite in the rhetorical schools. At a later period, Florus[5] could raise the question— Vergilius orator an poeta? The members of the literary circle that figures in Macrobius' *Saturnalia*, proclaim[6] the poet's excellences as an orator. He was said to furnish illustrations of the four types[7] of style recognised by the rhetorical theorists of the time. In the same spirit his ancient commentators[8] concentrated much of their attention on his rhetorical art. Claudius Donatus, at the beginning of his commentary on the *Aeneid*, declared[9] to his son that Virgil " tibi artem dicendi plenissimam demonstrabit."

[1] Cf. Schrader, op. cit., p. 566.

[2] Cf. Macrob. Sat. I. 16. 12 : " omnium disciplinarum peritus " ; Comment. in Somnium Scipionis, I. 6. 44.

[3] The system of allegorical interpretation came to be applied to the Aeneid also in the Middle Ages.

[4] *Vide supra*, p. 444.

[5] *Vide* Hirzel, op. cit., II. p. 64 *et seq.*, for some suggestions on the contents of Florus' Dialogue.

[6] I. 24. 8, *ib.* V. 1. 1 : " omnes . . . Vergilium non minus oratorem quam poetam habendum pronuntiabant."

[7] *Vide supra*, p. 76.

[8] *Vide* Georgii, op. cit., p. 5 *et seq.*, *ib.*, p. 106 *et seq.*, on Servius' comments on Sinon's speech ; Comparetti, Vergil in the Middle Ages, p. 56 *et seq.*

[9] Cf. also " inuenies in poeta rhetorem summum atque inde intelleges Vergilium non grammaticos, sed oratores praecipuos tradere debuisse " Proem. ed. Georgii, p. 4).

Eugraphius, in his commentary on Terence, also pays[1] a tribute to his skill as a rhetorician, and incidentally reveals the criterion by which he was guided in his judgment of the poets in general.

We have seen already that the poets were an important element in the reading recommended to the future orator. It was natural, then, for teachers of rhetoric to endeavour to sum up in a brief notice the salient characteristics of each author, and to emphasise such qualities as would be likely to prove of assistance to their students. It was with such a purpose[2] that Quintilian entered on his survey of Greek and Latin literature. The poets in general could be of service in the matter of style, while the dramatic poets in particular could be of benefit by reason of their skill in character-drawing, their emotional appeal, their portraiture of life, and even their capacity for dialectical argument. From what we have already seen of his outlook, it was natural for Quintilian to consider Homer[3] as an author of supreme importance for his purpose. Amongst the lyric poets, Alcaeus[4] is singled out as one who in the qualities of his style frequently resembles the orator. Of the writers of Tragedy, Euripides[5] would naturally make the strongest appeal to Quintilian, as being useful especially to the forensic orator by reason of his style, his wealth of striking reflections, his skill in altercation, and his power of stirring the emotions. Quintilian finds[6] the style of the Old Comedy particularly well adapted to the formation of the orator. Amongst the writers of the New Comedy, Menander, who

How poets may contribute to the formation of the orator

---

[1] Andria, Prol. : " cum omnes poetae virtutem oratoriam semper versibus exequantur, tum magis duo viri apud Latinos, Vergilius et Terentius."

[2] Cf. X. 1. 88 : " propiores alii (than Ennius) atque ad hoc de quo loquimur magis utiles."

[3] cf. Dionys. περὶ μιμ. II. p. 19 (Usener).

[4] X. 1. 63 ; cf. Dionys. op. cit., p. 20 : πολλαχοῦ γοῦν τὸ μέτρον τις εἰ περιέλοι, ῥητορείαν ἂν εὕροι πολιτικήν.

[5] X. 1. 67–68 ; cf. Dionys., op. cit., p. 21 : πολὺς ἐν ταῖς ῥητορικαῖς εἰσαγωγαῖς ; Dio. Chrys. 18. 7 : πολιτικῷ δὲ ἀνδρὶ πάνυ ὠφέλιμος.

[6] X. 1. 65 ; cf. I. 8. 7, *ib.* 11. 12, where Quintilian may have rather the New Comedy in mind.

had learned some lessons from Euripides, is specially[1] commended as likely to develop all the qualities which should distinguish the future orator. His style, his faithful transcription of life, his skill in character-drawing,[2] his power of invention,[3] the propriety with which he adapts his language to every circumstance, character, and emotion, all combine to make him a model of supreme importance for those who wish to attain success in the art of oratory. Quintilian considers that he shows his oratorical skill particularly in the judicial scenes, such as are found in the *Epitrepontes*[4] and other plays, and he is so impressed with this aspect of Menander's genius, that he will not reject the tradition which ascribed to him the authorship of the speeches of Charisius. Menander had the gift of being able to hold the mirror up to nature, while the variety and fidelity of his character-drawing made him in Quintilian's eyes a writer to be commended to declaimers, though the delicate art of the Greek dramatist would seem to be strangely out of place amidst the extravagances of the schools.

Quintilian dismisses in summary fashion the Roman poets whom he deemed unsuitable for his purpose, though

Quintilian's scale of values in fact he seems incapable of appreciating the genius of writers such as Ennius and Lucretius. Lucan, in whom the rhetorical element is strong, is considered[5] by him as more worthy of imitation by orators than by poets, and is acclaimed as " sententiis clarissimus," a quality that would naturally appeal to the young men who had been nurtured in the

---

[1] X. 1. 69 *et seq.*: " qui vel unus . . . diligenter lectus ad cuncta quae praecipimus effingenda sufficiat."

[2] Dio. Chrys. 18. 7, praises his μίμησις ἅπαντος ἤθους καὶ χάριτος ; cf. Wilamowitz-M, Menander, Das Schiedsgericht, p. 157 *et seq.*

[3] Dionys., op. cit., p. 22, recommends that he should be studied for τὸ πραγματικόν.

[4] We are now in a better position to appreciate Menander's skill as a pleader in the scene of the Epitrepontes, where Davus and Syriscus each pleads his cause, but unlike Quintilian we would probably consider that the least of Menander's merits.

[5] X. 1. 90 ; cf. St. Aug. De Consensu Evang. I. 30 : " Lucanus magnus in carmine declamator."

traditions of contemporary rhetoric, and dazzled by its epigrams. Quintilian has a word of praise[1] for the Roman tragedians Accius and Pacuvius, though they lacked the polish and perfection which they might have attained in a more cultured age. It may have been Accius' skill[2] in altercation that constituted in him the great source of attraction for Quintilian. Comedy is regarded as amongst the failures of Roman literature, in spite of the fact that Terence[3] had modelled himself so closely on Menander.[4] Here, indeed, Quintilian allows his view of the achievements of his own countrymen to be coloured by his admiration for the matchless grace and beauty[5] of the Greek originals. In the same spirit, Gellius tells[6] us that he considered the works of the Roman comic poets as endowed with a certain elegance and charm, until he had read the plays of their Greek prototypes. In comparison, his own countrymen seemed crude and lifeless.

I have dealt with only a few of the salient points in Quintilian's survey of Greek and Latin authors, with the object especially of indicating the tendencies **The formal** of such a method. Quintilian indeed, at **scheme of** **rhetoric** rare intervals seems to forget his real purpose, and indulges in disinterested criticism, but there was always the danger that, in emphasising the elements in a poet that might prove useful for rhetorical training, he might leave his readers under the impression that there was little else to look for, and so blind them to the finer qualities of poetry. The danger would become all the more real with every attempt to relate passages in the poets to the formal scheme of rhetoric. We find already before Quintilian's day that the poets were drawn[7] upon to furnish examples of the various classes of arguments[8] that came

---

[1] X. 1. 97.   [2] *Vide supra*, p. 455.
[3] To whom Quintilian pays a half-hearted tribute.
[4] Terence surely did not fail to reproduce some of the qualities which Quintilian praises so highly in Menander.
[5] Cf. X. 1. 100, XII. 10. 38.   [6] N.A. II. 23.
[7] Cic. De Inv. I. 83, 90–91, 95, Top. 61; Ad Her. II. 22–26; cf. Q. V. 10. 83, *ib.* 11. 14.
[8] We have seen that Aristotle had given a certain sanction to the practice, by relegating διάνοια (in tragedy) to the province of rhetoric.

under the head of " Inventio." This tendency is later seen in its extreme form in Donatus[1] and Eugraphius, who endeavour to co-ordinate certain passages in Terence with the doctrine of " status." In a similar spirit the poets were requisitioned[2] to illustrate the qualities that should prevail in the " partes orationis," such as the exordium, partitio, and narratio.

In the matter of style particularly, the rhetoricians found their closest affinity with the poets. Hence they were prone[3]

" Elocutio " to characterise this feature of a poet's work in terms that were current in their own domain. It is often difficult to determine how far the epithet " facundus," as applied[4] to the poets, carried with it rhetorical associations, but in the Silver Age, when rhetoric had established its supremacy in so many spheres of literature, even such an application of the word awakens the suspicion that its rhetorical significance may have been predominant. The doctrine of the Three Styles affords another example of how critics, in their estimate of the poets, thought[5] in terms of rhetorical theory, or at any rate based their criticisms on analogies with it. Varro evidently had the triad of rhetorical styles in mind in his characterisation[6] of Pacuvius, Lucilius, and Terence, though it would be a mistake to press in every case, as some modern authors have done, the terms[7] applied in criticism of a poet's style,

[1] Ad Andria, 51 ; Eugraph. ad Eun. 81, Ad Andria, 338, 872 ; cf. Georgii, Die antike Äneiskritik, p. 181 ; Schrader, op. cit., p. 564, on Telephus and Homer.

[2] Cic. De Inv. I. 27 (to illustrate the various kinds of " narratio "), ib. 33 ; cf. Q. VII. 10. 11.

[3] Vide supra, p. 449.

[4] Stat. Silvae, II. 1. 114 (applied to Menander) ; Mart. V. 30. 3 (Catullus), VII. 91. 1 (Juvenal) ; Q. X. 1. 65, ascribes to the Old Comedy " facundissima libertas."

[5] Gellius, VII. 14. 1.

[6] Ib. 6 : " ubertatis Pacuvium, gracilitatis Lucilius, mediocritatis Terentium," corresponding to the three Greek χαρακτῆρες ; ib. 1 ; vide supra, p. 24.

[7] e.g. " humilitas " (Petron. 4), " gracilis " (Fronto, II. 48), applied to the style of Lucilius ; vide supra, p. 56 ; an attempt has been made to bring even Horace's " molle atque facetum " into conformity with the tenets of the Plain Style ; cf. Ogle's protest, A.J. Ph. Vol. 37. p. 327 et seq. ; vide infra, p. 476 et seq.

into too close conformity with the doctrine of the Three
Styles as developed in rhetoric. Quintilian, however, was
evidently thinking of the stereotyped scheme, when he
described[1] Hesiod as the supreme representative of the
Middle style. The trend of such criticism is especially
well illustrated by Dionysius in some chapters[2] of his treatise
on Literary Composition, though he there concerns himself,
not with styles in the accepted sense, but with modes of
composition. He selects indiscriminately poets, orators,
and historians, to furnish illustrations of the three different
modes.

Before passing from this subject, I must deal briefly with
the alleged influence of Rhetorical theory on Horace's
Horace and criticism, especially as expounded in the
Rhetorical *Ars Poetica*. Hitherto, we have been mainly
theory concerned with the rhetorician's point of
view, while here we have a poet dealing with his own craft.
It will be of some interest to see how far it can be maintained[3]
that Horace's chief critical treatise was dependent for its
structure and content on the art of rhetoric, particularly as
it was taught in Hellenistic[4] times.

Some seeing in Cicero's rhetorical works the most faithful
reflex of Hellenistic theory,[5] lay great stress on the parallels
(even the verbal ones) supposed to exist
Parallels with between him and the *Ars Poetica*. It is
Cicero clear, of course, that Horace was a student[6]
of Cicero, and shows at times striking[7] resemblances to

---

[1] X. I. 52 : " daturque ei palma in illo medio genere dicendi " ; cf.
Dionys. De C.V. c. 23 ; περὶ μιμ. p. 22, where he ascribes to Euripides
κεκραμένη μεσότης τῆς λέξεως.

[2] C. XXI–XXIV, on the three ἁρμονίαι.

[3] Cf. Norden, Die Composition und Litteraturgattung der Horazischen
Epistula ad Pisones, Hermes, Vol. 40, p. 528 : " die Analyse zeigte das
Horaz die poetische Lehrsatze den rhetorischen nachgebildet hat."

[4] Barwick, Die Gliederung der rhetorischen τέχνη und die Horazische
Epistula ad Pisones, Hermes, Vol. 57, p. 44, holds that some features in the
Ars Poetica are derived from Heracleides Ponticus, through the medium of
Neoptolemus.

[5] Cf. especially, Grant and Fiske, Cicero's " Orator " and Horace's " Ars
Poetica," p. I *et seq.*

[6] *Vide supra*, p. 370 *et seq.*

[7] Cf. A.P. 68, Pro Marcello, II ; A.P. 89, De opt. gen. I. I ; A.P. 133-

him both in thought and diction. On the other hand, it is evident that Cicero's own speculations owed[1] something to poetic theory and practice. The parallels adduced are not always proof of the dependence of Horace on the Roman orator, as ultimately each was influenced by a body of doctrine that lay beyond himself. The recovery of substantial portions of Philodemus' treatise on Poetry has made it clear that the author of the *Ars Poetica* was indebted to the " Poetics " of Neoptolemus,[2] and has helped to confirm the Scholiast's statement that Horace borrowed from him " non quidem omnia sed eminentissima " (praecepta). The problem is thus carried back to an earlier time, and the more fundamental question arises as to how far Hellenistic " Poetic " was dependent on the scheme of rhetoric evolved in that period. The modern studies to which I have referred, for the most part examine the problem in so far as it immediately concerns the *Ars Poetica*, and convey the impression that they regard such dependence as almost complete. They would seem to leave little by way of original speculation to the writers of " Poetics," and they endeavour to force most of their theorisings into the moulds of conventional rhetoric. Though such writers may have followed the traditional scheme of rhetoric in some respects, yet it seems to me that more[3] of their theory was developed independently of it than they are given credit for. The attempt to force the *Ars Poetica*, at almost every turn, into the Procustean bed of Rhetoric, leads at times to some strange results.

Various views[4] have been expressed as to the character of that work, some seeing in it a series of desultory precepts

---

134, De opt. gen. 14 ; A.P. 147, De Rep. I. 38 ; A.P. 155, Cato Major, 70 : A.P. 325, Tusc. Disp. I. 5, on the utilitarian spirit in Rome.

[1] Cf. Or. 39, 66-68, 163, 174.

[2] I assume that Jensen, Philodemos, is right in ascribing to Neoptolemus the views discussed by Ph. in Bk. V. Col. 1-8, 11-12 ; cf. Col. 10. 33, where the name of Neoptolemus can be readily restored.

[3] Some of it, of course, was derived from the general theory of Aesthetics.

[4] Many of these have been summarised by Hack, op. cit., p. 5 *et seq.* ; cf. Birt, Über den Aufbau der Ars poetica, in Dieterich, Pulcinella, p. 279 *et seq.*

poured out with the unstudied ease of the Epistle, others
finding in it the rigorous formalism of a
Views on the scientific treatise. Norden approximates to
"Ars Poetica" the latter view, and regards it as an "isa-
gogic "[1] work, introductory to the art of poetry, and
designed to present the results of specialised investigation
in a form intelligible to beginners. In common with such
treatises, the subject of the *Ars Poetica* is dealt[2] with, according to him, under the heads[3] of " ars " and " artifex."
Though one might accept Norden's main division of the
poem, there would still be left abundant room for quarrel-
ling about the arrangement of details within the two chief
sections. Norden's main division has indeed received remarkable confirmation from Philodemus, who makes it
clear that Neoptolemus in his " Poetics " dealt with his
subject under the rubrics,[4] Poem, Poetry, and Poet. Philodemus, however, saw[5] the difficulty of maintaining rigidly
such a division, and evidently recognised the impossibility[6]
of placing the artist and his work in separate compartments.
A similar difficulty was experienced in the sphere of
Rhetoric, some,[7] for instance, contending that Invention,
Arrangement, and Style, should not be relegated to " ars,"
but classed as " opera oratoris."

How hard it is to obtain agreement about details, is
evident from modern studies of the *Ars Poetica*. Verses

---

[1] *Vide* Norden, op. cit., p. 508 *et seq.*, for illustrations of such treatises in
various arts.

[2] De Arte 1–294, De Artifice 306–476 (295–305 being transitional) ; it
is to be noted that Birt, op. cit., p. 281, had already before Norden recognised
the division " De Arte " and " De Artifice."

[3] Barwick, op. cit., p. 59, remarks that the division into " ars " and
" artifex " was natural in treatises dealing with a specific τέχνη.

[4] Such a treatment was a favourite one in dealing with the theory of
poetry ; cf. Jensen, op. cit., pp. 152, 171 ; Lucilius, fr. 338 (with Marx's
note) ; Ben Jonson, Spingarn, Critical Essays, Vol. I, p. 51, speaks of " the
thing fain'd, the faining, and the fainer " ; *vide supra*, p. 43.

[5] *Vide* Jensen, p. 19, on the difficulty of distributing the virtues of Style
between ars and artifex ; *ib.*, pp. 29–31, 102 *et seq.*, 118.

[6] *Vide* Hack, op. cit., p. 13.

[7] Q. III. 3. 11 ; Q. himself dealt with " imitatio " under " ars," while
others ranged it under " artifex."

1–37 are considered by some[1] to be a general introduction to the whole poem, while Norden relates[2]
them to the portion of the rhetorical scheme
Disagreement dealing with "tractatio argumentorum." In
on details
three different passages[3] Horace refers explicitly to subject-matter, but though it may be maintained
(as by Norden) that his point of view has altered on each
occasion, it can hardly be maintained that it has altered in
obedience to a stereotyped scheme. Again, we find him
dealing with character-drawing in different contexts.[4] The
plea can hardly be successfully advanced that in one passage
he is dealing with the question from the standpoint of
" ars," and in another from that of " artifex." The truth
seems to be that Horace was debarred from following a
rigid scheme, on the one hand by his desire to pay continual
homage to the principle of Decorum, and on the other by
his anxiety to develop and reinforce the critical creed which
he had already proclaimed to the world. For the latter,
the *Ars Poetica* should be read in conjunction with his
earlier works. However, Norden's and similar studies have
produced one good result, in showing that the *Ars Poetica*
was not devoid of plan, as some[5] scholars contended.

We now turn to consider some of the specific problems
of the poem, and see whether Horace in his discussion of
them was simply following the lead of
Ars v. Ingen- rhetorical theory. He raises[6] the question
ium
whether the merits of a poem depend more
on Nature than on Art. A similar question was debated in
the case of oratory. Plato considered[7] that natural endow-

---

[1] Barwick, op. cit., p. 48 (following Cauer) ; Horace certainly treats here
of one fundamental law, that of unity and simplicity, but he also touches on
the problem of defective styles, and breaches of Decorum.

[2] Op. cit., p. 489, though " tractatio " should naturally follow " inventio."

[3] A.P. 29, 40, 310.

[4] *Ib.* 114 *et seq.*, 156–178, 311 *et seq. ; vide supra,* pp. 405, 424.

[5] Scaliger spoke of it as " adeo sine arte ut Saturae propius esse videatur " ;
Lehrs attributed to it " form der formlosigkeit."

[6] A.P. 408 *et seq.*

[7] Phaedrus, 269 D, on φύσις, ἐπιστήμη, μελέτη ; Plato's phrase
ἔχειν ὥσπερ τἆλλα, shows that he is here applying a doctrine valid also
in other spheres than oratory ; Isocr. περὶ ἀντιδ. 187 *et seq.*, shows how

ments, knowledge, and practice were all essential to the formation of the perfect orator. The speculations of the Roman[1] theorists followed along the same lines.[2] The premier place as a rule was assigned to Nature, but it was agreed that Art should lend its aid, and help to bring it to perfection. Art is perfect, says the author[3] of the treatise *On the Sublime*, when it seems to be Nature, and Nature is most effective when she has Art hidden within her. At times there was a tendency[4] to exalt the part played by Art. Reaction was inevitable, and the cry of " Back to Nature " was raised,[5] as a protest against the cramping[6] effect of the rules of Art. Besides the body of technical precepts which constituted the " art " of Rhetoric in the narrower sense, there were other aids such as extended study, and the imitation of great models, that were recommended to develop a man's natural talents.

In poetry even more than in oratory, the rival claims of Nature and of Art were bound to be considered. In Greek literature, Pindar[7] seems to have been one

The realm of poetry

of the first to contrast the two, and to assign to the former the chief rôle in poetic creation, though, supreme artist that he was, he could not[8] altogether

---

universal was the application of the doctrine ; *ib.*, κατὰ σοφ. 14 *et seq.* ; cf. Dionys. περὶ μιμ. Usener, p. 14 ; cf. Thucyd. I. 138, for an early application of the doctrine to Themistocles.

[1] Q. II. 19. 1 *et seq., ib.* XI. 3. 11, where Quintilian discusses the question in connection with delivery.

[2] Ad Her. I. 2. 3, speaks only of ars, imitatio, exercitatio ; Cic. De. Or. I. 113 *et seq.*, where the rival claims of " ars " and " ingenium " are examined ; *ib.* II. 89, 232, Pro Archia, I. 1, Pro Coelio, 54, Br. 25 ; Q. III. 5. 1 ; cf. Tac. Dial. 33 ; *vide supra*, p. 170.

[3] 22. 1 ; cf. *ib.* 36. 4 ; Q. II. 17. 9, III. 2. 3, IX. 4. 7.

[4] Cf. Cic. De Fin. IV. 10 (in reference to oratory) : " ars tamen est dux certior quam natura."

[5] Q. XI. 3. 10 ; cf. Isocr. περὶ ἀντιδ. 197–198.

[6] *Vide supra*, pp. 121, 149 ; Q. II. 17. 5 *et seq.*, XI. 3. 180 ; περὶ ὕψους, 2. 1.

[7] Olymp. II. 86–87, *ib.* IX. 100 : τὸ δὲ φυᾷ κράτιστον ἅπαν ; cf. Nem. I. 25–26, III. 40–42, where a wider application is made of the contrast of Art and Nature ; cf., on the other hand, Epicharmus, fr. 284 (Kaibel, op. cit., I. p. 143) : ἁ δὲ μελέτα φύσιος ἀγαθᾶς πλέονα δωρεῖται ; Aly, op. cit., pp. 53–54.

[8] Olymp. IX. 107 ; cf. Butcher, Harvard Lectures, pp. 130–140.

ignore the function of Art. Many of the Ancients, however, considered that something more even than the union of these two was needed to explain the sublimity of the poet's imagination, and his gift of vision, which seemed to transcend so much the ordinary limits of the human mind. The theory of inspiration was invented to account for the phenomenon. In Homer[1] the Muse gives the bard the gift of sweet song, and inspires him to tell of the glorious deeds of warriors. Democritus seems to have been the first to enunciate[2] clearly the doctrine that the poet was an inspired madman, who without premeditation sang his sublimest lays in ecstatic frenzy. The poet was placed on a level with the seer[3], who utters many noble things without a knowledge of their meaning. In view of the ancient quarrel between Poetry and Philosophy, Plato naturally concerned himself with the character of the poet's[4] knowledge, especially in contrast with the absolute knowledge he demanded from the philosopher. He modified at times the extreme view of inspiration, or treated it with a touch of irony, but in general he held fast[5] to the theory, as accounting most adequately for the loftiest utterances of the poet. Aristotle, though he speaks[6] of poetry as inspired, was more guarded in his expressions than his master, when discussing the poet's powers. For him poetry had its origin[7] either in a strain of madness, or a happy endowment of nature which reminds us of the Roman conception of " ingenium." Such caution was natural in one who recognised that the poets had only gradually perfected their work through the test of experiment.

[1] Ody. VIII. 64. 73, XXII. 347 ; cf. Hesiod, Theogony, 30 *et seq.*

[2] *Vide* Diels, Die Fragmente, etc., Vol. I, p. 394, Clem. Alex. VI. 168 (there quoted) ; cf. Dio Chrys. 53. 1 (Arnim) ; Cic. De Div. I. 80, De Or. II. 194 ; Hor. A.P. 296.

[3] Plato, Apol. 22 C, Phaedrus, 244 B ; cf., however, Cic. De Div. II. 111, who says that the Sybil's verses owe more to art than to inspiration.

[4] Meno, 99 C–D ; cf. Chase Greene, Plato's view of Poetry, pp. 18, 56.

[5] Phaedrus, 238 D, 245 A, 265 B, Ion, 533 E, 534 B–C, Laws, 682 A, 719 C.

[6] Rhet. III. 7. 11.

[7] Poet. 17, 1455a ; cf. Bywater ad loc., on Ar's account of the effect of the melancholic temperament, Prob. 30. 1.

In Roman times, the theory of poetic inspiration in its crudest form was practically abandoned.[1]   Cicero regards[2]

The problem amongst the Romans the poet as having certain natural gifts that make him independent of art, and help him to rise above the common level, but the added words " quasi divino quodam spiritu inflari " are eloquent of the change of view-point.   Horace, at times, pays[3] lip service to the old theory, but the conception of the frenzied poet could make little appeal[4] to one who insisted so strongly on the labour of the file and perfection of technique.   The Romans, as a rule, preferred to look at the problem from the more prosaic point of view, and ask whether it was " ingenium " or " ars," that went most to the making of a poem.   In fact, the contrast between these two became a commonplace[5] in Roman criticism.   The early writers were acknowledged to possess " ingenium," but to lack the polish which art can bestow.   The position was reversed in the case[6] of some late authors who displayed more art than genius.   In face of the transcendent powers of Homer and Demosthenes, the Romans were compelled to claim[7] merely superiority in artistic finish for Virgil and Cicero, their counterparts in Latin literature.

In view of the prevalence of the discussion on the relative places of art and genius, we are not surprised at its appear-

Art and Nature in Horace's theory ance in Horace.   We find him paying generous homage to " ingenium," and recognising the divine qualities[8] of the great poet, but one might easily suppose that he is inclined to under-

---

[1] Cf., however, Sen. De Tranq. An. 15 ; Pliny, Ep. VII. 4. 10.

[2] Pro Archia, 18 ; cf. Tusc. Disp. I. 64 ; Q. X. 1. 81, *ib.*, 7. 13–14, for other guarded expressions on inspiration ; *vide supra*, p. 143.

[3] Cf. also Prop. IV. 1. 62, *ib.* 6. 75.

[4] Vide A.P. 296 *et seq.*, and his ironic picture of the " vesanus poeta," 453 *et seq.*

[5] *Vide supra*, pp. 286, 291 ; cf. Cic. Ad Q. Fr. II. 9 (11). 3 ; Ovid, Am. I. 15. 14, Trist. II. 424, V. 1. 27 ; Prop. II. 24. 23 ; Q.I. 8. 8 ; cf. Cic. De Or. I. 14 (on the early Roman orators), Or. 143 ; Q. X. 1. 40.

[6] Pliny, Ep. III. 7. 5, on Silius Italicus.

[7] Q. X. 1. 86. 106 ; cf. Hor. A.P. 323 ; Sikes, op. cit., p. 74 *et seq.*, 80 ; *vide supra*, p. 305.

[8] Sat. I. 4. 43.

rate the importance of genius, so insistently does he inculcate
the lesson that art must come to its assistance, if it is to be
brought to perfection. However, he does not propose[1]
mere technical finish as the goal towards which poets
should strive. His ideal was the happy union of art and
genius. It is interesting to note that Neoptolemus[2] championed the same ideal. Horace, in raising the question
as he does[3] in the *Ars Poetica*, may have been immediately
inspired by Neoptolemus,[4] but there is no need to assume
that either of these was indebted for the discussion of it to
rhetorical theory. Even if we had not Pindar as an early
witness in the case of poetry, Plato and Isocrates have
furnished evidence that the relative parts played by art
and genius were discussed in connection with most[5] human
activities.

An elaborate parallel is[6] worked out between the " genera
causarum "[7] (panegyric, deliberative, and forensic), and
the poetic genres treated by Horace. Even

**The poetic gen-
res and the
" genera cau-
sarum "** if the parallel is allowed to stand, it should
be noted that the writers of rhetorical
treatises covered the whole province of
rhetoric in dealing with these three genres, while Horace
did not aim at exhausting the poetic genres, but concentrated almost entirely[8] on Epic and the Drama.

We may admit that the *Ars Poetica* supplies analogies

---

[1] Cf. A.P. 320–322.

[2] Cf. Jensen, op. cit., p. 29, on the union of τέχνη and δύναμις ποιητική ;
ib., pp. 102–103 ; cf. *ib.*, pp. 21–23, on the distinction between εὖ ποιῶν
(the poet of good technique) and the ἀγαθὸς ποιητής.

[3] " Natura fieret laudabile carmen an arte, quaesitum est " (evidently by
one interested in the theory of poetry).

[4] Both he and Horace use the illustration of the flute-player in a similar
context ; cf. Jensen, p. 23, A.P. 414–415.

[5] Cf. Diog. Laert. V. 18 ; Vitruv. I. 1. 2 ; Süss, Ethos, p. 29, and the
interesting quotation from Hippocrates given by Thompson, Phaedrus,
269 D.

[6] Norden, op. cit., pp. 488, 494–496 ; Barwick, op. cit., pp. 45–46,
modifies somewhat Norden's scheme.

[7] Or " genera rhetorices," as some preferred to call them ; cf. Q. III.
3. 14–15.

[8] He touches incidentally on other genres, such as Lyric and Elegy, in
dealing with the development of appropriate metres, A.P. 73 *et seq.*

with the stereotyped divisions[1] of Rhetoric, such as Inventio, Dispositio, and Elocutio,[2] but here again one must distinguish the different positions of the poet and the orator. In the former, "invention" is concerned with a choice[3] of subject, in the latter, with the discovery of arguments that will be most telling for a case intrusted to his advocacy. Horace, in his precept[4] for "lucidus ordo," gives us something corresponding to the "dispositio" of the rhetorical scheme. It is, however, in the sphere of style (Elocutio) that one might expect to find many points of contact between the theory of poetry and that of rhetoric, inasmuch as it was generally recognised[5] that here at least there was ground that was common to both. Modern writers[6] discover an analogy between the Plain, the Middle, and the Grand styles of oratory, and the styles of Comedy, Satyric drama, and Tragedy. They are not content with pointing to a certain broad resemblance between them, but endeavour[7] to work out the analogy in detail, even to the length of instituting a comparison[8] between Cicero's " tenuis orator " and Horace's "tenuis poeta."[9] We are told[10] that "there is abundant evidence in the *Ars Poetica* that Horace still holds to the puristic virtues of the plain style," and that he "never quite conquered his distrust of the grand style."[11] Such epithets as " humilis," " parcus," " tenuis," are placed on a level with similar ones that figure in Cicero's character-

Analogies with Rhetoric

---

[1] Cf. Norden, p. 488, " de partibus artis poeticae."

[2] Horace does not deal explicitly with " Actio," though his discussion (A.P. 101 *et seq.*) involves it.

[3] Cf. A.P. 38 *et seq.*, 119 *et seq.* (on the alternatives of free invention or the choice of a traditional subject), 310 (more akin to the rhetorical " inventio ").

[4] A.P. 41.

[5] At any rate by those whose chief interest was rhetoric ; *vide supra*, p. 443.

[6] Norden, op. cit., p. 495.

[7] Grant and Fiske, op. cit., pp. 24, 39 *et seq.*, though we are told that there is no desire to press the evidence too far.

[8] *Ib.* p. 26.

[9] Whose existence seems to be based chiefly on A.P. 46.

[10] Grant and Fiske, p. 42.

[11] *Ib.* p. 41 ; it would be more true to say that he never conquered his aversion to the excess of the Grand style which led to bombast.

isation[1] of the Plain style. The qualities of the Middle style, including its humour, are discovered[2] in the Satyric drama, and even a reference[3] detected to the " dulcedo " which was one of its distinguishing marks. It seems to be forgotten that Horace was engaged on the peculiar problems of poetry, and, without preoccupation with the stylistic categories of the rhetorical schools, was endeavouring to show how, in accordance with Decorum, style should be adapted to the subjects of the Epic and of the various dramatic genres. It requires ingenuity to discover[4] anything in the *Ars Poetica* to correspond to the relation of the various styles to the " officia oratoris," while surely there is no suggestion[5] in it that the perfect poet will be master of every style, though Comedy may at times raise its tone, and Tragedy descend to the plainness of everyday speech. Such methods of exposition reveal how dangerous it is to stress overmuch what are often merely faint analogies.

One might, without exacting from him a strict technical accuracy, build up from Horace's criticism as a whole a

The "virtues" of Style

fairly coherent doctrine[6] of the " virtues "[7] of style. In passing judgment on Lucilius, he dealt incidentally with the virtue of " Latinitas," while he censured the same poet for a lack of clearness,[8] arising from his redundancy and his aversion to the labour of revision. In his precepts for brevity,[9] he was thinking of the special needs of the poet. He utters, it is

---

[1] Or. 76–90 ; *vide supra*, pp. 377, 379, 467.

[2] Fiske and Grant, pp. 42, 44 ; *vide supra*, p. 408.

[3] In A.P. 99 ; Kroll, Die historische Stellung von Horazens Ars poetica, p. 89, is, in view of what follows, nearer the mark in bringing the " dulcia " into relation with certain elements of πάθος, and the ψυχαγωγία effected by the poet ; cf. Cic. Part. Or. 32, 73 (quoted by him) ; Philodemus, Col. XXXIII, 22 *et seq.* (Jensen, p. 73) might be compared.

[4] Grant and Fiske, p. 63.

[5] *Ib.* p. 40.

[6] Much of it implicit rather than explicit ; here the analogy with Rhetoric is more strongly marked.

[7] It is interesting to note that Philodemus touched on the virtues of style in discussing the views of Neoptolemus and Crates ; *vide supra*, p. 375 *et seq.*

[8] Cf. also A.P. 26, *ib.* 41, on " lucidus ordo " ; Ep. II. 2. 120, the ideal poet will be " liquidus puroque simillimus amni."

[9] Cf. Jensen, op. cit., pp. 13–15, 61–65.

true, against the obscurity springing from over-conciseness
a warning which was a commonplace[1] with the rhetoricians,
but he enjoins brevity[2] in narration, and considers this virtue
also to be the soul of every useful maxim.[3]

The remaining virtues of ornateness and Decorum were
more complex and of wider range. As we saw, Theophrastus
under the heading of " ornatus " dealt with
choice of words, composition, and the use of
Figures. With the last element Horace does not concern
himself,[4] though it bulked large in the criticism of those who
judged poetry from the rhetorical point of view. In poetry,
composition would involve the handling of the various
metres,[5] while the poet's skill in it could serve to invest[6]
ordinary words with a new beauty, or to conceal their
natural harshness.[7] Horace, however, would despise mere
" nugae canorae,"[8] and condemn a style that was too
florid.[9]

Ornateness

---

[1] Cf. Cic. Br. 66 ; Sen. Ep. 114. 17 ; Q. IV. 2. 44, VIII. 2. 19, *ib*. 3. 82 ;
Dionys. De Thucyd. 24, Ep. ad Amm. II. 2 ; cf. De Lys. 4.

[2] With the Epic in view, A.P. 146 *et seq. ;* cf. Cic. De Rep. I. 38, for a
close parallel ; Q. X. 1. 49, on Homer's power in narration ; on brevity as
a quality of the " narratio " in rhetoric, cf. Ad Her. I. 9. 14, II. 22. 34
(illustrated from Ennius) ; Cic. De Inv. I. 28, De Or. II. 326, Or. 122 ;
Q. IV. 2. 31.

[3] A.P. 335 ; note context after " idonea dicere vitae " ; Horace seems
to be enjoining here an epigrammatic brevity, such as characterised the
" sententiae " of Publilius Syrus ; cf. Demetr. 9.

[4] Though Grant and Fiske, p. 44, find an implicit reference to metaphorical and figurative language in Horace's treatment of the diction of the
Satyric Drama, A.P. 234.

[5] A.P. 73 *et seq.*, where the metres are considered in connection with the
genres ; *ib.* 251 *et seq.*, where the metrical defects of Ennius and Accius are
criticised ; cf. Ep. I. 19. 23 *et seq.*

[6] *Vide supra*, p. 379 ; rhetoric, too, had its place for " apta junctura,"
Q. IX. 4. 27.

[7] Ep. II. 2. 122 : " nimis aspera sano levabit cultu," without aiming at
too much smoothness (A.P. 26) ; Horace is evidently here thinking chiefly
of the effect of composition ; cf. Dionys. De C.V. c. 12 ; Cic. De Or. III.
172, Or. 149–150.

[8] The quest for euphony, if too ardently pursued, might be a fault ; *vide
supra*, p. 397.

[9] The poet " luxuriantia compescet " (Ep. II. 2. 122), " ambitiosa recidet
ornamenta " (A.P. 447) ; cf. Q. X. 4. 1.

In his choice of words, as we have already seen,[1] he would have the poet reject those that are lacking in splendour,[2]

Choice of words

impressiveness, and vital force. Horace felt the charm of many of those " speciosa voca-bula "[3] that were current in earlier ages, and would have them restored to favour. The poet may coin new words, but must use the privilege with moderation. In his choice of diction generally, Horace, adopting the standpoint of the Anomalist, wishes to have regard for custom,[4] which he considers to be the chief arbiter in determining the development of language.

Now his treatment of the topic of ἐκλογὴ ὀνομάτων presents some striking analogies with its treatment in

The usage of poetry and prose

Rhetoric. We must not, however, forget that, though the theorists in this latter sphere pointed to the affinity between poetry and oratory, they yet recognised[5] certain differences between them. They excluded from prose certain words which poetry had consecrated to its own use. They allowed the prose-writer less licence than the poet in the use of archaisms, new coinages, and figurative language generally. It seems, indeed, as if in this portion of their theory the usage of poetry was their point of departure,[6] and their ultimate standard of comparison. Aristotle discussed in his *Poetics*[7] the diction proper to poetry and to its various genres, and to this discussion he refers in his *Rhetoric*,[8] as if he wished to keep it before him as a criterion in determining the

---

[1] *Vide supra*, p. 389 *et seq.*

[2] *Vide* Jensen, op. cit., p. 150, where Andromenides demands from the poet ῥημάτων κάλλη καὶ πρὸς ἀκοήν, καὶ γράμματα λαμπρά.

[3] Cf. Barfield, Poetic Diction, c. X, on archaism as an element in the language of poetry ; Barfield deals also with grammatical archaism ; cf. Lowes, op. cit., p. 130 *et seq.*

[4] *Vide supra*, p. 391 ; here Horace shows a marked resemblance to Cicero, who, except in the Brutus, generally championed Anomaly ; *vide supra*, p. 243 ; still one cannot conclude offhand that Horace was dependent on Cicero, as the question of Analogy *v.* Anomaly must have been constantly debated in Rome since the days of the Scipionic circle.

[5] *Vide supra*, p. 446 *et seq.*

[6] *Vide supra*, p. 441.

[7] C. XXI–XXII.

[8] III. 1. 10, *ib.* 2. 2, 5, 7.

measure of freedom to be granted in prose.[1] On the other hand, once a poet begins to dissect his own art, it seems inevitable that, in some form,[2] choice of diction will come up as a subject for his consideration. Though one might even concede that the writers of Poetics[3] owed something to the *formulation* of this element of style in the rhetorical schools, yet the poet's side of the question should not be ignored, nor should the attempt be made[4] to force this constituent of his art too violently into the traditional moulds of rhetoric.

With regard to Horace's treatment of the remaining virtue of Decorum, I need add little to what I have already said.[5] In dealing with this topic he shows

The virtue of Decorum some close parallels with Rhetoric, but the question might well be raised whether the poets did not deal with at least some aspects of the problem independently of rhetorical theory. The principle of propriety was almost universal in its range,[6] and, if we wished to be ingenious,[7] we might apply it to almost every sphere of human activity.[8] The principle was indeed a fundamental one for Horace, and was considered by him[9] an essential condition for success in literature. It lies at the basis of his teaching on the faults of style,[10] which sprang from a failure

[1] At any rate in elevated prose.

[2] *Vide supra*, p. 440.

[3] This would, perhaps, hold especially of the writers after Aristotle.

[4] As by Norden, op. cit., pp. 491–492 ; Grant and Fiske, p. 25 *et seq*

[5] *Vide supra*, p. 423 *et seq*.

[6] Cic. Or. 70, *ib*. 72, where Cicero says that among others who apply it, are " grammatici in poetis."

[7] Some of the modern writers on the Ars Poetica seem to me to be over-ingenious in their application of the principle ; cf. Hack, op. cit., p. 17 : " from this principle flow every word and phrase of the poem " ; *ib*. p.21 : " the rectius deducis, the five-act and three-actor rules, all these follow by hard necessity upon the doctrine of propriety " ; cf. Kroll, op. cit., p. 91 : " dasselbe gilt von dem Begriff, der sich vie ein roter Faden durch das Gedicht hindurchzieht, dem Prepon " ; *ib*. p. 94, where Kroll finds it illustrated even in Horace's precepts for the Chorus and Deus ex machina ; cf. Grant and Fiske, p. 15.

[8] Inasmuch as it embodied the concept of the Golden Mean.

[9] *Vide supra*, p. 423.

[10] A.P. 24 *et seq.*; Neoptolemus evidently discussed a kindred topic (Jensen, op. cit., p. 17), though unfortunately the passage is badly mutilated

to observe the Golden Mean, because a writer through defective judgment is misled by a false appearance of what is correct.[1] It is interesting to note that the faults stigmatised by Horace are those that are akin to virtues,[2] the brevity that through excess issues in obscurity, the smoothness that results in lack of vigour,[3] the effort after grandeur that ends in bombast.[4] Again, he prescribes that the poet in obedience to the dictates of Decorum should observe the law of the genre,[5] and adapt his style to his subject,[6] both as regards choice of words, and their metrical arrangement.[7] In all this he shows some striking analogies with Rhetoric.

Horace had the doctrine of Decorum also in mind in his treatment of character-drawing[8] ($\tilde{\eta}\theta os$), and the expression

Character-drawing and emotion

of emotion ($\pi\acute{a}\theta os$), both of which figured in rhetorical theory. As regards the former, it must first be noted that the aim of the poet and the orator was not always identical. The poet was aiming at dramatic Decorum,[9] which insured that the words and sentiments attributed to the personages of his play would be in harmony with their characters.[10] The orator[11] was primarily interested in employing a style of speech that would set his own character in a favourable light, as well as a style that would suit the character of his hearers, and make a deep impression upon them. Only rarely and incidentally

[1] Cf. Ad Her. IV. 10. 15 : " specie gravitatis falluntur " ; Cic. De Inv. I. 28 ; Q. VIII. 3. 56 (on $\kappa a\kappa\acute{o}\zeta\eta\lambda ov$) : " quidquid est ultra virtutem, quotiens ingenium judicio caret, et specie boni fallitur " ; *vide supra*, p. 138.

[2] Cf. Cic. Part. Or. 81 ; Sen. Controv. VII. pr. 5 ; Ovid, Ars Am. II. 662 ; Pliny, Ep. IX. 26. 5 ; Q. X. 2. 16, XII. 10. 73, 80.

[3] Cf. Q. IX. 4. 142 ; *vide supra*, p. 379.

[4] Cf. $\pi\epsilon\rho\grave{i}$ $\H{v}\psi ovs$, III. 3 ; Horace had himself many such examples before his mind ; Sat. I. 10. 36 : " turgidus Alpinus " ; Ep. I. 3. 13, A.P. 97, 230.

[5] *Vide supra*, p. 424.

[6] e.g. in Comedy, Tragedy, and the Satyric drama.

[7] Cf. Plato, Rep. III. 400 A *et seq.*, though Plato was viewing the question mainly from the ethical point of view.

[8] *Vide supra*, p. 423 *et seq.*

[9] *Vide supra*, p. 125 *et seq.*

[10] Cf. Cic. De Off. I. 97, where Cicero evidently regarded this aspect of Decorum as the special province of the poets.

[11] *Vide supra*, p. 122 *et seq.*

will he indulge in the dramatic exhibition of character,[1] and
for this he can learn most from the art of the dramatist.[2]
The same may be said to hold good as regards the element
of πάθος. The dramatic poet, in obedience to the law of
Decorum, was bound to see that the language employed by
his charcters was in keeping with their emotions,[3] though
here, in addition to the words of the drama, the actor's skill[4]
was invoked to interpret the mind of the poet. Horace,
moreover, insists[5] that the poet should feel the emotions
which he produces in others. This is in effect a plea for
sincerity in style. Cicero prescribes[6] a similar condition for
the orator, but it is worthy of note that he reinforces[7] his
precept by an appeal to the practice of both the actor and
the poet. As regards, then, both ἦθος and πάθος,[8] the
dramatic poets in particular were in a position to speculate
independently of rhetorical theory, and in these cases even
to lay it under a debt, though the rhetoricians might claim
that they were the first to formulate such matters with
clearness and precision.

By some,[9] Horace's precept for unity[10] is brought into
relation with the principle of Decorum. Such an interpretation is, of course, possible, if we take
The principle of unity Decorum in its widest sense, and acknowledge its sway in every department of life and
literature. Horace, however, was in this case merely proclaiming for his own domain what was a fundamental law
in Greek aesthetic theory. Plato first[11] clearly formulated

[1] *Vide supra*, p. 125 *et seq.*
[2] Cic. Cato Major, 65, where the influence of the Drama is apparent.
[3] A.P. 105 *et seq.*
[4] Cf. Cic. De Or. III. 216 *et seq.*, De Off. I. 114 ; Q. XI. 3. 4.
[5] A.P. 102 *et seq. ;* cf. Ar. Poet. 17. 1455a.
[6] *Vide supra*, p. 128.
[7] De Or. II. 193–195.
[8] Fiske and Grant, p. 35, declare that " it will be found that Horace's
theory of ἦθος is in complete conformity with such doctrines of Aristotle,
Hellenistic rhetoric, and Cicero " ; is the " complete conformity " meant to
suggest complete dependence ?
[9] Grant and Fiske, p. 17 ; cf. Kroll, op. cit., p. 92.
[10] *Vide supra*, pp. 405, 434.
[11] Menéndez Y Pelayo, op. cit., p. 8, says it was first formulated by Corax,
but I do not know on what authority.

the idea of unity[1] in the sphere of literature, and laid it down as a condition for every discourse. One may doubt if, as some have suggested, Plato was in a metaphysical mood in formulating the idea. It seems clear that he was thinking, not of the unity of Ideas as contrasted with the phenomenal world,[2] but rather of the analogy of the animal world, in which organic unity is maintained amidst variety.[3] Aristotle shared this conception of organic unity,[4] but, logician as he was, he insisted, too, on the need of maintaining the logical nexus between the different parts.[5] It is clear both from later Greek[6] and from the Roman writers,[7] how widespread was the application in literature of the idea of organic unity.

We turn now to consider certain aspects of the section which is treated by some modern writers under the heading "De artifice"; the poet's mission " de poeta."[8] Here an analogy is established[9] between the " officia poetae "[10] and the " officia oratoris," but it remains to be seen how far it can be pressed, or whether it can be maintained that the " officia poetae " are " a perfect analogue to Cicero's officia oratoris."[11] The perfect orator, as we have seen, will aim at three things—docere, delectare, movere. Horace declares that poets aim at affording either profit or pleasure, or at combining both in their works. He assigns the palm

[1] Phaedrus, 264 C (cf. Thompson ad loc., though his quotation from the Politicus is hardly relevant) ; ib. 268 D, where the conception is applied to tragedy ; cf. Laws, 752 A, Gorgias, 505 D ; Süss, Ethos, pp. 74–75.
[2] Cf. Grant and Fiske, loc. cit.
[3] Cf. A.P. 29, on a false variety.
[4] Poet. 23. 1459a ; cf. Rhet. III. 14. 8.
[5] Cf. Poet. VII. 1450b, on Tragedy.
[6] On its importance in History, cf. Polyb. I. 3. 4, III. 1. 4–5 ; Diodor. XX. 1. 5, compares History to ἐμψύχῳ σώματι ; cf. Lucian, Quomodo conscribenda sit historia, 23, on ἀκέφαλα τὰ σώματα εἰσάγοντες ; vide infra, p. 505 ; cf. περὶ ὕψους, X. 1.
[7] Cic. De Or. II. 325, Br. 208 ; Q. VII. pr. 2, ib. 10. 16 ; Evanthius, De Comoedia, Wessner, I. p. 20.
[8] The " artifex " as contrasted with the " ars."
[9] Vide Norden, op. cit., pp. 501–502 ; Grant and Fiske, pp. 49, 60–61 ; Barwick, op. cit., p. 51 et seq.
[10] Cf. A.P. 306 : " munus et officium, nil scribens ipse, docebo."
[11] Grant and Fiske, p. 20.

to those who achieve the latter result. The form[1] in which he expresses himself, shows that he had before his mind the debate that had been carried on for centuries on the nature of the poet's mission. Aristophanes seems to have been the first to discuss[2] the question explicitly,[3] but when he declared that the poet's function is to teach, he had in view moral teaching, whereas the " docere " of the orator was concerned with the instruction of judge or audience on the points of his case.

I need only recall the fact that the problem of the poet's mission was much in Plato's thoughts.[4] In constructing his Ideal Commonwealth, he naturally considered what rôle the poet should fill there, and what should be his relation to morality. Poetry shared in the condemnation which, on metaphysical grounds, he passed on Art generally, but it came under his lash mainly for ethical reasons,[5] as appealing to the lower element of the soul, and as feeding and watering the passions. Poets such as Homer and Hesiod are censured for demoralising men by their scandalous pictures of gods and heroes. Plato will then subject the poets admitted to his State to a rigorous censorship, and compel them to teach noble lessons, singing hymns to the gods and sounding the praises of great men. Yet, Puritan though he was, he could not altogether ignore the element of pleasure in poetry. Her advocates had declared that poetry was pleasurable, but was also profitable for States and for human life. Plato will listen favourably to this defence, for, as he says,[6] we shall be the gainers, if it can be established.

Aristotle conceded to the poet in his art greater freedom

[1] A.P. 333–334 ; note the triple " aut."

[2] Frogs, 1009, 1031, 1053 *et seq.*, *ib.* 685, on the function of the Chorus ; cf. his plea for Comedy, Achar. 500.

[3] Though it may have been implicitly before the mind of such critics of Homer as Xenophanes and Heraclitus.

[4] Barwick, op. cit., pp. 56–57, has conveniently collected the passages in which the two important words ἡδύ and ὠφέλιμον are used in reference to the end of poetry.

[5] Especially in Rep. II–III ; cf. *ib.* X. 606 ; Chase Greene, op. cit., pp. 29, 50, 65.

[6] Rep. X. 607 D–E.

than his master, though he condemns gratuitous wicked-
Later views on ness.[1] His judgments on Poetry were in the
the poet's main founded on aesthetic reasons, but at
mission times he is moved by ethical considerations.[2]
The issues in the debate were more clearly knit at a later
period when, on the one hand, Eratosthenes declared[3] that
the end of Poetry was to charm and not to teach, while, on
the other, the Stoics contended that the poet's chief aim was
to instruct.[4] In their view Poetry was a kind of elementary
philosophy,[5] and no one could be a good poet,[6] who was
not also a good man.[7] Amongst the poets, Homer was par
excellence the teacher of Greece, but, as many of his tales
of gods and heroes were felt to be prejudicial to morality,
the method of allegorical interpretation[8] was introduced to
safeguard his reputation. It became a favourite method
with the Stoics,[9] who laid such stress on the didactic
function of poetry, and would have revolted against the
doctrine of the moral indifference of Art. In spite of the
protests of Aristarchus, the allegorical interpretation of
Homer long continued to hold its ground, so that even so
discerning a critic as the author of the treatise *On the
Sublime*,[10] has recourse to it to save the poet from the im-
putation of impiety.

We find echoes of the discussion on the poet's function

[1] Poet. XV. 1454a, on the character of Menelaus in the Orestes.
[2] *Vide* Butcher, Aristotle's Theory of Poetry and Fine Art, p. 213, on
his requirement that the characters of a play shall be χρηστά.
[3] Strabo, I. 1. 10, I. 2. 3.
[4] Cf. Jensen, op. cit., p. 131 *et seq.*
[5] Cf. Strabo, loc. cit. ; Plut. De Aud. Poet. c. 14 ; the Stoics also maintained that the wise man alone is a poet ; cf. Padelford, Essays on the Study
and Use of Poetry, Introd., p. 28 *et seq.*
[6] Strabo, I. 2. 5 ; cf. Morr, op. cit., p. 48 *et seq. ; vide supra*, p. 161.
[7] Ben Jonson adopts this view, Spingarn, Crit. Essays, I. p. 12 ; cf.
Minturno's definition of the poet as " vir bonus imitandi peritus."
[8] Cf. Plato, Rep. II. 378 D ; cf. Xenoph. Mem. I. 3. 7 ; Dio Chrysos.
53. 4 (Arnim).
[9] Cf. Sen. Ep. 88. 5 *et seq. ;* the Stoics found in Homer examples of
both physical and moral allegory ; cf. Jensen, op. cit., p. 131 *et seq.*, 143
et seq., 166–168 ; cf. Wehrli, Zur Geschichte der allegorischen Deutung
Homers, p. 49 *et seq. ; vide supra*, p. 461.
[10] IX. 7.

in Philodemus. Neoptolemus required[1] that the perfect poet
should combine profit and delight. Philo-

Philodemus   demus finds fault with him for not defining
more clearly the kind of utility he demanded, as there were
numerous ways in which poetry might be instructive.[2]
Other aspects of the problem are discussed[3] in connection
with the views of the Stoic Ariston. He, in harmony with
the general attitude of his sect, emphasised the poet's duty
as a teacher, though Philodemus criticises him for applying
the terms " good " and " bad " to poetry, sometimes in
their ethical, sometimes in their aesthetic sense.

The Romans,[4] for the most part, would be inclined to
exact some useful service from the poet, though with their
practical common-sense they readily favoured

Roman views   a compromise[5] between Profit and Pleasure
as the end of Poetry. We have seen[6] that Cicero was somewhat unstable in his verdicts on the poets. He sometimes
judged their achievements from a strictly ethical standpoint,
and exhibited towards them some of Plato's rigid puritanism.
In the *Pro Archia*,[7] however, he manifested a fine enthusiasm
for the poet's calling, and depicted in vivid language the
delights of poetry, though even there, so anxious was he to
soothe Roman prejudices—he emphasised the utility to be
derived from it as a relaxation for one oppressed by the
routine of forensic duties. Quintilian, who would naturally
be inclined to dwell on the benefit that would accrue to the
student of rhetoric from the reading of poetry, startles us

[1] Horace in this matter very faithfully reproduces him ; cf. Jensen, op.
cit., p. 7 *et seq., ib.* p. 33 : δεῖν τῷ τελείῳ ποιητῇ μετὰ τῆς ψυχαγωγίας
τοῦ τοὺς ἀκούοντας ὠφελεῖν καὶ χρησμολογεῖν ; (cf. A.P. 334 :
" idonea dicere vitae ") ; *ib.* p. 108 *et seq.,* 123 ; on ψυχαγωγία, cf. A.P.
100 : " quocumque volent animum auditoris agunto " ; *vide supra,* p. 477.

[2] Amongst others by ethical teaching, Jensen, p. 7.

[3] *Ib.* p. 35 *et seq.,* 131 *et seq.*

[4] Sikes, op. cit., p. 35 *et seq.,* might be consulted for a good general discussion of the question ; cf. Tate's admirable article, " Horace and the
Moral Function of Poetry," C.Q. Vol. XXII, 1928, p. 65 *et seq.*

[5] Cf. Cic. De Leg. I. 5 (where History and Poetry are compared) :
" quippe, quom in illa omnia ad veritatem, Quinte, referantur, in hoc ad
delectationem pleraque ; cf. Pliny, Ep. IX. 33. 1.

[6] *Vide supra,* p. 147.

[7] *Vide supra,* p. 141 ; cf. p. 445.

at times[1] by declaring that the poet aims solely at giving pleasure, but, for all that, he would not relieve him of all moral responsibility.[2] It is interesting to note that Tacitus lays stress[3] rather on the personal pleasure enjoyed by the poet in the exercise of his craft.

We are here, however, concerned mainly with the views of Horace on the function of poetry, which has been so often impugned, and has in turn evoked so many "Apologies." Apart from other considerations, the Augustan critic felt bound to defend an art which had been debased by the numerous poetasters of the time, and to show that such a "levis insania"[4] could make some contribution to the commonweal. Hence he sets forth[5] the civilising influence of poetry in the primitive condition of the human race. He defends the Old Comedy and Satire,[6] on the ground that they perform a useful service to society. He, moreover, invests the poet[7] with a religious sanction[8] as the priest of the Muses, and presses poetry into the service of religion.[9] The worthy poet is the guardian of virtue,[10] and can guide the young into paths of goodness. The function that Horace assigns the Chorus,[11] is pre-eminently a religious and moral one. The poet can draw his best material from the "Socraticae chartae,"[12] which will teach him especially the various duties of life. We are not surprised to find Horace adopting the

---

[1] *Vide supra*, p. 446.

[2] Cf. X. 1. 100, on Afranius.

[3] Dial. 12.

[4] Ep. II. 1. 119.

[5] A.P. 391 *et seq.*; cf. Ar. Frogs, 1032; *vide supra*, p. 438.

[6] As he says of the Satirist: "quamquam ridentem dicere verum quid vetat" (Sat. I. 1. 24); *vide supra*, p. 355.

[7] Odes, III. 1. 3; cf. Pindar, fr. 118; Theocr. XVI. 29; *vide* Campbell, Horace, p. 61 *et seq.*, for some interesting remarks on this subject.

[8] A.P. 400: "divinis vatibus"; cf. Aen. VI. 662: "pii vates"; Pro Archia, 18; Ovid, Ars Am. III. 403, for the epithets "sanctus" and "sacer" applied to poets.

[9] Ep. II. 1. 132 *et seq.*

[10] *Ib.* 230; cf. *ib.* 126 *et seq.*

[11] A.P. 196 *et seq.*; cf. Ar. Frogs, 686–687; Steinmann, op. cit., p. 17 *et seq.*, 75.

[12] A.P. 310.

allegorical interpretation of the Stoics in his reading of Homer,[1] who, he declares, teaches more adequately than Chrysippus and Crantor the nature of the honourable and the expedient.[2] Poetry, too, can sing the praises of great men,[3] as Plato demanded of it, and has the power of conferring immortality.[4] In view of all this, Horace can claim with reason that the poet is " utilis urbi."[5] It was a claim particularly fitting in one who was the poet laureate of the new Imperial regime, and who, even in his *Odes*, could display in its interest some of the " high seriousness of poetry." Hence it is, that he assigns pride of place to the poet who unites profit with pleasure. In thus formulating his judgment in the *Ars Poetica*, Horace may have been following more immediately in the footsteps of Neoptolemus,[6] but we would like to think that his view of the poet's mission was not bounded by the limits of Hellenistic theory, especially in view of the fact that he elsewhere dwells[7] on it in so much detail. At any rate, it seems evident that the discussion of the poet's function was from the beginning conducted independently of rhetorical theory.[8] Whatever may be the analogy that exists between the " officia poetae " and the " officia oratoris," it should not be pressed so as to suggest that the former were formulated in imitation of the latter.

What can be said of the parallel supposed to exist between the perfect poet[9] and the perfect orator, as drawn by the theorists in their respective spheres ? It is **The perfect poet and the perfect orator** difficult, at any rate, to work out the parallel in detail. Horace rules out mediocrity in poetry,[10] though he does not look for a faultless genius.

[1] Ep. I. 2. 1 *et seq.*   [2] Discussed, as we know, in Cicero's De Officiis.

[3] Ep. II. 1. 249.   [4] Odes, IV. 8. 13 *et seq.*, *ib.* 9. 25 *et seq.*

[5] Ep. II. 1. 124.   [6] *Vide supra*, p. 486.

[7] Cf. Ep. II. 1 ; I am not, of course, here raising the question of the relative dates of this Epistle and the Ars Poetica.

[8] One might even raise the question whether the rhetoricians, in formulating their views on the " officia oratoris," were not influenced by poetic theory.

[9] Cf. Norden, op. cit., p. 502, who treats A.P. 347–415 under the rubric " De virtute poetae," A.P. 416–476 under the rubric " De vitiis poetae " (cf. A.P. 308) ; cf. Jensen, op. cit., pp. 123–124.

[10] A.P. 372 ; in all this section Horace is thinking of perfection of form ;

Cicero, taking account of actual conditions, finds a place in the scheme of things for the " mediocris orator."[1] He, however, outlines an ideal of eloquence[2] that may never be realised,[3] that of the orator who is inspired by lofty sentiments, who is master of every style, and has acquired an almost universal culture.[4] Horace does not postulate extensive learning in the poet,[5] and in this forms a strong contrast to Neoptolemus,[6] who demanded that the poet should have a knowledge of the various dialects, be versed in many sciences,[7] and be acquainted with human customs, if he is to depict life faithfully. No such ideal of the " doctus poeta " was before the mind of Horace. In his view, a study of the " Socraticae chartae " will enable the poet to achieve true and appropriate character-drawing, while a study of the great Greek models will teach him to esteem perfection of form, and avoid the slovenly workmanship that too often marred the glory of Roman poetry.

Finally, modern scholars[8] stress the analogy between Horace's " vesanus poeta " and Cicero's " insanus orator ";
but certain differences, as well as the diver-
The "vesanus sity of purpose of the two writers, should be
poeta" noted. The Horatian passage[9] is permeated with irony in its picture of the poet who, void of reason and

from another point of view, the poet is perfect, who combines the " utile " with the " dulce " ; cf. Jensen, p. 33.

[1] De Or. I. 117 (cf. 118, on the fastidiousness of our judgment in other arts), III. 213.

[2] Ib. I. 118, II. 85–86, Or. 7–8 ; cf. Q. I. 10. 4, XII. 2. 31, on " perfectus orator."

[3] Though Cicero hints plainly enough that it was realised in his own oratory.

[4] Vide supra, p. 150 et seq. ; cf. Vitruv. I. 1. 3 et seq., on the culture of the architect.   [5] Cf. Petron. Satyr. 118.

[6] Vide Jensen, op. cit., p. 11, 113–114 ; Jensen suggests that Neoptolemus, in his insistence on the study of dialects, shows the influence of the learned circles of Cos or Alexandria ; cf. Strabo, I. 2. 3 et seq., on Homer's learning.

[7] Cf. Dryden (in the postscript to the " Notes and Observations on the Empress of Morocco ") : " a man should be learned in several sciences . . . to be a complete and excellent poet."

[8] Vide Norden, op. cit., p. 506, who without decisive evidence says that Horace paints his mad poet in Stoic colours ; cf. Grant and Fiske, pp. 72–73 : " rhetorical analogies are unquestionably operative here."

[9] A.P. 453 et seq.

a sense of reality,[1] hastens to his own destruction. Such a one, wholly dominated by " ingenium,"[2] would refuse to live the laborious days which Horace had prescribed as essential for success in poetry, and thus would run counter to his most cherished ideals. Cicero's " insanus orator "[3] is one who is equipped with the dangerous weapon of oratorical power, but destitute of prudence and high purpose. In another passage[4] he has in mind the frenzied orators of the Asiatic school, who will employ the Grand style even when the audience is not attuned to it, or when it is wholly out of place. In criticising such a fault, Cicero's design was to parry the attacks of those who wished to affix the stigma of Asianism to his own oratory.

In reviewing the tendencies of these modern studies of the *Ars Poetica*, we must admit that one good service has Tendencies of been rendered by their insistence on some-modern studies thing approaching a well-defined plan in the of the " Ars poem, though it is sometimes forgotten how Poetica " difficult it would be in any event to make one of Horace's temperament adhere rigidly to it. Moreover, as I have said, we should examine his critical doctrine as a whole, and be prepared to find his interest in questions that were to him of vital importance, as well as his concern with contemporary movements in literature, overriding any stereotyped scheme. We may allow that there are some striking parallels between the *Ars Poetica* and what we might style the " schematism " of Rhetoric, especially as expounded in Greece in Hellenistic times, and in Rome by Cicero. We may even grant that, in the *formulation* of some of its precepts, poetic theory was indebted to the theory of rhetoric. In general, however, it seems to me that these modern studies, in their endeavour to bring the theory of poetry into almost complete conformity with that of rhetoric (and, for some at least, such

[1] Cf. *Ib.* 468 : " nec, si retractus erit, jam fiet homo."

[2] Cf. Kiessling-Heinze ad A.P. 453 ; we have thus a pendant to the discussion in 295 *et seq.*

[3] De Or. III. 55 (Stoic colouring is here evident) ; cf. Cicero's picture of Fimbria, Br. 233.

[4] Or. 99 ; the elder Seneca furnishes the best parallel in his reference to the " insania " of the declaimers ; *vide supra*, p. 241.

conformity connotes dependence), tend to work out the parallels between the two in too close detail, while they at times attach undue importance to mere vague analogies, disregard the peculiar problems of poetry, and take little account of principles that were considered fundamental in aesthetic theory generally.

History was another sphere to which Rhetoric extended its sway. The rhetorical point of view was often apparent
Rhetoric and History in the conception of it that prevailed among the Romans, who in this matter, as in so many others, were following the lead of the Greeks. It is necessary therefore, before I pass on to consider Roman opinion, to deal briefly with certain tendencies in Greek historical writing that will help to explain the invasion of Rhetoric into that domain.

Before the rise of historical writing in prose, the Epic[1] supplied its place, and helped to satisfy man's craving for
The Epic and History a knowledge of history, especially as regards primitive times, in which the border line between fact and legend was not clearly defined. The development of the historical Epic[2] shows how close the alliance between the two genres could become.[3] In later times, when conscientious investigation of fact and scrupulous regard for truth were regarded as the essential qualities in the historian, critics might proclaim[4] that poetry and history were bound by different[5] laws, but in the earlier period the historian was naturally drawn into rivalry with the Epic poet, and led to imitate his technique. After the manner of Homer, Herodotus[6] for the sake of variety

[1] Cf. Strabo, I. 2. 9, on the historical element in Homer; Bury, The Ancient Greek Historians, p. 2 *et seq.*; Norden, A.K. I. p. 35 *et seq.*, on the relation between Epic and History.

[2] On historical lays in Rome in primitive times, cf. Cic. Br. 75, Tusc. Disp. I. 3; Nonius on " assa voce," Mueller, I. p. 105; *vide supra*, p. 1.

[3] *Vide* Peter, Die geschichtliche Litteratur, Vol. I. p. 67 *et seq.*, on history in the poets.

[4] Lucian, Quomodo conscribenda sit historia, 8; Marcellinus, Life of Thucydides, 41; Cic. De Leg. I. 5; Ovid, Am. III. 12. 41; Pliny, Ep. IX. 33. 1; cf. Ad Her. I. 8. 13; Q. II. 4. 2.

[5] Though Q. (X. 1. 31), calls history " quodammodo carmen solutum," having in view the aim and style of historical composition.

[6] Cf. Dionys. Ad Pomp. c. 3; cf. Aly, op. cit., p. 64.

indulged in digressions, and at times abandoned direct narrative to allow his characters to speak for themselves. Set speeches (many of them fictitious) became, in spite of occasional protests,[1] an inseparable element in ancient historical writing, and were the chief factor in imparting to it a definitely rhetorical character.

Thucydides reacted[2] strongly against the methods of his predecessors, his critical instinct revolting especially against

Thucydides and his predecessors

their unqualified acceptance of the legendary. He contented himself with inserting a speech only when one was actually delivered, and, while keeping in mind the exigencies of the situation, he adhered as closely as possible to the general sense of the speaker.[3] He had no taste for empty rhetorical display, but he was no stranger to contemporary movements in rhetoric,[4] though he did not allow himself to become enslaved to their allurements. He had the merit, too, of raising (implicitly at least) the question whether the historian's aim should be profit or pleasure.[5] The answer given to it by particular historians had no little influence in determining how far they would seek to import into their writings the fascinations of rhetoric. For Thucydides[6] truth was the sovereign goddess that should preside over history. Impressed by the serious duty that confronted the historian, he proclaimed that his aim was not to tickle the ears by fine phrases, nor to charm by a pleasing narrative, but to make his history a school for statesmen,[7] and a guide for future generations. Hence, by critics who did not share his high

---

[1] Dionys. De Thucyd. 16; Diodorus, XX. 1, protests against long speeches as breaking the continuity of the narrative.

[2] I. 21–22; cf. Dionys. De Thucyd. 5–6; Jebb, Essays and Addresses, p. 359 *et seq.*

[3] Cf., however, Dionysius' criticism of the Melian Dialogue, De Thucyd. 41.

[4] Cf. Dionys. De Thucyd. 24, De Lys. 3, Ep. Ad Amm. II. c. 2, *ib.* 17; Cic. Or. 39, rather exaggerates in his tribute to Thucydides; Lamb, op. cit., C. III, V; Croiset, Thucydide I–II, Introd., p. 108 *et seq.; vide supra,* p. 259.

[5] Cf. the discussion in Lucian, op. cit. 8.

[6] Dionys. De Thucyd. 8; cf. Lucian, op. cit., 39, 61–63.

[7] Cf. Ar. Rhet. I. 4. 13; Dio Chrys. Or. 18. 9; Scheller, De Hellenistica Historiae Conscribendae Arte, p. 72 *et seq.; vide infra,* p. 501, on Polybius.

ideals,[1] he, with his severely practical aim, was adjudged inferior to Herodotus in the choice and treatment of his subject, and in all that made for grace and charm of style.

Others assigned a further didactic[2] purpose to history, which would insure the moral betterment of mankind, by

The didactic purpose of history

furnishing examples of illustrious men[3] whose lives would incite others to great deeds of virtue or of valour. Some historians, how-ever, made pleasure their chief aim,[4] and often with little regard for historical accuracy were ready to handle their subject-matter with a generous freedom, and employ every artifice of style, if only they could succeed in entertaining their readers.[5] They might reach this goal by an admixture of the legendary, or by digressions that would vary their narrative, but an alluring style arrayed in all the trappings of rhetoric was for them one of the surest means of gaining their end.

It is especially in this connection that Isocrates is a figure of importance. Though no historian himself, and

The import-ance of Isocrates

often indifferent to historical fact,[6] he was destined to influence the course of historical writing. His own treatment of events in Greek history, whenever the occasion arose, was strongly rhetorical in character.[7] He developed the ἐγκώμιον with its natural tendency to exaggeration,[8] though he pruned it

---

[1] Cf. Dionys. Ad Pomp. c. 3 ; Dio Chrysos. Or 18. 10 ; Hermog. περὶ ἰδ. Sp. II. p. 421 ; Cic. Hortensius, fr. 17 ; " quid enim Herodoto dulcius aut Thucydide gravius " ? Q. X. 1. 73.

[2] Cf. Polyb. I. 35. 9, II. 56. 11 (I quote from the Loeb ed.) ; Strabo, I. 1. 22–23 ; Ulrici, Characteristik der antiken Historiographie, p. 47 ; Wachsmuth, Einleitung in das Studium der alten Geschichte, p. 225.

[3] Cf. Isocr. I. 11, IX. 76 et seq. ; Polyb. II. 61. 3, XI. 10. 1 et seq. ; Diod. I. 2. 2.

[4] Duris demanded μίμησις καὶ ἡδονὴ ἐν τῷ φράσαι ; cf. Jacoby, Die Fragmente der Gr. Hist. II C. p. 117 ; Stemplinger, op. cit., p. 149.

[5] Cf. Polyb. IX. 2. 6, XXXVIII. 4 (1.d). 8 (reminiscent of Thucy-dides) ; Lucian, op. cit., 13.

[6] Cf. Panath. 246 ; Peter, Wahrheit und Kunst, p. 144 et seq. ; Blass, Die att. Bered. II. pp. 49–50.

[7] Vide Scala, Isokrates und die Geschichtschreibung, p. 108.

[8] Cf. Isocr. XI. 4 ; on the topics of ἔπαινος and ψόγος in history, cf. Polyb. VIII. 8 et seq. ; Dionys. Ad Pomp. 5 ; Scheller, op. cit., pp. 48–50 ;

of some of the absurdities which it exhibited in the hands of the Sophists. The Encomium in turn had its influence on biography, and on biographical details in history. It was, however, above all in the matter of style[1] that Isocrates was to leave his greatest impress on historical writing, through the medium of his pupils[2] Ephorus and Theopompus, the former of whom he characterised[3] as needing the spur,[4] the latter the rein.

Ephorus composed a treatise on Style,[5] and was interested in the theory of prose-rhythm.[6] One would naturally expect to find in him the marks of his training[7] in the school of Isocrates. However, though his fragments at times reveal a straining after effect[8] by the use of unusual words and strange compounds, he seems to have avoided the worst excesses of the rhetorical historians. It is, at any rate, significant that Polybius mentions[9] with approval the distinction that he drew between historians and speech-writers. He also pays a tribute to[10] him as being the first and only writer who undertook to compose a General History, while he praises his treatment of his subject, and his skill in digressions, which many were prone to regard

Ephorus

Leo, Die griechisch-römische Biographie, p. 91 *et seq.*; on these topics in epideictic oratory, cf. Ar. Rhet. I. 9, III. 14. 2; Gorgias, Helen, 1–2 (Immisch); *vide infra*, p. 519.

[1] By helping to import the panegyrical style into history; cf. Hermog. Περὶ ἰδ. Sp. II. p. 417.

[2] " Ex clarissima quasi rhetoris officina duo praestantes ingenio," Cic. De Or. II. 57; cf. Scala, op. cit., p. 115 *et seq.*

[3] Cic. De Or. III. 36, Ad Att. VI. 1. 12, Br. 204; Q. II. 8. 11, X. 1. 74; cf. Diog. Laert. V. 39, where the saying is applied by Aristotle to Theophrastus and Callisthenes; it was previously applied by Plato to Aristotle and Xenocrates.

[4] Cf. Dio Chrys. Or. 18. 10, on Ephorus' characteristics: τὸ δὲ ὕπτιον καὶ ἀνειμένον τῆς ἀπαγγελίας; Cic. Hortens. fr. 18: " quid enim . . . Ephoro mitius " ?

[5] Theon, Progym. Sp. II. 71.

[6] Cic. Or. 191, 192, 194, 218; Q. IX. 4. 87.

[7] Cf. Cic. Or. 172, *ib.* 191 : " levis ipse orator "; Sen. De Tranq. An. VI; Dionys. De C.V. c. 23.

[8] Cf. Blass, Die att. Bered. II. p. 436.

[9] XII. 28. 10–11.

[10] V. 33. 1; cf. Jacoby, op. cit., II A. pp. 38–39; Bury, op. cit., pp. 162–164.

chiefly as a vehicle for rhetorical display. In theory at least, Ephorus paid homage to Truth[1] as the essential quality in history, and was opposed[2] to those writers who sought for sensational effects by dwelling on the terrible and marvellous.

Theopompus generally reproduced[3] more faithfully than Ephorus the style of the Isocratic school,[4] though forcible character[5] that he was, he at times exhibited[6] something of vehemence of Demosthenes. He was given **Theopompus** to psychological studies of his characters, and, according to Dionysius, loved to reveal all the mysteries of seeming virtue and secret vice. Polybius, however, blamed him[7] for his unmeasured invective against Philip, while Lucian[8] saw in him rather the malignant critic than the impartial historian. It was especially in his acrimonious passages that he showed his gift of powerful and original expression,[9] though at times his efforts after forcefulness ended in feebleness and bathos.[10] He was a practical orator[11] as well as a historian, so that it is not surprising that the style of his history shows the impress of his training.[12] He

[1] Cf. fr. I (M); Jacoby, loc. cit., p. 52, Strabo, IX. 3. 11–12 (there quoted); Polyb. XII. 27. 7; cf., however, Sen. N.Q. VII. 16. 2 : " Ephorus vero non religiosissimae fidei ; saepe decipitur, saepe decipit."

[2] Strabo, VII. 3. 9; cf. Jacoby, loc. cit., pp. 54–55 ; ib. p. 41, fr. 22, for Duris' criticism of Ephorus.

[3] Dionys. Ad Pomp. c. 6 ; cf. Jacoby, op. cit., II A. p. 527 et seq.

[4] Hence the difficulty that many had about attributing to him the authorship of the Hellenica Oxyrhynchia ; cf. Walker, The Hellenica Oxyrhynchia, pp. 18, 70 (W. favours Ephorus) ; Peter, Wahrheit und Kunst, p. 136 ; Kalinka, H. Ox. Introd. p. 7, with some hesitation favours Cratippus as the author.

[5] Cic. Hortens. fr. 18 : " quid enim. . . . Theopompo acrius " ?

[6] Dionys. Ad Pomp. 6 ; cf. Norden, A.K. I. p. 122, Plut. Dem. 18 (there quoted).　　　　　　　　　　　　　　[7] VIII. 9 et seq.

[8] Op. cit. 59 ; cf. Dionys. Ant. Rom. I. 1 ; Cic. Ad Att. II. 6. 2.

[9] Cf. περὶ ὕψους, 31. 1 ; Cic. De Or. III. 36 : " exultantem verborum audacia " ; Br. 66.

[10] Demetr. 75, classes him with the δεινὰ οὐ δεινῶς λέγοντες ; cf. περὶ ὕψους, 43. 2 ; Dionys. περὶ μιμ, Usener, p. 26, for instances of frigidity in him.

[11] Cf. Gellius, X. 18. 6, for his panegyric on Mausolus ; Dionys. Ad Pomp. 6, attributes deliberative speeches also to him.

[12] Cf. Dio Chrys. Or. 18. 10, where he is recommended to the study of the orator ; Q. X. 1. 74 : " oratori magis similis."

reveals his affinity[1] with Isocrates by his meticulous care in avoiding hiatus, his elaborate periodic structure, his striving after rhythmical effects even at the cost of sacrificing the natural order of words, and by his frequent use of the Gorgianic figures. He thus displayed the chief characteristics of the epideictic style, though, according to Dionysius,[2] he fell short of the perfection of his master. Polybius finds fault[3] with him for allowing himself to be diverted from his main task of writing the history of Greece, in order to undertake the biography of Philip of Macedon. Dionysius, who is usually lavish in his praise of Theopompus, condemns some of his digressions as unnecessary,[4] childish, and inopportune. Such digressions, as well as the fables[5] with which he interspersed his history, would naturally offer a fair field for the display of his rhetorical powers.

The love of the fabulous was a rather common feature in Greek literature. It had already manifested itself in the geographical and ethnological speculations[6] of the early poets and historians. It received a fresh impetus when the Greeks began to write the history of the Orient,[7] and gave free rein to their imaginations in describing its marvels. Such a tendency was fostered all the more, when historians set themselves to chronicle the achievements of Alexander the Great. They had then an opportunity for painting in the richest colours the wonders of Eastern lands,[8] while they could employ all

The love of the fabulous

---

[1] Cf. Demetr. 27, 247, 250 ; Dionys. De C. V. 23 ; περὶ μιμ. Usener, p. 25 ; Cic. Or. 151, 207 ; Q. IX. 4. 35 ; Blass, Att. Ber. II. p. 419 *et seq.* ; *vide supra*, p. 97.

[2] De Isaeo, 19.   [3] VIII. 11 (13). 3 *et seq.*

[4] Ad Pomp. 6 ; cf. περὶ μιμ. Usener, p. 26, Jacoby, op. cit., II A. p. 533, on his fondness for digressions.

[5] Cf. Strabo, I. 2. 35 ; Cic. De Leg. I. 5 : " apud Theopompum sunt innumerabiles fabulae " ; cf. Susemihl, op. cit., I. p. 478 ; Jacoby, loc. cit., p. 547 *et seq.*, on his Θαυμάσια.

[6] Cf. Aesch. P. V. 708 *et seq.*, on the wanderings of Io ; Strabo, I. 2. 35 ; Gellius, IX. 4. 6 *et seq.*

[7] Ctesias wrote ' Persica ' and ' Indica,' ἃ μήτε αὐτὸς εἶδε μήτε ἄλλου εἰπόντος ἤκουσεν, Lucian, V. Hist. I. 3 ; Demetr. 215, calls him a poet ; cf. Gellius, IX. 4. 3.

[8] On Onesicritus *vide* Strabo, XV. 1. 28 ; Jacoby, op. cit., II A. p. 724 *et seq.*

their rhetorical skill in relating the almost superhuman exploits of the young monarch. Aristotle's nephew Callisthenes,[1] accompanied Alexander to Asia, and wrote a history of the expedition that was marred by all the defects of the rhetorical historian.[2] Though Aristotle himself paid a tribute to his gift of style, it is clear[3] that his efforts to reach sublimity often ended in bombast and frigidity. His frankness of speech brought him to a tragic death,[4] though, like others who followed in the train of Alexander,[5] he indulged at times in the most fulsome flattery of the monarch.[6]

Clitarchus' account of Alexander's expedition exhibited all the blemishes of similar histories, being marked by a

Clitarchus as historian

strong tendency to exaggeration,[7] and a love of the marvellous and sensational.[8] The inept character of the man was mirrored in his high-flown and turgid style.[9] He seems to have lost no opportunity of expending all the wealth of a meretricious rhetoric in describing the curiosities of the East,[10] and the pageantry of Eastern life. The popularity which his history enjoyed, must have helped to stereotype the tradition[11] of the King's campaigns, while its style proved a lure for many imitators,[12] including the Roman historian Sisenna.[13]

[1] Cf. Plut. Alex. 54, for Aristotle's opinion of him ; Jacoby, op. cit. II A. 632 et seq.

[2] Cf. Cic. De Or. II. 58, Ad Q. Fr. II. 11 (13). 4 ; Gellius, IX. 4. 3, on his love of the fabulous ; cf. Cic. De Div. II. 54, 57.

[3] περὶ ὕψους, III. 2.

[4] Many accounts are given of his punishment and death at the hands of Alexander, Jacoby, loc. cit., pp. 636–637 ; cf. Peter, Wahrheit und Kunst, p. 62.   [5] Cf. Lucian, Quomodo, etc., 12, on Aristobulus.

[6] Polyb. XII. 12b. 2 ; ib. 23. 4 ; Jacoby, loc. cit., p. 645.

[7] Q. X. 1. 75 : "probatur ingenium fides infamatur."

[8] Cf. Cic. Br. 42–43, for his highly-coloured account of the death of Themistocles.

[9] Cf. Demetr. 304 ; περὶ ὕψους, III. 2 ; Philod. Rhet. I. p. 180 ; Bury, op. cit., p. 176, who rightly sees in him a forerunner of Asianism ; Peter, Wahrheit und Kunst, p. 70 et seq.

[10] Cf. Jacoby, op. cit., II A. p. 747 et seq.

[11] A writer as late as Curtius Rufus is still awed by it ; cf. IX. 1. 4 : "equidem plura transcribo quam credo ; nam neque affirmare sustineo de quibus dubito neque subducere quae accepi" ; cf. Wachsmuth, op. cit., p. 574 et seq.   [12] Cf. Philod. Rhet. I. pp. 151–152.   [13] Cic. De Leg. I. 7.

How strongly the subject of Alexander and his exploits appealed to rhetoricians, is evident from the fact that it was treated also by the orator Hegesias.[1] His History was disfigured by all the flagrant faults that characterised his oratory. Plutarch quotes[2] from it a conceit frigid enough, as he says, to have stopped the conflagration of the temple of Diana. As we might expect, the element of the marvellous figured largely in the work, so that Gellius[3] numbers its author amongst the Greek writers who were " miraculorum fabularumque pleni." These examples will suffice to show with what an amount of false rhetoric the story of Alexander was invested. When those who professed to write sober history, presented a narrative so highly coloured and fantastic, we can imagine how the " legend " of the young monarch fared in the schools of declamation,[4] when the declaimers set out to embellish a theme that always had a powerful attraction for them.

The defects of Hegesias

There was a tendency amongst some historians[5] to imitate Tragedy in its aims and methods. They sought to thrill their readers by a dramatic vividness of narrative, and endeavoured to arouse the emotions of pity or terror, by setting forth in all the sombre hues of the tragic dramatist the vicissitudes of human fortune,[6] the deaths of great leaders,[7] or the fate of conquered cities.[8] Phylarchus was one of those who loved

The imitation of Tragedy

[1] Dionys. De C. V. 4 ; *ib.* 18, where his History is quoted to illustrate the ignoble rhythms he employed ; cf. Jacoby, op. cit., II A. p. 804 *et seq.*

[2] Alex. 3 ; cf. Cic. De. Nat. Deor. II. 69, where the conceit is ascribed to Timaeus.

[3] IX. 4. 3.

[4] Sen. Suas. I, IV, Controv. VII. 7 (22). 19 ; cf. Sen. Ep. 83. 19, 23.

[5] They, too, sought to achieve ἔκπληξις and ψυχαγωγία ; cf. Scheller, op. cit., p. 67 *et seq.* ; Ephorus criticised certain writers who dilated on the savagery of the Scythians, εἰδότες τὸ δεινὸν καὶ τὸ θαυμαστὸν ἐκπληκτικὸν ὄν ; cf. Jacoby, II A. p. 54, Strabo, VII. 3. 9 (there quoted) ; cf. Peter, Gesch. Lit. II. p. 317, on Tacitus.

[6] Cf. Dionys. De Thucyd. 5, on θεατρικαί τινες περιπέτειαι, found even in some of the older historians.

[7] Lucian, Quomodo, etc., 25 ; Cic. Br. 43.

[8] Dionys. De Thucyd. 15.

to deal in strong emotions, and seek for sensational effects[1] in his *History*. In criticising his efforts to play upon the feelings of his readers by a narrative full of harrowing details, Polybius protests[2] that the aim of the historian should not be that of the tragic poet. Duris also exhibited many features that would call for a similar protest. He is praised by Cicero[3] as a "homo in historia diligens," though, like many of his contemporaries, his writings contained a large admixture of the marvellous.[4] His criticism of Ephorus and Theopompus[5] for their failure in μίμησις, shows that he valued especially dramatic qualities in the historian. He grows particularly tragic in his tale of Athenian atrocities[6] on the capitulation of his native city of Samos, and fills it out with details which Plutarch considered to be figments of the writer's imagination. It is easy to see how methods such as were employed by Duris and Phylarchus,[7] might readily open the door to much spurious rhetoric.

Timaeus was one of the most important figures among the Hellenistic historians, and is worthy of notice, inasmuch

Timaeus

as he embodied[8] in his writings many of their most serious defects. His *History*, with all its faults, had a great vogue.[9] His unsparing criticism[10] of others, though it won for him the nickname of 'Επιτίμαιος[11],

---

[1] Cf. Polyb. II. 56–63 ; Plut. Them. 32 : ἀγῶνα βούλεται κινεῖν καὶ πάθος ; *ib.* Cleom. 30.

[2] II. 56. 10 *et seq.* ; cf. VII. 7. 1, XV. 34. 1 *et seq.*, 36, for methods similar to those of Phylarchus.

[3] Ad Att. VI. 1. 18.   [4] Cf. Pliny, N.H. I. 7, VII. 30.

[5] Jacoby, II A. p. 138, fr. 1 ; *vide supra*, p. 493 n. 4.

[6] Plut. Pericles, 28 ; cf. the story quoted from the Scholiast ad Eurip. Hec. 934, Jacoby, loc. cit., p. 145.

[7] Cf. Peter, Historicorum Rom. Reliquiae, Vol. I, Introd. p. 319, on the affinity of Valerius Antias with these historians.

[8] Polybius devotes a good portion of his 12th book to a criticism of him.

[9] Polyb. XII. 25c. 1, *ib.* 26d ; cf. Cic. De Or. II. 58 : "magnam eloquentiam ad scribendum attulit " ; Timaeus was a favourite with Atticus (Ad Att. VI. 1. 18).

[10] Cf. Polyb. XII. 4a, for his criticism of Ephorus and Theopompus ; *ib.* 6, 8. 2, on Aristotle (cf. Sandys, Constitution of Athens, Introd. p. 20) ; *ib.* XII. 12b, on Callisthenes ; cf. περὶ ὕψους, IV. 1.

[11] Diod. V. 1. 3.

carried with it a certain impress of sincerity. Though he professed to value truth as the most precious quality in the historian, he did not always live up to this profession. The calm judgment that should characterise the writer of history, was in his case often unbalanced by a rancorous animosity, which led him to indulge in unmeasured invective,[1] and even deliberate falsehood. He was careful enough in his chronology, while Polybius gives him credit[2] for an industrious study of documents, though in his reconstruction of past events he often fell into childish mistakes,[3] through defective judgment and the unfettered play of his imagination. Like so many of the Greek historians, he had a weakness for the fabulous, and was inclined[4] to intersperse his narrative with dreams and prodigies, and much that savoured of " base superstition and womanish love of the marvellous." He liked to display his ingenuity by recasting old traditions,[5] while he often indulged in extravagant paradoxes,[6] and was prone to hyperbole,[7] especially in his attempt to exalt his native land and its heroes. Polybius is especially severe[8] in his censure of the speeches which he introduced into his *History*. As a substitute for speeches actually delivered, he regales his readers with false rhetorical displays, and to men gifted with a capacity for ruling he attributes orations that are puerile, and bristling with absurdities. Such harangues were mostly on the level of school rhetoric,[9] and at times even fell below it. Though Timaeus himself drew[10] a distinction between history and

[1] Polyb. XII. 7. 1, *ib.* 13–15.

[2] XII. 26e. 3 ; cf., however, 25e. 7, 27. 3, where he is criticised for relying at times too much on documentary evidence.

[3] *Ib.* XII. 3. 5 *et seq.* ; cf. 4d. 1–2.

[4] XII. 24. 5.   [5] *Ib.* XII. 25. 4.

[6] *Ib.* 26b. 5, 26c. 1 ; cf. περὶ ὕψους, 4. 1, on his tendency ξένας νοήσεις ἀεὶ κινεῖν.

[7] Polyb. XII. 23, 26b. 4.

[8] *Ib.* 25a. 3 *et seq.*, 25b. 4. 25k, 26.

[9] *Ib.* 25a. 5, 25k. 8 ; Polyb. (26d. 6) calls the imitators of Timaeus μειρακιώδεις, διατριβικοί, καὶ τελέως ἀναλήθεις, a description that would well suit the " scholastici " of Roman days ; it is interesting to note how much Polybius had school rhetoric in mind in his criticism of Timaeus, as if he regarded him as a typical product of the rhetorical school.

[10] Polyb. XII. 28a. 1.

declamatory writing, he exhibited in his own work some of the most offensive features of the declamatory style. The tradition established by his countryman Gorgias, must have exerted its influence upon him,[1] though Dionysius[2] evidently regarded his attempt to reproduce the Isocratic manner as the origin of many of his most glaring faults. Cicero[3] found in him a representative of one type of Asianism, which aimed at elegance, epigrammatic pointedness, and rhythmical effects. Even this brief notice may serve to show how, in the hands of Timaeus, what should be the main purpose of the historian, was too often made subservient to a parade of rhetoric that was meretricious and unreal.

Polybius' criticism of the Hellenistic historians has prepared us for an understanding of his own conception[4] of historical writing. He belonged to the Stoic

The outlook of Polybius sect, and was a pupil of Panaetius. During his sojourn at Rome, as we have seen,[5] he was a member of the Scipionic circle, and shared its high ideals. In his critical spirit, his scientific outlook, his hostility to mere empty display, he reminds us of Thucydides, while his Stoic training may have helped him to value the virtue of dispassionateness even more highly than that historian. He likes to dwell on the utilitarian aspects[6] of history, as leading[7] to the moral advancement of mankind, or as a school[8] wherein statesmen may best learn the lessons of their craft. He is determined to search out for the causes of events, and the motives underlying actions, as the know-

---

[1] Cf. περὶ ὕψους, 4, where many examples of τὸ ψυχρόν are quoted from him.

[2] De Din. 8.

[3] Br. 325 ; cf. Norden, A.K. I. p. 139 ; Blass, Die griech. Beredsamkeit, p. 41 ; *vide supra*, p. 214.

[4] Amongst modern authors the following may be consulted : Wunderer, Polybios, c. V ; Strachan-Davidson, Hellenica, p. 353 *et seq.* ; Bury, op. cit., c. VI ; Susemihl, op. cit., II. p. 80 *et seq.*

[5] *Vide supra*, p. 29 *et seq.*

[6] Though he allows that both pleasure and profit may accrue from the study of history, XV. 36. 3 ; cf. Siegfried, Studien zur geschichtlichen Anschauung des Polybios, p. 29.

[7] *Vide supra*, p. 492.

[8] I. 1. 2, IX. 1. 4–5, XII. 25g. 2 ; cf. IX. 2. 6, XXXVIII. 4. 8.

ledge of these[1] may serve as a guide for succeeding ages. He, however, recognises[2] the influence of Fortune as a factor in human affairs.

There are, he tells us, many classes of readers,[3] some who are fond of a good story, others who are lovers of recondite lore, others again who are serious students

The duties of the historian

of political events. It is especially for the latter class that he wishes to write. There is probably no ancient writer that has set out more clearly and more fully than Polybius the duties and qualifications of the historian,[4] and the laborious training he must undergo to equip himself for his task. History, to have permanent value, should be written by those who have had practical experience in statesmanship,[5] and in the art of war, and who, as far as possible, have been able to see things for themselves. A man without such experience[6] will be largely beating the air, when he endeavours to elicit information from those who have themselves witnessed events, and even in his study of documents will be prone to draw unwarranted conclusions without due consideration of the evidence. Truth is often difficult to find,[7] but its discovery must be the historian's first care.[8] It is to history[9] what the eye is to the human body, and, if it be absent, all that is left is an unprofitable tale. The historian must scorn marvels and monsters,[10] prefer truth for its own sake, and tell nothing beyond it. The works of writers such as Chaereas and Sosylus rank not with sober history, but with the gossip of the barber's shop.[11] Subjectively as well as objectively, the

[1] XI. 19a. 1, XII. 25b. 1, 3, XXX. 6. 3–4.

[2] I. 4; cf. Siegfried, op. cit., p. 60, for a good analysis of the concept of Τύχη in Polybius; cf. Scala, Die Studien des Polybios, p. 159 et seq.

[3] φιλήκοι and φιλομαθοῦντες; cf. VII. 7. 8, IX. 1. 4, ib. 2. 5.

[4] XII. 25.

[5] XII. 25g. 1, 25h. 6, 28. 2 et seq., 28a. 4; cf. IX. 14. 1; cf. Lucian op. cit. 34, on the need of σύνεσις πολιτικὴ in the historian.

[6] XII. 28a. 10.

[7] VIII. 8. 8.

[8] XXXVIII. 4 (1d). 4 et seq.; cf. Strabo, I. 2. 17: τῆς μὲν οὖ ἱστορίας ἀλήθειαν εἶναι τέλος.

[9] I. 14. 6, XII. 12 (7). 3, XIII. 5. 4.

[10] III. 58. 9; cf. VII. 7. 1, XVI. 12. 3 et seq.

[11] III. 20. 5.

historian must make truth his highest aim ; he must distinguish history from encomium,[1] and be just and impartial[2] in his distribution of praise and blame. It is little wonder the Polybius, holding such ideals, proclaimed[3] himself the foe of the rhetorical historian, who was more concerned with the embellishment of his style than with discovery of truth. Even in their speeches, where historians are wont to allow themselves greater liberty for rhetorical display, he will have them record[4] the substance of what was really said, and will deny them any elaborate setting for such harangues. A brilliant style is an asset to the writer of history who is well equipped for his task, and conscientiously performs it, but Polybius, influenced by personal temperament and his Stoic training, distrusted the pursuit of stylistic ornament and beauty of expression, as likely to distract the historian from his duty of giving a plain, unvarnished tale of the truth as he had discovered it. He realised the importance of having a noble subject to treat, if one is to preserve a proper perspective,[5] and a due sense of proportion. He himself had selected a splendid subject,[6] when he set out to narrate how the world had fallen under Roman dominion, but he is conscious[7] that his self-denial has produced a work that many may consider austere and dull, owing to the uniformity of its composition.

It is clear from the criticisms of Polybius that there was a marked tendency towards a rhetorical treatment of history **The technique** in the Hellenistic period. In that age in **of historical** particular, when the laws of so many literary **writing** genres were hardening, a fairly well-defined theory was established to govern the technique of historical

---

[1] VIII. 8 (10). 6, X. 21 (24). 8 ; cf. Lucian, op. cit., 7, 11, 17, 59 ; *vide supra*, p. 493.

[2] I. 14. 5, VIII. 8 (10). 7, XVI. 14. 6 *et seq.* ; cf. Lucian, op. cit., 39–41.

[3] XVI. 17. 9 (on Zeno), *ib.* 18. 2 ; cf. XXIX. 12 (6a) ; XXXVIII. 4 (1d). 1, where he distinguishes the style of history from declamatory writing.

[4] II. 56. 10, XII. 25i. 8, on the principles that should govern the introduction of speeches ; cf. XXXVI. 1 (1a).

[5] I. 4. 3 *et seq.*, VII. 7. 6.

[6] I. 1. 5 ; cf. I. 13. 11, III. 1. 4, XXXVI. 1 (1a). 4.

[7] IX. 1. 2 ; Dionys. De C. V. 4, criticises him for faulty composition.

composition. We find echoes of such theorising in later authors such as Dionysius of Halicarnassus, and in certain Roman writers, who help to throw light on the constituents and characteristics that were usually looked for in the work of the historian. We shall find that many of the latter's duties were expected to give way before the exigencies of style.[1] Authors, particularly when they were dealing with ancient history, and traversing ground already covered, aimed[2] not so much to correct the mistakes of their predecessors by a more careful sifting and weighing of evidence, as to clothe old material in a new garb, and give a more brilliant presentation of events[3] than had hitherto been achieved.

Though Dionysius pays homage[4] to Truth as the deity to whom history should be consecrated, we find him censuring[5] Thucydides for revealing the misdeeds of Athens, and emphasising her shortcomings. He, moreover, requires[6] that the historian should deal out something like poetic justice in the course of his narrative. He attaches much importance to the historian's choice of a noble subject,[7] and one that will be pleasing to his readers. The story of a struggle that was epic in its character, and fraught with weighty issues, such as that treated by Herodotus, will naturally afford the fullest scope for the display of the historian's powers. It is evident[8] that merely local history made little appeal to Dionysius. Isocrates, viewing the question from the stand-

The views of Dionysius

---

[1] Cf. Lucian, op. cit. 51 ; Pliny, Ep. V. 8. 9 ; Fronto, II. 142 : " historia tamen potius splendide perscribenda."

[2] Cf. Livy, Praef. I ; Peter, Gesch. Lit. Vol. II. 190 *et seq.* ; Pliny, Ep. V. 8. 12 (there quoted).

[3] Cf. the ideal of Isocrates, Panegyr. 4, 8.

[4] De Thucyd. 8 ; cf. Lucian, op. cit. 39 : καὶ μόνῃ θυτέον τῇ ἀληθείᾳ ; *ib.* 61–63.

[5] Ad Pomp. 3 ; Lucian, op. cit. 38, is evidently a protest against this view.

[6] Cf. Scheller, op. cit., p. 34, on ἐπιείκεια.

[7] Ad Pomp. 3 ; *ib.* 4, where Xenophon is commended for his choice of subjects ; De Thucyd. 5, Antiq. Rom. I. 1. 2 : πρῶτον μὲν ὑποθέσεις αἱρεῖσθαι καλὰς καὶ μεγαλοπρεπεῖς ; cf. Diod. I. 3 ; Scheller, op. cit., p. 38 *et seq.*

[8] Cf. his criticism of Philistus, Ad Pomp. 5.

point of the rhetorician, had already proclaimed the value of a noble subject.[1] Even the prosaic Polybius was impressed with its importance, though he judged its worth rather from its human interest than from the possibilities it afforded of elaborate stylistic treatment. Too often, however, we find evidence of a tendency to make both the choice and treatment of a subject subservient to the demands of style. Dionysius will even have the historian exercise a principle of selection as regards his material, in order to render his narrative more attractive. At times historians, to prevent the even flow of their style being impeded, show reluctance[2] to enter into minute detail, and take refuge in a certain indefiniteness of statement. They aim especially at uniformity of style,[3] and thus for the most part prefer to set forth treaties and official acts in their own language, where a modern historian would consider it his duty to cite the original text. It was for the same reason that they hesitated[4] to reproduce a speech already published, as they were thereby precluded from giving it the impress of their own individuality.

Particularly when the annalistic treatment of history had become obsolete, stress was laid on the necessity of making an historical work an organic[5] whole like every other artistic creation in literature. Theorists, however, demanded that historians should combine variety with unity,[6] if they were to give adequate pleasure to their readers. Certain subjects[7] of their very nature possess an inherent variety of their own,

Unity and variety

---

[1] Philip. 10 ; cf. Panegyr. 4.

[2] Cf. Peter, Gesch. Lit. II. p. 276 *et seq.*, 282, Pliny, Ep. IX. 16. 1 (there quoted).

[3] *Vide* Peter, op. cit. I. p. 244 ; Stemplinger, op. cit., p. 248 *et seq. ;* Norden, A.K. I. p. 88 *et seq.*

[4] Cf. Livy, 45. 25. 3 ; Sall. Cat. 31. 6 ; Tac. Ann. XV. 63.

[5] Arist. Poet. 23. 1459a, contrasts from this point of view the Epic and the " ordinary histories " ; cf. Dionys. De Thucyd. 6, 9 ; Theon, Progym. Sp. II. 80, on the lack of unity in Thucydides ; Scheller, op. cit., p. 41 *et seq. ; vide supra*, p. 483.

[6] Cf. Dionys. Ad Pomp. 4–5, on variety in Xenophon, and the lack of it in Philistus ; cf. Diod. XX. 2.

[7] Cf. Polyb. I. 13. 11.

but writers could always impart variety to their narrative by the interweaving of a fabulous element,[1] and the many picturesque legends that, at least for their hoary antiquity, are entitled to some veneration.

In the speeches which he introduced, the historian found another means of relieving the tedium of his narrative. Here, too, he could best display his rhetorical

Rhetorical elements

powers. Theon declares[2] that a training in rhetoric is necessary for the historian, while Diodorus complains[3] that some have made history a mere appendix to oratory. The reading of certain historians was recommended[4] to the student of oratory, often it is true for the rhetorical colouring that pervaded their works as a whole, but more especially for the skill they displayed in the composition of their speeches. In general, whether a speech was fictitious, or adapted from one actually delivered, it was required that its tone be in harmony[5] with the occasion, and with the character of the speaker. Even in his adaptations, the historian allowed[6] himself a large measure of freedom in imparting to a speech his own qualities as a stylist.

The digression was another device employed by him to

Digressions

give variety to his narrative. It had its place also in the technique of the Epic poet,[7] and was beloved by the orator.[8] The latter's digressions

---

[1] Dionys. De Thucyd. 5–7 ; cf. Cic. Or. 65, on the practice of the Sophists ; Isocr. Panath. 246. [2] Progym. Sp. II. 70. [3] XX. 1.

[4] Dionys. Ad Pomp. 5–6, περὶ μιμ. Usener, p. 22 et seq., ib. p. 123, for the fragments of Cicero's Hortensius ; Dio Chrys. XVIII. 10 ; Q. X. 1. 74, ib. 5. 15 ; cf., however, X. 1. 31, 2. 21, for some pitfalls to be avoided ; in these latter passages, Q. emphasises certain differences between the historian and the orator.

[5] Dionys. De Thucyd. 36 ; Lucian, op. cit. 58 ; cf. Q. X. 1. 101, on Livy's speeches.

[6] Cf. Tac. Ann. XI. 24, for a free handling of a speech of Claudius ; Stemplinger, op. cit., p. 251, on the contrast between the last speech of Otho as it appears in Tac. Hist. II. 47, and in Plut. Otho, 15.

[7] Cf. Arist. Poet. 24. 1459b, on the nature of the Epic ; Dionys. Ad Pomp. 3, on Herodotus' imitation of Homer in this respect ; vide supra, p. 491.

[8] Isocr. Areop. 63, Panath. 74 ; Q. IV. 3. 12 ; Volkmann, op. cit., p. 164 et seq.

were required to have some bearing on the cause that he pleaded, and should not be so long drawn out as to break the main thread of his speech. Though the historians were fond of having recourse to what Livy styles[1] " deverticula amoena," they did not[2] all employ them with the same artistry.

The digression often took the form of a description (ἔκφρασις). Here again the historian could learn some-
The ἔκφρασις
thing from the practice of the Epic poet,[3] as well as from that of the orator,[4] who was able to expend all his art on such descriptions. The ἔκφρασις was, in fact, pre-eminently suited to the genius of the rhetorical historian. The later authors,[5] in particular, gave minute instructions regarding its scope and treatment. The style should be in harmony with the subject dealt with, and should above all exhibit the qualities of clearness and vividness. An abundant variety of topics[6] lay ready to hand. The history and character of cities, countries, and peoples, were favourite subjects[7] with historians, as they could be treated with a wealth of geographical or ethnographical detail, and offered the fullest scope for a writer's descriptive powers. Again, battle scenes, the deaths of famous leaders, the siege and capture of cities, the sufferings of the vanquished, could be painted[8] by them

---

[1] IX. 17. 1, though Livy himself is determined to use digressions only on rare occasions.

[2] Compare the criticisms passed on Ephorus and Theopompus in Polyb. XII. 28. 10, and Dionys. Ad Pomp. 6 ; cf. Theon. Progym. Sp. II. 80, on the proper use of digressions in history.

[3] *Ib.* 119, on Homer's description of the armour of Achilles ; on Virgil's practice, *vide* Heinze, op. cit., p. 77 *et seq.*, 396 *et seq. ;* Norden, Aen. VI. p. 120 *et seq.*, 133, 272, 295, 305 ; Aen. II, gives a typical description of a city's capture ; cf. Petron. 89 ; Hor. Ep. II. 1. 252 *et seq.*, on subjects for the ἔκφρασις ; A.P. 15 *et seq.*

[4] Q. III. 7. 27, IV. 3. 12, IX. 2. 44 ; cf. II. 4. 3, where " arcessitae descriptiones " are condemned ; cf. Dionys. Ars. Rhet. I. 3.

[5] Cf. Spengel, Rhetores Graeci, II. p. 16, 46, 118, III. 491.

[6] Ranged under the heads πρόσωπα, πράγματα, τόποι, χρόνοι.

[7] Cf. Cic. De Or. II. 63 ; cf. Ad Q. Fr. II. 15. 4 ; Sallust, B. Jug. 17 ; Tac. Ann. IV. 32–33, Agric. 10 ; Pliny, Ep. II. 5. 5.

[8] Cf. Polyb. XV. 34. 1 ; Cic. Or. 66 ; Plut. Alex. 75 ; Them. 32 ; cf. Brutus, 53, on the death of Porcia ; Val. Max. IV. 6. 5 ; *vide supra,* pp. 498–499.

in glorious or tragic colours as the occasion demanded. Many found material[1] for the ἔκφρασις in dreams, portents, and the marvels of nature generally. Dionysius praises[2] the comprehensiveness of the descriptions essayed by Theopompus, who " embodied in his work everything strange and wonderful found in every land and on every sea."

Such descriptions constituted[3] a point of contact between history and Sophistic rhetoric, and they had a great attraction for declaimers,[4] who could employ all their garish eloquence in the embellishment of themes so congenial to their nature. The Elder Pliny, in an interesting passage,[5] enumerates for us, by way of contrast with his Natural History, many of the ingredients that were usually employed in the composition of historical works : " nec admittunt excessus aut orationes sermonesve, aut casus mirabiles vel eventus varios, non alia jucunda dictu, aut legentibus blanda, sterili materia." Here we have several of the features which we have found to be associated with historical writing, particularly in the Hellenistic period. It was especially through such elements as speeches, digressions, and descriptions, that rhetoric was able to invade history, and thus suggest an affinity between the historian and the orator. That such an affinity was supposed to exist is clear from the words of Granius Licinianus,[6] who agrees with others in declaring that Sallust should be read not as a historian, but as an orator; " nam et tempora reprehendit sua et delicta carpit, et orationes inserit, et dat invicem loca, montes, flumina, et hoc genus alia."

Amongst Roman authors, Cicero deserves particular

History and Sophistic rhetoric

---

[1] Peter, Gesch. Lit. II. p. 314.
[2] Ad Pomp. 6; cf. *ib.* 5, on the commonplace character of Philistus' descriptions.
[3] Cic. Or. 65–66; St. Chrysostom, 49. 179. 8, censures the excessive use of the ἔκφρασις by the rhetoricians of his day; cf. Rohde, Griech Roman, p. 360.
[4] Sen. Suas. I. 15, Controv. II. pr. 3.
[5] Praef. 12.
[6] On this writer cf. Rosenberg, Einleitung und Quellenkunde zur röm. Geschichte, pp. 162–163.

attention, as he best serves to illustrate a conception of

Cicero's interest in history historical writing that must have been common amongst his countrymen, while at the same time he shows many traces of the influence of Greek, and especially of Hellenistic theory and practice, upon his views regarding this branch of literature. It is interesting to note the number of Hellenistic[1] historians that figure in his pages. It is difficult to decide how profound was his knowledge of the Greek historians, though their names came trippingly[2] off his tongue. However, his criticisms of them suggest at least a passing acquaintance.

No one has proclaimed the glories of history more clearly than Cicero, when he declares[3] that it is " testis temporum, lux veritatis, vita memoriae,

The glories of history magistra vitae," while no one has enunciated in nobler language the laws[4] that should govern historical writing. The historian should reveal the whole truth and nothing but the truth, and must not allow himself to be swayed by personal dislikes or predilections. Cicero represents[5] the writing of history as an arduous task, that requires serious preparation, and much leisure. When he styled it " magistra vitae,"[6] he probably considered it both as an ethical teacher, and as providing useful instruction for men in public life. In one passage[7] at least, he makes it clear that he did not regard history as written wholly for entertainment, while he stresses[8] the fact that it is bound by different laws from those of poetry, which makes pleasure its chief aim. Hence he would exclude

---

[1] Such as Callisthenes, Timaeus, Clitarchus, Duris, Polybius ; cf. De Or. II. 58–59, Ad Att. VI. 1. 18, Ad Fam. V. 12, Br. 42, 63, 325, De Leg. I. 7.

[2] Note the comment on Antonius, De Or. II. 59.

[3] *Ib.* 36.

[4] *Ib.* 62 : " nam quis nescit primam esse historiae legem ne quid falsi dicere audeat ? Deinde ne quid veri non audeat ? Ne quae suspicio gratiae sit in scribendo ? Ne quae simultatis ? " Cf. De Leg. I. 5 ; Sall. Cat. IV. 2–4 ; Tac. Ann. IV. 11 ; Pliny, Ep. VII. 17. 3.

[5] De Leg. I. 9.

[6] Cf. Livy, Praef. 10 ; Val. Max. Bk. I. praef. ; Tac. Ann. III. 65.

[7] De Fin. V. 51.

[8] De Leg. I. 5 ; cf. Lucian, op. cit., 8.

from it the element of the fabulous,[1] by which many historians[2] sought to enliven their narrative. He shows a critical spirit in his remarks[3] on the tendency of primitive peoples to create legends, and set them on a par with historical fact. He realised,[4] too, the difference between history and encomium, which allowed the writer to indulge in the language of hyperbole, and to treat many topics[5] that would be regarded as irrelevant in history. He knew[6] from his rhetorical training how highly-coloured could become the topics of praise and blame as treated in epideictic oratory, and how difficult it is, even for the most impartial historian, to control[7] them in his own domain. Roman history had been debased by private records, and by the attempts that were made to exalt particular families,[8] but, as Cicero saw, it had been corrupted especially by the funeral laudations,[9] inspired by affection, and delivered at the burial of illustrious men.

Cicero then had high ideals for historical writing, but unfortunately he was not always true to them. He forgets at times the distinction he had drawn between the laws of history and those of poetry, as when he appeals[10] to Ennius as a reliable historical source. He seems[11] to consider his own

A lowering
of ideals

[1] Cf. De Inv. I. 27, De Fin. V. 64.

[2] Cf. Livy, 39. 43. 1, on Val. Antias; Sen. N.Q. VII. 16; Tac. Hist. II. 50; C. Rufus, IX. 1. 4.

[3] De Rep. II. 10. 18–19, ib. 18. 33.

[4] Ad Att. I. 19. 10.

[5] On the topics treated, cf. Tac. Ann. XIII. 3; Varro seems to have caricatured such panegyrics in his Satire " Papiapapae," Riese, p. 183 et seq.; cf. Leo, Die griech-röm. Biographie, p. 90 et seq., 207 et seq., 227, 234 et seq.

[6] De Or. II. 341 et seq., Br. 47; cf. Ad Her. III. 6. 10 et seq.; Q. III. 7. 1 et seq.; vide supra, pp. 493, 503.

[7] Cf. Polyb. VIII. 11 (13). 1.

[8] Cf. Peter, Gesch. Lit. I. p. 299, on the labours of Atticus, and those of Varro and Hyginus, who wrote " De Familiis Trojanis "; cf. Nepos, Att. 18; Vell. II. 41. 2; Val. Max. IX. 15.

[9] Br. 61–62; cf. Livy, VIII. 40, XXVII. 27. 11, where Coelius rejects the account of Marcellus' death contained in " laudatione filii "; cf. Gellius, XIII. 19. 17; Polyb. VI. 54. 1 et seq.

[10] Br. 57, De Div. II. 116.

[11] Ad Att. I. 19. 10.

poem on his consulship as an historical work, though in it
he allowed himself all the license of the poet in the introduction of supernatural[1] agencies. We can imagine what
play his fancy would have made with the theme of Caesar's
expedition to Britain, if he had followed the promptings[2]
of his first enthusiasm. Here, however, he enjoyed the
privileges of the poet, but even when he refers to the treatment of historical subjects in prose, he generally displays a
hankering after a highly ornate and embellished style.

We must remember that Cicero, in the first instance, was
inclined to approach the study[3] of history from the standpoint of the orator. History had its use[4] as
The standpoint part of the wide culture demanded from the
of the orator orator, who could learn political wisdom
from the study of bygone ages, and could make effective
use of historical examples[5] in his speeches. But in other
respects Cicero's rhetorical training coloured his views on
history. Like so many[6] of the Ancients, he regarded a
brilliant style as of paramount importance for the historian.
Atticus credits[7] him with the view that history is an " opus
oratorium maxime." He himself comments[8] on the fact
that amongst the Greeks, in contrast with the Romans, it
was " eloquentissimi homines " who undertook the labour
of writing history. He appeals,[9] without any consciousness

---

[1] Cf. In Cat. III. 18, Ad Q. Fr. II. 7 (9). 1, De Div. I. 17 *et seq.* ; Plut.
Cic. 20.

[2] Ad Q. Fr. II. 13 (15a). 2 : " modo mihi date Britanniam quam pingam
coloribus tuis, penicillo meo " ; his first enthusiasm, however, seems to have
cooled remarkably, and he needed considerable spurring to complete the
poem ; cf. Ad Q. Fr. III. 8. 3, *ib.* 9. 6.

[3] In the ' Hortensius,' he had sounded the praise of history in the person
of Lucullus, and had evidently treated of the historians suitable for the
orator to study.

[4] De Or. I. 18, 158, 201, Br. 161, 322, Or. 120, Part. Or. 96 ; Q.
X. 1. 31.

[5] Hortens. frs. 15–16 ; cf. Ad Her. IV. 9. 13 ; Sen. Controv. I. pr. 18 ;
Q. III. 8. 66, X. 1. 34.

[6] *Vide supra,* p. 504.

[7] De Leg. I. 5 ; cf. De Or. II. 36 : " historia . . . qua voce alia nisi
oratoris immortalitati commendatur " ?

[8] De Or. II. 55.

[9] Br. 101, 228.

of incongruity, to the historical works of Fannius and Sisenna as evidence for their style of oratory.

Now, it will be interesting to examine certain ideas that were current as to the specific style in which history should

The style of history

be written, and to consider how far they were shaped by rhetorical theory. Some writers[1] presupposed the existence of a separate historical style. Others, though they spoke in general terms[2] of an historical style, refrained from classing it as a separate species. It is important to note that many who endeavoured to define the qualities of the historical style, appealed to the standards of oratorical prose, either by way of comparison, or contrast.[3] History required a certain fullness,[4] richness, and brilliance[5] of tone. Hence the historian will use[6] figures more freely than the orator, and have recourse at times to poetical ornament.[7] Some,[8] however, felt that the historian in his ordinary narrative should not strive after elaborate periodic structure or rhythmical effects, though they would allow him greater licence in his speeches. His style should generally[9] be characterised by a quiet, equable, unbroken flow.[10] It was

---

[1] Cf. Rufus, Sp. I. 463, where γένος ἱστορικὸν is enumerated as a separate style apart from the three oratorical styles ; ib. III. 483, where Nicolaus erroneously cites the authority of Aristotle for such a style ; cf. Vahlen, op. cit., p. 24.

[2] Dionysius speaks of πλάσμα ἱστορικὸν, De C. V. 4. Ad Pomp. 4,

[3] It should be noted that the contrast was often emphasised ; Colson has some interesting remarks on this, in a paper on the " Influence of Rhetoric on History," p. 168 et seq. (Class. Assoc., Vol. XIV).

[4] Cf. Q. X. 5. 15, on " historiae ubertas " ; Fronto, II. 158, where the conjecture " ubertatem " receives support from Quintilian.

[5] Q. X. 1. 33, on " historicus nitor " ; Pliny, Ep. I. 16. 4 ; Fronto, II. 142 ; Rufus, Sp. I. 463 ; Dionys. De Thucyd. 50.

[6] Q. X. 1. 31.

[7] Cf. Dionys. De Thucyd. 23, on Herodotus ; ib. 51, Ad Pomp. 3 ; Lucian, op. cit., 22, 45.

[8] Q. IX. 4. 18 ; cf. Demetr. 19, on the character of the historical period.

[9] Cic. De Or. II. 54, 58 ; Or. 66 ; cf. Q. IX. 4. 129 ; Pliny, Ep. V. 8. 10 ; Lucian, op. cit., 43, 55.

[10] Cf. Aq. Rom. Halm, op. cit., vol. I. p. 27, on " (oratio) perpetua, quam Graeci εἱρομένην λέξιν appellant," as suited to History.

this characteristic, in particular, that led critics[1] to contrast[2] strongly the style of history with that of forensic oratory, and to declare that the former was unsuited[3] for actual pleading in the law courts. Cicero compared[4] the historical style rather with that of Sophistic rhetoric and epideictic[5] oratory. Herein we can see the influence upon him of the school of Isocrates, and of the ideals of style evident in the works of the historians Ephorus and Theopompus.[6] Dionysius considered[7] Isocrates and his two chief pupils to have attained pre-eminence in the smooth or florid kind of composition, identified by some with the Middle style,[8] which made charm and sweetness its chief aim. In the *De Oratore*,[9] Cicero spoke with a certain note of reproof of the *History* of Callisthenes as written " rhetorico paene more." In the *Brutus*,[10] he professes admiration for the plain, unadorned style of Caesar's *Memoirs*, which men of sense will refrain from rehandling, though others in their folly may attempt to trick them out with the graces of rhetoric. However, in the *Orator*, one of his latest works, dazzled apparently by the glamour of the Isocratics, he favoured[11] the view that history should be treated with all

---

[1] Some probably had in mind Aristotle's distinction of ἀγωνιστική and γραφικὴ λέξις ; cf. Dionys. De Dem. 18, De Thucyd. 23.

[2] Cf. Cic. De Or. II. 64.

[3] A criticism often passed on the style of Thucydides ; *vide supra*, p. 230 ; Xenophon is also characterised as " a forensi strepitu remotissimus " ; cf. Dionys. De Thucyd. 50, Ad Pomp. 5, where Philistus is considered more suitable for ἀληθινοὺς ἀγῶνας ; cf., however, De Thucyd. 55 ; Dio Chrys. 18. 10.

[4] Or. 65–66.

[5] Cf. Hermog. περὶ ιδ. Sp. II. 417, 421–422 ; the epideictic and forensic styles were, of course, commonly contrasted ; Isocr. περὶ ἀντιδ. 46–47, Panegyr. 11, Panath. 11 ; cf. περὶ ὕψους, VIII. 3, Cic .Or. 37, 42, De op. gen. 17.

[6] Or. 207 ; cf. Br. 66.

[7] De C. V. 23 ; cf. De Dem. 40 ; Geigenmueller, op. cit., p. 80 *et seq.*

[8] Dionysius himself speaks of Theopompus' style as συγκειμένη κατὰ τὴν μέσην ἁρμονίαν ; cf. Lucian, op. cit., 46 ; *vide supra*, p. 73.

[9] II. 58.

[10] 262 ; *vide infra*, p. 518.

[11] Or. 207 : " ergo in aliis, id est in historia . . . placet *omnia* dici Isocrateo Theopompeoque more."

the splendour of the epideictic style.   He refers[1] specifically to the historian's use of speeches and descriptions, and
he would probably consider that on the adornment of both of
these the resources of rhetoric might well be lavishly expended.

How much he was preoccupied with considerations of
style in history to the neglect of other qualities, is evident
from his sketch of the development of
Considerations Roman historical writing, and his criticism
of style of the Roman historians.   Nothing, he
declares,[2] could be more dry and jejune than the *Annales
Pontificum*, the first step the Romans took to record the
history of their State.   The older Annalistic historians such
as Cato, Piso, and Fabius Pictor, were all characterised[3] by
the same baldness.   They made clearness and brevity their
chief aim, and, as Cicero significantly says, were " non
exornatores[4] rerum sed tantummodo narratores."   He
admits[5] that an advance in the writing of history was made
by Coelius and Sisenna, but the advance which he describes,
was wholly a matter of style.

Coelius was a teacher[6] of jurisprudence, and evidently
had also undergone a thorough training in rhetoric.   He
certainly introduced[7] a new note into the
Coelius writing of history, and pointed the way to
Antipater a more elegant treatment of it.   He followed
Silenus,[8] a native of Sicily, as his chief authority for his

[1] Or. 66 ; cf. De Or. II. 63.

[2] De Leg. I. 6 ; cf. De Or. II. 52, Ad Fam. V. 12. 5 ; Q. X. 2. 7.

[3] De Or. II. 52–53, De Leg. I. 6 : " quid tam exile quam isti omnes " ;
Br. 106, on Piso ; Peter, Historicorum Romanorum Reliquiae, Vol. I,
Introd. 174 *et seq.*, Frs., p. 112 *et seq. ;* cf. Gellius, V. 18, 8, on the differ-
ence between Annales and Historia.

[4] Cf. Pro Marcello, 4 ; with De Or. II. 52 *et seq.*, might be compared
Dionysius' account of the development of historical writing in Greece,
De Thucyd. 5, 23.

[5] De Leg. I. 6–7 ; De Or. II. 54 ; cf. Br. 66, for the advance made in
Greek history by Theopompus.

[6] Br. 102 ; *vide supra*, p. 183.

[7] On Coelius and his work, *vide* Peter, op. cit., I. Introd. p. 211 *et seq.*,
Frs., p. 158 *et seq.* ; Rosenberg, op. cit., p. 167 *et seq. ;* Marx, Ad Herennium,
Introd., p. 136 *et seq. ;* Cic. Ad Att. XIII. 8, for Brutus' Epitome of
Coelius ; Or. 230.

[8] Cic. De Div. I. 49 ; Nepos, Hann. XIII. 3 ; Silenus set out to glorify

account of the Second Punic war. In his fondness[1] for digressions and descriptions, in the use that he made of dreams[2] and portents,[3] he shows how potent was the influence of the Hellenistic historians upon his work. To thrill his readers, he magnified[4] the difficulties that Scipio experienced in his passage to Africa, and in the landing of his troops, while, according to Livy,[5] he represented him as transporting so great an army for his final encounter with Hannibal, that no one seemed to be left in Italy or Sicily. Coelius was probably[6] the first Roman historian to intersperse his history with fictitious speeches, on the elaboration of which he must have employed all the rhetorical skill at his command. He came under the spell of the Asianist school, and at times shows[7] some of the mannerisms of Hegesias. He paid particular attention to rhythm,[8] and sometimes[9] indulged in unnatural transpositions for the sake of rhythmical effects. He also displayed a leaning towards poetical[10] diction. Whatever judgment we may pronounce upon his taste, it is clear that he was assiduous in his quest after the embellishments of style. Though Cicero admits that, in form at least, he made a distinct advance upon his predecessors, yet he failed to satisfy the fastidiousness of the orator. In his earliest verdict upon him, Cicero considered that his style was lacking in variety, and had failed to attain that quiet, equable flow that was suited to historical writing. In the *Orator*,[11] where, for purposes of polemic, the defects

Hannibal, as other historians had glorified Alexander ; cf. Peter. op. cit., Vol. I, Introd., pp. 219–220.

[1] We find evidence of such digressions, and of topics suitable for the ἔκφρασις, in frs. 51–55, Peter, loc. cit., p. 174–175 ; cf. Lucilius, fr. 1079, for a possible reference to C.'s battle scenes.

[2] Cic. De Div. I. 48–49, 55–56.

[3] *Ib*. I. 78 ; cf. De Nat. Deor. II. 8.

[4] Livy, 29. 27. 13.   [5] *Ib*. 29. 25. 1.

[6] Peter, op. cit., I. Introd., p. 218 ; Jordan, op. cit., p. 196 *et seq*.

[7] Cf. Peter, frs. 9, 41 ; *ib*. Introd. p. 217 ; *vide supra*, p. 236.

[8] Peter, frs. 8, 25, 32 ; cf. 5, 24b, for verse effects ; cf. Leo, Gesch. der röm. Lit., p. 339 n. 4.

[9] Cic. Or. 229 ; Ad Her. IV. 12. 18.

[10] Cic. De Or. III. 153 ; cf. Fronto's reference (II. 48) to his use of "singula verba."

[11] 230.

of the Asianists are being decried, he is characterised as
" omnino rudis," though in the *Brutus* he is admitted to
possess a certain brilliance, considering the age in which
he wrote.

Sisenna was another historian who, by his history[1] of the
Marsic and Sullan wars, added some lustre[2] to Roman
historical writing. Still, he was guilty of
certain extravagances, due mainly to his
close imitation of Clitarchus.[3] He seems[4] to have flattered
Sulla no less fulsomely than the Greek historian had
flattered Alexander. Cicero mentions[5] the interesting fact
that he argued against dreams, but accepted portents. His
literary interests were varied, and led him to translate the
Milesian[6] tales of Aristides, and write a commentary on
Plautus. He was noted[7] for his use of novel and unusual
words and forms, which may have been due in part to his
adherence to the principle of Analogy, and in part to his
Plautine studies. He was an orator,[8] who carried his
rhetorical manner into his historical writings. Though
he easily surpassed the historians who had gone before
him, he still failed to come up to Cicero's ideals.

The same is true of Licinius Macer,[9] whose style was
generally verbose, and who, in spite of occasional animation, showed, especially in his speeches, the
effects of the narrow culture imparted by
the " rhetores Latini."[10] It is possible that
in his case Cicero's judgment was warped by personal and

Sisenna (margin note)

**Other his-
torians** (margin note)

---

[1] Sall. Jug. 95 ; Vell. II. 9. 4 ; cf. Gellius, XVI. 9. 5 ; Peter, op. cit., I.
Introd., p. 334 *et seq. ;* frs. *ib.*, p. 276 *et seq.*

[2] Cic. De Leg. I. 7, Br. 228.

[3] *Vide supra*, p. 497.

[4] Sall. Jug. 95. 2 ; cf. Peter, op. cit., I. Introd., p. 342.

[5] De Div. I. 99 ; cf. II. 54.

[6] Cf. Ovid, Trist. II. 443 ; Fronto, I. 4, on his use of " verba lasciva " ;
Peter, I. frs. p. 297.

[7] *Vide supra*, pp. 82, 237 ; cf. Peter, I. frs. p. 278 *et seq.*, for many
examples preserved by Nonius ; cf. Fronto, II. 48.

[8] Cic. In Verrem, Act. II. 110, IV. 43 ; Meyer. Or. Rom. Frag., p. 167.

[9] De Leg. I. 7 ; cf. Br. 238.

[10] Cf. Peter, op. cit., I. Introd. p. 354, on the interpretation of Cicero's
phrase " ex librariolis Latinis."

political rivalry. The temperament of the latter, and the ideal of historical writing which he favoured, would also explain his lack of esteem for the historians of the Stoic school. He considered[1] Fannius " exilis," while he is wholly silent on the historical work of Aelius Tubero.

Now, though Cicero admits that distinct progress had been made in the art of the historian before his time, we are told[2] that history has not yet been treated with the brilliancy needed to give it an honoured place in Latin literature. So far, the Romans had accomplished nothing that could vie with the glory of the Greeks in this genre. Cicero's friends urged him[3] to devote himself to such a task, as he alone could remove this reproach from his countrymen. As Nepos,[4] who evidently felt the glamour of his rhetoric,[5] expresses it: " ille enim fuit unus, qui potuerit et etiam debuerit historiam digna voce pronuntiare." Thus importuned by his friends, Cicero toyed[6] with the idea of essaying a great historical work. The publication of the *Liber Annalis*[7] of Atticus acted as a further incentive to him. He discussed[8] with his brother Quintus what period he should undertake to treat, his own inclination being to deal with contemporary[9] history, which he himself had helped to make. However, the great work was never written, it may be because he was dismayed by the magnitude of the task, or debarred from

" **Historiam digna voce pronuntiare** "

---

[1] De Leg. I. 6, Br. 101, Ad Att. XII. 5. 3, for Brutus' Epitome of F. ; Peter, op. cit., I. Introd. p. 193 *et seq.*, frs. p. 139 *et seq. ; vide supra*, p. 38.

[2] Br. 228; cf. De Leg. I. 5.

[3] *Ib.*; cf. Ad Att. XIV. 14. 5, XVI. 13c. 2.

[4] De Historicis Latinis, Koch, p. 98 ; Peter, op. cit., II. p. 40, fr. 17 ; Nepos tells us that History was left " omnino rude et incohatum " on Cicero's death.

[5] On the rhetorical elements in Nepos' own work, cf. Leo, Die griech-röm. Biogr., p. 216 *et seq. ;* Norden, A.K. I. p. 204 *et seq.*

[6] Br. 15 ; cf. Plut. Cic. 41, on the character of the projected work.

[7] *Vide supra*, p. 191.

[8] De Leg. I. 8 ; *vide* Häfner, Die literarischen Pläne Ciceros, p. 83 *et seq.*

[9] His 'Ανέκδοτα, written " Theopompio genere aut etiam asperiore multo," probably dealt with contemporary politics, and defended his own policy ; cf. Ad Att. II. 6. 2, XIV. 17. 6 ; Peter, op. cit., II. Introd. pp. 5–6 ; *vide* Häfner, p. 64 *et seq.*, for a good discussion of the probable character of the work, and the difficulties of its publication.

it by the multiplicity of his other occupations, and the diffi-culties of the political situation.

We get additional light on Cicero's ideals for historical writing, when we examine his own treatment of the story

Cicero's story
of his
consulship

of his consulship, and consider the manner in which he wished others to record it. He was anxious[1] that his achievements in that year should be set before the public in the fairest light, and he had evidently commissioned Archias to embellish the theme with all his poetic skill. Atticus wrote an account of that eventful year, but in a style which Cicero regarded[2] as uncouth and unadorned. The latter sent[3] a Memoir of the events in Greek to Poseidonius, " ut ornatius de isdem rebus scriberet," but Poseidonius, with the diplomacy of his race, declined the task, on the pretext that he despaired of improv-ing on Cicero's own narrative. The orator ingenuously calls this account a ὑπόμνημα, which usually[4] contained but the bare skeleton of facts, and the materials for history that were afterwards elaborated by another's hand. It is evident that, before he sent this " Memoir " to Poseidonius, he had taxed all his own resources in its embellishment, and, as he confesses[5] to Atticus, had exhausted on it the paint-boxes of Isocrates and his disciples, and some of the pigments of Aristotle. He had thus travelled far from the " pura et inlustris brevitas," which he had admired[6] in Caesar's *Memoirs*. How much he valued an ornate style, is apparent from his reference to a Geographical treatise which he had undertaken, but which he had quickly abandoned, because he found[7] the matter lacking in variety, and incapable of the adornment which he had at first considered possible.

---

[1] Pro Archia, 28 ; cf. Ad Att. I. 16. 15, where he expresses disappoint-ment with Archias ; cf. Ad Fam. V. 7. 3, for his sensitiveness to Pompey's opinion ; Pro Sulla 67 ; cf. Plut. Cic. 24, Caes. 8, Crassus, 13.

[2] Ad Att. II. 1. 1.

[3] *Ib.* 2 ; cf. *ib.* I. 19. 10, I. 20. 6.

[4] Cf. Br. 262 ; cf. Polyb. II. 40. 4, on Aratus' Memoirs ; Lucian, op. cit., 48.

[5] Ad Att. II. 1. 1.

[6] *Vide supra*, p. 513.

[7] *Ib.* II. 6. 1 : " et hercule sunt res difficiles ad explicandum et ὁμοειδεῖς, nec tam possunt ἀνθηρογραφεῖσθαι quam videbantur."

His famous letter[1] to Lucceius is an interesting document, which shows the influence of certain ideas we have already

His letter to Lucceius seen operative in our brief survey of the Greek historians. Lucceius was at the time engaged on a history of the Italic and Civil Wars. Cicero urges him not to wait for the completion of his projected work, but to write without delay a special monograph,[2] which, with the orator himself as the central[3] figure, would deal with events from the conspiracy of Catiline down to his return from exile. He requests[4] Lucceius to ignore the laws of history, and to set forth his achievements in a more favourable light that is warranted by a rigid regard for the truth. What he in fact demands[5] is that the laws of encomium,[6] rather than those of history proper, should be applied to the monograph, though he looks for a more impartial distribution of blame where he himself is not concerned. It is more interesting still to find him speaking of the proposed subject in terms[7] of the drama, and stressing the dramatic value of the events of those years as a further inducement to Lucceius to undertake the work. Besides possessing the great charm[8] of variety, such events can be shaped into a drama with many crises and vicissitudes[9] of fortune, and with elements of the sensational, capable[10] of casting a spell over the readers, and

---

[1] Ad Fam. V. 12 ; cf. Ad Att. IV. 6. 4, 9. 2, 11. 2.

[2] Ad Fam. V. 12. 4 : " modicum quoddam corpus."

[3] *Ib.* 2 : " si uno in argumento unaque in persona mens tua tota versabitur."

[4] *Ib.* 4.

[5] I find that Reitzenstein, Hellenistische Wundererzählungen, p. 84 *et seq.*, has already touched upon this question.

[6] The reference to Xen's Agesilaus, Ad Fam. V. 12. 7, is significant ; cf. Lucius Verus' request to Fronto (II. 196) to write an account of his Parthian campaign ; cf. Lucian, op. cit., 15 *et seq.*, 32 ; *vide supra*, p. 494.

[7] Cf. Ad. Fam. V. 12. 2, where " argumentum " is evidently used in its technical sense ; *ib.* 6 : " hanc quasi fabulam rerum eventorumque nostrorum " ; " habet enim varios actus."

[8] It is interesting to note that Vitruv. V. praef. 1, considers the element of novelty as one of the great charms of history.

[9] Cf. Hor. Odes, II. 1. 3 on " ludumque Fortunae," in reference to Pollio's History of the Civil Wars ; *vide supra*, p. 498.

[10] Ad Fam. V. 12. 4 : " quae vehementer animos hominum in legendo te scriptore tenere possit " (ψυχαγωγία).

awakening in them varied emotions.   We are moved to pity by the story of the death[1] of a great leader like Epaminondas, but the spectacle of a great man battling with perplexities amid manifold changes of fortune, will stir in succession feelings of wonder, suspense, joy, hope, or fear, and will give rise to the keenest pleasure, if his struggle is crowned with a glorious[2] issue.   Now that he is removed from the stress of the conflict, Cicero will be able to read with delight[3] the changing drama of his own fortunes in those eventful years.   In thus seeking to cast the subject proposed to Lucceius in the mould[4] of Tragedy, he shows that he had imbibed something of the spirit of the historians Duris and Phylarchus.

Though he had passed a noble eulogy upon history, and seemed fully alive to the seriousness of the historian's task,

The lure of style

yet it seems clear that, especially in his later years, the attainment of a brilliant style was regarded by him as the chief essential in historical writing.   The influence of the Isocratic school, and of Hellenistic theory, strongly affected his views.   It is evident, too, that both he and his friends shared the conviction that his rhetorical training had fitted him above all others to add a new glory to Latin letters by a great historical work.

There were two features in Roman life, the declamation

The influence of Declamation on history

and the practice of recitation, that might be considered briefly for their possible[5] reactions on historical writing, though the precise degree of their influence is difficult to gauge.   In their

---

[1] We have already seen how certain historians loved to work up the " clari ducum exitus " in tragic fashion ; *vide supra*, pp. 498, 507.

[2] I think " exitus notabilis " should be translated thus rather than " glorious death," as others take it ; it seems to me that Cicero meant the sentence in which it occurs, to stand as a description of his own struggles.

[3] Ad Fam. V. 12. 4 : " habet enim praeteriti doloris secura recordatio delectationem," the opposite of Dante's " nessun maggior dolore che ricordarsi del tempo felice nella miseria " (Inf. V. 121).

[4] Reitzenstein, op. cit., p. 90 *et seq.*, quoting Cic. De Inv. I. 27, Ad Her. I. 8. 12–13, endeavours to bring the suggested monograph into line with " narratio quae versatur in personis," and to show the affinity of this with the novel, but his attempt to work out a parallel is not convincing.

[5] Peter Die gesch. Lit. Vol. I. c. 1, on the place of history in Roman

debates, the declaimers often drew[1] their materials from history. Quintilian remarks[2] how useful to future poets and historians is the impersonation of historical characters, demanded especially in the handling of deliberative themes (suasoriae). The great figures of Greek and Roman history were staged, as it were, once more amid new surroundings. The exploits[3] of the Greeks in the Persian wars offered abundant scope for the florid rhetoric of the schools, while the expedition[4] of Alexander the Great constituted a theme that could be elaborated at will, especially if one indulged in speculation[5] on the possible limits of his achievements. Hannibal's campaign was another favourite[6] subject with the declaimers, who painted in vivid colours the difficulties of his passage over the Alps, or discussed his perplexities after his victory at Cannae. The heroes[7] of Ancient Rome figured in such debates, while attention was directed also to those who were prominent in the last struggle to preserve the liberty of the Republic. The declaimers considered[8] whether Cicero should have submitted to the humiliation of supplicating Antony for his life, or whether Brutus[9] should have begged for mercy at the hands of Caesar. Cato's "noble death" evidently made[10] as strong an appeal to them as it did to the poets.[11] Persius tells[12] us how when

education, might be consulted; I am indebted to him for several of my references here.

[1] Suet. De Rhet. I : " veteres controversiae aut ex historiis trahebantur, sicut sane nonnullae usque adhuc " ; Philost. V.S., also shows how attractive were historical subjects in the schools.

[2] III. 8. 49, ib. 52–53, on " controversiae " drawn from history, and the use of historical themes in the schools.

[3] Cic. De Off. I. 61 ; Sen. Suas. 2 ; cf. Philostr. V.S. 519.

[4] Vide supra, p. 498.

[5] Cf. Q. III. 8. 16–17, on " conjectura " ; Juv. X. 168 et seq.

[6] Juv. VII. 161 et seq., X. 166.

[7] Sen. Ep. III (24). 6, on M. Scaevola.

[8] Sen. Suas. VI, VII ; cf. Q. III. 8. 46, 49.

[9] Sen. De Ben. II. 20 ; cf. Sen. Suas. VI. 17.

[10] Suas. VI. 2, 4, 10, Controv. VIII. 4, X. 3 (32). 5 ; Sen. Ep. III (24). 6 et seq., 104. 29 et seq., where S. shows the influence of the schools.

[11] Hor. Odes, I. 12. 35, II. 1. 24 ; Lucan I. 128 ; cf. Tac. Dial. 2, on Maternus' tragedy " Cato,"

[12] III. 45.

a boy he tried to evade the task of reciting the dying speech of that hero, who under the Empire continued[1] to be revered as one of the greatest champions of Republican freedom.   Those who frequented the schools, loved to discuss the dangers[2] and temptations of absolute power, while they descanted on the cruelties[3] of tyrants, and sang the praises of tyrannicides.   In a work such as Valerius Maximus' *Facta ac Dicta Memorabilia*, the declaimers must have found abundant materials to satisfy their love of the sensational.

It is clear that history must have often taken strange shapes, when seen through the distorted[4] medium of declamatory rhetoric.   To it might aptly be applied Cicero's[5] dictum—"concessum est rhetoribus ementiri in historiis."   How far the Roman historians were influenced by the practice of declamation, is difficult to decide, and is too large a question to be discussed here at any length.   Both Asinius Pollio and Livy were habitués of the schools, while Tacitus had undergone a careful training in rhetoric.[6]   We might expect to find traces of their training, especially in their speeches, and in many of the topics[7] treated by them. The development[8] of Tacitus' art, to its culmination in the *Annals*, constitutes a problem in itself.   In his earlier[9] works,

The Roman historians and the Rhetorical Schools

[1] Tac. Ann. XVI. 22.   [2] Juv. I. 16, on Sulla ; cf. Q. III. 8. 53.

[3] Sen. Controv. II. 5 (13), IV. 7 ; Petron. Satyr. 1 ; Tac. Dial. 35 ; Q. VII. 3. 7, 4. 21, 8. 3, IX. 2. 81 ; Juv. VII. 151 ; cf. Boissier, op. cit., pp. 84, 94 *et seq. ; vide supra*, p. 460.

[4] Cf. Plut. Cleom. 30.

[5] Br. 42, though here Cicero had actually in mind such rhetorical historians as Clitarchus and Stratocles.

[6] Cf. Pliny, Ep. II. 1. 6, 11. 17, on his oratory.

[7] Cf. Livy, IX. 16 *et seq.*, on Alexander the Great ; one wonders how far Horace (Odes, II. 1) is reproducing topics actually occurring in Pollio's History ; some of them at least, would lend themselves to flamboyant rhetoric ; for the topics of the schools in Biography, cf. Peter, Hist. Rom. II. Introd. p. 48, on C. Nepos.

[8] Cf. Courbaud, Les Procédés d'Art de Tacite, c. 1, on its development as shown in his prefaces.

[9] Many of the topics in the speech of Calgacus (Agric. 30 *et seq. ;* cf. speech of P. Cerialis, Hist. IV. 73–74) are reminiscent of the schools ; cf. Ullmann, La Technique des Discours dans Salluste, Tite Live, et Tacite, p. 199 *et seq.*

he shows that he is still strongly under the spell of his masters in rhetoric. He never, perhaps, quite forgot their lessons, but he displayed his independence more and more as he progressed, and in his prose fashioned an instrument that was a perfect expression of his mordant genius. His epigrammatic terseness was almost certainly a legacy from the schools, but it is tempered by him to a finer point, whether he is employing it to stamp indelibly on our minds a salient feature in some historical personage, or to transfix some unworthy character with the bitter scorn of his cynicism. The rhetoric of the schools might have had an ill effect on history, in leading to exaggeration, and to a desire for sensational effects. How a historical theme could fare in the hands of a rhetorician, is well illustrated by Fronto's[1] flamboyant account of the Parthian campaign of Lucius Verus. The great Roman historians for the most part resisted the temptation to indulge in such extravagances. Though their training in the schools may have affected them in many subtle ways, it did not on the whole seriously impair their veracity.[2] The Elder Seneca gives[3] us one instance of how much Asinius Pollio valued truth in his *History*, though, in the point referred to, he had to overcome a deep-rooted prejudice. No one saw[4] more clearly than Tacitus the dangerous side of the declaimer's art. Though he may at times have been guilty of overstatement, while succumbing to the lure of some striking phrase or glittering epigram, he set before himself as an ideal to relate the truth to the best of his ability, and to write " sine ira et odio."

It is difficult to say how far it was customary to recite historical works at Rome. Asinius Pollio, who originated the " recitations," may[5] have recited his History of the Civil Wars. It was evidently not uncommon in the time of the Younger

The practice of recitation

---

[1] II. 198 *et seq.* ; cf. especially 208 *et seq.* ; Fronto is here giving us merely a Preface.

[2] Colson, Influence of Rhetoric on History, p. 159 *et seq.*, has some interesting remarks on this point.

[3] Suas. VI. 15.   [4] Dial. 35.

[5] Sen. Controv. IV. pr. 2, simply says " scripta sua recitavit " ; his friend Timagenes recited his own historical writings, Sen. De Ira, III. 23.

Pliny[1] for historians[2] to recite their works. The practice would naturally tend to impress on history, as it did on poetry, a rhetorical character. The narratives of the Parthian wars which Lucian[3] heard recited, give us a fair measure of the false rhetoric in which history was arrayed on such occasions.

[1] Ep. VII. 17. 3, IX. 27.
[2] Pliny does not preserve even their names.
[3] Op. cit., 14 *et seq.*

CHAPTER VIII

A RETROSPECT

IN THIS final chapter, my aim will be nothing more than
to stress certain tendencies in Roman literary theory and
criticism, to indicate the more important results gleaned in
the course of our survey, and endeavour to estimate their
value. The early period may seem to have yielded somewhat meagre results, but their value is enhanced if regarded
as a revelation of the first Roman essays in criticism. It is
always of interest to watch the awakening of the critical
spirit amongst a people. The problems of the early period
were those that would naturally arise, when a literature was
predominantly in the imitative stage, and a language was
little developed as a literary medium. The Romans were
then faced with many difficulties. They looked to the
Greeks for inspiration, but how was a Roman poet to
reproduce the stately manner of Greek Tragedy, or give a
reflex in his own tongue of the wealth and splendour of
Homeric diction ? He had to build up a poetical language
out of crude materials, and endeavour to impart to Latin
something of the richness and flexibility of his Greek prototype. If the epigram attributed to Naevius can be regarded
as authentic, he was evidently proud of his accomplishment
in moulding his native tongue for the purposes of poetry.
Ennius in turn, though he was styled by later critics " carens
arte " and " arte rudis," yet, even in that age of pioneer
work, felt that in the artistry of speech he had attained a
larger measure of success than any of his predecessors.
Accius and Pacuvius sought to enrich the Latin language by
some bold creations, but all enthusiasm for such ventures
must have been quickly chilled by the strong purist movement in the Scipionic circle, and by the unsparing ridicule
of Lucilius. It would be interesting to speculate how

Latin, and above all the language of Roman poetry, would have developed, if such experiments had been treated with a little more sympathy, if some indulgence had been shown even to Pacuvius' "repandirostrum." If it had travelled further along the path indicated by the older poets, the Latin of the Classical period would have been the gainer in becoming more vital, plastic, and varied, though it could never hope to emulate the suppleness and charm of Greek. The purist movement, however, continued to be a stumbling block for many generations, and engendered that morbid sensitiveness to criticism, and that shyness about attempting new coinages, which Quintilian noted as characteristic of his countrymen.

The critical problems that constituted the issue between Terence and his opponents, were also such as one would expect to find discussed in an imitative period, while other problems raised in Terence's Prologues would naturally confront one who was endeavouring to reproduce in a Latin dress the plays of the New Comedy. What was to be the relation of the Roman dramatist to his Greek model ? Was he to take as his standard the " obscura diligentia " of Luscius Lanuvinus and his followers, or allow himself a measure of liberty in the handling of his originals ? Terence vigorously defended his own practice of contamination, though he evidently considered a scene already adapted for the Roman stage to be inviolate. Again, what was the appropriate style for Comedy ? Terence clearly believed that his own language, purified and refined in the atmosphere of the Scipionic circle, was, compared with the defective style of his opponents, a more fitting medium for presenting to his countrymen some of the masterpieces of the New Comedy. Moreover, he probably regarded his own style as more in harmony with the spirit of Comedy. Particularly interesting is his condemnation of Luscius for a scene that transcended the limits of Comedy. It shows that Terence was influenced by that body of Greek critical opinion which had begun to lay down definite and rigid laws for the Comic drama. We need not, of course, be surprised that he was interested in the theoretical problems

(margin note: Terence's problems)

of his art. In this he was but following the lead of his Greek prototypes, who must have discussed numerous questions of a literary or technical character. The playwright of the New Comedy found himself beset by many difficulties, and Terence himself shows that he felt the hampering effect of certain stage conventions, as well as the continual recurrence of stock characters and similar situations. On the other hand, his abandonment of the Prologue of exposition proves his faith in his own powers as a dramatist. He was, it is true, compelled to such a course by the exigencies of literary polemic, but we would like to think that he was moved to it chiefly by his own sense of dramatic technique, and by his aversion to the crude device of the narrative Prologue. It is also possible that he was induced to reject such a prologue as inartistic by his friends in the Scipionic circle, who would have wished him to live up to the highest traditions of his art. Menander at times employed the narrative Prologue, but the allegorical personages that delivered it, invested it with an air of beauty and of mystery.

It would be difficult to overestimate the influence of the Scipionic circle in that early period. That was an age when there was a new ferment of ideas in the intellectual life of Rome. The first contact with Greek literature and philosophy had produced in some an unbalanced enthusiasm which tended to decry all native effort. The influence of Scipio and his associates must have acted as a strong antidote against Graecomania, though they themselves were the chief agents in the diffusion of a sane Hellenism amongst their countrymen. The activities of this coterie were many-sided. The speculations of Stoics such as Diogenes of Babylon, had impelled it to take a deep interest in linguistic and grammatical problems. The purist movement that grew up within it, cast, as we saw, a disapproving eye on novel experiments in language. We are, however, chiefly concerned with the reactions of this coterie on literary theory and criticism. Lucilius, though he could exhibit on occasion a sturdy independence of judgment, still in many of his criticisms was probably reflecting ideas current in his circle. Stoic

The Scipionic Circle

theories of style were predominant there, and naturally helped to foster a love of moderation and restraint. Though Lucilus himself was possessed of a fine critical instinct, yet, apart from its promptings, he may have imbibed from his associates that distaste for florid rhetoric, and for the turgid style of contemporary Tragedy, that is so marked in his fragments. We may take it that his friends shared his own lively interest in literary questions. Suetonius credits Crates[1] of Mallos with having given the first impulse to literary[2] studies in Rome during his enforced sojourn there. His lectures acted as an incentive to the Romans to undertake critical studies of their own poets, as is evidenced by the commentary which Lampadio published on the *Bellum Punicum* of Naevius. Indirectly at any rate, through his pupil Panaetius, the influence of Crates must have been potent in the Scipionic circle. As we know from Philodemus, the theory of poetry was attracting much attention in the second century B.C. Neoptolemus, Ariston, Andromenides, Crates, to mention the more important, were all busying themselves with its problems. It is particularly interesting to note Lucilius' acquaintance with Hellenistic theory. He makes a distinction between " poema " and " poesis," which finds a parallel in Neoptolemus.[3] But it was probably the speculations of Crates that had the most decisive influence on Lucilius. It may have been these that led him to discuss[4] the cacophonous effects of certain letters, and the general question of euphony[5] as a factor in the poet's style. It is clear that the element of euphony had engaged the attention of several of the Hellenistic theorists.

---

[1] Suet. De Gr. II ; cf. Sandys, A History of Classical Scholarship, I. pp. 156–160 ; Jensen, op. cit., p. 49 *et seq.*, 146 *et seq.*

[2] " Studium grammaticae," as Suetonius calls it.

[3] *Vide supra*, p. 43, Lucil. fr. 338 *et seq. ;* cf. discussion by Neoptolemus, who also used the Iliad as an illustration, Jensen, op. cit., pp. 29, 103 ; both Andromenides and Crates distinguished " poema " and " poesis," but from a somewhat different standpoint ; Jensen, pp. 152, 171.

[4] Fr. 377 on " r ", which is styled " cacosyntheton " ; cf. Jensen, p. 59, where there is a reference to Crates' views περὶ τῶν στοιχείων ; it is interesting to note that Catulus for his own purposes was making a scientific study of Greek sounds.

[5] Cf., fr. 1168, on " euphona."

Crates considered[1] that the appeal to the ear should be regarded as an important criterion in judging the merits of a poem, but, unlike the κριτικοί, he would appraise the poet's words, not merely for their sound values, but for their expressiveness as tested by the principles of Stoic Dialectic. It may have been Crates' Homeric studies that quickened Lucilius'[2] interest in Homer. In other respects, too, the Roman satirist was seemingly influenced by Hellenistic theory. From the days of Aristotle onwards, poetry tended more and more to become beset by formulism. Theorists made it their aim to define exactly the nature of each genre, to delimit its frontiers, and to prescribe the rules that should govern it. Lucilius was probably acting in this spirit, when he set out to formulate the laws of the genre in which he laboured, and to give us an analysis of the style and humour of Satire. In the modest claims which he makes for his *Satires*, and in his profession of inability to treat an epic theme, he evidently had before his mind a hierarchy of genres. Over and above all this, we have to note his acquaintance with the terms[3] of Greek rhetoric and literary criticism, though it is significant that he does not venture to seek Latin equivalents for them, but left that task for the Roman critics of a later age. From what we have seen of Lucilius and Terence, and of the activities of other members of the Scipionic circle, we begin to realise what a potent factor this coterie was in the development of Rome's intellectual life, and how numerous were the elements of Greek culture that became diffused through its agency.

If the critical works of Accius had survived as a whole, they would have shed further light on the methods of the critics in that early period. We have seen

Accius as critic

that he, too, occupied himself with the problems of grammar and of language, while in his fondness for etymology and for a nice dis-

[1] Cf. Jensen, op. cit., pp. 146, 153, 159, 171; *ib.* p. 151, on Andromenides and εὐφωνία.

[2] Cf. frs. 345–347, where Lucilius evidently has in mind the criticism of one trained in Stoic Dialectic; cf. frs. 480 *et seq.*, 540 (for Homeric epithets), 1375.

[3] Frs. 181 *et seq.*, 908.

crimination[1] in words, he provides further evidence of Stoic influence. However, his work on Plautus, his *Pragmatica*[2] and *Didascalica*, show that he had larger interests. Of special importance is the fragment[3] of the last-named work which emphasises the variety of the poetic genres, and the clear line of demarcation that separated them. It is probable that Accius, too, held fast to the conception of a hierarchy[4] of genres. From the fragments of the *Didascalica* one might conclude that he endeavoured to trace the history of Greek poetry from its earliest beginnings, and sought to work out the history of Latin poetry as far as possible on parallel lines.

In Porcius Licinus we have another critic who aimed at a systematic review of the Roman poets prior to his day. He was evidently an ardent Hellenist, who was interested chiefly in the progress of such Roman poetry as was inspired from Greek sources. He has the merit of being one of the first Roman critics to give us something approximating to aesthetic judgments on the poets. I dealt briefly with the Canon of Volcacius Sedigitus. It has little interest for us except as an attempt to emulate the methods of the Alexandrian critics, and as a further proof that in that age even Roman criticism was imitative. The leaven of Hellenistic theory was at work among the Romans, and the Roman critics were endeavouring to apply to the achievements of their own poets principles and methods already established amongst the Greeks. Unfortunately, in this early period we are mostly dependent on fragments, which fail to throw light on many of the dark places. If the works of such writers as Aelius Stilo and Varro were extant as a whole, they would be of immense help, as these authors were probably in the main carrying on the Hellenistic tradition, though they were

Study of the poets

---

[1] Cf. Funaioli, op. cit., frs. 15–17, 22.

[2] Dealing mainly with the problems of the theatre.

[3] Funaioli, fr. 8.

[4] Lucil. fr. 608, has been taken as referring to his contempt for the lowly genre of Satire ; on the conception of a hierarchy of genres, cf. Brunetière, Essays, p. 221 *et seq.* ; Ricardon, op. cit., pp. 235, 270–271 ; Babbitt, The New Laocoon, pp. 245–246.

applying its conceptions with some success in estimating the value of native literature.

It is to be noted that in this early period theory and criticism were mainly concerned with poetry. Prose, being **Interest in prose** a more difficult and elusive medium of expression, was but slowly winning its way to recognition as a separate branch of literature, and as an accomplishment that could enhance the reputation of the orator, the historian, or the philosopher. The visit of the three Greek philosophers to Rome in 155 B.C. must have done much to stimulate an interest in prose form. At any rate, the Romans were careful to note the different styles in which their discourses were delivered. The principles of Greek rhetoric began to be studied,[1] and must have helped considerably in the development of Latin oratorical prose. Stoic theories of style, as we saw, exerted a powerful influence on the members of the Scipionic circle, and taught its orators in particular to adopt a type of eloquence that was simple, restrained, and unimpassioned. However, from the Romans themselves in that period we have little in the way of positive theory. Cato dealt with rhetoric among other things in his scheme for the education of his son, but of his treatise only a few dicta have survived. In later years, Antonius published a manual of rhetoric,[2] which evidently dealt much with the dialectical side of oratory, though it was concerned also with the broader issues of its subject. However, no systematic attempt was apparently made to deal with the subtle problem of style before the *Auctor ad Herennium*, whose treatise, with all its shortcomings, marks an important stage in Roman rhetorical theory.

In my second chapter, I aimed at dealing with only the

[1] Cf. Cic. Br. 78, on Sulpicius Gallus ; *ib*. 96, for the probable effect of a study of Greek rhetoric on Lepidus ; *ib*. 104, on Diophanes of Mytilene, the teacher of Tib. Gracchus.

[2] In Cic. Br. 163, it is styled " de ratione dicendi libellus " ; in De Or. I. 208, it is said to be the fruit of Antonius' own experience, though we may take it for granted that it embodied much of Greek rhetorical theory ; cf. Q. III. 1. 19, III. 6. 45, VIII. pr. 13, XII. 1. 21, XII. 9. 5 ; Pliny, Ep. V. 20. 5.

more important aspects of the theory of style as expounded
by the Ancients. This difficult and elusive

The theory of style question was mainly treated as part of the
general theory of rhetoric. Naturally, atten-
tion was largely concentrated on oratorical style. Other
styles were occasionally discussed, but in terms reminiscent
of the rhetorical text-books. The method of handling the
general problem was of a piece with the methods employed
in the other departments of rhetoric. There was manifest a
desire to reduce everything to system, and to proceed by
way of fixed categories and stereotyped formulas. In oratory,
the distinction between the types of Forensic, Deliberative,
and Epideictic eloquence was recognised as fundamental,
and as conditioned chiefly by the aim of the speaker.[1] This
division of oratory naturally carried with it a certain differ-
entiation of styles. But the theorists on other grounds
sought to mark by nice gradations the various styles of
oratory. For the earlier theorists, the primary distinction[2]
lay between the style that is content to set forth the facts
of a case simply and without embellishment, and the style
that seeks to enthral an audience by appeals to the emotions,
and by the allurements of rhetoric. Again, of vital importance[3] is Aristotle's distinction between ἀγωνιστική and
γραφικὴ λέξις, as well as his further comment that the
epideictic style is the most suitable for written compositions.
Here we evidently have the germs of the distinction between
the style that has a practical aim, and one, the main object
of which is to give pleasure. The epideictic style thus held
a position analogous to that of the Fine Arts. In oratory,
it admitted whatever elaboration was within the writer's
power, and could be embroidered with all the ornaments
known to rhetoric. Its aim being display and the pleasure
of the hearers, it did not entail the same necessity upon an
orator to conceal his art, as when he was dealing with
practical issues in the law-courts, or before the public
assembly. The epideictic exercises of the Sophists must

---

[1] Cf. Ar. Rhet. I. 3. 5 ; Dionys. De Lys. 16.

[2] The distinction between the Plain and Grand styles, as it came to be
known.

[3] Cf. Rhys Roberts, Greek Rhetoric and Literary Criticism, p. 54 *et seq.*

have contributed not a little to the formulation of such a style.

We have seen that the division of oratorical styles into the Plain, the Middle, and the Grand, probably originated after the time of Theophrastus. Teachers of rhetoric found such categories useful in their attempts to classify various orators. They would have been especially helpful when the Atticist reaction set in, and when different models from among the Attic orators were being proposed for imitation. But, as Quintilian perceived, it is impossible to force all orators into these rigid categories, seeing that so many of them are different in genius, and exhibit such different characteristics. Hence later theorists felt constrained to formulate a fourth style, that was based chiefly on the predominant qualities of Demosthenes. However, the threefold division of styles could do little harm, if it was accepted in a general way, and regarded as helping to classify certain orators, and focus attention on their salient characteristics. The theorists were not content with that, but set out to assign very definite qualities[1] to each style, and to delimit sharply its boundaries. The formulation of the Plain style, for instance, was probably derived in large measure from the study of Lysias, though the theory and practice of the Stoics must also have contributed something to it. We can see that the mould[2] has become somewhat rigid by the time of Cicero, who can deal in a very detailed way with the diction, composition, and the precise degree of ornament, that distinguish the representatives of this style. Such a " formula," as Cicero calls it, could be made to subserve the Classical theory of imitation. When, for instance, Lysias was proposed as a model, it might have been at times convenient to direct attention to this abstract study of the Plain style as embodying his essential characteristics. It was not always realised that formulas may, at their best, capture only the external and superficial qualities of a writer, while they miss his inner spirit. Such a system laboured under other defects. Men

Rigid categories

---

[1] It was the same love of definiteness that inspired the Ancients to formulate the laws of the various genres.

[2] Cf. Or. 75 : " sequitur ut cujusque generis nota quaeratur et formula."

were often induced to imitate writers with whom they had no affinity, and thus evolved a style that bore the stamp of insincerity, as being in no way an emanation of their own inner consciousness. To force into the " Lysian " mould one whose genius was even somewhat akin to the Greek orator, involved a certain violence.

In the development of the ancient theory of style Theophrastus was a figure of prime importance. His treatise *On Style* is lost, but the fragments that survive, help us to reconstruct some of the main problems therein discussed. Like Aristotle, he applied to the sphere of literature the principle of the Golden Mean, which, as we saw, lay at the basis of Decorum, and on which depended the excellence of every good style. The faulty styles were conceived as so many aberrations from the Mean, either by way of excess or defect. It seems probable that Theophrastus set out to develop and systematise his master's teaching on style. He may thus be regarded as responsible for some at least of the formulism[1] which beset the stylistic theories of later times. Precepts and categories might be of considerable assistance to the student who was labouring on the dialectical side of rhetoric. They could help to equip him with the best methods of proof and refutation, and instruct him where to seek for his most telling arguments. Such rules were for the most part the fruit of observation and experiment, but, even in this department, a student might well be dismayed when he found rules multiplied, and confronting him, as it were, in serried array. Formulism, carried to such lengths, was soon bound to pall. More serious difficulties would arise when theorists attempted to weigh the imponderables, and to capture by rule[2] the subtle and intangible element of style. It may be admitted that the numerous rules drawn up by the Ancients to govern this department of a writer's energies, betoken a deep solicitude for perfection of detail. We may grant that many of their negative precepts are of value, as serving to restrain excess, or curb the exuberance of young writers.

The dangers of formulism

---

[1] As, for instance, in his elaborate precepts on the " virtues " of style.

[2] Some of De Gourmont's strictures on Albalat, in " Le Problème du Style," are interesting in this connection.

In this spirit, Aristotle, to use Stevenson's phrase, " made war upon the adjective," and sought to control the use of metaphor, having before his mind the extravagances of Sophistic prose. We may also admit as sound the Ancients' views on the virtues of clearness and correctness as essential to a good style. But the evil effects of formulism were seen especially, when they dealt with the third virtue of " ornatus," which Theophrastus resolved into choice of words, composition, and the use of Figures. The later theorists, in particular, set out to determine how far in each style it was permitted to go in the use of compounds, unusual words, archaisms, or new coinages. Here, it is true, Aristotle had supplied the hint, but, as happened in the case of the drama, those who followed in his wake, refined upon his teaching, and made it more stereotyped. He had, however, little to say about the Figures, though they evidently loomed large in Theophrastus' theory of style, and were regarded as an element of supreme importance in later rhetorical theory. When the doctrine of the three styles was fully evolved, the use or avoidance of certain Figures came to be a distinguishing mark of a particular style.[1] It is in developments such as this, that we realise how mechanical the theory of style could become, especially in the hands of its later exponents. As regards composition, however, the Ancients gave many precepts that are still of value. They themselves were alive to the danger that a meticulous care in this department might easily lead to artificiality. Yet, in their anxiety to attain to euphony, and to impart a rhythmical quality to speech, they showed extreme solicitude about details. This is evidenced by the attention which they paid even to the sound of individual letters, by their quest of " verba sonantia," and their elaborate rules for prose-rhythm. In the latter they were dealing with an element that was largely subjective, and that depended on the judgment of the ear, but they could at least point to certain rhythms that most men would find satisfying. In their anxiety to achieve rhythmical effects, and especially a harmonious cadence, they were ready to abandon at times the natural order of the words.

[1] Cf. Cic. Or. 82, on the Plain style ; *ib.* 92 *et seq.*, on the Middle style.

There were thus rules to govern almost every detail of expression. If we set out to separate form from matter (which many would regard as impossible), it is probable that our analysis of the constituents of style would follow the lines indicated by the Ancients. But with all this elaborate formulism, there was always the danger that the frame would become more important than the picture, and that the multiplication of precepts regulating the minutiae of style, would end by obstructing the free play of a writer's genius. Such a code might easily create the illusion that style was a mere " mechanic art," which could be acquired by the exact observance of rules. Most serious of all was the danger that the many elements involved in " ornatus," particularly the Figures, would be regarded as external ornament, which could be applied at will, and which bore no essential relation to a writer's thoughts and emotions. As Spingarn says[1] : " To deal with abstract classifications instead of artistic realities—versification instead of poetry, grammar instead of language, technique instead of painting —is to confuse form as concrete expression with form as an ornament or dead husk."

The Ancient theorists, it is true, endeavoured to counter-act some of the baneful effects of their system, by insisting that " a writer should conceal his art." They warned the orator, in particular, of the need of restraint in the employment of figurative language, prose rhythm, and elaborate periodic structure. The same lesson was inculcated by their principle of Decorum, which sprang from their love of order and due measure.[2] This principle involved, too, a constant adaptation of style to change of circumstances, and to the other factors which I have already discussed. It thus introduced an element of variety, and thereby helped to obviate the suspicion of artificiality. Moreover, the observance of Decorum was regarded as leaving on style the impress of sincerity,[3] which enabled it to carry conviction in its train.

Avoidance of artificiality

[1] Creative Criticism, p. 112.

[2] In this connection, it meant the transference of the principle of Sophrosyne to the sphere of literature.

[3] I have called this " objective sincerity," if the phrase may be allowed ;

When the Ancients spoke of the sincerity, or, if we wish, the " persuasiveness " of a style, it seems clear that it was a persuasiveness that was largely determined by factors external to the author. This is characteristic of a general tendency in Classical theory to set up objective standards, by which a writer's activities should be guided. When the Ancients stressed the need of avoiding any form of artificiality in style, they did so, not so much from the standpoint of the author, as from the standpoint of a rhetorical scheme that was rigidly predetermined. It is clear, however, that they looked at times upon the rules as a galling burden, and, in such moods, they exhibit something like the modern conception of sincerity as the free and unfettered expression of a writer's thoughts and emotions. It is in this spirit that Demetrius declares[1] that genuine passion needs no art. It was felt that vehement and overpowering emotion could override technical rules, and condone[2] almost any liberty of speech. As the author of the treatise *On the Sublime* realised,[3] divine genius cannot always be made subject to the reign of law, but its greatness, with all its attendant faults, is to be preferred to the unvarying accuracy of lesser minds, which so often ends in triviality.

The question might be raised how far the Ancients took into account individuality in style in our modern sense ; how far they recognised a style that was the direct outcome of an author's peculiar habits of thought and mental outlook. They, of course, took into account certain superficial idiosyncrasies[4] which quickly betray a writer. But the real problem goes deeper, and is concerned with the style[5] that can be regarded as a faithful reflex of a man's distinctive intellectual and emotional life. When the Ancients spoke of style as being

Individuality in style

---

in one of its aspects at least, it connoted an absence of artificiality, and begot that " persuasiveness " of which Aristotle speaks, Rhet. III. 7. 4.

[1] 27.

[2] Cf. Ar. Rhet. III. 7. 11 ; Q. IX. 3. 102, XI. 1. 49 *et seq.*

[3] C. 33.

[4] Easily learnt by those who set out to play the sedulous ape, as Seneca saw in the case of Sallust's imitators, Ep. 114. 17.

[5] Cf. Middleton Murry's acute analysis of the various meanings of the word " style," op. cit., p. 4 *et seq.*

a mirror of the man, they seem to have had in mind his moral character.[1] The dictum " qualis vita talis oratio "[2] is an echo of Plato, who, when enunciating the principle, was concerned with the question of moral training, and was seeking to determine what kind of art and literature should be admitted to his Ideal Commonwealth. The Stoics also, naturally emphasised the connection between style and character, and proclaimed that the good orator[3] should also be a good man. Seneca selects Maecenas as a typical example of the dictum quoted above, and traces the effeminate and disorderly character of his style to the corresponding traits in his character. If he had been equipped with the modern weapons of the psycho-analyst, he might have given us a still more piquant study of Maecenas' style. It is doubtful, however, if the literary idiosyncrasies of the latter were very deeply rooted. His style was probably at most a form of affectation, in which he was trying to outdo the extravagances of the rhetorical schools. Even if we admit the contention that there existed a close relation between an author's style and his moral character, the Ancients seem to have advanced little beyond this in their analysis of individuality in style. It is true that they recognised in a general way the factor of individuality. Cicero can proclaim[4] that the styles of oratory are as numerous as the orators themselves. Quintilian, as we saw, realised the impossibility of including all orators in the stereotyped divisions of style. However, though the Romans had before them examples of styles that seemed to emanate from a distinctive personality,[5] styles in which there was a perfect harmony between form and thought, they did not endeavour to analyse them as an expression of the writer's peculiar mentality. They had fixed categories,

[1] Cf. Ar. Rhet. III. 16. 9.

[2] Sen. Ep. 114. 1 ; Summers, *ad loc.*, remarks that the proverb, οἶος ὁ βίος τοιοῦτος καὶ ὁ λόγος, is by some ascribed to Socrates ; cf. Cic. Tusc. Disp. V. 45 (quoted by him).

[3] We have seen how in rhetorical theory the style was supposed to be in harmony with the ἦθος τοῦ λέγοντος.

[4] Cf. also Q. XII. 10. 10 : " totidem reperias ingeniorum quot corporum formas " ; *ib.* 11.

[5] e.g. Tacitus.

prescriptions, and formulae, that seemed to cover most phenomena in the world of style, and they usually rested content with these. It is to be noted that the law of Decorum, if rigidly applied, would seem to rule out almost completely individuality of style, in the sense which I have explained. It required the orator, in particular, to be a veritable Proteus, and to be master of many styles, which he could wield at will according to circumstances. Evidently his rhetorical training was expected to endow him with such a power, and teach him the nice adjustment to his ends of the various embellishments which rhetoric could furnish. But here again, we are dealing with factors that are largely external to the author.

In the questions which I have discussed in connection with the problem of style, we can discern something of the strength and weakness of Classical theory.

The Classical spirit This, for the most part, took account of the normal workings of the human mind, and was not so much concerned with the waywardness and eccentricity of genius. The Ancients had a passion for definiteness and order, which led them to draw up categories, and formulate laws in so many spheres of man's activity. In this spirit, they set out to define and prescribe the rules of the various literary genres, both in prose and in poetry. Such rules were usually derived from the practice of the best writers,[1] but critics were inclined to interpret them as fixed and inexorable laws, to which all who laboured in the genre had to conform. The various prescriptions for style were too often interpreted in a similar manner. In contrast to this we have the Romantic writer, who above all values his freedom, and feels the irksomeness[2] of hampering

[1] In this connection, Pope's statement in " A Discourse on Pastoral Poetry " is interesting : " It is by rules like these that we ought to judge of Pastoral. And since the instructions given in any art, are to be delivered as that art is in perfection . . . it is therefore from the practice of Theocritus and Virgil (the only undisputed authors of Pastoral) that the Criticks have drawn the foregoing notions concerning it."

[2] Even Ben Jonson, so much imbued with the Classical spirit, makes one of his characters plead not to " be tied to those strict and regular forms which the niceness of a few, who are nothing but form, would thrust upon us " ; cf. Moulton, The Ancient Classical Drama, pp. 434–435.

rules. Romanticism is devoted to the cult of the original and spontaneous, and, in its extreme form, would suffer no law above a writer's own caprice. On the other hand, the formulism involved in the Classical theory of style would seem to restrict[1] unduly a writer's liberty, and almost to stifle his originality. Yet, we can pay this homage to it that it was inspired by a love of precision, regularity, and proportion, and that it was designed especially as a check on undisciplined and unbridled idiosyncrasy. As we shall see, the Ancients themselves were at times inclined to rebel against a too rigorous formulism.

We have seen that much of Cicero's criticism ran on conventional lines. He was a keen student of the early **Cicero as critic of the poets** Roman poets, but his verdicts on them are rarely illuminating. His views were often coloured by the preoccupations of the orator, and he judged them by standards which he had learned from his teachers of rhetoric. He was not devoid of appreciation of the drama. He showed himself, in fact, keenly sensitive to the dramatic import of certain passages in the Roman dramatists, but rather from the standpoint of one who was interested in the art of delivery, and had seen such passages brilliantly interpreted by two of the greatest of Roman actors. At times, his attitude to poetry exhibits much of the Puritan spirit of Plato. He often shows himself devoid of settled principles of criticism, and consequently his judgments on the poets are vacillating. In general, it may be said that he displays little insight into the essential beauty of poetry, or the nature of its appeal.

In oratory Cicero was in a sphere that was peculiarly his own. The *De Oratore* was his first important work on the **The " pervulgata praecepta "** principles that should guide the orator in his art. It was in part the fruit of his own ripened experience, though in it he reproduces much of the traditional scheme of Greek rhetoric. However, he shows that his vision ranged beyond the

---

[1] Hence a Romantic critic like Spingarn, under the spell of Croce, would consign to the rubbish-heap the old Rules, the doctrine of the genres, the theory of style with metaphor, simile, and all the paraphernalia of Graeco-Roman rhetoric ; cf. Creative Criticism, p. 24 *et seq.*

boundaries of the rhetorical text-book. There was evidently a growing conviction in his mind that the " Rules " were not everything, and that by themselves they were incapable of producing the perfect orator. He thus came to despise his first essay on rhetorical theory,[1] not merely as immature, but as too narrow and pedantic, and as too much an echo of his school exercises. Here we have one amongst many signs of reaction against a scheme that had tended to become too stereotyped. Already Plato had directed the shafts of his keenest irony against the scholastic subtlety[2] which, with its refined division and sub-division,[3] and its strange terminology, sought to complicate the art of rhetoric, both on its dialectical and its stylistic side.[4] Even the analytic mind of Aristotle[5] could not endure the intricate divisions of their subject-matter introduced by certain rhetorical theorists. Amongst Roman writers, we find occasionally in Quintilian a healthy reaction against what he styles[6] the " superstitio praeceptorum." He realises[7] that the " arts " of rhetoric, composed in an academic atmosphere, sometimes sadly fail when confronted with the stern realities of life. Borrowing an idea from the Greeks, he likens respect for the tradition of petty rules to the solicitude of those who anxiously guard the coat their mother gave them. He protests[8] against the attempt to force the exordium into a uniform mould. On the other hand, as regards the elements of style, he notes[9] how certain theorists in their passion for novelty are impelled to refine upon the established classifications. He believes that the vigour of oratory is bound to be impaired by a meticulous attention to technical minutiae. There are more things[10] than

---

[1] The " De Inventione."

[2] Cf. Phaedrus, 266 D *et seq.*, on τὰ κομψὰ τῆς τέχνης.

[3] *Vide* Rhys Roberts, Greek Rhetoric, p. 116, for later developments.

[4] Phaedrus, 267 C, on Polus' devices for attaining εὐέπεια.

[5] Cf. Rhet. III. 13. 5, on the divisions of a speech adopted by Theodorus and his school ; *ib.* 16. 4, on rules for the " narratio."

[6] IV. 2. 85.

[7] V. 13. 59 *et seq.* ; *ib.* 14. 27, 31.

[8] IX. 4. 132.

[9] IX. 1. 17–18 ; *ib.* 2. 102, on the multiplication of Figures.

[10] IX. 4. 117 : " quaedam vero tradi arte non possunt."

are dreamt of in the stereotyped schemes of the rhetoricians. Cicero, too, had begun to realise the limitations of the " pervulgata praecepta," and of the conventional training in rhetoric. He saw that his ideal orator could not spring from the " rhetorum officinae," as he somewhat contemptuously calls them.[1] He points out how important it is for the orator not to rest content with a mere technical training, but to strive after a liberal education.[2] He vividly describes for us how the orator's range and vision are thus enlarged, how he is equipped with new weapons, which enable him to dazzle men's minds, and subdue them to his purpose.

We have seen some of the defects of Cicero's critical method in the *Brutus*, defects which were in a measure incidental to the plan he had adopted in that work. Considering the number of orators he undertook to review, it was inevitable that many of his criticisms would be superficial and perfunctory. The criticisms are at times reduced to the proportion of a mere label. In this, it is true, Cicero was but exhibiting a tendency common[3] among the Ancients. We find that in antiquity the " label " was prominent among the critic's stock-in-trade, whether he was dealing with poets,[4] orators,[5] or historians.[6] With their love of rigid categories, and their habit of defining the qualities of the various styles and the various literary genres,[7] many of the labels used by the Ancients may have had a deeper significance for them than they can have for the Moderns. There are certain labels with which even the modern critic can hardly dispense.[8] However, their theory of imitation made the Ancients

Labels in criticism

[1] Or. 12.

[2] He thus, as we saw, raises an educational problem that is very fundamental.

[3] *Vide* Saintsbury, op. cit., I. p. 383.

[4] Cf. Funaioli, op. cit., p. 203, on Varro ; Statius, Silvae, V. 3. 157 ; Gellius, VII. 14. 6, XIX. 9. 7 ; Fronto, II. 48.

[5] Cic. De Or. III. 28 ; Q. X. 2. 25, XII. 10. 11 ; Tac. Dial. 18 ; Apul. Apol. 95 ; cf. St. John Chrys. De Sacer. IV. 6 (424) ; St. Jerome, Ep. 125. 12.

[6] Cic. Ad Q. Fr. II. 11 (13). 4 ; cf. the fragments of the ' Hortensius,' Usener, op. cit., p. 123.

[7] Cf. Tac. Dial. 10, where the characteristics of several genres are ticketed.

[8] *Vide* Falls, The Critic's Armoury, pp. 15–16.

especially prone to exploit the label, as in it they were endeavouring to present the salient characteristic of the author whom they recommended. It is all to the good if an author's predominant quality (what Sainte-Beuve styles[1] his " trait saillant " and his " faculté maîtresse "), can be grasped within the narrow limits of a single epithet or phrase. We could well do with more labels such as " curiosa felicitas," " lactea ubertas," and " immortalis velo- citas,"[2] which seem inevitable[3] in their appropriateness. On the other hand, Cicero's labels often seem conventional and uninspired,[4] memories of his rhetorical training rather than the outcome of a profound acquaintance with the authors to whom he affixes them.

Though in the *De Oratore* Cicero showed signs of re- action against the elaborate precepts of the rhetoricians, yet,
Dogmatic criticism in most of his criticisms in the *Brutus,* he employs the framework of the traditional scheme of rhetoric. Ranging through the pre-requisites for the orator, the established divisions of oratory into judicial, deliberative, and forensic, the various parts of rhetoric,[5] the virtues of style with all that they implied, and the " officia oratoris," he could find in one or other of these a criterion by which to judge an orator, and at the same time a formula in which to embody his criticism. What he gives us for the most part is judicial or dogmatic criticism in its most extreme form, starting with fixed standards and established principles. In this, of course, he was following in the wake of the Classical critics generally, but we can see how mechanical the method could become, as it is often employed in the *Brutus.*

It is as well not to press the question as to how far certain of Cicero's criticisms were the fruit of an intimate knowledge

[1] Cf. MacClintock, op. cit., p. 134.
[2] Used by Q. X. 1. 102, of Sallust, whom Gellius styles " subtilis- simus brevitatis artifex."
[3] Vitruvius styled Pollio " nervosae vivacitatis exemplum," though we are not in a position to check the aptness of the description.
[4] One wonders whether Horace is not objecting as much to the system of labels, as to the criticisms they embody, in Ep. II. 1. 57 *et seq.*
[5] Such as Invention, Arrangement, etc.

of the authors or their works, where such a knowledge was possible. It is interesting to compare the results achieved by Dionysius in dealing with such an orator as Lysias. He had the advantage of making an extended study of his author, while many of Cicero's criticisms are in tabloid form. Though the Greek critic also, is tied to the traditional scheme of rhetoric, he at times contrives to get free of its shackles. Throughout, he maintains a certain enthusiasm for his subject, which makes us feel that he has got into personal touch with his author, that he has penetrated to the finer elements of his style, and has helped to reveal the secret of such success as Lysias had achieved. When he is in doubt concerning the genuineness of any of the speeches attributed to this orator, his judgment is finally determined[1] by the presence or absence of a peculiar indefinable charm which, for him at any rate, was the ultimate test of the true Lysian style. Dionysius furthermore gives us extracts[2] from particular speeches, a feature which we miss in the *Brutus*. Moreover, as I have said, Cicero often leaves the impression that he is not in contact with the personalities of the orators whom he is criticising. He was, it is true, profoundly interested in certain orators such as Crassus, Antonius, Calidius, and Hortensius, and his study of these marks a distinct advance in Roman criticism. But his judgments on many other orators are of the routine character that leaves us unsatisfied. They show little in the nature of a personal reaction to the specific qualities of their eloquence, and fail to explain the relation between the man and the orator.

Routine judgments

The modern critic aims at a more subtle analysis of an author's individuality, and seeks to penetrate to the secret springs of his thoughts. A lack of the personal note was, on the other hand, common among the ancient critics. Thus we find in Quintilian much criticism that is merely formulistic and

Other critics compared

---

[1] De Lysia, c. 11 ; the whole chapter is interesting, as Dionysius stresses the need of " impressionism," when a critic is dealing with certain departments of art and literature.

[2] Though they are mostly used as illustrations of other than stylistic qualities.

superficial. Some of his happiest touches are but skilful[1]
adaptations of judgments passed by his predecessors. At
times, however, his study of a particular author is more
elaborate and more incisive, especially when, as in the case
of Seneca, he is roused to a fierce antagonism, and is fighting
in defence of his most cherished ideals. But amongst
Roman critics, I would consider the Elder Seneca as occupy-
ing a place of distinction. He had, it must be admitted,
an easy task in stigmatising the extravagances of the schools.
At the same time, he has given us a striking analysis of the
psychology of the declaimers. He noted with the eye of
the trained observer their aims and methods, the influence
of their environment upon them, and the almost violent
transformation which some of them underwent in the
atmosphere of the declamation. Though he was himself
nurtured on other ideals, yet, being a critic of wide sympathies, he recognised that amidst much that was gaudy
and insipid in the style of the declaimers, there was often a
vigour and freshness that introduced a new note into Latin
prose. Some of Seneca's critical dicta[2] probably derived
their epigrammatic quality, and their incisiveness, from the
schools, while they often remind us of Joubert's *Pensées* in
their luminousness. He had the gift, too, of summing up
a man or a situation in a happy phrase. Thus he describes[3]
Ovid as deliberately hugging his defects, and says that
(with the true instinct of the declaimer) he was not content
to leave well enough alone. Seneca evidently tried to get
into close contact with the personalities of the men whom
he was portraying, and sought to throw some light on the
workings of their minds. He sets forth his own impressions
of their style in simple and unstudied language, and is not
endeavouring to frame his criticism in conformity with any
stereotyped scheme. We are thus attracted by his sym-

[1] Thus his phrase " verbis felicissime audax," used to describe Horace, is
an echo of Petronius ; so his description of Ovid as " nimium amator ingenii
sui," seems to be an echo of the Elder Seneca, C. II. 2 (10). 12.
[2] Cf. C. IX. pr. 2 : " sequitur hoc in forum declamatores ut necessaria
deserant dum speciosa sectantur " ; *ib*. X, pr. 10 : " multa donanda ingeniis
puto, sed donanda vitia non portenta sunt."
[3] C. II. 2 (10). 12, IX. 5 (28). 17.

pathetic study of the philosopher Fabianus, who seemed out of place among the declaimers, and alternated between a style that was plain and consonant with his profession, and one that in its floridness and unrestraint was designed to be in harmony with the spirit of the schools. Seneca draws for us vivid pictures of the characters and style of men such as Q. Haterius, Albucius, Montanus, " homo rarissimi etiamsi non emendatissimi ingenii,"[1] and Labienus. He describes[2] how Albucius abandoned the forum owing to the derision excited by his failure in a figure of speech. Labienus was a particularly interesting personality, inasmuch as he was a symbol of a transition period, and united in himself certain qualities of the old and new styles. In other respects, Seneca displays a sure grasp of the literary problems involved in the rise of the declamation. His prefaces alone would win for him a high rank among Roman critics. It is probable that he would not have achieved so much, if Cicero had not smoothed the path for him, but his judgments are generally characterised by a freshness and spontaneity that we often miss in Cicero.

The latter's application of the historical method must be set down as perhaps his greatest contribution to Roman criticism. It was no small achievement for The historical a critic at that time to trace, however im-method perfectly, the history of oratory from its first faint beginnings to what Cicero regarded as its culmination in his own day. He does not always clearly mark the stages of development, nor does he adequately define for us what constituted progress in the different epochs with which he deals. For all that, the use of the historical method enabled him to see that men are usually conditioned by the standards of contemporary culture. He did not therefore demand from the orators of the early period the polish and elegance of the Ciceronian age, but was prepared to see even in their shortcomings a striving towards higher things.

Cicero's quarrel with the Atticists was an incident of

[1] C. IX. 5 (28). 15.
[2] C. VII. pr. 7.

supreme importance for Roman criticism. The threat to
his supremacy as an orator acted as a power-
The Atticist controversy ful incentive to him to review his position,
and frame what he considered to be his
most effective defence against the charges of his adversaries.
The quarrel in Rome was an echo of a similar one in Greece,
which must have been carried on with almost equal bitterness, once the contrast between Attic refinement and restraint and Asiatic bombast and flamboyancy had been
noted by discerning critics. Besides stylistic considerations,
purity of speech was for the Greeks an important element in
the debate. The Roman Atticists were primarily concerned
with the problem of style, though the virtue of correctness
was also prominent among their ideals.

Cicero, being driven to the defensive, had to summon up
all his reserves. He borrowed some of his most potent
weapons from Greek, and especially from Hellenistic,
rhetorical theory. However, conceptions with which the
Greeks were long acquainted, had to be clothed in a Latin
dress ; equivalents for Greek critical terms had to be discovered ; unfamiliar problems discussed, or familiar ones
treated with more thoroughness[1] than was possible for any
of Cicero's predecessors. All this was a gain to Latin
prose, as it opened up a new storehouse of expression.
Cicero must have done much not merely to extend, but to
standardise, the critical vocabulary of his compatriots, and
thus placed succeeding Roman critics in his debt. We
noted instances in which he wavers about the use of a
particular term, but how readily he wielded the language
of the critic, is apparent from his brilliant characterisation
of some of the orators of his own day. We may doubt the
justice of some of his judgments ; we may despise many of
them as conventional, but we must admit that he taught
Roman criticism to speak in more varied accents than it
had known before his day.

The Atticist quarrel is, however, chiefly important as
revealing a divergence of ideals as regards
A divergence of ideals Latin oratorical prose. It is not easy to determine the reasons that led the Roman Atticists
to adopt their peculiar standpoint with such vehemence

[1] Cf. Cicero's claims concerning his discussion of prose-rhythm, Or. 226.

Education and environment[1] must have played their part, but in the last resort temperament was probably the decisive factor. Though the Atticists directed their main attack on Cicero, it would be interesting to speculate how far the earlier Atticists in particular, were led to react against excessive ornateness and redundancy by the spectacle of Hortensius still clinging to his Asiatic manner, even in his old age. The choice of models made by the protagonists in the quarrel is significant. It is at once indicative of their ideals, and shows how potent was the spell which the Greek writers continued to cast upon the Romans. Though Cicero professes his admiration for Demosthenes as an orator of unrivalled range and power, yet he declares that he is not always satisfied with his eloquence. In his longing for a richer and more rhythmical style of oratory, he was drawn to Isocrates as to a kindred spirit. The Atticists, on the other hand, were in general attracted to Lysias, an artist who exhibited restraint and discrimination in his prose, and who, while spurning[2] the garish ornaments of Sophistic rhetoric, could create enchantment out of the common speech of men.

Now, throughout the debate Cicero shows himself to be a skilful advocate, who is quick to seize on any point that could be of advantage for his own defence, or weaken the position of his opponents.

Debating points

For that purpose, he dwelt much on the " officia oratoris," and maintained that the Atticists failed conspicuously in the main function of the orator, the moving of his audience. In his contrast between " docere " and " movere," he introduced a distinction[3] which, as we saw, had its roots in Aristotle, and was later prominent in the theory of Theophrastus. Apart from its application to oratory,[4] the distinction is interesting, inasmuch as it serves

[1] From the first, the Atticists seem to have been an exclusive coterie.

[2] At any rate in his forensic speeches ; his Olympic oration shows that he could employ them in his panegyrical style ; cf. also the criticism passed on him by Theophrastus, Dionys. De Lys. c. 14.

[3] Ar. Rhet. III. 1. 1, 14. 8 ; Cic. Or. 124 ; Q. IV. 5. 6, V. 14. 30 ; Pliny, Ep. VI. 33. 9, IX. 16. 1.

[4] Where the question of delivery would also be involved.

to set in opposition a prose that is analytic, expository, and
unimpassioned, and one that pulsates with life, that is
warmed by the glow of a writer's emotions, and coloured
by his imagination. The latter is designed to achieve its
end chiefly through the feelings, while the former is primarily addressed to the intellect. In all this we are reminded
of De Quincey's distinction[1] between the " literature of
knowledge " and the " literature of power," the function of
the first, he tells us, being to *teach*, and the function of the
second being to *move*. Cicero demanded that the orator be
able to fulfil both[2] functions. It was, according to him,
when the Atticists were put to such a test, that their shortcomings were most fully revealed. Moreover, he declared
that it was vital for oratory to be popular in its appeal. The
polished, but attenuated style of Calvus, thus seemed to him
too delicate a fare to be set before the multitude. Employing
a similar criterion, he stressed the limitations of the Atticists' chief model Lysias, but though this might be considered a good debating point, it is evident that he missed
the finer implications in his opponents' contentions, and
their significance for prose style in general. Viewing the
problem from this latter standpoint, we are instinctively in
sympathy with the Atticists, who fought for an ideal of
style that was elegant and austere, and that did not depend
for its effect on a false brilliance or meretricious ornament.
The Atticist controversy as a whole helped to crystallise the
conceptions of Atticism and Asianism. These conceptions
still retain their value, as is evident from the use made of
them by modern[3] critics in their judgments on the prose
style of their contemporaries.

My chapter on the Ancients *v.* the Moderns might perhaps have been more correctly styled Ancient
v. Modern, as its aim was to study in certain
of its aspects the conflict of ideals between
Past and Present in Roman literature up to the days of

**Ancients v.
Moderns**

[1] Cf. Scott-James, op. cit., p. 22 *et seq.*

[2] As well as " delectare " or " conciliare," which, as we saw, was probably an offshoot of later theory that was endeavouring to define the function
of the Middle style.

[3] *Vide* MacClintock, op. cit., pp. 99–101, for Sainte-Beuve's application
of them,

Fronto. The conflict is interesting, if only as an index of the variations of literary taste at different periods. Such variations may be the fruit of a critical movement that is conscious and deliberate, and that proceeds according to well-defined principles, or again, they may spring[1] from factors that bear little relation[2] to literature. Men may desire change simply for the sake of change, or they may desire it because they are surfeited with a particular style, or a particular school, that, often for intangible reasons, has lost its appeal. But, throughout the controversy, we may see operative the two great forces of Tradition and Experiment, the one averse to change, or demanding at least orderly evolution, the other beckoning men on to strange paths, and hitherto uncharted regions.

It is not always easy to analyse the psychology of the protagonists in this literary quarrel. There are some who are naturally conservative, and who cling to the Past and its achievements with an often unreasoning devotion. This tendency is fortified, if it happens to coincide with a strong antiquarian movement, which idealises the Past, and invests, it may be, with a fictitious importance every vestige of antiquity. Such champions of the Ancients are inclined to view new movements with suspicion, and to regard as a sign of degeneracy everything that differs from the ideals which they themselves cherish. They look askance at the innovating genius, who has perhaps set out to break up the old moulds, and make new experiments with language. Sometimes we find in them a somewhat natural revolt against what they regard as the blatancy or garishness, or it may be the effeminacy, of modern art and literature. They profess to find a certain robustness in the Ancients, which with all its crudeness they welcome as a relief from modern prettiness and affectation. If the Ancients cannot rival the Modern in perfection of technique, their champions will

A problem of psychology

---

[1] Oratory seemed peculiarly susceptible to variations of this second kind ; the Dialogus of Tacitus supplies some illustrations.

[2] A point stressed by Kellett, in " The Whirligig of Taste " already referred to ; Kellett does not always clearly distinguish between taste and criticism proper ; cf. remarks by West, Deucalion, p. 27.

at any rate try to safeguard their position, by claiming for them superiority in natural talent.

The Moderns are often roused to action by the extravagant praise lavished on the Ancients by their advocates. They believe that such ardent zeal for their **The Moderns** cause is often inspired by jealousy of themselves, and is designed to disparage their achievements. Thus, as we saw, Horace strongly reacted against the enthusiasm manifested by the admirers of Lucilius, who discovered virtues in that poet which he could scarcely have attained to in his day. On the other hand, criticism begotten in such a mood of reaction is too often blind to the difficulties which the Ancients had to encounter, and to the real value of all they had accomplished. In particular, the Moderns who pose as the heralds of new ideas and of progress, often display an unreasonable contempt for tradition. "Passions[1] are engendered which form a sort of patriotism of the moment ; and what more natural for the partakers in the revolution than to despise the regime it seems to have overthrown ? " The Moderns sometimes forget that they themselves are building on foundations securely laid by former generations. Elated by their own discoveries, they tend to ignore the fact that well-established tradition is " no more than the fruit of successful experiment."[2] In poetry especially, they frequently claim to have made an advance in form, in greater mastery of technique, in the attainment of verse of smoother flow and more varied harmony. They deride the efforts of the Ancients as clumsy and ineffectual, forgetting that it was their pioneer work that made the way easy for themselves. Thus the Neoterics seemed oblivious of the noble services which Ennius had rendered to Roman poetry, when they spoke of him with a contempt which roused the ire of Cicero. Their own school was strongly imbued with the spirit of the Alexandrians. Its members loved to show their skill by experimenting with new metrical forms. Many of them concentrated their powers on the Epyllion, which seemed especially well adapted to admit the labour of the file within

---

[1] Lascelles Abercrombie, Progress in Literature, p. 25.
[2] *Vide* Tradition and Experiment, p. 99.

its narrow confines. Smoothness, elegance, and precision in every detail, they would probably consider as their great contribution to the poetical literature of Rome. Undoubtedly Latin in their hands became more subtle and delicate as a poetic medium. At a later period, it is interesting to find the amateur poets, contemporary with Persius, claiming[1] that they had attained to a verse of smoother flow than any who had gone before them. There is thus evidence of a continual quest after some advance, or some novelty, that will mark off one generation of poets from their predecessors. The modern exponents of " vers libre," we are told,[2] are engaged especially in making " experiments in the effect of texture on rhythm."

As a counterpart to the quest for advance in form, we have the quest for novelty in subject-matter. The Classical writers, as part of their tradition, loved to handle[3] and re-handle the same themes. In time, there inevitably ensues a satiety which causes a reaction against such traditional subjects. The old tales begin to suffer from a kind of natural exhaustion. They have lost the fine edge of their freshness and charm, so that even the highest skill of the poet or the dramatist cannot save them from becoming wearisome, or galvanise them into new life. The elegiac poets may use such legends as a picturesque setting for their thoughts, but they at times proclaim their contempt for them in face of the passion that has mastered them. The temperament of the Satirist is inclined to reject them for more realistic themes, and for the more vital interest of the life around him. He finds it a more congenial task to anatomise the evils of society, and hold its vices up to scorn, than to deal with subjects that can have no message for his contemporaries. As we saw, a moralist such as Seneca preferred to lay bare the ills of the soul, and prescribe remedies for minds diseased, rather than busy himself with antiquarian problems. Others

Novelty in subject-matter

---

[1] Cf. Persius, I. 63 *et seq.*, though one must make allowance for the exaggeration of the Satirist.

[2] Tradition and Experiment, p. 76.

[3] Cf. Hor. A.P. 132 ; Manilius, II. 50 ; Statius, Silvae, II. 7. 51, on " trita vatibus orbita."

again, recoil from the traditional legends, because their minds are possessed by a new-born enthusiasm for science. Thus poets such as Manilius and the author of the *Aetna*, filled with the spirit of Lucretius, believed that they were engaged in a nobler labour, and one fraught with more lasting benefit to mankind, when they set themselves to divine the secrets of Nature, and proclaim her marvels.

It is worth while to glance for a moment at certain variations of taste in Latin prose. Cicero, especially in the higher flights of his oratory, had set the example of a rich, elaborately embroidered, periodic style, that rivalled the splendour of Isocrates. Even in Cicero's time, there were some who found his oratory unpalatable, and who appealed against his advocacy of rhythmical prose to the simplicity and naturalness of the Ancients. In every age, as we have seen, there were many for whom the archaic colouring of the earlier writers possessed a powerful fascination. But, in the age following Cicero, there was a new form of reaction against Ciceronian prose. With changed conditions there came a stirring of new impulses. The schools of declamation, where in a measure was witnessed a rebirth of the Sophistic spirit, began to set the fashion. From the speaker were especially demanded greater brilliance, pointedness, and terseness, as well as the play of parodox and epigram that would add a new sparkle to his oratory. The stateliness and formal structure of the Ciceronian period were out of harmony with the spirit of the time. The Younger Seneca[1] found Cicero's prose too lumbering in its march, while its cadences had evidently begun to pall upon him. A taste was engendered for a style of greater pregnancy and allusiveness, a style that was more broken[2] and spasmodic, that showed a less obvious pattern than of old, and that seemed deliberately to despise rigid syntax and fixed rules. This new instrument could be wielded with great power by a master such as Tacitus, who learned to exploit its potentialities to the full. Seneca employed it as a medium

---

[1] He styles him " gradarius," Ep. 40. 11 ; cf. Ep. 100, 7–9, 114. 16.

[2] *Vide* Cazamian, Criticism in the Making, p. 63 *et seq.*, for an interesting discussion of the quest of discontinuity in modern art and literature.

for some vapid moralising, but his fondness for parodox
and epigram made his style irresistible in its appeal to the
young men[1] of his day.   Quintilian aimed at effecting at
least a moderate revival of Ciceronian ideals, but, though
he professes to regard Seneca as a spent force, his elaborate
criticism of his defects suggests that the spell of the Senecan
manner still continued to be potent.   We have noted that
Quintilian was one of those who were gifted with a sense of
historical perspective, which enabled him to maintain
generally a reasonable attitude in the quarrel of the Ancients
v. the Moderns.   Wedded as he was to the Ciceronian
tradition, he naturally found many elements in contemporary
prose that jarred upon him as false and meretricious, but,
for all that, he recognised that the modern style had often a
living energy that suited the genius of the age.

We witness a fresh reaction against Seneca and his ways
in Gellius and Fronto.   Their ideals ran counter to those of
the philosopher, who showed such scanty
Euphuism   respect for the Ancients.   Gellius and his
circle, partly impelled by the antiquarianism which was
fashionable under Hadrian, came to value inordinately all
that survived of early Roman literature.   They were
attracted by its quaintness, but they approached it, too,
with the ardent zeal of the grammarian, in whose eyes every
form that was obsolete or bizarre, became a pearl of great
price.   Fronto had his own uses for the primitive writers.
He abhorred the prettiness and artificiality of the modern
style, especially as represented by Seneca.   He evidently
considered that Roman prose should be set upon a new path,
if it was to be redeemed from its weaknesses.   I have
already described his efforts to build up his " elocutio
novella."   To impart a fresh vitality to the Latin language,
he was on the one hand led to a study of the early poets and
prose writers, and on the other induced to draw upon the
resources of the vulgar tongue.   Fronto's laboured efforts
could end only in a new form of artificiality, a euphuism[2]

[1] We have witnessed a similar cult of some modern writers who have
exploited the paradox and the epigram.
[2] Cf. the interesting description of the new style (as represented especially
by Apuleius) given by Pater in " Marius the Epicurean," Vol. I. c. 5–6.

that was bound to be short-lived, but his experiment is interesting as affording one more illustration of the strange variations of literary taste.

I have referred to the *Dialogus* of Tacitus as a document of cardinal importance for the quarrel, especially as it epitomises many of the principles that **The "Dialogus" of Tacitus** actuated the protagonists, and anticipates, implicitly at least, slogans that have been operative in criticism up to our own day. The notions of Relativity in literature, of Evolution, Progress, and Decadence, are all pressed into service in the course of the debate which Tacitus stages for us. His treatise thus possesses an interest that transcends the immediate problems which worried him and his contemporaries. In it, moreover, we find the main issues of the dispute clearly knit. Messalla might be styled a Classicist, who respects tradition, and has a profound admiration for the great authors of the Past. He regards his own age as decadent, when judged in the light of the ideals and achievements of former generations. Present-day literature is a reflex of a society that is undisciplined, and impervious to lofty motives. He insists, in particular, that no great oratory could flourish in an atmosphere so depraved. His opponent Aper is a typical product of the rhetorical schools, who had succumbed to the modern taste in oratory, and believed that " a truth looks freshest in the fashion of the day." He professed to find much even of late Republican eloquence dull and tedious. He makes a clever debating point in declaring that the terms " Ancient " and " Modern " are relative terms, which alter with the angle from which they are viewed. He claims that his age is a progressive one, and he will not have himself or his contemporaries branded as decadents. Literature, and oratory especially, are subject to an evolution of their own. They change with the times, and are in harmony with the prevailing taste, which now demands something polished and piquant, as compared with the crude efforts of the Ancients. Tacitus, in the person of Maternus, winds up the debate with a note of compromise, in which he urges men not to despise other ages, but to enjoy the blessings of their own. He evidently felt that each age could make a contribution to literature, the value of which it is not always easy to assess, and believed that in such an imponderable element it is difficult to strike a balance between the achievements of different epochs.

There is little that I need add to what I have already said upon Horace. I endeavoured to study him as a critic who **The spirit of** was a typical representative of the Classical **Horatian** tradition, and embodied in himself both its **criticism** strength and its weakness. His critical creed was, in its main outlines, well defined at the time of his first essays in poetry. The range of his criticism extended with the years, as new problems presented themselves for solution. In his theorising and in his judgments he assumed a more assured tone, and displayed a firmer grasp of principles, but there is a fundamental resemblance between the critic of the *Satires* and the critic of the *Epistles*. In his early years, in face of persistent attempts to exalt unduly the achievements of Lucilius, and probably equally persistent attempts to disparage his own, he was forced to review his position and that of his predecessor. He was not merely following the example of Lucilius, but acting in harmony with the general spirit of Classical theory, when he set out to define the " lex operis " for Satire, both as regards its style and its humour. He was thus endeavouring to satisfy the desire of the Ancients for fixed laws and formulae to govern each genre, but showing, too, how easy it was in antiquity to effect an alliance between the poet and the critic. If one conceives Satire to be like Comedy a " species vitae," much will follow from this fundamental conception. For one thing, the style of Satire must, in accordance with the law of Decorum, be based on the language of everyday life. Lucilius, as we saw, held to the conception of Satire as a mirror of life, but, both in his style and in his humour, fell short of Horatian ideals. Horace was no revolutionary. He sought for no violent break with tradition, but favoured rather an orderly evolution. It was in this spirit that he set out to formulate afresh the laws of Satire in the light of Augustan conditions. He conceived the humour of Satire as something more subtle, temperate, urbane, as more varied in tone, than was to be met with in the works of Lucilius. The admirers of the latter believed that their poet, in the entire spirit of his work, was in the direct line of descent from the Old Comedy writers. Horace admitted his predecessor's dependence on these, but considered that he had missed the finer element of the " exemplaria Graeca." He passed some severe strictures on the style of the older poet, who could pour out numerous[1] verses without effort. The supporters of Lucilius may have boasted that he never " blotted a line." We can imagine Horace retorting, " I would he had blotted a thousand," as Ben Jonson in his day replied to the enthusiastic admirers of Shakespeare. In the course of his criticism of his predecessor, Horace gives us a glimpse of his own ideal of style. It was an ideal that to the end remained substantially the same, though a riper experience enabled him to formulate it more fully in his later works. The poet must use the file with unwearying effort, if he is to attain perfection. It is only thus that he can eliminate redundancy, ensure polish and precision of language, and achieve that smoothness of verse which should be the goal of every poet worthy of the name. The poet's choice of words was naturally a question of first importance. He will select certain words for their beauty and sonority, but, if he is an artist, he may by a skilful setting transform into things of beauty the commonest materials of language. At times he may feel the need of an extension of the available vocabulary, but, whether he sets out to search for buried treasure in the language of the Past, or seeks to enrich his native tongue by new coinages, Horace will place severe restrictions[2] on his liberty. He will not countenance any violent experiments with language, nor any marked artificiality. Here, as elsewhere, the poet must exhibit that sense of due measure, which was such an important element in the Classical creed. Though Horace may pay a high tribute to " ingenium," though he may admire the greatness of

[1] His practice was thus in striking contrast with that of Virgil and of the new school of poets.
[2] I have spoken in this connection of the influence of the Purist movement ; Horace probably had in mind, too, the practice of such a supreme poet as Virgil.

Homer, even with its faults, and the rich, impetuous genius of Pindar, yet he will subject the poet to discipline and self-restraint in all things. Even in the realm of the imagination, he must feel the controlling hand of reason. To hold the balance equally between " ars " and " ingenium " was the aim of the greatest[1] Classical critics, though Horace at times seems to make it incline in favour of " ars." His precepts tend to curb overmuch the freedom of the poet's genius. Whatever shortcomings lay in Classical theory as expounded by Horace, were intensified by the Neo-classical critics who followed in his wake. They inclined to stereotype his principles, while their watch-words Correctness, Decorum, and Good Sense, which they might claim to have derived from him, were interpreted by them more rigidly and mechanically than Horace would have approved of.

With regard to the " law of the genre," we have seen how, for instance, the rules[2] for Tragedy and Comedy hardened as the result of Hellenistic theorising.

The law of the genre

Horace, in the main, adopted the conceptions of these genres prevailing in Hellenistic times, and thus helped to transmit them to the Neo-Classical critics. Though he would in general have insisted that each poetic genre should preserve its primary and essential nature, that did not preclude the possibility of one genre re-echoing another. Moreover, at any rate in secondary matters, it was open to a poet to interpret the law of the genre afresh in the light of modern conditions, as Horace himself wished to have the spirit of the Satyric drama brought more into conformity with the refinement of his own age, and the Roman sense of decorum.

The question of imitation was a vital one in Classical theory. Horace had his own use for the great models of the Past, especially those that were a legacy from the Golden

---

[1] The problem is well stated in περὶ ὕψους, c. 2.

[2] In this connection the material brought together by McMahon, in his article " Aristotelian Definitions of Tragedy and Comedy," is important, though he traces later definitions back to Aristotle's work " On Poets," and takes no account of the modifications of Aristotle's views in Hellenistic times.

Age of Greek literature. As the early Roman writers could
not teach the lessons which he wished to
The problem inculcate, he counsels the unceasing study
of imitation of the "exemplaria Graeca." These can
teach the aspiring poet to value perfection of form, and to
avoid that slovenly workmanship which an uncritical age
was disposed to view with a too indulgent eye. The
Romans may thus hope to infuse into their poetry something
of the delicate spirit of the Greek Muse. Horace, however,
would condemn the servile imitation of models no less than
naked plagiarism. As both his precepts and his practice
indicate, he demanded a vital form of imitation, that was not
incompatible with originality in the poet. He was thus
far from the standpoint of those later critics who urged the
writers of their time to pillage the Ancients without scruple,
or who encouraged them to desert Nature for the written
model.

In my chapter on the predominance of Rhetoric, I endeavoured to study the genesis of the rhetorical point of view
in judging the creations of the poets. The
Rhetoric and interactions of poetry and rhetoric in ancient
poetry times constitute a difficult problem in the
history of criticism. On the one hand, we are confronted
with the spectacle of Gorgias and his brother Sophists, who
borrowed freely from the resources of the poets, and helped
to place a definitely rhetorical impress on the ornament thus
acquired. On the other hand, we find many passages in
Euripides that, both in form and in thought, reveal the
influence of contemporary rhetoric. Again, it is evident
that those who, especially in Hellenistic times, set out to
draw up " arts " of rhetoric, studied the usage of the poets
no less than that of the prose-writers, when they were
endeavouring to analyse the constituents of style. They
directed their attention to the poet's choice of words, to his
rhythms, and to his use of figurative language. Though
they were prepared to recognise differences between the
poet and the orator, such differences often seem to have
been conceived as ones of degree rather than of kind. In
what were regarded as the externals of style, was discovered
ground that was in a measure common to poetry and oratory.

There were ornaments which both could employ, with due consideration, however, of their diverse aims and characters. The Figures afford an illustration, while at the same time they serve to show the effect of the method adopted by the rhetoricians. Those of them who composed technical treatises, endeavoured to make an exhaustive survey of the Figures, many of which must have been derived originally from the poets. Having found a place in the traditional scheme of rhetoric expounded in the schools, even those latter Figures came to be regarded as specifically " rhetorical "[1] ornament. But the theorists moving, as I have said, in a kind of vicious circle, employed such conventional schemes and formulas to test the achievements of the poets, even with regard to those elements for which they must have been originally indebted to them. It seems to me that we have an analogous proceeding in the verdict passed[2] by Dionysius on the exordium of Lysias' speech against Diogeiton. This exordium, we are told, will be found to be a model one, if tested by the rules laid down by the τεχνογράφοι, though these rules were in all probability based largely on the practice of Lysias[3] in this and other speeches. The later theorists in particular, inherited a stereotyped system of rhetoric, with the origin and development of which they were not seriously concerned. It was they, most of all, who helped to confuse the issues with regard to poetry, by employing indiscriminately their own peculiar standards in judging almost every phase of the poet's activities, and in seeking[4] to discover in him a complete art of rhetoric.

It is, of course, always a nice question how far the epithet " rhetorical " can be applied to a particular poet. Even the great poet may learn some useful lessons from formal rhetoric, without allowing himself to be dominated by it. The poet of lesser power often succumbs, however, to the allurements of rhetoric, and is led to strain after effects, and

[1] Which for many meant external or applied ornament.

[2] De Lys. 24.

[3] As being one of the earliest orators to bring to perfection the art of forensic eloquence.

[4] As critics did both in the case of Homer and Virgil.

employ ornament that stands apart from the body of his poem, and cannot be woven into its texture. The poet who has lived in the atmosphere[1] of the rhetorical schools, and has imbibed their spirit, will often be content with employing the devices he has mastered there, and will aim at little more than verbal dexterity. At a lower level still, stands the poetaster, who has been tempted to essay verse by the fatal facility which he has acquired during his rhetorical training.

The influence of rhetoric on history was the final question which I considered. In its early stages, history was indebted to the Epic and to the folk-tale for **Rhetoric and history** part of its technique, and never quite forgot its affiliations. The introduction of speeches by the historian, though it helped to give dramatic vividness to his narrative, in time opened the door to much spurious rhetoric. Thucydides endeavoured to establish a more scientific tradition in historical writing, but even in him the scientific historian is sometimes merged in the artist. He could not wholly escape the influence of contemporary[2] rhetoric, once he had decided to intersperse his narrative with speeches. But the historians of the school of Isocrates in particular, imparted a definitely rhetorical colouring to history, and subordinated most things to the exigencies of style. When we reach the Hellenistic period, we find that a well-defined technique for history has been evolved, and that rules have been formulated to govern its constituent elements. First of all, the historian was expected to make a selection of his materials, and to work them up into an artistic unity. Rhetoric was allowed free play in the speeches, digressions, and descriptions, in which he generally indulged. Polybius, in conformity with the spirit of Thucydides, advocated a more scientific treatment of history. He condemned the perversion of truth, the riot of false rhetoric, the love of the sensational and the marvellous, that characterised many of the Greek historians. The search for truth, and its accurate presentation, were for him the highest duties of the historian, and, though he

---

[1] Like so many of the poets of the Silver Age at Rome.
[2] Especially at a time when rhetoric was so much in the air.

would hardly go so far as to proclaim, like some of the modern scientific school, " that it is an idle superstition to suppose that history is a form of literature,"[1] yet he set comparatively little store by the literary art of the historian. His attitude is interesting as evidence of a struggle between the scientific and literary traditions in historical writing. The character of a historian's work is largely conditioned by his views on the scope, purpose, and essential factors of history.   Some of the Ancients, as we saw, made pleasure their chief aim, and for that reason sought to embellish their narrative with every ornament that rhetoric could supply. Polybius assigned a higher purpose to history, and, both in expounding his own views, and in his criticism of others, he touched on many fundamental problems connected with the functions of the historian.   There are, of course, certain questions which in this connection the Moderns have been able to formulate more fully, though it is doubtful if even they can provide an adequate answer to them.   Such are the questions, for instance, that concern the liberty to be conceded to an historian in selecting[2] and shaping his materials, in separating the relevant from the irrelevant, and the rôle to be assigned to the imagination in re-creating the Past.

Cicero, as one would expect, was in the line of the literary tradition where the writing of history was concerned.   We have seen how he discriminates between **Cicero's views on history** " exornatores rerum " and mere " narratores," and noted his insistence[3] on the fact that, even up to Sisenna's day, no Roman historian had achieved literary excellence.   A brilliant style should be accounted an added virtue in the historian, if he has conscientiously fulfilled his other functions.   Cicero's formulation of the laws of history showed that he had a fairly adequate conception of what those functions are.   Moreover, in dealing[4] with Caesar's *Memoirs*, he had before his

---

[1] Cf. Fortescue, The Writing of History, p. 40.

[2] We have an analogous problem in connection with Biography ; cf. Burdett, " Experiment in Biography " in " Tradition and Experiment," p. 161 *et seq.*

[3] Br. 228.   [4] *Ib.* 262 ; cf. Fortescue, op. cit., p. 61 *et seq.*

mind the distinction between history proper and the
materials for history, but his characterisation of history as an
" opus oratorium maxime " shows the real trend of his
mind. He did not, of course, intend by the phrase to make
history a mere department of rhetoric, but his use of it
shows how strongly he was under the spell of the rhetorical
tradition. He considered the style of history to exhibit a
close affinity with that of epideictic oratory, and saw in
Isocrates and his school the finest models of historical
composition. He regarded speeches and descriptions as
part of the historian's ordinary stock-in-trade, and evidently[1] saw in them opportunities for rhetorical display.
How lightly he took the duty of truthfulness and impar-
tiality in the historian, is seen from his suggestions to
Lucceius regarding his treatment of the proposed monograph. He wished him to apply therein the laws of Encomium rather than those of history, and to import into
his narrative an element of the poignant and sensational, by
methods resembling those of Duris and Phylarchus. Both
from his temperament and his training we may conclude
that, if Cicero had essayed the historical work which his
friends were eagerly awaiting from his pen, he would have
been more engrossed with the manner than with the
matter, and have shown more solicitude about the niceties
of style than about a true and impartial narrative.

In general, it may be said that the rhetorical tradition
was firmly established among the Roman historians, but it
Effects of the is difficult to decide how far it reacted
rhetorical adversely upon them. Modern standards
tradition of criticism may sometimes mislead us, when
we seek an answer to this question. It is not easy to
determine how far command over the resources of rhetoric,
and the gift of a brilliant style, were considered to relieve
the ancient historian from the more important duties of his
office, supposing that he was perfectly equipped to carry
them out. Again, how far did his pre-occupations with
rhetoric lure the historian to heighten his narrative, and

---

[1] Cf. Or. 66, where he sees in speeches and descriptions a point of contact
between history and Sophistic rhetoric.

traffic in the sensational ?[1]   The historian who frequented the schools of declamation, would be especially open to this temptation.   Lastly, one might ask how far speeches, descriptions, and digressions, were looked upon by the Ancients as mere conventions, and as spheres in which an historian might display his rhetorical powers, without impairing his essential veracity.

[1] Cf. Colson, Influence of Rhetoric on History, p. 159 *et seq*.

BIBLIOGRAPHY

The following abbreviations have been used in the notes : Val. = Valmaggi ;
A.K. = Die antike Kunstprosa (Norden) ; K. = Keil, Grammatici Latini ;
Sp. = Spengel, Rhetores Graeci ; Philod. = Philodemus, Rhetorica (Sudhaus).

N.B.—The Italics used in quotations are in every case my own.

ABERCROMBIE, LASCELLES. Progress in Literature. Cambridge University Press, 1929.

ALY, WOLF. Formprobleme der frühen griechischen Prosa. Leipzig, 1929.

ALLISON, F.G. Menander. The Principal Fragments (Loeb Classical Library). London, 1921.

ARCHER, W. Play-making, A Manual of Craftsmanship. London, 1913.

ARNIM, H. VON. Leben und Werke des Dio von Prusa. Berlin, 1898.

ARNIM, J. DE. Stoicorum Veterum Fragmenta, 4 vols. Leipzig, 1905–1924.

ARNIM, J. DE. Dionis Prusaensis (quem vocant Chrysostomum) quae extant omnia. Berlin, 1893.

BAILEY, J. Poetry and Commonplace (The British Academy Lecture on English Poetry, X). London, 1919.

BABBITT, IRVING. The New Laocoon. Boston and New York, 1910.

BABBITT, IRVING. Rousseau and Romanticism. Boston and New York, 1919.

BALDI, A. Die Gegner der griechischen Bildung in Rom (bis zum Ende der Republik) (II Teil). Burghausen, 1876.

BARFIELD, O. Poetic Diction. London, 1928.

BARWICK, K. Die Gliederung der rhetorischen τέχνη und die Horazische Epistula ad Pisones. Hermes, Vol. 57. 1 (1922), p. 1 et seq.

BASCOM, J. Philosophy of English Literature (Lowell Institute Lectures). London and New York, 1909.

BAUERSCHMIDT, HANS. Ergebnisse einer Vergleichung zwischen Ciceros Schriften " De Oratore " und " Orator " (Diss.). Erlangen, 1900.

BÉNARD, CH. L'Esthétique d'Aristote et de ses Successeurs. Paris, 1889.

BIRT, THEODOR. Zwei politische Satiren des alten Rom. Marburg, 1888.

BIRT, THEODOR. Über den Aufbau der Ars poetica des Horaz (Appendix in Dieterich, Pulcinella). Leipzig, 1897.

BLASS, F. Die attische Beredsamkeit, 3 vols. Leipzig, 1887–1898.

BLASS, F. Die griechische Beredsamkeit in dem Zeitraum von Alexander bis auf Augustus. Berlin, 1865.

BLASS, F. Die Rhythmen der asianischen und römischen Kunstprosa. Leipzig, 1905.

BLAKENEY, E. H. Horace on the Art of Poetry. Edited with revised text, translation, and commentary. London, 1928.

BOISSIER, GASTON. L'Opposition sous Les Césars. Paris, 1909.

BORNECQUE, M. H. Sénèque Le Rhéteur, Controverses et Suasoires, 2 vols. Paris, 1902.

BOURGERY, A. Sénèque Prosateur, Études Littéraires et Grammaticales sur la Prose de Sénèque Le Philosophe. Paris, 1922.

BOSANQUET, B. A History of Aesthetic. London, 1910.

BOURCIEZ, J. Le "Sermo cotidianus" dans les Satires d'Horace. Bordeaux and Paris, 1927.

BROCK, M. D. Studies in Fronto and his Age. Cambridge, 1911.

BRUNETIÈRE, F. Essays in French Literature. A selection translated by D. Nichol Smith. London, 1898.

BRUNETIÈRE, F. L'Évolution des Genres dans L'Histoire de la Littérature. Paris, 1914.

BRZOSKA, JULIUS. De Canone Decem Oratorum Atticorum Quaestiones. Breslau, 1883.

BRZOSKA, JULIUS. Art. "Fronto" in Pauly-Wissowa Realencyclopädie.

BURK, A. Die Pädagogik des Isokrates als Grundlegung des humanistischen Bildungsideals. Würzburg, 1923.

BURY, J. B. The Ancient Greek Historians (Harvard Lectures). London, 1909.

BUTCHER, S. H. Harvard Lectures on Greek Subjects. London, 1904.

BUTCHER, S. H. Aristotle's Theory of Poetry and Fine Art. London, 1895.

BUTLER, H. E. Post-Augustan Poetry from Seneca to Juvenal. Oxford, 1909.

BUTLER, H. E. The Institutio Oratoria of Quintilian, with an English Translation (Loeb Classical Library), 4 vols. London, 1920–1922.

BUTLER, H. E. and OWEN, A. S. Apulei Apologia sive Pro Se De Magia Liber. Oxford, 1914.

BÜTTNER, R. Porcius Licinus und der litterarische Kreis des Q. Lutatius Catulus. Leipzig, 1893.

BYWATER, INGRAM. Aristotle on the Art of Poetry. A Revised Text with Critical Introduction, Translation, and Commentary. Oxford (Clarendon Press), 1909.

CAMPBELL, A. Y. Horace. A New Interpretation. London, 1924.

CANTER, H. V. Rhetorical Elements in the Tragedies of Seneca (University of Illinois Studies, Vol. X). Illinois, 1925.

CAPPS, E. Four Plays of Menander. Ginn and Company, Boston and London, 1910.

CAUSERET, C. Étude sur La Langue de la Rhétorique et de la Critique Littéraire dans Cicéron. Paris, 1886.

CAZAMIAN, L. Criticism in the Making. London, 1929.

CENTERWALL, J. Spartiani Vita Hadriani Commentario Illustrata. Upsala, 1870

CICHORIUS, C. Untersuchungen zu Lucilius. Berlin, 1908.

CIMA, A. L'Eloquenza Latina prima di Cicerone. Rome, 1903.

COLIN, G. Rome et la Grèce de 200 à 146 avant Jésus-Christ. Paris, 1905.

COLSON, F. H. M. Fabii Quintiliani Institutionis Oratoriae Liber I. Edited with Introduction and Commentary. Cambridge, 1924.

COLSON, F. H. The Analogist and Anomalist Controversy. Class. Quarterly, XIII. 1, Jan., 1919.

COLSON, F. H. Some Considerations as to the Influence of Rhetoric on History. Proceedings of the Classical Association, Vol. XIV (Jan., 1917), pp. 149–173.

COMPARETTI, D. Vergil in the Middle Ages (English Translation by E. F. M. Benecke). London, 1908.

CONNINGTON, J. and NETTLESHIP, H. The Works of Virgil, Vol. I. Fifth Edition revised by F. Haverfield. London, 1898.

COOK, A. S. The Art of Poetry. The Poetical Treatises of Horace, Vida, and Boileau. Boston, 1892.

COOPER, LANE. An Aristotelian Theory of Comedy with an Adaptation of the Poetics and a Translation of the " Tractatus Coislinianus." Oxford (B. Blackwell), 1924.

COPE, E. M. The Rhetoric of Aristotle, with a Commentary (Revised and Edited by J. E. Sandys), 3 vols. Cambridge, 1877.

COPE, E. M. An Introduction to Aristotle's Rhetoric. London and Cambridge, 1867.

COURBAUD, E. Les Procédés d'Art de Tacite dans les " Histoires." Paris, 1918.

CROISET, A. Thucydide Livres I–II. Paris, 1886.

CURCIO, G. Le Opere Rhetoriche di M. Tullio Cicerone. Studio Critico. Acireale, 1900.

CURCIO, G. De Ciceronis et Calvi Reliquorumque Atticorum Arte Dicendi Quaestiones. Acide prope Cataniam, 1899.

DE GOURMONT, REMY. Decadence and other Essays on the Culture of Ideas (translated by W. Bradley). London, 1921.

DE GOURMONT, REMY. Le Problème du Style. Paris, 1902.

DE WITT, N. W. Virgil's Biographia Litteraria. Humphrey Milford, Oxford University Press, 1923.

DICK, A. Martianus Capella (text). Leipzig, 1925.

DIELS, H. Die Fragmente der Vorsokratiker, 2 vols. Berlin, 1906–1910.

DIETERICH, A. Pulcinella. Pompeianische Wandbilder und römische Satyrspiele. Leipzig, 1897.

DREW, D. L. Culex. Sources and their Bearing on the Problem of Authorship. Oxford (B. Blackwell), 1925.

DUCKETT, E. S. Studies in Ennius (Bryn Mawr College Monographs, Vol. 18). Bryn Mawr, 1915.

DUFF, J. WIGHT. A Literary History of Rome in the Silver Age. London, 1927.

DZIATZKO, K. Ausgewählte Komödien des P. Terentius Afer, Band I. Phormio (vierte Auflage bearbeitet von Dr. E. Hauler). Leipzig, 1913.

DZIATZKO, K. Ausgewählte Komödien, Band II. Adelphoe (zweite Auflage bearbeitet von Dr. R. Kauer). Leipzig, 1921.

EDWARD, W. A. The Suasoriae of Seneca the Elder. Introductory Essay, Text, Translation, and Explanatory Notes. Cambridge University Press, 1928.

EGGER, ÉMILE. Essai Sur l'Histoire de la Critique chez les Grecs (3rd ed.). Paris, 1887.

EGGER, MAX. Denys d'Halicarnasse. Essai sur la Critique Littéraire et la Rhétorique chez les Grecs au siècle d'Auguste. Paris, 1902.

ELLIS, ROBINSON. A Commentary on Catullus (2nd ed.). Oxford (Clarendon Press), 1889.

ELLIS, ROBINSON. Aetna. Oxford (Clarendon Press), 1901.

ERNESTI, J. C. T. Lexicon Technologiae Latinorum Rhetoricae. Leipzig, 1797.

FABIA, PH. Les Prologues de Térence. Paris–Avignon, 1888.

FAIDER, P. Études sur Sénèque. Gand, 1921.

FAIRCLOUGH, H. RUSHTON. Horace's View of the Relations of Satire and Comedy. Am. J. Phil. Vol. 34 (1913), p. 183 *et seq.*

FALLS, C. The Critic's Armoury. London, 1924.

FARRINGTON, B. Primum Graius Homo. An Anthology of Latin Translations from the Greek from Ennius to Livy. Cambridge University Press, 1927.

FISKE, G. C. Lucilius and Horace. A Study in the Classical Theory of Imitation. University of Wisconsin Studies, No. 7, 1920.

FLICKINGER, R. C. The Greek Theater and its Drama. University of Chicago Press, Illinois, 1918.

FORTESCUE, SIR JOHN. The Writing of History. London, 1926.

FRANK, TENNEY. Vergil. A Biography. Oxford (B. Blackwell), 1922.

FRANK, TENNEY. "Cicero and the Poetae Novi." Am. J. Phil. Vol. 40, p. 396 *et seq.*

FRIEDLÄNDER, L. Roman Life and Manners under the Early Empire, English Translation, Vols. I–III, by Leonard Magnus and J. H. Freese, Vol. IV (Appendices and Notes) by A. B. Gough. London, 1908–1913.

FRIEDLÄNDER, L. M. Valerii Martialis Epigrammaton Libri mit Erklärenden Anmerkungen. Leipzig, 1886.

FUNAIOLI, H. Grammaticae Romanae Fragmenta, Vol. I (all published). Leipzig, 1907.

GAFFIOT, F. La Prologue de l'Heautontimorumenos et la question de la Contamination. Revue de Phil. 1904, p. 128 *et seq.*

GARDNER, E. G. "Dante as Literary Critic," in Dante : Essays in Commemoration, 1321–1921. London, 1921.

GASELEE, S. The Love Romances of Parthenius and other Fragments (in volume with " Daphnis and Chloe "), Loeb Classical Library. London, 1924.

GAYLEY, C. M. and Scott, F. N. An Introduction to the Methods and Materials of Literary Criticism. Boston, 1901.

GEIGENMUELLER, P. Quaestiones Dionysianae de Vocabulis Artis Criticae. Leipzig, 1908.

GEORGII, H. Die antike Äneiskritik aus den Scholien und anderen Quellen. Stuttgart, 1891.

GEORGII, H. Tiberi Claudi Donati Interpretationes Vergilianae. Leipzig, 1905.

GERCKE, A. Seneca-Studien (Abdruck aus XXII Supplementband der Jahrb. für class. Phil.). Leipzig, 1895.

GERLACH, FR. D. C. Lucilii Saturarum Reliquiae. Zurich, 1846.

GILES, J. A. Valerii Catonis Carmina. Editio Putschiana repetita cum notis Putschii et Wernsdorfii omnibus. London, 1838.

GODLEY, A. D. "Senecan Tragedy " in English Literature and the Classics. Oxford (Clarendon Press), 1912.

GOELZER, H. Étude Lexicographique et Grammaticale de la Latinité de Saint Jérome. Paris, 1884.

GOLDBACHER, AL.   Der Hellenismus in Rom zur Zeit der Scipionen und seine Gegner (Inaugurationsrede).   Graz, 1891.

GOSSE, E.   Malherbe and the Classical Reaction in the Seventeenth Century (Taylorian Lecture).   Oxford (Clarendon Press), 1920.

GRANT, M. A.   The Ancient Rhetorical Theories of the Laughable. University of Wisconsin Studies, No. 21.   1924.

GRANT, M. A. and FISKE, G. C.   Cicero's " Orator " and Horace's " Ars Poetica."   Harvard Studies in Classical Philology, Vol. XXXV (1924).

GREENE, W. C.   Plato's View of Poetry.   Harvard Studies in Classical Philology, Vol. XXIX (1918).

GROEBE, P.   Art. " Asinius Pollio " in Pauly–Wissowa Realencyclopädie.

GUDEMAN, A.   P. Cornelii Taciti Dialogus De Oratoribus (zweite Auflage).   Leipzig, 1914.

GUGLIELMINO, F.   La Parodia nella Commedia Greca Antica. Catania, 1928.

GWYNN, A.   Roman Education from Cicero to Quintilian.   Oxford (Clarendon Press), 1926.

HACK, R. K.   The Doctrine of Literary Forms.   Harvard Studies in Classical Philology, Vol. XXVII (1916).

HAENNI, P. R.   Die litterarische Kritik in Ciceros " Brutus." Sarnen, 1905.

H¨FNER, SIEGFRIED.   Die literarischen Pläne Ciceros.   Coburg, 1928.

HAHN, L.   Rom und Romanismus im griechisch-römischen Osten bis auf die Zeit Hadrians.   Leipzig, 1906.

HAIGH, A. E.   The Tragic Drama of the Greeks.   Oxford (Clarendon Press), 1896.

HALM, C.   Rhetores Latini Minores, 2 vols.   Leipzig, 1863.

HAMILTON, CLAYTON.   Problems of the Playwright.   London, 1917.

HARDIE, W. R.   Res Metrica.   An Introduction to the Study of Greek and Roman Versification.   Oxford (Clarendon Press), 1920.

HARDIE, W. R.   The Culex.   Class. Quar. Jan., 1920.

HARNECKER, O.   Cicero und die Attiker.   Fleckeis. Jahrb. 125 (1882), p. 601 et seq.

HARTMANN, P.   De Canone Decem Oratorum.   Göttingen, 1891.

HECK, H.   Zur Entstehung des rhetorischen Attizismus.   Munich, 1917.

HEINZE, R.   De Horatio Bionis Imitatore.   Bonn, 1888.

HEINZE, R.   Virgils epische Technik (dritte Auflage).   Leipzig 1915.

HELM, R.   Lucian und Menipp.   Leipzig, 1906.

HENDERSON, B.W. The Life and Principate of the Emperor Hadrian. London, 1923.

HENDRICKSON, G. L. A Pre-Varronian Chapter in Literary History. Am. J. Phil. Vol. XIX (1898).

HENDRICKSON, G. L. The Peripatetic Mean of Style and the Three Stylistic Characters. Am. J. Phil. Vol. XXV (1904).

HENDRICKSON, G. L. The Origin and Meaning of the Ancient Characters of Style. Am. J. Phil. Vol. XXVI (1905).

HENDRICKSON, G. L. Literary Sources in Cicero's "Brutus." Am. J. Phil. Vol. XXVII (1906).

HENDRICKSON, G. L. The "De Analogia" of Julius Caesar, its Occasion, Nature, and Date, with Additional Fragments. Class. Phil. Vol. I (1906).

HENDRICKSON, G. L. The First Satire of Persius. Class. Phil. Vol. XXIII (1928).

HENDRICKSON, G. L. Horace and Valerius Cato. (I) Class. Phil. Vol. XI (1916), p. 249 et seq., (II) Vol. XII (1917), p. 77 et seq., (III) Ib. p. 329 et seq.

HENDRICKSON, G. L. Horace, Serm. I, 4 : A Protest and a Programme. Am. J. Phil. Vol. XXI (1900).

HENDRICKSON, G. L. Horace and Lucilius : A Study of Horace, Serm. I, 10, in Studies in Honor of Basil L. Gildersleeve. Baltimore, 1902.

HENNEQUIN, É. La Critique Scientifique. Paris, 1888.

HERTZ, M. Renaissance und Rococo in der römischen Literatur. Berlin, 1865.

HEVER, C. De Praeceptis Romanorum Euphonicis. Jena, 1909.

HIRZEL, R. Der Dialog. Ein literarhistorischer Versuchung, 2 vols. Leipzig, 1895.

HOWARD, W. G. Laokoon. Lessing Herder Goethe. Edited with an Introduction and Commentary. New York, 1910.

HUBBELL, H. M. The Influence of Isocrates on Cicero, Dionysius, and Aristides. Yale University Press, 1913.

HUBBELL, H. M. The Rhetorica of Philodemus. Translation and Commentary. (Transactions of the Connecticut Academy of Arts and Sciences, Vol. 23.) New Haven, Connecticut, 1920.

IMMISCH, O. Gorgiae Helena. Berlin and Leipzig (De Gruyter and Co)., 1927.

JACHMANN, G. "Die Composition des Plautinischen Poenulus," in Χάριτες F. Leo zum sechzigsten Geburtstag dargebracht. Berlin, 1911.

JACOBY, F. Die Fragmente der griechischen Historiker (in progress). Parts I, II, A, B, and C. Berlin, 1923–1930.

JAHN, O.   Ciceros Brutus bearbeitet von W. Kroll (5th ed.).   Berlin, 1908.

JEBB, R. C.   The Attic Orators from Antiphon to Isaeus, 2 vols. London, 1876.

JEBB, R. C.   The Characters of Theophrastus (2nd edition edited by J. E. Sandys).   London, 1909.

JEBB, R. C.   " The Speeches of Thucydides " in Essays and Addresses.   Cambridge University Press, 1907.

JENSEN, C.   Philodemos über die Gedichte (fünftes Buch).   Berlin, 1923.

JONES, H. L. and STERRETT, J. R. S.   The Geography of Strabo, Vols. I–VII (all published).   London, 1917–1930.

JORDAN, H.   Die Einleitung des Ciceronischen Brutus.   Hermes, Vol. VI, 1872.

KAIBEL, G.   Comicorum Graecorum Fragmenta, Vol. I.   Berlin, 1899.

KAIBEL, G.   Athenaei Naucratitae Dipnosophistarum Libri, 3 vols. Leipzig, 1887–1896.

KALINKA, E.   Hellenica Oxyrhynchia (Teubner Texts).   Leipzig, 1927.

KEIL, H.   Grammatici Latini, Vol. I.   Leipzig, 1857.

KELLETT, E. E.   The Whirligig of Taste (Hogarth Lectures, No. 8).   London, 1929.

KER, W. P.   The Art of Poetry (Inaugural Lecture).   Oxford (Clarendon Press), 1920.

KER, W. P.   Essays of John Dryden : Selected and Edited, 2 vols. Oxford (Clarendon Press), 1900.

KIESSLING, AD.   Annaei Senecae Oratorum et Rhetorum Sententiae Divisiones Colores (Teubner Texts).   Leipzig, 1922.

KIESSLING, AD.   Q. Horatius Flaccus. Satiren (fünfte Auflage erneuert von R. Heinze).   Berlin, 1921.

KIESSLING, AD.   Q. Horatius Flaccus. Briefe (dritte Auflage besorgt von R. Heinze).   Berlin, 1908.

KOCH, G. A.   Cornelii Nepotis Vitae.   Leipzig, 1855.

KOCK, TH.   Comicorum Atticorum Fragmenta, 3 vols.   Leipzig, 1880–1888.

KROLL, W.   Studien zum Verständnis der römischen Literatur. Stuttgart, 1924.

KROLL, W.   Randbemerkungen. Rhein. Mus. 1907, p. 86 *et seq.*

KROLL, W.   Die historische Stellung von Horazens Ars poetica. Sokrates, LXXII Band, 3–4 Heft.   Berlin, 1918.

KROLL, W.   M. Tullii Ciceronis Orator (als Ersatz der Ausgabe von O. Jahn).   Berlin, 1913.

KROLL, W. Cicero und die Rhetorik. N. Jahrb. für das klass. Altertum, VI (1903).

KROLL, W. C. Valerius Catullus (2nd ed.). Leipzig, 1929.

KUNST, K. Studien zur griechisch-römischen Komödie. Vienna and Leipzig, 1919.

LAFAYE, G. Catulle et ses Modèles. Paris, 1894.

LAMB, W. R. M. Clio Enthroned. A Study of Prose-form in Thucydides. Cambridge University Press, 1914.

LANDGRAF, G. Kommentar zu Ciceros Rede Pro Sex. Roscio Amerino (zweite Auflage). Leipzig, 1914.

LAURAND, L. Étude sur le Style des Discours de Cicéron. Paris, 1907.

LAURAND, L. De M. Tullii Ciceronis Studiis Rhetoricis. Paris, 1907.

LEGENDRE, P. Études Tironiennes. Commentaire sur la VIᵉ Églogue de Virgile (Bibliothèque de l'École des Hautes Études, Fascicule, 165). Paris, 1907.

LEGRAND, PH. E. The New Greek Comedy (translated by J. Loeb). London, 1917.

LEJAY, P. Histoire de la Littérature Latine des Origines à Plaute (Publiée par L. Pichard). Paris, 1923.

LEJAY, P. Plaute (Publiée par L. Pichard). Paris, 1925.

LEJAY, P. Oeuvres d'Horace. Satires. Paris, 1911.

LEO, F. Geschichte der römischen Literatur, Vol. I (all published). Berlin, 1913.

LEO, F. Plautinische Forschungen zur Kritik und Geschichte der Komödie. Berlin, 1912.

LEO, F. Die griechisch-römische Biographie nach ihrer litterarischen Form. Leipzig, 1901.

LESSING, G. E. Selected Prose Works (translated by E. C. Beasley and H. Zimmern). Bohn's Libraries. London, 1890.

LEWES, G. H. The Principles of Success in Literature. (Scott Library.)

LINCKE, E. P. Cornelius Scipio Ämilianus. Jahresbericht des Wettiner Gymnasiums zu Dresden, 1898.

LINTILHAC, E. De J.-C. Scaligeri Poetice. Paris, 1887.

LOWES, J. L. Convention and Revolt in Poetry (2nd ed.). London, 1930.

LUCAS, F. L. Seneca and Elizabethan Tragedy. Cambridge University Press, 1922.

LUCAS, F. L. Tragedy in Relation to Aristotle's Poetics (Hogarth Lectures, No. 2). London, 1927.

LUNDERSTEDT, P. De C. Maecenatis Fragmentis (Commentationes Philologae Jenenses). Leipzig, 1911.

MacClintock, L. Sainte-Beuve's Critical Theory and Practice after 1849. University of Chicago Press, 1920.

McMahon, A. P. " Seven Questions on Aristotelian Definitions of Tragedy and Comedy." Harvard Studies in Classical Philology, Vol. 40.

Mahaffy, J. P. The Silver Age of the Greek World. London, 1906.

Marchesi, C. Seneca. Messina, 1920.

Marx, F. C. Lucilii Carminum Reliquiae, 2 vols. Leipzig, 1904.

Marx, F. Art. " Accius," Pauly-Wissowa R.E.

Marx, F. Incerti Auctoris de Ratione Dicendi ad C. Herennium Libri IV. Leipzig, 1894.

Mayer, A. Theophrasti Περὶ Λέξεως Libri Fragmenta. Leipzig, 1910.

Merchant, F. I. Seneca the Philosopher and his Theory of Style. Am. J. Phil. Vol. XXVI (1905).

Meyer, W. Quaestiones Terentianae. Leipzig, 1902.

Meyer, H. Oratorum Romanorum Fragmenta. Zürich, 1832.

Michaut, G. Histoire de la Comédie Romaine—Sur les Trétaux latins. Paris, 1912.

Mommsen, Th. The History of Rome (translated by W. P. Dickson), 5 vols. New edition, London, 1894–1908.

Montague, C. E. Dramatic Values. London, 1911.

Moore, J. L. Servius on the Tropes and Figures of Vergil. Am. J. Phil. Vol. XII (1891), p. 157 *et seq.*, p. 267 *et seq.*

Morr, J. Poseidonios von Rhodos über Dichtung und Redekunst. Wiener Studien, XLV Band, 1926.

Moulton, R. G. The Modern Study of Literature. An Introduction to Literary Theory and Interpretation. University of Chicago Press, 1915.

Moulton, R. G. The Ancient Classical Drama. A Study in Literary Evolution. Oxford (Clarendon Press), 1890.

Moulton, R. G. World Literature and its Place in General Culture. New York, 1916.

Moulton, R. G. Shakespeare as a Dramatic Artist. Oxford (Clarendon Press), 1885.

Mueller, L. Quintus Ennius. Eine Einleitung in das Studium der römischen Poesie. St. Petersburg, 1884.

Mueller, L. Noni Marcelli Compendiosa Doctrina, 2 vols. Leipzig, 1888.

Mueller, L. Q. Horatii Flacci Sermonum et Epistularum Libri. I Theil : Satiren. Vienna (F. Tempsky), 1891.

Munro, H. A. J. T. Lucreti Cari De Rerum Natura Libri Sex, 2 vols. (4th ed.). Cambridge, 1886.

MURRAY, G. The Classical Tradition in Poetry. Oxford University Press, 1927.

MURRY, J. MIDDLETON. The Problem of Style. Oxford University Press, 1922.

MYERS, F. W. H. Wordsworth (English Men of Letters). London, 1906.

NASSAL, F. Aesthetisch-Rhetorische Beziehungen zwischen Dionysius von Halicarnass und Cicero. Tübingen, 1910.

NAVARRE, O. Essai sur la Rhétorique Grecque avant Aristote. Paris, 1900.

NETTLESHIP, H. The Noctes Atticae of Aulus Gellius. Am. J. Phil. Vol. IV (1883).

NISARD, D. Études de Moeurs et de Critique sur les Poëtes Latins de la Décadence, 2 vols. Paris, 1878.

NORDEN, E. Ennius und Vergilius. Leipzig, 1915.

NORDEN, E. Die antike Kunstprosa vom VI. Jahrhundert v. Chr. bis in die Zeit der Renaissance, 2 vols. Leipzig–Berlin, 1909.

NORDEN, E. P. Vergilius Maro. Aeneis Buch VI, (2nd ed.). Leipzig–Berlin, 1916.

NORDEN, E. In Varronis Saturas Menippeas Observationes Selectae. Leipzig, 1891.

NORDEN, E. Die Composition und Litteraturgattung des Horazischen Epistula ad Pisones. Hermes, Vol. XL.

NORWOOD, G. The Art of Terence. Oxford (B. Blackwell), 1923.

NORWOOD, G. Greek Tragedy. London, 1920.

Ogle, M. B. "Molle atque Facetum." Am. J. Phil. Vol. XXXVII (1916), p. 327 et seq.

OLTRAMARE, A. Les Origines de la Diatribe Romaine. Lausanne–Geneva (Payot & Co.), 1926.

PADELFORD, F. M. Essays on the Study and Use of Poetry by Plutarch and Basil the Great. Yale Studies in English, XV. New York, 1902.

Pascal, C. La Critica dei Poeti Romani in Orazio. Catania, 1920.

PASCAL, C. Scritti Varii di Letteratura Latina. Turin–Milan (Paravia & Co.), 1920.

PASQUALI, G. Orazio Lirico. Florence, 1920.

PATER, W. Appreciations. With an Essay on Style. London (Macmillan and Co.), 1890.

PATER, W. Marius the Epicurean, 2 vols. London (Macmillan and Co.), 1902.

PELAYO, MENÉNDEZ Y. Historia de las Ideas Estéticas en Espāna, Vol. I (Periodo Hispano-Romano), 3rd ed. Madrid, 1909.

PERRY, T. S. From Opitz to Lessing. Boston, 1885.

PETER, H. Historicorum Romanorum Reliquiae, 2 vols. Leipzig, 1914.

PETER, H. Wahrheit und Kunst. Geschichtschreibung und Plagiat im klassischen Altertum. Leipzig–Berlin, 1911.

PETER, H. Die geschichtliche Litteratur über die römische Kaizerzeit bis Theodosius I. und ihre Quellen, 2 vols. Leipzig, 1897.

PETERSON, W. M. Fabi Quintiliani Institutionis Oratoriae Liber Decimus. Oxford (Clarendon Press), 1891.

PETERSON, W. Cornelii Taciti Dialogus De Oratoribus. Oxford (Clarendon Press), 1893.

PIDERIT, W. Cicero De Oratore (sechste Auflage besorgt von O. Harnecker), 3 vols. Leipzig, 1886.

PLESSIS, F. Calvus. Avec un Essai sur la Polémique de Cicéron et des Attiques par J. Poirot. Paris, 1896.

POIRET, JULES. Essai sur L'Éloquence Judiciaire à Rome pendant la République. Paris, 1887.

POLHEIM, K. Die lateinische Reimprosa. Berlin, 1925.

POST, C. R. The Dramatic Art of Menander. Harvard Studies in Classical Philology, Vol. XXIV (1913).

PRESCOTT, H. W. The New Fragment of Callimachus' Coma Berenices. Class. Phil. Vol. XXIV. 3 (July, 1929).

PRICKARD, A. O. Aristotle on the Art of Poetry. London, 1891.

PRÜMM, C. Quaestionum Tullianarum ad Dialogi De Oratore Partes Philosophicas quae dicuntur spectantium Specimen. Saarbrück, 1927.

RADERMACHER, L. "Studien zur Geschichte der griechischen Rhetorik." Rhein. Mus. LIV (1899), p. 285 *et seq.; ib.* p. 351 *et seq.*, "Über die Anfänge des Atticismus."

RALEIGH, W. Style. London, 1911.

REGEL, G. De Vergilio Poetarum Imitatore Testimonia. Göttingen, 1907.

REICH, H. Der Mimus, 2 vols. Berlin, 1903.

REID, J. S. M. Tulli Ciceronis Academica. London, 1885.

REID, J. S. M. Tulli Ciceronis De Finibus Libri I, II. Cambridge University Press, 1925.

REITZENSTEIN, R. Werden und Wesen der Humanität im Altertum. Strassburg, 1907.

REITZENSTEIN, R. M. Terentius Varro und Johannes Mauropus von Euchaita. Eine Studie zur Geschichte der Sprachwissenschaft. Leipzig, 1901.

REITZENSTEIN, R. Scipio Aemilianus und die stoische Rhetorik. Strassburger Festschrift zur XLVI Versammlung deutscher Philologen. Strassburg, 1901.

REITZENSTEIN, R. Hellenistische Wundererzählungen. Leipzig, 1906.

RIBBECK, O. Tragicorum Latinorum Reliquiae. Leipzig, 1852.

RIBBECK, O. Alazon. Ein Beitrag zur antiken Ethologie und zur Kentniss der griechisch-römischen Komödie. Leipzig, 1882.

RIBBECK, O. Die römische Tragödie im Zeitalter der Republik. Leipzig, 1875.

RIDGEWAY, W. The Origin of Tragedy. Cambridge University Press, 1910.

RIESE, A. M. Terenti Varronis Saturarum Menippearum Reliquiae. Leipzig, 1865.

RIGAULT, M. H. Histoire de la Querelle des Anciens et des Modernes. Paris, 1856.

ROBERTS, W. RHYS. Dionysius of Halicarnassus. On Literary Composition. London, 1910.

ROBERTS, W. RHYS. Longinus. On the Sublime. Cambridge University Press, 1907.

ROBERTS, W. RHYS. Demetrius. On Style. Cambridge University Press, 1902.

ROBERTS, W. RHYS. Dionysius of Halicarnassus. The Three Literary Letters. Cambridge University Press, 1901.

ROBERTS, W. RHYS. Greek Rhetoric and Literary Criticism. London (Harrap and Co.), 1928.

ROBERTSON, J. M. Essays towards a Critical Method. London, 1889.

ROCHEBLAVE, S. De M. Fabio Quintiliano L. Annaei Senecae Judice. Paris, 1890.

ROHDE, E. Der griechische Roman und seine Vorläufer (3rd ed.). Leipzig, 1914.

ROHDE, E. Die asianische Rhetorik und die zweite Sophistik. Rhein. Mus. XLI (1886).

ROSENBERG, A. Einleitung und Quellenkunde zur römischen Geschichte. Berlin, 1921.

RUCKDESCHEL, F. Archaismen und Vulgarismen in der Sprache des Horaz. Munich, 1910.

SABINE, G. H. and SMITH, S. B. Marcus Tullius Cicero. On the Commonwealth. Columbus : The Ohio State University Press, 1929.

SAINTSBURY, G. A History of Criticism and Literary Taste in Europe from the Earliest Texts to the Present Day (3rd ed.), 3 vols. Edinburgh and London, 1908–1917.

SAINTE-BEUVE. Causeries de Lundi, 15 vols. Paris, 1857–1862.

SANDYS, J. E. M. Tulli Ciceronis Ad M. Brutum Orator. Cambridge University Press, 1885.

SANDYS, J. E.   Aristotle's Constitution of Athens.   London, 1893.
SANDYS, J. E.   A History of Classical Scholarship (2nd ed.), 3 vols.
Cambridge University Press, 1906–1908.
SCALA, RUDOLF V.   Die Studien des Polybios.   Stuttgart, 1890.
SCALA, RUDOLF V.   Isokrates und die Geschichtschreibung (Ver-
handlungen der XLI Versammlung deutscher Philologen und
Schulmänner in München, 1891).   Leipzig, 1892.
SCHANZ, M.   Geschichte der römischen Litteratur (3rd ed.), 4 vols.
(Handbuch Iwan Müller, VIII).   Munich, 1907–1920.
SCHELLER, P.   De Hellenistica Historiae Conscribendae Arte.
Leipzig, 1911.
SCHLITTENBAUER, S.   Die Tendenz von Ciceros Orator. Jahrb. für
klass. Phil. Supplementb. 28 (1903).
SCHMEKEL, A.   Die Philosophie der mittleren Stoa.   Berlin, 1892.
SCHMID, W.   Der Atticismus in seinen Haupvertretern von Diony-
sius von Halicarnass bis auf den zweiten Philostratus, 4 vols.
Stuttgart, 1887–1897.
SCHMID, W.   Über den kulturgeschichtlichen Zusammenhang und
die Bedeutung der griechischen Renaissance in der Römerzeit.
Leipzig, 1898.
SCHNEIDEWIN, M.   Die antike Humanität.   Berlin, 1897.
SCOTT, G.   The Architecture of Humanism.   A Study in the
History of Taste.   London, 1914.
SCOTT-JAMES, R. A.   The Making of Literature.   Some Principles
of Criticism examined in the light of Ancient and Modern
Theory.   London, 1928.
SCHRADER, H.   Telephos der Pergamener. Hermes, Vol. XXXVII,
p. 530 et seq.
SCHWIERCZINA, TH.   Frontoniana.   Breslau, 1883.
SHAIRP, J. C.   Aspects of Poetry.   Boston and New York (Houghton,
Mifflin Co.), 1881.
SHEEHAN, M.   De Fide Artis Rhetoricae Isocrati tributae.   Bonn,
1901.
SHEPPARD, J. T.   The Oedipus Tyrannus of Sophocles.   Cambridge
University Press, 1920.
SIEGFRIED, W.   Studien zur geschichtlichen Anschauung des Poly-
bios.   Leipzig–Berlin, 1928.
SIHLER, E. G.   The Collegium Poetarum at Rome.   Am. J. Phil.
XXVI (1905).
SIHLER, E. G.   Cicero of Arpinum.   A Political and Literary Bio-
graphy.   New Haven : Yale University Press, 1914.
SIKES, E. E.   Roman Poetry.   London, 1923.
SIMPSON, P.   Ben Jonson's Every Man in his Humour.   Oxford
(Clarendon Press), 1919.

SKUTSCH, F.   Aus Vergils Frühzeit.   Leipzig, 1901 ; Part II, Gallus und Vergil.   Leipzig, 1906.

SMILEY, C. N.   " Seneca and the Stoic Theory of Literary Style," in Classical Studies in honour of Charles Forster Smith.   Madison, 1919.

SPENGEL, L.   M. Terenti Varronis De Lingua Latina Libri.   Berlin, 1885.

SPENGEL, L.   Rhetores Graeci, 3 vols.   Leipzig, 1853–1856.

SPINGARN, J. E.   A History of Literary Criticism in the Renaissance.   New York (Columbia University Press), 1912.

SPINGARN, J. E.   Critical Essays of the Seventeenth Century, 3 vols.   Oxford (Clarendon Press), 1908–1909.

SPINGARN, J. E.   Creative Criticism.   New York, 1917.

SPRING, E.   A Study of Exposition in Greek Tragedy.   Harvard Studies in Classical Philology, Vol. XXVIII.

STARKIE, W. J. M.   The Acharnians of Aristophanes.   London, 1909.

STEINMANN, H.   De artis poeticae veteris parte quae est περὶ ἠθῶν.   Göttingen, 1907.

STEINTHAL, H.   Geschichte der Sprachwissenschaft bei den Griechen und Römern, 2 vols.   Berlin, 1890–1891.

STEMPLINGER, E.   Das Plagiat in der griechischen Literatur.   Leipzig-Berlin, 1912.

STEPHEN, LESLIE.   English Literature and Society in the Eighteenth Century (Ford Lectures).   London, 1904.

STEUART, E. M.   The Annals of Quintus Ennius.   Cambridge University Press, 1925.

STEVENSON, R. L.   " On Some Technical Elements of Style in Literature," in Essays Literary and Critical (Tusitala ed. vol. XXVIII, Heinemann, Ltd.).

STRACHAN-DAVIDSON, J. L.   " Polybius," in Hellenica.   Essays edited by Evelyn Abbott.   London, 1898.

STRILLER, F.   De Stoicorum Studiis Rhetoricis (Breslauer philologische Abhandlungen, Band I).   Breslau, 1886.

STROUX, J.   De Theophrasti Virtutibus Dicendi.   Leipzig, 1912.

SUDHAUS, S.   Philodemi Volumina Rhetorica (2 vols. and Supplementum).   Leipzig, 1902–1906.

SUESS, W.   Petronii Imitatio Sermonis Plebei qua necessitate conjungatur cum Grammatica illius aetatis Doctrina.   Dorpat, 1927.

SUMMERS, W. C.   The Silver Age of Latin Literature.   London, 1920.

SUMMERS, W. C.   Select Letters of Seneca.   London, 1910.

SUMMERS, W. C. The Declamations under the Empire. (Reprinted from Classical Association Proceedings, Vol. X. Jan., 1913.)

SUSEMIHL, F. Geschichte der griechischen Litteratur in der Alexandrinerzeit, 2 vols. Leipzig, 1891–1892.

SÜSS, W. Ethos. Studien zur älteren griechischen Rhetorik. Leipzig–Berlin, 1910.

TATE, J. Horace and the Moral Function of Poetry. Cl. Q. Vol. XXII. 2 (April, 1928).

TEMPEST, N. R. The Rhythm of English Prose. Cambridge University Press, 1930.

TERZAGHI, N. Fabula. Prolegomeni allo Studio del Teatro Antico, Vol. I. Milan (Remo Sandron), 1911.

Teuffel, W. S. History of Roman Literature. Revised and enlarged by Ludwig Schwabe. Translated from the Fifth German edition by G. C. W. Warr, 2 vols. London, 1900.

THOMPSON, W. H. The Phaedrus of Plato. London, 1868.

THOMPSON, W. H. The Gorgias of Plato (2nd ed.). London, 1894.

Tradition and Experiment in Present-day Literature. Addresses delivered at the City Literary Institute. London (Humphrey Milford), 1929.

ULLMANN, R. La Technique des Discours dans Salluste, Tite Live, et Tacite. Oslo, 1927.

ULRICI, H. Charakteristik der antiken Historiographie. Berlin, 1833.

USENER, H. Dionysii Halicarnassensis Librorum De Imitatione Reliquiae Epistulaeque Criticae Duae. Bonn, 1889.

VAHLEN, J. Ennianae Poesis Reliquiae (Anastatic Reprint). Leipzig, 1928.

VAHLEN, J. In M. Terentii Varronis Saturarum Menippearum Reliquias Conjectanea. Leipzig, 1858.

VALMAGGI, L. Q. Ennio. I Frammenti degli Annali. Turin, 1923.

VAN HOOK, L. The Metaphorical Terminology of Greek Rhetoric and Literary Criticism. Chicago University Press, 1905.

VOLKMANN, R. Die Rhetorik der Griechen und Römer (2nd ed.). Leipzig, 1885.

VAUGHAN, C. E. English Literary Criticism (The Warwick Library of English Literature). London.

VAUGHAN, C. E. The Romantic Revolt. Edinburgh and London, 1907.

WACHSMUTH, C. Einleitung in das Studium der alten Geschichte. Leipzig, 1895.

WALKER, R. J. The Ichneutae of Sophocles. London, 1919.

WALKER, E. M. The Hellenica Oxyrhynchia : its authorship and authority. Oxford (Clarendon Press), 1913.

WALSDORFF, F. Die antike Urteile über Platons Stil. Leipzig, 1927.

WALTZ, AD. Des Variations de la Langue et de la Métrique d' Horace dans ses différents ouvrages. Paris, 1881.

WARREN, T. H. Essays of Poets and Poetry, Ancient and Modern. London, 1909.

WEHRLI, F. Zur Geschichte der allegorischen Deutung Homers im Altertum. Borna–Leipzig (R. Noske), 1928.

WEINREICH, O. Senecas Apocolocyntosis. Berlin, 1923.

WESSNER, P. Aeli Donati quod fertur Commentum Terenti. Accedunt Eugraphi Commentum et Scholia Bembina, 3 vols. Leipzig, 1902–1908.

WEST, G. Deucalion or the Future of Literary Criticism. London, 1930.

WESTERMANN, A. Geschichte der Beredtsamkeit in Griechenland und Rom (2 parts). Leipzig, 1833–1835.

WILAMOWITZ-MOELLENDORFF, U. VON. Menander. Das Schiedsgericht (Epitrepontes). Berlin, 1925.

WILAMOWITZ-MOELLENDORFF, U. VON. " Asianismus und Attikismus." Hermes, Vol. XXXV (1900).

WILKINS, A. S. M. Tullii Ciceronis De Oratore Libri Tres, 3 vols. Oxford (Clarendon Press), 1888–1892.

WOODRUFF, L. B. Reminiscences of Ennius in Silius Italicus. New York (the Macmillan Company), 1910.

WORDSWORTH, W. Prefaces and Essays on Poetry (edited by A. G. George). Boston (Heath & Co.), 1892.

WUNDERER, C. Polybios. Lebens und Weltanschauung aus dem zweiten vorchristlichen Jahrhundert. Leipzig, 1927.

WYNDHAM, GEORGE. " Ronsard and La Pléiade " in Essays in Romantic Literature. London, 1919.

ZILLINGER, W. Cicero und die altrömischen Dichter. Würzburg, 1911.

INDEX

Brutus—*contd.*

Atticist leanings of, 256, 257; poetry, 452

Cicero on, 170, 256, 257; in Cicero's *Brutus*, 176, 178, 263–4, 323–4

Mentioned, 166, 191 *n.*³

βωμολόχος (or buffoon), 359–60, 361

Cacophony, 89

Cacozeli, 327

Cacozelia, 214 *and nn.*¹, ²

Caecilius, the comic poet, 8, 66, 67; and contamination, 17–18; style, 25

Plocium, 18

Cicero's criticism of, 50, 144, 147, 148, 285, 449

Varro on, 25 *n.*³, 297

Mentioned, 56 *n.*⁴

Caecilius Metellus Caprarius (the praetor), 41 *and n.*⁵

Caecilius of Caleacte, 215, 237 *n.*⁶

Caelius Rufus, 253–4, 273, 324; on Calidius, 220

Caesar, Julius, 254; tribute to Terence, 24 *and n.*³; tribute to Cicero, 176 *n.*², 203, 255; Atticist leanings of, 255, 256; character of his oratory, 255, 256 *and n.*; poetry of, 452

Commentaries, 256, 513, 562

De Analogia, 50 *n.*⁵, 243, 246, 254 *and n.*⁸, 255; dedicated to Cicero, 254, 255; Hendrickson's view of, 255

Caesar, Strabo Julius, 59, 61 *n.*⁴, 62–3, 186; oratorical style, 62–3, 256; dramas of, 449–50

Calidius, 217, 219, 224, 226; his style, 174, 219 *and n.*⁸, 220; care in composition, 381; association

with Roman Atticism, 217, 219, 243; view of the Grand style, 241

Cicero on, 174, 189, 204, 207, 218 *n.*³, 219–20, 234, 243, 544

Callaicus, D. Brutus, 51

Callimachus, 278, 286 *n.*³, 303, 412, 415 *n.*⁸, 416, 430 *n.*⁴

Callisthenes, 497 *and n.*⁴, 499 *n.*¹⁰

Cicero on, 513

Calvus, 218–19, 224, 228 *n.*⁴, 253, 254, 316, 324; style of, 86 *n.*⁹, 218, 228, 258, 262–3, 381, 549; Vatinian orations of, 262 *n.*³, 263 *and n.*³; and Roman Atticism, 217, 219, 220, 226, 227, 243, 324; influence of Alexandrian literature on, 218; treatises of, on oratory, 227 *and n.*⁶; attacks on Caesar, 256, 367; opposition to Cicero, 219; and the *De Oratore*, 225–6; correspondence with Cicero, 228 *and nn.*¹, ⁴, 229

Cicero on, 189, 218, 228 *and n.*¹, 229, 243, 262, 263, 381, 549; note of polemic, 220

Horace's animosity to, 302, 367

Canachus, 192

Canon of Orators, 66 *n.*¹

Canons of the poets, 65 *and nn.*⁴, ⁶, 66

Canutius, P., 184 *n.*⁴

Carbo, C., 181, 183

Carbo, Gaius, 189

Carneades the Academic, 30, 36 *n.*⁵, 44, 60, 140 *n.*¹, 160 *n.*⁴, 158–9

Castricius, 346

Cato, Porcius (the Elder), 200, 271, 346; and Hellenism, 29, 30, 32, 200; influence of, on Scipio, 32; his description of the orator, 161; oratory of, 189, 200, 201, 273, 324, 325, 327, 348, 349; style, 324, 349, 514; archaisms in, 81, 273; and Greek rhetorical theory, 200 *and n.*⁵; treatise on

Cicero, M. Tullius—*contd.*
Poetry, Poets—*contd.*
poets, 143, 145; Dramatic poets, 142, 146, 540; Lyric poetry,145,146–7,395,445; Poetry and the training of the orator, 146–7, 445; affinity between orator and poet, 143, 144, 147, 393, 443
See Writings, *infra*
Style, criticism and opinions on: the three styles, 68, 75, 85, 221; Grand style, 78, 222, 223; Middle style, 78, 140, 221; Plain style, 78, 163, 231–2, 533; the virtues of style, 77 *n*.⁵, 78, 136, 171–2, 222–3; ornateness, 78, 85, 172; archaisms, 81, 91 *n*.¹, 274 *and nn*.⁵, ⁶; metaphor, 94; prose rhythm, 99, 103, 105–6; list of the Figures, 109; on artificiality in style, 132; approximates to a definition of style, 136; matter and form, 136, 137; on faults in style, 138. *See also under* Subject headings
Writings, 176, 205; poetic compositions and translations, 143, 144, 451, 452, 511
Brutus, 167, 542, 543; aim in, 167, 323 *n*.³; historical method in, 141, 191 *et seq.*; critical terms in, 204; Latinitas, 197, 246; *cited or mentioned*, 141, 151, 153,167–9,176,179,180, 189, 191, 192, 199, 204, 208, 214, 234, 243, 255, 264, 449, 513, 516, 544 *and in notes passim*
De Finibus, 139, 140, 188; *De Inventione*, 144 *n*.¹, 149, 541 *and n*.¹; *De Officiis* 54, 362, 369, 488 *n*.²; *De Optimo Genere Oratorum*, 208

De Oratore, 149, 150, 151, 220, 244, 540, 543; scheme of education in, 153, 238; ideal of culture in, 158; polemic in, 224, 225–6, 232; account of development in Greek prose in, 230; treatment of Latinitas in, 245, 255; *cited or mentioned*, 45, 59, 60, 62, 144, 169, 171, 179, 180, 181, 184, 186, 222, 223, 228, 241, 344, 363, 513 *and in footnotes passim*
De Republica, 28, 30, 45; *Laelius*, 28, 45
Orator, 176–7, 204, 208; problem of composition in, 246; *cited or mentioned*, 45, 241, 256, 257, 363, 449, 513, 515
Pro Archia, 486; *Pro Caecina*, 137, 138, 177; *Pro Murena*, 166; *Pro Lege Manilia*, 177, 350; *Pro Rabirio*, 177
Fronto on, 350
Horace, parallels with, 468–9, 479 *n*.⁴
Otherwise mentioned, 45, 47, 88, 118, 123, 124 *n*.¹, 125, 156, 216, 342 *n*.⁸, 343, 344, 349, 439, 499, 522
See also under Names of Persons *and under* Subject headings
Cicero, Quintus, 145, 517; as verse maker, 451–2; version of Sophocles' *Banqueters*, 145, 407 *n*.³, 408 *n*.⁵, 451 *n*.⁷
Cimber, Annius, 274, 328
Cincius Alimentus, 347
Cinna, 288, 316 *and n*.⁹, 451
Zmyrna,285,286,302,381*n*.²,451
Clamor mulierum, 11
Claudius, Appius, 168, 270, 343
Cleanthes, 162
Climax, 113

606

INDEX

Style, aspects of—*contd.*

sincerity, 130–1, 536–7; individuality in style, 537–9; concealment of art in, 133–4; matter and form, 130, 136–8; defects of style, 138; doctrine of three styles, 68–9, 73, 74, 84, 467, 535 *See also under headings* Grand, Middle, Plain

Suetonius, *cited*, 5, 65, 256, 292, 332, 450, 452, 528; indebtedness to Varro, 296

σύγκρισις, method of, 183–4

Sulpicius Apollinaris, 311

Sulpicius Gallus, 23, 28, 193

Sulpicius, Servius, 151 *n*.³, 181, 184–5, 186, 187–8, 239 *n*.¹, 347; as orator, 185 *and nn.;* redundancy of, 185

Cicero on, 174, 184–8 *passim*, 225

TACITUS, 203, 522–3, 553; on oratory and party strife, 198; on Cicero and the Atticists, 227–8; and laudation of the Ancients, 270, 306; on Ancients *v.* Moderns controversy, 324–5, 340 *et seq.*, 555; on poetasters, 452; on the aim of the poet, 486

Annals, 522

Dialogus, 152, 339 *et seq.*, 550 *n*.¹, 555; Aper in, 256, 258, 280, 282, 324 *n*.⁸, 325, 340–3, 555; Maternus in, 280, 345, 555; Messalla in, 152, 328, 343–5, 555

Otherwise mentioned, 207, 261

Telephus, 462

Terence, 6 *et seq.*, 34, 67; connection with Scipionic circle, 23, 27, 64; literary polemic in prologues of, 7–27 *passim*, 298, 429, 526; ideal for the drama, 8 *and n*.¹, 26, 27; and the prologue of exposition, 8 *and n*.⁴, 9, 10, 11, 27, 527; method of exposition, 11–12;

use of the " prosopon protaticon," 12; attitude to the audience, 10, 24; appeal to the intellectuals, 11, 24, 299; relation to the Greek originals, 12–13, 20, 27, 429, 526; contamination, 12, 13–17, 20, 526; plagiarism, 15–20 *passim ;* reaction against conventions, 20–2, 27, 527; plays, authorship of, 23; preference of, for Menander, 24, 299, 466; style, 24–7, 299; claim to pure Latinity, 31, 34; indebtedness to rhetoricians, 455

Adelphi, 8, 13, 15, 16, 20, 296

Andria, 7, 12, 13, 22

Eunuch, 14–15, 19

Heautontimorumenos, 7, 11, 14, 21

Hecyra, 10, 12, 19, 20, 65

Phormio, 7, 12

Cicero on, 24, 144, 148

Horace on, 299

Varro on, 297, 467

Otherwise mentioned, 79, 142 *and n*.⁴, 321, 384, 464, 467, 529

Theocritus, 420

Theon, 160, 506, 507 *n*.²

Theophrastus, 69, 159, 534; doctrine of styles, 72, 533, 534; insistence on the Peripatetic Mean, 72, 135, 534; on virtues of style, 77, 78, 83, 135, 163, 171, 534 *n*.¹; ornatus, 85, 478, 535; and formulism, 534, 535

Characters, 372

Treatise on Style, 135, 534

Otherwise mentioned, 197 *n*.⁸, 209, 359 *n*.⁶, 362 *n*.¹, 445, 548

Theopompus, 494, 495–6, 499 *and n*.¹⁰, 507 *n*.², 508, 513; style, 496, 513; avoidance of hiatus, 97, 496

Thrasea, 269

Thrasymachus, 72, 73, 99, 249; prose rhythm, 99–100